The Romantic Tradition in American Literature

The Romantic Tradition in American Literature

Advisory Editor

HAROLD BLOOM
Professor of English, Yale University

ORATIONS

AND

SPEECHES,

ON

VARIOUS OCCASIONS

BY

EDWARD EVERETT

ARNO PRESS
A NEW YORK TIMES COMPANY
New York • 1972

Reprint Edition 1972 by Arno Press Inc.

Reprinted from a copy in The Wesleyan
University Library

The Romantic Tradition in American Literature
ISBN for complete set: 0-405-04620-0
See last pages of this volume for titles.

Manufactured in the United States of America

๛๛๛๛๛๛๛๛๛

Library of Congress Cataloging in Publication Data

Everett, Edward, 1794-1865.
  Orations and speeches.

  (The Romantic tradition in American literature)
  Reprint of the 1836 ed.
  1. American orations. I. Title. II. Series.
E337.8.E936   081   72-4963
ISBN 0-405-04634-0

ORATIONS

AND

SPEECHES

ORATIONS

AND

SPEECHES,

ON

VARIOUS OCCASIONS,

BY

EDWARD EVERETT.

BOSTON:
AMERICAN STATIONERS' COMPANY.
1836.

POWER PRESS OF WILLIAM S. DAMRELL,
39 Washington Street, Boston.

PREFACE.

THE following collection was made, at the suggestion of the respectable Association by whom it is published. It was at first intended, that it should consist of the materials of which this volume is composed, together with a selection of speeches in Congress, and articles in the North American Review, by the same author. It was found, on examination, that the addresses now submitted to the public would, of themselves, form a volume of ordinary size, and sufficient variety of matter. The collection has, accordingly, been confined to them, reserving for a future occasion, if deemed expedient, the preparation of another volume, to comprehend the speeches, essays, and other miscellaneous compositions not contained in this.

The orations and speeches contained in this volume, with the exception of the address delivered before the Massachusetts Agricultural Society, were printed at the time of their delivery; but advantage has been taken of the opportunity afforded by this republication, to revise and correct them, principally in matters of style.

It will be found, that some of the addresses, being on the same or similar occasions or subjects, exhibit a considerable similarity in the train of remark, and even

in the illustrations. This is particularly the case with
the orations delivered at Concord and Lexington, on
the 19th of April, 1825, and 1835. Such a similarity
was scarcely to be avoided. The general plan of the
two addresses is different, but they necessarily required
some description of the same memorable incidents ; and
any attempt to avoid the repetition must have been at
the sacrifice of topics consecrated to the occasion.

The author, being desirous, in submitting this collection
to the public, to make a contribution to the literature of
the country, which, however humble, might at least
possess the negative merit of being inoffensive, the
speeches delivered by him on political occasions have
been excluded, and nothing of a party character has
been knowingly admitted.

He is fully aware, that as the addresses which make
up the volume were in their origin occasional, the
collection of them cannot be expected to form a work
of permanent interest and importance. It would be all
he could hope, that they should be thought, at the time
of their separate appearance, not to fall below the line
of the indulgence usually extended to performances of
this character. He has been induced, more by the
encouragement of partial friends, than his own judgment
of their value, to submit them again to the public, in
their present form.

CHARLESTOWN, MASS., JULY, 1836.

CONTENTS.

viii CONTENTS.

ORATION

PRONOUNCED AT CAMBRIDGE, BEFORE THE SOCIETY OF PHI BETA
KAPPA, AUGUST 26, 1824.

—

MR. PRESIDENT AND GENTLEMEN,

IN discharging the honorable trust of being the public organ
of your sentiments on this occasion, I am anxious that the hour,
which we here pass together, should be occupied by those reflections exclusively, which belong to us as scholars. Our association in this fraternity is academical; we engaged in it before our
Alma Mater dismissed us from her venerable roof, to wander in
the various paths of life; and we have now come together in the
academical holidays, from every variety of pursuit, from almost
every part of our country, to meet on common ground, as the
brethren of one literary household. The professional cares of life,
like the conflicting tribes of Greece, have proclaimed to us a short
armistice, that we may come up in peace to our Olympia.

But from the wide field of literary speculation, and the innumerable subjects of meditation which arise in it, a selection must be
made. It has seemed to me proper that we should direct our
thoughts, not merely to a subject of interest to scholars, but to one,
which may recommend itself as peculiarly appropriate to us. If
'that old man eloquent, whom the dishonest victory of Cheronæa
killed with report,' could devote fifteen years to the composition of
his Panegyric on Athens, I shall need no excuse to a society of
American scholars, in choosing for the theme of my address on an
occasion like this, *the peculiar motives to intellectual exertion in
America.* In this subject, that curiosity, which every scholar feels
in tracing and comparing the springs of mental activity, is height-

1

ened and dignified, by the important connexion of the inquiry with the condition and prospects of our native land.

In the full comprehension of the terms, the *motives to intellectual exertion* in a country embrace the most important springs of national character. Pursued into its details, the study of these springs of national character is often little better than fanciful speculation. The question, why Asia has almost always been the abode of despotism, and Europe more propitious to liberty ; why the Egyptians were abject and melancholy ; the Greeks inventive, elegant, and versatile ; the Romans stern, saturnine, and, in matters of literature, for the most part servile imitators of a people, whom they conquered, despised, and never equalled ; why tribes of barbarians from the north and east, not known to differ essentially from each other at the time of their settlement in Europe, should have laid the foundation of national characters so dissimilar, as those of the Spanish, French, German, and English nations ;— these are questions to which a few general answers may be attempted, that will probably be just and safe, only in proportion as they are vague and comprehensive. Difficult as it is, even in the individual man, to point out precisely the causes, under the influence of which members of the same community and of the same family, placed apparently in the same circumstances, grow up with characters the most diverse ; it is infinitely more difficult to perform the same analysis on a subject so vast as a Nation ; where it is oftentimes first to be settled, what the precise character is, before you touch the inquiry into the circumstances by which it was formed.

But as, in the case of individual character, there are certain causes of undisputed and powerful operation ; there are also in national character causes equally undisputed of improvement and excellence, on the one hand, and of degeneracy, on the other. The philosophical student of history may often fix on circumstances, which in their operation on the minds of the people, in furnishing the motives and giving the direction to intellectual exertion, have had the chief agency in making them what they were or are. It is in the highest degree curious to trace physical and historical facts into their political, intellectual, and moral consequences ; and to show how the climate, the geographical position, and even the particular topography of a region connect themselves, by evident association, with the state of society, its leading pursuits, and characteristic institutions.

In the case of other nations, particularly of those, which in the great drama of the world, have long since passed from the stage, these speculations, however, are often only curious. The operation of a tropical climate in enervating and fitting a people for despotism; the influence of a broad river or a lofty chain of mountains, in arresting the march of conquest or of emigration, and thus becoming the boundary not merely of governments, but of languages, literature, institutions, and character; the effect of a quarry of fine marble on the progress of the liberal arts; the agency of popular institutions in promoting popular eloquence, and the tremendous reaction of popular eloquence on the fortunes of a state; the comparative destiny of colonial settlements, of insular states, of tribes fortified in nature's Alpine battlements, or scattered over a smiling region of olive gardens and vineyards; these are all topics indeed of rational curiosity and liberal speculation, but important only as they may illustrate the prospects of our own country.

It is, therefore, when we turn the inquiry to our country, when we survey its features, search its history, and contemplate its institutions, to see what the motives are, which are to excite and guide the minds of the people; when we dwell not on a distant, an uncertain, an almost forgotten past; but on an impending future, teeming with life and action, toward which we are rapidly and daily swept forward, and with which we stand in the dearest connexion, which can bind the generations of man together; a future, which our own characters, our own actions, our own principles, will do something to stamp with glory or shame; it is then that the inquiry becomes practical, momentous, and worthy the attention of every patriotic scholar. We then strive, as far as it is in the power of philosophical investigation to do it, to unfold our country's reverend auspices, to cast its great horoscope in the national sky, where many stars are waning, and many have set; to ascertain whether the soil which we love, as that where our fathers are laid, and we shall presently be laid with them, will be trod in times to come by a virtuous, enlightened, and free people.

I. The first of the circumstances which are acting and will continue to act, with a strong peculiarity among us, and which must prove one of the most powerful influences, in exciting and directing the intellect of the country, is the new form of political society, which has here been devised and established. I shall not wander so far from the literary limits of this occasion, nor into a field so oft trodden, as the praises of free political institutions. But the direct and appropriate influence on mental effort, of a political system like ours, has not yet, perhaps, received the attention, which, from every American scholar, it richly deserves. I have ventured to say, that a new form of polity has here been devised and established. The ancient Grecian republics, indeed, were free enough within the walls of the single city, of which many of them were wholly or chiefly composed; but to these single cities the freedom, as well as the power, was confined. Toward the confederated or tributary states, the government was generally a despotism, more capricious and not less severe, than that of a single tyrant. Rome, as a state, was never free; in every period of her history, authentic and dubious, royal, republican, and imperial, her proud citizens were the slaves of an artful, accomplished, wealthy aristocracy; and nothing but the hard fought battles of her stern tribunes can redeem her memory to the friends of liberty. In ancient and modern history, there is no example, before our own, of a purely elective and representative system. It is on an entirely novel plan, that, in this country, the whole direction and influence of affairs; all the trusts and honors of society; the power of making, abrogating, and administering the laws; the whole civil authority and sway, from the highest post in the government to the smallest village trust, are put directly into the market of merit. Whatsoever efficacy there is in high station and exalted honors, to call out and exercise the powers, either by awakening the emulation of aspirants, or exciting the efforts of incumbents, is here directly exerted on the largest mass of men, with the smallest possible deductions. Nothing is bestowed on the chance of birth, nothing flows through the channel of hereditary family interests; but whatever is desired must be sought in the way of a broad, fair, personal competition. It requires little argument to show, that such a system must most widely and most powerfully have the effect of appealing to whatever of energy the land contains; of searching out, with magnetic instinct, in the remotest quarters, the latent ability of its children.

It may be objected, and it has been, that for want of an hereditary government, we lose that powerful spring of action which resides in the patronage of such a government, and must emanate from the crown. With many individuals friendly to our popular institutions, it is nevertheless an opinion, that we must consent to lose something of the genial influence of princely and royal patronage on letters and arts, and find our consolation in the political benefits of our free system. It may be doubted, however, whether this view be not entirely false. As no one can suppose, that the mere fact of the existence of an hereditary government adds anything to the resources of a people, whatever is gained by concentrating an active patronage, in the metropolis, and in the central administration, must be lost by withdrawing the means of patronage from the distant portions of the state, and all its subordinate institutions. By the healthful action of our representative system, the public patronage is made to pervade the empire like the air ; to reach the farthest, descend to the lowest, and bind the distant together ; it is made not only to cooperate with the successful and assist the prosperous, but to cheer the remote, ' to remember the forgotten, to attend to the neglected, to visit the forsaken.' Before the rising of our republic in the world, the faculties of men had but one weary pilgrimage to perform,—to travel up to court. By an improvement on the Jewish polity, which enjoined on the nation a visit thrice a year to the holy city, the great, the munificent, the enlightened states of the ancient and modern world have required a constant residence on the chosen spot. *Provincial* has become another term for inferior and rude ; and *unpolite,* which once meant only *rural,* has got to signify, in all our languages, something little better than barbarous. But since, in the nature of things, a small part only of the population of a large state can, by physical possibility, be crowded within the walls of a city, and there receive the genial beams of metropolitan favor, it follows that the great mass of men are cut off from the operation of some of the strongest excitements to exertion. It is rightfully urged then, as a great advantage of our system, that the excitements of society are diffused as widely as its burdens, and search out and bring forward whatsoever of ability and zeal are comprehended within the limits of the land. The effect of this diffusion of privileges is all-powerful. Capacity and opportunity, the twin sisters, who can scarce subsist but with each other, are now brought together. The people who are to choose, and from whose number are to be chosen, by their neighbors, the highest officers of state, infallibly feel an impulse to mental activity; they read, think, and compare; they found village schools, they collect social libraries, they prepare their children for the higher establishments of education. The world has been grossly abused on the tendency of institutions perfectly popular. From the ill-organized states of antiquity, terrific examples of license and popular misrule are quoted, to prove that man requires to be protected from himself, without asking who is to protect him from the protector, himself also a man. While from the very first settlement of America to the present day, one of the most prominent traits of our character has been to cherish and diffuse the means of education. The village school-house, and the village church, are the monuments, which the American people have erected to their freedom; to read, and write, and think, are the licentious practices, which have characterized our democracy.

But it will be urged, perhaps, that, though the effect of our institutions be to excite the intellect of the nation, they excite it too much in a political direction; that the division and subdivision of the country into states and districts, and the equal diffusion throughout them of political privileges and powers, whatever favorable effect in other ways they may produce, are attended by this evil,— that they kindle a political ambition, where it would not and ought not to be felt; and particularly, that they are unfriendly in their operation on literature, as they call the aspiring youth, from the patient and laborious vigils of the student, to plunge prematurely into the conflicts of the Forum. It may, however, be doubted, whether there be any foundation whatever for a charge like this; and whether the fact, so far as it is one, that the talent and ambition of the country incline, at present, to a political course, be not owing to causes wholly unconnected with the free character of our institutions. It need not be said, that the administration of the government of a country, whether it be liberal or despotic, is the first thing to be provided for. Some persons must be employed in making and administering the laws, before any other interest can receive attention. Our fathers, the pilgrims, before they left the vessel, in which for five months they had been tossed on the ocean ; —before setting foot on the new world of their desire ;—drew up a simple constitution of government. As this is the first care in the order of nature, it ever retains its paramount importance. Society must be preserved in its constituted forms, or there is no safety for life, no security for property, no permanence for any institution, civil, moral, or religious. The first efforts, then, of social man are of necessity political. Apart from every call of ambition, honorable or selfish, of interest enlarged or mercenary, the care of the government is the first care of a civilized community. In the early stages of social progress, where there is little property and a scanty population, the whole strength of the society must be employed in its support and defence. Though *we* are constantly receding from these stages, we have not wholly left them. Even our rapidly increasing population is, and will for some time remain, small, compared with the space over which it is diffused ; and this, with the total absence of large hereditary fortunes, will create a demand for political services, on the one hand, and a necessity of rendering them, on the other.

There is then, no ground for ascribing the political tendency of the talent and activity of this country, to an imagined incompatibility of popular institutions with the profound cultivation of letters. It is the effect of other causes. Suppose our government were changed to-morrow ; that the five points of a strong government were introduced, an hereditary sovereign, an order of nobility, an established church, a standing army, and a military police ; and that these should take place of that admirable system, which now, like the genial air, pervades all, supports all, cheers all, and is nowhere seen. Suppose this change made, and other circumstances to remain the same ; our population no more dense, our boundaries as wide, and the accumulation of private wealth no more abundant. Would there, in the new state of things, be less interest in politics ? By the terms of the supposition, the leading class of the community, the nobles, are to be politicians by birth. By the nature of the case, a large portion of the remainder, who gain their livelihood by their industry and talents, would be engrossed, not indeed in the free political competition, which now prevails, but in pursuing the interests of rival court factions.   One class only, the peasantry, would remain, which would take less interest in politics than the corresponding class in a free state; or rather, this is a new class, which invariably comes in with a strong government; and no one can seriously think the cause of science and literature would be promoted, by substituting an European peasantry, in the place of, perhaps, the most substantial, uncorrupted population on earth, the American yeomanry.   Moreover, the evil in question is with us a self-correcting evil.   If the career of politics be more open, and the temptation to crowd it stronger, competition will spring up, numbers will engage in the pursuit; the less able, the less industrious, the less ambitious must retire, and leave the race to the swift and the battle to the strong.   But in hereditary governments no such remedy exists.   One class of society, by the nature of its position, must be rulers, magistrates, or politicians.   Weak or strong, willing or unwilling, they must play the game, though they, as well as the people pay the bitter forfeit.   The obnoxious king can seldom shake off the empoisoned purple; he must wear the crown of thorns, till it is struck off at the scaffold; and the same artificial necessity has obliged generations of nobles, in all the old states of Europe, to toil and bleed for a

Power too great to keep or to resign.

Where the compulsion stops short of these afflicting extremities, still, under the governments in question, a large portion of the community is unavoidably destined to the calling of the courtier, the soldier, the party retainer; to a life of service, intrigue, and court attendance; and thousands, and those the prominent individuals in society, are brought up to look on a livelihood gained by private industry as base; on study as the pedant's trade; on labor as the badge of slavery.   I look in vain, in institutions like these, for anything essentially favorable to intellectual progress.   On the contrary, while they must draw away the talent and ambition of the country, quite as much as popular institutions can do it, into pursuits foreign to the culture of the intellect, they necessarily doom to obscurity no small part of the mental energy of the land. For that mental energy has been equally diffused, by sterner levellers than ever marched in the van of a Revolution,—the nature of man and the Providence of God. Sterling native character, strength and quickness of mind, are not of the number of distinctions and accomplishments, that human institutions can monopolize within a city's walls. In quiet times, they remain and perish in the obscurity, to which a false organization of society consigns them. In dangerous, convulsed, and trying times, they spring up in the fields, in the village hamlets, and on the mountain tops, and teach the surprised favorites of human law, that bright eyes, skilful hands, quick perceptions, firm purpose, and brave hearts, are not the exclusive prerogative of courts.

Our popular institutions are therefore favorable to intellectual improvement, because their foundation is in dear nature. They do not consign the greater part of the social frame to torpidity and mortification. They send out a vital nerve to every member of the community, by which its talent and power, great or small, are brought into living conjunction and strong sympathy with the kindred intellect of the nation; and every impression on every part vibrates with electric rapidity through the whole. They encourage nature to perfect her work; they make education, the soul's nutriment, cheap; they bring up remote and shrinking talent into the cheerful field of competition; in a thousand ways they provide an audience for lips, which nature has touched with persuasion; they put a lyre into the hands of genius; they bestow on all who deserve it or seek it, the only patronage worth having, the only patronage that ever struck out a spark of 'celestial fire,'—the patronage of fair opportunity. This is a day of improved education; new systems of teaching are devised; modes of instruction, choice of studies, adaptation of text books, the whole machinery of means has been brought in our day, under severe revision. But were I to attempt to point out the most efficacious and comprehensive improvement in education,—the engine by which the greatest portion of mind could be brought and kept under cultivation, the discipline which would reach farthest, sink deepest, and cause the word of instruction, not to spread over the surface, like an artificial hue, carefully laid on, but to penetrate to the heart and soul of its subjects,

2

it would be popular institutions. Give the people an object in promoting education, and the best methods will infallibly be suggested by that instinctive ingenuity of our nature, which provides means for great and precious ends. Give the people an object in promoting education, and the worn hand of labor will be opened to the last farthing, that its children may enjoy means denied to itself. This great contest about black boards and sand tables will then lose something of its importance, and even the exalted names of Bell and Lancaster may sink from that very lofty height, where an over hasty admiration has placed them.

But though it be conceded to us, that the tendency, which is alleged to exist in this country toward the political career, is not a vicious effect of our free institutions, still it may be inquired, whether the new form of social organization among us is at least to produce no corresponding modification of our literature? As the country advances, as the population becomes denser, as wealth accumulates, as the various occasions of a large, prosperous, and polite community call into strong action and vigorous competition the literary talent of the country, will no peculiar form or direction be given to its literature, by the nature of its institutions? To this question an answer must, without hesitation, be given in the affirmative. Literature as well in its origin, as in its true and only genuine character, is but a more perfect communication of man with man and mind with mind. It is a grave, sustained, deliberate utterance of fact, of opinion, and feeling; or a free and happy reflection of nature, of character, or of manners; and if it be not these, it is poor imitation. It may, therefore, be assumed as certain, that the peculiarity of our condition and institutions will be reflected in some peculiarity of our literature; but what that shall be it is as yet too early to say.* Literary history informs us of many studies, which

* The peculiar natural features of the American continent are of themselves sufficient to produce some strong peculiarity in its literature; but this topic is comprehensive and curious enough for a separate Essay. It has, I am permitted to say, been made the subject of one, by M. de Salazar, the minister from the Colombian Republic to the United States, which will shortly be presented to the friends of American letters. An essay on such a subject, from an accomplished citizen of a free State, established in what was lately a Spanish colony, is itself an admirable illustration of the genial influence of popular institutions on Intellectual Improvement.

have been neglected as dangerous to existing governments ; and many others which have been cultivated because they were prudent and safe. We have hardly the means of settling from analogy, what direction the mind will most decisively take, when left under strong excitements to action, wholly without restraint from the arm of power, throughout a vastly extensive and highly prosperous country. It is impossible to anticipate what garments our native muses will weave for themselves. To foretell our literature would be to create it. There was a time before an epic poem, a tragedy, or a historical composition had ever been produced by the wit of man. It was a time of vast and powerful empires, of populous and wealthy cities. Greece had been settled a thousand years, before the golden age of her literature began. But these new and beautiful forms of human thought and feeling all sprang up under the excitement of her free institutions. Before they appeared in the world, it would have been idle for the philosopher to form conjectures, as to the direction, which the kindling genius of the age was to assume. He, who could form, could and would realize the anticipation, and it would cease to be an anticipation. Assuredly, epic poetry was invented then and not before, when the gorgeous vision of the Iliad, not in its full detail of circumstance, but in the dim conception of its leading scenes and bolder features, burst into the soul of Homer. Impossible, indeed, were the task, fully to foresee the course of the mind, under the influence of institutions as new, as peculiar, and far more animating than those of Greece. But if, as no one will deny, our political system bring more minds into action on equal terms, if it provide a prompter circulation of thought throughout the community, if it give weight and emphasis to more voices, if it swell to tens of thousands and millions, those ' sons of emulation, who crowd the narrow strait where honor travels,' then it seems not too much to foretell some peculiarity at least, if we may not call it improvement, in that literature, which is but the voice and utterance of all this mental action. There is little doubt that the instrument of communication itself will receive great improvements ; that the written and spoken language will acquire force and power ; possibly, that forms of address, wholly new, will be struck out, to meet the universal demand for new energy. When the improvement or the invention, (whatever it be,) comes, it will come unlooked for, as well to its happy author as the world. But where great interests are at stake, great concerns rapidly succeeding each other, depending on almost innumerable wills, and yet requiring to be apprehended at a glance, and explained in a word; where movements are to be given to a vast empire, not by transmitting orders, but by diffusing opinions, exciting feelings, and touching the electric cord of sympathy, there language and expression will become intense, and the old processes of communication must put on a vigor and a directness, adapted to the aspect of the times. Our country is called, as it is, practical; but this is the element for intellectual action. No strongly marked and high toned literature; poetry, eloquence, or ethics, ever appeared but in the pressure, the din, and crowd of great interests, great enterprises, and perilous risks, and dazzling rewards. Statesmen, and warriors, and poets, and orators, and artists, start up under one and the same excitement. They are all branches of one stock. They form, and cheer, and stimulate; and, what is worth all the rest, understand each other ; and it is as truly the sentiment of the student, in the recesses of his cell, as of the soldier in the ranks, which breathes in the exclamation :

> To all the sons of sense proclaim,
> One glorious hour of *crowded life*
> Is worth an age without a name.

But we are brought back to the unfavorable aspect of the subject, by being reminded out of history, of the splendid patronage which arbitrary governments have bestowed on letters, and which, from the nature of the case, can hardly be extended even to the highest merit under institutions like our own. We are told of the munificent pensions, the rich establishments, the large foundations ; of the museums erected, the libraries gathered, the endowments granted, by Ptolemies, Augustuses, and Louises, of ancient and modern days. We are asked to remark the fruit of this noble patronage ; wonders of antiquarian or scientific lore, Thesauruses and Corpuses, efforts of erudition, from which the emulous student, who would read all things, weigh all things, surpass all things, recoils in horror ; volumes and shelves of volumes, before which meek-eyed patience folds her hands in despair.

When we have contemplated these things, and turn our thoughts back to our poor republican land, to our frugal treasury, and the caution with which it is dispensed ; to our modest fortunes, and the thrift with which they are hoarded ; to our scanty public libraries, and the plain brick walls within which they are deposited ; we may be apt to form gloomy auguries of the influence of free political institutions on our literature. It is important then, that we examine more carefully the experience of former ages, and see how far their institutions, as they have been more or less popular, have been more or less marked by displays of intellectual excellence. When we make this examination, we shall be gratified to find, that the precedents are all in favor of liberty. The greatest efforts of human genius have been made, where the nearest approach to free institutions has taken place. There shone not forth one ray of intellectual light, to cheer the long and gloomy ages of the Memphian and Babylonian despots. Not a historian, not an orator, not a poet is heard of in their annals. When we ask, what was achieved by the generations of thinking beings, the millions of men, whose natural genius was as bright as that of the Greeks, nay, who forestalled the Greeks in the first invention of many of the arts, we are told that they built the pyramids of Memphis, the temples of Thebes, and the tower of Babylon, and carried Sesostris and Ninus upon their shoulders, from the West of Africa to the Indus. Mark the contrast in Greece. With the first emerging of that country into the light of political liberty, the poems of Homer appear. Some centuries of political misrule and literary darkness follow, and then the great constellation of their geniuses seems to rise at once. The stormy eloquence and the deep philosophy, the impassioned drama and the grave history, were all produced for the entertainment of that 'fierce democratie' of Athens. Here then, the genial influence of liberty on letters is strongly put to the test. Athens was certainly a free state ; free to licentiousness, free to madness. The rich were arbitrarily pillaged to defray the expenses of the state, the great were banished to appease the envy of their rivals, the wise sacrificed to the fury of the populace. It was a state, in short, where liberty existed with most of the imperfections, which have led men to love and praise despotism. Still, however, it was for this lawless, merciless people, that the most chastised and accomplished literature, which the world has known, was produced. The philosophy of Plato was the attraction, which drew to a morning's walk in the olive gardens of the academy, the young men of this factious city. Those tumultuous assemblies of Athens, the very same, which rose in their wrath, and to a man, and clamored for the blood of Phocion, required to be addressed, not in the cheap extemporaneous rant of modern demagogues, but in the elaborate and thrice repeated orations of Demosthenes. No! the noble and elegant arts of Greece grew up in no Augustan age, enjoyed neither royal nor imperial patronage. Unknown before in the world, strangers on the Nile, and strangers on the Euphrates, they sprang at once into life, in a region not unlike our own New-England,— iron bound, sterile, and free. The imperial astronomers of Chaldæa went up almost to the stars in their observatories; but it was a Greek, who first foretold an eclipse, and measured the year. The nations of the East invented the alphabet, but not a line has reached us of profane literature, in any of their languages; and it is owing to the embalming power of Grecian genius, that the invention itself has been transmitted to the world. The Egyptian architects could erect structures, which, after three thousand five hundred years, are still standing, in their uncouth original majesty; but it was only on the barren soil of Attica, that the beautiful columns of the Parthenon and the Theseum could rest, which are standing also.

With the decline of liberty in Greece, began the decline of all her letters and all her arts, though her tumultuous democracies were succeeded by liberal and accomplished princes. Compare the literature of the Alexandrian with that of the Periclean age; how cold, pedantic, and imitative! Compare, I will not say, the axes, the eggs, the altars, and the other frigid devices of the pensioned wits in the museum at Alexandria; but compare their best productions with those of independent Greece; Callimachus with Pindar, Lycophron with Sophocles, Aristophanes of Byzantium with Aristotle, and Apollonius the Rhodian with Homer. When we descend to Rome, to the Augustan age, the exalted era of Mæcenas, we find one uniform work of imitation, often of translation. The choicest geniuses seldom rise beyond a happy transfusion of the Grecian masters. Horace translates Alcæus, Terence translates Menander, Lucretius translates Epicurus, Virgil translates

Homer, and Cicero,—I had almost said,—translates Demosthenes and Plato. But the soul of liberty did burst forth from the lips of Cicero, 'her form had not yet lost all its original brightness,' her inspiration produced in him the only specimens of a purely original literature, which Rome has transmitted to us. After him, their literary history is written in one line of Tacitus; *gliscente adulatione, magna ingenia deterrebantur.* The fine arts revived a little under the princes of the Flavian house, but never rose higher than a successful imitation of the waning excellence of Greece. With the princes of this line, the arts of Rome expired, and Constantine the great, was obliged to tear down an arch of Trajan for sculptures, wherewithal to adorn his own. In modern times the question is more complicated. Civilized states have multiplied; political institutions have varied in different states, and at different times in the same state; some liberal institutions have existed in the bosom of societies otherwise despotic; and a great addition of new studies has been made to the encyclopædia, which have all been cultivated by great minds, and some of which, as the physical and experimental sciences, have little or no direct connexion with the state of liberty. These circumstances perplex, in some degree, the inquiry into the effect of free institutions on intellectual improvement in modern times. There are times and places, where it would seem, that the muses, both the gay and the severe, had been transformed into court ladies. Upon the whole, however, the modern history of literature bears but a cold testimony to the genial influence of the governments, under which it has grown up. Dante and Petrarch composed their beautiful works in exile; Boccacio complains in the most celebrated of his, that he was transfixed with the darts of envy and calumny; Macchiavelli was pursued by the party of the Medici, for resisting their tyrannical designs; Guicciardini retired in disgust, to compose his history in voluntary exile; Galileo confessed in the prisons of the Inquisition, that the earth did not move; Ariosto lived in poverty; and Tasso died in want and despair.* Cervantes, after he had immortalized himself in his great work, was obliged to write on for bread. The whole

---

* Martinelli, in his edition of the Decamerone, cited in the Introduction to Sidney's Discourses on Government, Edition of 1751, p. 34.

French academy was pensioned to crush the great Corneille. Racine, after living to see his finest pieces derided as cold and worthless, died of a broken heart. The divine genius of Shakspeare owed but little surely to patronage, for it raised him to no higher rank than that of a subaltern actor in his own and Ben Jonson's plays. The immortal Chancellor was sacrificed to the preservation of a worthless minion, and is said, (falsely I trust,) to have begged a cup of beer in his old age, and begged in vain. The most valuable of the pieces of Selden were written in that famous resort of great minds, the tower of London. Milton, surprised by want in his infirm old age, sold the first production of the human mind for five pounds. The great boast of English philosophy was expelled from his place in Oxford, and kept in banishment, 'the king having been given to understand,' to use the words of Lord Sunderland, who ordered the expulsion, 'that *one Locke* has, upon several occasions, behaved himself very factiously against the government.' Dryden sacrificed his genius to the spur of immediate want. Otway was choked with a morsel of bread, too ravenously swallowed after a long fast. Johnson was taken to prison for a debt of five shillings; and Burke petitioned for a Professorship at Glasgow, and was denied. When we survey these facts, and the innumerable others, of which these are but a specimen, we may perhaps conclude that, in whatever way the arbitrary governments of Europe have encouraged letters, it has not been in that of a steady, cheering patronage. We may think there is abundant reason to acknowledge, that the ancient lesson is confirmed by modern experience, and that popular institutions are most propitious to the full and prosperous growth of intellectual excellence.

II. If the perfectly organized system of liberty, which here prevails, be thus favorable to intellectual progress, various other conditions of our national existence are not less so, particularly the extension of one language, government, and character over so vast a space as the United States of America. Hitherto, in the main, the world has seen but two forms of political government, free governments in small states, and arbitrary governments in large ones. Though various shades of both have appeared, at different times, in the world, yet on the whole, the political ingenuity of man has never found out the mode of extending liberal institutions beyond small districts, or of governing large empires, by any other means than the visible demonstration and exercise of absolute power. The effect in either case has been unpropitious to the growth of intellectual excellence. Free institutions, though favorable to the growth of intellectual excellence, are not the only thing needed. In order that free institutions may have their full and entire effect, in producing the highest attainable degree of intellectual improvement, they require to be established in an extensive region, and over a numerous people. This constitutes a state of society entirely new among men; a vast empire, whose institutions are wholly popular. While we experience the genial influence of those principles, which belong to all free states, and in proportion as they are free; independence of thought, and the right of expressing it; we are to feel in this country, we and those who succeed us, all that excitement, which, in various ways, arises from the reciprocal action upon each other of the parts of a great empire. Literature as has been already hinted, is the voice of the age and the state. The character, energy, and resources of the country, are reflected and imaged forth in the conceptions of its great minds. They are the organs of the time; they speak not their own language, they scarce think their own thoughts; but under an impulse like the prophetic enthusiasm of old, they must feel and utter the sentiments which society inspires. They do not create, they obey the Spirit of the Age; the serene and beautiful spirit descended from the highest heaven of liberty, who laughs at our little preconceptions, and with the breath of his mouth, sweeps before him the men and the nations, that cross his path. By an unconscious instinct, the mind in the strong action of its powers, adapts itself to the number and complexion of the other minds, with which it is to enter into communion or conflict. As the voice falls into the key, which is suited to the space to be filled, the mind, in the various exercises of its creative faculties, strives with curious search for that master-note, which will awaken a vibration from the surrounding community, and which, if it do not find it, is itself too often struck dumb.

For this reason, from the moment in the destiny of nations, that they descend from their culminating point, and begin to decline, from that moment the voice of creative genius is hushed, and at

3

best, the age of criticism, learning, and imitation, succeeds. When
Greece ceased to be independent, the forum and the stage became
mute. The patronage of Macedonian, Alexandrian, and Perga-
mean princes was lavished in vain. They could not woo the
healthy Muses of Hellas, from the cold mountain tops of Greece,
to dwell in their gilded halls. Nay, though the fall of greatness,
the decay of beauty, the waste of strength, and the wreck of power
have ever been among the favorite themes of the pensive muse,
yet not a poet arose in Greece to chant her own elegy; and it is
after near three centuries, and from Cicero and Sulpicius, that we
catch the first notes of pious and pathetic lamentation over the
fallen land of the arts. The freedom and genius of a country are
invariably gathered into a common tomb, and there

> can only strangers breathe
> The name of that which was beneath.

It is when we reflect on this power of an auspicious future, that
we realize the prospect, which smiles upon the intellect of America.
It may justly be accounted the great peculiarity of ancient days,
compared with modern, that in antiquity there was, upon the whole,
but one civilized and literary nation at a time in the world. Art
and refinement followed in the train of political ascendency, from
the East to Greece, and from Greece to Rome. In the modern
world, under the influence of various causes, intellectual, political,
and moral, civilization has been diffused throughout the greater
part of Europe and America. Now mark a singular fatality as
regards the connexion of this enlarged and diffused civilization,
with the progress of letters and the excitement to intellectual exertion in any given state. Instead of one sole country, as in antiquity,
where the arts and refinements find a home, there are, in modern
Europe, seven or eight equally entitled to the general name of cultivated nations, and in each of which some minds of the first order
have appeared. And yet, by the multiplication of languages, an
obstacle all but insuperable has been thrown in the way of the free
progress of genius, in its triumphant course, from region to region.
The muses of Shakspeare and Milton, of Camoens, of Lope de
Vega and Calderon, of Corneille and Racine, of Dante and Tasso,
of Gœthe and Schiller, are strangers to each other.

This evil was so keenly felt in the sixteenth and seventeenth centuries, that the Latin language was widely adopted as a dialect common to scholars. We see men like Luther, Calvin, and Erasmus, Bacon, Grotius, and Thuanus, who could scarce have written a line without exciting the admiration of their contemporaries, driven to the use of a tongue, which none but the learned could understand. For the sake of addressing the scholars of other countries, these great men, and others like them, in many of their writings, were obliged to cut themselves off from all sympathy with the mass of those, whom as patriots they must have wished most to instruct. In works of pure science and learned criticism, this is of the less consequence; for, being independent of sentiment, it matters less how remote from real life the symbols, by which ideas are conveyed. But when we see a writer like Milton, who, as much as any other whom England ever produced, was a master of the music of his native tongue, who, besides all the eloquence of thought and imagery, knew better than any other man how to clothe them, according to his own beautiful expression,

> In notes, with many a winding bout
> Of linked sweetness, long drawn out,
> With wanton heed and giddy cunning,
> The melting voice through mazes running,
> Untwisting all the chains that tie
> The hidden soul of harmony;

when we see a master of English eloquence thus gifted, choosing a dead language, the dialect of the closet, a tongue without an echo from the hearts of the people, as the vehicle of his defence of that people's rights ; asserting the cause of Englishmen in the language, as it may be truly called, of Cicero ; we can only measure the incongruity, by reflecting what Cicero would himself have thought and felt, if called to defend the cause of Roman freedom, not in the language of the Roman citizen, but in that of the Chaldeans or Assyrians, or some people still farther remote in the history of the world. There is little doubt that the prevalence of the Latin language among modern scholars, was a great cause not only of the slow progress of letters among the lower ranks, but of the stiffness and constraint formerly visible in the vernacular style of most scholars themselves. That the reformation in religion advanced with such rapidity, is doubtless in no small degree to be attributed to the translations of the Scriptures, and the use of liturgies in the modern tongues. While the preservation in England of a strange language,—I will not sin against the majesty of Rome by calling it Latin,—in legal acts, down to so late a period as 1730, may be one cause, that the practical forms of administering justice have not been made to keep pace with the popular views that have triumphed in other things. With the erection of popular institutions under Cromwell, among various other legal improvements,* very many of which were speedily adopted by our plain dealing forefathers, the records of the law were ordered to be kept in English ; 'A novelty,' says the learned commentator on the English laws, 'which at the restoration was no longer continued, practisers having found it very difficult to express themselves so concisely or significantly in any other language but Latin.'†

Nor are the other remedies more efficacious, which have been attempted for the evil of a multiplicity of tongues. Something is done by translations, and something by the acquisition of foreign languages. But that no effectual transfusion of the higher literature of a country can take place, in the way of translation is matter of notoriety ; and it is a remark of one of the few, who could have courage to make such a remark, Madame de Stael, that it is impossible fully to comprehend the literature of a foreign tongue. The general preference given to Young's Night Thoughts and Ossian over all the other English poets, in many parts of the continent of Europe, seems to confirm the justice of the observation.

There is, indeed, an influence of exalted genius co-extensive with the earth. Something of its power will be felt, in spite of the obstacles of different languages, remote regions, and other times. But its true empire and its lawful sway, are at home, and over the hearts of kindred men. A charm, which nothing can borrow, nothing counterfeit, nothing dispense with, resides in the simple sound of our mother tongue. Not analyzed, nor reasoned upon, it unites the earliest associations of life with the maturest conceptions

* See a number of them in Lord Somers' Tracts, vol. I.
† Blackstone's Commentaries, vol. III. 422.

of the understanding. The heart is willing to open all its avenues to the language, in which its infantile caprices were soothed ; and by the curious efficacy of the principle of association, it is this echo from the feeble dawn of life, which gives to eloquence much of its manly power, and to poetry much of its divine charm. This feeling of the music of our native language is the first intellectual capacity that is developed in children, and when by age or misfortune,

> ' the ear is all unstrung,
> Still, still, it loves the lowland tongue.'

What a noble prospect is opened in this connexion for the circulation of thought and sentiment in our country! Instead of that multiplicity of dialect, by which mental communication and sympathy are cut off in the old world, a continually expanding realm is opened and opening to American intellect, in the community of our language, throughout the wide spread settlements of this continent. The enginery of the press will here, for the first time, be brought to bear, with all its mighty power, on the minds and hearts of men, in exchanging intelligence, and circulating opinions, unchecked by diversity of language, over an empire more extensive than the whole of Europe.

And this community of language, all important as it is, is but a part of the manifold brotherhood, which unites and will unite the growing millions of America. In Europe, the work of international alienation, which begins in diversity of language, is carried on and consummated by diversity of government, institutions, national descent, and national prejudices. In crossing the principal rivers, channels, and mountains, in that quarter of the world, you are met, not only by new tongues, but by new forms of government, new associations of ancestry, new and generally hostile objects of national boast and pride. While on the other hand, throughout the vast regions included within the limits of our Republic, not only the same language, but the same laws, the same national government, the same republican institutions, and a common ancestral association prevail, and will diffuse themselves. Mankind will here exist, move, and act in a kindred mass, such as was never before congregated on the earth's surface. The necessary consequences of such

a cause overpower the imagination.   What would be the effect on
the intellectual state of Europe, at the present day, were all her
nations and tribes amalgamated into one vast empire, speaking the
same tongue, united into one political system, and that a free one,
and opening one broad unobstructed pathway for the interchange
of thought and feeling, from Lisbon to Archangel?   If effects are
to bear a constant proportion to their causes ; if the energy of
thought is to be commensurate with the masses which prompt it,
and the masses it must penetrate ; if eloquence is to grow in fervor
with the weight of the interests it is to plead, and the grandeur of
the assemblies it addresses ; if efforts rise with the glory that is to
crown them ; in a word, if the faculties of the human mind, as we
firmly believe, are capable of tension and achievement altogether
indefinite ;

Nil actum reputans, dum quid superesset agendum,

then it is not too much to say, that a new era will open on the
intellectual world, in the fulfilment of our country's destinies.   By
the sovereign efficacy of the partition of powers between the
national and state governments, in virtue of which the national
government is relieved from all the odium of internal administration, and the state governments are spared the conflicts of foreign
politics, all bounds seem removed from the possible extension of
our country, but the geographical limits of the continent.   Instead
of growing cumbrous, as it increases in size, there never was a
moment since the first settlement in Virginia, when the political
system of America moved with so firm and bold a step as at the
present day.   If there is any faith in our country's auspices, this
great continent, in no remote futurity, will be filled up with a
homogeneous population ; with the mightiest kindred people known
in history ; our language will acquire an extension, which no other
ever possessed ; and the empire of the mind, with nothing to resist
its sway, will attain an expansion, of which as yet we can but
partly conceive.   The vision is too magnificent to be fully borne ;
—a mass of two or three hundred millions, not chained to the oar
like the same number in China, by a brutalizing despotism, but
held in their several orbits of nation and state, by the grand representative attraction ; bringing to bear on every point the concen-

trated energy of such a host; calling into competition so many minds; uniting into one great national feeling the hearts of so many freemen; all to be guided, persuaded, moved, and swayed, by the master spirits of the time!

III. Let me not be told that this is a chimerical imagination of a future indefinitely removed; let me not hear repeated the ribaldry of an anticipation of ' two thousand years,'—of a vision that requires for its fulfilment a length of ages beyond the grasp of any reasonable computation. It is the last point of peculiarity in our condition, to which I invite your attention as affecting the progress of intellect, that the country is growing with a *rapidity* hitherto entirely without example in the world. For the two hundred years of our existence, the population has doubled itself, in periods of less than a quarter of a century. In the infancy of the country, and while our numbers remained within the limits of a youthful colony, a progress so rapid as this, however important in the principle of growth disclosed, was not yet a circumstance strongly to fix the attention. But arrived at a population of ten millions, it is a fact of the most overpowering interest, that, within less than twenty-five years, these ten millions will have swelled to twenty; that the younger members of this audience will be citizens of the largest civilized state on earth; that in a few years more than one century, the American population will equal the fabulous numbers of the Chinese empire. This rate of increase has already produced the most striking phenomena. A few weeks after the opening of the Revolutionary drama at Lexington, the momentous intelligence, that the first blood was spilt, reached a party of hunters beyond the Alleghanies, who had wandered far into the western wilderness. In prophetic commemoration of the glorious event, they gave the name of Lexington to the spot of their encampment in the woods. That spot is now the capital of a state larger than Massachusetts; from which, in the language of one of her own citizens, whose eloquence is the ornament of his country, the tide of emigration still farther westward is more fully pouring than from any other in the Union.*

* Mr Clay's Speech on Internal Improvement.

I need not say that this astonishing increase of numbers, is by
no means the limit and measure of our country's growth. Arts,
agriculture, all the great national interests, all the sources of national wealth, are growing in a ratio still more rapid. In our cities
the intensest activity is apparent; in the country every spring of
prosperity, from the smallest improvement in husbandry to the
construction of canals and rail-roads across the continent, is in
vigorous action. Abroad, our vessels are beating the pathways of
the ocean white; on the inland frontier, the nation is journeying
on, like a healthy giant, with a pace more like romance than
reality.

These facts, and thousands like them, form one of those
peculiarities in our country's condition, which will have the most
powerful influence on the minds of its children. The population
of several states of Europe has reached its term. In some it is
declining, in some stationary; and in the most prosperous, under
the extraordinary impulse of the last part of the eighteenth century, it doubles itself but about once in seventy-five years. In
consequence of this, the process of social transmission is heavy and
slow. Men, not adventitiously favored, come late into life, and
the best years of existence are exhausted in languishing competition.
The man grows up, and in the stern language of one of their most
renowned economists,* finds no cover laid for him at Nature's table.
The smallest official provision is a boon, at which great minds are
not ashamed to grasp; the assurance of the most frugal subsistence
commands the brightest talents and the most laborious studies;
poor wages pay for the unremitted labor of the most curious hands;
and it is the smallest part of the population only that is within the
reach even of these humiliating springs of action. We need not
labor to contrast this state of things with the teeming growth and
noble expansion of all our institutions and resources. Instead of
being shut up, as it were, in the prison of a stationary, or a very
slowly progressive community, the emulation of our countrymen is
drawn out and tempted on, by a horizon constantly receding before
them. New nations of kindred freemen are springing up in successive periods, shorter even than the active portion of the life of

* Mr Malthus.

man. 'While we spend our time,' says Burke on this topic, 'in deliberating on the mode of governing two millions in America, we shall find we have millions more to manage.'* Many individuals are in this house, who were arrived at years of discretion when these words of Burke were uttered, and the two millions, which Great Britain was then to manage, have grown into ten, exceedingly unmanageable. The most affecting view of this subject is, that it puts it in the power of the wise, and good, and great, to gather, while they live, the ripest fruits of their labors. Where, in human history is to be found a contrast like that, which the last fifty years have crowded into the lives of those favored men, who raising their hands or their voices, when our little bands were led out to the perilous conflict with one of the most powerful empires on earth, have lived to be crowned with the highest honors of the Republic, which they established? Honor to their grey hairs, and peace and serenity to the evening of their eventful days !

Though it may never again be the fortune of our country to bring within the compass of half a century a contrast so dazzling as this, yet in its grand and steady progress, the career of duty and usefulness will be run by all its children, under a constantly increasing excitement. The voice, which, in the morning of life, shall awaken the patriotic sympathy of the land, will be echoed back by a community, incalculably swelled in all its proportions, before that voice shall be hushed in death. The writer, by whom the noble features of our scenery shall be sketched with a glowing pencil, the traits of our romantic early history gathered up with filial zeal, and the peculiarities of our character seized with delicate perception, cannot mount so entirely and rapidly to success, but that ten years will add new millions to the numbers of his readers. The American statesman, the orator, whose voice is already heard in its supremacy, from Florida to Maine, whose intellectual empire already extends beyond the limits of Alexander's, has yet new states and new nations starting into being, the willing tributaries to his sway.

This march of our population westward has been attended with consequences in some degree novel, in the history of the human

* Speech on Conciliation with America, March 22, 1775.

4

mind. It is a fact somewhat difficult of explanation, that the
refinement of the ancient nations seemed almost wholly devoid of
an elastic and expansive principle. The arts of Greece were
enchained to her islands and her coasts; they did not penetrate the
interior, at least not in every direction. The language and literature of Athens were as much unknown, to the north of Pindus, at
a distance of two hundred miles from the capital of Grecian refinement, as they were in Scythia. Thrace, whose mountain tops
may almost be seen from the porch of the temple of Minerva at
Sunium, was the proverbial abode of barbarism. Though the
colonies of Greece were scattered on the coasts of Italy, of France,
of Spain, and of Africa, no extension of their population far into
the interior took place, and the arts did not penetrate beyond the
walls of the cities, where they were cultivated. How different is
the picture of the diffusion of the arts and improvements of civilization, from the coast to the interior of America! Population
advances westward with a rapidity, which numbers may describe
indeed, but cannot represent, with any vivacity, to the mind. The
wilderness, which one year is impassable, is traversed the next by
the caravans of the industrious emigrants, who go to follow the
setting sun, with the language, the institutions, and the arts of
civilized life. It is not the irruption of wild barbarians, sent to
visit the wrath of God on a degenerate empire; it is not the inroad
of disciplined banditti, marshalled by the intrigues of ministers
and kings. It is the human family, led out to possess its broad
patrimony. The states and nations, which are springing up in the
valley of the Missouri, are bound to us, by the dearest ties of a
common language, a common government, and a common descent.
Before New England can look with coldness on their rising
myriads, she must forget that some of the best of her own blood
is beating in their veins; that her hardy children, with their axes
on their shoulders, have been literally among the pioneers in this
march of humanity; that young as she is, she has become the
mother of populous states. What generous mind would sacrifice
to a selfish preservation of local preponderance, the delight of
beholding civilized nations rising up in the desert; and the language, the manners, the institutions, to which he has been reared,
carried with his household gods to the foot of the Rocky Moun-

tains? Who can forget that this extension of our territorial limits is the extension of the empire of all we hold dear; of our laws, of our character, of the memory of our ancestors, of the great achievements in our history? Whithersoever the sons of the thirteen states shall wander, to southern or western climes, they will send back their hearts to the rocky shores, the battle fields, and the intrepid councils of the Atlantic coast. These are placed beyond the reach of vicissitude. They have become already matter of history, of poetry, of eloquence:

> The love, where death has set his seal,
> Nor age can chill, nor rival steal,
> Nor falsehood disavow.

Divisions may spring up, ill blood may burn, parties be formed, and interests may seem to clash; but the great bonds of the nation are linked to what is passed. The deeds of the great men, to whom this country owes its origin and growth, are a patrimony, I know, of which its children will never deprive themselves. As long as the Mississippi and the Missouri shall flow, those men and those deeds will be remembered on their banks. The sceptre of government may go where it will; but that of patriotic feeling can never depart from Judah. In all that mighty region, which is drained by the Missouri and its tributary streams—the valley co-extensive with the temperate zone—will there be, as long as the name of America shall last, a father, that will not take his children on his knee and recount to them the events of the twenty-second of December, the nineteenth of April, the seventeenth of June, and the fourth of July?

This then is the theatre, on which the intellect of America is to appear, and such the motives to its exertion; such the mass to be influenced by its energies, such the crowd to witness its efforts, such the glory to crown its success. If I err, in this happy vision of my country's fortunes, I thank God for an error so animating. If this be false, may I never know the truth. Never may you, my friends, be under any other feeling, than that a great, a growing, an immeasurably expanding country is calling upon you for your best services. The name and character of our Alma Mater have already been carried by some of our brethren thousands of miles from her venerable walls; and thousands of miles still farther westward, the communities of kindred men are fast gathering, whose minds and hearts will act in sympathy with yours.

The most powerful motives call on us, as scholars, for those efforts, which our common country demands of all her children. Most of us are of that class, who owe whatever of knowledge has shone into our minds, to the free and popular institutions of our native land. There are few of us, who may not be permitted to boast, that we have been reared in an honest poverty or a frugal competence, and owe every thing to those means of education, which are equally open to all. We are summoned to new energy and zeal by the high nature of the experiment we are appointed in Providence to make, and the grandeur of the theatre on which it is to be performed. When the old world afforded no longer any hope, it pleased Heaven to open this last refuge of humanity. The attempt has begun, and is going on, far from foreign corruption, on the broadest scale, and under the most benignant prospects; and it certainly rests with us to solve the great problem in human society, to settle, and that forever, the momentous question— whether mankind can be trusted with a purely popular system? One might almost think, without extravagance, that the departed wise and good of all places and times, are looking down from their happy seats to witness what shall now be done by us; that they who lavished their treasures and their blood of old, who labored and suffered, who spake and wrote, who fought and perished, in the one great cause of Freedom and Truth, are now hanging from their orbs on high, over the last solemn experiment of humanity. As I have wandered over the spots, once the scene of their labors, and mused among the prostrate columns of their Senate Houses and Forums, I have seemed almost to hear a voice from the tombs of departed ages; from the sepulchres of the nations, which died before the sight. They exhort us, they adjure us to be faithful to our trust. They implore us, by the long trials of struggling humanity, by the blessed memory of the departed; by the dear faith, which has been plighted by pure hands, to the holy cause of truth and man; by the awful secrets of the prison houses, where the sons of freedom have been immured; by the noble heads which have been brought to the block; by the wrecks of time, by the eloquent ruins of nations, they conjure us not to quench the light which is rising on the world. Greece cries to us, by the convulsed lips of her poisoned, dying Demosthenes; and Rome pleads with us, in the mute persuasion of her mangled Tully. They address us each and all in the glorious language of Milton, to one, who might have canonized his memory in the hearts of the friends of liberty, but who did most shamefully betray the cause: 'Reverere tantam de te expectationem, spem patriæ de te unicam. Reverere vultus et vulnera tot fortium virorum, quotquot pro libertate tam strenue decertârunt, manes etiam eorum qui in ipso certamine occubuerunt. Reverere exterarum quoque civitatum existimation-em de te atque sermones; quantas res de libertate nostrâ tam fortiter partâ, de nostrâ republicâ tam gloriose exortâ sibi polliceantur; quæ si tam cito quasi aborta evanuerit, profecto nihil æque dedecorosum huic genti atque periculosum fuerit.'*

Yes, my friends, such is the exhortation which calls on us to exert our powers, to employ our time, and consecrate our labors in the cause of our native land. When we engage in that solemn study, the history of our race; when we survey the progress of man, from his cradle in the East to these limits of his wandering; when we behold him forever flying westward from civil and religious thraldom, over mountains and seas, seeking rest and finding none, but still pursuing the flying bow of promise, to the glittering hills which it spans in Hesperian climes, we cannot but exclaim with Bishop Berkeley, the generous prelate of England, who bestowed his benefactions, as well as blessings, on our country;

> Westward the Star of Empire takes its way;
> The four first acts already past,
> The fifth shall close the drama with the day;
> Time's noblest offspring is the last.

In that high romance, if romance it be, in which the great minds of antiquity sketched the fortunes of the ages to come, they pictured to themselves a favored region beyond the ocean; a land of equal laws and happy men. The primitive poets beheld it in the islands of the blest; the Doric bards fancied it in the Hyper-

* Milton's Defensio Secunda.

borean regions ; the sage of the academy placed it in the lost
Atlantis ; and even the sterner spirit of Seneca could discern a
fairer abode of humanity, in distant regions then unknown. We
look back upon these uninspired productions, and almost recoil
from the obligation they imply. By us must these fair visions be
realized, by us must be fulfilled these high visions, which burst in
trying hours upon the longing hearts of the champions of truth.
There are no more continents or worlds to be revealed ; Atlantis
hath arisen from the ocean, the farthest Thule is reached, there
are no more retreats beyond the sea, no more discoveries, no more
hopes.

Here then a mighty work is to be fulfilled, or never, by the race
of mortals. The *man*, who looks with tenderness on the sufferings
of good men in other times ; the *descendant of the pilgrims*, who
cherishes the memory of his fathers ; the *patriot*, who feels an
honest glow at the majesty of the system of which he is a member ;
the *scholar*, who beholds with rapture the long sealed book of un-
prejudiced truth opened for all to read ; these are they, by whom
these auspices are to be accomplished. Yes, brethren, it is by the
intellect of the country, that the mighty mass is to be inspired ;
that its parts are to communicate and sympathize with each other,
its bright progress to be adorned with becoming refinements, its
strong sense uttered, its character reflected, its feelings interpreted
to its own children, to other regions, and to after ages.

Meantime, the years are rapidly passing away and gathering
importance in their course. With the present year, will be completed the half century from that most important era in human
history, the commencement of our revolutionary war. The jubilee of our national existence is at hand. The space of time, that
has elapsed since that momentous date, has laid down in the dust,
which the blood of many of them had already hallowed, most of
the great men to whom, under Providence, we owe our national
existence and privileges. A few still survive among us, to reap
the rich fruits of their labors and sufferings ; and ONE has yielded
himself to the united voice of a people, and returned in his age, to
receive the gratitude of the nation, to whom he devoted his youth.
It is recorded on the pages of American history, that when this

friend of our country applied to our commissioners at Paris, in 1776, for a passage in the first ship they should despatch to America, they were obliged to answer him, (so low and abject was then our dear native land,) that they possessed not the means nor the credit sufficient for providing a single vessel, in all the ports of France. 'Then,' exclaimed the youthful hero, 'I will provide my own;' and it is a literal fact, that when all America was too poor to offer him so much as a passage to her shores, he left, in his tender youth, the bosom of home, of happiness, of wealth, of rank, to plunge in the dust and blood of our inauspicious struggle!

Welcome, friend of our fathers, to our shores! Happy are our eyes that behold those venerable features. Enjoy a triumph, such as never conqueror nor monarch enjoyed, the assurance that throughout America, there is not a bosom, which does not beat with joy and gratitude at the sound of your name. You have already met and saluted, or will soon meet, the few that remain, of the ardent patriots, prudent counsellors, and brave warriors, with whom you were associated in achieving our liberty. But you have looked round in vain for the faces of many, who would have lived years of pleasure on a day like this, with their old companion in arms and brother in peril. Lincoln, and Greene, and Knox, and and Hamilton, are gone; the heroes of Saratoga and Yorktown have fallen, before the only foe they could not meet. Above all, the first of heroes and of men, the friend of your youth, the more than friend of his country, rests in the bosom of the soil he redeemed. On the banks of his Potomac, he lies in glory and peace. You will revisit the hospitable shades of Mount Vernon, but him whom you venerated as we did, you will not meet at its door. His voice of consolation, which reached you in the Austrian dungeons, cannot now break its silence, to bid you welcome to his own roof. But the grateful children of America will bid you welcome, in his name. Welcome, thrice welcome to our shores; and whithersoever throughout the limits of the continent your course shall take you, the ear that hears you shall bless you, the eye that sees you shall bear witness to you, and every tongue exclaim, with heartfelt joy, welcome, welcome La Fayette!

ORATION

DELIVERED AT PLYMOUTH, DECEMBER 22, 1824.

———

AMIDST all the proud and grateful feelings, which the return of this anniversary must inspire, in the bosom of every child of New-England, a deep solicitude oppresses me, lest I should fail in doing justice to the men, to the day, and to the events, which we are met to commemorate. This solicitude, I would hope, is no mere personal feeling. I should be unworthy to address you, on this occasion, could I, from the selfish desire of winning your applause, devote any of the moments of this consecrated day to any cold speculations, however ingenious or original. Gladly would I give utterance to the most familiar commonplaces, could I be so happy in doing it, as to excite or strengthen the feelings, which belong to the time and the place. Gladly would I repeat to you those sentiments, which a hundred times have been uttered and welcomed on this anniversary; sentiments, whose truth does not change in the change of circumstances; whose power does not wear out with time. It is not by pompous epithets or lively antithesis, that the exploits of the pilgrims are to be set forth by their children. We can only do this worthily, by repeating the plain tale of their sufferings, by dwelling on the circumstances under which their memorable enterprise was executed, and by cherishing and breathing that spirit, which led them across the ocean, and guided them to the spot where we stand. We need no voice of artificial rhetoric to celebrate their names. The bleak and deathlike desolation of nature proclaims, with touching eloquence, the fortitude and patience of the meek adventurers. On the bare and wintry fields around us, their exploits are written in characters, which will last, and tell their tale to posterity, when brass and marble have crumbled into dust.

The occasion which has called us together is certainly one, to which no parallel exists in the history of the world. Other countries, and our own also, have their national festivals. They commemorate the birth-days of their illustrious children; they celebrate the foundation of important institutions: momentous events, victories, reformations, revolutions awaken, on their anniversaries, the grateful and patriotic feelings of posterity. But we commemorate the birth-day of all New-England; the foundation, not of one institution, but of all the institutions, the settlements, the establishments, the communities, the societies, the improvements, comprehended within our broad and happy borders.

Were it only as an act of rare adventure; were it a trait in foreign, or ancient history; we should fix upon the achievement of our fathers, as one of the noblest deeds, in the annals of the world. Were we attracted to it, by no other principle than that sympathy we feel, in all the fortunes of our race, it could lose nothing,—it must gain,—in the contrast, with whatever history or tradition has preserved to us of the wanderings and settlements of the tribes of man. A continent for the first time, effectually explored; a vast ocean traversed by men, women, and children, voluntarily exiling themselves from the fairest portions of the old world; and a great nation grown up, in the space of two centuries, on the foundations so perilously laid, by this pious band: —point me to the record, to the tradition, nay to the fiction of anything, that can enter into competition with it. It is the language not of exaggeration, but of truth and soberness to say, that there is nothing in the accounts of Phenician, of Grecian, or of Roman Colonization, that can stand in the comparison.

What new importance then, does not the achievement acquire for us, when we consider that it was the deed of our fathers; that this grand undertaking was accomplished on the spot where we dwell; that the mighty region they explored is our native land; that the unrivalled enterprise they displayed, is not merely a fact proposed to our admiration, but is the source of our being; that their cruel hardships are the spring of our prosperity; that their

5

weary banishment gave us a home; that to their separation from everything which is dear and pleasant in life, we owe all the comforts, the blessings, the privileges, which make our lot the envy of mankind!

These are the well known titles of our ancestors to our gratitude and veneration.

But there seems to me this peculiarity in the nature of their enterprise, that its grand and beneficent consequences are, with the lapse of time, constantly unfolding themselves, in an extent, and to a magnitude, beyond the reach of the most sanguine promise. In the frail condition of human affairs, we have generally nothing left us to commemorate, but heroic acts of valor, which have resulted in no permanent effect; great characters, that have struggled nobly, but in vain, against the disastrous combinations of the times; and brilliant triumphs of truth and justice, rendered unproductive, by the complication of untoward and opposite events. It is almost the peculiar character of the enterprise of our pilgrim forefathers,— successful indeed in its outset,—that it has been more and more successful, at every subsequent point in the line of time. Accomplishing all they projected; what they projected was the least part of what has been accomplished. Forming a design, in itself grand, bold, and even appalling, for the risks and sacrifices it required; the fulfilment of that design is the least thing, which in the steady progress of events, has flowed from their counsels and their efforts. Did they propose to themselves a refuge beyond the sea, from the religious and political tyranny of Europe? They achieved not that alone, but they have opened a wide asylum to all the victims of tyranny throughout the world. We ourselves have seen the statesmen, the generals, the kings of the elder world, flying for protection to the shadow of our institutions. Did they look for a retired spot, inoffensive for its obscurity, and safe in its remoteness, where the little church of Leyden might enjoy the freedom of conscience? Behold the mighty regions over which, in peaceful conquest,—*victoria sine clade*,—they have borne the banners of the cross. Did they seek, beneath the protection of trading charters, to prosecute a frugal commerce in reimbursement of the expenses of their humble establishment? The fleets and navies of their descendants are on the farthest ocean; and the wealth of the

Indies is now wafted with every tide to the coasts, where with hook and line they painfully gathered up their little adventures. In short, did they, in their brightest and most sanguine moments, contemplate a thrifty, loyal, and prosperous colony, portioned off, like a younger son of the imperial household, to an humble and dutiful distance? Behold the spectacle of an independent and powerful Republic, founded on the shores where some of those are but lately deceased, who saw the first-born of the pilgrims!

And shall we stop here? Is the tale now told; is the contrast now complete; are our destinies all fulfilled; are we declining, or even stationary? My friends, I tell you, we have but begun; we are in the very morning of our days; our numbers are but an unit; our national resources but a pittance; our hopeful achievements in the political, the social, and the intellectual nature, are but the rudiments of what the children of the Pilgrims must yet attain. If there is anything certain in the principles of human and social progress; if there is anything clear in the deductions from past history; if there is any, the least, reliance to be placed on the conclusions of reason, in regard to the nature of man,—the existing spectacle of our country's growth, magnificent as it is, does not suggest even an idea of what it must be. I dare adventure the prediction, that he who shall stand where I stand, two centuries hence, and look back on our present condition from a distance equal to that from which we contemplate the first settlement of the Pilgrims, will sketch a contrast far more astonishing; and will speak of our times as the day of small things, in stronger and juster language, than any in which we can depict the poverty and wants of our fathers.

But we ought to consecrate this day, not to the promise, nor even the present blessings of our condition, except so far as these are connected with the memory of the Pilgrims. The twenty-second of December belongs to them; and we ought, in consistency, to direct our thoughts to the circumstances, under which their most astonishing enterprise was achieved. I shall hope to have contributed my mite towards our happy celebration, if I can succeed in pointing out a few of those circumstances of the first emigration to our country, and particularly of the first emigration to New-England, from which, under a kind Providence, has flowed not only the immediate success of the undertaking, but the astonishing train of consequences auspicious to the cause of liberty, humanity, and truth.

I. Our forefathers regarded, with natural terror, the passage of the mighty deep. Navigation, notwithstanding the great advances which it had made in the sixteenth century, was yet, comparatively speaking, in its infancy. The very fact, that voyages of great length and hazard were successfully attempted in small vessels, (a fact, which, on first view, might seem to show a high degree of perfection in the art,) in reality proves that it was as yet but imperfectly understood. That the great Columbus should put to sea, for the discovery of a new passage across the Western Ocean to India, with two out of three vessels unprovided with decks, may indeed be considered the effect, not of ignorance of the art of navigation, but of bitter necessity. But that Sir Francis Drake, near a hundred years afterwards, the first naval commander who ever sailed round the earth, enjoying the advantage of the royal patronage, and aided by the fruits of no little personal experience, should have embarked on his voyage of circumnavigation, with five vessels, of which the largest was of one hundred, and the smallest of fifteen tons,* must needs be regarded as proof, that the art of navigation, in the generation preceding our ancestors, had not reached that point, where the skilful adaptation of means to ends supersedes the necessity of extraordinary intrepidity, aided by not less extraordinary good fortune. It was therefore the first obstacle, which presented itself to the project of the Pilgrims, that it was to be carried into execution, across the ocean, which separates our continent from the rest of the world. Notwithstanding, however, this circumstance, and the natural effect it must have had on their minds, there is no doubt, that it is one of those features in our natural situation, to which America is indebted, not merely for the immediate success of the enterprise of settlement, but for much of its subsequent prosperity.

The rest of the world, though nominally divided into three continents, in reality consists of but one. Europe, Asia, and Africa are separated by no natural barriers, which it has not been easy in every age, for an ambitious invader to pass; and apart from this

* Biographia Britannica, III. 1782.

first consequence of the juxtaposition of their various regions, a sympathy of principle and feeling, of policy and passion, may be propagated, at all times, even to their remote and seemingly inaccessible communities. The consequence has been, on the whole, unfavorable to social progress. The extent of country inhabited or rather infested by barbarous tribes, has generally far outweighed the civilized portions; and more than once, in the history of the world, refinement, learning, arts, laws, and religion, with the wealth and prosperity they have created, have been utterly swept away, and the hands moved back on the dial plate of time, in consequence of the irruption of savage hordes into civilized regions. Were the early annals of the East as amply preserved as those of the Roman empire, they would probably present us with accounts of revolutions, on the Nile and the Euphrates, as disastrous as those, by which the civilized world was shaken, in the first centuries of the Christian era. Till an ocean interposes its mighty barrier, no citadel of freedom or truth has been long maintained. The magnificent temples of Egypt were demolished in the sixth century before our Saviour, by the hordes, which Cambyses had collected from the *steppes* of Central Asia. The vineyards of Burgundy were wasted in the third century of our era, by roving savages from beyond the Caucasus. In the eleventh century, Gengis Khan and his Tartars swept Europe and Asia from the Baltic to the China Sea. And Ionia and Attica, the gardens of Greece, are still, under the eyes of the leading Christian powers of Europe, beset by remorseless barbarians, whose fathers issued a few centuries ago, from the Altai Mountains.

Nor is it the barbarians alone, who have been tempted by this facility of communication, to a career of boundless plunder. The Alexanders and the Cæsars, the Charlemagnes and the Napoleons, the founders of great empires, the aspirers at universal monarchy, have been enabled, by the same circumstance, to turn the annals of mankind into a tale of war and misery. When we descend to the scrutiny of single events, we find that the nations, who have most frequently and most immediately suffered, have been those most easily approached and overrun;—and that those who have longest or most uniformly maintained their independence, have done it by virtue of lofty mountains, wide rivers, or the surrounding sea.

In this state of things, the three united continents of the old world do not contain a single spot, where any grand scheme of human improvement could be attempted, with a prospect of fair experiment and full success, because there is no spot safe from foreign interference; and no member of the general system so insignificant, that his motions are not watched with jealousy by all the rest. The welfare and progress of man in the most favored region, instead of proceeding in a free and natural course, dependent on the organization and condition of that region alone, can only reach the point, which may be practicable in the general result of an immensely complicated system, made up of a thousand jarring members.

Our country accordingly opened, at the time of its settlement, and still opens, a new theatre of human development.—Notwithstanding the prodigious extent of commercial intercourse, and the wide grasp of naval power among modern states, and their partial effect in bringing us into the political system of Europe, we are yet essentially strangers to it;—placed at a distance, which retards, and for every injurious purpose, neutralizes all peaceful communication, and defies all hostile approach. To this it was owing that so little was here felt of the convulsions of the civil wars, which followed in England soon after the expulsion of our fathers. To this, in a more general view, we are indebted for many of our peculiarities as a nation, for our steady colonial growth, our establishment of independence, our escape amidst the political storms, which, during the last thirty years, have shaken the empires of the earth.—To this we shall still be indebted, and more and more indebted, with the progress of our country, for the originality and stability of national character. Hitherto the political effects of our seclusion, behind the mighty veil of waters, have been the most important. Now, that our political foundations are firmly laid; that the work of settlement, of colonization, of independence, and of union is all done, and happily done, we shall reap, in other forms, the salutary fruits of our remoteness from the centres of foreign opinion and feeling.

I say not this in direct disparagement of foreign states; their institutions are doubtless as good, in many cases, as the condition of things now admits; or when at the worst, could not be remedied by any one body, nor by any one generation of men. But without disparaging foreign institutions, we may be allowed to prefer our own; to assert their excellence, to seek to maintain them on their original foundations, on their true principles, and in their unmingled purity. That great word of Independence, which, if first uttered in 1776, was most auspiciously anticipated in 1620, comprehends much more than a mere absence of foreign jurisdiction. I could almost say, that if it rested there, it would scarcely be worth asserting. In every noble, in every true acceptation, it implies not merely an American government, but an American character, an American feeling. To the formation of these, nothing will more powerfully contribute than our geographical distance from other parts of the world.

In these views there is nothing unsocial; nothing hostile to a friendly and improving connexion of distant regions with each other, or to the profitable interchange of the commodities, which a bountiful Providence has variously scattered over the earth. For these and all other desirable ends, the perfection, to which the art of navigation is brought, affords abundant means of conquering the obstacles of distance. At this moment, the reward of American skill is paid by the chieftains of inner Tartary, wrapped up in the furs, which in our voyages of circumnavigation, we have collected on the North Western Coast of our Continent. The interest on American capital is paid by the haughty viziers of Anatolia, whose opium is cultivated and gathered for our merchants. The wages of American labor are paid by the princes of Hindostan, whose plantations of indigo depend on us for a portion of their market. While ambition and policy, by intrigue and bloodshed, are contesting the possession of a few square miles of territory, our peaceful commerce has silently extended its jurisdiction from island to island, from sea to sea, from continent to continent, till it holds the globe in its grasp.

But while no one can doubt the mutual advantages of a judiciously conducted commerce, or be insensible of the good, which has resulted to the cause of humanity, from the cultivation of a peaceful and friendly intercourse with other climes, it is yet beyond question, that the true principle of American policy, to which the whole spirit of our institutions, not less than the geographical features of the country, invites us, is *separation from Europe*. Next to UNION AT HOME, which ought to be called not so much the essential condition of our national existence, as our existence itself, separation from all other countries, is the great principle, by which we are to prosper. It is toward this that our efforts, public and private, ought to strain ; and we shall rise or decline in strength, improvement, and worth, as we observe or desert this principle. This is the voice of nature, which did not in vain disjoin our continent from the old world ; nor reserve it beyond the ocean for fifty centuries, only that it might become a common receptacle for the exploded principles, the degenerate examples, and the remediless corruptions of other states. This is the voice of our history, which traces every thing excellent in our character and prosperous in our fortunes, to dissent, nonconformity, departure, resistance, and revolution. This is taught us by the marked peculiarity, the wonderful novelty which, whether we will it or not, displays itself in our whole physical, political, and social existence.

And it is a matter of sincere congratulation, that, under the healthy operation of natural causes, very partially accelerated by legislation, the current of our pursuits and industry, without deserting its former channels, is throwing a broad and swelling branch into the interior. Foreign commerce, the natural employment of an enterprising people, whose population is accumulated on the seacoast, and whose neutral services were invited by a world in arms, is daily reverting to a condition of more equal participation among the various maritime states, and is in consequence becoming less productive to any one. While America remains, and will always remain, among the foremost commercial and naval states, an ample portion of our resources has already taken a new direction. We profited of the dissensions of Europe, which threw her trade into our hands. We are now profiting of the pacification of Europe, in the application to our own soil, our own mineral and vegetable products, our water courses and our general internal resources, of a part of the capital thus accumulated.

This circumstance is, in a general view, most gratifying ; inasmuch as it creates a new bond of mutual dependence, in the variety of our natural gifts, and in the mutual benefits rendered each other by the several sectional interests of the country. The progress is likely to be permanent and sure, because it has been mainly brought about in the natural order of things, and with little legislative interference. Within a few years what a happy change has taken place! The substantial clothing of our industrious classes is now the growth of the American soil, and the texture of the American loom; the music of the water-wheel is heard on the banks of our thousand rural streams; and enterprise and skill, with wealth, refinement, and prosperity in their train, having studded the seashore with populous cities, are making their great ' progress ' of improvement through the interior, and sowing towns and villages, as it were broadcast, through the country !

II. If our remote position be so important among the circumstances, which favored the enterprise of our fathers, and have favored the growth of their settlements, scarcely less so was the point of time at which those settlements were commenced.

When we cast our eyes over the annals of our race, we find them to be filled with a tale of various fortunes; the rise and fall of nations;—periods of light and darkness;—of great illumination, and of utter obscurity;—and of all intermediate degrees of intelligence, cultivation, and liberty. But in the seeming confusion of the narrative, our attention is arrested by three more conspicuous eras, at unequal distances in the lapse of ages.

In Egypt we still behold, on the banks of the Nile, the monuments of a polished age;—a period, no doubt, of high cultivation, and of great promise. Beneath the influence of causes, which are lost in the depth of antiquity, but which are doubtless connected with the debasing superstitions and political despotism, which prevailed in that country, this period passed away, and left scarce a trace of its existence, beyond the stupendous and mysterious structures,—the temples, the obelisks, and the pyramids,—which yet bear witness to an age of great power and cultivated art, and mock the curiosity of mankind by the records inscrutably carved on their surfaces.

Passing over an interval of one thousand years, we reach the second epoch of light and promise. With the progress of freedom

6

in Greece, that of the mind kept pace; and an age both of achievement and of hope succeeded, of which the influence is still felt in the world. But the greater part of mankind were too barbarous to improve by the example of this favored corner; and though the influence of its arts, letters, and civilization was wonderfully extensive and durable,—though it seemed to revive at the court of the Roman Cæsars, and still later, at that of the Arabian Caliphs, yet not resting on those popular institutions and popular principles, which can alone be permanent because alone natural, it slowly died away, and Europe and the world relapsed into barbarity.

The third great era of our race is the close of the fifteenth century. The use of the mariner's compass and the invention of the art of printing, had furnished the modern world, with two engines of improvement and civilization, either of which was far more efficacious than all united, known to antiquity. The reformation also, about this time, disengaged Christianity, itself one of the most powerful instruments of civilization, from those abuses, which had hitherto greatly impaired its beneficent influence on temporal affairs; and at this most chosen moment in the annals of the world, America was discovered.

It would not be difficult, by pursuing this analysis, to show that the very period, when the settlement of our coasts began, was peculiarly auspicious to the foundation of a new and hopeful system.

Religious reformation was the original principle, which kindled the zeal of our pilgrim fathers; as it has been so often acknowledged to be the master principle of the greatest movements in the modern world. The religions of Greece and Rome were portions of the political systems of these countries. The Scipios, the Crassuses, and Julius Cæsar himself, were high priests. It was, doubtless, owing in part to this example, that at an early period after the first introduction of Christianity, the heads of the church so entirely mistook the spirit of this religion, that, in imitation of the splendid idolatry, which was passing away, they aimed at a new combination of church and state, which received but too much countenance from the policy of Constantine. This abuse, with ever multiplying and aggravated calamitous consequences, endured, without any effectual check, till the first blow was aimed at the supremacy of the papal power, by Philip the Fair of France, in the fourteenth century, who laid the foundation of the liberties of the Gallican church, by what may be called the Catholic Reformation.

After an interval of two hundred years, this example was followed and improved upon by the Princes in Germany, who espoused the protestant reformation of Luther, and in a still more decisive manner by Henry the Eighth in England; at which period we may accordingly date the second great step in the march of religious liberty.

Much more, however, was yet to be effected toward the dissolution of the unnatural bond between Church and State. Hitherto a domestic was substituted for a foreign yoke, and the rights of private conscience had, perhaps, gained but little in the exchange. In the middle of the sixteenth century, and among the exiles, whom the tyranny of Queen Mary had driven to the free cities on the Rhine, the ever memorable sect of Puritans arose. On their return to England, in the reign of Queen Elizabeth, they strenuously opposed themselves to the erection and peculiarities of the English national church.

Nearly as we have now reached, both in simplicity of principle and point of time, to our pilgrim forefathers, there is one more purifying process to go through, one more generation to pass away. The major part of the Puritans themselves, while they rejected some of the forms, and disliked the organization of the English church, adhered in substance to the constitution of the Genevan church, and their descendants were willing, a century later, to accept of an establishment by law in Scotland.

It remained, therefore, to shake off the last badge of subjection, and take the last step in the progress of reform, by asserting the independence of each single church. This principle may be considered as firmly established, from the time of John Robinson, who may be called the father of the *Independent* churches. His own at Leyden was the chief of these, and fidelity to their principles was the motive of their departure from Holland, and the occasion of their settlement at Plymouth.

But all may not be disposed to unite, in so exact a specification of the beginning of the seventeenth century, as the period, when religious reform had reached its last perfection, and consequently, as the era most favorable to the establishment of a new and free state.   None, however, on a larger view of the subject, will be unwilling to allow, that this was the great age of general improvement.   It was the age, when the discoveries of the Spanish, Portuguese, and English navigators had begun to exert a stimulating influence on the world at large; and the old continent and the new, like the magnetic poles, commenced those momentous processes of attraction and repulsion, from which so much of the activity of both has since proceeded.   It was the period when the circulation of knowledge had become general; and books in all languages were in the hands of a very large class in every country. The history of Europe, in all its states, shows the extent and vehemence of the consequent fermentation.   With their new engines of improvement and new principles of right, the communities of men rushed forward in the course of reform; some with firmness and vigor, proportioned to the greatness of the object in view,—most with tumult and desperation, proportioned to the duration and magnitude of their injuries,—and none with entire success.   The most that was effected, in the most fortunate states, was a compromise between the new claims and the old abuses. Absolute kings stipulated to be no longer absolute; and free citizens preferred what they called petitions of right.   In this way, and after infinite struggles, a tolerable foundation for considerable practical liberty was laid on two principles, in the abstract false, as principles of government; that of acquiescence on the part of the sovereign, and prescription in favor of the people.   So firmly established are these principles, by consent of the statesmen of the freest country in Europe, as the best and only foundation of civil rights, that so late as the last years of the eighteenth century, a work of ingenuity seldom, of eloquence never, surpassed, was written by Mr Burke, to prove, that the people of England have not a right to appoint and to remove their rulers; and that if they ever had the right, they deliberately renounced it at what is called the glorious revolution of 1688, for themselves and their posterity forever.

The work of reform is of course rendered exceedingly difficult

in Europe, by the length of time for which great abuses have existed, and the extent to which these abuses are interwoven with
the whole system.   We cannot but regard it as the plain interposition of Providence, that, at the critical point of time, when the
most powerful springs of improvement were in operation, a chosen
company of pilgrims, who were actuated by these springs of improvement, in all their strength, who had purchased the privilege
of dissent at the high price of banishment from the civilized world,
and who, with the dust of their feet, had shaken off the antiquated
abuses and false principles, which had been accumulating for
thousands of years, came over to these distant, unoccupied shores.
I know not that the work of thorough reform could be safely trusted
to any other hands.   I can credit their disinterestedness, when
they maintain the equality of ranks ; for no rich forfeitures of
attainted lords await them in the wilderness.   I need not question
the sincerity with which they assert the rights of conscience ; for
the plundered treasures of an ancient hierarchy are not to seal
their doctrine.   They rested the edifice of their civil and religious
liberties on a foundation as pure as the snows around them.   Blessed be the spot, the only one on earth, where such a foundation
was ever laid !   Blessed be the spot, the only one on earth, where
man has attempted to establish the good, without beginning with the
sad, the odious, the often suspicious task of pulling down the bad !

III.   Under these auspices, the Pilgrims landed on the coast of
New-England.   They found it a region of moderate fertility,
offering an unsubdued wilderness to the hand of labor, with a
climate temperate indeed, but compared with that which they had
left, verging somewhat near to either extreme ; and a soil which
promised neither gold nor diamonds, nor any thing but what should
be gained from it by patient industry.   This was but a poor reality
for that dream of oriental luxury, with which America had filled
the imaginations of men: The visions of Indian wealth, of mines
of silver and gold, and fisheries of pearl, with which the Spanish
adventurers in Mexico and Peru had astonished the ears of Europe,
were but poorly fulfilled on the bleak, rocky, and sterile plains of
New-England.   No doubt, in the beginning of the settlement,
these circumstances operated unfavorably on the growth of the
colony.   In the nature of things, it is mostly adventurers, who

incline to leave their homes and native land, and risk the uncertainty of another hemisphere; and a climate and soil like ours furnished but little attraction to the adventuring class. Captain Smith, in his zeal to promote the growth of New-England, is at no little pains to show that the want of mineral treasures was amply compensated by the abundant fishery of the coast; and having sketched in strong colors the prosperity and wealth of the states of Holland, he adds, 'Divers, I know, may allege many other assistances, but this is the chiefest mine, and the sea the source of those silver streams of their virtue, which hath made them now the very miracle of industry, the only pattern of perfection for these affairs; and the benefit of fishing is that *primum mobile* that turns all their spheres to this height of plenty, strength, honor and exceeding great admiration.'*

While we smile at this overwrought panegyric on the primitive resource of our fathers, we cannot but acknowledge that it has foundation in truth. It is doubtless to the untempting qualities of our climate and soil, and the conditions of industry and frugality, on which alone the prosperity of the colony could be secured, that we are to look for a full share of the final success of the enterprise.

To this it is to be ascribed that the country itself was not preoccupied by a crowded population of savages, like the West India Islands and Mexico, who, placed upon a soil yielding almost spontaneously a superabundance of food, had multiplied into populous empires, and made a progress in the arts, which served no other purpose, than to give strength and permanence to some of the most frightful systems of despotism, that ever afflicted humanity; systems uniting all that is most horrible in depraved civilization and wild barbarity. The problem indeed is hard to be solved, in what way and by what steps a continent, possessed by savage tribes, is to be lawfully occupied and colonized by civilized man. But this question was divested of much of its practical difficulty by the scantiness of the native population, which our fathers found in New-England, and the migratory life to which the necessity of the chace reduced them. It is owing to this, that the annals of New-England exhibit no scenes like those which were acted in Hispaniola,

* Smith's Generall Historie, &c. Vol. II. p. 185, Richmond Edit.

in Mexico, and Peru ; no tragedies like those of Anacoana, of Guatimozin, and of Atahualpa ; no statesman like Bovadilla ; no heroes like Pizarro and Cortes ;

"No dark Ovando, no religious Boyle."

The qualities of our climate and soil enter largely in other ways into that natural basis, on which our prosperity and our freedom have been reared. It is these which distinguish the smiling aspect of our busy, thriving villages from the lucrative desolation of the sugar islands, and all the wide spread, undescribed, indescribable miseries of the colonial system of modern Europe, as it has existed beyond the barrier of these mighty oceans, in the unvisited, unprotected, and unavenged recesses of either India. We have had abundant reason to be contented with this austere sky, this hard, unyielding soil. Poor as it is, it has left us no cause to sigh for the luxuries of the tropics, nor to covet the mines of the southern regions of our hemisphere. Our rough and hardly subdued hill-sides and barren plains have produced us that, which neither ores, nor spices, nor sweets could purchase,—which would not spring in the richest gardens of the despotic East. The compact numbers and the strength, the general intelligence and the civilization, which, since the world began, were never exhibited beneath the sultry line, have been the precious product of this iron bound coast. The rocks and the sands, which would yield us neither the cane nor the coffee tree, have yielded us, not only an abundance and a growth in resources, rarely consistent with the treacherous profusion of tropical colonies, but the habits, the manners, the institutions, the industrious population, the schools and the churches, beyond all the wealth of all the Indies.

' Man is the nobler growth our soil supplies,
And souls are ripened in our northern skies.'

Describe to me a country rich in veins of the precious metals, that is traversed by good roads. Inform me of the convenience of bridges, where the rivers roll over golden sands. Tell me of a thrifty, prosperous village of freemen, in the miserable districts where every clod of the earth is kneaded up for diamonds, beneath the lash of the task-master. No, never! while the constitution,

not of states, but of human nature, remains the same; never, while
the laws, not of civil society, but of God are unrepealed, will there
be a hardy, virtuous, independent yeomanry, in regions where two
acres of untilled banana will feed a hundred men.   It is idle to call
that *food*, which can never feed a free, intelligent, industrious
population.   It is not food; it is dust; it is chaff; it is ashes;—there
is no nourishment in it, if it be not carefully sown, and painfully
reaped, by laborious freemen, on their own fee-simple acres.

IV. Nor ought we to omit to say, that if our forefathers found,
in the nature of the region to which they emigrated, the most favorable spot for the growth of a free and happy state, they themselves
sprang from the land, the best adapted to furnish the habits and
principles essential to the great undertaking.   In an age that speculates, and speculates to important purpose, on the races of fossil
animals, of which no living specimen has existed since the deluge,
and which compares, with curious criticism, the dialects of languages
which ceased to be spoken a thousand years ago, it cannot be called
idle to inquire, which of the different countries of modern Europe
possesses the qualities, that best adapt it to become the parent nation
of a new and free state.   I know not in fact, what more momentous question in human affairs could be asked, than that which
regards the most hopeful lineage of a collective empire.   But without engaging in so extensive a discussion, I may presume that there
is not one who hears me, that does not feel it a matter of congratulation and joy, that our fathers were Englishmen.

No character is perfect among nations, more than among men;
but it must needs be conceded, that after our own country, England is the most favored abode of liberty; or rather, that besides
our own, it is the only land where liberty can be said to exist; the
only land where the voice of the sovereign is not stronger than
the voice of the law.   We can scarce revolve with patience, the
idea, that we might have been a Spanish colony, a Portuguese
colony, or a Dutch colony; we can scarcely compare with coolness, the inheritance of those institutions, which were transmitted
to us by our fathers, with that which we must have received from
almost any other country; absolute government, military despotism, and the holy inquisition.   What would have been the condition of this flourishing and happy land, had these been the institu-

tions, on which its settlement was founded? There are, unfortunately, too many materials for answering this question, in the history of the Spanish and Portuguese settlements on the American continent, from the first moment of unrelenting waste and desolation, to the distractions and conflicts, of which we ourselves are the witnesses. What hope can there be for the colonies of nations, which possess themselves no spring of improvement; and tolerate none in the regions over which they rule; whose administration sets no bright examples of political independence; whose languages send out no reviving lessons of sound and practical science, (afraid of nothing that is true,) of manly literature, of free speculation; but repeat, with every ship that crosses the Atlantic, the same debasing voice of despotism, credulity, superstition, and slavery?

What citizen of our republic is not grateful, in the contrast which our history presents? Who does not feel, what reflecting American does not acknowledge, the incalculable advantages derived to this land, out of the deep foundations of civil, intellectual, and moral truth, from which we have drawn in England? What American does not feel proud, that he is descended from the countrymen of Bacon, of Newton, and of Locke? Who does not know, that while every pulse of civil liberty in the heart of the British empire beat warm and full in the bosom of our fathers; the sobriety, the firmness, and the dignity with which the cause of free principles struggled into existence here, constantly found encouragement and countenance from the sons of liberty there? Who does not remember, that when the Pilgrims went over the sea, the prayers of the faithful British confessors, in all the quarters of their dispersion, went over with them, while their aching eyes were strained, till the star of hope should go up in the western skies? And who will ever forget, that in that eventful struggle, which severed this mighty empire from the British crown, there was not heard, throughout our continent in arms, a voice which spoke louder for the rights of America, than that of Burke or of Chatham, within the walls of the British parliament, and at the foot of the British throne? No, for myself, I can truly say, that after my native land, I feel a tenderness and a reverence for that of my fathers. The pride I take in my own country makes me respect that from which we are sprung. In touching the soil of England, I seem to return, like a

7

descendant, to the old family seat ;—to come back to the abode of
an aged and venerable parent. I acknowledge this great consanguinity of nations. The sound of my native language beyond the
sea, is a music to my ear, beyond the richest strains of Tuscan
softness, or Castilian majesty. I am not yet in a land of strangers,
while surrounded by the manners, the habits, the forms, in which
I have been brought up. I wander delighted through a thousand
scenes, which the historians, the poets, have made familiar to us,—
of which the names are interwoven with our earliest associations.
I tread with reverence, the spots, where I can retrace the footsteps
of our suffering fathers ; the pleasant land of their birth has a claim
on my heart. It seems to me a classic, yea, a holy land, rich in
the memory of the great and good ; the martyrs of liberty, the
exiled heralds of truth ; and richer, as the parent of this land of
promise in the west.

I am not,—I need not say I am not,—the panegyrist of England. I am not dazzled by her riches, nor awed by her power.
The sceptre, the mitre, and the coronet,—stars, garters, and blue
ribbons,—seem to me poor things for great men to contend for.
Nor is my admiration awakened by her armies mustered for the
battles of Europe ; her navies, overshadowing the ocean ; nor her
empire grasping the farthest East. It is these, and the price of
guilt and blood by which they are maintained, which are the cause
why no friend of liberty can salute her with undivided affections.
But it is the refuge of free principles, though often persecuted ; the
school of religious liberty, the more precious for the struggles to
which it has been called ; the tombs of those who have reflected
honor on all who speak the English tongue ; it is the birth-place
of our fathers, the home of the Pilgrims ; it is these which I love
and venerate in England. I should feel ashamed of an enthusiasm
for Italy and Greece, did I not also feel it for a land like this. In
an American it would seem to me degenerate and ungrateful, to
hang with passion upon the traces of Homer and Virgil, and follow
without emotion the nearer and plainer footsteps of Shakspeare and
Milton ; and I should think him cold in his love for his native land,
who felt no melting in his heart for that other native land, which
holds the ashes of his forefathers.

V. But it was not enough, that our fathers were of England : the masters of Ireland, and the lords of Hindostan are of England too. But our fathers were Englishmen, aggrieved, persecuted, and banished. It is a principle, amply borne out by the history of the great and powerful nations of the earth, and by that of none more than the country of which we speak, that the best fruits and choicest action of the commendable qualities of the national character, are to be found on the side of the oppressed few, and not of the triumphant many. As in private character, adversity is often requisite to give a proper direction and temper to strong qualities, so the noblest traits of national character, even under the freest and most independent of hereditary governments, are commonly to be sought in the ranks of a protesting minority, or of a dissenting sect. Never was this truth more clearly illustrated than in the settlement of New-England.

Could a common calculation of policy have dictated the terms of that settlement, no doubt our foundations would have been laid beneath the royal smile. Convoys and navies would have been solicited to waft our fathers to the coast ; armies, to defend the infant communities ; and the flattering patronage of princes and lords, to espouse their interests in the councils of the mother country. Happy, that our fathers enjoyed no such patronage ; happy, that they fell into no such protecting hands ; happy, that our foundations were silently and deeply cast in quiet insignificance, beneath a charter of banishment, persecution, and contempt ; so that when the royal arm was at length outstretched against us, instead of a submissive child, tied down by former graces, it found a youthful giant in the land, born amidst hardships, and nourished on the rocks, indebted for no favors, and owing no duty. From the dark portals of the star chamber, and in the stern text of the acts of uniformity, the Pilgrims received a commission, more efficient than any that ever bore the royal seal. Their banishment to Holland was fortunate ; the decline of their little company in the strange land was fortunate ; the difficulties which they experienced in getting the royal consent to banish themselves to this wilderness were fortunate ; all the tears and heart breakings of that ever memorable parting at Delfthaven, had the happiest influence on the rising destinies of New-England. All this purified the ranks of the settlers.

These rough touches of fortune brushed off the light, uncertain, selfish spirits. They made it a grave, solemn, self-denying expedition. They cast a broad shadow of thought and seriousness over the cause, and if this sometimes deepened into melancholy and bitterness, can we find no apology for such a human weakness?

It is sad indeed to reflect on the disasters, which this little band of Pilgrims encountered. Sad to see a portion of them the prey of unrelenting cupidity, treacherously embarked in an unseaworthy ship, which they are soon obliged to abandon, and crowd themselves into one vessel; one hundred persons, besides the ship's company, in a vessel of one hundred and sixty tons. One is touched at the story of the long, cold, and weary autumnal passage; of the landing on the inhospitable rocks at this dismal season; where they are deserted before long by the ship, which had brought them, and which seemed their only hold upon the world of fellow men, a prey to the elements and to want, and fearfully ignorant of the numbers, the power, and the temper of the savage tribes, that filled the unexplored continent, upon whose verge they had ventured. But all this wrought together for good. These trials of wandering and exile, of the ocean, the winter, the wilderness, and the savage foe, were the final assurance of success. It was these that put far away from our fathers' cause all patrician softness, all hereditary claims to preeminence. No effeminate nobility crowded into the dark and austere ranks of the Pilgrims. No Carr nor Villiers desired to lead on the ill-provided band of despised Puritans. No well endowed clergy were on the alert, to quit their cathedrals, and set up a pompous hierarchy in the frozen wilderness. No craving governors were anxious to be sent over to our cheerless El Dorados of ice and of snow. No, they could not say they had encouraged, patronized, or helped the Pilgrims. They could not afterwards fairly pretend to reap where they had not strewn; and as our fathers reared this broad and solid fabric with pains and watchfulness, unaided, barely tolerated, it did not fall, when the arm, which had never supported, was raised to destroy.

Methinks I see it now, that one solitary, adventurous vessel, the Mayflower of a forlorn hope, freighted with the prospects of a future state, and bound across the unknown sea. I behold it pursuing, with a thousand misgivings, the uncertain, the tedious voyage.

Suns rise and set, and weeks and months pass, and winter surprises them on the deep, but brings them not the sight of the wished for shore. I see them now scantily supplied with provisions, crowded almost to suffocation in their ill-stored prison, delayed by calms, pursuing a circuitous route ;—and now driven in fury before the raging tempest, on the high and giddy waves. The awful voice of the storm howls through the rigging. The laboring masts seem straining from their base ;—the dismal sound of the pumps is heard ;—the ship leaps, as it were, madly, from billow to billow ;— the ocean breaks, and settles with engulphing floods over the floating deck, and beats with deadening weight, against the staggered vessel. I see them, escaped from these perils, pursuing their all but desperate undertaking, and landed at last, after a five months' passage, on the ice clad rocks of Plymouth,—weak and weary from the voyage,—poorly armed, scantily provisioned, depending on the charity of their ship-master for a draft of beer on board, drinking nothing but water on shore,—without shelter,—without means,—surrounded by hostile tribes. Shut now the volume of history, and tell me, on any principle of human probability, what shall be the fate of this handful of adventurers. Tell me, man of military science, in how many months were they all swept off by the thirty savage tribes, enumerated within the early limits of New-England? Tell me, politician, how long did this shadow of a colony, on which your conventions and treaties had not smiled, languish on the distant coast ? Student of history, compare for me the baffled projects, the deserted settlements, the abandoned adventures, of other times, and find the parallel of this. Was it the winter's storm, beating upon the houseless heads of women and children ; was it hard labor and spare meals ;—was it disease,— was it the tomahawk,—was it the deep malady of a blighted hope, a ruined enterprise, and a broken heart, aching in its last moments, at the recollection of the loved and left, beyond the sea ; was it some, or all of these united, that hurried this forsaken company to their melancholy fate ?—And is it possible, that neither of these causes, that not all combined, were able to blast this bud of hope ? Is it possible, that from a beginning so feeble, so frail, so worthy, not so much of admiration as of pity, there has gone forth a progress so steady, a growth so wonderful, a reality so important, a promise yet to be fulfilled, so glorious ?

Such, in a very inadequate statement, are some of the circumstances under which the settlement of our country began. The historian of Massachusetts, after having given a brief notice of Carver, of Bradford, of Winslow, of Brewster, of Standish, and others, adds, 'These were the founders of the colony of Plymouth. The settlement of this colony occasioned the settlement of Massachusetts Bay; which was the source of all the other colonies of New-England. Virginia was in a dying state, and seemed to revive and flourish from the example of New-England. I am not preserving from oblivion,' continues he, 'the names of heroes whose chief merit is the overthrow of cities, of provinces, and empires; but the names of the founders of a flourishing town and colony, if not of the whole British empire in America.'* This was the judicious reflection of Hutchinson, sixty years ago, when the greatest tribute to be paid to the Fathers of Plymouth was, that they took the lead in colonizing the British possessions in America. What then ought to be our emotions, as we meet on this anniversary, upon the spot where the first successful foundations of the great American republic were laid ?

Within a short period, an incident has occurred, which of itself connects, in the most gratifying association, the early settlement of New-England with the present growth and prosperity of our wide extended republic. Within the past year the sovereign hand of this great confederacy of States has been extended for the restoration and security of the harbor, where, on the day we celebrate, the germ of the future growth of America was comprehended within one weather-beaten vessel, tossing upon the tide, on board of which, in the words of Hutchinson, the fathers of New-England by a solemn instrument, 'formed themselves into a proper democracy.' Two centuries only have elapsed, and we behold a great American representation convened, from twenty-four independent and flourishing republics, taking under their patronage the local interests of the spot where our fathers landed, and providing in the same act of appropriation, for the removal of obstacles in the Mis-

* Hutchinson's History of Massachusetts Bay, vol. II. Appendix, p. 463.

sissippi and the repair of Plymouth beach. I know not in what words a more beautiful commentary could be written, on our early infancy or our happy growth. There were members of the national Congress which made that appropriation, I will not say from distant states, but from different climates ; from regions which the sun in the heavens does not reach in the same hour that he rises on us. Happy community of protection ! Glorious brotherhood ! Blessed fulfilment of that first timorous hope, that warmed the bosoms of our fathers !

Nor is it even our mighty territory, to which the influence of the principles and example of the fathers of New-England is confined. While I utter the words, a constitution of republican government, closely imitated from ours, is going into operation in the states of the Mexican confederation, a region more extensive than all our territories east of the Mississippi. Farther south, one of the provinces of central America, the republic of Guatimala, has sent its envoys to solicit a union with us. Will posterity believe, that such an offer was made and refused, in the age that saw England and Spain rushing into war, for the possession of a few uninhabited islets on the coast of Patagonia ? Pass the isthmus of Darien, and we behold the sister republic of Colombia, a realm two thirds as large as Europe, ratifying her first solemn treaty of amity and commerce with the United States ; while still onward to the south, in the valleys of the Chilian Andes, and on the banks of La Plata, in states not less vast than those already named, constitutions of republican government are in prosperous operation, founded on our principles, and modelled on our forms. When our commissioners visited those countries in 1817, they found the books most universally read among the people, were the constitutions of the United States and of the several states, translated into the language of the country ; while the public journals were filled with extracts from the celebrated ' Defence ' of these constitutions, written by that venerable descendant of the Pilgrims, who still lives to witness the prosperous operation of the governments, which he did so much to establish.

I do not fear that we shall be accused of extravagance in the enthusiasm we feel at a train of events of such astonishing magnitude, novelty, and consequence, connected by associations so intimate, with the day we now hail ; with the events we now celebrate ; with the pilgrim fathers of New-England.   Victims of persecution ! how wide an empire acknowledges the sway of your principles ! Apostles of liberty ! what millions attest the authenticity of your mission !   Meek champions of truth, no stain of private interest or of innocent blood is on the spotless garments of your renown ! The great continents of America have become, at length, the theatre of your achievements ; the Atlantic and the Pacific, the highways of communication, on which your principles, your institutions, your example are borne.   From the oldest abodes of civilization, the venerable plains of Greece, to the scarcely explored range of the Cordilleras, the impulse you gave at length is felt. While other regions revere you as the leaders of this great march of humanity, we are met on this joyful day, to offer to your memory our tribute of filial affection.   The sons and daughters of the Pilgrims, we have assembled on the spot where you, our suffering fathers, set foot on this happy shore.   Happy indeed, it has been for us.   O that you could have enjoyed those blessings, which you prepared for your children !   Could our comfortable homes have shielded you from the wintry air ; could our abundant harvests have supplied you in time of famine ; could the broad shield of our beloved country have sheltered you from the visitations of arbitrary power !   We come, in our prosperity, to remember your trials ; and here, on the spot where New-England began to be, we come, to learn of you, our pilgrim fathers, a deep and lasting lesson of virtue, enterprise, patience, zeal, and faith !

ORATION

—

FELLOW CITIZENS,

THE subject which the present occasion presents to our consideration, is of the highest interest. The appearance of a new state in the great family of nations is one of the most important topics of reflection, that can ever be addressed to us. In the case of America, the magnitude and the difficulty of this subject are immeasurably increased. Our progress has been so rapid, the interval has been so short between the first plantations in the wilderness and the full development of our political system; there has been such a visible agency of single characters in affecting the condition of the country, such an almost instantaneous expansion of single events into consequences of incalculable importance, that we find ourselves deserted by almost all the principles and precedents, drawn from the analogy of other states. Men have here seen, felt, and acted themselves, what in most other countries has been the growth of centuries.

Take your station for instance on Connecticut river. Every thing about you, whatsoever you behold or approach, bears witness, that you are a citizen of a powerful and prosperous state. It is just seventy years, since the towns, which you now contemplate with admiration as the abodes of a numerous, refined, enterprising population, safe in the enjoyment of life's best blessings, were wasted and burned by the savages of the wilderness; and their inhabitants by hundreds,—the old and the young, the minister of the gospel, and the mother with her new born babe,—were wakened at midnight by the warwhoop, dragged from their beds, and

8

marched with bleeding feet across the snow-clad mountains,—to be sold as slaves into the cornfields and kitchens of the French in Canada. Go back eighty years farther; and the same barbarous foe is on the skirts of your oldest settlements,—at your own doors. As late as 1676, ten or twelve citizens of Concord were slain or carried into captivity, who had gone to meet the savage hordes in their attack on Sudbury, in which the brave Captain Wadsworth and his companions fell.

These contrasts regard the political strength of our country; the growth in national resources presents a case of increase still more astonishing, though less adapted to move the feelings. By the last valuation, the aggregate property of Massachusetts is esti- mated at something less than three hundred millions. By the valuation made in 1780, the property of Massachusetts and Maine was estimated at only eleven millions!

This unexampled rapidity of our national growth, while it gives to our history more than the interest of romance, leaves us often in doubt, what is to be ascribed to the cooperation of a train of inci- dents and characters, following in long succession upon each other; and what is to be referred to the vast influence of single important events.

That astonishing incident in human affairs, the Revolution of America, as seen on the day of its portentous, or rather let me say, of its auspicious commencement, is the theme of our present con- sideration. To what shall we direct our thoughts? On the one hand, we behold a connexion of events; the time and circum- stances of the original discovery; the system of colonization; the settlements of the pilgrims; their condition, temper, and institu- tions; their singular political relation with the mother country; their long and doubtful struggle with the savage tribes; their col- lisions with the royal governors; their cooperation in the British wars; with all the influences of their geographical and physical condition; uniting to constitute what I may call the national edu- cation of America. When we take this survey, we feel that we ought to divide the honors of the Revolution with the great men of the colony in every generation; with the Winslows and the Pep- perells, the Cookes and the Mathers, the Winthrops and the Bradfords, and all who labored and acted in the cabinet, the desk, or the field, for the one great cause. On the other hand, when we dwell upon the day itself, every thing else seems lost in the comparison. Had our forefathers failed, on that day of trial, which we now celebrate; had their votes and their resolves, (as was tauntingly predicted on both sides of the Atlantic,) ended in the breath, in which they began; had the rebels laid down their arms, as they were commanded; and the military stores, which had been frugally treasured up for this crisis, been, without resistance, destroyed ;— then the Revolution had been at an end, or rather never had been begun; the heads of Hancock and Adams and their brave colleagues would have been exposed in ghastly triumph on Temple-bar; a military despotism would have been firmly fixed in the colonies; the patriots of Massachusetts would have been doubly despised, the scorn of their enemies, the scorn of their deluded countrymen ; the cry of liberty, which they had raised from the shore to the mountains, would have been turned back in a cry of disdain; and the heart of this great people, then beating and almost bursting for freedom, would have been struck cold and dead, and, for aught we can now reason, forever.

There are those, who object to such a celebration as this, as tending to keep up a hostile sentiment toward England. But I do not feel the force of this scruple. In the first place, it was not England, but the English ministerial party of the day, and a small circle in that party, which projected the measures that resulted in our Revolution. The rights of America found steady and powerful asserters in England. Lord Chatham declared to the House of Peers that he was glad America had resisted; and, alluding to the fact that he had a son in the British army, he added, 'that none of his blood should serve in this detested cause.' Nay, even the ministers that imposed the stamp duty, the measure which hastened the spirit of America to a crisis, which it might not have reached in a century, Lord Mansfield, the Duke of Grafton, the Earl of Shelburne, Lord Camden, rose, one after another, and asserted in the House of Lords, that they had no share in the measures which were proposed by the very cabinet, of which they were leading members.

But I must go further. Did faithful history compel us to cast on all England united the reproach of those measures, which drove our fathers to arms ; and were it, in consequence, the unavoidable effect of these celebrations to revive the feelings of revolutionary times in the bosoms of the aged ; to kindle those feelings anew, in the susceptible hearts of the young ; it would still be our duty, on every becoming occasion, in the strongest colors, and in the boldest lines we can command, to retrace the picture of the times that tried men's souls. We owe it to our fathers, we owe it to our children. A pacific and friendly feeling towards England is the duty of this nation ; but it is not our only duty, it is not our first duty. America owes an earlier and a higher duty to the great and good men, who caused her to be a nation ; who, at an expense of treasure, a contempt of peril, a prodigality of blood—as pure and noble as ever flowed,—of which we can now hardly conceive, vindicated to this continent a place among the nations of the earth. I cannot consent, out of tenderness to the memory of the Gages, the Hutchinsons, the Grenvilles and Norths, the Dartmouths and Hillsboroughs, to cast a veil over the labors and the sacrifices of the Quincys, the Adamses, the Hancocks, and the Warrens.

There is not a people on earth so abject, as to think that national courtesy requires them to hush up the tale of the glorious exploits of their fathers and countrymen. France is at peace with Austria and Prussia ; but she does not demolish her beautiful bridges, baptized with the names of the battle fields, where Napoleon annihilated their armies ; nor tear down the columns, moulten out of the heaps of their captured artillery. England is at peace with France and Spain, but does she suppress the names of Trafalgar and the Nile ; does she overthrow the towers of Blenheim castle, eternal monuments of the disasters of France ; does she tear down from the rafters of her chapels, where they have for ages waved in triumph, consecrated to the God of battles, the banners of Cressy and Agincourt ?—No ; she is wiser ; wiser, did I say ? she is truer, juster to the memory of her fathers and the spirit of her children. The national character, in some of its most important elements, must be formed, elevated, and strengthened from the materials which history presents. Are we to be eternally ringing the changes upon Marathon and Thermopylæ ; and going back to find in obscure texts of Greek and Latin the great exemplars of patriotic virtue ? I rejoice that we can find them

nearer home, in our own country, on our own soil;—that strains
of the noblest sentiment, that ever swelled in the breast of man,
are breathing to us out of every page of our country's history, in
the native eloquence of our mother tongue ;—that the colonial and
the provincial councils of America, exhibit to us models of the
spirit and character, which gave Greece and Rome their name
and their praise among the nations. Here we ought to go for our
instruction ;—the lesson is plain, it is clear, it is applicable. When
we go to ancient history, we are bewildered with the difference of
manners and institutions. We are willing to pay our tribute of
applause to the memory of Leonidas, who fell nobly for his country,
in the face of the foe. But when we trace him to his home, we
are confounded at the reflection, that the same Spartan heroism to
which he sacrificed himself at Thermopylæ, would have led him to
tear his only child, if it happened to be a sickly babe,—the very
object for which all that is kind and good in man rises up to plead,
—from the bosom of its mother, and carry it out to be eaten by
the wolves of Taygetus. We feel a glow of admiration at the
heroism displayed at Marathon, by the ten thousand champions of
invaded Greece ; but we cannot forget that the tenth part of the
number were slaves, unchained from the work-shops and door-posts
of their masters, to go and fight the battles of freedom. I do not
mean that these examples are to destroy the interest with which
we read the history of ancient times ; they possibly increase that
interest, by the singular contrast they exhibit. But they do warn
us, if we need the warning, to seek our great practical lessons of
patriotism at home ; out of the exploits and sacrifices, of which
our own country is the theatre ; out of the characters of our own
fathers. Them we know, the high-souled, natural, unaffected,—
the citizen heroes. We know what happy firesides they left for
the cheerless camp. We know with what pacific habits they
dared the perils of the field. There is no mystery, no romance,
no madness, under the name of chivalry, about them. It is all
resolute, manly resistance,—for conscience' and liberty's sake,—
not merely of an overwhelming power, but of all the force of long-
rooted habits, and the native love of order and peace.

Above all, their blood calls to us from the soil which we tread ;
it beats in our veins ; it cries to us, not merely in the thrilling

words of one of the first victims in the cause,—'My sons, scorn to
be slaves;'—but it cries with a still more moving eloquence,—
'My sons, forget not your fathers.' Fast, oh, too fast, with all our
efforts to prevent it, their precious memories are dying away.
Notwithstanding our numerous written memorials, much of what is
known of those eventful times dwells but in the recollection of a
few revered survivors, and with them is rapidly perishing, unre-
corded and irretrievable. How many prudent counsels, conceived
in perplexed times ; how many heart-stirring words, uttered when
liberty was treason ; how many brave and heroic deeds, performed
when the halter, not the laurel, was the promised meed of patriotic
daring,—are already lost and forgotten in the graves of their authors.
How little do we,—although we have been permitted to hold converse with the venerable remnants of that day,—how little do we
know of their dark and anxious hours ; of their secret meditations ;
of the hurried and perilous events of the momentous struggle.
And while they are dropping round us like the leaves of autumn,
and scarce a week passes that does not call away some member of
the veteran ranks, already so sadly thinned, shall we make no
effort to hand down the traditions of their day to our children ; to
pass the torch of liberty, which we received in all the splendor of
its first enkindling, bright and flaming, to those who stand next us
in the line ; so that when we shall come to be gathered to the dust
where our fathers are laid, we may say to our sons and our grand-
sons, 'If we did not amass, we have not squandered your inheritance of glory?'

Let us then faithfully go back to those all-important days. Let
us commemorate the events, with which the momentous revolutionary crisis was brought on ; let us gather up the traditions which
still exist ; let us show the world, that if we are not called to follow
the example of our fathers, we are at least not insensible to the
worth of their characters ; nor indifferent to the sacrifices and trials,
by which they purchased our prosperity.

Time would fail us to recount the measures by which the way
was prepared for the Revolution ;—the stamp act ; its repeal, with
the declaration of the right to tax America ; the landing of troops
in Boston, beneath the batteries of fourteen vessels of war, lying
broadside to the town, with springs on their cables, their guns

loaded, and matches smoking; the repeated insults, and finally the massacre of the fifth of March, resulting from this military occupation; and the Boston Port-Bill, by which the final catastrophe was hurried on. Nor can we dwell upon the appointment at Salem, on the seventeenth of June, 1774, of the delegates to the continental congress; of the formation at Salem, in the following October, of the provincial congress; of the decided measures, which were taken by that noble assembly, at Concord and at Cambridge; of the preparations they made against the worst, by organizing the militia, providing stores, and appointing commanders. All this was done by the close of the year 1774.

At length the memorable year of 1775 arrived. The plunder of the provincial stores at Medford, and the attempt to seize the cannon at Salem, had produced a highly irritated state of the public mind. The friends of our rights in England made a vigorous effort, in the month of March, to avert the crisis that impended. On the twenty-second of that month, Mr Burke spoke the last word of conciliation and peace. He spoke it in a tone, and with a power befitting the occasion and the man;—he spoke it to the north-west wind. Eight days after, at that season of the year when the prudent New-England husbandman repairs the enclosures of his field, for the protection of the fruits of nature's bounty which ere long will cover them, General Gage sent out a party of eleven hundred men to overthrow the stone walls in the neighborhood of Boston, by way of opening and levelling the arena for the bloody contest he designed to bring on. With the same view, in the months of February and March, his officers were sent in disguise to traverse the country, to make military surveys of its roads and passes, to obtain accounts of the stores at Concord and Worcester, and to communicate with the small number of disaffected Americans. These disguised officers were here at Concord, on the twentieth of March; and received treacherous or unsuspecting information of the places where the provincial stores were concealed. I mention this, only to show, that our fathers, in their arduous contest, had every thing to contend with; secret as well as open foes; treachery in the cabinet, as well as power in the field. But I need not add, that they possessed not only the courage and the resolution, but the vigilance and care demanded for the crisis. In

November, 1774, a society had been formed at Boston, principally
of the mechanics of that town,—a class of men to whom the revolutionary cause was as deeply indebted, as to any other in America,—for the express purpose of closely watching the movements
of the open and secret foes of the country. In the long and
dreary nights of a New-England winter, they patrolled the streets;
and not a movement, which concerned the cause, escaped their
vigilance. Not a measure of the royal governor, but was in their
possession, in a few hours after it was communicated to his confidential officers. Nor was manly patriotism alone aroused in the
cause. The daughters of America were inspired with the same
noble temper that animated their fathers, their husbands, and their
brethren. The historian tells us, that the first intimation communicated to the patriots, of the impending commencement of hostilities, came from a ' daughter of liberty, unequally yoked with an
enemy of her country's rights.'

With all these warnings, and all the vigilance with which the
royal troops were watched, none supposed the fatal moment was
hurrying on so rapidly. On Saturday, April fifteenth, the provincial Congress adjourned their session in this place, to meet on the
tenth of May. On the very same day, Saturday, the fifteenth of
April, the companies of grenadiers and light infantry in Boston,
the flower not merely of the royal garrison, but of the British army,
were taken off their regular duty, under the pretence of learning
a new military exercise. At the midnight following, the boats of
the transport ships, which had been previously repaired, were
launched, and moored for safety under the sterns of the vessels of
war. Not one of these movements,—least of all, that which took
place beneath the shades of midnight,—was unobserved by the
vigilant sons of liberty. The next morning Colonel Paul Revere,
a very active member of the patriotic society just mentioned, was
despatched by Dr Joseph Warren to John Hancock and Samuel
Adams, then at Lexington, whose seizure was threatened by the
royal governor. So early did these distinguished patriots receive
the intelligence, that preparations for an important movement were
on foot. Justly considering, however, that some object besides the
seizure of two individuals was probably designed, in the movement
of so large a force, they counselled the Committee of Safety to

order the distribution into the neighboring towns, of the stores collected at Concord. Colonel Revere, on his return from this excursion on the sixteenth of April, in order to guard against any accident, which might make it impossible at the last moment to give information from Boston of the departure of the troops, concerted with his friends in Charlestown, that whenever the British forces should embark in their boats to cross into the country, two lanterns should be lighted in the North Church steeple, and one, should they march out by Roxbury.

Thus was the meditated blow prepared for before it was struck ; and we almost smile at the tardy prudence of the British commander, who, on Tuesday the eighteenth of April, despatched ten sergeants, who were to dine at Cambridge, and at nightfall scatter themselves on the roads from Boston to Concord, to prevent notice of the projected expedition from reaching the country.

At length the momentous hour arrives, as big with consequences to man, as any that ever struck in his history. The darkness of night is still to shroud the rash and fatal measures, with which the liberty of America is hastened on. The highest officers in the British army are as yet ignorant of the nature of the meditated blow. At nine o'clock in the evening of the eighteenth, Lord Percy is sent for by the governor, to receive the information of the design. On his way back to his lodgings, he finds the very movements, which had been just communicated to him in confidence by the commander in chief, a subject of conversation in a group of patriotic citizens in the street. He hastens back to General Gage, and tells him he is betrayed ; and orders are instantly given to permit no American to leave the town. But the order is five minutes too late. Dr Warren, the President of the Committee of Safety, though he had returned at nightfall from the meeting at West Cambridge, was already in possession of the whole design ; and instantly despatched two messengers to Lexington, Mr William Dawes, who went out by Roxbury, and Colonel Paul Revere, who crossed to Charlestown. The Colonel received this summons at ten o'clock on Tuesday night ; the lanterns were immediately lighted up in North Church steeple ; and in this way, before a man of the soldiery was embarked in the boats, the news of

9

their coming was travelling with the rapidity of light, through the country.*

Having accomplished this precautionary measure, Colonel Revere repaired to the north part of the town, where he constantly kept a boat in readiness, in which he was now rowed by two friends across the river, a little to the eastward of the spot where the Somerset man-of-war was moored, between Boston and Charlestown. It was then young flood, the ship was swinging round upon the tide, and the moon was just rising upon this midnight scene of solemn anticipation. Colonel Revere was safely landed in Charlestown, where his signals had already been observed. He procured a horse from Deacon Larkin for the further pursuit of his errand. That he would not be permitted to accomplish it without risk of interruption was evident from the information which he received from Mr Richard Devens, a member of the Committee of Safety, that on his way from West Cambridge, where the Committee sat, he had encountered several British officers, well armed and mounted, going up the road.

At eleven o'clock, Colonel Revere started upon his errand. After passing Charlestown neck, he saw two men on horseback under a tree. On approaching them, he perceived them by the light of the moon to be British officers. One of them immediately tried to intercept, and the other to seize him. The Colonel instantly turned back toward Charlestown, and then struck into the Medford road. The officer in pursuit of him, endeavoring to cut him off, plunged into a clay pond, in the corner between the two roads, and the Colonel escaped. He according pursued his way to Medford, awoke the captain of the minute men there, and giving the alarm at every house on the road, passed on through West Cambridge to Lexington. There he delivered his message to Messrs Hancock and Adams,† and there also he was shortly after joined by Mr William Dawes, the messenger who had gone out by Roxbury.

After staying a short time at Lexington, Messrs Revere and Dawes, at about one o'clock of the morning of the nineteenth of April, started for Concord, to communicate the intelligence there.

* See note A.   † See note B.

They were soon overtaken on the way by Dr Samuel Prescott of Concord, who joined them in giving the alarm at every house on the road. About half way from Lexington to Concord, while Dawes and Prescott were alarming a house on the road, Revere, being about one hundred rods in advance, saw two officers in the road, of the same appearance as those he had escaped in Charlestown. He called to his companions to assist him in forcing his way through them, but was instantly surrounded by four officers. These officers had previously thrown down the wall of an adjoining field, and the Americans, prevented from forcing their way onward, passed into the field. Dr Prescott, although the reins of his horse had been cut in the struggle with the officers, succeeded, by leaping a stone wall, in making his escape from the field, and reaching Concord. Revere aimed at a wood, but was there encountered by six more officers, and was with his companion made prisoner. The British officers, who had already seized three other Americans, having learned from their prisoners, that the whole country was alarmed, thought it best for their own safety to hasten back, taking their prisoners with them. Near Lexington meetinghouse, on their return, the British officers heard the militia, who were on parade, firing a volley of guns. Terrified at this, they compelled Revere to give up his horse, and then pushing forward at a full gallop, escaped down the road.

The morning was now advanced to about four o'clock, nor was it then known at Lexington, that the British were so near at hand. Colonel Revere again sought Messrs Hancock and Adams at the house of the Reverend Mr Clark, and it was thought expedient by their friends, who had kept watch there during the night, that these eminent patriots should remove toward Woburn. Having attended them to a house on the Woburn road, where they proposed to stop, Colonel Revere returned to Lexington to watch the progress of events. He soon met a person at full gallop, who informed him that the British troops were coming up the road. Hastening now to the public house, to secure some papers of Messrs Hancock and Adams, Colonel Revere saw the British troops pressing forward in full array.

It was now seven hours since these troops were put in motion. They were mustered at ten o'clock of the night preceding, on the

Boston Common, and embarked, to the number of eight hundred grenadiers and light infantry, in the boats of the British squadron. They landed at Phipps' Farm, a little to the south of Lechmere's Point, and on disembarking, a day's provision was dealt out to them. Pursuing the path across the marshes, they emerged into the old Charlestown and West Cambridge road.

And here let us pause a moment in the narration, to ask, who are the men, and what is the cause? Is it an army of Frenchmen and Canadians, who in earlier days had often run the line between them and us, with havoc and fire, and who have now come to pay back the debt of recent defeat and subjugation? Or is it their ancient ally of the woods, the stealthy savage,—borne in his light canoe, with muffled oars, over the midnight waters,—creeping like the felon wolf through our villages, that he may start up at dawn, to wage a war of surprise, of plunder, and of horror against the slumbering cradle and the defenceless fireside? O no! It is the disciplined armies of a brave, a christian, a kindred people; led by gallant officers, the choice sons of England; and they are going to seize, and secure for the halter, men whose crime is, that they have dared to utter in the English tongue, on this side of the ocean, the principles which gave, and give England her standing among the nations; they are going to plunge their swords in the breasts of men, who fifteen years before, on the plains of Abraham, stood, and fought, and conquered by their side. But they go not unobserved; the tidings of their approach are travelling before them; the faithful messengers have aroused the citizens from their slumbers; alarm guns are answering to each other, and spreading the news from village to village; the tocsin is heard, at this unnatural hour, from steeples that never before rung with any other summons than that of the gospel of peace; the sacred tranquillity of the hour is startled with all the mingled sounds of preparation,—of gathering bands, and resolute though unorganized resistance.

The Committee of Safety, as has been observed, had set, the preceding day, at West Cambridge; and three of its respected members, Gerry, Lee, and Orne, had retired to sleep, in the public house, where the session of the committee was held. So difficult was it, notwithstanding all that had passed, to realize that a state of things could exist, between England and America, in which

American citizens should be liable to be torn from their beds by an armed force at midnight, that the members of the Committee of Safety, though forewarned of the approach of the British troops, did not even think it necessary to retire from their lodgings. On the contrary, they rose from their beds and went to their windows to gaze on the unwonted sight, the midnight march of armies through the peaceful hamlets of New England. Half the column had already passed, when a flank guard was promptly detached to search the public house, no doubt in the design of arresting the members of the Committee of Safety, who might be there. It was only at this last critical moment, that Mr Gerry and his friends bethought themselves of flight, and without time even to clothe themselves, escaped naked into the fields.

By this time Colonel Smith, who commanded the expedition, appears to have been alarmed at the indications of a general rising throughout the country. The light infantry companies were now detached and placed under the command of Major Pitcairne, for the purpose of hastening forward, to secure the bridges at Concord; and thus cut off the communication between this place and the towns north and west of it. Before these companies could reach Lexington, the officers already mentioned, who had arrested Colonel Revere, joined their advancing countrymen, and reported that five hundred men were drawn up in Lexington, to resist the king's troops. On receiving this exaggerated account, the British light infantry was halted, to give time for the grenadiers to come up, that the whole together might move forward to the work of death.

The company assembled on Lexington Green, which the British officers, in their report, had swelled to five hundred, consisted of sixty or seventy of the militia of the place. Information had been received about nightfall, both by private means and by communications from the Committee of Safety, that a strong party of officers had been seen on the road, directing their course toward Lexington. In consequence of this intelligence, a body of about thirty of the militia, well armed, assembled early in the evening; a guard of eight men under Colonel William Munroe, then a sergeant in the company, was stationed at the house of the Rev. Mr Clark; and three men were sent off to give the alarm at Concord. These

three messengers were however stopped on their way, as has been
mentioned, by the British officers, who had already passed onward.
One of their number, Elijah Sanderson, has lately died at Salem
at an advanced age.   A little after midnight, as has been observed,
Messrs Revere and Dawes arrived with the certain information,
that a very large body of the royal troops was in motion.   The
alarm was now generally given to the inhabitants of Lexington,
messengers were sent down the road to ascertain the movements of
the troops, and the militia company under Captain John Parker
appeared on the green to the number of one hundred and thirty.
The roll was duly called at this perilous midnight muster, and some
answered to their names for the last time on earth.   The company
was now ordered to load with powder and ball, and awaited in
anxious expectation the return of those who had been sent to
reconnoitre the enemy.   One of them, in consequence of some
misinformation, returned and reported that there was no appearance
of troops on the road from Boston.   Under this harrassing uncertainty and contradiction, the militia were dismissed, to await the
return of the other expresses, and with orders to be in readiness at
the beat of the drum.   One of these messengers was made prisoner by the British, whose march was so cautious, that they
remained undiscovered till within a mile and a half of Lexington
meetinghouse, and time was scarce left for the last messenger to
return with the tidings of their approach.

The new alarm was now given; the bell rings, alarm guns are
fired, the drum beats to arms.   Some of the militia had gone home,
when dismissed; but the greater part were in the neighboring
houses, and instantly obeyed the summons.   Sixty or seventy
appeared on the green and were drawn up in double ranks.   At
this moment the British column of eight hundred gleaming bayonets
appears, headed by their mounted commanders, their banners
flying and drums beating a charge.   To engage them with a
handful of militia of course was madness,—to fly at the sight of
them, they disdained.   The British troops rush furiously on ; their
commanders, with mingled threats and execrations, bid the Americans lay down their arms and disperse, and their own troops to fire.
A moment's delay, as of compunction, follows.   The order with
vehement imprecations is repeated, and they fire.   No one falls,

and the band of self-devoted heroes, most of whom had never seen such a body of troops before, stand firm in the front of an army, outnumbering them ten to one. Another volley succeeds ; the killed and wounded drop, and it was not till they had returned the fire of the overwhelming force, that the militia were driven from the field. A scattered fire now succeeded on both sides while the Americans remained in sight; and the British troops were then drawn up on the green to fire a volley and give a shout in honor of the victory.*

While these incidents were taking place, and every moment then came charged with events, which were to give a character to centuries; Hancock and Adams, though removed by their friends from the immediate vicinity of the force sent to apprehend them, were apprized, too faithfully, that the work of death was begun. The heavy and quick repeated vollies told them a tale, that needed no exposition,—which proclaimed that Great Britain had renounced that strong invisible tie which bound the descendants of England to the land of their fathers, and had appealed to the right of the strongest. The inevitable train of consequences burst in prophetic fulness upon their minds; and the patriot Adams, forgetting the scenes of tribulation through which America must pass to realize the prospect, and heedless that the ministers of vengeance, in overwhelming strength, were in close pursuit of his own life, uttered that memorable exclamation, than which nothing more sublime can be found in the records of Grecian or Roman heroism, —" O, what a glorious morning is this ! "

Elated with its success, the British army took up its march toward Concord. The intelligence of the projected expedition had been communicated to this town by Dr Samuel Prescott, in the manner already described; and from Concord had travelled onward in every direction. The interval was employed in removing a portion of the public stores to the neighboring towns, while the aged and infirm, the women and children, sought refuge in the surrounding woods. About seven o'clock in the morning, the glittering arms of the British column were seen advancing on the Lincoln road. A body of militia, from one hundred and fifty to two hun-

* See note C.

dred men, who had taken post for observation on the heights above
the entrance to the town, retire at the approach of the army of the
enemy, first to the hill a little farther north, and then beyond the
bridge.   The British troops press forward into the town, and are
drawn up in front of the courthouse.   Parties are then ordered out
to the various spots where the public stores and arms were supposed to be deposited.   Much had been removed to places of safety,
and something was saved by the prompt and innocent artifices of
individuals.   The destruction of property and of arms was hasty
and incomplete, and considered as the object of an enterprise of
such fatal consequences, it stands in shocking contrast with the
waste of blood by which it was effected.

I am relating events, which though they can never be repeated
more frequently than they deserve, are yet familiar to all who hear
me.   I need not, therefore, attempt, nor would it be practicable
did I attempt it, to recall the numerous interesting occurrences of
that ever memorable day.   The reasonable limits of a public discourse must confine us to a selection of the more prominent incidents.

It was the first care of the British commander to cut off the
approach of the Americans from the neighboring towns, by destroying or occupying the bridges.   A party was immediately sent to
the south bridge and tore it up.   A force of six companies, under
Captains Parsons and Lowrie, was sent to the north bridge.   Three
companies under Captain Lowrie were left to guard it, and three
under Captain Parsons proceeded to Colonel Barrett's house, in
search of provincial stores.   While they were engaged on that
errand, the militia of Concord, joined by their brave brethren from
the neighboring towns, gathered on the hill opposite the north
bridge, under the command of Colonel Robinson and Major Buttrick.   The British companies at the bridge were now apparently
bewildered with the perils of their situation, and began to tear up
the planks of the bridge; not remembering, that this would expose
their own party, then at Colonel Barrett's, to certain and entire
destruction.   The Americans, on the other hand, resolved to keep
open the communication with the town, and perceiving the attempt
which was made to destroy the bridge, were immediately put in
motion, with orders not to give the first fire.   They drew near to

the bridge, the Acton company in front, led on by the gallant Davis. Three alarm guns were fired into the water, by the British, without arresting the march of our citizens. The signal for a general discharge is then made;—a British soldier steps from the ranks, and fires at Major Buttrick. The ball passed between his arm and his side, and slightly wounded Mr Luther Blanchard, who stood near him. A volley instantly followed, and Captain Davis was shot through the heart, gallantly marching at the head of the Acton militia against the choice troops of the British line. A private of his company, Mr Hosmer of Acton, also fell at his side. A general action now ensued, which terminated in the retreat of the British party, after the loss of several killed and wounded, toward the centre of the town, followed by the brave band who had driven them from their post. The advance party of British at Colonel Barrett's was thus left to its fate ; and nothing would have been more easy than to effect its entire destruction. But the idea of a declared war had yet scarcely forced itself, with all its consequences, into the minds of our countrymen ; and these advanced companies were allowed to return unmolested to the main band.

It was now twelve hours since the first alarm had been given, the evening before, of the meditated expedition. The swift watches of that eventful night had scattered the tidings far and wide ; and widely as they spread, the people rose in their strength. The genius of America, on this the morning of her emancipation, had sounded her horn over the plains and upon the mountains ; and the indignant yeomanry of the land, armed with the weapons which had done service in their fathers' hands, poured to the spot where this new and strange tragedy was acting. The old New-England drums, that had beat at Louisburgh, at Quebec, at Martinique, at the Havana, were now sounding on all the roads to Concord. There were officers in the British line, that knew the sound ;—they had heard it, in the deadly breach, beneath the black, deep-throated engines of the French and Spanish castles, and they knew what followed, where that sound went before. With the British it was a question no longer of protracted contest, nor even of halting long enough to rest their exhausted troops, after a weary night's march, and all the labor, confusion, and dis-

10

tress of the day's efforts. Their dead were hastily buried in the public square; their wounded placed in the vehicles which the town afforded; and a flight commenced, to which the annals of warfare will hardly afford a parallel. On all the neighboring hills were multitudes from the surrounding country, of the unarmed and infirm, of women and of children, who had fled from the terrors and the perils of the plunder and conflagration of their homes; or were collected, with fearful curiosity, to mark the progress of this storm of war. The panic fears of a calamitous flight, on the part of the British, transformed this inoffensive, timid throng into a threatening array of armed men; and there was too much reason for the misconception. Every height of ground, within reach of the line of march, was covered with the indignant avengers of their slaughtered brethren. The British light companies were sent out to great distances as flanking parties; but who was to flank the flankers? Every patch of trees, every rock, every stream of water, every building, every stone wall, was *lined*, (1 use the words of a British officer in the battle,) with an unintermitted fire. Every cross road opened a new avenue to the assailants. Through one of these the gallant Brooks led up the minute men of Reading. At another defile, they were encountered by the Lexington militia, under Captain Parker, who, undismayed at the loss of more than a tenth of their number in killed and wounded in the morning, had returned to the conflict. At first the contest was kept up by the British, with all the skill and valor of veteran troops. To a military eye it was not an unequal contest. The commander was not, or ought not to have been taken by surprise. Eight hundred picked men, grenadiers and light infantry, from the English army, were no doubt considered by General Gage a very ample detachment to march eighteen or twenty miles through an open country; and a very fair match for all the resistance which could be made by unprepared husbandmen, without concert, discipline, or leaders. With about ten times their number, the Grecian commander had forced a march out of the wrecks of a field of battle and defeat, through the barbarous nations of Asia, for thirteen long months, from the plains of Babylon to the Black Sea, through forests, defiles, and deserts, which the foot of civilized man had never trod. It was the American cause,—its holy foundation in truth and right, its strength and

life in the hearts of the people, that converted what would naturally have been the undisturbed march of a strong, well provided
army, into a rabble rout of terror and death. It was this, which
sowed the fields of our pacific villages with dragon's teeth ; which
nerved the arm of age ; called the ministers and servants of the
church into the hot fire ; and even filled with strange passion and
manly strength the heart and the arm of the stripling. A British
historian, to paint the terrific aspect of things that presented itself
to his countrymen, declares that the rebels swarmed upon the hills,
as if they dropped from the clouds. Before the flying troops had
reached Lexington, their rout was entire. Some of the officers had
been made prisoners, some had been killed, and several wounded,
and among them the commander in chief, Colonel Smith. The
ordinary means of preserving discipline failed ; the wounded, in
chaises and wagons, pressed to the front and obstructed the road ;
wherever the flanking parties, from the nature of the ground, were
forced to come in, the line of march was crowded and broken ; the
ammunition began to fail ; and at length the entire body was on a
full run. 'We attempted,' says a British officer already quoted,
'to stop the men and form them two deep, but to no purpose ; the
confusion rather increased than lessened.' An English historian
says, the British soldiers were driven before the Americans like
sheep ; till, by a last desperate effort, the officers succeeded in
forcing their way to the front, 'when they presented their swords
and bayonets against the breasts of their own men, and told them,
if they advanced they should die.' Upon this they began to form,
under what the same British officer pronounces 'a very heavy fire,'
which must soon have led to the destruction or capture of the
whole corps. At this critical moment a reinforcement arrived.
Colonel Smith had sent back a messenger from Lexington to apprize General Gage of the check he had there received, and of the
alarm which was running through the country. Three regiments
of infantry and two divisions of marines with two fieldpieces, under
the command of Brigadier General Lord Percy, were accordingly
detached. They marched out of Boston, through Roxbury and
Cambridge,* and came up with the flying party, in the hour of

* See note D.

their extreme peril. While their fieldpieces kept the Americans at bay, the reinforcement drew up in a hollow square, into which, says the British historian, they received the exhausted fugitives, ' who lay down on the ground, with their tongues hanging from their mouths, like dogs after a chase.'

A half hour was given to rest; the march was then resumed; and under cover of the fieldpieces, every house in Lexington, and on the road downwards, was plundered and set on fire. Though the flames in most cases were speedily extinguished, several houses were destroyed. Notwithstanding the attention of a great part of the Americans was thus drawn off, and although the British force was now more than doubled, their retreat still wore the aspect of a flight. The Americans filled the heights that overhung the road, and at every defile the struggle was sharp and bloody. At West Cambridge, the gallant Warren, never distant when danger was to be braved, appeared in the field, and a musket ball soon cut off a lock of hair from his temple. General Heath was with him, nor does there appear till this moment, to have been any effective command among the American forces.

Below West Cambridge, the militia from Dorchester, Roxbury, and Brookline came up. The British fieldpieces began to lose their terror. A sharp skirmish followed, and many fell on both sides. Indignation and outraged humanity struggled on the one hand, veteran discipline and desperation on the other ; and the contest, in more than one instance, was man to man, and bayonet to bayonet.

The British officers had been compelled to descend from their horses to escape the certain destruction, which attended their exposed situation. The wounded, to the number of two hundred, now presented the most distressing and constantly increasing obstruction to the progress of the march. Near one hundred brave men had fallen in this disastrous flight; a considerable number had been made prisoners ; a round or two of ammunition only remained ; and it was not till late in the evening, nearly twenty-four hours from the time when the first detachment was put in motion, that the exhausted remnant reached the heights of Charlestown. The boats of the vessels of war were immediately employed to transport the wounded ; the remaining British troops in Boston came over to Charlestown to protect their weary countrymen during the night ; and before the close of the next day the royal army was formally besieged in Boston.

Such, fellow citizens, imperfectly sketched in their outline, were the events of the day we celebrate ; a day as important as any recorded in the history of man. It is a proud anniversary for our neighborhood. We have cause for honest complacency, that when the distant citizen of our own republic, when the stranger from foreign lands, inquires for the spots where the noble blood of the Revolution began to flow, where the first battle of that great and glorious contest was fought, he is guided through the villages of Middlesex, to the plains of Lexington and Concord. It is a commemoration of our soil, to which ages, as they pass, will add dignity and interest; till the names of Lexington and Concord, in the annals of freedom, will stand by the side of the most honorable names in Roman or Grecian story.

It was one of those great days, one of those elemental occasions in the world's affairs, when the people rise and act for themselves. Some organization and preparation had been made ; but, from the nature of the case, with scarce any effect on the events of that day. It may be doubted, whether there was an efficient order given the whole day to any body of men, as large as a regiment. It was the people, in their first capacity, as citizens and as freemen, starting from their beds at midnight, from their firesides, and from their fields, to take their own cause into their own hands. Such a spectacle is the height of the moral sublime ; when the want of every thing is fully made up by the spirit of the cause ; and the soul within stands in place of discipline, organization, resources. In the prodigious efforts of a veteran army, beneath the dazzling splendor of their their array, there is something revolting to the reflective mind. The ranks are filled with the desperate, the mercenary, the depraved; an iron slavery, by the name of subordination, merges the free will of one hundred thousand men, in the unqualified despotism of one ; the humanity, mercy, and remorse, which scarce ever desert the individual bosom, are sounds without a meaning to that fearful, ravenous, irrational monster of prey, a mercenary army. It is hard to say, who are most to be commiserated, the wretched people, 'on whom it is let loose, or the still more wretched people,

whose substance has been sucked out, to nourish it into strength
and fury.   But in the efforts of the people,—of the people struggling for their rights, moving not in organized, disciplined masses,
but in their spontaneous action, man for man, and heart for heart,
—there is something glorious.   They can then move forward without orders, act together without combination, and brave the flaming
lines of battle, without entrenchments to cover, or walls to shield them.
No dissolute camp has worn off from the feelings of the youthful soldier the freshness of that home, where his mother and his sisters sit
waiting, with tearful eyes and aching hearts, to hear good news
from the wars; no long service in the ranks of a conqueror has
turned the veteran's heart into marble ; their valor springs not from
recklessness, from habit, from indifference to the preservation of a
life, knit by no pledges to the life of others.   But in the strength
and spirit of the cause alone they act, they contend, they bleed.
In this, they conquer.   The people always conquer.   They always
must conquer.   Armies may be defeated; kings may be overthrown,
and new dynasties imposed by foreign arms on an ignorant and
slavish race, that care not in what language the covenant of their
subjection runs, nor in whose name the deed of their barter and
sale is made out.   But the people never invade ; and when they
rise against the invader, are never subdued.   If they are driven from
the plains, they fly to the mountains.   Steep rocks and everlasting
hills are their castles ; the tangled, pathless thicket their palisado,
and nature,—God, is their ally.   Now he overwhelms the hosts of
their enemies beneath his drifting mountains of sand ; now he buries
them beneath a falling atmosphere of polar snows ; he lets loose
his tempests on their fleets ; he puts a folly into their counsels, a
madness into the hearts of their leaders ; and never gave and never will give a full and final triumph over a virtuous, gallant people,
resolved to be free.

    There is another reflection, which deserves to be made, while
we dwell on the events of the nineteenth of April.   It was the
work of the *country*.   The *cities* of America, particularly the
metropolis of our own state, bore their part nobly in the revolutionary contest.   It is not unjust to say, that much of the spirit which
animated America, particularly before the great appeal to arms,
grew out of the comparison of opinions and concert of feeling,

which might not have existed, without the convenience of assembling which our large towns afford. But if we must look to the city for a part of the impulse, we must look to the country at large, for the heart to be moved,—for the strength and vigor to persevere in the motion. It was the great happiness of America, that her cities were no larger, no more numerous, no nearer to each other; that the strength, the intelligence, the spirit of the people were diffused over plains, and encamped on the hills.

In most of the old and powerful states of Europe, the nation is identified with the capital, and the capital with the court. France must fall with the city of Paris, and the city of Paris with a few courtiers, cabinet ministers, and princes. No doubt the English ministry thought that by holding Boston, they held New-England; that the country was conquered in advance, by the military occupation of the great towns. They did not know, that every town and village in America had discussed the great questions at issue for itself; and in its town-meetings, and committees of correspondence and safety, had come to the resolution, that America must not be taxed by England. The English government did not understand,—we hardly understood, ourselves, till we saw it in action, —the operation of a state of society, where every man is or may be a freeholder, a voter for every elective office, a candidate for every one; where the means of a good education are universally accessible; where the artificial distinctions of society are known but in a slight degree; where glaring contrasts of condition are rarely met with; where few are raised by the extreme of wealth above their fellow men, and fewer sunk by the extreme of poverty beneath it. The English ministry had not reasoned upon the natural growth of such a soil; that it could not permanently bear either a colonial, or a monarchical government; that the only true and native growth of such a soil was a perfect independence and an intelligent republicanism. Independence, because such a country must disdain to go over the water to find another to protect it; Republicanism, because the people of such a country must disdain to look up for protection to any one class among themselves. The entire action of these principles was unfolded to the world on the nineteenth of April, 1775. Without waiting to take an impulse from any thing but their own breasts, and in defiance of the whole exerted powers of the British empire, the yeomanry of the country rose as a man, and set their lives on this dear stake of liberty.

When we look back on the condition in which America stood on the 19th of April, 1775 ; and compare it with that in which it stands this day, we can find no language of gratitude with which to do justice to those, who took the lead in the revolutionary cause. The best gratitude, the best thanks will be an imitation of their example. It would be an exceedingly narrow view of the part assigned to this country on the stage of the nations, to consider the erection of an independent and representative government as the only political object at which the Revolution aimed, and the only political improvement which our duty requires. These are two all-important steps, indeed, in the work of meliorating the state of society. The first gives the people of America the sovereign power of carrying its will into execution ; the second furnishes an equitable and convenient mode of ascertaining what the will of the people is. But shall we stop here ? Shall we make no use of these two engines, by whose combined action every individual mind enjoys a share in the sovereign power of this great nation ? Most of the civil and social institutions which still exist in the country, were brought by our fathers from the old world, and are strongly impressed with the character of the state of society which there prevails. Under the influence of necessity, these institutions have been partially reformed, and rendered, to a certain degree, harmonious with the nature of a popular government. But much remains to be done, to make the work of revolution complete. Many portions of our social and political system yet need,—so to say,—to be revolutionized ; that is, to be revised, and made entirely conformable to the interests and wishes of the great mass. It is time, in short, to act upon the maxim in which the wisdom of all ages is wrapped up,—THE VOICE OF THE PEOPLE IS THE VOICE OF GOD. Apart from inspired revelation, there is no way, in which the will of heaven is made known, but by the sound, collective sense of the majority of men. It is given to no privileged family, to no hereditary ruler; it is given to no commanding genius ; it is given to no learned sage ; it is given to no circle of men to pronounce this sacred voice. It must be uttered by the people, in their own capacity : and whensoever it is uttered, I say not it ought to be, but that it will be obeyed.

But it is time to relieve your patience. I need not labor to impress you with a sense of the duty, which devolves on those, whose sires achieved the ever memorable exploits of this day. The lesson, I know, has not been lost upon you. Nowhere have the spirit and principles of the Revolution preserved themselves in greater purity ; nowhere have the institutions, to which the Revolution led, been more firmly cherished. The toils and sufferings of that day were shared by a glorious band of patriots, whose name was your boast while living ; whose memory you will never cease to cherish. The day we commemorate called the noble farmer of Middlesex,—the heroic Prescott,—to the field, and impelled him not to accept, but to solicit the post of honor and danger, on the 17th of June :—noble, I call him, for when did coronet or diadem ever confer distinction, like the glory which rests on that man's name ? In the perils of this day, the venerable Gerry bore his part. This was the day, which called the lamented Brooks and Eustis to their country's service ; which enlisted them, blooming in the freshness and beauty of youth, in that sacred cause, to which the strength of their manhood and the grey hairs of their age were devoted. The soil which holds their honored dust shall never be unworthy of them.

What pride did you not justly feel in that soil, when you lately welcomed the nation's guest,—the venerable champion of America, —to the spot, where that first note of struggling freedom was uttered, which sounded across the Atlantic, and drew him from all the delights of life, to enlist in our cause ! Here, you could tell him, our fathers fought and fell, before they knew whether another arm would be raised to second them. No Washington had appeared to lead, no Lafayette had hastened to assist, no charter of independence had yet breathed the breath of life into the cause, when the nineteenth of April called our fathers to the field.

What remains, then, but to guard the precious birthright of our liberties ; to draw from the soil which we inhabit, a consistency in the principles so nobly vindicated, so sacredly sealed thereon ? It shall never be said, while distant regions, wheresoever the temples

11

of freedom are reared, are sending back their hearts to the plains of
Lexington and Concord, for their brightest and purest examples of
patriotic daring, that we, whose lives are cast on these favored spots,
can become indifferent to the exhortation, which breathes to us
from every sod of the valley. Those principles, which others may
adopt on the colder ground of their reason and their truth, we are
bound to support by the dearest and deepest feelings. Wheresoever the torch of liberty shall expire, wheresoever the manly simplicity of our land shall perish beneath the poison of luxury, wheresoever the cause which called our fathers this day to arms, and the
principles which sustained their hearts in that stern encounter, may
be deserted or betrayed,—it shall not, fellow citizens, it shall not
be, on the soil which was moistened with their blood. The names
of Marathon and Thermopylæ, after ages of subjection, still nerve
the arm of the Grecian patriot; and should the foot of a tyrant, or
of a slave, approach these venerated spots, the noble hearts that
bled at Lexington and Concord, 'all dust as they are,' would beat
beneath the sod with indignation.

Honor, this day, to the venerable survivors of that momentous
day, which tried men's souls. Great is the happiness they are
permitted to enjoy, in uniting, within the compass of their own
experience, the doubtful struggles and the full blown prosperity of
our happy land. May they share the welfare they witness around
them; it is the work of their hands, the fruit of their toils, the
price of their lives freely hazarded, that their children might live
free. Bravely they dared; patiently,—aye, more than patiently,
—heroically, piously, they suffered; largely, richly, may they enjoy. Most of their companions are already departed; let us renew
our tribute of respect this day to their honored memory. Numbers
present will recollect the affecting solemnities, with which you
accompanied to his last home, the brave, the lamented Buttrick.
With trailing banners, and mournful music, and all the touching
ensigns of military sorrow, you followed the bier of the fallen soldier, over the ground where he led the determined band of patriots
on the morn of the Revolution.

But chiefly to those who fell; to those who stood in the breach,
at the breaking of that day of blood at Lexington; to those who
joined in battle, and died honorably, facing the foe at Concord; to

those who fell in the gallant pursuit of the flying enemy ;—let us this day pay a tribute of grateful admiration. The old and the young ; the gray-haired veteran, the stripling in the flower of youth; husbands, fathers, brethren, sons ;—they stood side by side, and fell together, like the beauty of Israel, on their high places.

We have founded this day a monument to their memory. When the hands that rear it are motionless, when the feeble voice is silent, which speaks our father's praise, the engraven stone shall bear witness to other ages, of our gratitude and their worth. And ages still farther on, when the monument itself, like those who build it, shall have crumbled to dust, the happy aspect of the land which our fathers redeemed, the liberty they achieved, the institutions they founded, shall remain, one common, eternal monument to their memory.

NOTES.

Note A, page 74.

THAT the lanterns were observed in Charlestown, we are informed by Colonel Revere, in the interesting communication in the Collections of the Historical Society, from which this part of the narrative is chiefly taken. A tradition by private channels has descended, that these lanterns in the North Church were quickly noticed by the officers of the British army, on duty on the evening of the 18th. To prevent the alarm being communicated by these signals into the country, the British officers, who had noticed them, hastened to the church to extinguish them. Their steps were heard on the stairs in the tower of the church, by the sexton, who had lighted the lanterns. To escape discovery, he himself extinguished the lanterns, and passing by the officers on the stairs, concealed himself in the vaults of the church. He was, a day or two after, arrested, while discharging the duties of his office at a funeral, tried, and condemned to death; but respited on a threat of retaliation from Gen. Washington, and finally exchanged. This anecdote was related to me, with many circumstances of particularity, by one who had often heard it from the sexton himself.

Note B, page 74.

The manner in which Colonel Revere was received at Lexington, which is not related in his own letter, will appear from the following extract from the deposition of Colonel William Munroe, which, with several other similar interesting documents, forms a part of the Appendix to the pamphlet alluded to in the next note.

"About midnight, Colonel Paul Revere rode up and requested

admittance. I told him the family had just retired, and requested they might not be disturbed by any noise about the house. ' Noise!' said he, ' you 'll have noise enough before long. The regulars are coming out.' We then permitted him to pass." p. 33.

Note C, page 79.

It will be perceived, that, in drawing up the account of the transactions at Lexington, reference has been had to the testimony contained in the pamphlet lately published, entitled, ' History of the Battle at Lexington, on the morning of the 19th of April, 1775. By Elias Phinney.' While in this pamphlet several interesting facts are added, on the strength of the depositions of surviving actors in the scene, to the accounts previously existing, there is nothing, perhaps, in them, which may not be reconciled with those previously existing accounts, if due allowance be made for the sole object for which the latter were originally published,—(to show that the British were the aggressors,)—for the hurry and confusion of the moment; and for the different aspect of the scene as witnessed by different persons, from different points of view. It has, however, been my aim not to pronounce on questions in controversy; but to state the impression left on my own mind, after an attentive examination of all the evidence.

Note D, page 83.

An interesting anecdote relative to this march of Lord Percy has been communicated to me by a veteran of the Revolution, who bore his part in the events of the day. Intelligence having been promptly received of Lord Percy's being detached, the Selectmen of Cambridge, by order of the Committee of Safety, caused the planks of the Old Bridge to be taken up. Had this been effectually done, it would have arrested the progress of Lord Percy. But the planks, though all taken up, instead of being thrown into the river or removed to a distance, were piled up on the causeway, at the Cambridge end of the bridge. But little time was therefore lost by Lord Percy, in sending over men upon the string-pieces of the bridge, who replaced the planks, so as to admit the passage of the troops. This was, however, so hastily and insecurely done, that when a convoy of provision wagons, with a sergeant's guard, which had followed in the rear of the reinforcement, reached the bridge, the planks were found to be too loosely laid to admit a safe passage; and a good deal of time was consumed in adjusting them. The convoy at length passed; but after such a delay, that Lord Percy's army was out of sight. The officer who commanded the convoy was unacquainted with the roads, and was misdirected by the inhabitants at Cambridge; having at last, after much lost time, been put into the right road, the body of troops under Lord Percy was so far advanced, as to afford the convoy no protection. A plan was accordingly laid and executed by the citizens of West Cambridge (then Menotomy) to arrest this convoy. The alarum-list, or body of exempts, under Captain Frost, by whom this exploit was effected, acted under the direction of a negro, who had served in the French war; and who, on this occasion, displayed the utmost skill and spirit. The history of Gordon, and the other accounts which follow him, attribute the capture of the convoy to the Rev. Dr Payson of Chelsea. Those who have farther information alone can judge between the two accounts. The Rev. Mr Thaxter of Edgartown, in a letter lately (1825) published in the United States Literary Gazette, has ascribed the same exploit to the Rev. Edward Brooks of Medford. Mr Brooks early hastened to the field as a volunteer that day; and is said to have preserved the life of Lieut. Gould of the 18th regiment, who was made prisoner at Concord Bridge; but there is, I believe, no ground for ascribing to him the conduct of the affair in question.

ORATION

DELIVERED AT CAMBRIDGE, ON THE FOURTH OF JULY, 1826.

FELLOW CITIZENS,

IT belongs to us, with strong propriety, to celebrate this day. The town of Cambridge, and the county of Middlesex, are filled with the vestiges of the Revolution; whithersoever we turn our eyes, we behold some memento of its glorious scenes. Within the walls, in which we are now assembled, was convened the first provincial Congress, after its adjournment at Concord. The rural magazine at Medford, reminds us of one of the earliest acts of British aggression. The march of both divisions of the Royal army, on the memorable nineteenth of April, was through the limits of Cambridge; in the neighboring towns of Lexington and Concord, the first blood of the Revolution was shed; in West Cambridge, the Royal convoy of provisions was, the same day, gallantly surprised by the aged citizens, who staid to protect their homes, while their sons pursued the foe. Here the first American army was formed; from this place, on the seventeenth of June, was detached the Spartan band, that immortalized the heights of Charlestown; consecrated that day, with blood and fire, to the cause of American liberty. Beneath the venerable elm, which still shades the southwestern corner of the common, General Washington first unsheathed his sword at the head of an American army; and to *that* seat* he was wont every Sunday to repair, to join in the supplications which were made for the welfare of his country.

---

* The first wall pew, on the right hand of the pulpit.

How changed is now the scene! The foe is gone! The din and the desolation of war are passed; Science has long since resumed her station in the shades of our venerable University, no longer glittering with arms. The anxious war-council is no longer in session, to offer a reward for the discovery of the best mode of making saltpetre,—an unpromising stage of hostilities, when an army of twenty thousand men is in the field in front of the foe. The tall grass now waves in the trampled sallyports of some of the rural redoubts, that form a part of the simple lines of circumvallation, within which a half-armed American militia held the flower of the British army blockaded; the plough has done, what the English batteries could not do,—and levelled others of them with the earth; and the MEN, the great and good men,—their warfare is over, and they have gone quietly down to the dust they redeemed from oppression!

At the close of a half century since the declaration of our Independence, we are assembled to commemorate that great and happy event. We come together, not because it needs, but because it deserves these acts of celebration. We do not meet each other, and exchange our felicitations, because we should otherwise fall into forgetfulness of this auspicious era; but because we owe it to our fathers and to our children, to mark its return with grateful festivities. The major part of this assembly is composed of those, who had not yet engaged in the active scenes of life, when the Revolution commenced. We come not to applaud our own work, but to pay a filial tribute to the deeds of our fathers. It was for their children, that the heroes and sages of the Revolution labored and bled. They were too wise not to know, that it was not personally their own cause, in which they were embarked; they felt that they were engaging in an enterprise, which an entire generation must be too short to bring to its mature and perfect issue. The most they could promise themselves was, that, having cast forth the seed of liberty; having shielded its tender germ from the stern blasts that beat upon it; having watered it with the tears of waiting eyes, and the blood of brave hearts; their children might gather the fruit of its branches, while those who planted it should moulder in peace beneath its shade.

Nor was it only in this, that we discern their disinterestedness,

and their heroic forgetfulness of self.   Not only was the independence, for which they struggled, a great and arduous adventure, of
which they were to encounter the risk, and others to enjoy the
benefits; but the oppressions, which roused them, had assumed, in
their day, no worse form than that of a pernicious principle.   No
intolerable acts of oppression had ground them to the dust.   They
were not slaves, rising in desperation from beneath the agonies of
the lash; but free men, snuffing from afar 'the tainted gale of
tyranny.'   The worst encroachments on which the British ministry had ventured, might have been borne, consistently with the
practical enjoyment of many of the advantages, resulting from
good government.   On the score of calculation alone, that generation had much better have paid the duties on glass, painters'
colors, stamped paper, and tea, than have plunged into the expenses of the Revolutionary war.   But they thought not of shuffling
off upon posterity the burden of resistance.   They well understood the part, which Providence had assigned to them.   They
perceived that they were called to discharge a high and perilous
office to the cause of Freedom; that their hands were elected to
strike the blow, for which near two centuries of preparation—never
remitted, though often unconscious—had been making, on one side
or the other of the Atlantic.   They felt that the colonies had now
reached that stage in their growth, when the difficult problem of
colonial government must be solved.   Difficult, I call it, for such
it is to the statesman, whose mind is not sufficiently enlarged for
the idea, that a wise colonial government must naturally and rightfully end in independence; that even a mild and prudent sway, on
the part of the mother country, furnishes no reason for not severing
the bands of the colonial subjection; and that when the rising
state has passed the period of adolescence, the only alternate which
remains, is that of a peaceable or violent separation.

    The British ministry, at that time weaker than it had ever been
since the infatuated reign of James II, had no knowledge of political science, but that which they derived from the text of official
records.   They drew their maxims, as it was happily said of one
of them, that he did his measures, from the file.   They heard that
a distant province had resisted the execution of an act of parliament.   Indeed, and what is the specific, in cases of resistance?—
    12

a military force ;—and two more regiments are ordered to Boston. Again they hear, that the General Court of Massachusetts Bay has adopted measures, subversive of the allegiance due to the crown. A case of a refractory corporation ;—what is to be done? First try a mandamus ; and if that fails, seize the franchises into his majesty's hands. They never asked the great question, whether Providence has assigned no laws to regulate the changes in the condition of that most astonishing of human things, a nation of kindred men. They did not inquire, I will not say whether it were rightful and expedient, but whether it were practicable, to give law across the Atlantic, to a people who possessed within themselves every imaginable element of self-government ;—a people rocked in the cradle of liberty, brought up to hardship, inheriting little but their rights on earth, and their hopes in heaven.

But though the rulers of Britain appear not to have caught a glimpse of the great principles involved in these questions, our fathers had asked and answered them. They perceived, with the rapidity of intuition, that the hour of separation had come ; because a principle was assumed by the British government, which put an instantaneous check to the further growth of liberty. Either the race of civilized man happily planted on our shores, at first slowly and painfully reared, but at length auspiciously multiplying in America, is destined never to constitute a free and independent state ; or these measures must be resisted, which go to bind it, in a mild but abject colonial vassalage. Either the hope must be forever abandoned, that had been brightening and kindling toward assurance, like the glowing skies of the morning,—the hope that a new centre of civilization was to be planted on the new continent, at which the social and political institutions of the world may be brought to the standard of reason and truth, after thousands of years of degeneracy,—either this hope must be abandoned, and forever, or the battle was now to be fought, first in the political assemblies, and then, if need be, in the field.

It can scarcely be said, that the battle was fought, in the halls of legislation. A spectacle indeed seemed to be promised to the civilized world, of breathless interest, and uncalculated consequence. ' You are placed,' said the provincial Congress of Massachusetts, in their address to the inhabitants, of December 4th, 1774, promulgated at the close of a session held in the very house, where we are now convened, 'You are placed by Providence in a post of honor, because it is a post of danger; and while struggling for the noblest objects, the liberties of our country, the happiness of posterity, and the rights of human nature, the eyes, not only of North America and the whole British empire, but of all Europe, are upon you.'* A mighty question of political right was at issue, between the two hemispheres. Europe and America, in the face of mankind, are going to plead the great cause, on which the fate of popular government forever is suspended. One circumstance, and one alone exists, to diminish the interest of the contention—the perilous inequality of the parties,—an inequality far exceeding that, which gives animation to a contest; and so great as to destroy the hope of an ably waged encounter. On the one side were arrayed the two houses of the British parliament, the modern school of political eloquence, the arena where great minds had for a century and a half strenuously wrestled themselves into strength and power, and in better days the common and upright chancery of an empire, on which the sun never set. Upon the other side rose up the colonial assemblies of Massachusetts and Virginia, and the continental congress of Philadelphia, composed of men trained within a small provincial circuit;—unaccustomed to the inspiration, which the consciousness of a station before the world imparts; who brought no power into the contest, but that which they drew from their cause and their bosoms. It is by champions like these, that the great principles of representative government, of chartered rights, and constitutional liberty, are to be discussed; and surely never, in the annals of national controversy, was exhibited a triumph so complete of the seemingly weaker party, a rout so disastrous of the stronger.

Often as it has been repeated, it will bear another repetition; it never ought to be omitted in the history of constitutional liberty; it ought especially to be repeated this day;—the various addresses, petitions, and appeals, the correspondence, the resolutions, the legislative and popular debates, from 1764, to the declaration of independence, present a maturity of political wisdom, a strength of

* Massachusetts State Papers, p. 416.

argument, a gravity of style, a manly eloquence, and a moral courage, of which unquestionably the modern world affords no other
example.   This meed of praise, substantially accorded at the time
by lord Chatham, in the British parliament, may well be repeated
by us.   For most of the venerated men to whom it is paid, it is
but a pious tribute to departed worth.   The Lees and the Henrys,
Otis, Quincy, Warren, and Samuel Adams, the men who spoke
those words of thrilling power, which raised and directed the storm
of resistance, and rang like the voice of fate across the Atlantic,
are beyond the reach of our praise.   To most of them it was
granted to witness some of the fruits of their labors; such fruits as
revolutions do not often bear.   Others departed at an untimely
hour, or nobly fell in the onset; too soon for their country, too soon
for liberty, too soon for every thing but their own undying fame.
But all are not gone; some still survive among us; the favored,
enviable men, to hail the jubilee of the independence they declared.
Go back, fellow citizens, to that day, when Jefferson and Adams
composed the sub-committee, who reported the Declaration of
Independence.   Think of the mingled sensations of that proud
but anxious day, compared to the joy of this.   What reward, what
crown, what treasure, could the world and all its kingdoms afford,
compared with the honor and happiness of having been united in
that commission, and living to see its most wavering hopes turned
into glorious reality.   Venerable men! you have outlived the dark
days, which followed your more than heroic deed; you have outlived your own strenuous contention, who should stand first among
the people, whose liberty you had vindicated.   You have lived to
bear to each other the respect, which the nation bears to you both;
and each has been so happy as to exchange the honorable name
of the leader of a party, for that more honorable one, the Father
of his Country.   While this our tribute of respect, on the jubilee
of our independence, is paid to the grey hairs of the venerable sur-
vivor in our neighborhood; let it not less heartily be sped to him,
whose hand traced the lines of that sacred charter, which, to the
end of time, has made this day illustrious.   And is an empty profession of respect all that we owe to the man, who can show the
original draught of the Declaration of the Independence of the
United States of America, in his own handwriting?   Ought not a

title-deed like this to become the acquisition of the nation? Ought
it not to be laid up in the archives of the people? Ought not the
price, at which it is bought, to be a provision for the ease and comfort of the old age of him who drew it? Ought not he, who at the
age of thirty declared the independence of his country, at the age
of eighty, to be secured by his country in the enjoyment of his
own?

Nor would we, on the return of this eventful day,* forget the
men, who, when the conflict of counsel was over, stood forward in
that of arms. Yet let me not by faintly endeavoring to sketch, do
deep injustice to the story of their exploits. The efforts of a life
would scarce suffice to paint out this picture, in all its astonishing
incidents, in all its mingled colors of sublimity and woe, of agony
and triumph. But the age of commemoration is at hand. The
voice of our fathers' blood begins to cry to us, from beneath the
soil which it moistened. Time is bringing forward, in their proper
relief, the men and the deeds of that high-souled day. The generation of contemporary worthies is gone; the crowd of the
unsignalized great and good disappears; and the leaders in war as
well as counsel, are seen, in Fancy's eye, to take their stations on
the mount of Remembrance. They come from the embattled
cliffs of Abraham; they start from the heaving sods of Bunker's
Hill; they gather from the blazing lines of Saratoga and Yorktown, from the blood-dyed waters of the Brandywine, from the
dreary snows of Valley Forge, and all the hard fought fields of
the war! With all their wounds and all their honors, they rise
and plead with us, for their brethren who survive; and command
us, if indeed we cherish the memory of those, who bled in our
cause, to show our gratitude, not by sounding words but by stretching out the strong arm of the country's prosperity, to help the
veteran survivors gently down to their graves!

But it is time to turn from sentiments, on which it is unavailing
to dwell. The fiftieth return of this all-important day, appears to
enjoin on us to reassert the principles of the Declaration of Independence. Have we met, fellow-citizens, to commemorate merely the

* About the time these words were uttered, Thomas Jefferson breathed his last,
and toward the close of the afternoon of the same day, John Adams also expired.
See the following Address.

successful termination of a war?   Certainly not ; the war of 1756 was, in its duration, nearly equal, and signalized in America by the most brilliant achievements of the provincial arms.   But no one attempts to prevent that war, with all its glorious incidents, from gradually sinking into the shadows, which time throws back on the deeds of men.   Do we celebrate the anniversary of our independence, merely because a vast region was severed from an European empire, and established a government for itself ?   Scarcely even this ; the acquisition of Louisiana, a region larger than the old United States,—the almost instantaneous conversion of a vast Spanish colonial waste, into free and prosperous members of our republican federation,—the whole effected by a single happy exercise of the treaty-making power,—this is an event, in nature not wholly unlike, in importance not infinitely beneath the separation of the colonies from England, regarded merely as an historical transaction.   But no one thinks of commemorating with festivals the anniversary of this cession ; perhaps not ten who hear me recollect the date of the treaty by which it was effected ; although it is perhaps the most important occurrence in our history, since the declaration of independence, and will render the administration of Mr Jefferson memorable, as long as our republic shall endure.

But it is not merely nor chiefly the military success nor the political event, which we commemorate on these patriotic anniversaries.   We mistake the principle of our celebration when we speak of its object, either as a trite theme, or as one among other important and astonishing incidents, of the same kind in the world.   The declaration of the independence of the United States of America, considered, on the one hand as the consummation of a long train of measures and counsels,—preparatory, even though unconsciously of this event,—and on the other hand, as the foundation of the systems of government, which have happily been established in our beloved country, deserves commemoration, as forming the era, from which the establishment of government on a rightful foundation is destined universally to date.   Looking upon the declaration of independence as the one prominent event which is to represent the American system, (and history will so look upon it,) I deem it right in itself and seasonable this day to assert, that, while all other political revolutions, reforms, and improvements have been in various ways of the nature of palliatives and alleviations of systems essentially and irremediably vicious, this alone is the great discovery in political science ; the practical fulfilment of all the theories of political perfection, which had amused the speculations and eluded the grasp of every former period and people. Although this festive hour affords but little scope for dry disquisition, and shall not be engrossed by me with abstract speculation, yet I shall not think I wander from the duties of the day, in dwelling briefly on the chain of ideas, by which we reach this great conclusion.

The political organization of a people is of all matters of temporal concernment the most important. Drawn together into that great assemblage, which we call a nation, by the social principle, some mode of organization must exist among men ; and on that organization depends more directly, more collectively, more permanently, than on any thing else, the condition of the individual members that make up the community. On the political organization, in which a people shall for generations have been reared, it mainly depends, whether we shall behold in our fellow man the New Hollander, making a nauseous meal from the worms which he extracts from a piece of rotten wood ;*—the African cutting out the under jaw of his captive to be strung on a wire, as a trophy of victory, while the mangled wretch is left to bleed to death, on the field of battle ;†—or whether we shall behold him social, civilized, christian ; scarcely faded from that perfect image, in which

> ' —— in beauty clad,
> With health in every vein,
> And reason throned upon his brow,
> Stepped forth immortal man.'

Such is the infinite importance to the nations of men of the political organization which prevails among them. The most momentous practical question, therefore, of course, is, in what way a people shall determine the political organization under which it will live ; or, in still broader terms, what is a right foundation of government. Till the establishment of the American constitutions, this question had received but one answer in the world ; I mean but

---

* Malthus's Essay on Population, vol. I. p. 33. Amer. ed.
† Edwards's History of the West Indies, vol. II. p. 68. 3d ed.

one, which obtained for any length of time and among any numerous people ; and that answer was, *force.* The right of the strongest was the only footing on which the governments of the ancient and modern nations were in fact placed ; and the only effort of the theorists was, to disguise the simple and somewhat startling doctrine of the right of the strongest, by various mystical or popular fictions, which in no degree altered its real nature. Of these the only two worthy to detain us, on the present occasion, are those of the two great English political parties, the whigs and the tories, as they are called, by names not unlike, in dignity and significance, to the doctrines which are designated by them. The tories taught, that the only foundation of government was ' divine right ;' and this is substantially the same notion, which is still inculcated on the continent of Europe ; though the delicate ears of the age are flattered by the somewhat milder term, *legitimacy.* The whigs maintained, that the foundation of government was an ' original contract ;' but of this contract the existing organization was the record and the evidence ; and the obligation was perpetually binding. It may deserve the passing remark, therefore, that in reality the doctrine of the whigs in England is a little less liberal than that of the tories. To say, that the will of God is the warrant, by which the king and his hereditary counsellors govern the land, is, to be sure, in a practical sense, what the illustrious sage of the Revolution, surviving in our neighborhood, dared, as early as 1765, to pronounce it, ' dark ribaldry.' But in a merely speculative sense, it may, without offence, be said, that government, like every thing else, subsists by the Divine will ; and in this acceptation, there is a certain elevation and unction in the sentiment. But to say, that the form of government is matter of original compact with the people ; that my ancestors, ages ago, agreed that they and their prosperity, to the end of time, should give up to a certain line of princes the rule of the state ; that no right remains of revising this compact ; that nothing but extreme necessity, a necessity which it is treasonable even to attempt to define beforehand, justifies a departure from this compact, in which no provision is made, that the will of the majority should prevail, but the contrary ;—seems to me to be a use of language, not in itself more rational, and obnoxious to the charge, of affecting a liberality which it does not possess.

And now, fellow citizens, I think I speak the words of truth, without exaggeration, when I say, that before the establishment of our American constitutions, this tory doctrine of the divine right was the most common, and this whig doctrine of the original contract was professedly the most liberal doctrine, ever maintained by any political party in any powerful state. I do not mean, that in some of the little Grecian republics, during their short-lived noon of liberty and glory, nothing better was practised ; nor that, in other times and places, speculative politicians had not in their closets dreamed of a better foundation of government. But I do mean, that, whereas the whigs in England are the party of politicians who have enjoyed, by general consent, the credit of inculcating a more liberal system, this notion of the compact is the extent to which their liberality went.

It is plain, whichever of these phrases,—' divine right,' or ' original compact,'—we may prefer to use, that the right of the strongest lies at the foundation of both, in the same way, and to the same degree. The doctrine of the divine right gives to the ruler authority to sustain himself against the people, not merely because resistance is unlawful, but because it is sacrilegious. The doctrine of the compact denounces every attempted change in the person of the prince as a breach of faith, and as such also not only treasonable but immoral. When a conflict ensues, force alone, of course, decides which party shall prevail ; and when force has so decided, all the sanctions of the divine will and of the social compact revive in favor of the successful party. Even the statute legislation of England allows the successful usurper to claim the allegiance of the subject, in as full a manner as it could be done by a lawful sovereign.

Nothing is wanting to fill up this sketch of other governments, but to consider what is the form in which force is exercised to sustain them ; and this is that of a standing army ;—at this moment, the chief support of every government on earth, except our own. As popular violence, the unrestrained and irresistible force of the mass of men, long oppressed and late awakened, and bursting in its wrath all barriers of law and humanity,—is unhappily the usual instrument by which the intolerable abuses of a corrupt government are removed ; so the same blind force of the same fearful

13

multitude, systematically kept in ignorance both of their duty and
their privileges as citizens, employed in a form somewhat different
indeed, but far more dreadful,—that of a mercenary standing army,
—is the instrument by which corrupt governments are sustained.
The deplorable scenes which marked the earlier stages of the French
Revolution have called the attention of this age to the fearful effects
of popular violence ; and the minds of men have recoiled from the
horrors which lead the van, and the desolation which marks the
progress of an infuriated mob.   But the power of the mob is transient ; the rising sun most commonly scatters its mistrustful ranks ;
the difficulty of subsistence drives its members asunder ; and it is
only while it exists in mass, that it is terrible.   But there is a form,
in which the mob is indeed portentous ; when to all its native terrors it adds the force of a frightful permanence ; when, by a regular
organization, its strength is so curiously divided, and by a strict
discipline its parts are so easily combined, that each and every portion of it carries in its presence the strength and terror of the whole ;
and when, instead of that want of concert which renders the common mob incapable of arduous enterprises, it is despotically swayed
by a single master mind, and may be moved in array across the
globe.

I remember, (if, on such a subject, I may be pardoned an illustration approaching the ludicrous,) to have seen the two kinds of
mob brought into direct collision.   I was present at the second great
meeting of the populace of London in 1819, in the midst of a
crowd of I know not how many thousands, but assuredly a vast
multitude, which was gathered together in Smithfield market.   The
universal distress was extreme ; it was a short time after the scenes
at Manchester, at which the public mind was exasperated ;—deaths
by starvation were said not to be rare ;—ruin by the stagnation of
business was general ;—and some were already brooding over the
dark project of assassinating the ministers, which was not long after
matured by Thistlewood and his associates ; some of whom, on the
day to which I allude, harangued this excited, desperate, starving
assemblage.   When I considered the state of feeling prevailing in
the multitude around me,—when I looked in their lowering faces,
—heard their deep, indignant exclamations,—reflected on the
physical force concentrated, probably that of thirty or forty thousand

able-bodied men; and added to all this, that they were assembled
to exercise an undoubted privilege of British citizens; I did suppose that any small number of troops, who should attempt to
interrupt them, would be immolated on the spot. While I was
musing on these things, and turning in my mind the commonplaces
on the terrors of a mob, a trumpet was heard to sound,—an uncertain, but a harsh and clamorous blast. I looked that the surrounding stalls, in the market, should have furnished the unarmed multitude at least with that weapon, with which Virginius sacrificed his
daughter to the liberty of Rome; I looked that the flying pavement should begin to darken the air. Another blast is heard,—a
cry of 'The horse-guards!' ran through the assembled thousands;
the orators on the platform were struck mute; and the whole of
that mighty host of starving, desperate men incontinently took to their
heels; in which, I must confess,—feeling no call, on that occasion,
to be faithful found, among the faithless,—I did myself join them.
We had run through the Old Bailey and reached Ludgate hill,
before we found out that we had been put to flight by a single
mischievous tool of power, who had come triumphing down the
opposite street on horseback, blowing a stage-coachman's horn.

We have heard of those midnight scenes of desolation, when the
populace of some overgrown capital, exhausted by the extremity of
political oppression, or famishing at the gates of luxurious palaces,
or kindled by some transport of fanatical zeal rushes out to find the
victims of its fury; the lurid glare of torches, casting their gleams
on faces dark with rage; the ominous din of the alarm bell, striking with affright on the broken visions of the sleepers; the horrid
yells, the thrilling screams, the multitudinous roar of the living
storm, as it sweeps onward to its objects;—but oh, the disciplined,
the paid, the honored mob; not moving in rags and starvation to
some act of blood or plunder; but marching, in all the pomp and
circumstance of war, to lay waste a feebler state; or cantoned at
home among an overawed and broken-spirited people! I have
read of granaries plundered, of castles sacked, and their inmates
cruelly murdered, by the ruthless hands of the mob. I have read
of friendly states ravaged, governments overturned, tyrannies founded and upheld, proscriptions executed, fruitful regions turned into

trampled deserts, the tide of civilization thrown back, and a line of generations cursed, by a well organized system of military force.

Such was the foundation in theory and in practice of all the governments which can be considered as having had a permanent existence in the world, before the Revolution in this country. There are certainly shades of difference between the oriental despotisms, ancient and modern,—the military empire of Rome,—the feudal sovereignties of the middle ages,—and the legitimate monarchies of the present day. Some were and are more, and some less, susceptible of melioration in practice ; and of all of them it might perhaps be said,—being all in essence bad,

'That, which is best administered, is best.'

In no one of these governments, nor in any government, was the truth admitted, that the only just foundation of all government is the will of the people. If it ever occurred to the practical or theoretical politician, that such an idea deserved examination, the experiment was thought to have been made in the republics of Greece, and to have failed ; as fail it certainly did, from the physical impossibility of conducting the business of the state by the actual intervention of every citizen. Such a plan of government must of course fail ; if for no other reason, at least for this, that it would prevent the citizen from pursuing his own business, which it is the object of all government to enable him to do. It was considered then as settled, that the citizens, each and all, could not be the government ; some one or more must discharge its duties for them. Who shall do this ;—how shall they be designated ?

The first king was a fortunate soldier, and the first nobleman was one of his generals ; and government has passed by descent to their posterity, with no other interruption than has taken place, when some new soldier of fortune has broken in upon this line of succession, in favor of himself and of his generals. The people have passed for nothing in the plan ; and whenever it has occurred to a busy genius to put the question, By what right is government thus exercised and transmitted ? the common answer, as we have seen, has been, By divine right ; while in times of rare illumination, men have been consoled with the assurance, that such was the original contract.

But a brighter day and a better dispensation were in reserve. The founders of the feudal system, barbarous, arbitrary, and despotic as they were, and profoundly ignorant of political science, were animated by a spirit of personal liberty ; out of which, after ages of conflict, grew up a species of popular representation. In the eye of the feudal system, the king was the first baron, and standing within his own sphere, each other baron was as good as the first. From this important relation, in which the feudal lords of England claimed to stand to their prince, arose the practice of their being consulted by him, in great and difficult conjunctures of affairs ; and hence the cooperation of a grand council, (subsequently convened in two houses under the name of *parliament*,) in making the laws and administering the government. The formation of this body has proved a great step in the progress of popular rights ; its influence has been decisive in breaking the charm of absolute monarchy, and giving to a body partially elegible by the people a share in the government. It has also operated most auspiciously on liberty, by exhibiting to the world, on the theatre of a conspicuous nation, a living example, that in proportion as the rights and interests of a people are represented in a government, in that degree the state becomes strong and prosperous. Thus far the science and the practice of government had gone in England, and here it had come to a stand. An equal representation, even in the House of Commons, was unthought of ; or thought of only as one of the exploded abominations of Cromwell. It is asserted by Mr Hume, writing about the middle of the last century, and weighing this subject with equal moderation and sagacity, that ' the tide has run long and with some rapidity, to the side of popular government, and is just beginning to turn toward monarchy.' And he maintains that the British constitution is, though slowly, yet gradually verging toward an absolute government.

Such was the state of political science, when the independence of our country was declared, and its constitution organized on the basis of that declaration. The precedents in favor of a popular system were substantially these,—the short-lived prosperity of the republics of Greece, where each citizen took part in the conduct of affairs ; and the admission into the British government of one branch of the legislature nominally elective, and operating, rather by opinion than power, as a partial check on the other branches. What lights these precedents gave them, our fathers had; beyond this, they owed every thing to their own wisdom and courage, in daring to carry out and apply to the executive branch of the government that system of delegated power, of which the elements existed in their own provincial assemblies.   They assumed, at once, not as a matter to be reached by argumentation, but as the dictate of unaided reason,—as an axiom too obvious to be discussed, though never in practice applied,—that where the state is too large to be governed by an actual assembly of all the citizens, the people shall elect those, who will act for them, in making the laws and administering the government.   They, therefore, laid the basis of their constitutions in a proportionate delegation of power from every part of the community; and regarding the declaration of our independence as the true era of our institutions, we are authorized to assert, that from that era dates the establishment of the only perfect organization of government, that of a Representative Republic, administered by persons freely chosen by the people.

The plan of government is therefore, in its theory, perfect; and in its operation it is perfect also;—that is to say, no measure of policy, public or private, domestic or foreign, can long be pursued, against the will of a majority of the people.   Farther than this the wisdom of government cannot go.   The majority of the people may err.   Man collectively, as well as individually, is man still; but whom can you more safely trust than the majority of the people? who is so likely to be right, always right, and altogether right, as the collective majority of a great and civilized nation, represented in all its interests and pursuits, and in all its communities?

Thus has been solved the great problem in human affairs; and a frame of government, perfect in its principles, has been brought down from the airy regions of Utopia, and has found ' a local habitation and a name ' in our country.   Henceforward we have only to strive that the practical operation of our systems may be true to their spirit and theory.   Henceforth it may be said of us, what never could be said of any people, since the world began,—be our sufferings what they will, no one can attribute them to our frame of government; no one can point out a principle in our political system, of which he has had reason to complain; no one can sigh for a change in his country's institutions, as a boon to be desired for himself or for his children. There is not an apparent defect in our constitutions which could be removed without introducing a greater one; nor a real evil, whose removal would not be rather a nearer approach to the principles on which they are founded, than a departure from them.

And what, fellow citizens, are to be the fruits to us and to the world, of the establishment of this perfect system of government? I might partly answer the inquiry, by reminding you what have been the fruits to us and to the world; by inviting you to compare our beloved country, as it is, in extent of settlement, in numbers and resources, in the useful and ornamental arts, in the abundance of the common blessings of life, in the general standard of character, in the means of education, in the institutions for social objects, in the various great industrious interests, in public strength and national respectability, with what it was in all these respects fifty years ago. But the limits of this occasion will not allow us to engage in such an enumeration; and it will be amply sufficient for us to contemplate in its *principle*, the beneficial operation on society, of the form of government bequeathed to us by our fathers. This principle is Equality; the equal enjoyment by every citizen of the rights and privileges of the social union.

The principle of all other governments is monopoly, exclusion, favor. They secure great privileges to a small number, and necessarily at the expense of all the rest of the citizens.

In the keen conflict of minds, which preceded and accompanied the political convulsions of the last generation, the first principles of society were canvassed with a boldness and power before unknown in Europe; and, from the great principle that *all men are equal*, it was for the first time triumphantly inferred, as a necessary consequence, that the will of a majority of the people is the rule of government. To meet these doctrines, so appalling in their tendency to the existing institutions of Europe, new ground was also taken by the champions of those institutions, and particularly by a man, whose genius, eloquence, and integrity gave a currency, which nothing else could have given, to his splendid paradoxes. In one of his renowned productions,* this great man,—for great, almost beyond

* The Appeal from the New to the Old Whigs.

rivalry, even in his errors, most assuredly he was,—in order to meet the inference drawn from the equality of man, that the will of the majority must be the rule of government, has undertaken, as he says, ' to fix, with some degree of distinctness, an idea of what it is we mean, when we say, the PEOPLE ; ' and in fulfilment of this design, he lays it down, ' that in a state of rude nature, there is no such thing as a people. A number of men, in themselves, can have no collective capacity. The idea of a people is the idea of a corporation ; it is wholly artificial, and made like all other legal fictions, by common agreement.'

' In a state of rude nature, there is no such thing as a people ! ' I would fain learn in what corner of the earth, rude or civilized, men are to be found, who are not a people, more or less improved. ' A number of men in themselves have no collective capacity ! ' I would gladly be told where,—in what region, I will not say of geography, but of poetry or romance,—a number of men has been placed, by nature, each standing alone, and not bound by any of those ties of blood, affinity, and language, which form the rudiments of a collective capacity. ' The idea of a people is the idea of a corporation ; it is wholly artificial, and made like all other legal fictions, by common agreement.' Indeed, is the social principle artificial ? is the gift of articulate speech, which enables man to impart his condition to man, the organized sense, which enables him to comprehend what is imparted ? is that sympathy, which subjects our opinions and feelings, and through them our conduct, to the influence of others, and their conduct to our influence ? is that chain of cause and effect, which makes our characters receive impressions from the generations before us, and puts it in our power, by a good or bad precedent, to distil a poison or a balm into the characters of posterity,—are these, indeed, all by-laws of a corporation ? Are all the feelings of ancestry, posterity, and fellow-citizenship ; all the charm, veneration and love, bound up in the name of *country ;* the delight, the enthusiasm, with which we seek out, after the lapse of generations and ages, the traces of our fathers' bravery or wisdom, are these all ' a legal fiction ? ' Is it, indeed, a legal fiction, that moistens the eye of the solitary traveller, when he meets a countryman in a foreign land ? Is it a ' common agreement,' that gives its meaning to my mother tongue, and enables me to speak to the hearts of my kindred men, beyond the rivers and beyond the mountains? Yes, it is a common agreement; recorded on the same registry with that, which marshals the winged nations, that,

> In common, ranged in figure, wedge their way,
> Intelligent of seasons; and set forth
> Their aery caravan, high over seas
> Flying, and over lands, with mutual wing
> Easing their flight.

The mutual dependence of man on man, family on family, interest on interest, is but a chapter in the great law, not of corporations, but of nature. The law, by which commerce, manufactures, and agriculture support each other, is the same law, in virtue of which the thirsty earth owes its fertility to the rivers and the rains; and the clouds derive their high-travelling waters from the rising vapors; and the ocean is fed from the secret springs of the mountains; and the plant that grows derives its increase from the plant that decays; and all subsist and thrive, not by themselves but by others, in the great political economy of nature. The necessary cohesion of the parts of the political system is no more artificial, than the gravity of the natural system, in which planet is bound to planet, and all to the sun, and the sun to all. And yet the great political, intellectual, moral system, which we call a People, is a legal fiction! 'O that mine enemy had said it,' the admirers of Mr Burke may well exclaim. O that some ruthless Voltaire, some impious Rousseau had uttered it. Had uttered it? Rousseau did utter the same thing; and more rebuked than any other error of this misguided genius, is his doctrine of the Social Contract, of which Burke has reasserted, and more than reasserted the principle, in the sentences I have quoted.

But no, fellow citizens; political society exists by the law of nature. Man is formed for it; every man is formed for it; every man has an equal right to its privileges; and to be deprived of them, under whatever pretence, is so far to be reduced to slavery. The authors of the declaration of independence saw this, and taught that all men are born free and equal. On this principle, our constitutions rest; and no constitution can bind a people on any other principle. No original contract, that gives away this right, can

14

bind any but the parties to it. My forefathers could not, if they had wished, have stipulated to their king, that his children should rule over their children. By the introduction of this principle of *equality* it is, that the declaration of independence has at once effected a before unimagined extension of social privileges. Grant that no new blessing (which, however, can by no means with truth be granted) be introduced into the world on this plan of equality, still it will have discharged the inestimable office of communicating, in equal proportion, to all the citizens, those privileges of the social union, which were before partitioned in an invidious gradation, profusely among the privileged orders, and parsimoniously among the rest. Let me instance in the right of suffrage. The enjoyment of this right enters largely into the happiness of the social condition. I do not mean, that it is necessary to our happiness actually to exercise this right at every election ; but I say, the right itself to give our voice in the choice of public servants, and the management of public affairs, is so precious, so inestimable, that there is not a citizen who hears me, that would not lay down his life to assert it. This is a right unknown in every country but ours ; I say unknown, because in England, whose institutions make the nearest approach to a popular character, the elective suffrage is not only incredibly unequal and capricious in its distribution,—but extends, after all, only to the choice of a minority of one house of the legislature.* Thus then the people of this country are, by their constitutions of government, endowed with a new source of enjoyment, elsewhere almost unknown ; a great and substantial happiness ; a real happiness. Most of the desirable things of life bear a high price in the world's market. Every thing usually deemed a great good, must, for its attainment, be weighed down, in the opposite scale, with what is as usually deemed a great evil,—labor, care, danger. It is only the unbought, spontaneous, essential circumstances of our nature and condition, that yield a liberal enjoyment. Our religious hopes, intellectual meditations, social sentiments, family affections, political privileges, these are springs of unpurchased happiness ; and to condemn men to live under an arbitrary government, is to cut

---

* These remarks, it will be observed from the date of the address, were made several years before the Reform of the House of Commons.

them off from nearly all the satisfaction, which nature designed should flow from those principles within us, by which a tribe of kindred men is constituted a people.

But it is not merely an extension to all the members of society, of those blessings, which, under other systems, are monopolized by a few ;—great and positive improvements, I feel sure, are destined to flow from the introduction of the republican system. The first of these will be, to make wars less frequent, and finally to cause them to cease altogether. It was not a republican, it was the subject of a monarchy, and no patron of novelties, who said,

> War is a game, which, were their subjects wise,
> Kings would not play at.

A great majority of the wars, which have desolated mankind, have been caused by the disputed titles and rival claims of sovereigns, or by their personal characters, particularly their ambition, or the character of their favorites, or by some other circumstance evidently incident to a form of government, which withholds from the people the ultimate control of affairs. And the more civilized men grow, strange as it may seem, the more universally is this the case. In the barbarous ages the people pursued war as an occupation ; its plunder was more profitable, than their labor at home, in the state of general insecurity. In modern times, princes raise their soldiers by conscription, their sailors by impressment, and drive them at the point of the bayonet and dirk, into the battles they fight for reasons of state. But in a republic, where the people, by their representatives, must vote the declaration of war, and afterwards raise the means of its support, none but wars of just and necessary defence can be easily waged. Republics, we are told, indeed, are ambitious,—a seemingly wise remark, devoid of meaning. Man—man is ambitious ; and the question is, where will his ambition be most likely to drive his country into war ; in a monarchy where he has but to ' cry havoc, and let slip the dogs of war,' or in a republic, where he must get a vote of a strong majority of the nation ? Let history furnish the answer. The book, which promised you, in its title, a picture of the progress of the human family, turns out to be a record, not of the human family, but of the Macedonian family, the Julian family, the families of York and Lancaster, of Lorraine and Bourbon. We need not go to the ancient annals to confirm this remark. We need not speak of those, who reduced Asia and Africa, in the morning of the world, to a vassalage from which they have never recovered. We need not dwell on the more notorious exploits of the Alexanders and the Cæsars, the men who wept for other worlds to visit with the pestilence of their arms. We need not run down the bloody line of the dark ages, when the barbarous North disgorged her ambitious savages on Europe, or when at a later period, barbarous Europe poured back her holy ruffians on Asia ; we need but look at the dates of modern history,—the history of civilized, balanced Europe. We here behold the ambition of Charles V, involving the continent of Europe in war, for the first half of the sixteenth century, and the fiendlike malignity of Catherine de' Medici and her kindred, distracting it the other half. We see the haughty and cheerless bigotry of Philip, persevering in a conflict of extermination for one whole age in the Netherlands, and darkening the English channel with his armada ; while France prolongs her civil dissensions, because Henry IV was the twenty-second cousin of Henry III. We enter the seventeenth century, and again find the pride and bigotry of the House of Austria wasting Germany and the neighboring powers with the Thirty Years' war ; and before the peace of Westphalia is concluded, England is plunged, by the Stuarts, into the fiery trial of her militant liberties. Contemporaneously, the civil wars are revived in France, and the kingdom is blighted by the passions of Mazarin. The civil wars are healed, and the atrocious career of Louis XIV begins ; a half century of bloodshed and woe, that stands in revolting contrast with the paltry pretences of his wars. At length the peace of Ryswic is made in 1697, and bleeding Europe throws off the harness and lies down like an exhausted giant to repose. In three years, the testament of a doating Spanish king gives the signal for the Succession war; till a cup of tea spilt on Mrs Masham's apron, restores peace to the afflicted kingdoms. Meantime the madman of the North had broken loose upon the world, and was running his frantic round. Peace at length is restored, and with one or two short wars, it remains unbroken, till, in 1740, the will of Charles VI occasions another testamentary contest; and in the gallant words of the stern but relenting moralist,

The Queen, the beauty, sets the world in arms.

Eight years are this time sufficient to exhaust the combatants, and the peace of Aix-la-Chapelle is concluded; but, in 1755, the old French war is kindled in our own wilderness, and through the united operation of the feuds in England, which sprang from the disputed succession to the Crown, the corruption of the French court, and the ambition of Frederic, spreads throughout Europe. The wars of the last generation I need not name, nor dwell on that signal retribution, by which the political ambition of the cabinets at length conjured up the military ambition of the astonishing individual, who seems, in our day, to have risen out of the ranks of the people, to chastise the privileged orders with that iron scourge, with which they had so long afflicted mankind; to gather with his strong Plebeian hands the fragrance of those palmy honors, which they had reared for three centuries in the bloody gardens of their royalty. It may well be doubted, whether, under a government like ours, one of all these contests would have taken place. Those that arose from disputed titles, and bequests of thrones, could not of course have existed; and making every allowance for the effect of popular delusion, it seems to me not possible, that a representative government would have embarked in any of the wars of ambition and aggrandizement, which fill up the catalogue.

Who then are these families and individuals—these royal *lanistæ* —by whom the nations are kept in training for a long gladiatorial combat? Are they better, wiser than we? Look at them in life; what are they? 'Kings are fond,' says Mr Burke, no scoffer at thrones, 'Kings are fond of low company.'* What are they when gone? *Expende Hannibalem.* Enter the great cathedrals of Europe, and contemplate the sepulchres of the men, who claimed to be the lords of each successive generation. Question your own feelings, as you behold where the Plantagenets and Tudors, the Stuarts and those of Brunswick lie mournfully huddled up in the

* Speech on Economical Reform.

chapels of Westminster Abbey; and compare those feelings with the homage you pay to Heaven's aristocracy,—the untitled learning, genius, and wit that moulder by their side. Count over the sixty-six emperors and princes of the Austrian house, that lie gathered in the dreary pomp of monumental marble, in the vaults of the Capuchins at Vienna; and weigh the worth of their dust against the calamities of their Peasants' war, their Thirty Years' war, their Succession war, their wars to enforce the Pragmatic Sanction, and of all the other uncouth pretences for destroying mankind, with which they have plagued the world.

But the cessation of wars, to which we look forward as the result of the gradual diffusion of republican government, is but the commencement of the social improvements, which cannot but flow from the same benignant source. It has been justly said that he was a great benefactor of mankind, who could make two blades of grass grow, where one grew before. But our fathers were the great benefactors of mankind, who brought into action such a vast increase of physical, political, and moral energy; who have made not two citizens to live only, but hundreds, yea, unnumbered thousands, to live and to prosper in regions, which but for their achievements would have remained for ages unsettled, and to enjoy those rights of men, which but for their institutions would have continued to be arrogated, as the exclusive inheritance of a few. I appeal to the fact. I ask any sober judge of political probability to tell me, whether more has not been done to extend the domain of civilization, in fifty years, since the declaration of independence, than would have been done in five centuries of continued colonial subjection. It is not even a matter of probability; the king in council had adopted it, as a maxim of his American policy, that no settlements in this country should be made beyond the Alleghanies;—that the design of Providence in spreading out the fertile valley of the Mississippi, should not be fulfilled.

I know that it is said, in palliation of the restrictive influence of European governments, that they are as good as their subjects can bear. I know it is said, that it would be useless and pernicious to call on the half savage and brutified peasantry of many countries, to take a share in the administration of affairs, by electing or being elected to office. I know they are unfit for it; it is the very curse of the system. What is it that unfits them? What is it that makes slavish labor, and slavish ignorance, and slavish stupidity,- their necessary heritage? Are they not made of the same Caucasian clay? Have they not five senses, the same faculties, the same passions? And is it any thing but an aggravation of the vice of arbitrary governments, that they first deprive men of their rights, and then unfit them to exercise those rights; profanely construing the effect into a justification of the evil?

The influence of our institutions on foreign nations is,—next to their effect on our own condition,—the most interesting question we can contemplate. With our example of popular government before their eyes, the nations of the earth will not eventually be satisfied with any other. With the French Revolution as a beacon to guide them, they will learn, we may hope, not to embark too rashly on the mounting waves of reform. The cause, however, of popular government is rapidly gaining in the world. In England, education is carrying it wide and deep into society. On the continent, written constitutions of governments, nominally representative, —though as yet, it must be owned, nominally so alone,—are adopted in eight or ten late absolute monarchies; and it is not without good grounds that we may trust, that the indifference with which the Christian powers contemplate the sacrifice of Greece, and their crusade against the constitutions of Spain, Piedmont, and Naples, will satisfy the mass of thinking men in Europe, that it is time to put an end to these cruel delusions, and take their own government into their own hands.

But the great triumphs of constitutional freedom, to which our independence has furnished the example, have been witnessed in the southern portion of our hemisphere. Sunk to the last point of colonial degradation, they have risen at once into the organization of free republics. Their struggle has been arduous; and eighteen years of chequered fortune have not yet brought it to a close. But we must not infer, from their prolonged agitation, that their independence is uncertain; that they have prematurely put on the *toga virilis* of Freedom. They have not begun too soon; they have more to do. Our war of independence was shorter;—happily we were contending with a government, that could not, like that of

Spain, pursue an interminable and hopeless contest, in defiance of the people's will. Our transition to a mature and well-adjusted constitution was more prompt than that of our sister republics ; for the foundations had been long settled, the preparation long made. And when we consider that it is our example, which has aroused the spirit of Independence from California to Cape Horn ; that the experiment of liberty, if it had failed with us, most surely would not have been attempted by them ; that even now our counsels and acts will operate as powerful precedents in this great family of republics, we learn the importance of the post which Providence has assigned us in the world. A wise and harmonious administration of the public affairs,—a faithful, liberal, and patriotic exercise of the private duties of the citizen,—while they secure our happiness at home, will diffuse a healthful influence through the channels of national communication, and serve the cause of liberty beyond the Equator and the Andes. When we show a united, conciliatory, and imposing front to their rising states, we show them, better than sounding eulogies can do, the true aspect of an independent republic. We give them a living example that the fireside policy of a people is like that of the individual man. As the one, commencing in the prudence, order, and industry of the private circle, extends itself to all the duties of social life, of the family, the neighborhood, the country ; so the true domestic policy of the republic, beginning in the wise organization of its own institutions, pervades its territories with a vigilant, prudent, temperate administration ; and extends the hand of cordial interest to all the friendly nations, especially to those which are of the household of liberty.

It is in this way, that we are to fulfil our destiny in the world. The greatest engine of moral power, which human nature knows, is an organized, prosperous state. All that man, in his individual capacity, can do,—all that he can effect by his fraternities,—by his ingenious discoveries and wonders of art,—or by his influence over others,—is as nothing, compared with the collective, perpetuated influence on human affairs and human happiness of a well constituted, powerful commonwealth. It blesses generations with its sweet influence ;—even the barren earth seems to pour out its fruits under a system where property is secure, while her fairest gardens are blighted by despotism. Men, thinking, reasoning men, abound beneath its benignant sway. Nature enters into a beautiful accord, a better, purer *asiento* with man, and guides an industrious citizen to every rood of her smiling wastes ;—and we see, at length, that what has been *called* a state of nature, has been most falsely, calumniously so denominated ; that the nature of man is neither that of a savage, a hermit, nor a slave ; but that of a member of a well-ordered family, that of a good neighbor, a free citizen, a well-informed, good man, acting with others like him. This is the lesson which is taught in the charter of our independence ; this is the lesson which our example is to teach the world.

15

ADDRESS

DELIVERED AT CHARLESTOWN, AUGUST 1, 1826, IN COMMEMORA-
TION OF JOHN ADAMS AND THOMAS JEFFERSON.

———

FRIENDS AND FELLOW CITIZENS,

WE are assembled, beneath the weeping canopy of the
heavens, in the exercise of feelings, in which the whole family of
Americans unites with us.   We meet to pay a tribute of respect to
the revered memory of those, to whom the whole country looks up
as to its benefactors; to whom it ascribes the merit of unnumbered public services, and especially of the inestimable service of
having led in the councils of the Revolution.   It is natural, that
these feelings, which pervade the whole American people, should
rise into peculiar strength and earnestness in your hearts.   In meditating upon these great men, your minds are unavoidably carried
back to those scenes of suffering and of sacrifice into which, at the
opening of their arduous and honored career, this town and its
citizens were so deeply plunged.   You cannot but remember, that
your fathers offered their bosoms to the sword, and their dwellings
to the devouring flames, from the same noble spirit which animated
the venerable patriarchs whom we now deplore.   The cause they
espoused was the same which strewed your streets with ashes, and
drenched your hill-tops with blood.   And while Providence, in
the astonishing circumstances of their departure, seems to have
appointed that the revolutionary age of America should be closed
up, by a scene as illustriously affecting, as its commencement was
appalling and terrific; you have justly felt it your duty,—it has
been the prompt dictate of your feelings,—to pay, within these

hallowed precincts, a well-deserved tribute to the great and good men to whose counsels, under God, it is in no small degree owing, that your dwellings have risen from their ashes, and that the sacred dust of those who fell reposes in the bosom of a free and happy land.

It was the custom of the primitive Romans, to preserve in the halls of their houses the images of all the illustrious men, whom their families had produced. These images are supposed to have consisted of a mask exactly representing the countenance of each deceased individual, accompanied with habiliments of like fashion with those worn in his time, and with the armor, badges, and insignia of his offices and exploits; all so disposed around the sides of the hall as to present in the attitude of living men the long succession of the departed ; and thus to set before the Roman citizen, whenever he entered or left his habitation, the venerable array of his ancestors revived in this imposing similitude. Whenever, by a death in the family, another distinguished member of it was gathered to his fathers, a strange and awful procession was formed. The ancestral masks, including that of the newly deceased, were fitted upon the servants of the family, selected in the size and appearance of those whom they were intended to represent, and drawn up in solemn array to follow the funeral train of the living mourners, first to the market-place, where the public eulogium was pronounced, and then to the tomb. As he thus moved along, with all the dark fathers of his name, resuscitated in the lineaments of life, and quickening, as it were, from their urns, to enkindle his emulation, the virtuous Roman renewed his vows of pious respect to their memory, and his resolution to imitate the fortitude, the frugality, and the patriotism of the great heads of his family.*

Fellow citizens, the great heads of the American family are fast passing away; of the last, of the most honored, two are now no more. We are assembled not to gaze with awe on the artificial and theatric images of their features, but to contemplate their venerated characters, to call to mind their invaluable services, to cherish their revered memory ; to lay up the image of their virtues in our hearts. The two men, who stood in a relation, in which no

* Polyb. Historiar. lib. VI.

others now stand to this whole continent, have fallen. The men whom Providence marked out among the first of the favored instruments, to lead this chosen people into the holy land of liberty, have discharged their high office, and are no more. The men, whose ardent minds prompted them to take up their country's cause, when there was nothing else to prompt, and every thing to deter them; the men who afterwards, when the ranks were filled with the brave and resolute, were yet in the front of those brave and resolute ranks; the men, who, when the wisest and most sagacious were needed to steer the newly launched vessel through the broken waves of the unknown sea, sat calm and unshaken at the helm; the men, who, in their country's happier days, were found most worthy to preside over the great interests of the land they had so powerfully contributed to rear into greatness,—these men are now no more.

They have left us not singly and in the sad but accustomed succession, in which the order of nature calls away the children of men; but having lived, and acted, and counselled, and dared, and risked all, and triumphed, and enjoyed together, they have gone together to their great reward. In the morning of life,—without previous concert, but with a kindred spirit,—they plunged together into a conflict, which put to hazard all which makes life precious. When the storm of war and revolution raged, they stood side by side, on such perilous ground, that, had the American cause failed, though all else had been forgiven, they were of the few whom an incensed empire's vengeance would have pursued to the ends of the earth. When they had served through their long career of duty, forgetting the little that had divided them, and cherishing the great communion of service, and peril, and success, which had united them, they walked, with honorable friendship, the declining pathway of age; and now they have sunk down together, in peace, into the bosom of a redeemed and grateful country. Time, and their country's service, and kindred hearts, a like fortune and a like reward united them; and the last great scene confirmed the union. They were useful, honored, prosperous, and lovely in their lives, and in their deaths, they were not divided.

Happiest at the last, they were permitted almost to choose the hour of their departure; to die on that day, on which those who loved them best could have wished they might die. It is related as a singular felicity of the great philosopher Plato, that he died, at a good old age, at a banquet, surrounded with flowers and perfumes, amidst festal songs, on his birth-day. Our Adams and Jefferson died on the birth-day of the nation; the day which their own deed had immortalized, which their own prophetic spirit had marked out, as the great festival of the nation; not amidst the festal songs of the banquet, but amidst the triumphal anthems of a whole grateful people. At the moment that Jefferson expired, his character was the theme of eulogy, in every city and almost every village of the land; and the lingering spirit of his great co-patriot fled, while his name was pronounced with grateful recollection, at the board of patriotic festivity, throughout a country, that hailed him as among the first and boldest of her champions, even in the days when friends were few and hearts were faint.

Our jubilee, like that of old, is turned into sorrow. Among the crumbling ruins of Rome, there is a shattered arch, reared by the emperor Vespasian, when his son Titus returned from the destruction of Jerusalem. On its broken pannels and falling frieze are still to be seen, represented as borne aloft in the triumphal procession of Titus, the well known spoils of the second temple, the sacred vessels of the holy place, the candlestick with seven branches, and, in front of all, the silver trumpets of the jubilee, in the hands of captive priests, proclaiming not now the liberty, but the humiliation and the sorrows of Judah. From this mournful spectacle, it is said, the pious and heart-stricken Hebrew, even to the present day, turns aside in sorrow. He will not enter Rome, through the gate of the arch of Titus, but winds his way through the by-paths of the Palatine, and over the broken columns of the palace of the Cæsars, that he may not behold the sad image of the trumpets of the jubilee, borne aloft in the captive train.

The jubilee of America is turned into mourning. Its joy is mingled with sadness; its silver trumpet breathes a mingled strain. Henceforward and forever, while America exists among the nations of the earth, the first emotion on the fourth of July shall be of joy and triumph in the great event which immortalizes the day,—the second shall be one of chastised and tender recollection of the venerable men, who departed on the morning of the jubilee. This

mingled emotion of triumph and sadness has sealed the moral
beauty and sublimity of our great anniversary. In the simple
commemoration of a victorious political achievement, there seems
not enough to occupy all our purest and best feelings. The fourth
of July was before a day of unshaded triumph, exultation, and
national pride; but the angel of death has mingled in the all-glorious pageant, to teach us we are men. Had our venerated fathers
left us on any other day, the day of the united departure of two
such men would henceforward have been remembered but as a day
of mourning. But now, while their decease has gently chastened
the exultations of the triumphant festival; the banner of independence will wave cheerfully over the spot where they repose. The
whole nation feels, as with one heart, that since it must sooner or
later have been bereaved of its revered fathers, it could not have
wished that any other had been the day of their decease. Our
anniversary festival was before triumphant; it is now triumphant
and sacred. It before called out the young and ardent, to join in
the public rejoicings; it now also speaks, in a touching voice, to
the retired, to the grey-headed, to the mild and peaceful spirits, to
the whole family of sober freemen. With some appeal of joy, of
admiration, of tenderness, it henceforth addresses every American
heart. It is henceforward, what the dying Adams pronounced it,
a great and a good day. It is full of greatness, and full of goodness.
It is absolute and complete. The death of the men, who declared
our independence,—their death on the day of the jubilee, was all that
was wanting to the fourth of July. To die on that day, and to
die together, was all that was wanting to Jefferson and Adams.

Think not fellow-citizens, that, in the mere formal discharge of
my duty this day, I would overrate the melancholy interest of the
great occasion. Heaven knows, I do any thing but intentionally
overrate it. I labor only for words, to do justice to your feelings and to mine. I can say nothing, which does not sound as
cold, as tame, and as inadequate to myself as to you. The theme
is too great and too surprising, the men are too great and good to
be spoken of, in this cursory manner. There is too much in the
contemplation of their united characters, their services, the day
and coincidence of their death, to be properly described, or to be
fully felt at once. I dare not come here and dismiss, in a few

summary paragraphs, the characters of men, who have filled such a space in the history of their age. It would be a disrespectful familiarity with men of their lofty spirits, their rich endowments, their deep counsels, and wise measures, their long and honorable lives, to endeavor thus to weigh and estimate them. I leave that arduous task, to the genius of kindred elevation, by whom to-morrow it will be discharged.* I feel the mournful contrast in the fortunes of the first and best of men, that after a life in the highest walks of usefulness ; after conferring benefits, not merely on a neighborhood, a city, or even a state, but on a whole continent, and a posterity of kindred men ; after having stood in the first estimation for talents, services, and influence, among millions of fellow citizens, a day should come, which closes all up ; pronounces a brief blessing on their memory ; gives an hour to the actions of a crowded life ; describes in a sentence what it took years to bring to pass, and what is destined for years and ages to continue and operate on posterity ; forces into a few words the riches of busy days of action and weary nights of meditation ; passes forgetfully over many traits of character, many counsels and measures, which it cost perhaps years of discipline and effort to mature ; utters a funeral prayer ; chants a mournful anthem ; and then dismisses all into the dark chambers of death and forgetfulness.

But no, fellow citizens, we dismiss them not to the chambers of forgetfulness and death. What we admired, and prized, and venerated in them, can never die, nor dying, be forgotten. I had almost said that they are now beginning to live ; to live that life of unimpaired influence, of unclouded fame, of unmingled happiness, for which their talents and services were destined. They were of the select few, the least portion of whose life dwells in their physical existence ; whose hearts have watched, while their senses have slept ; whose souls have grown up into a higher being ; whose pleasure is to be useful ; whose wealth is an unblemished reputation ; who respire the breath of honorable fame ; who have deliberately and consciously put what is called life to hazard, that they may live in the hearts of those who come after. Such men do

* A Eulogy was delivered on Adams and Jefferson, on the following day, in Faneuil Hall, by Daniel Webster.

not, cannot die. To be cold, and motionless, and breathless; to feel not and speak not; this is not the end of existence to the men who have breathed their spirits into the institutions of their country, who have stamped their characters on the pillars of the age, who have poured their hearts' blood into the channels of the public prosperity. Tell me, ye, who tread the sods of yon sacred height, is Warren dead? Can you not still see him, not pale and prostrate, the blood of his gallant heart pouring out of his ghastly wound, but moving resplendent over the field of honor, with the rose of Heaven upon his cheek, and the fire of liberty in his eye? Tell me, ye, who make your pious pilgrimage to the shades of Vernon, is Washington indeed shut up in that cold and narrow house? That which made these men, and men like these, cannot die. The hand that traced the charter of independence is indeed motionless, the eloquent lips that sustained it, are hushed; but the lofty spirits that conceived, resolved, matured, maintained it, and which alone to such men, ' make it life to live,' these cannot expire;—

> These shall resist the empire of decay,
> When time is o'er, and worlds have passed away;
> Cold in the dust, the perished heart may lie,
> But that, which warmed it once, can never die.

This is their life, and this their eulogy. In these our feeble services of commemoration, we set forth not their worth, but our own gratitude. The eulogy of those, who declared our independence, is written in the whole history of independent America. I do not mean, that they alone wrought out our liberties; nor should we bring a grateful offering to their tombs, in sacrificing at them the merits of their contemporaries. But no one surely, who considers the history of the times, the state of opinions, the power of England, the weakness of the colonies, and the obstacles that actually stood in the way of success, can doubt that, if John Adams and Thomas Jefferson had thrown their talents and influence into the scale of submission, the effect would have been felt to the cost of America, for ages. No, it is not too much to say, that ages on ages may pass, and the growing millions of America may overflow the uttermost regions of this continent, but never can there be an American citizen, who will not bear in his condition, in his pursuits, in his welfare, some trace of what was counselled, and said, and done by these great men. This is their undying praise ; a praise, which knows no limits but those of America, and which is uttered, not merely in these our eulogies, but in the thousand inarticulate voices of art and nature. It sounds from the woodman's axe in the distant forests of the west ; for what was it that unbarred to him the portals of the mountains? The busy water-wheel echoes back the strain ; for what was it that released the industry of the country from the fetters of colonial restriction ? Their praise is borne on the swelling canvass of America to distant oceans, where the rumor of acts of trade never came ; for what was it that sent our canvass there ? and it glistens at home, in the eyes of the happy population of a prosperous and grateful country. Yes, the people, the people rise up and call them blessed. They invoke eternal blessings on the men, who could be good as well as great, whose ambition was their country's welfare, who did not ask to be rewarded by oppressing themselves the country they redeemed from oppression.

The day we have separated to the remembrance of our departed fathers is indeed but a fleeting moment ; its swift watches will soon run out, and the pausing business of life start again into motion. But every day of our country's succeeding duration, every age as it comes forward with its crowded generations, to enjoy the blessings of our institutions, will take up the surprising theme. Though its affecting novelty will pass away for us, it will strike the hearts of our children ; and the latest posterity, looking back on the period of the Revolution as the heroic age of America, will contemplate, with mingled wonder and tenderness, this great and closing scene.

I shall not, fellow citizens, on this occasion, attempt a detailed narrative of the lives of these distinguished men. To relate their history at length, would be to record the history of the country, from their first entrance on public life to their final retirement. Even to dwell minutely on the more conspicuous incidents of their career, would cause me to trespass too far on the proper limits of the occasion, and to repeat what is well known to most who hear me. Let us only enumerate those few leading points in their lives and characters, which will best guide us to the reflections we ought

16

to make, while we stand at the tombs of these excellent and honored men.

Mr Adams was born on the 30th of October, 1735, and Mr Jefferson on the 13th of April, 1743. One of them rose from the undistinguished mass of the community, while the other, born in higher circumstances, voluntarily descended into its ranks. Although happily in this country it cannot be said of any one, that he owes much to birth or family, yet it sometimes happens, even under the perfect equality which fortunately prevails among us, that a certain degree of deference follows in the train of family connexions, apart from all personal merit. Mr Adams was the son of a New-England yeoman, and in this alone, the frugality and moderation of his bringing up are sufficiently related. Mr Jefferson owed more to birth. He inherited a good estate from his respectable father; but instead of associating himself with the opulent interest in Virginia,—at that time, in consequence of the mode in which their estates were held and transmitted, an exclusive and powerful class, and of which he might have become a powerful leader,—he threw himself into the ranks of the people.

It was a propitious coincidence, that of these two eminent statesmen, one was from the north, and the other from the south; as if, in the happy effects of their joint action, to give us the first lesson of union. The enemies of our independence, at home and abroad, relied on the difficulty of uniting the colonies in one harmonious system. They knew the difference in our local origin; they exaggerated the points of dissimilarity in our sectional character. They thought the south would feel no sympathy in the distresses of the north; that the north would look with jealousy on the character and institutions of the south. It was therefore most auspicious, in the great dispositions of the Revolution, that while the north and the south had each its great rallying point, in Virginia and Massachusetts, the wise and good men, whose influence was most felt in each, moved forward in brotherhood and concert. Mr Quincy, in a visit to the southern colonies, had entered into an extensive correspondence with the friends of liberty in that part of the country. Richard Henry Lee and his brother Arthur maintained a constant intercourse with Samuel Adams. Dr Franklin, though a citizen of Pennsylvania, was a native of

Boston ; and from the first moment of their meeting at Philadelphia, Jefferson and Adams began to cooperate cordially, in that
great work of independence to which they were both devoted.
While the theoretical politicians of Europe were speculating on
our local peculiarities, and the British ministry were building their
best hopes upon the maxim, divide and conquer, they might well
have been astonished to see the declaration of independence reported into Congress, by the joint labor of the son of a Virginia planter
and of a New-England yeoman.

The education of Adams and Jefferson was within the precincts
of home. They received their academical instruction at the seminaries of their native States, the former at Cambridge, the latter
at William and Mary. At these institutions, they severally laid
the foundation for very distinguished attainments as scholars, and
formed a taste for letters, which was fresh and craving to the last.
They were both familiar with the ancient languages, and the literature they contain. Their range in the various branches of general
reading was perhaps equally wide, and was uncommonly extensive ;
and it is, I believe, doing no injustice to any other honored name
to say, that, in this respect, they stood without an equal in the
band of revolutionary worthies.

Their first writings were devoted to the cause of their country.
Mr Adams, in 1765, published his Essay on the Canon and
Feudal Law, which two years afterwards was republished in London, and was there pronounced one of the ablest performances
which had crossed the Atlantic.* It expresses the boldest and

* The copy I possess of this work was printed by Almon, at London, in 1768,
as a sequel to some other political pieces, with the following title, and preliminary
note: ' The following dissertation which was written at Boston, in New-England, in
the year 1765, and then printed there in the Gazette, being very curious, and having
connexion with this publication, it is thought proper to reprint it.'

' The author of it is said to have been Jeremy Gridley, Esq. Attorney General of
the Province of Massachusetts Bay, member of the General Court, colonel of the
first regiment of militia, president of the marine society, and grand master of the
Free Masons. He died at Boston, Sept. 7, 1767.

' *A Dissertation on the Canon and Feudal Law.*'

This copy formerly belonged to Dr Andrew Eliot, to whom it was presented by
Thomas Hollis. Directly above the title is written, apparently in Dr A. Eliot's
hand-writing, ' The author of this dissertation is John Adams, Esq.' And at the

most elevated sentiments, in language most vigorous and animating ; and might have taught in its tone, what it taught in its doctrine, that America must be unoppressed, or must become independent. Among Mr Jefferson's first productions was, in like manner, a political essay, entitled 'A Summary View of the Rights of British America.' It contains, in some parts, a near approach to the ideas and language of the declaration of independence; and its bold spirit and polished, but at the same time, powerful execution, are known to have had their effect, in causing its author to be designated for the high trusts confided to him in the continental Congress. At a later period of life, Mr Jefferson became the author of the Notes on Virginia, a work equally admired in Europe and America ; and Mr Adams of the Defence of the American Constitutions, a performance that would do honor to the political literature of any country. But, in enumerating their literary productions, it must be remembered, that they were both employed, the greater part of their lives, in the active duties of public service ; and that the fruits of their intellect are not to be sought in the systematic volumes of learned leisure, but on the files of office, in the archives of state, and in a most extensive public and private correspondence.

The professional education of these distinguished statesmen had been in the law ; and was therefore such as peculiarly fitted them for the contest, in which they were to act as leaders. The law of England, then the law of America, is closely connected with the history of the liberty of England. Many of the questions at issue between the Parliament of Great Britain and the Colonies, were questions of constitutional, if not of common law. For the discussion of these questions, the legal profession furnished the best preparation. In general, the contest was, happily for the colonies, at first forensic ; a contest of discussion and of argumentation ; affording

foot of the page is the following note, in the same hand-writing, but marked with inverted commas, as a quotation, and signed T. H.

'The Dissertation on the Canon and Feudal Law is one of the very finest productions ever seen from N. America.'

'By a letter from Boston in N. E. signed SUI JURIS, inserted in that valuable newspaper, the London Chronicle, July 19, *it should seem the writer of it happily yet lives!*' T. H.

This was said fifty-eight years ago!

time, and opportunity, and excitement to diffuse throughout the people, and stamp deeply on their minds the great principles, which having first been triumphantly sustained in the argument, were then to be confirmed in the field. This required the training of the patriot lawyer, and this was the office which, in that capacity, was eminently discharged by Jefferson and Adams, to the doubtful liberties of their country. The cause, in which they were engaged, abundantly repaid the service and the hazard. It gave them precisely that amplitude of view and elevation of feeling, which the technical routine of the profession is too apt to stifle. Their practice of the law was not in the narrow litigation of the courts, but in the great forum of contending empires. It was not nice legal fictions they were there employed to balance, but sober realities of indescribable weight. The life and death of their country was the all-important issue. Nor did their country afterwards afford them leisure for the ordinary practice of their profession. Mr Jefferson indeed, in 1776 and 1777, was employed with Wythe and Pendleton in an entire revision of the code of Virginia; and Mr Adams was offered about the same time the first seat on the bench of the Superior Court of his native State. But each was shortly afterwards called to a foreign mission, and spent the rest of the active years of his life, with scarce an interval, in the political service of his country.

Such was the education and quality of these men, when the revolutionary contest came on. In 1774, and on the 17th of June, a day destined to be in every way illustrious, Mr Adams was elected a member of the continental Congress, of which body he was signalized, from the first, as a distinguished leader. In the month of June in the following year, when a commander in chief was to be chosen for the American armies, and when that appointment seemed in course to belong to the commanding general of the brave army from Massachusetts and the neighboring States, which had rushed to the field, Mr Adams recommended George Washington to that all-important post, and was thus far the means of securing the blessing of his guidance to the American armies. In August, 1775, Mr Jefferson took his seat in the continental Congress, preceded by the fame of being one of the most accomplished and powerful champions of the cause, though among the youngest members of that body.   It was the wish of Mr Adams, and probably of Mr Jefferson, that independence should be declared in the fall of 1775 ; but the country seemed not then ripe for the measure.

At length the accepted time arrived.   In May, 1776, the colonies, on the proposition of Mr Adams, were invited by the General Congress, to establish their several State governments.   On the 7th of June, the resolution of independence was moved by Richard Henry Lee.   On the 11th, a committee of five was chosen to announce this resolution to the world ; and Thomas Jefferson and John Adams stood at the head of this committee.   From their designation by ballot to this most honorable duty, their elevated standing in the Congress might alone be inferred.   In their amicable contention and deference each to the other of the great trust of composing the all-important document, we witness their patriotic disinterestedness, and their mutual respect.   This trust devolved on Jefferson, and with it rests on him the imperishable renown of having penned the declaration of independence of America.   To have been the instrument of expressing, in one brief, decisive act, the concentrated will and resolution of a whole family of States ; of unfolding, in one all-important manifesto, the causes, the motives, and the justification of the great movement in human affairs, which was then taking place ; to have been permitted to give the impress and peculiarity of his own mind, to a charter of public right, destined, or rather let me say already elevated to an importance, in the estimation of men, equal to any thing human, ever borne on parchment, or expressed in the visible signs of thought, this is the glory of Thomas Jefferson.   To have been among the first of those who foresaw, and foreseeing, broke the way for this great consummation ; to have been the mover of numerous decisive acts, its undoubted precursors ; to have been among many able and generous spirits, that united in this perilous adventure, by acknowledgment unsurpassed in zeal, and unequalled in power ; to have been exclusively associated with the author of the declaration ; and then, in the exercise of an eloquence as prompt as it was overwhelming, to have taken the lead in inspiring the Congress to adopt and proclaim it, this is the glory of John Adams.

Nor was it among common and inferior minds, that these men

enjoyed their sublime pre-eminence.   In the body that elected Mr
Jefferson to draft the declaration of independence, there sat a patriot
sage, than whom the English language does not possess a better
writer, Benjamin Franklin.   And Mr Adams was pronounced by
Mr Jefferson himself the ablest advocate of independence, in a
Congress, which could boast among its members such men as Patrick Henry, Richard Henry Lee, and our own Samuel Adams.
They were great and among great men ; mightiest among the
mighty ; and enjoyed their lofty standing in a body, of which half
the members might with honor have presided over the deliberative
councils of a nation.

   All glorious as their office in this council of sages has proved,
they beheld the glory only, in distant vision, while the prospect
before them was shrouded with darkness and lowering with terror.
'I am not transported with enthusiasm,' is the language of Mr
Adams, the day after the resolution was adopted, 'I am well aware
of the toil, the treasure, and the blood it will cost, to maintain this
declaration, to support and defend these States.   Yet through all
the gloom, I can see a ray of light and glory.   I can see that the
end is worth more than all the means.'   Nor was it the rash
adventure of uneasy spirits, who had every thing to gain and
nothing to risk by their enterprise.   They left all for their country's
sake.   Who does not see that Adams and Jefferson might have
risen to any station in the British empire?   They might have
revelled in the royal bounty ; they might have stood within the
shadow of the throne which they shook to its base.   It was in the
full understanding of their all but desperate choice, that they chose
for their country.   Many were the inducements, which called
them to another choice.   The dread voice of authority ; the array
of an empire's power ; the pleadings of friendship ; the yearning
of their hearts towards the land of their fathers' sepulchres ; the
land which the great champions of constitutional liberty still made
venerable ; the ghastly vision of the gibbet, if they failed ; all the
feelings which grew from these sources were to be stifled and kept
down, for a dearer treasure was at stake.   They were any thing
but adventurers, any thing but malecontents.   They loved peace,
they loved order, they loved law, they loved a manly obedience to
constitutional authority ; but they chiefly loved freedom and their

country ; and they took up the ark of her liberties with pure hands, and bore it through in triumph, for their strength was in Heaven.

And how shall I attempt to follow them through the succession of great events, which a rare and kind Providence crowded into their lives ; how shall I attempt to count all the links of that bright chain, which binds the perilous hour of their first efforts for freedom, with the rich enjoyment of its consummation ? How shall I attempt to enumerate the posts they filled and the trusts they discharged at home and abroad, both in the councils of their native States, and of the confederation ; both before and after the adoption of the federal constitution : the codes of law and systems of government they aided in organizing ; the foreign embassies they sustained ; the alliances with powerful States they contracted, when America was weak ; the loans and subsidies, they procured from foreign powers, when America was poor ; the treaties of peace and commerce, which they negotiated ; their participation in the federal government on its organization, Mr Adams as the first Vice-President, Mr Jefferson as the first Secretary of State ; their mutual possession of the confidence of the only man, to whom his country accorded a higher place ; and their successive administrations in chief of the interests of this great republic ? These all are laid up in the annals of the country ; her archives are filled with the productions of their fertile and cultivated minds ; the pages of her history are bright with the lustre of their achievements ; and the welfare and happiness of America pronounce, in one general eulogy, the just encomium of their services.

Nor need we fear, fellow-citizens, to speak of their political dissensions. If they who opposed each other, and arrayed the nation, in their arduous contention, were able in the bosom of private life to forget their former struggles, we surely may contemplate them, even in this relation, with calmness. Of the counsels adopted and the measures pursued in the storm of political warfare, I presume not to speak. I knew these great men, not as opponents, but as friends to each other ; not in the keen prosecution of a political controversy, but in the cultivation of a friendly correspondence. As they respected and honored each other, I respect and honor both. Time too has removed the foundation of their dissensions. The principles on which they contended are settled, some in favor of one and some in favor of the other: the great foreign interests, that lent ardor to the struggle have happily lost their hold on the American people; and the politics of the country now turn on questions not agitated in their days. Meantime, I know not whether, if we had it in our power to choose between the recollection of these revered men, as they were, and what they would have been without their great struggle, we could wish them to have been other than they were, even in this respect. Twenty. years of friendship succeeding ten of rivalry, appear to me a more amiable and certainly a more instructive spectacle, even than a life of unbroken concert. As a friend to both their respected memories, I would not willingly spare the attestation, which they were pleased to render to each other's characters. We are taught, in the valedictory lessons of our Washington that 'the spirit of of party is the worst enemy of a popular government;' shall we not rejoice that we are taught, in the lives of our Adams and our Jefferson, that the most embittered contentions, which as yet have divided us, furnish no ground for lasting disunion. In their lives did I say? Oh, not in their lives alone, but in that mysterious and lovely union which has called them together to the grave.

The declining period of their lives presents their own characters, in the most delightful aspect, and furnishes the happiest illustration of the perfection of our political system. We behold a new spectacle of moral sublimity; the peaceful old age of the retired chiefs of the republic; an evening of learned, useful, and honored leisure following upon a youth of hazard, a manhood of service, a whole life of alternate trial and success. We behold them indeed active and untiring, even to the last. At the advanced age of eighty-five years, our venerable fellow citizen and neighbor is still competent to take a part in the convention for revising the state constitution, to whose original formation, forty years before, he so essentially contributed; and Mr Jefferson, at the same protracted term of life, was able to project and carry on to their completion, the extensive establishments of the University of Virginia.

But it is the great and closing scene, which appears, by higher allotment, to crown their long and exalted career, with a consummation almost miraculous. Having done so much and so happily

17

for themselves, so much and so beneficially for their country; at that last moment, when man can no more do any thing for his country or for himself, it pleased a kind Providence to take their existence into his hands, and to do that for both of them, which, to the end of time, will cause them to be deemed, not more happy in the renown of their lives than in the opportunity of their death.*

I could give neither force nor interest to the account of these sublime and touching scenes, by any thing beyond the simple recital of the facts, already familiar to the public. The veil of eternity was first lifted up, from before the eyes of Mr Jefferson. For several weeks his strength had been gradually failing, though the vigor of his mind remained unimpaired. As he drew nearer to the last, and no expectation remained that his term could be much protracted, he expressed no other wish, than that he might live to breathe the air of the fiftieth anniversary of independence. This he was graciously permitted to do. But it was evident, on the morning of the fourth, that Providence intended that this day, consecrated by his deed, should be solemnized by his death. On some momentary revival of his wasting strength, the friends around would have soothed him with the hope of continuing; but he answered their kind encouragements only by saying, he did not fear to die. Once, as he drew nearer to his close, he lifted up his languid head and murmured with a smile, 'it is the fourth of July;' while his repeated exclamation, on the last great day was, *Nunc dimittis, Domine,* 'Lord, now lettest thou thy servant depart in peace.' He departed in peace, a little before one o'clock of this memorable day; unconscious that his co-patriot, who fifty years before had shared its efforts and perils, was now the partner of its glory.

Mr Adams' mind had also wandered back, over the long line of great things, with which his life was filled, and found rest on the thought of Independence. When the discharges of artillery proclaimed the triumphant anniversary, he pronounced it 'a Great and a Good day.' The thrilling word of Independence, which, fifty years before, in the ardor of his manly strength he had sounded out to the nations, from the hall of the revolutionary Congress, was

* Tacit. J. Agricol. Vit. c. XLV.

now among the last that dwelt on his quivering lips; and when, toward the hour of noon, he felt his noble heart growing cold within him, the last emotion which warmed it was, that ' Jefferson still survives.' But he survives not; he is gone: They are gone together!

Friends, fellow-citizens, free, prosperous, happy Americans! The men who did so much to make you so, are no more. The men who gave nothing to pleasure in youth, nothing to repose in age, but all to that country, whose beloved name filled their hearts as it does ours, with joy, can now do no more for us; nor we for them. But their memory remains, we will cherish it; their bright example remains, we will strive to imitate it; the fruit of their wise counsels and noble acts remains, we will gratefully enjoy it.

They have gone to the companions of their cares, of their dangers, and their toils. It is well with them. The treasures of America are now in heaven. How long the list of our good, and wise, and brave, assembled there! how few remain with us! There is our Washington; and those, who followed him in their country's confidence, are now met together with him, and all that illustrious company.

The faithful marble may preserve their image; the engraven brass may proclaim their worth; but the humblest sod of Independent America, with nothing but the dew-drops of the morning to gild it, is a prouder mausoleum than kings or conquerors can boast. The country is their monument. Its independence is their epitaph. But not to their country is their praise limited. The whole earth is the monument of illustrious men. Wherever an agonizing people shall perish, in a generous convulsion, for want of a valiant arm and a fearless heart, they will cry, in the last accents of despair, Oh, for a Washington, an Adams, a Jefferson. Wherever a regenerated nation, starting up in its might, shall burst the links of steel that enchain it, the praise of our venerated Fathers shall be the prelude of their triumphal song!

The contemporary and successive generations of men will disappear. In the long lapse of ages, the Tribes of America, like those of Greece, and Rome, may pass away. The fabric of American Freedom, like all things human, however firm and fair, may crumble into dust. But the cause in which these our Fathers shone is immortal. They did that, to which no age, no people of reasoning men, can be indifferent. Their eulogy will be uttered in other languages, when those we speak, like us who speak them, shall be all forgotten. And when the great account of humanity shall be closed, in the bright list of those who have best adorned and served it, shall be found the names of our Adams and our Jefferson!

ORATION

DELIVERED BEFORE THE CITIZENS OF CHARLESTOWN, ON THE
4TH OF JULY, 1828.

—

FELLOW CITIZENS,

THE event, which we commemorate, is all-important, not merely in our own annals, but in those of the world. The sententious English poet has declared, that ' the proper study of mankind is man ;' and of all inquiries, which have for their object the temporal concerns of our nature, the history of our fellow beings is unquestionably among the most interesting. But not all the chapters of human history are alike important. The annals of our race have been filled up with incidents, which concern not, or at least ought not to concern the great company of mankind. History, as it has often been written, is the genealogy of princes,—the field-book of conquerors,—and the fortunes of our fellow men have been treated, only so far as they have been affected by the influence of the great masters and destroyers of our race. Such history is, I will not say a worthless study, for it is necessary for us to know the dark side, as well as the bright side of our condition. But it is a melancholy and heartless study, which fills the bosom of the philanthropist and the friend of liberty with sorrow.

But the History of Liberty,—the history of men struggling to be free,—the history of men who have acquired, and are exercising their freedom,—the history of those great movements in the world, by which liberty has been established, diffused, and perpetuated, form a subject, which we cannot contemplate too closely,—to which we cannot cling too fondly. This is the real history of man,—of the human family,—of rational, immortal beings.

This theme is *one;*—the *free* of all climes and nations, are themselves *a people.* Their annals are the history of freedom. Those who fell victims to their principles, in the civil convulsions of the short-lived republics of Greece, or who sunk beneath the power of her invading foes ; those who shed their blood for liberty amidst the ruins of the Roman republic ; the victims of Austrian tyranny in Switzerland, and of Spanish tyranny in Holland ; the solitary champions or the united bands of high-minded and patriotic men, who have, in any region or age, struggled and suffered in this great cause, belong to that PEOPLE OF THE FREE, whose fortunes and progress are the most noble theme which man can contemplate.

The theme belongs to us. We inhabit a country, which has been signalized in the great history of freedom. We live under institutions, more favorable to its diffusion, than any which the world has elsewhere known. A succession of incidents, of rare curiosity, and almost mysterious connexion, has marked out America as the great theatre of political reform. Many circumstances stand recorded in our annals, connected with the assertion of human rights, which, were we not familiar with them, would fill even our own minds with amazement.

The theme belongs to the day. We celebrate the return of the day on which our separate national existence was declared ; the day when the momentous experiment was commenced, by which the world, and posterity, and we ourselves were to be taught, how far a nation of men can be trusted with self-government,—how far life, and liberty, and property are safe, and the progress of social improvement is secure, under the influence of laws made by those who are to obey the laws ; the day, when, for the first time in the world, a numerous people was ushered into the family of nations, organized on the principle of the political equality of all the citizens.

Let us then, fellow citizens, devote the time which has been set apart for this portion of the duties of the day, to a hasty review of the history of Liberty, especially to a contemplation of some of those astonishing incidents, which preceded, accompanied, or have followed the settlement of America, and the establishment of our political institutions ; and which plainly indicate a general tendency and cooperation of things, toward the erection, in this country, of the great monitorial school of human freedom.

We hear much, in our early days, of the liberty of Greece and Rome ;—a great and complicated subject, which this is not the time nor the place to attempt to disentangle.   True it is, that we find, in the annals of both these nations, bright examples of public virtue ;—the record of faithful friends of their fellow men ;—of strenuous foes of oppression at home or abroad ;—and admirable precedents of popular strength.   But we nowhere find in them the account of a populous and extensive region, blessed with institutions securing the enjoyment and transmission of regulated liberty. In freedom, as in most other things, the ancient nations, while they made surprisingly near approaches to the truth, yet for want of some one great and essential principle or instrument, came utterly short of it in practice.   They had profound and elegant scholars, but for want of the art of printing, they could not send information out among the people, where alone it is of great use, in reference to human happiness.   Some of them ventured boldly to sea, and possessed an aptitude for commerce ; yet for want of the mariner's compass, they could not navigate distant oceans, but crept for ages along the shores of the Mediterranean.   In respect to freedom, they established popular institutions in single cities ; but for want of the representative principle, they could not extend these institutions over a large and populous country.   But as a large and populous country, generally speaking, can alone possess strength enough for self-defence, this want was fatal.   The freest of their cities, accordingly fell a prey, sooner or later, to the invading power, either of a foreign tyrant or of a domestic traitor.

In this way, liberty made no firm progress in the ancient states. It was a speculation of the philosopher, and an experiment of the patriot ; but not a natural state of society.   The patriots of Greece and Rome had indeed succeeded in enlightening the public mind, on one of the cardinal points of freedom, the necessity of an elected executive.   The name and the office of a king were long esteemed not only something to be rejected, but something rude and uncivilized, belonging to savage nations, ignorant of the rights of man, as understood in cultivated states.   The word *tyrant,* which originally meant no more than *monarch,* was soon made, by the Greeks, synonymous with oppressor and despot, as it has continued ever since.   When the first Cæsar made his encroachments on the liberties of Rome, the patriots even of that age, did boast that they had

> ——————' heard their fathers say,
> There was a Brutus once, that would have brooked
> The eternal devil, to keep his state in Rome,
> As easily as a King.'

So deeply rooted was this horror of the very name of king in the bosom of the Romans, that under their worst tyrants, and in the darkest days, the forms of the republic were preserved.   There was no name, under Nero and Caligula, for the office of monarch. The individual who filled the office was called Cæsar and Augustus, after the first and second of the line.   The word *emperor* implied no more than general.   The offices of consul and tribune were kept up ; although, if the choice did not fall, as it frequently did, on the emperor, it was conferred on his favorite officer, and sometimes on his favorite horse.   The senate continued to meet, and affected to deliberate ; and in short, the empire began and continued a pure military despotism, engrafted by a sort of permanent usurpation, on the forms and names of the ancient republic. The spirit indeed of liberty had long since ceased to animate these ancient forms ; and when the barbarous tribes of Central Asia and Northern Europe burst into the Roman Empire, they swept away the poor remnant of these forms, and established upon their ruins, the system of feudal monarchy, from which all the modern kingdoms are descended.   Efforts were made, in the middle ages, by the petty republics of Italy, to regain the inherent rights, which a long prescription had wrested from them.   But the remedy of bloody civil wars between neighboring cities, was plainly more disastrous than the disease of subjection.   The struggles of freedom in these little states, resulted much as they had done in Greece ; exhibiting brilliant examples of individual character, and short intervals of public prosperity, but no permanent progress in the organization of liberal institutions.

At length a new era seemed to begin.   The art of printing was discovered. The capture of Constantinople, by the Turks, drove the learned Christians of that city into Italy, and letters revived. A general agitation of public sentiment, in various parts of Europe, ended in the religious reformation. A spirit of adventure had awakened in the maritime nations, and projects of remote discovery were started; and the signs of the times seemed to augur a great political regeneration. But, as if to blast this hope in its bud; as if to counterbalance at once the operation of these springs of improvement; as if to secure the permanence of the arbitrary institutions which existed in every country in that part of the globe, at the moment when it was most threatened; the last blow at the same time was given to the remaining power of the Great Barons,—the sole check on the despotism of the monarch which the feudal system provided; and a new institution was firmly established in Europe, prompt, efficient, and terrible in its operation, beyond any thing which the modern world had seen,—I mean the system of standing armies;—in other words, a military force, organized and paid to support the king on his throne, and retain the people in their subjection.

From this moment, the fate of freedom in Europe was sealed. Something might be hoped, from the amelioration of manners, in softening down the more barbarous parts of political despotism; but nothing was to be expected, in the form of liberal institutions, founded on principle.

The ancient and the modern forms of political servitude were thus combined. The Roman emperors, as I have hinted, maintained themselves simply by military force, in nominal accordance with the forms of the republic. Their power, (to speak in modern terms,) was no part of the constitution, even in their own times. The feudal sovereigns possessed a constitutional precedence in the state, which, after the diffusion of Christianity, they claimed by the grace of God; but their power, in point of fact, was circumscribed by that of their brother barons. With the firm establishment of standing armies, was consummated a system of avowed despotism, transcending all forms of the popular will, existing by divine right, unbalanced by any effectual check in the state, and upheld by military power. It needs but a glance at the state of Europe, in the beginning of the sixteenth century, to see, that, notwithstanding the

18

revival and diffusion of letters, the progress of the reformation, and
the improvement of manners, the tone of the people, in the most
enlightened countries, was more abject than it had been since the
days of the Cæsars.   England was certainly not the least free of
all the countries in Europe ; but who can patiently listen to the
language with which Henry the VIII chides, and Elizabeth scolds
the lords and commons of the Parliament of Great Britain.

All hope of liberty then seemed lost; in Europe all hope was
lost.   A disastrous turn had been given to the general movement
of things ; and in the disclosure of the fatal secret of standing
armies, the future political servitude of man was apparently decided.

But a change is destined to come over the face of things, as
romantic in its origin, as it is wonderful in its progress.   All is not
lost ; on the contrary, all is saved, at the moment, when all seemed
involved in ruin.   Let me just allude to the incidents, connected
with this change, as they have lately been described, by an accomplished countryman, now beyond the sea.*

About half a league from the little sea-port of Palos, in the
province of Andalusia, in Spain, stands a convent dedicated to
St Mary.   Sometime in the year 1486, a poor wayfaring stranger,
accompanied by a small boy, makes his appearance, on foot, at the
gate of this convent, and begs of the porter a little bread and water for his child.   This friendless stranger is COLUMBUS.   Brought
up in the hardy pursuit of a mariner, with no other relaxation from
its toils but that of an occasional service in the fleets of his native
country, with the burden of fifty years upon his frame, the unprotected foreigner makes his suit to the sovereigns of Portugal and
Spain.   He tells them that the broad flat earth on which we tread,
is round ;—he proposes, with what seems a sacrilegious hand, to
lift the veil which had hung, from the creation of the world, over
the floods of the ocean ;—he promises, by a western course, to
reach the eastern shores of Asia,—the region of gold, and diamonds,
and spices ; to extend the sovereignty of Christian kings over
realms and nations hitherto unapproached and unknown ;—and
ultimately to perform a new crusade to the Holy Land, and ran-

* Irving's Life of Columbus.

som the sepulchre of our Saviour, with the new found gold of the East.

Who shall believe the chimerical pretension? The learned men examine it, and pronounce it futile. The royal pilots have ascertained by their own experience, that it is groundless. The priesthood have considered it, and have pronounced that sentence so terrific where the inquisition reigns, that it is a wicked heresy;— the common sense, and popular feeling of men, have been roused first into disdainful and then into indignant exercise, toward a project, which, by a strange new chimera, represented one half of mankind walking with their feet toward the other half.

Such is the reception which his proposal meets. For a long time the great cause of humanity, depending on the discovery of this fair continent, is involved in the fortitude, perseverance, and spirit of the solitary stranger, already past the time of life, when the pulse of adventure beats full and high. If he sink beneath the indifference of the great, the sneers of the wise, the enmity of the mass, and the persecution of a host of adversaries, high and low, and give up the fruitless and thankless pursuit of his noble vision, what a hope for mankind is blasted! But he does not sink. He shakes off his paltry enemies, as the lion shakes the dew-drops from his mane. That consciousness of motive and of strength, which always supports the man who is worthy to be supported, sustains him in his hour of trial; and at length, after years of expectation, importunity, and hope deferred, he launches forth upon the unknown deep, to discover a new world, under the patronage of Ferdinand and Isabella.

The patronage of Ferdinand and Isabella!—Let us dwell for a moment on the auspices under which our country was brought to light. The patronage of Ferdinand and Isabella! Yes, doubtless, they have fitted out a convoy, worthy the noble temper of the man, and the gallantry of his project. Convinced at length, that it is no day-dream of a heated visionary, the fortunate sovereigns of Castile and Arragon, returning from their triumph over the last of the Moors, and putting a victorious close to a war of seven centuries' duration, have no doubt prepared an expedition of well-appointed magnificence, to go out upon this splendid search for other worlds. They have made ready, no doubt, their proudest galleon to waft the heroic adventurer upon his path of glory, with a whole armada of kindred spirits, to share his toils and honors.

Alas, from his ancient resort of Palos, which he first approached as a mendicant,—in three frail barks, of which two were without decks,—the great discoverer of America sails forth on the first voyage across the unexplored waters. Such is the patronage of kings. A few years pass by ; he discovers a new hemisphere ; the wildest of his visions fade into insignificance, before the reality of their fulfilment ; he finds a new world for Castile and Leon, and comes back to Spain, loaded with iron fetters. Republics, it is said, are ungrateful ;—such are the rewards of monarchs !

With this humble instrumentality, did it please Providence to prepare the theatre for those events, by which a new dispensation of liberty was to be communicated to man. But much is yet to transpire, before even the commencement can be made, in the establishment of those institutions, by which this great advance in human happiness was to be effected. The discovery of America had taken place under the auspices of the government most disposed for maritime adventure, and best enabled to extend a helping arm, such as it was, to the enterprise of the great discoverer. But it was not from the same quarter, that the elements of liberty could be derived, to be introduced, expanded, and reared in the new world. Causes, upon which I need not dwell, made it impossible, that the great political reform should go forth from Spain. For this object, a new train of incidents was preparing in another quarter.

The only real advances which modern Europe had made in freedom, had been made in England. The cause of liberty in that country was persecuted, was subdued ; but not annihilated, nor trampled out of being. From the choicest of its suffering champions, were collected the brave band of emigrants, who first went out on the second, the more precious voyage of discovery,—the discovery of a land where liberty, and its consequent blessings might be established.

A late English writer* has permitted himself to say, that the original establishment of the United States, and that of the colony

---

* London Quarterly Review, for January, 1828.

of Botany Bay, were pretty nearly modelled on the same plan. The meaning of this slanderous insinuation, is, that the United States were settled by deported convicts, in like manner as New South Wales has been settled by felons, whose punishment by death has been commuted into transportation. It is doubtless true, that, at one period, the English government was in the habit of condemning to hard labor as servants, in the colonies, a portion of those, who had received the sentence of the law. If this practice makes it proper to compare America with Botany Bay, the same comparison might be made of England herself, before the practice of transportation began, and even now ; inasmuch as a large portion of her convicts are held to labor within her own bosom. In one sense, indeed, we might doubt whether the allegation were more of a reproach or a compliment. During the time that the colonization of America was going on the most rapidly, the best citizens of England,—if it be any part of good citizenship to resist oppression,—were immured in her prisons of state, or lying at the mercy of the law.*

Such were the convicts by which America was settled :—men convicted of fearing God, more than they feared man ; of sacrificing property, ease, and all the comforts of life, to a sense of duty, and the dictates of conscience ;—men, convicted of pure lives, brave hearts, and simple manners. The enterprise was led by RALEIGH, the chivalrous convict, who unfortunately believed that his royal master had the heart of a man, and would not let a sentence of death, which had slumbered for sixteen years, revive and take effect, after so long an interval of employment and favor. But *nullum tempus occurrit regi.* The felons who followed next, were the heroic and long-suffering church of ROBINSON, at Leyden,— CARVER, BREWSTER, BRADFORD, and their pious associates, convicted of worshipping God according to the dictates of their consciences, and of giving up all,—country, property, and the tombs of their fathers,—that they might do it, unmolested. Not content with having driven the Puritans from her soil, England next enacted, or put in force, the oppressive laws, which colonized Maryland

* See Mr Walsh's ' United States and Great Britain,' Sec. II.

with Catholics, and Pennsylvania with Quakers. Nor was it long before the American plantations were recruited by the Germans, convicted of inhabiting the Palatinate, when the merciless armies of Louis XIV were turned into that devoted region ; and by the Huguenots, convicted of holding what they deemed the simple truth of Christianity, when it pleased the mistress of Louis XIV to be very zealous for the Catholic faith. These were followed, in the next century, by the Highlanders, convicted of the enormous crime under a monarchical government, of loyalty to their hereditary prince, on the plains of Culloden ; and the Irish, convicted of supporting the rights of their country, against what they deemed an oppressive external power. Such are the convicts by whom America was settled.

In this way, a fair representation of whatsoever was most valuable in European character, the resolute industry of one nation, the inventive skill and curious arts of another,—the courage, conscience, principle, self-denial of all, were winnowed out, by the policy of of the prevailing governments, little knowing what they did, as a precious seed, wherewith to plant the soil of America. By this singular coincidence of events, our beloved country was constituted the great asylum of suffering virtue and oppressed humanity. It could now no longer be said,—as it was of the Roman Empire,— that mankind were shut up, as if in a vast prison-house, from whence there was no escape. The political and ecclesiastical oppressors of the world, allowed their persecution to find a limit, at the shores of the Atlantic. They scarce ever attempted to pursue their victims beyond its protecting waters. It is plain, that, in this way alone, the design of Providence could be accomplished, which provided for one catholic school of freedom in the western hemisphere. For it must not be a freedom of too sectional and peculiar a cast. On the stock of the English civilization, as the general basis, were to be engrafted the languages, the arts, and the tastes of the other civilized nations. A tie of consanguinity must connect the members of every family of Europe, with some portion of our happy land ; so that in all their trials and disasters, they may look safely beyond the ocean for a refuge. The victims of power, of intolerance, of war, of disaster, in every other part of the world, must feel, that they may find a kindred home, within our limits.

Kings, whom the perilous convulsions of the day have shaken from their thrones, must find a safe retreat; and the needy emigrant must at least not fail of his bread and water, were it only for the sake of the great Discoverer, who was himself obliged to beg them. On this corner stone the temple of our freedom was laid from the first;—

> ' For here the exile met, from every clime,
> And spoke in friendship, every distant tongue;
> Men, from the blood of warring Europe sprung,
> Were here divided by the running brook.'

This peculiarity of our population, which some have thought a misfortune, is in reality one of the happiest features of the American character. Without it, there would have been no obvious means of introducing a new school of civilization into the world. Had we been the unmixed descendants of any one nation of Europe, we should have retained a moral and intellectual dependence on that nation, even after the dissolution of our political connexion should have taken place. It was sufficient for the great purposes in view, that the earliest settlements were made by men, who had fought the battles of liberty in England, and who brought with them the rudiments of constitutional freedom, to a region, where no deep-rooted prescriptions would prevent their development. Instead of marring the symmetry of our social system, it is one of its most attractive and beautiful peculiarities, that, with the prominent qualities of the Anglo-Saxon character, inherited from the English settlers, we have an admixture of almost every thing that is valuable in the character of most of the other states of Europe.

Such was the first preparation for the great political reform, of which America was to be the theatre. The colonies of England, —of a country, where the sanctity of laws and the constitution is professedly recognized,—the North American colonies,—were protected, from the first, against the introduction of the unmitigated despotism, which prevailed in the Spanish settlements;—the continuance of which, down to the moment of their late revolt, prevented the education of those provinces, in the exercise of political rights; and, in that way, has thrown them into the revolution, inexperienced and unprepared,—victims, some of them, to a domestic anarchy, scarcely less grievous than the foreign yoke they have thrown off. While, however, the settlers of America brought with them the principles and feelings, the political habits and tem- per, which defied the encroachments of arbitrary power, and made it necessary, when they were to be oppressed, that they should be oppressed under the forms of law; it was an unavoidable con- sequence of the state of things,—a result perhaps of the very nature of a colonial government,—that they should be thrown into a position of controversy with the mother country; and thus become familiar with the whole energetic doctrine and discipline of resistance. This formed and hardened the temper of the colonists, and trained them up to a spirit, meet for the conflict of separation.

On the other hand, by what I had almost called an accidental circumstance, but one which ought rather to be considered as a leading incident in the great train of events, connected with the establishment of constitutional freedom in this country, it came to pass, that nearly all the colonies,—(founded as they were on the charters, granted to corporate institutions in England, which had for their object the pursuit of the branches of industry and trade, pertinent to a new plantation,)—adopted a regular representative system; by which,—as in ordinary civil corporations,—the affairs of the community are decided by the will and voices of its mem- bers, or those authorized by them. It was no device of the parent government, which gave us our colonial assemblies. It was no refinement of philosophical statesmen, to which we are indebted for our republican institutions of government. They grew up, as it were, by accident, on the simple foundation I have named. ' A house of burgesses,' says Hutchinson, ' broke out in Virginia, in 1620;' and ' although there was no color for it in the charter of Massachusetts, a house of deputies appeared suddenly in 1634.' ' Lord Say,' observes the same historian, ' tempted the principal men of Massachusetts, to make themselves and their heirs, nobles and absolute governors of a new colony; but under this plan, they could find no people to follow them.'

At this early period, and in this simple, unpretending manner, was introduced to the world, that greatest discovery in political science, or political practice, a representative republican system. ' The discovery of the system of the representative republic,' says

M. de Chateaubriand, 'is one of the greatest political events that ever occurred.' But it is not *one* of the greatest, it is the very greatest ;—and, combined with another principle, to which I shall presently advert, and which is also the invention of the United States, it marks an era in human things ;—a discovery in the great science of social happiness compared with which every thing, that terminates in the temporal interests of man, sinks into insignificance.

Thus then was the foundation laid, and thus was the preparation commenced, of the grand political regeneration. For about a century and a half, this preparation was carried on. Without any of the temptations, which drew the Spanish adventurers to Mexico and Peru, the colonies throve almost beyond example, and in the face of neglect, contempt, and persecution. Their numbers, in the substantial middle classes of life, increased with singular rapidity. There were no prerogatives to invite an aristocracy, no vast establishments to attract the indigent.—There was nothing but the rewards of labor and the hope of freedom.

But at length this hope, never adequately satisfied, began to turn into doubt and despair. The colonies had become too important to be overlooked ;—their government was a prerogative too important to be left in their own hands ;—and the legislation of the mother country decidedly assumed a form, which announced to the patriots, that the hour at length had come, when the chains of the great discoverer were to be avenged ; the sufferings of the first settlers to be compensated ; and the long deferred hopes of humanity were to be fulfilled.

You need not, friends and fellow citizens, that I should dwell upon the incidents of the last great act in the colonial drama. This very place was the scene of some of the earliest, and the most memorable of them ;—their recollection is a part of the inheritance of honor, which you have received from your fathers. In the early councils, and first struggles of the great revolutionary enterprise, the citizens of this place were among the most prominent. The measures of resistance which were projected by the patriots of Charlestown, were opposed but by one individual. An active cooperation existed between the political leaders in Boston and this place. The beacon light, which was kindled in the towers of

19

Christ Church, in Boston, on the night of the eighteenth, was answered from the steeple of the church, in which we are now assembled. The intrepid messenger, who was sent forward to convey to HANCOCK and ADAMS the intelligence of the approach of the British troops, was furnished with a horse, for his eventful errand, by a respected citizen of this place. At the close of the following momentous day, the British forces,—the remnant of its disastrous events,—found refuge, under the shades of night, upon the heights of Charlestown;—and there, on the ever memorable seventeenth of June, that great and costly sacrifice, in the cause of freedom, was awfully consummated with fire and blood. Your hilltops were strewed with the illustrious dead; your peaceful homes were wrapped in devouring flames; the fair fruits of a century and a half of civilized culture were reduced to a heap of bloody ashes;—and two thousand men, women, and children, turned houseless upon the world. With the exception of the ravages of the nineteenth of April, the chalice of woe and desolation was in this manner first presented to the lips of the citizens of Charlestown; and they were called upon, at that early period, to taste of its extreme bitterness. Thus devoted, as it were, to the cause, it is no wonder that the spirit of the revolution should have taken possession of their bosoms, and been transmitted to their children. The American, who, in any part of the Union, could forget the scenes and the principles of the revolution, would thereby prove himself unworthy of the blessings, which he enjoys; but the citizen of Charlestown, who could be cold on this momentous theme, must hear a voice of reproach from the walls, which were reared on the ashes of the seventeenth of June; a piercing cry from the very sods of the sacred hill, where our fathers shed their blood.

The revolution was at length accomplished. The political separation of the country from Great Britain, was effected; and it now remained to organize the liberty, which had been reaped on bloody fields;—to establish, in the place of the government, whose yoke had been thrown off, a government at home, which should fulfil the great design of the revolution, and satisfy the demands of the friends of liberty at large. What manifold perils awaited the step! The danger was incalculable, that too little or too much would be done. Smarting under the oppressions of a government, of which the residence was remote, and the spirit alien to their feelings, there was great danger, that the colonies, in the act of declaring themselves sovereign and independent states, would push to an extreme the prerogative of their separate independence, and refuse to admit any authority, beyond the limits of the particular commonwealths which they severally constituted. On the other hand, achieving their independence beneath the banners of the continental army, ascribing, and justly, a large portion of their success, to the personal qualities of the beloved Father of his Country, there was danger not less imminent, that those, who perceived the evils of the opposite extreme, would be inclined to confer too much strength on one general government; and would, perhaps, even fancy the necessity of investing the hero of the revolution, in form, with that sovereign power, which his personal ascendency gave him in the hearts of his countrymen. Such and so critical was the alternative, which the organization of the new government presented, and on the successful issue of which, the entire benefit of this great movement in human affairs was to depend.

The first effort to solve the great problem, was made in the progress of the revolution, and was without success. The articles of confederation verged to the extreme of a union too weak for its great purposes ; and the moment the pressure of the war was withdrawn, the inadequacy of this first project of a government was felt. The United States found themselves overwhelmed with debt, without the means of paying it. Rich in the materials of an extensive commerce, they found their ports crowded with foreign ships, and themselves without the power to raise a revenue. Abounding in all the elements of national wealth, they wanted resources, to defray the ordinary expenses of government.

For a moment, and, to the hasty observer, this last effort for the establishment of freedom, had failed. No fruit had sprung from this lavish expenditure of treasure and blood. We had changed the powerful protection of the mother country, into a cold and jealous amity, if not into a slumbering hostility. The oppressive principles, against which our fathers had struggled, were succeeded by more oppressive realities. The burden of the British navigation act was removed, but it was followed by the impossibility of protecting our shipping, by a navigation law of our own. A state of general prosperity, existing before the revolution, was succeeded by universal exhaustion;—and a high and indignant tone of militant patriotism, by universal despondency.

It remained then to give its last great effect to all that had been done, since the discovery of America, for the establishment of the cause of liberty in the western hemisphere; and by another more deliberate effort, to organize a government, by which not only the present evils, under which the country was suffering, should be remedied, but the final design of Providence should be fulfilled. Such was the task, which devolved on the council of sages, who assembled at Philadelphia, on the second day of May, 1787, of which General Washington was elected President, and over whose debates your townsman, Mr Gorham, presided, for two or three months, as chairman of the committee of the whole, during the discussion of the plan of the federal constitution.

The very first step to be taken, was one of pain and regret. The old confederation was to be given up. What misgivings and grief must not this preliminary sacrifice have occasioned to the patriotic members of the convention! They were attached, and with reason, to its simple majesty. It was weak then, but it had been strong enough to carry the colonies through the storms of the revolution. Some of the great men, who led up the forlorn hope of their country, in the hour of her dearest peril, had died in its defence. Its banner over us had been not love alone, but triumph and joy. Could not a little inefficiency be pardoned to a Union, with which France had made an alliance, and England had made peace? Could the proposed new government do more or better things than this had done? And above all, when the flag of the old thirteen was struck, which had never been struck in battle, who could give assurance, that the hearts of the people could be rallied to another banner?

Such were the misgivings of some of the great men of that day,—the Henrys, the Gerrys, and other eminent anti-federalists, to whose scruples, it is time that justice should be done. They were the sagacious misgivings of wise men, the just forebodings of

brave men ; who were determined not to defraud posterity of the
blessings, for which they had all suffered, and for which some of
them had fought.

The members of that convention, in going about the great work
before them, deliberately laid aside the means, by which all preceding legislators had aimed to accomplish a like work. In founding a strong and efficient government, adequate to the raising up of a
powerful and prosperous people, their first step was, to reject the
institutions to which other governments traced their strength and
prosperity. The world had settled down into the sad belief, that
an hereditary monarch was necessary to give strength to the
executive. The framers of our constitution provided for an elective chief magistrate, chosen every four years. Every other
country had been betrayed into the admission of a distinction of
ranks in society, under the absurd impression, that privileged orders
are necessary to the permanence of the social system. The framers
of our constitution established every thing on the pure natural
basis of a uniform equality of the elective franchise, to be exercised by all the citizens, at fixed and short intervals. In other
countries, it had been thought necessary to constitute some one
political centre, toward which all political power should tend, and
at which, in the last resort, it should be exercised. The framers
of the constitution devised a scheme of confederate and representative sovereign republics, united on a happy distribution of powers,
which, reserving to the separate states all the political functions
essential to the public peace and private justice,—bestowed upon
the general government those and those only, required for the
service of the whole.

Thus was completed the great revolutionary movement ; thus
was perfected that mature organization of a free system, destined to
stand forever as the exemplar of popular government. Thus was
discharged the duty of our fathers to themselves, to the country, to
the world.

The power of the example thus set up, in the eyes of the nations, was instantly and widely felt. It was immediately made
visible to sagacious observers, that a constitutional age had begun.
It was in the nature of things, that, where the former evil existed
in its most inveterate form, the reaction should also be the most

violent.   Hence the dreadful excesses that marked the progress of
the French revolution, and for a while almost made the name of
liberty odious.   But it is not less in the nature of things, that,
when the most indisputable and enviable political blessings stand
illustrated before the world,—not merely in speculation and in
theory, but in living practice and bright example,—the nations of
the earth, in proportion as they have eyes to see, and ears to hear,
and hands to grasp, should insist on imitating the example.   Imitated it they have, and imitate it they will.   France clung to the hope
of constitutional liberty through thirty years of appalling tribulation,
and now enjoys the freest constitution in Europe.   Spain, Portugal, the two Italian kingdoms, and several of the German states
have entered on the same path.   Their progress has been and must
be various ; modified by circumstances ; by the interests and passions of governments and men, and in some cases seemingly arrested.
But their march is as sure as fate.   If we believe at all in the
political revival of Europe, there can be no really retrograde movement in this cause ; and that which seems so, in the revolutions of
government, is like those of the heavenly bodies, a part of their
eternal orbit.

     There can be no retreat, for the great exemplar must stand, to
convince the hesitating nations, under every reverse, that the
reform they strive at, is practicable, is real, is within their reach.
Institutions may fluctuate ; they may be pushed onward, as they
were in France, to a premature simplicity, and fall back to a similitude of the ancient forms.   But there is an element of popular
strength abroad in the world, stronger than forms and institutions,
and daily growing in power.   A public opinion of a new kind has
arisen among men,—the opinion of the civilized world.   Springing
into existence on the shores of our own continent, it has grown
with our growth and strengthened with our strength ; till now, this
moral giant, like that of the ancient poet, marches along the earth
and across the ocean, but his front is among the stars.   The course
of the day does not weary, nor the darkness of night arrest him.
He grasps the pillars of the temple where oppression sits enthroned,
not groping and benighted, like the strong man of old, to be crushed himself beneath the fall ; but trampling, in his strength, on the
massy ruins.

Under the influence, I might almost say the unaided influence, of public opinion, formed and nourished by our example, three wonderful revolutions have broken out in a generation. That of France, not yet consummated, has left that country, (which it found in a condition scarcely better than Turkey,) in the possession of the blessings of a representative constitutional government. Another revolution has emancipated the American possessions of Spain, by an almost unassisted action of moral causes. Nothing but the strong sense of the age, that a government like that of Ferdinand, ought not to subsist, over regions like those which stretch to the south of us, on the continent, could have sufficed to bring about their emancipation, against all the obstacles, which the state of society among them, opposes at present, to regulated liberty and safe independence. When an eminent British statesman said of the emancipation of these States, that 'he had called into existence a new world in the West,' he spoke as wisely as the artist, who, having tipped the forks of a conductor with silver, should boast that he had created the lightning, which it calls down from the clouds. But the greatest triumph of public opinion is the revolution of Greece. The spontaneous sense of the friends of liberty at home and abroad, —without armies, without navies, without concert, and acting only through the simple channels of ordinary communication, principally the press,—has rallied the governments of Europe to this ancient and favored soil of freedom. Pledged to remain at peace, they have been driven, by the force of public sentiment, into the war. Leagued against the cause of revolution, as such, they have been compelled to send their armies and navies, to fight the battles of revolt. Dignifying the barbarous oppressor of Christian Greece, with the title of 'ancient and faithful ally,' they have been constrained, by the outraged feeling of the civilized world, to burn up, in time of peace, the navy of their ally, with all his antiquity and all his fidelity ; and to cast the broad shield of the Holy Alliance over a young and turbulent republic.

This bright prospect may be clouded in ; the powers of Europe, which have reluctantly taken, may speedily abandon the field. Some inglorious composition may yet save the Ottoman empire from dissolution, at the sacrifice of the liberty of Greece, and the power of Europe. But such are not the indications of things. The pros-

pect is fair, that the political regeneration, which commenced in
the West, is now going backward to resuscitate the once happy
and long deserted regions of the older world. The hope is not
now chimerical, that these lovely islands, the flower of the Levant,
—the shores of that renowned sea, around which all the associations of antiquity are concentrated,—are again to be brought back
to the sway of civilization and Christianity. Happily the interest
of the great powers of Europe seems to beckon them onward in
the path of humanity. The half-deserted coasts of Syria and
Egypt, the fertile but almost desolated Archipelago, the empty
shores of Africa, the granary of ancient Rome, seem to offer themselves as a ready refuge for the crowded, starving, discontented
millions of South Western Europe. No natural nor political obstacle
opposes itself to their occupation. France has long cast a wistful
eye on Egypt. Napoleon derived the idea of his expedition, which
was set down to the unchastened ambition of a revolutionary soldier,
from a memoir found in the cabinet of Louis XVI. England has
already laid her hand,—an arbitrary, but a civilized and Christian
hand,—on Malta ; and the Ionian Isles and Cyprus, Rhodes, and
Candia must soon follow ;—while it is not beyond the reach of
hope, that a representative republic may be established in Central
Greece and the adjacent islands. In this way, and with the example of what has here been done, to extend the reign of civilization
and freedom, it is not too much to anticipate, that many generations
will not pass, before the same benignant influence will revisit the
awakened East, and thus fulfil, in the happiest sense, the vision of
Columbus, by restoring a civilized population to the primitive seats
of our holy faith.

    Fellow citizens, the eventful pages in the volume of human for-
tune are opening upon us, with sublime rapidity of succession. It
is two hundred years this summer, since a few of that party, who,
in 1628, commenced in Salem the first settlement of Massachusetts,
were sent by Governor Endicott, to explore the spot where we stand.
They found that one pioneer, of the name of WALFORD, had gone
before them, in the march of civilization, and had planted himself
among the numerous and warlike savages in this quarter. From
them, the native lords of the soil, these first hardy adventurers derived their title to the lands, on which they settled ; and by the

arts of civilization and peace, opened the way for the main body of the colonists of Massachusetts, under Governor Winthrop, who two years afterwards, by a coincidence which you will think worth naming, arrived in Mystic River, and pitched his patriarchal tent, on Ten Hills, upon the *seventeenth day of June,* 1630. Massachusetts, at that moment, consisted of six huts at Salem, and one at this place. It seems but a span of time, as the mind ranges over it. A venerable individual is living, at the seat of the first settlement, whose life covers one half of the entire period :* but what a destiny has been unfolded before our country!—what events have crowded your annals!—what scenes of thrilling interest and eternal glory have signalized the very spot where we stand!

In that unceasing march of things, which calls forward the successive generations of men to perform their part on the stage of life, we at length are summoned to appear. Our fathers have passed their hour of visitation;—how worthily, let the growth and prosperity of our happy land, and the security of our firesides attest. Or if this appeal be too weak to move us, let the eloquent silence of yonder venerated heights,—let the column, which is there rising in simple majesty, recall their venerated forms, as they toiled, in the hasty trenches, through the dreary watches of that night of expectation, heaving up the sods, where many of them lay in peace and in honor, ere the following sun had set. The turn has come to us. The trial of adversity was theirs; the trial of prosperity is ours. Let us meet it as men who know their duty, and prize their blessings. Our position is the most enviable, the most responsible, which men can fill. If this generation does its duty, the cause of constitutional freedom is safe. If we fail : if we fail ;—not only do we defraud our children of the inheritance which we received from our fathers, but we blast the hopes of the friends of liberty throughout our continent, throughout Europe, throughout the world, to the end of time.

History is not without her examples of hard-fought fields, where the banner of liberty has floated triumphantly on the wildest storm of battle. She is without her examples of a people, by whom the dear-bought treasure has been wisely employed, and safely handed

---

* The late venerable Dr Holyoke of Salem.

20

down. The eyes of the world are turned for that example to us. It is related by an ancient historian,* of that Brutus who slew Cæsar, that he threw himself on his sword, after the disastrous battle of Philippi, with the bitter exclamation, that he had followed virtue as a substance, but found it a name. It is not too much to say, that there are, at this moment, noble spirits in the elder world, who are anxiously watching the practical operation of our institutions, to learn whether liberty, as they have been told, is a mockery, a pretence, and a curse,—or a blessing, for which it becomes them to brave the rack, the scaffold, and the scimetar.

Let us then, as we assemble, on the birth day of the nation, as we gather upon the green turf, once wet with precious blood, let us devote ourselves to the sacred cause of CONSTITUTIONAL LIBERTY. Let us abjure the interests and passions, which divide the great family of American freemen. Let the rage of party spirit sleep to-day. Let us resolve, that our children shall have cause to bless the memory of their fathers, as we have cause to bless the memory of ours.

* Dio Cassius, lib. XLVII. in fin.

ADDRESS

DELIVERED AT THE ERECTION OF A MONUMENT TO JOHN HAR-
VARD, SEPTEMBER 26, 1828.

———

WE are assembled, fellow students, and fellow citizens, to witness the erection of a simple monument to the memory of John
Harvard.   It is known to you all, with what ready forethought our
pilgrim fathers provided for the education of those who should
come after them.   Six years only had elapsed, from the time that
Governor Winthrop, with the charter of the colony, set his foot on
the banks of Mystic river, when the General Court appropriated four hundred pounds, out of the scanty resources at its command, for the erection of a school or college, at Cambridge, then
called Newtown.*   The views of our worthy fathers, at this time,
probably did not extend beyond the establishment of a grammar
school.

But that Providence, which, on so many other occasions watched over the infancy of America, and gave the right direction to its
first beginnings, was vigilant here.   In the year 1637, (the year
following that in which the school at Newtown was established,)
the Reverend John Harvard arrived in the colony.   As he was
admitted a freeman in November, 1637, it is supposed that he
came over in the autumn of that year.

This ever memorable benefactor of learning and religion in
America, had been educated at the university of Cambridge in
England ; was a master of arts of Emanuel College in that uni-

* See note A, at the end.

versity; and afterwards a minister of the gospel.   But in what part
of England, or in what year he was born; where he was settled
in the ministry; and what were the circumstances of his life, before leaving his native land, are matters as yet unknown to us. We
are not without hopes, that in answer to inquiries addressed to the
institution in England, where our founder was educated, we may
yet derive some information on these interesting points.

The scanty notices which our early histories contain of him,
lead us to suppose that he brought to this country the disease,
which soon proved fatal to him. He engaged, however, in the
duties of his profession, and was employed as a preacher in the
church in this place. But his usefulness in that calling, was destined to a short duration. He died on the 14th of September of
the year following his arrival, corresponding in the new style, to
the 26th of September; performing in his last act a work of liberality, destined, we trust, to stand while America shall endure, and
with a usefulness as wide as its limits.

By his last will, he bequeathed to the colony, for the endowment
of the school at Newtown, one moiety of his estate, amounting to
a sum little short of eight hundred pounds; a bequest which, even
in the present prosperous state of the country, would be thought
liberal, and which, in its condition at that period, may truly be
called munificent.

This donation gave an instantaneous impulse to the projected
establishment.   It was determined, by the Court, to erect the school
into a college.   In filial commemoration of the place where several
of our fathers had been educated, the name of Newtown was
changed to that of Cambridge; and the college itself was called
by that of Harvard.

And thus did our worthy founder become the instrument in the
hand of Providence, of effecting the design, which the pious leaders
of the colony had most at heart. Such he was felt to be by his
contemporaries. In a letter written by some of them, in 1642,
they say, 'After God had carried us safe to New-England, and
we had builded our houses, provided necessaries for our livelihood,
reared convenient places for God's worship, and settled the civil
government; one of the next things we longed for and looked after,
was to advance learning, and perpetuate it to posterity, dreading

to leave an illiterate ministry to the churches, when our present ministers should lie in the dust. And as we were thinking and consulting how to effect this great work, it pleased God to stir up the heart of one Mr Harvard, (a godly gentleman and lover of learning, then living amongst us,) to give the one half of his estate towards the erecting of a college, and all his library.'*

The college instantly went into operation, on the footing of the ancient institutions of Europe; and in 1642, four years only after the decease of Harvard, sent forth its first class of graduates into the community; men who rose to eminence in the ministry of the gospel, in professional life, and in the public service, both at home and abroad. One of the first class graduated at Cambridge, was sent, both by Cromwell and Charles II, as minister to the States General of Holland. One became a fellow of a College at Oxford; two received degrees of medicine at Leyden and Padua; one received a degree of divinity at Dublin; and on one was conferred the degree of doctor of divinity at Oxford, then as now, the greatest academical distinction to which an English theologian can attain.† Nor was it without example, that young men were sent from England, to receive their education at Harvard college, within a few years after its foundation.‡

With such energy and spirit did our *Alma Mater* spring into being; and so decisive is the evidence that, even in that first stage of the existence of the college, it furnished an education adequate to every department of the civil or sacred service of the country, and not inferior to that of the distinguished schools in Europe.

But it would belong rather to a history of the college than to a eulogy on its founder, to pursue this narrative. I will only add, that till about the end of the seventeenth century, it remained the only college in America, and consequently, up to that period, almost the only source of liberal education accessible to its children, this side of the Atlantic.

It is, then, fellow students, one hundred and ninety years, this day, since the death of the man, who was recognized by his con-

* New-England's First Fruits. Mass. Hist. Coll. I. p. 202. Old Series.
† See note B, at the end.
‡ Johnson's Wonder-Working Providence. Mass. Hist. Coll. New Series. VII. 29.

temporaries as the founder of the most ancient seminary in the country, the college where we received our education. In paying these honors to his single name, we do no injustice to other liberal benefactors of earlier or later times. It is a part of the merit of those, who go forward in works of public usefulness and liberality, that they construct a basis, on which others of kindred temper, who come after them, may build ; and awaken a spirit, which may lead to services still more important than their own.

But considering the penury of the colony, the exhaustion of its first settlers, and the extreme difficulty which must, in consequence, have attended the foundation of a college, it is not easy to estimate the full importance of the early and liberal benefactions of the man whom we commemorate. But for his generosity, the people might have been depressed for the want of the hopes which they built on such an institution, and from the fear of an uneducated posterity ; and society might so far have yielded to the various causes of degeneracy, incident to a remote and feeble colony, as never afterwards to have felt the importance of learning, nor made provision for the education of the people; a result, we may safely say, which would have been fatal to the character of this community.

But it was otherwise ordered for our welfare. A generous spirit was guided to our shores for no other purpose, as it would seem, but to dispense the means requisite for the foundation of the college. Less than two hundred years have elapsed, and not much less than six thousand names are borne on the catalogue of the institution, whose venerable walls are indeed a noble monument to their founder. There is a tradition, that, till the revolutionary war, a grave-stone was standing on the hill, over the spot where his ashes repose. With other similar memorials, it was destroyed at that period ; and nothing but the same tradition remains, to guide us to the hallowed spot. On that spot we have erected a plain and simple, but, at the same time, we apprehend, a permanent memorial. It will add nothing to the renown of him who is commemorated by it, but it will guide the grateful student and the respectful stranger to the precincts of that spot, where all that is mortal rests, of one of the earliest of the country's benefactors.

It is constructed of our native granite, in a solid shaft of fifteen feet elevation, and in the simplest style of ancient art. On the

eastern face of the shaft, and looking towards the land of his birth
and education, we have directed his name to be inscribed upon the
solid granite; and we propose to attach to it, in a marble tablet,
this short inscription, in his mother tongue :—

On the twenty-sixth day of September, A. D. 1828, this Stone
was erected by the Graduates of the University at Cambridge, in
honor of its Founder, who died at Charlestown, on the twenty-sixth
day of September, A. D. 1638.

On the opposite face of the shaft, and looking westward, toward
the walls of the university which bears his name, we have provided another inscription, which, in consideration of his character as
the founder of a seat of learning, is expressed in the Latin tongue :

In piam et perpetuam memoriam JOHANIS HARVARDII, annis fere
ducentis post obitum ejus peractis, academiæ quæ est Cantabrigiæ
Nov-Anglorum alumni, ne diutius vir de litteris nostris optime me-
ritus sine monumento quamvis humili jaceret, hunc lapidem ponen-
dum curaverunt.

And now let no man deride our labor, however humble, as useless or insignificant. With what interest should we not gaze upon
this simple and unpretending shaft, had it been erected at the decease of him whom it commemorates, and did we now behold it
gray with the moss, and beaten with the storms of two centuries!
In a few years, we, who now perform this duty of filial observance,
shall be as those who are resting beneath us; but our children and
our children's children, to the latest generation, will prize this simple memorial, first and chiefly for the sake of the honored name,
which is graven on its face, but with an added feeling of kind
remembrance of those who have united to pay this debt of gratitude.

And when we think of the mighty importance, in our community, of the system of public instruction, and regard the venerable
man whom we commemorate, as the first to set the example of
contributing liberally for the endowment of places of education, (an
example faithfully imitated in this region, in almost every succeeding age,) we cannot, as patriots, admit, that any honor, which it is
in our power to pay to his memory, is beyond his desert. If we

further dwell on our own obligation, and consider that we ourselves
have drank of the streams, that have flowed from this sacred well;
that in the long connexion of cause and effect, which binds the
generations of men, as with links of steel, to each other, it is perhaps owing to his liberality, that we have enjoyed the advantages
of a public education, we shall surely feel, as students, that the
poor tribute we have united to render to his memory, falls infinitely
below the measure either of his merit or of our obligation.

But, humble as they are, let these acts of acknowledgment
impress on our bosoms a just estimate of desert. Of all the first
fathers of New-England, the wise and provident rulers, the grave
magistrates, the valiant captains,—those who counselled the people in peace, and led them in war,—the gratitude of this late posterity has first sought out the spot, where this transient stranger
was laid to rest, scarce a year after his arrival in America. It is
not that we are insensible to the worth of *their* characters, nor that
we are ungrateful for *their* services. But it was given to the venerated man, whom we commemorate this day, first to strike the
key-note in the character of this people:—first to perceive with a
prophet's foresight, and to promote with a princely liberality, considering his means, that connexion between private munificence
and public education, which, well understood and pursued by others, has given to New-England no small portion of her name and
her praise in the land.   What is there to distinguish our community
so honorably as its institutions for general education,—beginning
with its public schools, supported wholly by the people, and continued through the higher institutions, in whose establishment and
dotation public and private liberality has gone hand in hand? What
so eminently reflects credit upon us, and gives to our institutions a
character not possessed by those of many other communities, as
the number and liberality of the private benefactions, which have
been made to them?   The excellent practice of *liberal giving*
has obtained a currency here, which, if I mistake not, it possesses
in few other places.   Men give, not merely from their abundance,
but from their competence; and following the great example,
which we now celebrate, of John Harvard, who gave half his
fortune and all his books, it is no uncommon thing for men to
devote a very considerable portion of estates, not passing the bounds
of moderation, to the endowment of public institutions.

And well does the example of Harvard teach us, that what is thus given away, is, in reality, the portion best saved and longest kept. In the public trusts to which it is confided, it is safe, as far as any thing human is safe, from the vicissitudes to which all else is subject. Here neither private extravagance can squander, nor personal necessity exhaust it. Here, it will not perish with the poor clay, to whose natural wants it would else have been appropriated. Here, unconsumed itself, it will feed the hunger of mind, the only thing on earth that never dies; and endure, and do good for ages, after the donor himself has ceased to live, in aught but his benefactions.

There is, in the human heart, a natural craving to be remembered by those who succeed us. It is not the first passion which awakens in the soul, but it is the strongest which animates, and the last which leaves it. It is a sort of instinctive philosophy, which tells us, that we who live, and act, and move about the earth, and claim it for our own, are not *the human race;* that we are but a small part of it; that those who are to follow us, when we are gone, and those that here lie slumbering beneath our feet, are with us but one company, of which we are the smallest part. It tells us, that the true glory of man is not that which blazes out for a moment, and dazzles the contemporary spectator; but that which lives when the natural life is gone; which is acknowledged by a benefitted and grateful posterity, whom it brings back, even as it does at this moment, with thankful offerings at an humble tomb; and gives to an otherwise obscure name a bright place in the long catalogue of ages.

We stand here amidst the graves of some of the earliest and best of the fathers and sons of New-England. Men of usefulness and honor in their generation, are gathered around us, and among them, no doubt, not a few, whose standing in the community, whose public services, and whose fortune placed them, in the estimate of their day, far above the humble minister of the gospel, who landed on our shores but to leave them forever. But were it given to man to live over the life that is passed, and could the voice of a superior being penetrate the clay on which we stand, and call on the sleepers to signify, whether they would not gladly exchange the wealth, the honors, and the influence they enjoyed, for the death-

21

less name of this humble stranger, they would start up as one man, from beneath the sods that cover them.

We have now, fellow students, discharged our duty to the memory of a great benefactor of our country. In this age of commemoration, as it has been called, it was not meet that the earliest of those, to whom we all are under obligations, should be passed over. Nor is it we, who are here assembled, nor the immediate inhabitants of this vicinity, who are alone united in this act of grateful commemoration. It is not the least of the prerogatives of the intellectual service, that its influence is as little bounded by space as by time. Not a few of the sons of Harvard, in the distant parts of the Union, have promptly contributed their mite towards the erection of this humble structure. While the college which he founded, shall continue to the latest posterity a monument not unworthy of the most honored name, we trust that this plain memorial also will endure ; and while it guides the dutiful votary to the spot where his ashes are deposited, will teach to those who survey it, the supremacy of intellectual and moral desert, and encourage them too, by a like munificence, to aspire to a name, as bright as that which stands engraven on its shaft :

clarum et venerabile nomen
Gentibus, et multum nostræ quod proderat urbi.

NOTES.

Note A, to page 163. Almost all the information in our possession, on the subject of Harvard, is found in the following interesting Note of the learned and accurate editor of Winthrop's Journal. ' We must regret that Winthrop has taken no notice of the ever honored name of Rev. John Harvard, except in the loose memoranda at the end of his MSS. From our Colony Records I find, he was made free 2d November, 1637, at the same time with Rev. John Fiske. By a most diligent antiquary, John Farmer, Esq. of Concord, N. H., this information is given me from Rev. Samuel Danforth's Almanac for 1648: " 7mo. 14 day, 1638, John Harvard, Master of Arts, of Emmanuel College in Cambridge, deceased, and, by will, gave the half of his estate, (which amounted to about 700 pounds,) for the erecting of the College." My correspondent adds, " I do not recollect that any other authority gives the exact *time* of his death, or the *college* at which he was educated." Johnson, lib. II. c. 12 and 19, has favored us with more than any other book. It is peculiarly vexatious to learn from Mather, of the founder of the college, which he so much and so often desired, happily in vain, to rule, only the amount of his bequest, and that he died of consumption. The sons of the oldest university in our country will be pleased with my extract, from our Colony Records, I. 179, of the first motion in this blessed work. " The court agreed to give 400 pounds toward a school or college, whereof 200 pounds to be paid the next year, and 200 pounds when the work is finished, and the next court to appoint where and what building." This was in October, 1636, in the midst of the war with the Pequots, and the beginning of the Antinomian controversy, and we should remember that the appropriation was equal to a year's rate, of the whole colony.—Harvard's will was probably nuncuapative, as it is nowhere recorded.'—*Savage's edition of Winthrop's Journal*, vol. II. pp. 87, 88.

Cotton Mather mentions £779 17s. 2d. as the precise sum

bequeathed by Harvard. Governor Winthrop says about £800.
In *New-England's First Fruits*, Harvard's estate is said to have
been ' in all about £1700.' It is probable, therefore, that in the
foregoing extract from Danforth's Almanac, we ought, instead of
£700, to read £1700. A Latin elegy to the memory of Harvard,
written by John Wilson, is subjoined by Mather to his account of
the foundation of the college. In this elegy (in which Harvard is
represented as speaking) the following lines occur:

> Me (licet indignum) selegit gratia Christi
> Fundarem musis, qui pia tecta piis.
> (Non quod vel chara moriens uxore carerem
> Aut hœres alius quod mihi nullus erat);
> Hœredes vos ipse meos sed linquere suasit
> Usque ad dimidium sortis opumque Deus;
> Sat ratus esse mihi sobolis, pietatis amore
> Educet illustres si schola nostra viros.

From these lines it might be inferred as probable, that Harvard
left a widow, and some other heir, who was not his son.

———

Note B, to page 165.—The following is the first class of Harvard College, as it stands in the catalogue:

1642.

Benjamin Woodbridge, M. Oxon. S. T. D.
GEORGIUS DOWNING, Eques; Oliv. Crom. et Caro. II. leg. apud
    Resp. Bat.
Johannes Bulkley, Mr.
Gulielmus Hubbard, Mr.
SAMUEL BELLINGHAM, M. M. D. Lugd.
Johannes Wilson, Mr.
HENRICUS SALTONSTALL, M. D. Pad. et Oxon. Soc.
TOBIAS BARNARD.
Nathaniel Brewster, Th. Bac. Dublin.

Of these graduates at Harvard College, Woodbridge was
settled in the ministry at Newbury in Berkshire, England. Curious particulars of Sir George Downing* are given in Hutchinson,
Vol. I. p. 107, but particularly in Savage's edition of Winthrop's

———
* He has recently been made the subject of two very learned and interesting
lectures, delivered before the Massachusetts Historical Society, by the Rev. C. W.
Upham, of Salem.

Journal, Vol. II. p. 241, 242. A descendant of Sir George Downing, of the same name, founded Downing College, at Cambridge, in England, on a more liberal foundation than any other college in that university. Bulkley was settled as a clergyman at Fordham in England, and after his ejectment as a non-conformist, practised physic with success in London. He was the son of the eminent divine of the same name, the founder of Concord in Middlesex county. Hubbard was the minister of Ipswich, the famous historian of New-England and of the Indian Wars. Wilson was minister of Dorchester, and is, with several others of this class, among whom are Barnard and Brewster, particularly commemorated by Johnson.

APPENDIX.

On the 6th of September, 1827, a few gentlemen, graduates of Harvard University, happened to be assembled, at the house of Dr George Parkman, in Boston. Some conversation took place, on the propriety of erecting a monument to the memory of JOHN HARVARD, the founder of the University at Cambridge. The proposal met with the hearty concurrence of the gentlemen present, and was believed to be one, which would prove acceptable to the graduates at large. In order to carry it into effect, without unnecessary delay, it was determined to proceed immediately to the adoption of the steps, necessary to be taken to bring the subject before the alumni of the college. The Meeting was accordingly organized, and in pursuance to the resolutions adopted by it, the following *Circular* was issued.

' A meeting of a few individuals, who have received their education at Harvard College, was held in Boston, on the 6th instant. The Hon. F. C. Gray was called to the chair, and Mr E. Everett appointed Secretary.

The object of the meeting was stated to be, to consider the propriety of paying a tribute of respect to the memory of John Harvard, founder of the University at Cambridge, by erecting a suitable monument, in the grave-yard, at Charlestown, where he lies buried: and, on motion, it was

Resolved, That the Chairman and Secretary of this meeting be requested to prepare a statement on this subject, to be submitted to the graduates of Harvard College, inviting a subscription of one dollar each, for the object proposed.

Resolved, That the Hon. P. O. Thatcher be requested to act as Treasurer of the Fund to be raised; and, that the Chairman, Secretary, and Treasurer, adopt the requisite measures for the erection of the monument.

The meeting was then dissolved.

Copy from the Record.

Attest, EDWARD EVERETT, Secretary.'

In pursuance of the foregoing resolutions, the undersigned beg leave to submit the following statement to the graduates of Harvard College:

John Harvard was educated at Emmanuel College, in the University of Cambridge, in England, and, having received the degree of Master of Arts, was settled as a minister in that country. He came over to America, as is supposed, in 1637, having been admitted a freeman of the Colony, on the 2d of November, in that year. After his arrival in this country, he preached a short time at Charlestown, but was laboring under consumption, and died September 14th, 1638. By his Will, he left the half of his estate, (which amounted in the whole to 1559*l.* 14*s.* 4*d.*) as an endowment of the College, which the General Court, two years before, had determined to establish; and which, in honor of this singular liberality, was, by order of the Court, thenceforward called by his name.

These few facts are all, which our histories have preserved to us, relative to this ever-honored name. The previous life of the stranger, who, in the short space of a year passed in a state of declining health, was able to lay this great foundation of good, for remote posterity, is unknown. Of his brief ministry in Charlestown nothing is recorded. We are unacquainted even with the age at which he died; and no memorial exists to point out the spot, where his ashes rest, upon the burying hill in Charlestown.

In our ancient and venerable University, a most illustrious, and, we trust, imperishable monument has been reared to his memory. But it has appeared to many of the children of our *Alma Mater*, that common respect toward the name of a public benefactor, suggests the propriety of marking out, by a suitable memorial, the spot where his mortal remains are deposited. It seems unbecoming that the stranger, who inquires for such a memorial of the earliest benefactor of the cause of education in the country, should be told that none such has been raised.

Under the influence of these feelings, the undersigned have been directed to submit to the consideration of those who have received their education at Harvard College, the propriety of erecting a simple and suitable monument to the memory of its founder, on the burying hill in Charlestown. It is proposed, that it should be a plain, substantial, permanent work, of moderate cost, to be executed in hewn granite. With a view to unite, in this dutiful act, as many of the sons of Harvard as approve the object, it has been thought proper to limit the proposed subscription to one dollar from each individual. Although it is only to the sons of Harvard, that the undersigned have thought themselves authorized directly to address this invitation, yet, as the College at Cambridge may be regarded as the parent stock of nearly all the New England seminaries, we shall cordially welcome the cooperation of those among us, who, although not educated at Cambridge, share with us, in our respect for the memory of the first benefactor of American Letters.

As soon as the requisite arrangements can take place, personal application will be made to the alumni of the College resident in Boston and other large towns, with a view of receiving the subscriptions, to the amount of one dollar from each individual, of those who may be inclined to unite in this act of dutiful commemoration. Gentlemen to whom, from their remote and dispersed places of residence, it may not be practicable to make this personal application, are invited to transmit their subscription by letter, addressed to the Secretary. A list of the subscribers, with a memorandum of the proceedings towards effecting the object proposed, will be deposited in the archives of Harvard College.

The suitable steps for erecting the work will be taken without unnecessary delay.

Meantime it is requested, as this statement is not addressed to the public, that it may not find its way into the newspapers.

F. C. GRAY, *Chairman.*

EDWARD EVERETT, *Secretary.*

Boston, 14th September, 1827.

In consequence of this invitation, a considerable number of the graduates of the college subscribed the sum proposed, toward the erection of the monument. In the summer of 1828, the committee of arrangements found themselves enabled to proceed to the execution of their trust. They applied to the selectmen of Charlestown, for permission to erect the monument, on the burying hill in that town, which request was promptly granted. A contract was then entered into, between the treasurer of the fund and Mr Solomon Willard, architect, for the immediate execution of the work. In pursuance of this contract, the monument was hewn, by permission, from the quarry of the Bunker Hill Monument Association, at Quincy. Mr Almoran Holmes was employed by the architect to transport it from the quarry to the burying hill. For this purpose nineteen yoke of oxen were employed. Its weight is between twelve and thirteen tons. It was raised to its position on the hill, by Mr Holmes, on the 26th of the month by the application of a powerful apparatus, by which the mass was held suspended freely in the air, till, at a signal given, it was lowered to its destined place.

The monument is a solid obelisk, fifteen feet in height, four feet square at the larger extremity, and two at the smaller, and rises from a substantial foundation, without a base, from the surface of the ground. On the eastern face is inscribed the name of Harvard, in large letters and in high relief; the first experiment, it is believed, of this kind, in working the granite of this country. Beneath this name is an English inscription, and on the opposite face an inscription in Latin, wrought in white marble tablets by Mr A. Carey, and attached to the shaft. The monument is enclosed in a simple iron railing, surrounding a space nine feet square, and stands on a beautiful and commanding position, on the top of the burying hill in Charlestown.

The 26th day of September, being the anniversary of the decease of Harvard, was fixed upon for the erection of the monument, of which notice was given in the public papers the day before. The

Corporation and Faculty of Harvard College, the President of the United States, the Rev. Dr Kirkland, the Committee appointed by the citizens of Charlestown, on the subject of the monument, Hon. T. H. Perkins, president of the Bunker Hill Monument Association, and S. Willard, Esq. architect of the monument, had been invited by the Committee of Arrangements to attend on this occasion. A large company of spectators, students of the university, and citizens at large, were also present. At eleven o'clock precisely, the Rev. Dr Walker, pastor of the second congregational church in Charlestown, introduced the ceremonial by a prayer, and the monument was then lowered to its permanent position.

The President of the United States, having been obliged to return to Washington, and being thereby prevented from attending on this occasion, had addressed the following letter to Dr Parkman, a member of the Committee of Arrangements, which was now read.

WASHINGTON, 21st September, 1828.

DEAR SIR,

Among the many privations incident to my sudden but necessary departure from home, to return to my family here, was that of the pleasure which I had indulged the hope of enjoying, by personal participation in that act of filial reverence to the memory of our common benefactor, 'one Mr Harvard,' in which you are so worthily engaged.

In compliance with your request, I had I believe rashly promised to address a few remarks to the spectators who may be assembled to witness the erection of this tardy monument,—a monument creditable to the feelings of those by whom it is now raised, but which can add little to the renown of him whom it is intended to honor.

The name of Harvard is not one of those, towards which his own age, or their posterity can be chargeable with ingratitude. From the very interesting printed paper enclosed in your letter, it appears that from the first institution of the college it received his *name*, an honor far beyond the reach of brass, marble, or granite. A single act of posthumous benevolence has enrolled him among the benefactors of mankind: and of the thousands, who in the lapse of two centuries have drank from the fountain of living waters opened in the rock of the desert at the touch of his staff, what soul so insensible has there been among them, as not to cherish the memory of him, to whose bounty they have been indebted for so much of their intellectual cultivation, and of their moral refinement? His name, identified from the first, with the university which he founded, shares in all the honors of all her sons; and his bequest, the amount of which must be measured by the spirit with which it was bestowed, has erected to his honor a monument, in the heart of every pupil admitted within her walls, which renewed from year to year, and multiplied from age to age, will endure long after granite, brass, and marble shall have crumbled into dust.

22

I do not think it surprising that the cotemporary memorials of the person and character of Mr Harvard are so scanty.   Your ' New-England's First Fruits ' mention him with honor as a godly gentleman, and a lover of learning; but these were qualities very common among the first settlers of New-England.   All the principal founders both of the Plymouth and Massachusetts colonies were persons of family, education, and high intellectual refinement.   Neither trading, speculation, nor romantic adventure, had any share in the motives of their emigration.   There might be, and doubtless was, some mixture of worldly ambition interwoven with the purposes of individuals among them, but in the annals of the world New-England stands alone, as emphatically the colony of conscience.   Mr Harvard was not one of the original settlers.   He came eight or ten years after them, when provision had been amply made for the first wants of nature and of society.   Food, raiment, shelter, the worship of God, and civil government, had all been successively acquired and instituted.   These are the first necessities of civilized man, and these having been supplied, the next in natural course was *education.*   Harvard came with a considerable estate, precisely at the time when this want was pressing most heavily upon them.   Other colonies have fallen into the practice of sending their children to be educated in the schools and colleges of the mother country.   But it was precisely *against* the doctrines of those schools and colleges, that the New-England colonies had been settled.   They were therefore debarred of that resource, and constrained to rely for the education of their children upon themselves.

Harvard was himself a clergyman.   Possessed of a fortune competent to a comfortable subsistence in his native country, his emigration could have been dictated only by principles of moral and religious duty.   But these motives were common to the great mass of the first settlers, whose sincerity had been tested by greater sacrifices and sufferings, than appear to have been required or endured by him.   He probably was not involved in those vehement religious controversies upon questions unintelligible to us and to them, but upon which they wasted their understanding and their affections.   He was not distinguished among the divines of the age as a disputant.   He took a less beaten path to the veneration of after times, and a shorter road to heaven.

I shall assuredly be with you at the performance of your truly filial duties, in spirit and inclination.   For your kind good wishes accept the hearty return and thanks of your friend and brother pupil of Harvard,

J. Q. ADAMS.

To Dr George Parkman, Boston.

The foregoing Address was then delivered by Mr E. EVERETT, a member of the Committee of Arrangements, and at their request.

SPEECH

DELIVERED AT A PUBLIC DINNER AT NASHVILLE, TENNESSEE, 2D JUNE, 1829.

Mr President and Gentlemen,

THE sentiment which has just been announced, and the kind attention, of which I find myself, on this occasion, the object, demand my particular acknowledgments. Coming among you from a remote district of the country; personally acquainted, on my arrival, with but a single individual, besides your distinguished representative in Congress; possessing none of those public and political claims on your notice, which are usually acknowledged by courtesies of this kind, I find myself the honored guest of this day; cordially greeted by so large a company, where I could have expected only to form a few acquaintances; and made to feel myself at home in the land of strangers. I should feel that sense of oppression, which unmerited honor ought always to produce, did I look within myself for the reason of this flattering distinction. It is not there, gentlemen, that I look for it. I know that it flows from a much higher source; from your ready hospitality;—from your liberal feeling, which is able to take in those parts of the Republic which are the most remote from you; and which disposes you, even toward the person of an individual stranger, to strengthen the bonds of good will, between all the brethren of the great American family. It is in this view of the subject alone, that I could reconcile my accepting this kind proffer of your public attentions, with the inoffensive privacy, which it is my study to preserve in my present journey; for the sake of which I have been led, on more than one occasion, since I left home, to express a wish to be excused from similar attentions on the part of political friends; attentions which would have implied a public standing which I do not possess; and would have caused my excursion to be ascribed to another than its real motive.

That motive, gentlemen, is the long cherished wish to behold, with my own eyes, this western world, not of promise merely, but of most astonishing and glorious fulfilment. The wonders, as they may justly be called, of the West; the prodigious extent of the territory; the magnitude of the streams, that unite into one great system the remotest parts of this boundless region;—the fertility of its soil, of which the accounts, till they are verified by actual observation, seem rather like the fables of romance than sober narrative, were among the earliest objects that attracted my youthful curiosity. While visiting some of the most ancient abodes of civilization in the elder world, I had frequent occasion to observe, (and I have no doubt, Mr President,* that your observation confirmed the fact,) that the curiosity of the intelligent men of Europe is more awake, on the subject of this than of any other portion of our country. Of the Atlantic coast they have some general knowledge, arising from the length of time since it was settled, and the political events of which it has been the theatre; but the valley of the Mississippi seems to have presented itself, as it were suddenly, to their imaginations, as a most peculiar, important, and hitherto comparatively unknown region. But from the time, that I have been led more particularly to reflect on the Western country, in its social relations to the rest of the Union, I have felt an irresistible desire to endeavor to understand, from personal observation, the stupendous work of human advancement, which is here going on, and of which the history of mankind certainly affords no other example. I cannot but think it the most interesting subject of contemplation, which the world at present affords. Apart from the grand natural features of the scene,—the aspect of populous towns springing like an exha-

* Hon. Geo. W. Campbell, formerly Secretary of the Treasury, and minister of the United States at St Petersburg.

lation from the soil, of a vacant or savage wilderness transmuted
in one generation, into a thickly inhabited territory,—must certainly appeal as strongly to the inquisitive mind, as the sight of
crumbling towers,—of prostrate columns,—of cities once renowned
and powerful reduced to miserable ruins,—and crowded provinces
turned into deserts. While these latter objects are thought sufficient to reward the traveller for a distant pilgrimage to foreign
countries, he may well be pardoned for feeling himself attracted by
the opposite spectacle which is presented to him at home ; a scene
not of decay, but of teeming life ; of improvement almost too rapid
to seem the result of human means.

It is a remark often quoted of a celebrated foreign statesman,
(M. de Talleyrand,) that America presents, as you travel westward, in point of space, the same succession of appearances, which
may be traced in Europe, as you go back in point of time ;—that
as you move from the coast toward the interior, on this continent,
you pass through those stages of civilization, which are found in
Europe as you follow its history back to the primitive ages. If we
take the aboriginal tribes of our continent into the survey, there is
some foundation for the remark ; but applied to our own population, it is rather ingenious than solid. The scene presented, by our
western country, is not that of a barbarous race, growing up like
the primitive tribes of Europe, into civilized nations ; but it is the
far more rapid and intelligent progress of a civilized people, extending itself through a rude wilderness, and transplanting the mature
arts of life into the hidden recesses of the forest. The traveller,
who penetrates a thousand or two thousand miles from the coast
to the interior, may find, it is true, the log hut of the first settler,
as he may find within the limits of Philadelphia and New-York,
aye, of Paris or London, many a wretched hovel far less commo-
dious ; but he will also find here substantial dwellings,—spacious
and even magnificent mansions,—the abodes of competence and
of abundance,—surrounded by all the indications of the improved
arts of life. I have learned, to my astonishment, that within
twenty years the city of Nashville has grown up, from not exceeding four or five brick houses, to its present condition, as a large,
populous, and thriving capital ; the mart of a great and increasing
commerce, exhibiting, for the number of its inhabitants, as many

costly edifices, as any city in the Union. The log houses have
disappeared, not in the lapse of two thousand, or even of two
hundred years, but in the lapse of twenty years. The primitive
forts of the old hunters are gone, not by the decay of age, but in
the progress of society for a single generation. Far as we are from
the coast, we walk abroad and find ourselves, not in the rude infancy of society, but in the midst of its arts, its refinements, and
its elegancies,—the product not of centuries, but of the life of
man. We are told, that

> ' A thousand years scarce serve to form a state,
> An hour may lay it in the dust.'

The reverse seems almost true. While we contemplate in
Europe the fate of kingdoms, that have been tottering for ages on
the brink of decay, slowly dying for a thousand years, we behold
our own republics rising into maturity, within the experience of a
generation. Were they not our countrymen, our fathers; did not
the grey hairs of a few surviving veterans carry conviction to our
minds, we could scarce credit the narrative of the pioneers of the
western settlements. It was not till 1764, that even Daniel Boone,
whose flight from wilderness to wilderness forms a sort of Hegira
in the West, made his appearance in East Tennessee. The first
cession of land obtained by treaty of the Indians in this State, is
of no older date than April, 1775,—a momentous month, as if the
great order of events in the country's progress required, that simul-
taneously as the blow was struck, which gave independence to
America, the portals of the western mountains should be thrown
open to her sons, who had hitherto been forbidden, by authority
from the Crown, to extend their settlements beyond the Ohio. All
those high-spirited adventurers cannot have passed off the stage,
who moved forward at the head of the column of the first emigrants.
It is related, that in the year 1766, not a white man was found
settled on the Tennessee or the Cumberland, by a party, who, in
that year, descended these rivers. The population of the State,
at the present period, cannot be less than 600,000.

But it is not merely the rapid growth of the western settlements
into populous States, that surprises the traveller from the sea-coast.
For this growth he must be prepared, because he finds it set down

in the statistical tables of the country, and because, as a mere matter of figures, he cannot but comprehend it. That which strikes him with astonishment is the advanced state of the community,—the social improvement which he witnesses. He finds this great region abounding not merely with fertile lands, but with highly cultivated farms, filled, not with wild hunters, but with a substantial yeomanry. The forests are interspersed, like the regions he has left, with villages active with all the arts of life:—he descends the mighty rivers in one of those floating castles,—half ware-house and half palace,—which the genius of Fulton has launched on all our waters; built here in greater numbers than in the East, and with at least equal magnificence; and on these rivers he finds, from Pittsburg down to New-Orleans, a succession of large towns surpassed only by a few of the Atlantic cities; growing fast into rivalry with some of them;—and already rich not merely in wealth, but in all the refinements of life, and in all the institutions that adorn the nature of social, intellectual, moral, and religious man.

Such a spectacle cannot be contemplated, without mingled feelings of astonishment and gratification. I am sure you will pardon me for adding, that it enhances the pleasure with which a son of New-England contemplates it, to find that among those who have swelled the numbers of this great family,—who have come not merely to share your prosperity, but in former days to partake the more doubtful fortunes of the early settlements,—are not a few of the children of that distant region. He rejoices that he is able, in addition to the ties of common language, government, and laws, to trace those of common origin and kindred blood. Nor does he rejoice alone. The feeling, I am sure, is mutual. This festive occasion, gentlemen, is a pledge that you too are not less willing to seize an opportunity however slight, of promoting that mutual good will, which is more important for the perpetuity of the Union, than all the forms of the Constitution.

The beloved land of my birth, gentlemen, compared with yours, is, generally speaking, a barren region. Our rocks and sands yield not those rich harvests which clothe your more fertile soil with plenty; nor are we connected with our sister states by noble streams like yours, which penetrate the country for thousands of miles, and bind the deepest interior to the marts on the coast. But I may venture to assure you, on behalf of my fellow citizens at home, that we behold, not with envy, but with pride, your natural advantages and wonderful progress. When we are visited by strangers from Europe, after we have shown them what is most worthy of notice among ourselves, we habitually add, that this is little, compared with the astonishing advancement of the West. We boast of your improvements as more surprising than our own. We are in the habit of contrasting our comparatively tardy progress under a foreign colonial system with your more rapid growth, beneath the cheering influence of American Independence. We look to you to complete the great undertaking, which was but begun by the fathers of the American people, who settled the Atlantic coast. Reflecting men in that region never regarded the great work to be performed in America, as confined to the settlement of the strip along the shore. It was to open the whole western world as an abode of civilized freemen, and we wish you God-speed in accomplishing your share of the noble work. Two centuries have passed away since the first settlers of the Atlantic coast were struggling with those hardships, which the generation immediately preceding you was here called to encounter; and we cordially rejoice, that a period of thirty years has purchased for you that security and prosperity, which were with us the growth of a century and a half. We feel happy in the belief, that in your further advancement you will not forget the cradles of the American race, and that you will bear in kindly remembrance the men and the deeds, which are among the dearest titles of our glory. In casting the eye over the map of your State, we behold among the names of your counties, those of our Lincoln, Greene, Knox, Warren and Perry. We feel that our hearts are thus linked together by the tie of common devotion to the precious memory of our great and good men; and we confidently rest in the assurance, that when the present generation, with us as with you, shall have passed away, our children will unite with yours, in the tribute of gratitude to those, who, whether at the North or South, the East or the West, have triumphed or bled, have stood or fallen, in their country's cause.

Gentlemen, it has been justly stated, that when the next census shall be taken, the valley of the Mississippi will probably be found to contain a population larger than that with which the old thirteen

States plunged into the revolutionary war, and when, after a period of ten years more, yet another enumeration shall be made, you will then perhaps outvote us in the councils of the nation. The sceptre will then depart from Judah, never to return. We look forward to that event without alarm, as in the order of the natural growth of this great republic. We have a firm faith that our interests are mutually consistent; that if you prosper we shall prosper, if you suffer we shall suffer; that our strength will grow with the closeness of our union; and that our children's welfare, honor, and prosperity will not suffer in the preponderance, which, in the next generation, the West must possess in the balance of the country.

One word more, Gentlemen, and I will relieve your patience. In the course of human events, it is certain that we, who are now assembled, shall never *all* be assembled together again. It is probable, that when we shall part this evening, the most of us will do it to meet no more on earth. Allow me, with the seriousness inseparable from that feeling, to assure you, that this unexpected and flattering mark of your kindness will never be forgotten by me or mine; but at whatever distance of time or place, and in whatever vicissitudes of fortune, will be remembered, as one of the most grateful incidents of my life. Permit me, in taking my seat, to reciprocate the sentiment last announced, by proposing,—

THE INHABITANTS OF NASHVILLE, MAY THEIR PROSPERITY, LIKE THEIR CITY, BE FOUNDED ON A ROCK.

23

SPEECH

DELIVERED AT A PUBLIC DINNER AT LEXINGTON, KENTUCKY,
17TH JUNE, 1829.

———

MR PRESIDENT AND GENTLEMEN,

CUSTOM and propriety forbid me to remain silent ; but I hope
it would be superfluous, as I am sure it would be unavailing, to
attempt to express my feelings, on receiving the kind attentions of
this company.　No gentleman, who has himself had occasion,
while absent from home, to experience the value of acts of private
or public hospitality, will doubt the sentiments excited in me, by
these testimonials of your favorable opinion.　If the voice of welcome, that awaits him beneath his own roof, on his return home,
make the most direct appeal to the sensibilities of the traveller, it
is with a satisfaction scarcely inferior, heightened by a sense of
obligation, that he receives, in a distant region, those proofs of
kindness and assurances of good will, in which he seems to recover
some of the best endearments of home in the land of strangers.　I
would spare you, Gentlemen,—I would spare myself,—the effort
to describe, in set phrases, what, if felt, needs no explanation ;
what, if it be not felt, cannot be explained ; and beg you, with
the plainness of a sincere and grateful heart, to believe, that I place
the proper value on this public and cordial manifestation of your
friendly feeling ; and that, while I take to myself,—and feel honored in doing so,—so much of it as flows from your hospitable
regard toward a stranger, I rejoice more specially in this festive

meeting, as a pledge of good will between the distant sections of the Union, to which we respectively belong. That Union, gentlemen, resting as it does on a political basis, must derive much of its strength and value from harmony and cordiality between the distant members. In a despotic government, resting on the principle of the immediate subordination of all the parts to one head, this harmony among the subjects is not necessary. It may even be the interest of the sovereign to play off the jealousies of the different parts of the state against each other; thus preventing them from combining against himself. But in a popular government, where every thing is ultimately referred to the will of the citizens, mutual good will between them is all-important.

It is therefore most fortunate for us, that the basis, on which our Union rests, is natural, broad, and stable. The several parts of which it is composed, have not been bound to each other, by the measures of a preponderating political power, exerted by the stronger members to attach the weaker to their sovereignty. Nor do we owe our gathering together into this family of States, to the intermarriage of northern Ferdinands with southern Isabellas.— Our Union was not cemented by the sealing wax of diplomatic congresses,—where foreign statesmen sit in judgment, to parcel out reluctant provinces among rival empires;—nor by the blood of disastrous battle fields. Had such been the origin of our association, we might have expected, that incurable antipathies would exist between the discordant members, and that a union, commenced in power, violence, or intrigue, would continue in disgust while it lasted, and end in civil war. On the contrary, among numerous instructive aspects, in which our political system presents itself to the contemplation of the friends of Liberty, none is more important than that, in which it teaches the most auspicious mode of extending a popular government over a vast region of country, filled by a rapidly increasing population, by means of a confederation of States. The superficial observer, not merely abroad, but at home, may regard the multiplication of States, with their different local interests, as an alarming source of dissension, threatening eventual destruction to the Republic. But had the sagacity of the most profound politician been exercised, to contrive a mode in which the continent of North America should become one broad theatre, for the exercise of the rights and the enjoyment and perpetuation of the privileges of republican government and rational liberty, it may well be doubted, whether any other so effectual, so prompt, and at the same time so simple, could have been devised by him, as the creation of a number of separate States, successively formed, as a population becoming dense in the older settlements, had poured itself into the newer fields of adventure and promise; united by a confederacy in the pursuit of all objects of common and general interest; and separate, independent, and sovereign, as to all of individual concern. It is thus, that our Union is extending itself, not as a mere matter of political arrangement, still less by compulsion and power, but by the choice and act of the individual citizens.

What have we seen in all the newly settled portions of the Union? The hardy and enterprising youth finds society in the older settlements comparatively filled up. His portion of the old family farm is too narrow to satisfy his wants or his desires, and he goes forth, with the paternal blessing, and generally with little else, to take up his share of the rich heritage, which the God of nature has spread before him in this western world. He quits the land of his fathers, —the scenes of his early days,—with tender regret glistening in his eye, though hope mantles on his cheek. He does not, as he departs, shake off the dust of the venerated soil from his feet; but he goes on the bank of some distant river, to perpetuate the remembrance of the home of his childhood. He piously bestows the name of the spot where he was born, on the spot to which he has wandered; and while he is laboring with the difficulties, struggling with the privations, languishing perhaps under the diseases incident to the new settlement and the freshly opened soil, he remembers the neighborhood whence he sprang; the roof that sheltered his infancy; the spring that gushed from the rock by his father's door; where he was wont to bathe his heated forehead, after the toil of his youthful sports; the village school-house; the rural church; the graves of his father and his mother. In a few years a new community has been formed; the forest has disappeared, beneath the sturdy arm of the emigrant; his children have grown up, the hardy offspring of the new clime; and the rising settlement is already linked in all its partialities and associations with that from which its fathers and founders had wandered. Such, for the most

part, is the manner in which the new States have been built up ;
and in this way a foundation is laid, *by nature herself,* for peace,
cordiality, and brotherly feeling, between the ancient and recent
settlements of the country.

It is, however, the necessary course of things, that as the newly
settled portion of the country is organized into States, possessing
each the local feeling and local interests of separate political communities, some prejudices,—like the domestic dissensions of the
members of the same family,—should spring up among them, or
between them and the older States.   These may owe their origin
to the more exclusive settlement of some of the new States, from
some of the old ones respectively ; to supposed inconsistency of
the interests of different sections of the country ; to the diversity of manners incident to the peculiarity of geographical and social
position, and the leading pursuits of life ; or to the conflicts of
party politics, which are of necessity, in a free country, often
capricious, and as violent as they are uncertain.   From these and
other causes, on which I need not dwell, and without any impeachment of the prosperous operation of our system, prejudices may
arise between the different sections of the country, calculated to
disturb that harmony, for which a deep foundation is laid in nature,
and which it is all-important to preserve, and if possible to increase.
To remove these prejudices, to establish kind feelings, to promote
good will between the different members of the political family,
appears to me, without exception, the most important object at
which a patriotic citizen, in any portion of the country, can aim.
Our union is our strength, and our weakness too : Our strength,
so long as it exists unimpaired and cherished ; our weakness, whenever discord shall expose a vulnerable point to hostile art or power.
Even the *separate* prosperity of the States, supposing they could
prosper separately, which they cannot, is not enough : I had almost
said, is to be deprecated.   They ought, for their perfect safety, to
owe their prosperity, in some degree, to each other ; to mutual
dependence ; to common interest, and the common feeling derived
from it, or strengthened by it.

It is with these sentiments, (if I may be permitted to allude to
my own public conduct before a company of gentlemen of various
political opinions, and on an occasion consecrated to the oblivion

of every topic of party strife,) that since I have been a member of Congress, I have supported the policy, which aims to open or to perfect the communication between the distant sections of the country, particularly by the extension and preservation of the National Road. The State of which I am a citizen, has already paid between one and two hundred thousand dollars toward the construction and repair of that road; and I doubt not she is prepared to contribute her proportion towards its extension to the place of its destination, as well as toward the completion of the full design, by constructing a lateral branch, through this State, and the States south of Kentucky, to the gulf of Mexico. The friends of internal improvement in the Atlantic States, do not pretend to be indifferent to their own interest. They know that the National Road is a highway for the products of their factories, their fisheries, and their commerce. But I trust also they act upon higher principles,—a regard to the national Union; that they perceive what Washington perceived, and began to inculcate, in the very moment of cessation from war,—almost before he had put off his harness,— that nothing is more essential to the strength of this Union, than an easy communication from East to West.

Subsidiary, in no small degree, to this, and every other measure of legislative enactment aiming at the same end, is that interchange of the courtesies of social life, by which kind feelings are to be awakened or fostered. As between individuals, so between States, which are composed of individuals, there is a temper and a feeling, as important to be rightly directed as the course of legislation or the public policy. On this topic, although perhaps more appropriate to the occasion, I could not, within any reasonable limits, nor without going beyond the bounds of delicacy towards the audience I address, express all that I feel; all that has been inspired in my bosom, by what I have witnessed of the courtesy, the cordiality, the hospitality of the West. I would not, to be sure, be thought to have been so uninformed of any part of the country, as to be wholly ignorant of the state of public sentiment prevailing in it, on any important point. But it will not, I hope, be thought impertinent, if I say, that it has been, not without some surprise, as well as the highest gratification, that I have made a journey of between three and four thousand miles in the West, in the public conveyances by land and water, always without a companion, often unknown; and without having heard a syllable, which could give pain to the feelings of (what I trust I shall ever show myself,) a dutiful son of New-England. I cannot but cherish the hope, that improving means of communication between the States, will put it in the power of increasing numbers of our brethren in other parts of the Union, to give as good an account of that portion of it, to which I belong, and from an experience as agreeable.

Gentlemen, there is no place in the West, I have taken a greater interest in visiting, than your hospitable town; an interest strengthened by the former residence of a beloved and lamented brother among you, and his connexion with the university here established, which has already done so much, and is destined, I am sure, to do so much more, for the public good in this part of the country. Every patriot, every reflecting man, who considers that useful knowledge, widely diffused, is the only sure basis of enlightened freedom, sympathizes with you in your regret for that disaster, which has reduced its well provided apartments and stately walls to melancholy ruins. The public spirit, which raised, will, I doubt not, speedily restore those walls, and infuse new energy into an institution, justly ranked among the most respectable in the country, an honor to this town and to the State, and a public benefit to the West. Indeed, in the early care, which in this and some of the neighboring States, has been had for the establishment of places of education, though much is naturally still to be done, I recognize the spirit which animated the pilgrim fathers of New-England, (never to be mentioned by their descendants without praise,) in the same cause. You have had your Morrison, as we had our Harvard. As a community, you have already given pledges, that you are determined your posterity shall have cause to bless your memory, as we have to bless the memory of our ancestors. Let but the foundations be deeply laid in a liberal public and private patronage, and the intellectual edifice,—the solid fabric of an enlightened community,—will stand firm, though the brick and the marble may, for a time, sink beneath the devouring flames, and the scientific treasures they contained, be reduced to dust and ashes.

There is one association recalled to my mind, in visiting this place, to which it would be unpardonable, were I insensible; an association, which has perpetuated, in the name of your city, that of an ever memorable village in the county I inhabit, and in the near neighborhood of my residence. When the news of the battle of Lexington, on the 19th of April, 1775, reached a party of hunters, assembled at the spring in this place, they resolved, in prophetic commemoration of that event, to give the name of Lexington to the place of their encampment, and the town that should there be founded. Not more than fifty years, I believe, have passed away, since the actual laying out of this town; and in that period, what a monument have not you and your fathers reared to the brave and good men, who, at that doubtful crisis of the country's fate, on the morn of her independence, offered up their lives in her sacred cause! They were not of your kindred, except in the kindred of struggling liberty, and by the blood which they shed for your freedom, as for their own. They lie in their humble graves, in the beautiful village where they fell; and a simple stone marks the scene of their costly sacrifice; but how worthily, in the remote West, has their pious self-devotion been commemorated, in the ample streets, the sightly dwellings, the substantial public edifices, in the charitable, the literary, the religious foundations of this important town!

The day of our present meeting carries us back, by a natural and most interesting coincidence, to the same eventful period, to the battle fields, which have rendered so many portions of the Atlantic coast a classic soil, and to those historical recollections, which are a rich portion of the moral treasures of United America. It is the 17th of June. On that day, fifty-four years ago, the heights of Charlestown, the place of my residence, were the scene of that great and costly sacrifice to the cause of American Liberty. The precious blood there shed, flowed not alone for the ancient colonies, by whom the revolutionary war was fought, but for you also, their hopeful offspring. Oh, that the brave and devoted spirits, who there offered up their lives, could have caught a glimpse, in their dying moments, of the prosperity they were achieving for regions then beyond the line of American colonization, and for the millions, that are springing up in the mighty West. Oh, that they could have anticipated, in the last agony, the tribute of gratitude, which beams in your glistening eyes!

But little more than half a century has elapsed since that momentous event, and meantime, in the astonishing progress of our country, this State, then an almost pathless wilderness, half explored, untilled, or tilled only by the bold hunter, who went to the field with a spade in one hand and a rifle in the other, has become itself the parent of other rising States. Beyond the Wabash,—beyond the Mississippi,—there are now large communities, who look to these their native fields, with the same feelings, with which your fathers looked back to their native homes in Virginia. I have myself, within a week or two, heard an individual, who had been to explore for himself a new home in Illinois, and was on his return to take out his family to the chosen spot, even while commending the abundance and fertility of the vast prairies in that region, check himself, as we were passing by some of the prosperous settlements, the comfortable houses, the rich corn-fields, the pleasant meadows, the beautiful woodland pastures of his native State, and exclaim, ' after all, there is nothing on God's earth like old Kentucky ! '

And thus, gentlemen, it is, that civilization, improvement, and our republican institutions of government are making their auspicious, progress from region to region, throughout the continent founded on the happiest conception of political wisdom, and confirmed by the dear ties of nature and kindred. The rapid growth of the country has brought into unusual association those opposite feelings and relations, which belong respectively to ancient and modern States, and were never before combined in one. And the torch of enlightened liberty, originally kindled at the altars of Jamestown and Plymouth, and long ago transmitted across the mountains, is still travelling onward and onward, through the wide West. It requires no great stretch of the imagination, to trace its auspicious path to regions yet lying in the untenanted solitude of nature ; nor to apply to it, with still happier augury, the beautiful language, by which the poet has described the revival of freedom, among the nations of the elder world :—

> I saw the expecting regions stand,
> To catch the coming flame in turn;
> I saw, from ready hand to hand,
> The bright but struggling glory burn.

24

And each, as she received the flame,
Lighted her altar with its ray;
Then, smiling, to the next who came,
Speeded it on its sparkling way.

But, Mr President, I must check myself, on this delightful theme, and spare your patience. Allow me, in sitting down, to renew my thanks to this respectable company, for their friendly and hospitable attentions, and to propose the following sentiment :—

THE EASTERN AND WESTERN STATES :—ONE IN ORIGIN, ONE IN INTEREST :—UNITED IN GOVERNMENT, MAY THEY BE STILL MORE UNITED BY MUTUAL GOOD WILL.

SPEECH

DELIVERED AT A PUBLIC DINNER, AT THE YELLOW SPRINGS, IN
OHIO, 29TH JUNE, 1829.

—

MR CHAIRMAN,

PERMIT me to thank you and this respectable company, for
the sentiment just announced; although I find it difficult to do so
in any suitable terms. It is known to most of the company, that
I arrived here two or three hours since, with my worthy friend,
your fellow citizen, (Mr Fales, of Dayton,) with no other anticipation, than that of enjoying the natural beauties of this lovely
spot, where every thing seems combined, that can delight the eye,
afford recreation, and promote health. To meet, in addition to the
gratification of a visit to so agreeable a retreat, the kind and unexpected welcome of such a company, inspires me, I need not say,
with emotions, which I had better leave to your indulgence to
imagine, than attempt to express. Allow me, therefore, to pass
from a topic so unimportant as my private feelings, and dwell a few
moments on those views, which present themselves to the mind of
the stranger, in visiting your prosperous State.

My first distinct impressions relative to this State were formed
some thirteen years ago, in the interior of the continent of Europe,
from a work which had then just been published by your distinguished fellow citizen, Dr Drake,—*The Picture of Cincinnati*.
Having, at that time, an opportunity, through the pages of one of
the literary journals of Germany, to call the attention of the reading public in that quarter, to the wonderful progress you had made

196

and were making, as set forth in the work alluded to, I found the
account to be received almost with incredulity. Nor was this
wonderful. I remember to have passed eighteen months in that
country, traversing it, to a considerable extent, in several directions,
before I had seen one new house, in progress of erection. With
such a state of things about them, (the consequence of the disastrous political condition of Europe,) you can easily conceive, that
they found it difficult to credit the statement, when they were told
that Ohio contained in 1787 not a single white settlement, in 1790
three thousand inhabitants, in 1800 forty-two thousand, in 1810
two hundred and thirty thousand, and in 1815 at least four hundred thousand; and that this was not merely the overpouring of
the whole redundant population of the old States, into one favorite
resort of emigration; but that half a dozen other new States had
been growing up, with nearly equal rapidity, at the same time,
while the old States also had been steadily on the increase. It is
not surprising, that such facts, told to a community, whose population is nearly stationary, should scarcely gain credence.

Such was the impression produced by the condition of your State
in 1815. The next time my attention was more particularly called
to the subject, was about two years since, by another interesting
work, the well-known pamphlet, entitled 'Cincinnati in 1826,' in
which some general views are given of the progress of Ohio.
From this it appeared, that in the interval between the two publications, new wonders of advancement had been made; and farther
strides had been taken, astonishing even to the eye, familiarized to
the improvements by which you are surrounded. In this short
period, regular communications by stage coaches had been established; the National Road had entered your limits; your rivers had
become thronged with steamboats; and your population had
doubled. But your progress did not stop at this period. On the
contrary, it now received perhaps, its most powerful stimulus.
Your canal policy,—the glory and prosperity of the State,—had
been determined upon, and a commencement made in its vigorous
execution. In the latest publications relative to your State, particularly in '*The Geography and the History of the Valley of the
Mississippi*,' the still farther and still more rapid progress produced
by this new stimulus is indicated. But even this does not bring it

down to the present hour. On the points, where the system of communication is complete, the effect has been magical. The population of Cincinnati, by accurate estimate, has risen since 1825 from sixteen to twenty-five thousand ; and, as I have been informed, on the best authority, an increase in the value of its real property has taken place, equal to the whole expense of the Miami canal. But no book can describe your State, farther down than to the moment when it is written. Its condition changes, while the geographer is casting up the figures that represent it. As well might you, by the theoretical rules of navigation, attempt to designate the position of a steamboat on the Ohio, when it is swollen by the floods of spring. While you are fixing your quadrant, the bôat is swept downwards for miles on the bosom of the rushing stream.

These and similar facts, sir, would the less merit frequent repetition were the rapid progress of the country occasioned merely by the abundance of fertile land, operating as a temptation to the adventurer in search of fortune. But when we contrast the progress of the Western States of our Union, with that of the British possessions in their immediate neighborhood, we see that other causes have been at work, to produce this unparalleled state of things. It is well known, that the British Government has held out very strong temptations to persons disposed to emigrate to its North American possessions. The expense of crossing the ocean has been defrayed, grants of land have been made, freedom from taxes guarantied, and implements of husbandry furnished, (if we are not misinformed,) at the public expense. Some portion of the land itself, in those possessions, for natural fertility, climate, and geographical position is equal to any part of the Western States. But while some of those States have been adding to their numbers from thirty to one hundred thousand inhabitants yearly, it has been publicly stated, of late, by an inhabitant of Upper Canada, that the increase of that province, emigration included, has not for ten years exceeded four thousand five hundred per annum.

We learn, from this contrast, that the growth of your western country is not merely the progress of its citizens in numerical multiplication. It is civilization personified and embodied, going forth to take possession of the land. It is the *principle* of our institutions, advancing not so much with the toilsome movement of human agency, but rather like the grand operations of sovereign Providence. It seems urged along its stupendous course, as the earth itself is propelled in its orbit, silent and calm, like the moving planet, with a speed we cannot measure ; yet not like that, without a monument to mark its way through the vacant regions of space, but scattering hamlets, and villages, and cities on its path,—the abodes of civilized and prosperous millions.

The ties of interest, which connect all the States of this Union, are innumerable ; and those of mutual good will are destined, I trust, to add all their strength to the compact. It ought to be the desire and the effort of every true patriot, to merge, in one comprehensive feeling, all discordant sectional preferences. But the circumstances of first settlement and geographical proximity will produce associations, not inconsistent with the one great principle of union, and resting on a basis too natural to be discredited. It cannot be expected, that New-England and the Middle States should not feel complacency, in reflecting, that the foundations of Ohio were laid by some of their citizens ; that the germs of your growth were derived from our soil. Acknowledging the high traits of character, to be found in the various strongly marked sections of the country, we cannot be insensible to the prevailing affinity between your population and ours. In the leading characteristics of society here, we recognize the qualities to which we have been familiarized at home. While we witness your auspicious progress we take pride in reflecting, that it is the extension of our own immediate kindred ; the ripening of a fruit, which our fathers planted.

Nor is this similarity confined to things of a superficial nature, belonging rather to the province of manners than institutions. In many concerns of highest moment, and particularly in the system of public schools commenced in Ohio, we behold an assurance, that your vast community is destined to grow up into a still nearer resemblance of what we deem the best features of ours. Regarding the *mind* of the citizens as the most precious part of the public capital, we have felt, that an efficient plan of general education is one of the first elements of public wealth. The diffusion of intelligence has furnished us our best compensation for our narrow limits and moderately fertile soil ; and the tax which has effected it, has returned with the richest interest to the citizens. We rejoice to see you adopting the same policy, and providing for a posterity, instructed in the necessary branches of useful knowledge. Such a policy, besides all its other benefits, binds the different members of the body politic by the strongest ties. It lays the rich under contribution, for the education of the poor; and it places the strong watchman of public intelligence and order at the door of the rich. In the first adoption of such a system, difficulties are to be expected; it cannot go equally well into operation in every quarter; perhaps not perfectly in any quarter. But the man, or the body of men, that shall effectually introduce it, will perform a work of public utility, of which the blessing and the praise will never die.

It has been frequently remarked that our beloved country is set up by Providence, as a great exemplar to the world, from which the most enlightened and best governed of the ancient nations have much to learn. When we think how recently our continent itself was discovered, that almost ever since it has been subjected to foreign rule, and left unshielded, to receive every impression that could be stamped on it by foreign ascendency, we must feel that is extraordinary that we have been able to constitute ourselves an acknowledged subject of envy and imitation, to all the communities on earth. But when we of the old States turn our attention to the spectacle beneath our eyes at home, we are astonished to find, that our comparatively ancient commonwealths, monitors as we deemed them in the great school of improvement, are obliged to come in turn, and take a most important lesson from you. In your great works of internal improvement,—in the two canals, one of which you have completed and the other of which you are pushing to its completion, at large public expense and under circumstances requiring no ordinary measure of legislative courage,—you are setting an example to the oldest states of the confederacy. Forty years since, and the only white population, connected with Ohio, was on its way, in a single wagon, from Massachusetts to this place.* You have now a

---

* The reference is to an incident, alluded to, in the following manner, in a speech of the author, at the celebration of the Second Centennial Anniversary of the settlement of Salem, 18th September, 1828:—

" But, sir, while on this happy occasion we contemplate, with mingled feelings of

system of artificial navigation of nearly four hundred miles rapidly advancing to its completion ; while the Massachusetts rail road is still locked up in the port folio of the commissioners, who have surveyed the route.   It is however, one of the happy effects of our separation into different States, that it gives scope for a generous emulation, in objects of public utility.   It is hardly to be believed, that the ancient settlements on the coast will consent to be long behind the younger States of the West in the march of improvement ; or fearful, with their abundant capital, to commence those great public enterprises, which have not been found beyond the reach of your infant resources.   Happy the region where such are the objects of competition between neighboring States !

pride and joy, the lovely and august form of our America, rising as it were, from the waves of the ocean, with the grace of youth in all her steps, and the heaven of liberty in her eye, there is another aspect, under which we are led by natural association to regard her, as we consider the family of republics which have sprung into being beyond the mountains.   The graceful and lovely daughter has become the mother of rising States.   While our thoughts, on this day, are carried back to the tombs of our fathers beyond the sea, there are millions of kindred Americans beyond the rivers and mountains, whose hearts are fixed on the Atlantic coast, as the cradle of their political existence.   If the States of the coast were struck from existence, they would already have performed their share of the great duty, as it has been called, of social transmission.   A mighty wilderness has been colonized, almost within our own day, by the young men of the Atlantic coast; not driven by the arm of persecution from the land of their birth, but parting, with tearful eyes, from their pleasant homes, to follow the guiding hand of Providence to the Western realms of promise.

It is just forty years this summer, since a long, ark-like looking wagon was seen traversing the roads and winding through the villages of Essex and Middlesex, covered with black canvass, inscribed on the outside, in large letters, ' To Marietta on the Ohio.'   That expedition under Dr Cutler of this neighborhood, was the first germ of the settlement of Ohio, which now contains near a million of inhabitants. Forty years have scarce passed by, since this great State, with all its settlements, improvements, its mighty canals and growing population, was covered up, (if I may so say,) under the canvass of Dr Cutler's wagon.   Not a half century, and a State is in existence, (twice as large as our old Massachusetts,) to whom not Old England but New-England, is the land of ancestral recollection.   Yes, sir, on richer soils and broader plains than ours, there is a large community of men, to whom our rocks and our sands will be forever dear.   Ten years ago, there were thirteen or fourteen settlements west of the Alleghanies, bearing the name of Salem, the city of peace; one in Kentucky, one in Indiana, eight or nine in Ohio, all bearing the name of the spot, where we are now assembled,—where the fathers of Massachusetts first set foot, two hundred years ago.' '

Permit me in conclusion, gentlemen, to revert to the idea, with which I commenced,—the astonishing and marvellous progress of the West. The settlement of Ohio and the other North-Western States, may be considered as dating from the Ordinance of 1787. The individual, who drew that ever memorable statute is still living, a most respected citizen and eminent jurist of Massachusetts, Nathan Dane. Of those also, who first emigrated to this region, and encountered the hardships of the wilderness, and the perils of the savage foe, all have not passed away. What events have been crowded into the lives of such men! It is only when we consider what they found the country, and what they handed it down to this generation, that we learn the efficacy of public and private virtue, —of wise counsel,—of simple manners,—a firm purpose,—and an inborn love of liberty! But I forbear, sir, to enlarge on considerations so familiar to this respected company, and only ask permission to propose to its acceptance, the following sentiment :—

THE STATE OF OHIO:—FOUNDED BY THE VIRTUES OF THE LAST GENERATION, SUSTAINED BY THE PUBLIC SPIRIT OF THIS, ITS PROSPERITY IS SURE.

25

ADDRESS

DELIVERED BEFORE THE CHARLESTOWN LYCEUM, ON THE 28TH
OF JUNE, 1830, THE ANNIVERSARY OF THE ARRIVAL OF GOV-
ERNOR WINTHROP.

THIS day completes the second century, since Governor Winthrop explored the banks of the Mystic River. From his arrival
at Charlestown, accompanied by a large number of settlers, furnished with a supply of every thing necessary for the foundation of
the colony, and especially, bringing with them the Colonial Charter, may, with great propriety, be dated the foundation of Massachusetts, and in it, that of New-England. There are other interesting events, in our early history, which have, in like manner,
been justly commemorated, for their connexion with the same great
era. The landing of the Pilgrims at Plymouth, has been regarded,
from the first, as a period, from which we may with propriety,
compute the settlement of New-England ; and has been celebrated,
with every demonstration of pious and grateful respect. The completion of the second century, from the arrival of Governor Endecott at Salem, was noticed two years since, by our fellow citizens
of that place, in a manner worthy of the interest and magnitude
of the event ; and the anniversary of the commencement of the
settlement of Boston, is reserved for a like celebration, in the
autumn of the present year.

Were these celebrations a matter of mere ceremonial observance,
their multiplication would be idle and oppressive. But they are
all consecrated to events of real interest. They have a tendency
to extend the knowledge of the early history of the country.
They are just tributes to the memory of worthy men, to whom we

are under everlasting obligations. They furnish fit occasions for inculcating the great principles which led to the settlement of our happy country; and by connecting some interesting associations with the spots familiar to us, by daily visitation, they remind us that there is something worthy to be commemorated, in the soil which we inhabit; and thus furnish food for an enlightened patriotism. The genius of our institutions has made this the chief means of perpetuating, by sensible memorials, the fame of excellent men and great achievements. Wisely discarding those establishments, which have connected with hereditary possessions in the soil, and transmissible dignities in the State, the name and family of discoverers and conquerors, it has been, with us, left to the affection and patriotism, by which the observance of these occasions is prompted, to preserve the worth of our forefathers from forgetfulness.

For these considerations, it was thought expedient by the members of the Charlestown Lyceum, that the arrival of Governor Winthrop on our shores, with the charter of the colony, should not pass unnoticed. When I was first requested to deliver an address on the occasion, it was my expectation, that it would be done with no greater publicity, than that with which the lectures before this institution have been usually delivered. The event, however, has been considered as of sufficient importance to receive a more public notice; and in this opinion of the members of the Charlestown Lyceum and our fellow citizens who unite with them, I have cheerfully acquiesced. It will not, however, be expected of me, wholly to abandon the form which my address, in its origin, was intended to assume, although less adapted than I could wish, to the character of this vast audience, before which I have the honor to appear.

In performing the duty which devolves upon me in consequence of this arrangement, I propose briefly to narrate the history of the event which we celebrate, and then to dwell on some of the general topics, which belong to the day and the occasion.

When America was discovered, the great and interesting questions presented themselves, what right had the European discoverers in the new found continent, and in what way were its settlement and colonization to proceed.

The first discovery was made, under the auspices of European governments, which admitted the right of the Head of the Catholic Church to dispose of all the kingdoms of the earth ; and of course, of all newly discovered regions, which had not before been appropriated. This right of the Head of the Catholic Church was recognized by Protestant princes, only so far as it might be backed by that of actual discovery ;—and although the Kings of Spain and Portugal had received from the Pope a distributive grant of all the newly discovered countries on the globe, the sovereign of England claimed the right of making his own discoveries, and appropriating them as he pleased, to the benefit of his own subjects and government. Under this claim, and in consequence of the discoveries of Cabot, our mother country invested herself with this great and ultimate right of disposing of the American continent, from the gulf of Mexico, northwardly, till it reached the limits covered by the like claim of actual discovery, on the part of other governments.*

It is not my intention to enter into the discussion of the nature and extent of this right of discovery. If we admit, that it was the will of Providence, and for the interest of humanity, that America should be settled by a civilized race of men, we admit, at the same time, a perfect right, in some way or other, to effect that settlement. And though it may be out of our power to remove all the difficulties which attend the question,—although we cannot perhaps, on the received principles of natural law, theoretically reconcile the previous rights of the aboriginal population with the accruing rights of the discoverers and settlers, yet we must either allow that those rights are not, upon the whole, irreconcilable, or, we must maintain that it was the will of Providence, and for the greatest good of mankind, that America should remain in the condition in which the discoverers found it.

No judicious person, at the present day, will maintain this ; and no such opinion was entertained by the governments of Europe, nor by the enterprising, patriotic, and liberal men, on whom it

---

* Opinion of the Supreme Court of the United States, in the case of Johnson & Graham's Lessees vs. McIntosh; 8th Wheaton.

EVERETT'S ORATIONS. 205

devolved to deal practically with this great subject. How great it was,—it is true,—they did not feel; as we, with a like subject thrown practically into our hands,—I mean the settlement of our own vacant public domain, are equally insensible to its importance. Although there is a great lodgment of civilized men on this continent, which is rapidly extending itself, yet there is still a vast region wholly unsettled, and presenting very nearly the same aspect to us, which the whole North American continent did to our forefathers, in Great Britain. But no man, I think, who analyzes either the popular sentiment of this community, or the legislative policy of this government, will deny, that the duty to be performed by the people of this generation, in settling these unsettled regions of our country, has scarce ever presented itself in its magnitude, grandeur, and solemnity, to the minds either of people or of rulers. It was justly remarked, more than once this winter, in the great debate in the Senate of the United States, nominally on the subject of the public domain, that this subject was the only one not glanced at in the discussion; and that subject, I may say without fear of contradiction, is as important to the people of the United States, and to the cause of liberty throughout the world, as the question of colonizing America, which presented itself to the nations and governments of Europe, in the fifteenth and sixteenth centuries.

These questions are never comprehended, till it is too late. Experience alone unfolds their magnitude. We may strain our minds to grasp them, but they are beyond our power. There is no political *calculus*, which can deal with the vast elements of a nation's growth. Providence, or destiny, or the order of things, in which, while we think ourselves the agents, we are humble instruments,—aided by some high impulses from the minds and hearts of wise and great men, catching a prophetic glimpse of the future fortunes of our race,—these decide the progress of nations; and educe consequences the most stupendous, from causes seemingly least proportionate to the effect.

But, though we do not find any traces in the public sentiment, or in the legislation of Europe, in the sixteenth and seventeenth centuries, of an accurate foresight of the great work which that age was called upon to perform, yet there was unquestionably a dis-

tinct perception, that the enclosure of the civilized families of the
earth had been suddenly enlarged.   Spain and Portugal poured
themselves forth impetuously into the new found region ; and Great
Britain, though with something of a constitutional tardiness, followed
the example.

The first British patents, for the settlement of the discoveries on
the North American continent, were those of Sir Humphrey Gilbert and Sir Walter Raleigh, in the latter quarter of the sixteenth
century.   These and some similar grants were vacated, from inability to fulfil their conditions ; or from other causes, failed to take
permanent effect.   When Queen Elizabeth died in 1603, not a
European family was known to exist on the continent of America,
north of the gulf of Mexico.   On the tenth of April, 1606, King
James granted a patent, dividing that portion of North America,
which lies between the thirty-fourth and forty-fifth degrees of latitude, into two nearly equal districts.   The southern, called the first
colony, he granted to the London Company.   The northern, called
the second colony, he granted to the Plymouth Company, and
allotted it as a place of settlement, to several knights, gentlemen,
and merchants of Bristol, Plymouth, and other parts of the west
of England.   This patent conveyed a grant of the property of the
land along the coast for fifty miles, on each side from the place of
their first habitation, and extending one hundred miles into the
interior.

Under these charters, various attempts at colonization and settlement were made, and at first, with very doubtful success, by the
Virginia Company.   These, of course, it is no part of our present
business to pursue.   In 1614, the adventurous Captain Smith,
famous in his connexion with the settlement of Virginia, was sent
out by four individuals in England, who were disposed to engage
in an enterprise on these distant shores, to explore the coast of
North Virginia.   He arrived on the coast of Maine at the end of
April, 1614, and in the course of the following summer, he visited
the North Eastern shores of America, from the Penobscot river to
Cape Cod ; entered and examined the rivers, surveyed the country,
and carried on a trade with the natives.   Having, on his return to
England, constructed from his surveys a map of the country, it
was submitted to Prince Charles, who gave the name of New-

England to the region explored by Smith, and bestowed his own name on what was then supposed to be its principal river. The season in which Captain Smith visited the country, is that in which it appears in its greatest beauty. His account of it was such as to excite the attention and kindle the imagination of men in England, and the profitable returns of his voyage united with these impressions to strengthen the disposition which was felt, to colonize the newly explored region. Several attempts were accordingly made, to carry this design into effect, for the benefit and under the auspices of the Plymouth Company, but all without success. The great enterprise was reserved to be accomplished by a very different instrumentality.

In 1617, the church of Mr Robinson at Leyden, had come to the resolution of exiling themselves to the American wilderness. As the principal attempts at settlement had been made in the Southern colony or Virginia, their thoughts were turned to that quarter, and they sent two of their number to London, to negotiate with the Virginia Company on the terms of their settlement; and to ascertain whether liberty of conscience would be granted them, in the new country. The Virginia Company was disposed to grant them a patent, with as ample privileges as it was in their power to convey. The king, however, could not be induced to patronize the design, and promised only a connivance in it, so long as they demeaned themselves peaceably. In 1619, the arrangement was finally made with the Virginia Company; and in the following year, the ever-memorable emigration to Plymouth took place. In consequence of the treacherous and secret interference of the Dutch, who had their own designs upon that part of the coast which had been explored by Hudson, the captain of the vessel which transported the first company to America, conveyed them to a place without the limits of the patent of the Virginia company; and where of course the Pilgrims were set down beyond the protection of any grant and the pale of any law. In three or four years a patent was obtained of the Plymouth Company, and on this sole basis, the first New-England settlement rested, till its incorporation with the colony of Massachusetts Bay.

In the year 1620, the old patent of the Plymouth Company was revoked, and a new one was granted to some of the highest nobility and gentry of England, and their associates, constituting them and their successors, 'the council established at Plymouth, in the County of Devon, for the planting, ruling, ordering and governing of New-England in America.' By this patent, that part of America, which lies between the fortieth and forty-eighth degrees of north latitude in breadth, and in length by all the breadth aforesaid, throughout the main, from sea to sea, was given to them, in absolute property. Civil and jurisdictional powers, like those which had been granted by the Virginia patent, were conferred on the council established by this charter; on which as, on a basis, rested all the subsequent patents and grants of this portion of the country. By this grant, a considerable part of the British colonies in North America; the whole of the New-England States, and of New York; about half of Pennsylvania; two thirds of New Jersey and Ohio; a half of Indiana and Illinois, the whole of Michigan, Huron, and the territory of the United States westward of them, and on both sides of the Rocky mountains, and from a point considerably within the Mexican dominions on the Pacific Ocean, nearly up to Nootka Sound, were liberally granted by King James, 'to the council established at Plymouth, in the County of Devon.'

From the period of the landing of the Pilgrims at Plymouth, the intolerance of the established church in England become daily more oppressive. The non-conforming ministers were silenced, ejected, imprisoned, and exiled; and numerous examples of the extremest rigor of the law, were made, both of them and the laity. The entire extent, to which these severities were carried, may be estimated, from their amount in a single instance. On the impeachment of Bishop Wren, it was charged that during two years and a half, for which he administered the diocese of Norwich, fifty ministers were deprived of their places, for not complying with the prescribed ceremonies, and three thousand of the laity compelled to leave the kingdom.

These increasing severities, and the necessity, under which conscientious men were laid, of abandoning their principles or their homes, turned the thoughts of many persons of consideration and property toward a permanent asylum in New-England. The first steps were restrained and gradual; but a few years witnessed the fulfilment of the design. In 1624, Mr White of Dorchester, in England, a celebrated non-conforming minister, induced a number of merchants and other gentlemen to attempt another settlement, as a refuge for those whose religious principles exposed them to oppression at home; and by their contributions, under a license obtained from the Plymouth settlers, an establishment was commenced at Cape Ann. The care of this establishment was the following year committed by the proprietors to Mr Roger Conant, a person of great worth, who had, however, retired from the colony at Plymouth. After a short residence at Cape Ann, Roger Conant removed a little further to the westward, and fixed upon a place called by the Indians Naumkeag, as a more advantageous place of settlement, and as a spot well adapted for the reception of those, who were disposed to imitate the example of their brethren, and seek a refuge from tyranny in the western wilderness. The accounts of this place circulated in England, among those who were maturing this design; and Mr Conant, though deserted by almost all his brethren, was induced by Mr White to remain at Salem, by the promise of procuring a patent and a reinforcement of settlers. Accordingly, on the 19th of March, 1628, an agreement was concluded between the council of Plymouth, and certain gentlemen associated in the neighborhood of Dorchester in England, under the auspices of Mr White, of that place; and a patent was conveyed to these associates, of all the tract of country, lying between three miles north of the Merrimack and three miles south of Charles rivers, and extending from the Atlantic to the Pacific ocean. These associates were Sir Henry Roswell, Sir John Young, Thomas Southcoat, John Humphrey, John Endecott and Simon Whetcomb; and the patent ran to them, their heirs, and associates.

Mr White, in pursuit of his project for establishing a colony for the non-conformists, was in communication with persons of that description, in different parts of England, and, through his agency, the six patentees, whose names I have just mentioned, were brought into connexion with several religious persons in London and the neighboring country, who at first associated with them, and afterwards purchased out the right of the three first named of the six

26

patentees.* Among these new associates were John Winthrop, Isaac Johnson, and Sir Richard Saltonstall.

Thus reinforced, the strength of the company was vigorously bent upon the establishment of the colony in New England. They organized themselves, by choosing Matthew Cradock, governor of the colony, and Thomas Goff, deputy governor, and eighteen assistants. By this company, and in the course of the same summer of 1628, John Endecott was sent over, with a considerable number of planters and servants, to 'establish a plantation at Salem, to make way for settling the colony, and be their agent to order all affairs, till the patentees themselves should come.' Endecott sailed from Weymouth on the 20th of June, and his first letter to the company, in London, bears date 13th September, 1628.

In the same year of 1628, the foundation of the town of Charlestown was laid, under the patronage of Governor Endecott, but not, I apprehend, by any of the members of his party. As this is a matter of some local importance, I shall dwell for a moment upon it. It is well known, that Ralph, William, and Richard Sprague, in the course of the summer of 1628, traversed the country, between Salem and Charles river, and made a settlement at Charlestown ; and it is commonly supposed, that as they came from Salem, with Governor Endecott's consent, they were of the company which he brought over.†

On looking, however, into our ancient records, I find the following remark. After relating the arrival of Endecott at Salem, the record goes on to say :—'Under whose wing, there were a few also that settle and plant up and down, scattering in several places of the Bay ; where, though they meet with the dangers, difficulties, and wants, attending new plantations in a solitary wilderness, so far remote from their native country, yet were they not long without

---

* See the detail in Governor Dudley's most interesting letter, to the Countess of Lincoln, of 12th March 1630, written, as he says, 'rudely, having yet no table, nor other room to write in, than by the fire side, on my knee, in this sharp winter.'— Historical Collections, First Series. Vol. VIII. p. 36.

† 'The Spragues, (who went thither [to Charlestown,] from Endecott's company at Salem.)'—Winthrop's Journal, Savage's edition, Vol. I. p. 53. *Note.*—And so other writers.

company, for in the year of our Lord one thousand six hundred and twenty-eight, came over from England several people at their own charges, and arrived at Salem. After which, people came over yearly in great numbers ; in —— years many hundreds arrived, and settled not only in the Massachusetts Bay, but did suddenly spread themselves into other colonies also.

'Among those, who arrived at Salem, *at their own charge,* were Ralph Sprague, with his brethren Richard and William, who, with three or four more, by joint consent and approbation of Mr John Endecott, governor, did the same summer of Anno 1628, undertake a journey from Salem, and travelled the woods, about twelve miles, to the westward, and lighted of a place, situate and lying on the north bank of Charles river, full of Indians, called Aberginians. Their old chief sachem being dead, his eldest son, by the English called John Sagamore, was their chief; a man naturally of gentle and good disposition, by whose free consent they settled about the hill of the same place, by the natives called Mishawum ; where they found one English pallisadoed and thatched house, wherein lived Thomas Walford, a smith, situate on the south end of the westernmost hill of the east field, a little way from Charles river side ; and upon surveying, they found it was a neck of land generally full of stately timber, as was the main, and the land lying on the east side of the river called Mistick river, (from the farm Mr Cradock's servants had planted, called Mistick, which this river led up into,) indeed, generally all the country round about was an uncouth wilderness, full of timber.'

This passage seems to establish the fact, that the three Spragues, the founders of the settlement in this place, were not members of Governor Endecott's company, but independent adventurers, who came over to Salem, at their own cost. They were persons of character, substance, and enterprise ; excellent citizens, generous public benefactors ; and the heads of a very large and respectable family of descendants.

The patent from the council of Plymouth gave to the associates as good a right to the soil as the council possessed, but no powers of government. For this object, the royal charter was necessary. An humble petition for such a charter was presented to the king in council, and on the 4th of March, 1629, the charter passed the seals, confirming the patent of the council of Plymouth, and creating the Governor and Company of the Massachusetts Bay, in New-England, a body politic and corporate, in deed, fact, and name. By this charter, the company were empowered to elect forever, out of the freemen of said company, a governor, deputy governor, and eighteen assistants annually, on the fourth Wednesday of Easter term, and to make laws not repugnant to the laws of England.*

At a meeting, or court, as it was called, of this company, held at London, on the 30th of April following, a form of government was adopted for the colony. By this form of government, the direction of affairs was committed to thirteen individuals, to be resident in the colony, one of whom shall be governor. Mr Endecott was, by the same instrument, appointed governor, and six individuals were named councillors. These seven persons were authorized to choose three more, and the remaining two, requisite to make up the number of twelve, were to be designated by the *old planters*, as they were called, or persons who had settled in New-England previous to the Massachusetts patent;—and whose rights, though not provided for by that instrument, were treated with tenderness by the patentees. These magistrates were to continue in office one year. The mode in which their successors were to be chosen, is not specified by this form of government, but was probably intended to be the same, as that observed in the first election.†

In the course of this summer of 1629, six ships, in the service of the company, sailed for the infant colony, carrying with them an ample supply of provisions, and three hundred settlers. Mr Francis Higginson, who was named first on the list of the councillors chosen by the company, and the other ministers sent out for the spiritual instruction of the colony, embarked for Naumkeag or Salem, in this fleet.

The position at Salem, not being thought adapted to become the capital, Mr Thomas Graves, an engineer in the service of the company, with about one hundred of the company's servants under his care, removed to this place in the course of the summer of

---

* Hazard's State Papers, Vol. I. pp. 239—255.

† Hazard, Vol. I. p. 263. From Massachusetts Records, A. Folio 9.

1629, where the Spragues and their companions had established themselves the year before; and at this time, from the name of the river on which it stands, they called the place Charlestown.*

Thus far the proceedings of the company were conducted on the footing of a trading corporation, organized in England, for the purpose of carrying on a commercial establishment in a foreign and dependent region. Whatever higher motive had been proposed to themselves, by the active promoters of the colony, the royal government of Great Britain, in granting the charter of the company, had probably no design to lay the foundation of a new commonwealth, established on principles at war with those of the mother country. But larger designs were entertained on the part of some of the high-minded men, who engaged in the undertaking. The civil and ecclesiastical oppression of the times had now reached that point of intolerable severity, to which the evils of humanity are sometimes permitted to extend, when Providence designs to apply to them a great and strange remedy. It was at this time, to all appearance, the reluctant but deliberate conviction of the thinking part of the community,—of that great class in society, which constitutes the strength of England as of America,—that Old England had ceased to be a land for men of moderate private fortunes to live in. Society was tending rapidly to that disastrous division of master and dependent, which is fatal to all classes of its members. The court was profligate, corrupt, and arbitrary, beyond example,—and it remained to be seen, whether the constitution of the government contained any check on its power and caprice. In the ʻ*Considerations for the Plantation of New-England,*ʼ drawn up a year or two before, by those who took the lead in founding the colony of Massachusetts Bay, it was forcibly stated, ʻthat England grew weary of her inhabitants; insomuch that man, which is the most precious of all creatures, was there more vile and base than the earth he trod on; and children and families, (if unwealthy) were accounted a burdensome incumbrance, instead of the greatest blessing.ʼ

---

* This event, and that of the arrival of Governor Winthrop, are by a very singular anachronism, dated, the one in 1628, and the other in 1629, in our Charlestown Records.

From such a state of things, and the assurance of a perfect remedy in New-England, for some of the evils which they suffered, a
considerable number of persons of great respectability, of good fortune, and of consideration in society, came to the resolution of
leaving their native land, and laying the foundation of a better
social system on these remote and uninhabited shores.   As a preliminary to this, however, they required a total change of the
footing, on which the attempts at colonization had hitherto proceeded.
It fell far short of their purpose, to banish themselves to the new
world, as the dependent servants of a corporation in London; and
they required, as a previous condition, that the charter of the colony, and the seat of its government should be transferred from
London to America.   This was the turning point in the destiny of
New-England.   Doubting the legality of such a step, they took
the advice of counsel learned in the law, and from them received
the opinion, that the proposed transfer of the charter was legal.
Against this opinion, there is, at the present day, a pretty general
consent of the writers on America, both in England and the United States; and it may therefore be deemed presumptuous in me,
to express an opposite judgment.   But, though the removal of the
charter was not probably contemplated, I find in it, no condition
prescribed, that the meetings of the corporation, or the place of
deposit of the charter itself, should be in London, or any other
particular place.   The very design, for which the charter was
granted to the company, implied, of course, the possibility that a part
of the freemen that compose it, should reside in New-England, and
I perceive nothing in the instrument, forbidding them all to reside
in that part of the king's dominions.

Those, whose professional advice had been taken on the subject
of removing the charter, having decided in favor of the legality of
that measure, its expediency was submitted, at a court of the company, held at London, on the 28th of July, 1629; and on the
29th of August, after hearing the reports of two committees, raised
to consider the arguments for and against the removal, it was, by
the generality of the company voted, that the patent and government of the company be transferred to New-England.   At a subsequent meeting, held October 20th, 'the court having received
extraordinary great commendation of Mr John Winthrop, both for

his integrity and sufficiency, as being one very well fitted for the place, with a full consent, choose him governor for the ensuing year, to begin this day.' On the same day, the deputy governor and assistants were chosen, of persons at that time purposing to emigrate, some of whom, however, never executed this design.

John Winthrop was a gentleman of good fortune, and was born at Groton, in the county of Suffolk, on the 12th of January, 1587,* and was educated by his father, who was himself eminent for skill in the law, to that profession. John Winthrop was so early distinguished for his gravity, intelligence, and learning, that he was introduced into the magistracy of his county at the age of eighteen, and acquitted himself with great credit, in the discharge of its duties.

His family had, for two generations at least, distinguished itself for its attachment to the reformed religion, and John Winthrop was of that class of the English church, who thought that the work had not all been accomplished, in throwing off their allegiance to Rome. I believe we have no account of the circumstances, by which he was first led to take an interest in the settlement of New-England, nor does his name occur in connexion with the early history of the colony, till we find it mentioned among those, who, in 1628, united themselves with the Dorchester adventurers. Having been, in October 1629, elected governor of the new colony, for such it is henceforward to be regarded, he prepared himself to enter on this great enterprise, by disposing of his patrimony in England, which was valued at a rent of six or seven hundred pounds sterling per annum. The feelings with which he addressed himself to the noble work may be partly conceived from the nature of the enterprise and the character of the man, and they are more fully set forth in his most admirable letters to his wife and son, with which the world has lately been favored.

On the 22d of March, 1629, we find the governor with two of his sons, on board a vessel at the Isle of Wight, bound for America, with Dudley, the deputy governor, and several of the assistants,

---

* Mather says June. I am inclined to think that this, with numerous other errors, which have exposed Mather to severe reprehension, was a misprint arising from the circumstance, that his work was printed in London, and consequently not corrected by him.

and with a large number of emigrants, embarked in a fleet which, with the vessels that preceded and followed them, the same season, amounted in the whole to seventeen sail, all of which reached New-England.

From the period, at which Governor Winthrop set sail for New-England, till a short time before his death, he kept a journal of his life from day to day,—which has fortunately been preserved to us, partly in the original manuscript, of which a portion was brought to light, and for the first time published, a few years ago.* The voyage of Governor Winthrop was unattended with any considerable incident, and on the 12th June, after a passage of about six weeks, the vessel in which he sailed, came to anchor off Salem. On landing, they found the colony there in a disheartening condition, eighty of their number having died the preceding winter, and the survivors looking for support to the supplies expected by the governor, which unfortunately did not arrive, in the vessel which brought him.

The intention had been already taken not to establish the seat of government at Salem.—After lying a few days at anchor off that place, Governor Winthrop undertook to explore the Massachusetts Bay, "to find a place for sitting down." On the 17th June, old style, he proceeded up the Mistick river, as far as the spot, which he occupied as a country residence during his life, and which has preserved to the present day the name of the Ten Hills, given to it by him.

Our records give but a melancholy account of the condition of things, which the colonists were called to encounter in their establishment at this place. We there read, that

'The governor and several of the assistants dwelt in the *great house*, which was last year built in this town, by Mr Graves and the rest of their servants. The multitude set up cottages, booths, and tents about the town-hill. They had long passage. Some of the ships were seventeen, some eighteen weeks a coming. Many people arrived sick of the scurvy, which also increased much after their arrival, for want of houses, and by reason of wet lodgings, in

* By Hon. James Savage, with learned annotations on the whole work, now for the first time published entire, in two volumes.

their cottages, &c. Other distempers also prevailed, and although people were generally very loving and pitiful, yet the sickness did so prevail, that the *whole* were not able to tend the *sick* as they should be tended; upon which many perished and died, and were buried about the town-hill;—by which means, the provisions were exceedingly wasted, and no supplies could now be expected by planting: besides, there was miserable damage and spoil of provisions by sea, and divers came not so well provided as they would, upon a report whilst they were in England, that now there was enough in New-England.'

It was the intention of the governor and the chief part of those who accompanied him, to establish themselves permanently in this place, and to this end the governor made preparation for building his house here. But, as our records proceed, 'the weather being hot, many sick, and others faint, after their long voyage, people grew discontented for want of water, who generally notioned no water good for a town but running springs; and though this neck do abound in good water, yet for want of experience and industry, none could then be found to suit the humor of that time, but a brackish spring in the sands, by the water side, on the west side of the north-west field, which could not supply half the necessities of the multitude, at which time the death of so many was concluded to be much the more occasioned by this want of good water.'

In consequence of this difficulty, numbers of those who had purposed to settle themselves at Charlestown, sought an establishment at other places, as Watertown and Dorchester, and still more removed to the other side of the river, and laid the foundation of Boston.

'In the mean time,' continue our records, 'Mr Blackstone dwelling on the other side of Charles River alone, at a place by the Indians called *Shawmut*, where he only had a cottage, at or not far off the place called Blackstone's Point, he came and acquainted the governor of an excellent spring there, withal inviting him and soliciting him thither, whereupon, after the death of Mr Johnson and divers others, the governor, with Mr Wilson, and the greatest part of the church, removed thither.'

Such were the inconveniences and distresses of the first settlement, which bore so heavily on the health and spirits of the colo-

27

nists, that on the return of the vessels which brought them out, more than a hundred went back to England.

But the necessary limits of this address will not permit me to pursue the narrative, and I can only ask your attention to a few of those reflections, which are suggested by the occasion.

What our country is, which has sprung from these beginnings, we all see and know :—its numbers bordering upon twelve millions, if they do not exceed it ; its great abundance in all that composes the wealth and the strength of nations ; its rich possession of the means of private happiness ; its progress in the useful and refined arts of life ; its unequalled enjoyment of political privileges ; its noble provision of literary, social, charitable, and religious establishments,—constituting, altogether, a condition of prosperity, which I think, has never been equalled on earth.   What our country was, on the day we commemorate, it is difficult to bring distinctly home to our minds.   There was a feeble colony in Virginia ; a very small Dutch settlement in New-York ; a population of about three hundred at Plymouth ; about as many more English inhabitants, divided between Salem and Charlestown ; a few settlers scattered up and down the coast ; and all the rest a vast wilderness, the covert of wild beasts and savages.

In this condition of things, the charter of the colony was brought over, and the foundations were laid of a new state.   In the motives which led to this enterprise, there were unquestionably two principles united.   The first projects of settling on the coast of New-England had their origin in commercial adventure ; and without the direction given by this spirit to the minds of men, and the information brought home by fishing and trading vessels, the attempt would probably have never been made, to establish a colony.   It deserves to be remarked, therefore, in an age like the present, when it is too much the practice to measure the value of all public enterprises by the returns in money which they bring back to their projectors, that probably a more unprofitable speculation in a financial light, than that of the council of Plymouth, was never undertaken. In a few years, they gladly surrendered their patent to the crown, and it is doubtful whether, while they held it, they divided a farthing's profit.   Yet, under their patent, and by their grant, was undertaken and accomplished perhaps the greatest work on record the annals of humanity.

Mixed with this motive of commercial speculation, (itself liberal and praiseworthy,) was another, the spring of all that it truly great in human affairs, the conservative and redeeming principle of our natures, I mean the *self-denying enthusiasm* of our forefathers, sacrificing present ease for a great end. I do not mean to say, that even they had an accurate foresight of the work, in which they were engaged. What an empire was to rise on their humble foundations, imagination never revealed to them, nor could they, nor did they, conceive it. They contemplated an obscure and humble colony, safe beneath the toleration of the crown, where they could enjoy, what they prized above all earthly things, the liberty of conscience, in the worship of God. Stern as they are pourtrayed to us, they entertained neither the bitterness of an indignant separation from home, nor the pride of an anticipated and triumphant enlargement here. Their enthusiasm was rather that of fortitude and endurance ; passive and melancholy. Driven though they were from their homes, by the oppression of the established church, they parted from her as a dutiful child from a severe but venerated parent. 'We esteem it our honor,' say they, in their inimitable letter from on board the Arbella, 'to call the church of England, from which we rise, our dear mother ; and we cannot part from our native country, where she specially resideth, without much sadness of heart, and many tears in our eyes, ever acknowledging, that such hope and part as we have obtained in the common salvation, we have received in her bosom, and sucked it from her breasts.' And, having, in this same pathetic appeal, invoked the prayers of their brethren in England, for their welfare, they add, 'What goodness you shall extend to us, in this or any other christian kindness, we, your brethren, shall labor to repay, in what duty we are or shall be able to perform ; promising, so far as God shall enable us, to give him no rest on your behalf, wishing our heads and hearts may be fountains of tears for your everlasting welfare, when we shall be in our poor cottages in the wilderness, overshadowed with the spirit of supplication, through the manifold necessities and tribulations, which may not altogether unexpectedly, nor, we hope, unprofitably befall us.'*

* Hutchinson, Vol. I. Appendix, No. 1.

In the spirit that dictated these expressions,—the disinterested enthusiasm of men, giving up home, and friends, and their native land, for a conscientious principle,—we behold not merely the cause of the success of their enterprise, but the secret source of every great and generous work, especially in the founding of social institutions, that was ever performed. One trading company after another had failed ; charters had been given, enlarged, and vacated ; well appointed fleets had been scattered or returned without success, and rich adventures had ended in ruin ; when a few aggrieved gentlemen, turning their backs on plenty, at home, and setting their faces towards want and danger, in the wilderness, took up and accomplished the work.

The esteem, in which we of the present day hold their characters, and the sympathy we feel in their trials, are, perhaps, qualified, by finding, that this enthusiasm, which inspired them, was almost wholly expended on the concerns of the church, and was associated in that respect, with opinions and feelings,—as we may think, —not the most enlarged and liberal. This prejudice, however, for such I regard it, ought not to be permitted to establish itself, in the minds of any generation of the descendants of the fathers of New-England. The spirit that actuated them was the great principle of disinterested enthusiasm,—the purest and best that can warm the heart and govern the conduct of man. It took a direction toward the doctrines and forms of the church, partly, of course, because religion is a matter, on which tender and ardent minds feel, with the greatest sensibility ; but mainly because they were, in that respect, oppressed and aggrieved. It was precisely the same spirit, which animated our fathers in the revolution, assuming then the form of the passion for civil liberty, and struggling against political oppression, because this was the evil which *they* suffered : And it is the same principle, which, in every age, wars against tyranny, sympathizes with the oppressed, kindles at the report of generous actions, and, rising above selfish calculation and sensual indulgence, learns ' to scorn delights and live laborious days,' and is ready, when honor and duty call, to sacrifice property, and ease, and life.

There is another thing, that must be borne in mind, when we sit in judgment on the character of our fathers. The *opinions* which men entertain, especially on great social institutions, and the duties which grow out of them, depend very much on the degree of intelligence prevailing in the world. Great men go beyond their age, it is true; but there are limits to this power of anticipation. They go beyond it in some things, but not in all, and not often, in any, to the utmost point of improvement. Lord Bacon laid down the principles of a new philosophy, but did not admit the Copernican system. Men who have been connected with the establishment of great institutions, ought to be judged, by the general result of their work. We judge of St Peter's by the grandeur of the elevation, and the majesty of the dome, not by the flaws in the stone, of which the walls are built. The fathers of New-England, a company of private gentlemen, of moderate fortunes, bred up under an established church, and an arbitrary and hereditary civil government, came over the Atlantic two hundred years ago. They were imperfect, they had faults, they committed errors. But they laid the fonndations of the state of things, which we enjoy;—of political and religious freedom; of public and private prosperity; of a great, thriving, well-organized republic. What more could they have done? What more could any men do? Above all, what lesson should we have given them, had we been in existence, and called to advise on the subject? Most unquestionably we should have discouraged the enterprise altogether. Our political economists would have said, abandon this mad scheme of organizing your own church and state, when you can have all the benefit of the venerable establishments of the mother country, the fruit of the wisdom of ages, at a vastly less cost. The capitalists would have said, do not be so insane, as to throw away your broad acres and solid guineas, in so wild a speculation. The man of common sense, that dreadful foe of great enterprises, would have discredited the whole project. Go to any individual of the present day, situated as Governor Winthrop was, at his family mansion, at Groton, in England, in the bosom of a happy home, surrounded by an affectionate, prosperous family, in the enjoyment of an ample fortune, and tell him, inasmuch as the government has ordained that the priest should perform a part of the sacred service in a white surplice, and make the sign of the cross in baptism, that therefore he had better convert his estate

into money, and leave his home and family, and go and settle a
colony, on one of the islands of the Pacific ocean, or establish
himself at the mouth of Columbia river, where he would have
liberty of conscience.   I think he would recommend to his *adviser,*
to go and establish *himself,* at a certain mansion, which benevolence has provided, a little to the north of Lechmere's Point.

I do not say the cases are wholly parallel: But such would be
the view now taken, on the principles which govern men in our
state of society, of such a course as that which was pursued by
Governor Winthrop and his associates.

I deduce from this, not that they were high-minded, and we, base
and degenerate ; I will not so compliment the fathers at the expense of the sons.   On the contrary, let the crisis arrive ; let a
state of things present itself, (hardly conceivable, to be sure, but
within the range of possibility,) when our beloved New-England
no longer afforded us the quiet possession of our rights, I believe
we should then show ourselves the worthy descendants of the pilgrims ; and if the earth contained a region, however remote, a
shore, however barbarous, where we could enjoy the liberty denied
us at home, that we should say, 'where liberty is, there is my
country,' and go and seek it.   But let us not meantime, nourished
as we are out of the abundance which they, needy and suffering
themselves, transmitted to us, deride their bigotry, which turned
trifles into consequence, or wonder at their zeal, which made great
sacrifices for small inducements.   It is ungrateful.

Nor let us suppose, that it would be too safe to institute a
comparison, between our fathers and ourselves, even on those
points, with regard to which, we have both been called to act.   It
has so happened, that the government of the United States has, in
the course of the last year, been obliged to consider and act on
a subject, which was one of the first and most anxious, that
presented itself to the early settlers of New-England,—I mean our
relations with the Indian tribes.   In alluding to this subject, I freely
admit that, in the infancy of the colonies, when the Indians were
strong and the colonists weak,—when the savage, roaming the
woods, with the tomahawk and scalping knife, was a foe to the
New-England settlements, alike dangerous and dreadful,—some
actions were committed in the settlements, in moments of excite-

ment, which we cannot too deeply condemn, nor too sadly deplore. In allusion to these actions, and in vindicating the course, which during the past year, has been pursued toward the tribes of civilized Indians, resident within the United States, it has been argued, that they have not been treated with greater severity, by the government of the United States, or of any of the separate States, than they were treated by the fathers of New-England. But it would seem not enough for an age, which is so liberal of its censures of the puritans, to show itself *only not more* oppressive than they. Has civilization made no progress, in two hundred years? Will any statesman maintain, that the relation of our Union, to the feeble and dependent tribes, within its limits, is the same, as that of the infant colonies, toward the barbarous nations, which surrounded them? It was the opinion of that age, that the royal patents gave a perfect right to the soil. We have *hitherto* professed to believe, that nothing can give a perfect right to the soil occupied by the Indian tribes, but the free consent of these tribes, expressed by public compact, to alienate their right, whatever it be. They believed, that heathen nations, as such, might be rightfully dispossessed, by christian men. We have professed to believe, that this would be a very equivocal way of showing our christianity. And yet, notwithstanding these opinions, I do not recollect that, in a single instance, our fathers claimed a right to eject the native population. For a long time, they were the weaker party. Among the first acts of the Plymouth colony, was an amicable treaty with the nearest and most powerful Indian chieftain, who lived and died their friend. The colonists of Massachusetts, in a letter of instructions,* from the company, of 28th May, 1629, were directed to make a reasonable composition with the Indians, who claimed lands within their patent. The worthy founders of Charlestown, an enterprising handful of men, settled down here, with the free consent of the powerful tribe in their neighborhood, whose chief remained the friend of the English to the last.—In a word, the opinions of our forefathers, on this interesting subject, are expressed, by Mr Pinchon, of Springfield, with a discrimination and pointed-

---

* Hazard's State Papers, Vol. I. p. 277; to the same effect also a still earlier letter of instructions.

ness, almost prophetic of the present contest. 'I grant,' says he, in reference to a particular case, ' that all these Indians* are within the line of the patent ; but yet, you cannot say they are your subjects, nor yet within your jurisdiction, till they have fully subjected themselves, (which I know they have not,) and until you have bought their land. Until this be done, they must be esteemed as an independent, free people.'

Contrast these doctrines with those latterly advanced by the government, both of the United States and several of the individual States :—That the State charters give a perfect right to the soil and sovereignty, within their nominal limits, and that the Indians have only a right of occupancy, and that by permission ; that the treaties with them, negotiated for fifty years, with all the forms of the constitution, bind them as far as the treaties contain cessions of land, but do not bind us, when we guaranty the remainder of the land to them :—that when the Indians, on the faith of these treaties, cry to us for protection against State laws, unconstitutionally passed, with the known design and to the admitted effect, of compelling them to leave their homes, it is within the competence of the executive, without consulting the National Legislature, to withhold this protection, and advise the Indians as they would escape destruction, to fly to the distant wilderness :—and all this, in the case, not of savage, unreclaimed tribes, such as our forefathers had to deal with, who lived by the chase, without permanent habitations, to whom one tract of the forest was as much a home as another, but tribes, whom we have trained to civilization, whom we have converted to our religion ; who live, as we do, by the industrious arts of life, and who, in their official papers, written by themselves, plead for their rights, in better English, than that of the high officers of the government, who plead against them.

But I protest against bringing the actions of men, in one age, to the standard of another, in things that depend on the state of civilization and public sentiment throughout the world. Try our fathers by the only fair test, the standard of the age in which they lived ; and I believe that they admit a very good defence, even on

* See the case referred to in Winthrop's Journal, Savage's edition, Vol. II. p. 384.

the point, where they are supposed to be most vulnerable,—that of religious freedom. I do not pretend, that they were governed by an enlightened spirit of toleration. Such a spirit, actuating a large community, made up of men of one mind, and possessing absolute power to compel the few dissenters to conform, is not so common, even at the present day, as may be thought. I have great doubts, whether the most liberal sect of Christians, now extant, if it constituted as great a majority as our forefathers did of the community, and if it possessed an unlimited civil and ecclesiastical power, would be much more magnanimous than they were, in its use. They would not, perhaps, use the scourge, or the halter; humanity proscribes them altogether, except for the most dangerous crimes; but that they would allow the order of the community to be disturbed by the intrusion of opposite opinions, distasteful to themselves, I have great doubts. With all the puritanical austerity, and,— what is much more to be deplored,—the intolerance of dissent, which are chargeable to our fathers, they secured, and we are indebted to them for, two great principles, without which all the candor and kindness we may express towards opponents, go but a short step toward religious freedom. One of these is the independent character, which they ascribed to each individual church; the other, the separation of church and state. Our fathers were educated under an ecclesiastical system, which combined all the churches into one body. They forbore to imitate that system here, though the hierarchy of the new churches would have been composed of themselves, with John Cotton at its head. They were educated in a system, where the church is part of the state, and vast endowments are bestowed, in perpetuity, upon it. This, too, our fathers could have imitated, securing to themselves while they lived, and those who thought with them, when they were gone, the usufruct of these endowments, as far as the law could work such assurance. They did neither, although they had purchased the fair right of doing what they pleased, by banishing themselves, for that very reason, from the world. They did neither, although they lived in an age, when, had they done both, there was no one who could rightfully cast reproach upon them. In all the wide world, there was not a government, nor a people, that could rebuke them, by precept or example. Where was there?

28

In England, the fires of papacy were hardly quenched, when tyrannies scarcely less atrocious against the Puritans began. In France, the Protestants were at the mercy of a capricious and soon revoked toleration. The Catholics, in Germany, were unchaining their legions against the Lutherans; and in Holland, *reformed* Holland, fine and imprisonment were the reward of Grotius, the man, in whom that country will be remembered, ages after the German ocean has broken over her main dyke. Had our forefathers laid the foundation of the most rigid ecclesiastical system, that ever oppressed the world, and locked up a quarter part of New-England in mortmain, to endow it, there was not a community in Christendom to bear witness against them.

If we would, on a broad, rational ground, come to a favorable judgment, on the whole, of the merit of our forefathers, the founders of New-England, we have only to compare what they effected, with what was effected by their countrymen and brethren in Great Britain. While the fathers of New-England, a small band of individuals, for the most part of little account in the great world of London, were engaged, on this side of the Atlantic, in laying the foundations of civil and religious liberty, in a new Commonwealth, the patriots in England undertook the same work of reform in that country. There were difficulties, no doubt, peculiar to the enterprise, as undertaken in each country. In Great Britain, there was the strenuous opposition of the friends of the established system; in New-England, there was the difficulty of creating a new State, out of materials the most scanty and inadequate. If there were fewer obstacles here, there were greater means there. They had all the improvements of the age, which the Puritans are said to have left behind them; all the resources of the country, while the Puritans had nothing but their own slender means; and, at length, all the patronage of the government;—and with them they overthrew the church; trampled the House of Lords under foot; and brought the King to the block. The fathers of New-England, from first to last, struggled against almost every conceivable discouragement. While the patriots at home were dictating concessions to the king and tearing his confidential friends from his arms, the patriots of America could scarcely keep their charter out of his grasp. While the former were wielding a resolute majority in parliament, under the lead of the boldest spirits that ever lived, combining with Scotland, and subduing Ireland, and striking terror into the continental governments, the latter were forming a frail union of the New-England colonies, for immediate defence, against a savage foe. While the 'Lord General Cromwell,' (who seems to have picked up this modest title among the spoils of the routed aristocracy,) in the superb flattery of Milton,

> ' Guided by faith, and matchless fortitude,
> To peace and truth his glorious way had ploughed,
> And on the neck of crowned fortune proud
> Had reared God's trophies,'

our truly excellent and incorruptible Winthrop was compelled to descend from the chair of state, and submit to an impeachment.

And what was the comparative success?—There were, to say the least, as many excesses committed in England as in Massachusetts Bay. There was as much intolerance, on the part of men just escaped from persecution; as much bigotry, on the part of those, who had themselves suffered for conscience' sake; as much unreasonable austerity; as much sour temper; as much bad taste; as much for charity to forgive, and as much for humanity to deplore. The temper, in fact, in the two Commonwealths, was much the same; and some of the leading spirits played a part in both. And to what effect? On the other side of the Atlantic, the whole experiment ended in a miserable failure. The Commonwealth became successively oppressive, hateful, contemptible: a greater burden than the despotism, on whose ruins it was raised. The people of England, after sacrifices incalculable, of property and life, after a struggle of thirty years' duration, allowed the general, who happened to have the greatest number of troops at his command, to bring back the old system,—King, Lords, and Church,—with as little ceremony, as he would employ, in issuing the orders of the day. After asking, for thirty years, What is the will of the Lord concerning his people? what is it becoming a pure church to do? what does the cause of liberty demand, in the day of its regeneration?—there was but one cry in England, What does General Monk think? what will General Monk do? will he bring back the king with conditions, or without? And General Monk concluded to bring him back without.

On this side of the Atlantic, and in about the same period, the work which our fathers took in hand was, in the main, successfully done. They came to found a republican colony ; they founded it, They came to establish a free church, They established what they called a free church ; and transmitted to us, what we call a free church. In accomplishing this, which they did anticipate, they brought also to pass what they did not so distinctly foresee, what could not, in the nature of things, in its detail and circumstance, be anticipated,—the foundation of a great, prosperous, and growing republic. We have not been just to these men. I am disposed to do all justice to the memory of each succeeding generation. I admire the indomitable perseverance, with which the contest for principle was kept up, under the second charter. I reverence, this side idolatry, the wisdom and fortitude of the revolutionary and constitutional leaders, but I believe we ought to go back beyond them all, for the real framers of the Commonwealth. I believe that its foundation stones, like those of the Capitol of Rome, lie deep and solid, out of sight, at the bottom of the walls,—Cyclopean work,—the work of the Pilgrims,—with nothing below them but the rock of ages. I will not quarrel with their rough corners, or uneven sides ; above all, I will not change them for the wood, hay, and stubble of modern builders.

But, it is more than time, fellow citizens, that I should draw to a close. These venerable foundations of our republic were laid on the *very spot*, where we stand ; by the fathers of Massachusetts. *Here*, before they were able to erect a suitable place for worship, they were wont, beneath the branches of a spreading tree, to commend their wants, their sufferings, and their hopes to Him, that dwelleth not in houses made with hands; *here*, they erected their first habitations ; *here*, they gathered their first church ; *here*, they made their first graves.

Yes, on the very spot where we are assembled ; now crowned with this spacious church ; surrounded by the comfortable abodes of a dense population ; there were, during the first season after the landing of Winthrop, fewer dwellings for the living, than graves for the dead. It seemed the will of Providence, that our fathers should be tried by the extremities of either season. When the

Pilgrims approached the coast of Plymouth, they found it clad with all the terrors of a northern winter :—

> The sea around was black with storms,
> And white the shores with snow.

We can scarcely now think, without tears, of a company of men, women, and children, brought up in tenderness, exposed, after several months' uncomfortable confinement on ship-board, to the rigors of our November and December sky, on an unknown, barbarous coast, whose frightful rocks, even now, strike terror into the heart of the returning mariner; though he knows that the home of his childhood awaits him, within their enclosure.

The Massachusetts Company arrived at the close of June. No vineyards, as now, clothed our inhospitable hill-sides; no blooming orchards, as at the present day, wore the livery of Eden, and loaded the breeze with sweet odors;—no rich pastures, nor waving crops, stretched beneath the eye, along the way side, from village to village, as if Nature had been spreading her halls with a carpet, fit to be pressed by the footsteps of her descending God! The beauty and the bloom of the year had passed. The earth, not yet subdued by culture, bore upon its untilled bosom nothing but a dismal forest, that mocked their hunger with rank and unprofitable vegetation. The sun was hot in the heavens. The soil was parched, and the hand of man had not yet taught its secret springs to flow from their fountains. The wasting disease of the heart-sick mariner was upon the men;—and the women and children thought of the pleasant homes of England, as they sunk down from day to day, and died at last for want of a cup of cold water, in this melancholy land of promise. From the time the company sailed from England, in April, up to the December following, there died not less than two hundred persons,—nearly one a day.

They were buried, say our records, about the Town-hill. This is the Town-hill. We are gathered over the ashes of our forefathers.

It is good, but solemn, to be here. We live on holy ground; all our hill-tops are the altars of precious sacrifice :

This is stored with the sacred dust of the first victims in the cause of liberty.

And *that** is rich from the life stream of the noble hearts, who bled to sustain it.

Here, beneath our feet, unconscious that we commemorate their worth, repose the meek and sainted martyrs, whose flesh sunk beneath the lofty temper of their noble spirits ; and there, rest the heroes, who presented their dauntless foreheads to the God of battles, when he came to his awful baptism of blood and of fire.

Happy the fate, which has laid them so near to each other, the early and the latter champions of the one great cause ! And happy we, who are permitted to reap in peace the fruit of their costly sacrifice ! Happy, that we can make our pious pilgrimage to the smooth turf of that venerable summit, once ploughed with the wheels of maddening artillery, ringing with all the dreadful voices of war, wrapped in smoke, and streaming with blood ! Happy, that here, where our fathers sank, beneath the burning sun, into the parched clay, we live, and assemble, and mingle sweet counsel, and grateful thoughts of them, in comfort and peace !

* Bunker Hill.

A

DISCOURSE

ON THE IMPORTANCE TO PRACTICAL MEN OF SCIENTIFIC KNOWL-
EDGE, AND ON THE ENCOURAGEMENTS TO ITS PURSUIT.*

———

THE object of the Mechanics' Institute is, to diffuse useful
knowledge among the mechanic class of the community. It aims,
in general, to improve and inform the minds of its members; and
particularly to illustrate and explain the principles of the various arts
of life, and render them familiar to that portion of the community,
who are to exercise these arts as their occupation in society. It is
also a proper object of the Institute, to point out the connexion
between the mechanic arts and the other pursuits and occupations,
and show the foundations, which exist in our very nature, for a cordial union between them all.

These objects recommend themselves strongly and obviously to
general approbation. While the cultivation of the mind, in its
more general sense, and in connexion with morals, is as important
to mechanics as to any other class of the community, nothing is
plainer than that those whose livelihood depends on the skilful practice
of the arts, ought to be instructed, as far as possible, in the scientific principles and natural laws, on which the arts are founded.
This is necessary, in order that the arts themselves should be pursued to the greatest advantage; that popular errors should be erad-

* The following Essay is compiled from a discourse delivered by the author, at
the opening of the Mechanics' Institute in Boston, in November, 1827; an address
before the Middlesex County Lyceum, at Concord, in November, 1829; and an
oration before the Columbian Institute at Washington, January, 1830.

icated; that every accidental improvement in the processes of industry, which offers itself, should be readily taken up and pursued to its principle; that false notions, leading to waste of time and labor, should be prevented from gaining or retaining currency; in short, that the useful, like the ornamental arts of life, should be carried to the point of attainable perfection.

The history of the progress of the human mind shows us, that for want of a diffusion of scientific knowledge among practical men, great evils have resulted, both to science and practice. Before the invention of the art of printing, the means of acquiring and circulating knowledge were few and ineffectual. The philosopher was, in consequence, exclusively a man of study, who, by living in a monastic seclusion, and by delving into the few books which time had spared,—particularly the works of Aristotle and his commentators,—succeeded in mastering the learning of the day; learning, mostly of an abstract and metaphysical nature. Thus, living in a world not of practice, but speculation, never bringing his theories to the test of observation, his studies assumed a visionary character. Hence the projects for the transmutation of metals; a notion not originating in any observation of the qualities of the different kinds of metals, but in reasoning, *a priori,* on their supposed identity of substance. So deep rooted was this delusion, that a great part of the natural science of the middle ages consisted in projects to convert the baser metals into gold. It is plain, that such a project would no more have been countenanced, by intelligent, well-informed persons, practically conversant with the nature of the metals, than a project to transmute pine into oak, or fish into flesh.

In like manner, by giving science wholly up to the philosophers, and making the practical arts of life merely a matter of traditionary repetition from one generation to another of uninformed artisans, much evil of an opposite kind was occasioned. Accident, of course, could be the only source of improvement; and for want of acquaintance with the leading principles of mechanical philosophy, the chances were indefinitely multiplied against these accidental improvements. For want of the diffusion of information among practical men, the principles prevailing in an art in one place were unknown in other places; and processes existing at one period were liable to be forgotten in the lapse of time. Secrets and mysteries, easily kept in such a state of things, and cherished by their possessor as a source of monopoly, were so common, that *mystery* is still occasionally used as synonymous with *trade*. This also contributed to the loss of arts once brought to perfection, such as that of staining glass, as practised in the middle ages. Complicated machinery was out of the question; for it requires, for its invention and improvement, the union of scientific knowledge and practical skill. The mariner was left to creep along the coast, while the astronomer was casting nativities; and the miner was reduced to the most laborious and purely mechanical processes, to extract the precious metals from the ores that really contained them, while the chemist, who ought to have taught him the method of amalgamation, could find no use for mercury, but as a menstruum, by which baser metals could be turned into gold.

At the present day, this state of things is certainly changed. A variety of popular treatises and works of reference have made the great principles of natural science generally accessible. It certainly is in the power of almost every one, by pains and time properly bestowed, to acquire a decent knowledge of every branch of practical philosophy. But still, it would appear, that, even now, this part of education is not on the right footing. Generally speaking, even now, all actual instruction in the principles of natural science is confined to the colleges; and the colleges are, for the most part, frequented only by those intended for professional life. The elementary knowledge of science, which is communicated at the colleges, is indeed useful in any and every calling; but it does not seem right, that none but those intended for the pulpit, the bar, or the profession of medicine, should receive instruction in those principles, which regulate the operation of the mechanical powers, and lie at the foundation of complicated machinery; which relate to the navigation of the seas, the smelting and refining of metals, the composition and improvement of soils, the reduction to a uniform whiteness of the vegetable fibre, the mixture and application of colors, the motion and pressure of fluids in large masses, the nature of light and heat, the laws of magnetism, electricity, and galvanism. It would seem, that this kind of knowledge was more immediately requisite for those who are to construct or make use of labor-saving machinery, who are to traverse the ocean, to lay out and direct the

29

excavation of canals, to build steam-engines and hydraulic presses, to work mines, and to conduct large agricultural and manufacturing establishments. Hitherto, with some partial exceptions, little has been done, systematically, to afford to those engaged in these pursuits, that knowledge, which, however convenient to others, would seem essential to them. There has been scarce any thing, which could be called education for practical life ; and those persons, who, in the pursuit of any of the useful arts, have signalized themselves, by the employment of scientific principles, for the invention of new processes, or the improvement of the old, have been self-educated men.

I am aware, that it is often made an argument against scientific education, that the greatest discoveries and inventions have been either the production of such self-educated men, or have been struck out by accident. There certainly is some truth in this. So long as no regular system of scientific education for the working classes exists, it is a matter of necessity, that, if any great improvement be made, it must be either the result of accident, or the happy thought of some powerful native genius, which forces its way without education, to the most astonishing results. This, however, is no more the case, with respect to the useful arts and the mechanical pursuits, than with respect to all the other occupations of society; and it would continue to be the case, after the establishment of the best system of scientific education. We find, in every pursuit and calling, some instances of remarkable men, who, without an early education adapted to the object, have raised themselves to great eminence. Lord Chancellor King, in England, was a grocer at that period of life, which is commonly spent in academical study, by those destined for the profession of the law. Chief Justice Pratt, of New York, having been brought up a carpenter, was led, by a severe cut from an axe, which unfitted him for work, to turn his attention to the law. Franklin, who seemed equally to excel in the conduct of the business of life, in the sublimest studies of philosophy, and in the management of the most difficult state affairs, was bred a printer. All these callings are quite respectable, but no one would think of choosing either of them as the school of the lawyer, judge, or statesman. The fact, that the native power of genius sometimes forces its way against all obstacles, and under every discouragement, proves nothing as to the course which it is expedient for the generality of men to pursue. The safe path to excellence and success, in every calling, is that of appropriate preliminary education, diligent application to learn the art, and assiduity in practising it. And I can perceive no reason, why this course should not be followed, in reference to the mechanical, as well as the professional callings. The instances of eminent men, like those named, and many others that might be named, such as Arkwright and Harrison, who have sprung from the depths of poverty to astonish and benefit mankind, no more prove that education is useless to the mechanic, than the corresponding examples prove, that it is useless to the statesman, jurist, or divine.

Besides, it will perhaps be found, that the great men, like those I have named, instead of being instances to show that education is useless, prove only, that, occasionally, men, who commence their education late, are as successful as those who commence it early. This shows, not that an early education is no benefit, but that the want of it may sometimes be made up in later years. It might be so made up, no doubt, oftener than it is ; and it is, in this country, much more frequently than in any other.

The foundation of a great improvement is also often a single conception, which suggests itself occasionally to strong and uneducated minds ; and who have the good fortune, afterwards, to receive from others that aid, in executing their projects, without which the most promising conception might have perished undeveloped. Thus Sir Richard Arkwright was without education, but endowed with a wonderful quickness of mind. What particular circumstances awakened his mechanical taste, we are not told. There is some reason to think, that this, like other strongly-marked aptitudes, may partly depend on the peculiar organization of the body, which is exactly the same in no two men. The daily observation of the operation of the spinning-wheel, in the cottages of the peasantry of Lancashire, gave him a full knowledge of the existing state of the art, which it was his good fortune to improve to a degree which is even yet the wonder of the world. He conceived, at length the idea of an improved machine for spinning. And in this conception,—not improbably a flash across the mind, the work of an instant,—lay all his original merit. But this is every thing.

America was discovered from the moment that Columbus firmly grasped the idea that, the earth being spherical, the Indies might be reached by sailing on a westerly course. If the actual discovery had not been made for ages after the death of Columbus, he would, nevertheless, in publishing this idea to the world, have been the pilot that led the way, whoever had followed his guidance. Sir Richard Arkwright, having formed the conception of his spinning machine, had recourse to a watchmaker to execute his idea. But how rarely could it happen, that circumstances would put it in the power of a person, ignorant, and poor, to engage the cooperation of an intelligent watchmaker!

Neither is it intended, that the education which we recommend, should extend to a minute acquaintance with the practical application of science to the details of every art. This would be impossible, and does not belong to preparatory education. We wish only that the general laws and principles should be so taught, as greatly to multiply the number of persons competent to carry forward such casual suggestions of improvement as may present themselves, and to bring their art to that state of increasing excellence, which all arts reach by long-continued, intelligent cultivation.

It may further be observed, with respect to those great discoveries which seem to be produced by happy accidents and fortuitous suggestion, that such happy accidents are most likely to fall in the way of those, who are on the look out for them,—those whose mental eyesight has been awakened and practised to behold them. The world is informed of all the cases in which such fortunate accidents have led to useful and brilliant results; but their number would probably appear smaller than it is now supposed to be, were such a thing possible as the *negative history* of discovery and improvement. No one can tell us what might have been done, had every opportunity been faithfully improved, every suggestion sagaciously caught up and followed out. No one can tell how often the uneducated or unobservant mind has approached to the very verge of a great discovery,—has had some wonderful invention almost thrust upon it,—but without effect. The ancients, as we learn from many passages in the Greek and Latin classics, were acquainted with convex lenses, but did not apply them to the construction of magnifying glasses or telescopes. They made use of seal-rings with inscriptions; and they marked their flocks with brands, containing the owner's name. In each of these practices, faint rudiments of the art of printing are concealed. Cicero, in one of his moral works, (*De Natura Deorum,*) in confuting the error of those philosophers, who taught that the world was produced by the fortuitous concourse of wandering atoms, uses the following language, as curious, in connexion with the point I would illustrate, as it is beautiful in expression, and powerful in argument :—' Here,' says he, ' must I not wonder, if there should be a man who can persuade himself, that certain solid and separate bodies are borne about by force or weight, and that this most beautiful and finished world is formed by their accidental meeting ? Whoever can think this possible, I do not see why he cannot also believe that, if a large number of *forms* of the one and twenty letters (of gold or any like substance) were thrown any where together, that the annals of Ennius might be made out from them, as they are cast on the ground, so as to be read in order ; a thing which I know not if it be within the power of chance to effect, even in a single verse.' How very near an approach is made, in this remark, to the invention of the art of printing, fifteen hundred years before it took place !

How slight and familiar was the occurrence which gave to Sir Isaac Newton the first suggestion of his system of the universe ! This great man had been driven by the plague from London to the country, and had left his library behind him. Obliged to find occupation in the activity of his own mind, he was led, in his meditations, to trace the extent of the principle which occasioned the fall of an apple from the tree, in the garden where he passed his solitary hours. Commencing with this familiar hint, he followed it out to that universal law of gravity, which binds the parts of the earth and ocean together, which draws the moon to the earth, the satellites to the planets, the planets to the sun, and the sun itself, with its attendant worlds, toward some grand and general point of attraction for that infinity of systems, of which the several stars are the centres. How many hundreds of thousands of men, since the creation of the world, had seen an apple falling from a tree ! How many philosophers had speculated profoundly, on the system

of the universe! But it required the talent of a man, placed by
general consent at the head of the human race, to deduce from this
familiar occurrence, on the surface of the earth, the operation of
the primordial law of nature which governs the movements of the
heavens, and holds the universe together. Nothing less than his
sagacity could have made the deduction, and nothing less than a
mathematical skill, and an acquaintance with the previously ascertained principles of science,—such as falls to the lot of very few,—
would have enabled Newton to demonstrate the truth of his
system.

Let us quote another example, to show that the most obvious
and familiar facts may be noticed for ages without effect, till they
are observed by a sagacious eye, and scrutinized with patience and
perseverance. The appearance of lightning in the clouds is as old
as creation ; and certainly no natural phenomenon forces itself more
directly on the notice of men. The existence of the electric fluid,
as excited by artificial means, was familiarly known to philosophers
a hundred years before Franklin ; and there are a few vague hints,
prior to his time, that lightning is an electrical appearance. But
it was left for Franklin distinctly to conceive that proposition, and
to institute an experiment by which it should be demonstrated.
The process, by which he reached this great conclusion is worth
remembering. Dr Franklin had seen the most familiar electrical experiments performed at Boston, in 1745, by a certain Dr Spence, a
Scotch lecturer. His curiosity was excited by witnessing these experiments, and he purchased the whole of Dr Spence's apparatus, and
repeated the experiments at Philadelphia. Pursuing his researches
with his own instruments, and others which had been liberally presented to the province of Pennsylvania, by the proprietor, Mr
Penn, and by Dr Franklin's friend, Mr Collinson, our illustrious
countryman rapidly enlarged the bounds of electrical science, and
soon arrived at the undoubting conviction, that the electrical fluid
and lightning are identical. But he could not rest till he had
brought this truth to the test of demonstration, and he boldly set
about an experiment, upon the most terrific element in nature. He
at first proposed, by means of a spire, which was erecting in Philadelphia, to form a connexion between the region of the clouds
and an electrical apparatus ; but the appearance of *a boy's kite* in

the air, suggested to him a readier method. Having prepared a kite adapted for the purpose, he went out into a field, accompanied by his son, to whom alone he had imparted his design. The kite was raised, having a key attached to the lower end of the cord, and being insulated by means of a silken thread, by which it was fastened to a post. A heavy cloud, apparently charged with lightning, passed over the kite ; but no signs of electricity were witnessed in the apparatus. Franklin was beginning to despair, when he saw the loose fibres bristling from the hempen cord. He immediately presented his knuckle to the key, and received the electrical spark. Overcome by his feelings, at the consummation of this great discovery, 'he heaved a deep sigh, and, conscious of an immortal name, felt that he could have been content, had that moment been his last.' How easily it might have been his last, was shown by the fact, that when Professor Richman, a few months afterwards, was repeating this experiment at St Petersburgh, a globe of fire flashed from the conducting rod to his forehead, and killed him on the spot.

Brilliant as Dr Franklin's discoveries in electricity were, and much as he advanced the science by his sagacious experiments and unwearied investigations, a rich harvest of farther discoveries was left by him to the succeeding age. The most extraordinary of these is the discovery of a modification of electricity, which bears the name of the philosopher by whom it was made known to the world ;—I refer, of course, to Galvanism. Lewis Galvani was an anatomist in Bologna. On a table in his study, lay some frogs, which had been prepared for a broth for his wife, who was ill. An electrical machine stood on the table. A student of Galvani accidentally touched the nerve on the inside of the leg of one of the frogs, and convulsions immediately took place in the body of the animal. Galvani himself was not present at the moment, but this curious circumstance caught the attention of his wife,—a lady of education and talent,—who ascribed it to some influence of the electrical machine. She informed her husband of what had happened, and it was his opinion also, that the electrical machine was the origin of the convulsions. A long-continued and patient course of investigation corrected this error, and established the science of galvanic electricity, nearly as it now exists ; and which has proved, in the hands of Sir Humphrey Davy, the agent of the most brilliant and astonishing discoveries. Frogs have been a common article of food in Europe for ages; but it was only when they were brought by accident into the study of the anatomist, and fell beneath the notice of a sagacious eye, that they became the occasion of this brilliant discovery.

In all these examples, we see that, whatever be the first origin of a great discovery or improvement, science and study are required to perfect and illustrate it. The want of a knowledge of the principles of science has often led men to waste much time on pursuits, which a better acquaintance with those principles would have taught them were hopeless. The patent office, in every country where such an institution exists, contains, perhaps, as many machines, which show the want, as the possession, of sound scientific knowledge. Besides unsuccessful essays at machinery, holding forth a promise of feasibility, no little ingenuity, and much time and money, have been lavished on a project, which seems, in modern times, to supply the place of the philosopher's stone of the alchemists ;—I mean a contrivance for perpetual motion ; a contrivance inconsistent with the law of gravity. A familiar acquaintance with the principles of science is useful, not only to guide the mind to the discovery of what is true and practical, but to protect it from the delusions of an excited imagination, ready to waste itself, in the ardor of youth, enterprise, and conscious ingenuity, on that which the laws of Nature herself have made unattainable.

Such are some of the considerations, which show the general utility of scientific education, for those engaged in the mechanical arts. Let us now advert to some of the circumstances, which ought, particularly in the United States of America, to act as encouragements to the young men of the country to apply themselves earnestly, and, as far as it can be done, systematically, to the attainment of such an education.

1. And, first, it is beyond all question, that what are called the mechanical trades of this country are on a much more liberal footing than they are in Europe. This circumstance not only ought to encourage those who pursue them, to take an honest pride in improvement, but it makes it their incumbent duty to do so. In almost every country of Europe, various restraints are imposed on

the mechanics, which almost amount to slavery. A good deal of censure has been lately thrown on the journeymen printers of Paris, for entering into combinations not to work for their employers, and for breaking up the power-presses, which were used by the great employing printers. I certainly shall not undertake to justify any acts of illegal violence, and the destruction of property. But when you consider, that no man can be a master printer in France without a license, and that only eighty licenses were granted in Paris, it is by no means wonderful that the journeymen, forbidden by law to set up for themselves, and prevented by the power-presses from getting work from others, should be disposed, after having carried through one revolution for the government, to undertake another for themselves. Of what consequence is it to a man, forbidden by the law to work for his living, whether Charles X or Louis Philip is king?

In England, it is exceedingly difficult for a mechanic to obtain a settlement, in any town except that in which he was born, or where he served his apprenticeship. The object of imposing these restrictions is, of course, to enforce on each parish the maintenance of its native poor; and the resort of mechanics from place to place, is permitted only on conditions with which many of them are unable to comply. The consequence is, they are obliged to stay where they were born; where, perhaps, there are already more hands than can find work; and, from the decline of the place, even the established artisans want employment. Chained to such a spot, where chance and necessity have bound him, the young man feels himself but half free. He is thwarted in his choice of a pursuit for life, and obliged to take up with an employment against his preference, because there is no opening in any other. He is depressed in his own estimation, because he finds himself unprotected in society. The least evil likely to befall him is, that he drags along a discouraged and unproductive existence. He more naturally falls into dissipation and vice, or enlists in the army or navy; while the place of his nativity is gradually becoming a decayed, and finally a rotten borough, and, as such, enables some rich nobleman to send two members to parliament, to make laws against combinations of workmen.

30

In other countries, singular institutions exist, imposing oppressive burdens on the mechanical classes. I refer now more particularly to the corporations, guilds, or crafts, as they are called, that is, to the companies formed by the members of a particular trade. These exist, with great privileges, in every part of Europe; in Germany, there are some features in the institution, as it seems to me, peculiarly oppressive. The different crafts in that country are incorporations recognized by law, governed by usages of great antiquity, with funds to defray the corporate expenses, and in each considerable town, a house of entertainment is selected, as the house of call, (or harbor, as it is styled,) of each particular craft. No one is allowed to set up as a master workman, in any trade, unless he is admitted as a freeman or member of the craft; and such is the stationary condition of most parts of Germany, that I understand that no person is admitted as a master workman in any trade, except to supply the place of some one deceased or retired from business. When such a vacancy occurs, all those desirous of being permitted to fill it, present a piece of work, which is called their master-piece, being offered to obtain the place of a master workman. Nominally, the best workman gets the place; but you will easily conceive, that, in reality, some kind of favoritism must generally decide it. Thus is every man obliged to submit to all the chances of a popular election, whether he shall be allowed to work for his bread; and that, too, in a country where the people are not permitted to have any agency in choosing their rulers. But the restraints on journeymen, in that country, are still more oppressive. As soon as the years of apprenticeship have expired, the young mechanic is obliged, in the phrase of the country, to *wander* for three years. For this purpose he is furnished by the master of the craft in which he has served his apprenticeship, with a duly authenticated wandering book, with which he goes forth to seek employment. In whatever city he arrives, on presenting himself, with this credential, at the house of call, or harbor, of the craft in which he has served his time, he is allowed, gratis, a day's food and a night's lodging. If he wishes to get employment in that place, he is assisted in procuring it. If he does not wish to, or fails in the attempt, he must pursue his wandering; and this lasts for three years, before he can be any where admitted as a master. I have heard it argued, that this system had the advantage of circulating knowledge from place to place, and imparting to the young artisan the fruits of travel and intercourse with the world. But however beneficial travelling may be, when undertaken by those who have the taste and capacity to profit by it, I cannot but think, that to compel every young man, who has just served out his time, to leave his home, in the manner I have described, must bring his habits and morals into peril, and be regarded rather as a hardship than as an advantage. There is no sanctuary of virtue like home.

You will see, from these few hints, the nature of some of the restraints and oppressions to which the mechanical industry of Europe is subjected. Wherever governments and corporations thus interfere with private industry, the spring of personal enterprise is unbent. Men are depressed with a consciousness of living under control. They cease to feel a responsibility for themselves, and, encountering obstacles whenever they step from the beaten path, they give up improvement as hopeless. I need not, in the presence of this audience, remark on the total difference of things in America. We are apt to think, that the only thing in which we have improved on other countries, is our political constitution, whereby we choose our rulers, instead of recognizing their hereditary right.— But a much more important difference between us and foreign countries is wrought into the very texture of our society ; it is that generally pervading freedom from restraint, in matters like those I have just specified. In England, it is said that forty days' undisturbed residence in a parish gives a journeyman mechanic a settlement, and consequently entitles him, should he need it, to support from the poor rates of that parish. To obviate this effect, the magistrates are on the alert, and instantly expel a new comer from their limits, who does not possess means of giving security, such as few young mechanics command. A duress like this, environing the young man, on his entrance into life, upon every side, and condemning him to imprisonment for life on the spot where he was born, converts the government of the country,—whatever be its name,—into a despotism.

2. There is another consideration, which invites the artisans of this country to improve their minds ; it is the vastly wider field

which is opened to them, as the citizens of a new country; and the proportionate call which exists for labor and enterprise in every department. In the old world, society is full. In every country but England, it has long been full. It was in that country not less crowded, till the vast improvements in machinery and manufacturing industry were made, which have rendered it, in reference to manufactures and commerce,—what ours is, still more remarkably, in every thing,—a new country,—a country of urgent and expansive demand, where new branches of employment are constantly opening, new kinds of talent called for, new arts struck out, and more hands employed in all the old ones. In different parts of our country, the demand is of a different kind, but it is active and stirring every where.

It may not be without use to consider the various causes of this enlargement of the field of action, in this country.

The first, and perhaps the main cause, is the great abundance of good land, which lies open, on the easiest conditions, to every man who wishes to avail himself of it. One dollar and twenty-five cents will enable any man to purchase an acre of first rate land. This circumstance alone acts like a safety-valve to the great social steam-engine. There can be no very great pressure any where in a community, where, by travelling a few miles into the interior, a man can buy an acre of land for a day's work. This was the first stimulus applied to the condition of things in this country, after the revolutionary war, and it is still operating in full force.

The next powerful spring to our industry was felt in the navigating interest. This languished greatly under the old confederation, being crushed by foreign competition. The adoption of the constitution breathed the breath of life into it. By the duty on foreign tonnage, and by the confinement of the privilege of an American vessel to an American built ship, our commercial marine sprang into existence with the rapidity of magic, and,—under a peculiar state of things in Europe,—appropriated to itself the carrying trade of the world.

Shortly after this stimulus was applied to the industry of the Northern and Middle States, the Southern States acquired an equally prolific source of wealth, unexpected and rapid beyond example in its operation ;—I mean the cultivation of cotton. In 1789, the hope was expressed by southern members of congress, that, if good seed could be procured, cotton might be raised in the Southern States, where, before that time, and for several years after, not a pound had been raised for exportation. The culture of this beautiful staple was encouraged by a duty of three cents a pound on imported cotton ; but it languished for some time, on account of the difficulty of separating the seed from the fibre. At length, Eli Whitney, of Connecticut, invented the saw-gin ; and so prodigiously has this culture increased, that it is calculated that the cotton crop of last year amounted to one million of bales, of at least three hundred pounds each.

In 1807, the first successful essays were made with steam navigation. The progress at first was slow. In 1817, there was not such a thing as a regular line of steamboats on the western waters. Two hundred steamboats now ply those waters, and half as many navigate the waters of the Atlantic coast.

The embargo and war created the manufactures of the United States. Before that period, nothing was done, on a large scale, in the way of manufactures. With some fluctuations in prosperity, they have succeeded in establishing themselves on a firm basis. A laboring man can now buy two good shirts, well made, for a dollar. Fifteen years ago, they would have cost him three times that sum.

Still more recently, a system of internal improvements has been commenced, which will have the effect, when a little further developed, of crowding within a few years the progress of generations. Already, Lake Champlain, from the north, and Lake Erie, from the west, have been connected with Albany. The Delaware and Chesapeake Bays have been united. A canal is nearly finished in the upper part of New Jersey, from the Delaware to the Hudson, by which coal is already despatched to our market. Another route is laid out across the same State, to connect New York, by a rail-road, with Philadelphia. A water communication has been opened by canals half way from Philadelphia to Pittsburgh. Considerable progress is made both on the rail-road and the canal, which are to unite Baltimore and Washington with the Ohio river. A canal of sixty miles in length is open from Cincinnati to Dayton, in the State of Ohio; and another, of more than three hundred miles in extent, to connect Lake Erie with the Ohio, is two thirds completed.*

I mention these facts, (which, though among the most considerable, are by no means all of the same character which might be quoted,) not merely as being in themselves curious and important; though this they are in a high degree. My object is, to turn your attention to their natural effect, in keeping up a constant and high demand for labor, art, skill, and talent of all kinds, and their accumulated fruits, that is, capital; and thereby particularly inviting the young to exert themselves strenuously to take an active, industrious and honorable part in a community, which has such a variety of employments and rewards for all its members. The rising generation beholds before it *not a crowded* community, but one where labor, both of body and mind, is in greater request, and bears a higher relative price, than in any other country. When it is said that labor is dear in this country, this is not a mere commercial proposition, like those which fill the pages of the price current; but it is a great *moral fact*, speaking volumes as to the state of society, and reminding the American citizen, particularly the young man who is beginning life, that he lives in a country where every man carries about with him the thing in greatest request; where the labor and skill of the human hands, and every kind of talent and acquisition, possess a relative importance elsewhere unknown,—in other words, where an *industrious man* is of the greatest consequence.

These considerations are well calculated to awaken enterprise, to encourage effort, to support perseverance; and we behold on every side that such is their effect. I have already alluded to the astonishing growth of our navigation after the adoption of the federal constitution. It affords an example, which will bear dwelling upon, of American enterprise, placed in honorable contrast with that of Europe. In Great Britain, and in other countries of Europe, the India and China trade was, and to a great degree still is, locked up by the monopoly enjoyed by affluent companies, protected and patronized by the state, and clothed, themselves, in

* Most of the works here mentioned as being in progress, are now (1836) completed, and innumerable others have since been undertaken or projected.

some cases, with imperial power. The territories of the British East India Company are computed to embrace a population of one hundred and fifteen millions of souls. The consequence of this state of things was not the activity, but the embarrassment, of the commercial intercourse with the East. Individual enterprise was not awakened. The companies sent out annually their unwieldy vessels of twelve hundred tons burden, commanded by salaried captains, to carry on the commerce which was secured to them by a government monopoly, and which, it was firmly believed, could not be carried on in any other way. Scarcely was American independence declared, when our moderate-sized merchant vessels, built with economy, and navigated with frugality, doubled both the great capes of the world. The north-western coast of America began to be crowded. Not content with visiting old markets, our intelligent ship-masters explored the numerous islands of the Indian Archipelago. Vessels from Salem and Boston, of two and three hundred tons, went to ports in those seas, that had not been visited by a foreign ship since the days of Alexander the Great. The intercourse between Boston and the Sandwich Islands was uninterrupted. A man would no more have thought of boasting that he had been round the world, than that he had been to Liverpool. After Lord Anson and Captain Cook had, by order and at the expense of the British government, made their laborious voyages of discovery and exploration in the Pacific ocean, and on the coast of America, it still remained for a merchant vessel from Boston, to discover and enter the only considerable river that flows into the Pacific, from Behring's Strait to Cape Horn. Our fellow citizen, Captain Gray, piloted the British admiral Vancouver into the Columbia river ; and, in requital of this service, the British government now claims jurisdiction over it, partly on the ground of prior discovery !

This is a single instance of the propitious effect on individual enterprise of the condition of things under which we live. But the work is not all done ; it is, in fact, hardly begun. This vast continent is as yet no where fully stocked,—almost every where thinly peopled. There are yet mighty regions of it, in which the settler's axe has never been heard. These remain, and portions of them will long remain, open for coming generations, a sure pre-

servative against the evils of a redundant population on the sea-
board. The older parts of the country, which have been settled
by the husbandman, and reclaimed from the state of nature, are
now to be settled again by the manufacturer, the engineer, and the
mechanic. First settled by a civilized, they are now to be settled
by a dense population. Settled by the hard labor of the human
hands, they are now to be settled by the labor-saving arts, by
machinery, by the steam-engine, and by internal improvements.
Hitherto, the work to be done, was that which nothing but the
tough sinews of the arm of man could accomplish. This work, in
most of the old States, and some of the new ones, has been done,
and is finished. It was performed under incredible hardships, fearful dangers, with heart-sickening sacrifices, amidst the perils of
savage tribes, and of the diseases incident to a soil on which deep
forests, for a thousand years, had been laying their deposit, and
which was now for the first time opened to the sun. The kind,
the degree, the intensity of the labor, which has been performed
by the men who settled this country, have, I am sure, no parallel
in history. I believe, if a thrifty European farmer from Norfolk, in
England, or Flanders, a vine-dresser from Burgundy, an olive-
gardener from Italy,—under the influence of no stronger feelings
than those which actuate the mass of the stationary population of
those countries,—were set down in a North American forest, with
an axe on his shoulder, and told to get his living, that his heart
would fail him at the sight. What has been the slow work of two
thousand years in Europe, has here been effected in two hundred,
unquestionably under the cheering moral effect of our free institutions. We have now, in some parts of the United States, reached
a point in our progress, where, to a considerable degree, a new
form of society will appear; in which the wants of a settled country and a comparatively dense population will succeed to those of
a thin population, scattered over a soil as yet but partially reclaimed.
We shall henceforth feel, more and more, the want of improved
means of communication. We must, in every direction, have turnpike roads, unobstructed rivers, canals, rail-roads, and steamboats.
The mineral treasures of the earth, metals, coals, ochres, fine clay,
limestone, gypsum, salt, are to be brought to light, and applied to the
purposes of the arts, and the service of man. Another immense

capital, which nature has invested for us in the form of water power, (a natural capital, which I take to be fully equal to the steam capital of Great Britain,) is to be turned to account, by being made to give motion to machinery. Still another vast capital, lying unproductive, in the form of land, is to be realized, and no small part of it, for the first time, by improved cultivation. All the manufactures are to be introduced on a large scale ; the coarser, —where it has not been done,—without delay ; and the finer, in rapid succession, and in proportion to the acquisition of skill, the accumulation of capital, and the improvement of machinery. With these will grow up, or increase, the demand for various institutions for education ; the call for every species of intellectual service ; the need for every kind of professional assistance,—a demand rendered still more urgent, by a political organization, of itself in the highest degree favorable to the creation and diffusion of energy throughout the commonwealth.

These are so many considerations, which call on the rising generation of those destined for the active and mechanical arts, *to improve their minds*. It is only in this manner, that they can effectually ascertain the true bent of their own faculties, and, having ascertained it, employ themselves with greatest success in the way for which Providence has fitted them. It is only in this manner that they can make themselves highly respected in society, and secure to themselves the largest share of those blessings, which are the common objects of desire. In most of the countries of the older world, the greatest part of the prizes of life are literally distributed by the lottery of birth. Men are born to wealth, which they cannot alienate ; to power, from which they cannot, without a convulsion of the body politic, be removed ; or to poverty and depression, from which, generally speaking, they cannot emerge. Here, it rarely happens, that, even for a single generation, an independence can be enjoyed without labor and diligence bestowed on its acquisition and preservation ; while, as a general rule, the place to which each individual shall rise in society is precisely graduated on the scale of capacity and exertion,—in a word, of merit. Every thing, therefore, that shows the magnitude and growth of the country,—its abundance and variety of resources,— its increasing demand for all the arts, both of ornament and utility,

31

—is another reason, calling upon the emulous young men of the working classes to enter into the career of improvement, where there is the fullest scope for generous competition, and every talent of every kind is sure to be required, honored, and rewarded.

There is another reflection, which ought not to be omitted. The rapid growth and swift prosperity of the country have their peculiar attendant evils, in addition to those inseparable from humanity. To resist the progress of these evils, to provide, seasonably and efficaciously, the moral and reasonable remedy of those disorders of the social system, to which it may be more particularly exposed, is a duty to be performed by the enlightened and virtuous portion of the mass of the community, quite equal in importance to any other duty, which they are called to discharge. In Europe, it is too much the case, that the virtuous influences, which operate on the working classes, come down from the privileged orders, while the operatives themselves, as they are called, are abandoned to most of the vices of the most prolific source of vice,—ignorance. It is of the utmost importance, in this country, that the active walks of life should be filled by an enlightened class of men, with a view to the security and order of the community, and to protect it from those evils, which have been thought, in Europe, to be inseparable from the great increase of the laboring population. What is done in other countries by *gens d'armes* and horse-guards, must here be done by public sentiment, or not at all. It is an enlightened moral public sentiment, that must spread its wings over our dwellings, and plant a watchman at our doors. It is perfectly well known to all who hear me, that as a class, the mechanic and manufacturing population of Europe is regarded as grossly depraved; while the agricultural population,—with as little exception,—is set down as incurably stupid. This conviction was so prevalent, that many of the most patriotic of *our* citizens were opposed to the introduction of manufactures among us, partly on the ground, that factories are, in their nature, seminaries of vice and immorality. Thus far, this fear has been most happily relieved by experience; and it is found that those establishments are as little open to reproach, on the score of morals, as any other in the community. Our mechanic and agricultural population will, in this part of the country, support the comparison, for general intelligence and morality with any in the world. This state of things, if it can be rendered permanent, is a great social triumph, and will be to America a juster subject of self-gratulation than any thing belonging merely to the political, economical, and physical growth of the community. It deserves the consideration of every patriot, that the surest way of perpetuating and diffusing this most enviable state of things,—this most desirable of all the advantages, which we can have over the old world,—is to multiply the means of improving the mind, and put them within the reach of all classes. An intelligent class can scarce ever be, as a class, vicious; never, as a class, indolent. The excited mental activity operates as a counterpoise to the stimulus of sense and appetite. The new world of ideas; the new views of the relations of things; the astonishing secrets of the physical properties and mechanical powers, disclosed to the well-informed mind, present attractions, which,—unless the character is deeply sunk,—are sufficient to counterbalance the taste for frivolous or corrupt pleasures; and thus, in the end, a standard of character is created in the community, which, though it does not invariably save each individual, protects the virtue of the mass.

3. I am thus brought to the last consideration, which I shall mention, as an encouragement to the mechanic classes to improve their minds; and that is, the comparatively higher rank which our institutions assign to them in the political system. One of the great causes, no doubt, of the enterprise and vigor which have already distinguished our countrymen, in almost every pursuit, is the absence of those political distinctions, which are independent of personal merit and popular choice. It is the strongest motive that we can suggest, for unremitted diligence in the acquisition of useful knowledge, on the part of the laborious classes, that they have a far more responsible duty to discharge to society than ever devolved on the same class in any other community. Every book of travels, not less than every opportunity of personal observation, instructs us of the deplorable ignorance of a great part of those by whom the work of the community is done, in foreign countries. In some parts of England, this class is more enlightened than it is on the continent of Europe; and in that country, great efforts are making, at the present time,—and particularly through the instru-

mentality of institutions like that under the auspices of which we
are now assembled,—to extend the means of education to those
who have hitherto been deprived of them.   But it is a party question among them, not how far it is right and proper, but how far it is
prudent and safe, to enlighten the people ; and while the liberal
party in England are urgent for the diffusion of useful knowledge, to
prevent the people from breaking out into violence and revolution,
the government party exclaim against a farther diffusion of knowledge, as tending to make the people discontented with their condition.   I remember to have seen, not long since, a charge to the
grand jury by a very eminent English judge, in which the practice
of boxing is commended, and the fear is expressed, that popular
education has been pushed too far !

The man who should, in this country, express the opinion, that
the education of the people foreboded ill to the state, would merely
be regarded as wanting common judgment and sagacity.   We are
not only accustomed to that state of things, but we regard it as our
great blessing and privilege, to which the higher orders in Europe
look forward, as the fearful result of bloody revolutions.   The
representative system, and our statute of distributions, are regarded
by us, not as horrors consequent upon a convulsion of society, but
as the natural condition of the body politic.

This condition of the country, however, is not to be regarded
merely as a topic of lofty political declamation.   Its best effects
are, and must be, those which are not immediately of a political
character.   If the mass of the people behold no privileged class
placed invidiously above them ; if they choose those who make
and administer the laws ; if the extent of public expenditure is
determined by those who bear its burden,—this surely is well ;
but if the mass of the people here were what it is in most parts
of Europe, it may be doubted whether such a system would not
be too good for them.   Who would like to trust his life and fortune
to a Spanish jury, or a Neapolitan jury ?   Under the reign of
Napoleon, an attempt was made to introduce the trial by jury, not
only into France, but into some of the dependent kingdoms.   It
has been stated, that when the peasants of some of these countries
were impanneled in the jury-box, they not only considered it an

excessively onorous and irksome duty, but showed themselves utterly incapable of discharging it with sufficient discretion and intelligence.

The great use, then, to be made of popular rights should be popular improvement. Let the young man, who is to gain his living by his labor and skill, remember that he is a citizen of a free state ; that on him and his contemporaries it depends, whether he will be happy and prosperous himself in his social condition, and whether a precious inheritance of social blessings shall descend, unimpaired, to those who come after him ; that there is no important difference in the situation of individuals, but that which they themselves cause, or permit to exist ; that if something of the inequality in the goods of fortune, which is inseparable from human things, exist in this country, it ought to be viewed only as another excitement to that industry, by which, nine times out of ten, wealth is acquired ; and still more to that cultivation of the mind, which, next to the moral character, makes the great difference between man and man. The means are already ample and accessible ; and it is for the majority of the community, by a tax, of which the smallest proportion falls on themselves, to increase these means to any desirable extent.

These remarks apply, with equal force, to almost every individual. There are some considerations, which address themselves more exclusively to the ardent mind emulous of the praise of excelling. Such cannot realize too soon, that we live in an age of improvement ; an age, in which investigation is active and successful in every quarter ; and in which what has been effected, however wonderful, is but the brilliant promise of what may further be done. The important discoveries which have been made in almost every department of human occupation, speculative and practical, within less than a century, are almost infinite. To speak only of those which minister most directly to the convenience of man,— what changes have not been already wrought in the condition of society ; what addition has not been made to the wealth of nations, and the means of private comfort, by the inventions, discoveries and improvements of the last hundred years ? High in importance among these are the increased facilities for transportation. By the use of the locomotive steam-engine upon a rail-road, passengers and merchandise may now be conveyed from place to place, at the rate of fifteen and even twenty miles an hour. Although not to be compared with this, the plan of M'Adam is eminently useful, consisting, as it does, of a method, by which a surface as hard as a rock can be carried along, over any foundation, at an expense not much greater, and, under some circumstances, not at all greater, than that of turnpike roads on the old construction. By the chemical process of bleaching, what was formerly done by exposure to the sun and air for weeks, is now done under cover, in a few days. By the machinery for separating the seed from the staple of cotton, the value of every acre of land, devoted to the culture of this most important product, has, to say the least, been doubled. By the machinery for carding, spinning, and weaving cotton, the price of a yard of durable cotton cloth has been reduced from half a dollar to a few cents. Lithography and stereotype printing are probably destined to have a very important influence in enlarging the sphere of the operations of the press. By the invention of gas lights, an inflammable air, yielding the strongest and purest flame, is extracted in a laboratory, and conducted, under ground, all over a city, and brought up wherever it is required, in the street, in the shop, in the dwelling-house. The safety-lamp enables the miner to walk unharmed through an atmosphere of explosive gas. And, last and chiefest, the application of steam, as a general moving power, is rapidly extending its effect from one branch of industry to another, from one interest to another, of the community, and bids fair, within no distant period, to produce the most essential changes in the social condition of the world. All these beautiful, surprising, and most useful discoveries and improvements have been made within less than a century ; most of them within less than half that time.

What must be the effect of this wonderful multiplication of ingenious and useful discoveries and improvements ? Undoubtedly *this*, that, in addition to all their immediate beneficial consequences, they will lead to further discoveries and still greater improvements. Of that vast system, which we call Nature, and of which none but its Author can comprehend the whole, the laws and the properties, that have as yet been explored, unquestionably form but a few parts connected with a grand succession of parts yet undiscovered, by an indissoluble, although an unseen chain. Each new truth that is found out, besides its own significance and value, is a step to the knowledge of further truth, leading off the inquisitive mind on a new track, and upon some higher path; in the pursuit of which new discoveries are made, and the old are brought into new and unexpected connexions.

The history of human science is a collection of facts, which, while it proves the connexion with each other of truths and arts, at first view remote and disconnected, encourages us to scrutinize every department of knowledge, however trite and familiar it may seem, with a view to discovering its relation with the laws and properties of nature, comprehended within it, but not yet disclosed. The individual, who first noticed the attractive power of magnetic substances, was gratified, no doubt, with observing a singular and inexplicable property of matter, which he may have applied to some experiments rather curious than useful. The man, who afterwards observed the tendency of a magnetized body toward the poles of the earth, unfolded a far more curious and important law of nature, but one which, resting there, was productive of no practical consequences. Then came the sagacious, or most fortunate person, who, attaching the artificial magnet to a traversing card, contrived the means of steering a vessel in the darkest night across the high seas. To him we cannot suppose that the important consequences of his discovery were *wholly* unperceived; but since, in point of history, near two centuries passed away before they began to be developed, we can hardly suppose that the inventor of the mariner's compass caught more than a glimpse of the nature of his invention. The Chinese are supposed to have been acquainted with it, as also with the art of printing, from time immemorial, without having derived from either any of those results, which have changed the aspect of modern Europe. Then came Columbus. Guided by the faithful pilot, who watches when the eye of man droops,—the patient little steersman, whom darkness does not blind, nor the storm drive from his post,—Columbus discovered a new world;—a glorious discovery, as he, no doubt, felt it to be, both in anticipation and achievement. But it does not appear, that even Columbus had indulged a vision more brilliant than that of a princely inheritance for his own family, and a rich colony for Spain ;—a vision fulfilled in his own poverty and chains, and in the corruption and degeneracy of the Spanish monarchy. And yet, from his discovery of America, so disastrous to himself and country, have sprung, directly or indirectly, most of the great changes of the political, commercial, and social condition of man in modern times. It is curious, also, to reflect, that as the Chinese, from time immemorial, (as has just been remarked,) have possessed the mariner's compass, and the art of printing, to little purpose; so they, or some people in their neighborhood, on the north-eastern coast of Asia, either with the aid of the compass, or merely by coasting from island to island, appear to have made the discovery of America, on the western side of the continent, a thousand years before it was discovered by Columbus, on the eastern side,—without, however, deriving from this discovery any beneficial consequences to the old world or the new. It was left for the spirit of civilization, awakened in western Europe toward the close of the fifteenth century, to develope, and put in action, the great elements of power and light, latent in this discovery.

Its first effect was the establishment of the colonial system, which, with the revolution in the financial state of Europe, occasioned by the opening of the American mines, gave, eventually, a new aspect to both hemispheres. What the sum total of all these consequences has been, may be partly judged from the fact, that the colonization of the United States is but one of them. The further extension of adventures of discovery was facilitated by new scientific inventions and improvements. The telescope was contrived, and, from the more accurately observed movements of the heavenly bodies, tables of longitude were constructed, which gave new confidence to the navigator. He now visits new shores, lying under different climates, whose productions, transplanted to other regions, or introduced into the commerce of the world, give new springs to industry, open new sources of wealth, and lead to the cultivation of new arts. It is unnecessary to dwell on particulars; but who can estimate the full effect on social affairs of such products as sugar, coffee, tea, rice, tobacco, the potato, cotton, indigo, the spices, the dye-woods, the mineral and fossil substances, newly made to enter into general use and consumption; the discovery, transportation, and preparation of which are so many unforeseen effects of former discoveries? Each of these, directly or indirectly, furnished new materials for mind to act upon; new excitement to its energies. Navigation, already extended, receives new facilities from the use of the chronometer. The growing wealth of the community increases the demand for all the fabrics of industry; the wonderful machinery for carding, spinning, and weaving, is contrived; water and vapor are made to do the work of human hands, and almost of human intellect; as the cost of the fabric decreases, the demand for it multiplies, geometrically, and furnishes an ever-growing reward for the exertions of the ever-active spirit of improvement. Thus a mechanical invention may lead to a geographical discovery; a physical cause to a political or an intellectual effect. A discovery results in an art; an art produces a comfort; a comfort, made cheaply accessible, adds family on family to the population; and a family is a new creation of thinking, reasoning, inventing, and discovering beings. Thus, instead of arriving at the end, we are at the beginning of the series, and ready to start, with recruited numbers, on the great and beneficent career of useful knowledge.

What, then, are these great and beneficial discoveries in their origin? What is the process which has led to them? They are the work of rational man, operating upon the materials existing in nature, and observing the laws and properties of the physical world. The Creator of the universe has furnished us the material; it is all around us, above us, and beneath us; in the ground under our feet; the air we breathe; the waters of the ocean, and of the fountains of the earth; in the various subjects of the kingdoms of nature. We cannot open our eyes, nor stretch out our hands, nor take a step, but we see, and handle, and tread upon the things, from which the most wonderful and useful discoveries and inventions have been deduced. What is gunpowder, which has changed the character of modern warfare? It is the mechanical mixture of some of the most common and least costly substances. What is the art of printing? A contrivance less curious, as a piece of mechanism, than a musical box. What is the steam-engine? An apparatus for applying the vapor of boiling water. What is vaccination? A trifling ail, communicated by a scratch of the lancet,

32

and capable of protecting human life against one of the most dreadful maladies to which it is exposed.

And are the properties of matter all discovered? its laws all found out? the uses to which they may be applied all detected? I cannot believe it. We cannot doubt, that truths now unknown are in reserve, to reward the patience and the labors of future lovers of truth, which will go as far beyond the brilliant discoveries of the last generation, as these do beyond all that was known to the ancient world. The pages are infinite in that great volume, which was written by the hand divine, and they are to be gradually turned, perused, and announced, to benefited and grateful generations, by genius and patience; and especially by patience; by untiring, enthusiastic, self-devoting patience. The progress which has been made in art and science is indeed vast. We are ready to think a pause must follow; that the goal must be at hand. But there is no goal; and there can be no pause; for art and science are in themselves progressive and infinite. They are moving powers, animated principles: they are instinct with life; they are themselves the intellectual life of man. Nothing can arrest them, which does not plunge the entire order of society into barbarism. There is no end to truth, no bound to its discovery and application; and a man might as well think to build a tower, from the top of which he could grasp Sirius in his hand, as prescribe a limit to discovery and invention. Never do we more evince our arrogant ignorance, than when we boast our knowledge. True Science is modest; for her keen, sagacious eye discerns that there are deep, undeveloped mysteries where the vain sciolist sees all plain. We call this an age of improvement, as it is. But the Italians, in the age of Leo X, and with great reason, said the same of their age; the Romans, in the time of Cicero, the same of theirs; the Greeks in the time of Pericles, the same of theirs; and the Assyrians and Egyptians, in the flourishing periods of their ancient monarchies, the same of theirs. In passing from one of these periods to another, prodigious strides are often made; and the vanity of the present age is apt to flatter itself, that it has climbed to the very summit of invention and skill. A wiser posterity at length finds out, that the discovery of one truth, the investigation of one law of nature, the contrivance of one machine, the perfection of one art, instead of narrowing, has widened the field of knowledge still to be acquired, and given, to those who came after, an ampler space, more numerous data, better instruments, a higher point of observation, and the encouragement of living and acting in the presence of a more intelligent age. It is not a century since the number of fixed stars was estimated at about three thousand. Newton had counted no more. When Dr. Herschel had completed his great telescope, and turned it to the heavens, he calculated that two hundred and fifty thousand stars passed through its field in a quarter of an hour!

It may not irreverently be conjectured to be the harmonious plan of the universe, that its two grand elements of mind and matter should be accurately adjusted to each other; that there should be full occupation in the physical world, in its laws and properties, and in the moral and social relations connected with it, for the contemplative and active powers of every created intellect. The imperfection of human institutions has, as far as man is concerned, disturbed the pure harmony of this great system. On the one hand, much truth, discoverable even at the present stage of human improvement, as we have every reason to think, remains undiscovered. On the other hand, thousands and millions of rational minds, for want of education, opportunity and encouragement, have remained dormant and inactive, though surrounded on every side by those qualities of things, whose action and combination, no doubt, still conceal the sublimest and most beneficial mysteries.

But a portion of the intellect, which has been placed on this goodly theatre, is wisely, intently, and successfully active; ripening, even on earth, into no mean similitude of higher natures. From time to time, a chosen hand, sometimes directed by chance, but more commonly guided by reflection, experiment, and research, touches, as it were, a spring until then unperceived; and, through what seemed a blank and impenetrable wall,—the barrier to all farther progress,—a door is thrown open into some before unexplored hall in the sacred temple of truth. The multitude rushes in, and wonders that the portals could have remained concealed so long. When a brilliant discovery or invention is proclaimed, men are astonished to think how long they have lived on its confines, without penetrating its nature.

It is now a hundred years since it was found out that the vapor of boiling water is, as we now think it, the most powerful mechanical agent within the control of man. And yet, even after the contrivance of the steam-engine on a most improved construction, and although the thoughts of numerous ingenious mechanicians were turned to the subject, and various experiments made, it was left for our fellow-citizen Fulton, in a successful application of this agent, as brilliant as its first discovery, to produce another engine,—the steamboat,—of incalculable utility and power. The entire consequences of this discovery cannot yet be predicted; but there is one prediction relative to it, and that among the first ever made, which has been most calamitously fulfilled. When the interests of Mr Fulton, under the laws of New York, were maintained by Mr Emmet at the bar of the legislature of that State, at the close of his argument, he turned to his client, in an affecting apostrophe. After commending the disinterestedness with which he devoted his time, talents and knowledge to enterprises and works of public utility, to the injury of his private fortunes, he added: ' Let me remind you, however, that you have other and closer ties. I know the pain I am about to give, and I see the tears I make you shed. But by that love I speak,—by that love, which, like the light of heaven, is refracted in rays of different strength, upon your wife and children, which, when collected and combined, forms the sunshine of your soul ;—by that love I do adjure you, provide in time for those dearest objects of your care. Think not I would instil into your mind a mean or sordid feeling; but now, that wealth is passing through your hands, let me entreat you to hoard it while you have it.' And then, after sketching the dangers which threatened his interests as guarantied by the laws of the State, Mr Emmet prophetically added: ' Yes, my friend, my heart bleeds while I utter it, but I have fearful forebodings, that you may hereafter find in public faith a broken staff for your support, and receive from public gratitude a broken heart for your reward.' From the time this prediction was uttered, the stupendous consequences of the invention of Fulton have been, every day, more and more amply developed. It has brought into convenient neighborhood with each other some of the remotest settlements on the waters of the United States. It has made the Mississippi navigable up stream as well as down, (which it hardly was before,) in credibly accelerating, in time of peace, the settlement of its mighty valley, and making it henceforth invulnerable in time of war. It has added beyond all estimate to the value of the time, and to the amount of the capital, of a large portion of the population of the country ; and, without impairing the importance of these benefits to America, has as signally imparted them, or similar benefits, to Europe, and the rest of the civilized world. While these grand developments of the character of Fulton's invention have been taking place, the life, the estate, the family of the great inventor, have, one after another, been sacrificed and crushed. Within a few months after the eloquent appeal just recited was made, Fulton actually died of disease contracted by exposure in the gratuitous service of the public. In a few years, a decision of the Supreme Court of the United States scattered the remains of his property to the winds ; and twice or thrice, since that period, has an appeal been made to Congress, on behalf of his orphan children, for such a provision as would spare them from the alternative of charity or starvation—and has been made in vain.*

But it is time to return to the facts with which I was illustrating the wonderful advances made, from time to time, in the cultivation or application of the most familiar arts. As far back as human history runs, the use of the distaff and loom is known ; but it is not yet one hundred years since Sir Richard Arkwright was born ; the poor journeyman barber, the youngest of thirteen children, who began and perfected the most important improvements in the machinery for manufacturing cotton, which (as has been stated on the most respectable English authority) 'bore the English nation triumphantly through the wars of the French revolution,' and are unquestionably of greater value to her than all her colonies, from Hindostan to Labrador.

The ocean which lies between America and Europe may be crossed in a fortnight ; but, after the fleets of Tyre, of Carthage, of Rome, and of the maritime powers of the middle ages, had been, for thousands of years, accustomed to navigate the sea, it was

---

* An application in favor of the family of Fulton was before Congress, at the time this discourse was pronounced, before the Columbian Institute, in the hall of the House of Representatives.

reserved for a poor Genoese pilot, begging his way from court to court, and by the simple process of sailing on one course as long as he had water to float his ship, to discover a new world.

Our geographical knowledge shows us that we do not, like so many generations of our predecessors, live within the reach of other undiscovered continents ; but we do unquestionably live, act, and speculate, within the reach of properties and powers of things, whose discovery and application (when they take place) will effect changes in society, as great as those produced by the magnet, the discovery of America, the art of printing, or the steamboat. We do doubtless live within the reach of undiscovered worlds of science, art, and improvement. No royal permission is requisite to launch forth on the broad sea of discovery that surrounds us,— most full of novelty where most explored,—and it may yet be reserved for the modest and secluded lover of truth and votary of science, in the solitude of his humble researches, to lay open such laws of matter, as will affect the condition of the civilized world.

This, then, is the encouragement we have to engage in any well-conceived enterprise for the diffusion of useful knowledge and the extension of general improvement. Wherever there is a human mind possessed of the common faculties, and placed in a body organized with the common senses, there is an active, intelligent being, competent, with proper cultivation, to the discovery of the highest truths, in the natural, the social, and the political world. It is susceptible of demonstration,—if demonstration were necessary,—that the number of useful and distinguished men, which are to benefit and adorn society around us, will be exactly proportioned, upon the whole, to the means and encouragements to improvement existing in the community ; and every thing, which multiplies these means and encouragements, tends, in the same proportion, to the multiplication of inventions and discoveries useful and honorable to man. The mind, although it does not stand in need of high cul-.ture, to the attainment of great excellence, does yet stand in need of some culture, and cannot thrive and act without it. When it is once awakened, and inspired with a consciousness of its own powers, and nourished into vigor by the intercourse of kindred minds, either through books or living converse, it does not disdain, but it needs not, further extraneous aid. It ceases to be a pupil ;

it sets up for itself; it becomes a master of truth, and goes fearlessly onward, sounding its way, through the darkest regions of investigation. But it is almost indispensable, that, in some way or other, the elements of truth should be imparted from kindred minds; and if these are wholly withheld, the intellect, which, if properly cultivated, might have soared with Newton to the boundaries of the comet's orbit, is chained down to the wants and imperfections of mere physical life, unconscious of its own capacities, and unable to fulfil its higher destiny.

Contemplate, at this season of the year, one of the magnificent oak trees of the forest, covered with thousands and thousands of acorns. There is not one of those acorns that does not carry within itself the germ of a perfect oak, as lofty and as wide spreading as the parent stock; which does not enfold the rudiments of a tree that would strike its roots in the soil, and lift its branches toward the heavens, and brave the storms of a hundred winters. It needs for this but a handful of soil, to receive the acorn as it falls, a little moisture to nourish it, and protection from violence till the root is struck. It needs but these; and these it does need, and these it must have; and for want of them, trifling as they seem, there is not one out of a thousand of those innumerable acorns, which is destined to become a tree.

Look abroad through the cities, the towns, the villages of our beloved country, and think of what materials their population, in many parts already dense, and every where rapidly growing, is, for the most part, made up. It is not lifeless enginery, it is not animated machines, it is not brute beasts, trained to subdue the earth: it is rational, intellectual beings. There is not a mind, of the hundreds of thousands in our community, that is not capable of making large progress in useful knowledge; and no one can presume to tell or limit the number of those who are gifted with all the talent required for the noblest discoveries. They have naturally all the senses and all the faculties—I do not say in as high a degree, but who shall say in no degree?—possessed by Newton, or Franklin, or Fulton. It is but a little which is wanted to awaken every one of these minds to the conscious possession and the active exercise of its wonderful powers. But this little, generally speaking, is indispensable. How much more wonderful an instrument is an eye than a telescope! Providence has furnished this eye; but art must contribute the telescope, or the wonders of the heavens remain unnoticed. It is for want of the little, that human means must add to the wonderful capacity for improvement born in man, that by far the greatest part of the intellect, innate in our race, perishes undeveloped and unknown. When an acorn falls upon an unfavorable spot, and decays there, we know the extent of the loss;—it is that of a tree, like the one from which it fell;—but when the intellect of a rational being, for want of culture, is lost to the great ends for which it was created, it is a loss which no one can measure, either for time or for eternity.

LECTURE

ON THE WORKING MEN'S PARTY, DELIVERED BEFORE THE CHARLES-
TOWN LYCEUM, 6TH OCTOBER, 1830.

MAN is, by nature, an active being. He is made to labor. His whole organization,—mental and physical,—is that of a hard-working being. Of his mental powers we have no conception, but as certain capacities of intellectual action. His corporeal faculties are contrived for the same end, with astonishing variety of adaptation. Who can look only at the muscles of the hand, and doubt that man was made to work? Who can be conscious of judgment, memory, and reflection, and doubt that man was made to act? He requires rest, but it is in order to invigorate him for new efforts; to recruit his exhausted powers; and, as if to show him, by the very nature of rest, that it is Means, not End:—that form of rest, which is most essential and most grateful, sleep, is attended with the temporary suspension of the conscious and active powers,—an image of death. Nature is so ordered, as both to require and encourage man to work.—He is created with wants, which cannot be satisfied without labor; at the same time, that ample provision is made by Providence, to satisfy them with labor. The plant springs up and grows on the spot, where the seed was cast by accident. It is fed by the moisture, which saturates the earth, or is held suspended in the air; and it brings with it a sufficient covering to protect its delicate internal structure. It toils not, neither doth it spin, for clothing or food. But man is so created, that, let his wants be as simple as they will, he must labor to sup-

33

ply them. If, as is supposed to have been the case in primitive ages, he lives upon acorns and water, he must draw the water from the spring; and, in many places, he must dig a well in the soil; and he must gather the acorns from beneath the oak, and lay up a store of them for winter. He must, in most climates, contrive himself some kind of clothing of barks or skins; must construct some rude shelter; prepare some kind of bed, and keep up a fire. In short, it is well known, that those tribes of our race, which are the least advanced in civilization, and whose wants are the fewest, have to labor the hardest for their support; but, at the same time, it is equally true, that, in the most civilized countries, by far the greatest amount and variety of work are done; so that the improvement, which takes place in the condition of man, consists, not in diminishing the amount of labor performed, but in enabling men to work more, or more efficiently, in the same time.—A horde of savages will pass a week in the most laborious kinds of hunting; following the chase day after day; their women, if in company with them, carrying their tents and their infant children on their backs; and all be worn down by fatigue and famine; and, in the end, they will, perhaps, kill a buffalo. The same number of civilized men and women would, probably, on an average, have kept more steadily at work, in their various trades and occupations, but with much less exhaustion; and the products of their industry would have been vastly greater; or, what is the same thing, much more work would have been done.

It is true, as man rises in improvement, he would be enabled, by his arts and machinery, to satisfy the primary wants of life, with less labor; and this may be thought to show, at first glance, that man was not intended to be a working being; because, in proportion as he advances in improvement, less work would be required to get a mere livelihood. But here we see a curious provision of nature. In proportion as our bare natural wants are satisfied, artificial wants, or civilized wants, show themselves. And, in the very highest state of improvement, it requires as constant an exertion to satisfy the new wants, which grow out of the habits and tastes of civilized life, as it requires, in savage life, to satisfy hunger and thirst, and keep from freezing. In other words, the innate desire of improving our condition keeps us all in a state of want. We cannot be so well off that we do not feel obliged to work, either to ensure the continuance of what we now have, or to increase it.— The man, whose honest industry just gives him a competence, exerts himself, that he may have something against a rainy day;— and how often do we not hear an affectionate father say, he is determined to spare no pains,—to work in season and out of season,—in order that his children may enjoy advantages denied to himself?

In this way, it is pretty plain, that Man, whether viewed in his primitive and savage state, or in a highly improved condition, is a working being. It is his destiny—the law of his nature—to labor. He is made for it,—and he cannot live without it; and the Apostle Paul summed up the matter, with equal correctness and point, when he said, that "if any would not work, neither should he eat."

It is a good test of principles like these, to bring them to the standard of general approbation or disapprobation. There are, in all countries, too many persons, who, from mistaken ideas of the nature of happiness, or other less reputable causes, pass their time in idleness, or in indolent pleasures; but I believe no state of society ever existed, in which the energy and capacity of labor were not commended and admired, or in which a taste for indolent pleasure was commended or admired by the intelligent part of the community. When we read the lives of distinguished men, in any department, we find them almost always celebrated for the amount of labor they could perform. Demosthenes, Julius Cæsar, Henry the Fourth of France, Lord Bacon, Sir Isaac Newton, Franklin, Washington, Napoleon,—different as they were in their intellectual and moral qualities,—were all renowned as hard workers. We read how many days they could support the fatigues of a march; how early they rose, how late they watched; how many hours they spent in the field, in the cabinet, in the court, in the study; how many secretaries they kept employed; in short, how hard they worked. But who ever heard of its being said of a man, in commendation, that he could sleep fifteen hours out of the twenty-four, that he could eat six meals a day, and that he never got tired of his easy-chair?

It would be curious to estimate, by any safe standard, the amount in value of the work of all kinds done in a community. This, of course, cannot be done with any great accuracy. The pursuits of men are so various, and the different kinds of labor performed are so different in the value of their products, that it is scarcely possible to bring the aggregate to any scale of calculation. If we would form a kind of general judgment of the value of the labor of a community, we must look about us. All the improvements, which we behold, on the face of the earth; all the buildings of every kind in town and country; all the vehicles employed on the land and water; the roads, the canals, the wharfs, the bridges; all the property of all kinds, which is accumulated throughout the world; and all that is consumed, from day to day and from hour to hour, to support those who live upon it,—all this is the product of labor; and a proportionate share is the product of the labor of each generation.—It is plain that this comprehensive view is one, that would admit of being carried out into an infinity of details, which would furnish the materials rather for a folio than a lecture. But as it is the taste of the present day, to bring every thing down to the standard of figures, I will suggest a calculation, which will enable us to judge of the value of the labor performed in the community in which we live.—Take the population of Massachusetts, for the sake of round numbers, at six hundred thousand souls. I presume it will not be thought extravagant to assume, that one in six performs every day a good day's work, or its equivalent. If we allow nothing for the labor of five out of six, (and this certainly will cover the cases of those too young and too old to do any work, or who can do only a part of a day's work,) and if we also allow nothing for those whose time is worth more than that of the day-laborer, we may safely assume, that the sixth person performs daily a vigorous efficient day's work of body or mind, by hand or with tools, or partly with each, and that this day's work is worth one dollar. This will give us one hundred thousand dollars a day, as the value of the work done in the State of Massachusetts. I have no doubt that it is a good deal more,—for this would be very little more than it costs the population to support itself, and allows scarce any thing for accumulation, a good deal of which is constantly taking place. It will, however, show sufficiently the great amount of the labor done in this State, to take it as coming up, at least, to one hundred thousand dollars per day.

I have thus far laid down two propositions :—

First, that man is, by his nature, a working being; and, second, that the daily value of his work, estimated merely in money, is immensely great in any civilized community.

I have made these preliminary remarks, as an introduction to some observations, which I propose to submit, in the remainder of this lecture, on the subject of 'a working men's party.'—Towards the organization of such a party, steps have been taken in various parts of the country. It is probable, that a great diversity of views exists, among those who have occupied themselves upon the subject, in different places. This circumstance, and the novelty of the subject in some of its aspects, and its importance in all, have led me to think, that we might pass an hour profitably, in its contemplation.

I will observe upon it, in the first place, then, that if, as I have endeavored to show, man is by nature a working being, it would follow, that a working men's party is founded in the very principles of our nature.—Most parties may be considered as artificial in their very essence; many are local, temporary and personal. What will all our political parties be, a hundred years hence? What are they now, in nine tenths of the habitable globe? Mere nonentities. —But the working men's party, however organized, is one that must subsist, in every civilized country, to the end of time. In other words, its first principles are laid in our nature.

It secondly follows, from what I have remarked above, that the working men's party concerns a vast amount of property, in which almost every man is interested; and in this respect it differs from all controversies and parties, which end merely in speculation, or which end in the personal advancement and gratification of a few individuals.

The next question, that presents itself, is, What is the general object of a working men's party? I do not now mean, what are the immediate steps, which such a party proposes to take; but what is the main object and end, which it would secure. To this I suppose I may safely answer, that it is not to carry this or that political election; not to elevate this or that candidate for office, but to promote the prosperity and welfare of working men; that is, to secure to every man disposed to work, the greatest freedom in the choice of his pursuit, the greatest encouragement and aid in pursuing it, the greatest security in enjoying its fruits:—in other words, to make *work*, in the greatest possible degree, produce *happiness*.

The next inquiry seems to be, Who belong to the working men's party? The general answer here is obvious,—All who do the work, or are actually willing and desirous to do it, and prevented only by absolute inability, such as sickness or natural infirmity. Let us try the correctness of this view, by seeing whom it would exclude and whom it would include.

This rule, in the first place, would exclude all bad men; that is, those who may work indeed, but who work for immoral and unlawful ends. This is a very important distinction, and if practically applied, and vigorously enforced, it would make the working men's party the purest society, that ever existed since the time of the primitive Christians. It is greatly to be feared, that scarce any of the parties, that divide the community, are sufficiently jealous on this point; and for the natural reason, that it does not lie in the very nature of the parties.—Thus, at the polls, the vote of one man is as good as the vote of another. The vote of the drunkard counts one; the vote of the temperate man counts *but* one. For this reason, the mere party politician, if he can secure the vote, is apt not to be very inquisitive about the temperance of the voter. He may even prefer the intemperate to the temperate; for to persuade the temperate man to vote with him, he must give him a good reason;—the other will do it for a good drink.

But the true principles of the working men's party require, not merely that a man should work, but that he should work in an honest way and for a lawful object. The man, who makes counterfeit money, probably works harder than the honest engraver, who prepares the bills, for those authorized by law to issue them. But he would be repelled with scorn, if he presented himself as a member of the working men's party. The thief, who passes his life, and gains a wretched, precarious subsistence, by midnight trespasses on his neighbor's grounds; by stealing horses from the stall, and wood from the pile; by wrenching bars and bolts at night, or picking pockets in a crowd, probably works harder, (taking uncertainty and anxiety into the calculation, and adding, as the usual consequence, four or five years in the compulsory service of the state,) than the average of men pursuing honest industry, even of the most laborious kind: but this hard work would not entitle him to be regarded as a member of the working men's party.

If it be inquired, who is to be the judge, what kind of work is not only no title, but an absolute disqualification for admission to the working men's party, on the score of dishonesty, we answer, that, for all practical purposes, this must be left to the law of the land. It is true, that under cover and within the pale of the law, a man may do things morally dishonest, and such as ought to shut him out of the party. But experience has shown, that it is dangerous to institute an inquisition into the motives of individuals; and so long as a man does nothing which the law forbids,—in a country where the people make the laws,—he ought, if not otherwise disqualified, to be admitted as a member of the party.

There ought, however, perhaps, to be two exceptions to this principle; one, in the case of those who pursue habitually a course of life, which, though contrary to law, is not usually punished by the law, such as persons habitually intemperate. It is plain, that these men ought not to be allowed to act with the party, because they would always be liable, by a very slight temptation, to be made to act in a manner hostile to its interests; and because they are habitually in a state of incapacity to do any intelligent and rational act.

The other exception ought to be of men who take advantage of the law to subserve their own selfish and malignant passions. This is done in various ways, but I will allude to but one. The law puts it in the power of the creditor, not merely to seize the property of the debtor, in payment of the debt, but to consider every case of inability as a case of fraudulent concealment, and to punish it, as such, by imprisonment. This is often done in a way to inflict the greatest possible pain, and in cases in which not only no advantage but additional cost accrues to the creditor. A man who thus takes the advantage of the law, to wreak upon others his malignant passions, ought to be excluded not merely from the working men's party, but from the pale of civilized society.

The next question regards idlers. If we exclude from the working men's party all dishonest and immoral workers, what are we to say to the case of the idlers?—In general terms, the answer to this question is plain; they too must be excluded. With what pretence of reason can an idler ask to be admitted into the association of working men, unless he is willing to qualify himself by going to work? and then he ceases to be an idler. In fact, the man who idles away his time, acts against the law of his nature, as a working being. It must be observed, however, that there are few cases where a man is *merely* an idler. In almost every case, he must be something worse,—such as a spendthrift, a gamester, or an intemperate person; a bad son, a bad husband, and a bad father. If there are any persons dependent on him for support; if he idles away the time which he ought to devote to maintaining his wife, or his children, or his aged parents, he then becomes a robber; a man that steals the bread out of the mouths of his own family, and rends the clothes off their backs; and he is as much more criminal than the common highway robber, who takes the stranger's purse on the turnpike road, as the ties of duty to our parents and children are beyond those of common justice between man and man. But I suppose it would not require much argument to show, that the person, who leaves to want those whom he ought to support, even if he does not pass his idle hours in any criminal pursuit, has no right to call himself a working man.

There is a third class of men, whose case deserves consideration, and who are commonly called busy-bodies.—They are as different from real working men, as light is from darkness. They cannot be called idlers, for they are never at rest; nor yet workers, for they pursue no honest, creditable employment. So long as they are merely busy-bodies, and are prompted in their officious, fluttering, unproductive activity, by no bad motive and no malignant passion, they cannot, perhaps, be excluded from the party, though they have really no claim to be admitted into it. But here, too, the case of a *mere* busy-body scarce ever occurs. This character is almost always something more; a dangerous gossip, a tattling mischief-maker, a propagator, too frequently, an inventor of slander. He repeats at one fire-side, with additions, what he heard at another, under the implied obligation of confidence; he is commonly in the front rank of all uneasy and inconsiderate movements, safely entrenched behind his neighbor, whom he pushes into trouble; and he is very fond of writing anonymous libels in the newspapers, on men of whom he knows nothing. Such men—and there are too many of them—ought to be excluded from the party.

Shutting out, then, all who work dishonestly, and all who do not work at all, and admitting the busy-bodies with great caution, the working men's party comprehends all those by whom the work of the community is really done ;—all those who, by any kind of honest industry, employ the talent which their Creator has given them. All these form one great party, one comprehensive society, and this by the very law of our nature. Man is not only, as I observed in the beginning, a working being; but he is a being formed to work in society ; and if the matter be carefully analyzed, it will be found, that civilization, that is, the bringing men out of a savage into a cultivated state, consists in multiplying the number of pursuits and occupations ; so that the most perfect society is one where the largest number of persons are prosperously employed, in the greatest variety of ways. In such a society, men help each other, instead of standing in each other's way. The farther this division of labor is carried, the more persons must unite, harmoniously, to effect the common ends. The larger the number, on which each depends, the larger the number to which each is useful.

This union of different kinds of workmen in one harmonious society seems to be laid, in the very structure and organization of man. Man is a being consisting of a body and a soul. These words are *soon* uttered, and they are so *often* uttered, that the mighty truth which is embraced in them, scarce ever engages our attention.—But man is composed of body and soul. What is body ? It is material substance ; it is clay, dust, ashes. Look at it, as you tread it, unorganized, beneath your feet ; contemplate it, when, after having been organized and animated, it is, by a process of corruption, returning to its original state. Matter, in its appearance to us, is an unorganized, inanimate, cold, dull, and barren thing. What it is in its essence, no one but the Being who created it knows. The human mind can conceive of it, but in a negative way. We say, that the body of man is formed of the clay or dust ; because these substances seem to us to make the nearest approach

34

to the total privation of all the properties of intellect. Such is the *body* of man.—What is his *soul?*—Its essence is as little known to us as that of body ; but its qualities are angelic, divine. It is soul, which thinks, reasons, invents, remembers, hopes, and loves. It is the soul which lives ; for when the soul departs from the body, all its vital powers cease ; and it is dead ;—and what is the body then ?

Now the fact, to which I wish to call your attention, is, that these two elements, one of which is akin to the poorest dust on which we tread, and the other of which is of the nature of angelic and even of divine intelligence, are, in every human being, without exception, brought into a most intimate and perfect union. We can conceive, that it might have been different. God could have created matter by itself and mind by itself. We believe in the existence of incorporeal beings, of a nature higher than man ; and we behold beneath us, in brutes, plants, and stones, various orders of material nature, rising, one above another, in organization ; but none of them (as we suppose) possessing mind.—We can imagine a world so constituted, that all the intellect would have been by itself, pure and disembodied ; and all the material substance by itself, unmixed with mind ; and acted upon by mind, as inferior beings are supposed to be acted upon by angels. But in constituting our race, it pleased the Creator to bring the two elements into the closest union ; to take the body from the dust ; the soul from the highest heaven ; and mould them into one.

The consequence is, that the humblest laborer, who works with his hands, possesses within him a soul, endowed with precisely the same faculties as those which, in Franklin, in Newton, or Shakspeare, have been the light and the wonder of the world ; and, on the other hand, the most gifted and ethereal genius, whose mind has fathomed the depths of the heavens and comprehended the whole circle of truth, is enclosed in a body, subject to the same passions, infirmities, and wants, as the man whose life knows no alternation but labor and rest, appetite and indulgence.

Did it stop here, it would be merely an astonishing fact in the constitution of our natures ;—but it does not stop here. In consequence of the union of the two principles in the human frame, every act that a man performs, requires the agency both of body

and mind.   His mind cannot see, but through the optic eye-glass ;
nor hear, till the drum of his ear is affected by the vibrations of the
air.   If he would speak, he puts in action the complex machinery
of the vocal organs ; if he writes, he employs the muscular system
of the hands ; nor can he even perform the operations of pure
thought, except in a healthy state of the body.   A fit of the tooth-
ache, proceeding from the irritation of a nerve about as big as a
cambric-thread, is enough to drive an understanding, capable of
instructing the world, to the verge of insanity.   On the other hand,
there is no operation of manual labor so simple, so mechanical,
which does not require the exercise of perception, reflection,
memory, and judgment ; the same intellectual powers, by which
the highest truths of science have been discovered and illustrated.

The degree to which any particular action (or series of actions
united into a pursuit) shall exercise the intellectual powers, on the
one hand, or the mechanical powers on the other, of course, depends on the nature of that action.   The slave, whose life, from
childhood to the grave, is passed in the field ; the New Zealander,
who goes to war, when he is hungry, devours his prisoners, and
leads a life of cannibal debauch till he has consumed them all, and
then goes to war again ; the Greenlander, who warms himself with
the fragments of wrecks and drift-wood thrown upon the glaciers,
and feeds himself with blubber ; seem all to lead lives requiring
but little intellectual action ; and yet, as I have remarked, a careful
reflection would show that there is not one, even of them, who
does not, every moment of his life, call into exercise, though in an
humble degree, all the powers of the mind.   In like manner, the
philosopher who shuts himself up in his cell, and leads a contemplative existence, among books or instruments of science, seems to
have no occasion to employ, in their ordinary exercise, many of
the capacities of his nature for physical action ;—although he also,
as I have observed, cannot act, or even think, but with the aid of
his body.

The same Creator who made man a mixed being, composed of
body and soul, having designed him for such a world as that in
which we live, has so constituted the world, and man who inhabits
it, as to afford scope for great variety of occupations, pursuits,
and conditions, arising from the tastes, characters, habits, virtues,

and even vices, of men and communities. For the same reason, that,—though all men are alike composed of body and soul, yet no two men probably are exactly the same in respect to either;—*so* provision has been made, by the Author of our being, for an infinity of pursuits and employments, calling out, in degrees as various, the peculiar powers of both principles.

But I have already endeavored to show, that there is no pursuit and no action that does not require the united operation of both; and this of itself is a broad natural foundation for the union into one interest of all, in the same community, who are employed in honest work of any kind; viz., that, however various their occupations, they are all working with the same instruments,—the organs of the body and the powers of the mind.

But we may go a step farther, to remark the beautiful process, by which Providence has so interlaced and wrought up together the pursuits, interests, and wants of our nature, that the philosopher, whose home seems less on earth than among the stars, requires, for the prosecution of his studies, the aid of numerous artificers in various branches of mechanical industry; and, in return, furnishes the most important facilities to the humblest branches of manual labor. Let us take, as a single instance, that of astronomical science. It may be safely said, that the wonderful discoveries of modern astronomy, and the philosophical system depending upon them, could not have existed, but for the *telescope*. The want of the telescope kept astronomical science in its infancy among the ancients. Although Pythagoras, one of the earliest Greek philosophers, by a fortunate exercise of sagacity, conceived the elements of the Copernican system, yet we find no general and practical improvement resulting from it. It was only from the period of the discoveries, made by the telescope, that the science advanced, with sure and rapid progress. Now the astronomer does not make telescopes. I presume it would be impossible for a person, who employed in the abstract study of astronomical science time enough to comprehend its profound investigations, to learn and practise the trade of making glass. It is mentioned, as a remarkable versatility of talent in a few eminent observers, that they have superintended the cutting and polishing the glasses or mirrors of their own telescopes. But I presume, if there never had been a telescope, till some scientific astronomer had learned to mix, melt, and mould glass, such a thing would never have been heard of. It is not less true, that those employed in making the glass could not, in the nature of things, be expected to acquire the scientific knowledge, requisite for carrying on those arduous calculations, applied to bring into a system the discoveries, made by the magnifying power of the telescope. I might extend the same remark to the other materials, of which a telescope consists. It cannot be used to any purpose of nice observation, without being very carefully mounted, on a frame of strong metal ; which demands the united labors of the mathematical instrument-maker and the brass-founder. Here then, in taking but one single step out of the philosopher's observatory, we find he needs an instrument, to be produced by the united labors of the mathematical instrument-maker, the brass-founder, the glass-polisher, and the maker of glass,—four trades.* He must also have an astronomical clock, and it would be easy to count up half a dozen trades, which directly or indirectly are connected in making a clock. But let us go back to the *object-glass* of the telescope. A glass factory requires a building and furnaces. The man who makes the glass, does not make the building. But the stone and brick mason, the carpenter, and the blacksmith, must furnish the greater part of the labor and skill, required to construct the building. When it is built, a large quantity of fuel, wood and wood-coal, or mineral coal of various kinds, or all together, must be provided ; and then the materials of which the glass is made, and with which it is colored, some of which are furnished by commerce from different and distant regions, and must be brought in ships across the sea. We cannot take up any one of *these* trades, without immediately finding that it connects itself with numerous others. Take, for instance, the mason who builds the furnace. He does not make his own bricks, nor burn his own lime ; in common cases, the bricks come from one place, the lime from another, the sand from another. The brick-maker does not cut down his own wood. It is carted or brought in boats to his brick-yard. The man who carts it, does not make his own wagon ; nor does the person, who

---

* The allusion is here to the simplest form of a telescope. The illustration would be stronger in the case of a reflector.

brings it in boats, build his own boat. The man, who makes the wagon, does not make its tire. The blacksmith, who makes the tire, does not smelt the ore; and the forgeman, who smelts the ore, does not build his own furnace (and there we get back to the point whence we started), nor dig his own mine. The man, who digs the mine, does not make the pick-axe, with which he digs it; nor the pump, with which he keeps out the water. The man, who makes the pump, did not discover the principle of atmospheric pressure, which led to pump-making; that was done by a mathematician at Florence, experimenting in his chamber, on a glass tube. And here we come back again to our glass; and to an instance of the close connexion of scientific research with practical art. It is plain, that this enumeration might be pursued, till every art and every science were shown to run into every other. No one can doubt this, who will go over the subject in his own mind, beginning with any one of the processes of mining and working metals, of ship-building, and navigation, and the other branches of art and industry, pursued in civilized communities.

If then, on the one hand, the astronomer depends for his telescope on the ultimate product of so many arts; in return, his observations are the basis of an astronomical system, and of calculations of the movements of the heavenly bodies, which furnish the mariner with his best guide across the ocean. The prudent shipmaster would no more think of sailing for India, without his Bowditch's *Practical Navigator*, than he would without his compass; and this Navigator contains tables, drawn from the highest walks of astronomical science. Every first mate of a vessel, who works a lunar observation, to ascertain the ship's longitude, employs tables, in which the most wonderful discoveries and calculations of La Place, and Newton, and Bowditch, are interwoven.

I mention this as but one of the cases, in which astronomical science promotes the service and convenience of common life; and perhaps, when we consider the degree to which the modern extension of navigation connects itself with industry in all its branches, this may be thought sufficient. I will only add, that the cheap convenience of an almanac, which enters into the comforts of every fireside in the country, could not be enjoyed, but for the labors and studies of the profoundest philosophers. Not that great learning or talent is now required to execute the astronomical calculations of an almanac, although no inconsiderable share of each is needed for this purpose; but because, even to perform these calculations requires the aid of tables, which have been gradually formed on the basis of the profoundest investigations of the long line of philosophers, who have devoted themselves to this branch of science. For, as we observed on the mechanical side of the illustration, it is not one trade alone, which is required to furnish the philosopher with his instrument, but a great variety; so, on the other hand, it is not the philosopher in one department, who creates a science out of nothing. The observing astronomer furnishes materials to the calculating astronomer, and the calculator derives methods from the pure mathematician; and a long succession of each for ages, must unite their labors, in a great result. Without the geometry of the Greeks, and the algebra of the Arabs, the infinitesimal analysis of Newton and Leibnitz would never have been invented.

Examples and illustrations equally instructive might be found in every other branch of industry. The man who will go into a cotton mill, and contemplate it from the great water-wheel, that gives the first movement, (and still more, from the steam-engine, should that be the moving power,) who will observe the parts of the machinery, and the various processes of the fabric, till he reaches the hydraulic press, with which it is made into a bale, and the canal or rail-road by which it is sent to market, may find every branch of trade and every department of science literally crossed, intertwined, interwoven with every other, like the woof and the warp of the article manufactured. Not a little of the spinning machinery is constructed on principles drawn from the demonstrations of transcendental mathematics; and the processes of bleaching and dying, now practised, are the results of the most profound researches of modern chemistry. And if this does not satisfy the inquirer, let him trace the cotton to the plantation, where it grew, in Georgia or Alabama; the indigo to Bengal; the oil to the olive-gardens of Italy, or the fishing-grounds of the Pacific ocean; let him consider Whitney's cotton-gin; Whittemore's carding-machine; the power-loom; and the spinning apparatus; and all the arts, trades, and sciences, directly or indirectly connected with these; and I believe he will soon agree, that one might start from a yard of coarse printed cotton, which costs ten cents, and prove out of it, as out of a text, that every art and science under heaven had been concerned in its fabric.

I ought here to allude, also, to some of those pursuits which require the ability to exercise, at the same time, on the part of the same individual, the faculties, both of the intellectual and physical nature,—or which unite very high and low degrees of mental power. I have no doubt, that the talent for drawing and painting, possessed by some men to such an admirable degree, depends partly on a peculiar organic structure of the eye, and of the muscles of the hand, which gives them their more delicate perceptions of color, and their greater skill in delineation. These, no doubt, are possessed by many individuals, who want the intellectual talent,—the poetic fire, —required for a great painter. On the other hand, I can conceive of a man's possessing the invention and imagination of a painter, without the eye and the hand required to embody on the canvass the ideas and images in his mind. When the two unite, they make a Raphael or a Titian ; a Wilkie or an Allston. An accomplished statuary, such as Canova or Chantrey, must, on the one hand, possess a soul filled with all grand and lovely images, and have a living conception of ideal beauty ; and, on the other hand, he must be a good stone-cutter, and able to take a hammer and a chisel in his hand, and go to work on a block of marble, and chip it down to the lip of Apollo, or the eyelid of Venus. The architect must be practically acquainted with all the materials of building,—wood, brick, mortar and stone ; he must have the courage and skill to plant his moles against the heaving ocean, and to hang his ponderous domes and gigantic arches in the air ; while he must have taste to combine the rough and scattered blocks of the quarry into beautiful and majestic structures ; and discern clearly in his mind's eye, before a sledge-hammer has been lifted, the elevation and proportions of the temple. The poet must know, with a schoolmaster's precision, the weight of every word, and what vowel follows most smoothly on what consonant ; at the same time, that his soul must be stored with images, feelings, and thoughts, beyond the power of the boldest and most glowing language to do more than faintly shadow out. The surgeon must, at once, have a mind naturally gifted and diligently trained, to penetrate the dark recesses of organic life; and a nerve and tact, which will enable him to guide his knife among veins and arteries, out of sight, in the living body of an agonizing, shrieking fellow creature, or to take a lancet in his left hand, and cut into the apple of the eye. The lawyer must be able to reason from the noblest principles of human duty, and the most generous feelings of human nature; he must fully comprehend the mighty maze of the social relations; he must carry about with him a stock of learning almost boundless; he must be a sort of god to men and communities, who look up to him, in the hour of the dearest peril of their lives and fortunes; and he must, at the same time, be conversant with a tissue of the most senseless fictions and arbitrary technology, that ever disgraced a liberal science. The merchant must be able to look, at the same moment, at the markets and exchanges of distant countries and other hemispheres, and combine considerations of the political condition, the natural wants, the tastes and habits of different parts of the world; and he must be expert at figures,—understand bookkeeping by double entry,—and know as well how to take care of a quarter chest of tea as a cargo of specie. The general-in-chief must be capable of calculating, for a twelve-month in advance, the result of a contest, in which all the power, resource, and spirit of two great empires enter and struggle, on land and by sea; and he must have an eye, that can tell, at a glance, and on the responsibility of his life, how the stone walls, and trenched meadows, the barns, and the woods, and the cross-roads of a neighborhood, will favor or resist the motions of a hundred thousand men, scattered over a space of five miles, in the fury of the advance, the storm of battle, the agony of flight, covered with smoke, dust and blood.

It was my intention to subject the art of printing to an analysis of the trades, arts and sciences connected with it; but I have not time to do it full justice, and the bare general idea need not be repeated. I will only say that, beginning with the invention which bears, in popular tradition, the name of Cadmus,—I mean the invention of alphabetical signs to express sounds,—and proceeding to the discovery of convenient materials for writing, and the idea of written discourse; thence to the preparation of manuscript books; and thence to the fabric, on a large scale, of linen and cotton pa-

35

per, the invention of movable types, and the printing press, the art of engraving on metal, of stereotype printing, and of the power press,—we have a series of discoveries, branching out into others in every department of human pursuit; connecting the highest philosophical principles with the results of mere manual labor, and producing, in the end, that system of diffusing and multiplying the expression of thought, which is, perhaps, the glory of our human nature. Pliny said, that the Egyptian reed was the support on which the immortal fame of man rested. He referred to its use in the manufacture of paper. We may, with greater justice, say as much of the manufacture of paper from rags, and of the printing press, neither of which was known to Pliny. But with all the splendor of modern discoveries and improvements in science and art, I cannot but think that he who, in the morning of the world, first conceived the idea of representing sounds by visible signs, took the most important step in the march of improvement. This sublime conception was struck out in the infancy of mankind. The name of its author, his native country, and the time when he lived, are known only by very uncertain tradition; but though all the intelligence of ancient and modern times, and in the most improved countries, has been concentred into a focus, burning and blazing upon this one spot, it has never been able to reduce it to any simpler elements, nor to improve, in the slightest degree, upon the original suggestion of Cadmus.

In what I have thus far submitted to you, you will probably have remarked, that I have illustrated chiefly the connexion with each other of the various branches of science and art; of the intellectual and physical principles. I have not distinctly shown the connexion of the moral principle, in all its great branches, with both. This subject would well form the matter of a separate essay. But its elementary ideas are few and plain. The arts and sciences, whose connexion we have pointed out, it is plain, require for their cultivation a civilized state of society. They cannot thrive in a community which is not in a state of regular political organization, under an orderly system of government, uniform administration of laws, and a general observance of the dictates of public and social morality. Farther, such a community cannot exist without institutions of various kinds for elementary, professional, and moral education; and connected with these, are required the services of a large class of individuals, employed in various ways, in the business of instruction; from the meritorious schoolmaster, who teaches the little child its A, B, C, to the moralist, who lays down the great principles of social duty for men and nations, and the minister of divine truth, who inculcates those sanctions, by which God himself enforces the laws of reason. There must also be a class of men, competent by their ability, education, and experience, to engage in the duty of making and administering the law; for, in a lawless society, it is impossible that any improvement should be permanent. There must be another class competent to afford relief to the sick, and thus protect our frail natures from the power of the numerous foes that assail them.

It needs no words to show, that all these pursuits are, in reality, connected with the ordinary work of society, as directly as the mechanical trades by which it is carried on. For instance, nothing would so seriously impair the prosperity of a community, as an unsound and uncertain administration of justice. This is the last and most fatal symptom of decline in a state. A community can bear a very considerable degree of political despotism, if justice is duly administered between man and man. But where a man has no security, that the law will protect him in the enjoyment of his property; where he cannot promise himself a righteous judgment in the event of a controversy with his neighbor; where he is not sure, when he lies down at night, that his slumbers are safe, there he loses the great motives to industry and probity; credit is shaken; enterprise disheartened, and the state declines. The profession, therefore, which is devoted to the administration of justice, renders a service to every citizen of the community, as important as to those whose immediate affairs require the aid of counsel.

In a very improved and civilized community, there are also numerous individuals, who, without being employed in any of the common branches of industry, or of professional pursuit, connect themselves, nevertheless, with the prosperity and happiness of the public, and fill a useful and honorable place in its service. Take, for instance, a man like Sir Walter Scott, who, probably, never did a day's work in his life, in the ordinary acceptation of the term, and who has for some years retired from the subordinate station he filled in the profession of the law, as sheriff of the county and clerk of the Court. He has written and published at least two hundred volumes of wide circulation. What a vast amount of the industry of the community is thereby put in motion!—The book-sellers, printers, paper-makers, press-makers, type-makers, book-binders, leather-dressers, ink-makers, and various other artisans re-quired, to print, publish, and circulate the hundreds and thousands of volumes of the different works which he has written, must be almost numberless. I have not the least doubt, that, since the se-ries of his publications begun, if all whose industry,—directly or remotely,—has been concerned in them, not only in Great Britain, but in America, and on the continent of Europe, could be brought together, and stationed side by side, as the inhabitants of the same place, they would form *a very considerable town.* Such a person may fairly be ranked as a working man.

And yet I take this to be the least of Sir Walter Scott's deserts. I have said nothing of the service rendered to every class, and to every individual in every class, by the writer, who beguiles of their tediousness the dull hours of life; who animates the principle of goodness within us, by glowing pictures of struggling virtue; who furnishes our young men and women with books, which they may read with interest, and not have their morals poisoned as they read them. Our habits, our principles, our characters,—whatever may be our pursuit in life,—depend very much on the nature of our youthful pleasures, and on the mode in which we learn to pass our leisure hours. And he who, with the blessing of Providence, has been able, by his mental efforts, to present virtue in her strong at-tractions, and vice in her native deformity, to the rising generation, has rendered a service to the public, greater even than his, who in-vented the steam-engine, or the mariner's compass.

I have thus endeavored to show, in a plain manner, that there is a close and cordial union between the various pursuits and occupa-tions, which receive the attention of men in a civilized community: —that they are links of the same chain, every one of which is essential to its strength.

It will follow, as a necessary consequence; as the dictate of rea-son and as the law of nature;—that every man in society, whatev-er his pursuit, who devotes himself to it, with an honest purpose, and in the fulfilment of the social duty which Providence devolves upon him, is entitled to the good fellowship of each and every other member of the community ;—that all are the parts of one whole, and that between those parts, as there is but one interest, so there should be but one feeling.

Before I close this lecture, permit me to dwell for a short time on the principle, which I have had occasion to advance above, that the immortal element of our nature,—the reasoning soul,—is the inheritance of all our race. As it is this which makes man superior to the beasts that perish; so it is this, which, in its moral and intellectual endowments, is the sole foundation for the only distinctions between man and man, which have any real value. This consideration shows the value of institutions for education and for the diffusion of knowledge. It was no magic, no miracle, which made Newton, and Franklin, and Fulton. It was the patient, judicious, long-continued cultivation of powers of the understanding, eminent, no doubt, in degree, but not differing in kind, from those which are possessed by every individual in this assembly.

Let every one, then, reflect, especially every person not yet past the forming period of his life, that he carries about in his frame, as in a casket, the most glorious thing, which, this side heaven, God has been pleased to create,—an intelligent spirit. To describe its nature, to enumerate its faculties, to set forth what it has done, to estimate what it can do, would require the labor of a life devoted to the history of man. It would be vain, on this occasion, and in these limits, to attempt it. But let any man compare his own nature with that of a plant, of a brute beast, of an idiot, of a savage ; and then consider that it is in mind alone, and the degree to which he improves it, that he differs essentially from any of them.

And let no one think he wants opportunity, encouragement, or means. I would not undervalue these, any or all of them; but, compared with what the man does for himself, they are of little account. Industry, temperance, and perseverance are worth more than all the patrons that ever lived in all the Augustan ages. It is these that create patronage and opportunity. The cases of our Franklin and Fulton are too familiar to bear repetition. Consider that of Sir Humphrey Davy, who died last year, and who was, in some departments of science, the first philosopher of the age.* He was born at Penzance in Cornwall, one of the darkest corners of England ; his father was a carver of wooden images for signs, and figure-heads, and chimney-pieces. He himself was apprenticed to an apothecary, and made his first experiments in chemistry with his master's phials and gallipots, aided by an old syringe, which had been given him by the surgeon of a French vessel, wrecked on the Land's End. From the shop of the apothecary, he was transferred to the office of a surgeon ; and never appears to have had any other education than that of a Cornish school, in his boyhood. Such was the beginning of the career of the man, who, at the age of twenty-two, was selected, by our own countryman, Count Rumford, (himself a self-taught benefactor of mankind,) to fill the chair of chemistry at the Royal Institution, in London ; such was the origin and education of the man who discovered the metallic basis of the alkalis and the earths ; invented the safety-lamp ; and placed himself, in a few years, in the chair of the Royal Society of London, and at the head of the chemists of Europe. Sir Humphrey Davy's most brilliant discoveries were effected by his skilful application of the galvanic electricity,—a principle, whose existence had been detected, a few years before, by an Italian philosopher, from noticing the contractions of a frog's limb ;—a fact, which shows how near us, in every direction, the most curious facts lie scattered by nature. With an apparatus, contrived by himself, to collect and condense this powerful agent, Sir Humphrey succeeded in decomposing the earths and the alkalis ; and in extracting from common potash, the metal (before unknown) which forms it base ;— possessing, at 70° of the thermometer, the lustre and general appearance of mercury ; at 50°, the appearance of polished silver, and the softness of wax ; so light that it swims in water ; and so inflammable that it takes fire when thrown on ice.

These are, perhaps, but brilliant novelties ; though connected, no doubt, in the great chain of cause and effect, with principles of art and science, conducive to the service of man. But the invention of the safety-lamp, which enables the miner to walk with safe-

---

* The sketch of Sir Humphrey Davy, which follows, to the end of the lecture, is abridged from the article in the Annual Biography, for 1830.

ty through an atmosphere of explosive gas, and has already preserved the lives of hundreds of human beings, is a title to glory and the gratitude of his fellow men, which the most renowned destroyer of his race might envy.

The counsels of such a man, in his retirement and meditation, are worth listening to. I am sure you will think I bring this lecture to the best conclusion, by repeating a sentence from one of his moral works :—

' I envy,' says he, ' no quality of the mind or intellect in others ; not genius, power, wit, or fancy ; but if I could choose what would be most delightful, and I believe, most useful to me, I should prefer A FIRM RELIGIOUS BELIEF to every other blessing.'

AN

ADDRESS

DELIVERED AS THE INTRODUCTION TO THE FRANKLIN LECTURES,
IN BOSTON, NOVEMBER 14, 1831.

———

NOTWITHSTANDING the numerous institutions, for promoting useful knowledge, in our community, it was still found, that many were excluded from the benefit of them. The number of persons that can be accommodated in any one hall, is, of course, limited ; and it has been thought desirable to make the attempt to provide an additional course of lectures, on the various branches of useful knowledge, for the benefit of those, who have not had it in their power, for this or any other reason, to obtain access to the other institutions, which have set so praiseworthy an example, in this work of public utility. We are assembled, this evening, to make the beginning of this new course of popular instruction.

The plan of this course of lectures was suggested at so late a period, this year, that it may not, perhaps, be possible, the present season, to carry it fully into effect, in such a manner as is wished and designed, in reference to the choice and variety of subjects. It is intended, eventually, that it should extend to the various branches of natural science. It will impart useful information, relative to the Earth, the Air, and the Ocean ; the wonders of the heavens ; and the mineral treasures beneath the surface of the globe. It may extend to the different branches of natural history, and acquaint you with the boundless variety of the animated creation. The various properties of natural bodies will form a prominent subject of consideration, as the basis of so many of the arts and trades, and the sources from which so many of the wants of man are supplied. In like manner, those natural powers and properties of matter, the agency of fire, water, steam, and weight, which, in their various combinations, produce the wonders of improved machinery, by which industry is facilitated, and the most important fabrics are furnished cheaply and abundantly, will not be overlooked. It may be supposed, that a due share of attention will be paid to the geographical survey of the globe, to the history of our own race, the fortunes of the several nations, into which mankind have been divided, and the characters of great and good men, who, long after they have departed from life, survive in the gratitude and admiration of their fellow-men. A general and intelligible view of the constitution and laws of the country, in which we have the happiness to live, tending, as it will, to enlighten us in the discharge of our duties as citizens, will no doubt be presented to you, by some, who will take a part in these lectures. Nor will they, I venture to hope, be brought to a close, without having occasionally directed your thoughts to those views of our common nature, which belong to us as rational and immortal beings, and to those duties and relations which appertain to us as accountable agents.

The general plan of these lectures extends to these and all other branches of sound and useful knowledge; to be treated in such order, as circumstances may suggest; and with such variety and selection of subjects and fulness of detail, as the convenience of the lecturers and the advantage of the audience may dictate. They have been called the *Franklin Lectures*, in honor of our distinguished townsman, the immortal Franklin, the son of a tallow-chandler, and the apprentice to a printer in this town;—a man, who passed all his early years, and a very considerable portion of his life, in manual industry; and who was chiefly distinguished by his zealous and successful efforts for the promotion of useful knowledge. His name has given lustre to the highest walks of science, and adorns one of the proudest pages of the history of our country, and the world. But we have thought it was still more a name of hope and promise, for an institution like this, which aims to promote useful knowledge, (the great study of his life,) among that

36

class of our fellow-citizens, from which it was ever his pride himself to have sprung.

It would seem, at the commencement of a course of public instruction of this kind, a pertinent inquiry, *Why* should we endeavor to cultivate and inform our minds, by the pursuit of knowledge?

This question, to which the good sense of every individual furnishes, without meditation, some general reply, demands a full and careful answer. I shall endeavor, in this address, to state some of the reasons, which go to furnish such an answer.

All men should seek to cultivate and inform their minds, by the pursuit of useful knowledge, as the great means of happiness and usefulness.

All other things being equal, the pursuit and attainment of knowledge are, at the time, the surest source of happiness. I do not mean, that knowledge will make up for the want of the necessaries and comforts of life : it will not relieve pain, heal sickness, nor bring back lost friends. But if knowledge will not do this, ignorance will do it still less. And it may even be affirmed, and all who have made the experiment themselves will testify to the truth of the remark, that nothing tends more to soothe the wounded feelings, to steal away the mind from its troubles, and to fill up the weariness of a sick chamber and a sick bed, than, for instance, some intelligible, entertaining, good book, read or listened to.

But knowledge is still more important, as the means of being useful ; and the best part of the happiness, which it procures us, is of that purer and higher kind, which flows from the consciousness that, in some way or other, by good example or positive service, we have done good to our fellow-men. One of the greatest modern philosophers said, that *knowledge is power;* but it is power because it is usefulness. It gives men influence over their fellow-men, because it enables its possessors to instruct, to counsel, to direct, to please, and to serve their fellow-men. Nothing of this can be done, without the cultivation and improvement of the mind.

It is the mind, which enables us to be useful, even with our bodily powers. What is strength without knowledge to apply it ? What are the curiously organized hands, without skill, to direct their motion ? The idiot has all the bodily organs and senses of the most intelligent and useful citizen.

It is through mind, that man has obtained the mastery of nature and all its elements, and subjected the inferior races of animals to himself. Take an uninformed savage, a brutalized Hottentot, in short, any human being, in whom the divine spark of reason has never been kindled to a flame ; and place him on the sea-shore, in a furious storm, when the waves are rolling in, as if the fountains of the deep were broken up. Did you not know, from certain experience, that man, by the cultivation of his mind, and the application of his useful arts, had actually constructed vessels, in which he floats securely on the top of these angry waves, you would not think it possible that a being, like that we have mentioned, could for one moment resist their fury. It is actually related of some of the North American Indians, a race of men, who are trained, from their infancy, to the total suppression of their emotions of every kind, and who endure the most excruciating torments, at the stake, without signs of suffering, that when they witnessed, for the first time, on the western waters of the United States, the spectacle of a steamboat under way, moving along without sails or oars, and spouting fire and smoke, even they could not refrain from exclamations of wonder. Hold out a handful of wheat, or Indian corn, to a person wholly uninformed of their nature, and ignorant of the mode of cultivating them, and tell him, that by scattering these dry kernels abroad, and burying them in the cold damp earth, you can cause a harvest to spring up, sufficient for a winter's supply of food, and he will think you are mocking him, by vain and extravagant tales. But it is not the less true, that in these, and in every other instance, it is the mind of man, possessed of the necessary knowledge and skill, that brings into useful operation, for the supply of human want, and the support and comfort of human life, the properties and treasures of the natural world, the aid of inferior animals, and even our own physical powers.

When, therefore, we improve our minds, by the acquisition of useful knowledge, we appropriate to ourselves, and extend to others, to whom we may impart our knowledge, a share of this natural control over all other things, which Providence has granted to his rational children.

It cannot, it is true, be expected to fall to the lot of many individuals, by extending their knowledge of the properties and laws of the natural world, to strike out new discoveries and inventions, of the highest importance. It is as much as most men can hope, and promise themselves, to be enabled to share the comfort and benefit of the unnumbered improvements, which, from the beginning of time, have been made by others; and which, taken together, make up the civilization of man. Still, there are examples, in almost every age, of men, who, by the happy effects of their individual pursuit of useful knowledge, have conferred great benefits upon all mankind. I presume, that in consequence of the success of Arkwright, in inventing the machinery for spinning cotton, of Cartwright, in inventing the power-loom, and our own countryman Whitney, in inventing a machine for preparing cotton, the expense of necessary clothing is diminished two thirds for every man in Europe and America. In other words, the useful knowledge acquired and imparted to the world, by these three men, has enabled every man, woman, and child in the civilized world, as far as clothing is concerned, to live at one third of the former cost. We are struck with astonishment when we behold these curious machines; when we look, for instance, at a watch, and see a few brass wheels, put in motion by a little bit of elastic steel, counting out the hours and minutes, by night and by day, and even enabling the navigator to tell how many miles he has sailed, upon the waste ocean, where there are no marks or monuments, by which he can measure his progress. But how much more wonderful is the mind of man, which, in the silence of the closet, turned in upon itself, and deeply meditating upon the properties and laws of matter, has contrived this wonderful machine!

The invention of the power-loom, by Mr Cartwright, beautifully illustrates the strength and reach of the intellectual principle, resolutely applied to a given object. In consequence of Arkwright's machinery for spinning, it was soon found, that there would be a difficulty in weaving all the yarn that could be spun. It was remarked in a company, where Mr Cartwright was present, in 1784, that, in order to remedy this evil, Mr Arkwright must exercise his ingenuity, and invent a weaving mill, in order to work up the yarn, which should be spun in his spinning mills. The subject was discussed; and it was pronounced by the gentlemen present, who were manufacturers from Manchester, in England, to be impossible. Mr Cartwright thought otherwise: he said there had been lately exhibited in London, a machine for playing chess; and he felt quite sure, that it could not be more difficult to construct a machine to weave cloth, than a machine, which could go through all the movements of such a complicated game. Mr Cartwright was a clergyman, forty years old, and had never given his attention to the subject of machinery. This subject, however, was so strongly on his mind, that some time afterwards, he resolved to make the attempt, to invent a weaving machine. He had not, at that time, it appears, ever seen even a common loom. But reasoning upon the nature of the processes, necessary to be gone through to cross the threads, in such a way as to make a piece of cloth, he hit upon the plan of a loom, and, with the assistance of a carpenter and blacksmith, he made one. It was a very rude machine. 'The warp,' says Mr Cartwright, 'was laid perpendicularly; the reed fell with a force of at least half a hundred weight, and the springs which threw the shuttle, were strong enough to throw a congreve rocket.' Besides this, it required the strength of two powerful men to work it, and that at a slow rate, and for a short time. But the principle was there. Mr Cartwright now went and examined the looms of common form, and soon succeeded in constructing one very nearly resembling the power-looms which are now in use. In the account of this interesting invention, which I am quoting,* it is said that 'Dr Cartwright's children still remember often seeing their father, about this time, walking to and fro, in deep meditation, and occasionally throwing his arms from side to side, on which they used to be told, that he was thinking of weaving and throwing the shuttle.' Some time after he had brought his first loom to perfection, a manufacturer, who had called upon him to see it at work, after expressing his admiration at the ingenuity displayed in it, remarked, that wonderful as Mr Cartwright's mechanical skill was, there was one thing that would effectually baffle him, and that was the weaving of patterns in checks, or, in other words, the combining in the same

* Library of Entertaining Knowledge, Vol. viii, p. 347. Second American edition.

web, of a pattern or fancy figure, with the crossing colors that make the check. Mr Cartwright made no reply to this observation, at the time ; but, some weeks after, on receiving a second visit, from the same person, he had the pleasure of showing him a piece of muslin, of the description mentioned, beautifully woven by machinery. The man was so much astonished, that he declared, that something more than human agency must have been concerned in the fabric.

The wonderful results of the sagacity and perseverance of Fulton, in carrying into effect the conceptions of his mind, on the subject of steam navigation, still more nobly illustrate the creative power of the human intellect ; but it is a matter too familiar to need comment.

But it must not be supposed, from the instances I have chosen, to show the amount of good, which may be done by the exercise of the mental powers, that it is confined to the material comforts of life ; to steamboats, looms, or machinery for spinning. Far from it. The true and most peculiar province of its efficacy is the moral condition. Think of the inestimable good conferred on all succeeding generations, by the early settlers of America, who first established the system of public schools, where instruction should be furnished, *gratis*, to all the children in the community. No such thing was before known in the world. There were schools and colleges, supported by funds, which had been bequeathed by charitable individuals ; and, in consequence, most of the common schools of this kind in Europe, were regarded as a kind of pauper establishments, to which it was not respectable to have recourse. So deep-rooted is this idea, that, when I have been applied to for information, as to our public schools, from those parts of the United States, where no such system exists, I have frequently found it hard to obtain credit, when 1 have declared, that there was nothing disreputable, in the public opinion here, in sending children to schools supported at the public charge. The idea of such schools, therefore, when it first crossed the minds of our forefathers, was entirely original ; but how much of the prosperity and happiness of their children, and posterity, has flowed from this living spring of public intelligence ! So, too, the plan of Sunday schools, which have proved a blessing of inestimable value, in Europe and America, and particularly to thousands, who are deprived of the advantages of other institutions. It is probable, that instruction is now given, in the Sunday schools, to more than a million and a half of pupils, by more than one hundred and fifty thousand teachers. This plan was the happy suggestion of an humble individual,—a printer,—who contemplated, at first, nothing but the education of the destitute and friendless children in his immediate neighborhood. After laboring in this noble field of usefulness for twenty years, and among the class of population most exposed to the temptations to crime, he had the satisfaction of being able to say, that out of three thousand scholars, he had heard of but one, who had been sent to jail, as a criminal.* Who would not be ashamed to compare the pure and happy renown of the man, who had extended, by the suggestion of this simple, but before untried plan of education, the blessings of instruction to a million and a half of his fellow-creatures, with the false and unmerited glory, which has been awarded to conquerors, whose wars have hurried their millions of victims to cruel and untimely death !

This topic might be illustrated, perhaps, still more powerfully, by depicting the evils which flow from ignorance. These are deplorable enough in the case of the individual; although, if he

* See a very interesting address, at the celebration of the Sunday School jubilee, or the fiftieth year from the institution of Sunday schools, by Robert Raikes: delivered at Charleston, S. C., Sept. 14, 1831, by the Hon. Thomas Smith Grimke. I find, however, the following statement in a public print, of the accuracy of which I have no means of judging:—

'The credit of originating these institutions has usually been given to Mr Raikes, a newspaper proprietor of Gloucester, who died some years ago. It now appears, however, from statements and documents of unquestionable authenticity, that the plan of the first school of this description, which was established in Gloucester, in 1780, originated with the Rev. Thomas Stock, head master of the cathedral school of that city. Mr Stock, who was in narrow circumstances, communicated the details of his plan to Mr Raikes, when the latter assisted him with his purse; and, having taken a very active and zealous part, in promoting the establishment of Sunday schools, he ultimately obtained all the merit of being their founder. Mr Raikes, who is undoubtedly entitled to much credit, for his benevolent exertions in the cause of education, lived to see 250,000 children enrolled in these schools. The number now enjoying the benefit of instruction on the Sabbath, in England, is 1,250,000. At Birmingham, the system has been carried to a much greater extent, than in any other town in England, nearly 13,000 Sunday school pupils having been mustered there, on the occasion of the late jubilee.'

live surrounded by an intelligent community, the disastrous consequences are limited. But the general ignorance of large numbers and entire classes of men, acting under the unchastened stimulus of the passions, and excited by the various causes of discontent, which occur in the progress of human affairs, is often productive of scenes, which make humanity shudder. I know not, that I could produce a more pertinent illustration of this truth, than may be found in the following extract from a foreign journal. It relates to the outrages, committed by the peasantry, in a part of Hungary, in consequence of the ravages of the cholera in that region.

'The suspicion, that the cholera was caused by poisoning the wells, was universal among the peasantry of the counties of Zips and Zemplin, and every one was fully convinced of its truth. The first commotion arose in Klucknow, where, it is said, some peasants died in consequence of taking the preservatives; whether by an immoderate use of medicine, or whether they thought they were to take chlorate of lime internally, is not known. This story, with a sudden and violent breaking out of cholera at Klucknow, led the peasants to a notion of the poisoning of the wells, which spread like lightning. In the sequel, upon the attack of the estate of Count Czaki, a servant of the chief bailiff was on the point of being murdered, when, to save his life, he offered to disclose something important. He said, that he received from his master two pounds of poisonous powder, with orders to throw it into the wells, and, with an axe over his head, took oath publicly in the church, to the truth of his statement. These circumstances, and the fact, that the peasants, when they forcibly entered the houses of the land-owners, every where found chlorate of lime, which they took for the poisonous powder, confirmed their suspicions, and drove the people to madness. In this state of excitement, they committed the most appalling excesses. Thus, for instance, when a detachment of thirty soldiers, headed by an ensign, attempted to restore order in Klucknow, the peasants, who were ten times their number, fell upon them; the soldiers were released, but the ensign was bound, tortured with scissors and knives, then beheaded, and his head fixed on a pike, as a trophy. A civil officer, in company with the military, was drowned, his carriage broken, and chlorate of lime being found in the carriage, one of the inmates was compelled to eat it till he vomited blood, which again confirmed the notion of poison. On the attack of the house of the Lord at Klucknow, the Countess saved her life by piteous entreaties ; but the chief bailiff, in whose house chlorate of lime was unhappily found, was killed, together with his son, a little daughter, a clerk, a maid, and two students, who boarded with him. So the bands went from village to village ; wherever a nobleman or a physician was found, death was his lot ; and in a short time, it was known that the high constable of the county of Zemplin, several counts, nobles, and parish priests had been murdered. A clergyman was hanged, because he refused to take an oath that he had thrown poison into the well ; the eyes of a countess were put out, and innocent children cut to pieces. Count Czaki, having first ascertained that his family was safe, fled from his estate, at the risk of his life, but was stopped at Kirchtrauf, pelted with stones, and wounded all over, torn from his horse, and only saved by a worthy merchant, who fell on him, crying, " Now I have got the rascal." He drew the count into a neighboring convent, where his wounds were dressed, and a refuge afforded him. His secretary was struck from his horse with an axe, but saved in a similar manner, and in the evening conveyed, with his master, to Leutschau. But enough of these horrible scenes.'

It is by no means my purpose, on this occasion, to attempt even a sketch of what the judicious exercise of the intelligent principle has enabled men to do, for the improvement of their fellow-men. Enough, I venture to hope, has been said, to put all who favor me with their attention, upon the reflection, that it is only by its improvement, that it is possible for a man to render himself useful to man ; and, consequently, that it is in this way alone, that he can taste the highest and purest pleasure, which our natures can enjoy, that which proceeds from the consciousness, of having been useful to others.

But it is time that I should make a few remarks on another subject, which would seem appropriately to belong to this occasion.

An idea, I fear, prevails, that truths, such as I have now attempted to illustrate, are obvious enough in themselves, but that they

37

apply only to men of literary education, to professional characters, and persons of fortune and leisure; and that it is out of the power of the other classes of society, and those who pass most of their time in manual labor and mechanical industry, to engage in the pursuit of knowledge, with any hope of being useful to themselves and others.

This I believe to be a great error. I trust we may regard the meeting of this numerous audience, as a satisfactory proof, that you consider it an error; and that you are persuaded, that it is in your power, to enjoy the pleasures and the benefits which flow from the pursuit of useful knowledge.

What is it that we wish to improve? The mind.—Is this a thing monopolized by any class of society? God forbid: it is the heritage with which he has endowed all the children of the great family of man. Is it a treasure belonging to the wealthy? It is talent bestowed alike on rich and poor; high and low. But this is not all; mind is, in all men, and in every man, the same active, living and creative principle; it is the man himself. One of the renowned philosophers of heathen antiquity beautifully said of the intellectual faculties, I call them not *mine*, but *me*. It is these, which make the man; which are the man. I do not say, that opportunities, that wealth, leisure, and great advantages for education are nothing; but I do say, they are much less than is commonly supposed; I do say, as a general rule, that the amount of useful knowledge which men acquire, and the good they do with it, are by no means in direct proportion to the degree to which they have enjoyed what are commonly called the great advantages of life. Wisdom does sometimes, but not most commonly, feed her children with a silver spoon. I believe it is perfectly correct to say, that a small proportion only of those, who have been most distinguished for the improvement of their minds, have enjoyed the best advantages for education. I do not mean to detract, in the least degree, from the advantages of the various seminaries for learning, which public and private liberality has founded in our country. They serve as places, where a large number of persons are prepared for their employment in the various occupations, which the public service requires. But, I repeat it, of the great benefactors of our race; the men, who, by wonderful inventions, remarkable discoveries, and extraordinary improvements, have conferred the most eminent service on their fellow-men, and gained the highest names in history, —by far the greater part have been men of humble origin, narrow fortunes, small advantages, and self-taught.

And this springs from the nature of the mind of man, which is not, like natural things, a vessel to be filled up from without; into which you may pour a little or pour much; and then measure, as with a gage, the degrees of knowledge imparted. The knowledge that *can* be *so* imparted, is the least valuable kind of knowledge; and the man who has nothing but this, may be very learned, but cannot be very wise. We do not invite you to these lectures, as if their object would be attained, when you have heard the weekly address. It is to kindle the understanding to the consciousness of its own powers; to make it feel within itself, that it is a living, spiritual thing; to feed it, in order that it may itself begin to act and operate, to compare, contrive, invent, improve, and perfect. This is our object;—an object, as much within the reach of every man who hears me, as if he had taken a degree in the best college in Christendom.

In this great respect,—the most important that touches human condition,—we are all equal. It is not more true, that all men possess the same natural senses and organs, than that their minds are endowed with the same capacities for improvement, though not, perhaps, all in the same degree. The condition in which they are placed, is certainly not a matter of entire indifference. The child of a savage, born in the bosom of a barbarous tribe, is, of course, shut out from all chance of sharing the improvements of civilized communities. So, in a community, like our own, an infant condemned, by adverse circumstances, to a life of common street beggary, must be considered as wholly out of the reach of all improving influences. But Shakspeare, whose productions have been the wonder and delight of all who speak the English language, for two hundred years, was a runaway youth, the son of a wool-comber, who got his living in London, by holding horses at the door of the theatre, for those who went to the play; and Sir Richard Arkwright, who invented the machinery for spinning cotton, of which I have already spoken, was the youngest of thirteen children of a poor peasant, and, till he was thirty years of age, followed the business of a travelling barber.

As men bring into the world with them an equal intellectual endowment; that is, minds equally susceptible of improvement; so in a community, like that in which we have the happiness to live, the means of improvement are much more equally enjoyed, than might, at first, be supposed. Whoever has learned to read, possesses the keys of knowledge; and can, whenever he pleases, not only unlock the portals of her temple, but penetrate to the inmost halls and most secret cabinets. A few dollars, the surplus of the earnings of the humblest industry, are sufficient to purchase the use of books, which contain the elements of the whole circle of useful knowledge.

It may be thought that a considerable portion of the community *want time* to attend to the cultivation of their minds. But it is only necessary to make the experiment, to find *two things;* one, how much useful knowledge can be acquired in a very little time; and the other, how much time can be spared, by good management, out of the busiest day. Generally speaking, our duties leave us time enough, if our passions would but spare us; our labors are much less urgent, in their calls upon us, than our indolence and our pleasures. There are very few pursuits in life, whose duties are so incessant, that they do not leave a little time, every day, to a man, whose temperate and regular habits allow him the comfort of a clear head and a cheerful temper, in the intervals of occupation; and then there is one day in seven, which is redeemed to us, by our blessed religion, from the calls of life, and affords us all time enough, for the improvement of our rational and immortal natures.

It is a prevalent mistake to suppose, that any class of men have much time to spend, or do spend much time, in mere contemplation and study. A small number of literary men may do this; but the very great majority of professional men,—lawyers, doctors, and ministers, men in public station, rich capitalists, merchants,—men, in short, who are supposed to possess eminent advantages, and ample leisure to cultivate their minds, are all very much occupied with the duties of life, and constantly and actively employed in pursuits very uncongenial to the cultivation of the mind and the attainment of useful knowledge. Take the case of an eminent lawyer, in full practice. He passes his days in his office, giving advice to clients, often about the most uninteresting and paltry details of private business, or in arguing over the same kind of business in court; and when it comes night, and he gets home, tired and harassed, instead of sitting down to rest or to read, he has to study out another perplexed cause, for the next day; or go before referees; or attend a political meeting, and make a speech; while every moment, which can be regarded, in any degree, as leisure time, is consumed by a burdensome correspondence. Besides this, he has his family to take care of. It is plain, that he has no more leisure for the free and improving cultivation of his mind, independent of his immediate profession, than if he had been employed the same number of hours, in mechanical or manual labor. One of the most common complaints of professional men, in all the professions, is, that *they* have no time to read; and I have no doubt, there are many such, of very respectable standing, who do not, in any branch of knowledge, not connected with their immediate professions, read the amount of an octavo volume in the course of a season.

There is, also, a time of leisure, which Providence, in this climate, has secured to almost every man, who has any thing which can be called a home; I mean *our long winter evenings*. This season seems provided, as if expressly, for the purpose of furnishing those who labor, with ample opportunity for the improvement of their minds. The severity of the weather, and the shortness of the days, necessarily limit the portion of time, which is devoted to out-doors' industry; and there is little to tempt us abroad, in search of amusement. Every thing seems to invite us to employ an hour or two of this calm and quiet season, in the acquisition of useful knowledge, and the cultivation of the mind. The noise of life is hushed; the pavement ceases to resound with the din of laden wheels, and the tread of busy men; the glaring sun has gone down, and the moon and the stars are left to watch in the heavens, over the slumbers of the peaceful creation. The mind of man should keep its vigils with them; and while his body is reposing from the labors of the day, and his feelings are at rest from its excitements, he should seek, in some amusing and instructive page, a substantial food for the generous appetite for knowledge.

If we needed any encouragement to make these efforts to improve our minds, we might find it in every page of our country's history. Nowhere do we meet with examples, more numerous and more brilliant, of men, who have risen above poverty and obscurity, and every disadvantage, to usefulness and an honorable name. Our whole vast continent was added to the geography of the world, by the persevering efforts of an humble Genoese mariner, the great Columbus, who, by the steady pursuit of the enlightened conception which he had formed of the figure of the earth, before any navigator had acted upon the belief that it was round, discovered the American continent. He was the son of a Genoese pilot; a pilot and seaman himself; and, at one period of his melancholy career, was reduced to beg his bread at the doors of the convents in Spain. But he carried within himself, and beneath an humble exterior, a spirit, for which there was not room in Spain, in Europe, nor in the then known world; and which led him on to a height of usefulness and fame, beyond that of all the monarchs that ever reigned.

The story of our Franklin cannot be repeated too often;—the poor Boston boy; the son of an humble tradesman, brought up a mechanic himself; a stranger at colleges, till they showered their degrees upon him; who rendered his country the most important services, in establishing her independence; enlarged the bounds of philosophy, by a new department of science; and lived to be pronounced, by Lord Chatham, in the British house of peers, an honor to Europe, and the age in which he lived.

Why should I speak of Green, who left his blacksmith's furnace, to command an army in the revolutionary war; the chosen friend of Washington, and, next to him, perhaps, the military leader, who stood highest in the confidence of his country?

West, the famous painter, was the son of a Quaker in Philadelphia; he was too poor, at the beginning of his career, to purchase canvass and colors; and he rose, eventually, to be the first artist in Europe, and president of the Royal Academy at London. Count Rumford was the son of a farmer, at Woburn: he never had the advantage of a college education, but used to walk down to Cambridge, to hear the lectures on natural philosophy. He became one of the most eminent philosophers in Europe; founded the royal institution in London, and had the merit of bringing forward Sir Humphrey Davy, as the lecturer on chemistry, in that establishment. Robert Fulton was a portrait painter in Pennsylvania, without friends or fortune. By his successful labors in perfecting steam navigation, he has made himself one of the greatest benefactors of man. Whitney, the son of a Massachusetts farmer, was a machinist. His cotton-gin, according to Judge Johnson, of the Supreme Court of the United States, has trebled the value of all the cotton lands at the South, and has had an incalculable influence on the agricultural and mechanical industry of the world. Whittemore, of West Cambridge, the person who invented the machinery for the manufacture of cards, possessed no other means of improvement than those which are within the reach of every temperate and industrious man. Several in this audience were probably acquainted with the modest and sterling merit of the late Paul Moody. To the efforts of his self-taught mind, the early prosperity of the great manufacturing establishments at Waltham and Lowell, is, in no small degree, owing. I believe I may say, with truth, that not one of these individuals enjoyed, at the outset, superior opportunities for acquiring useful knowledge, to those in the reach of every one who hears me.

These are all departed; but we have, living among us, illustrious instances of men, who, without early advantages, but by the resolute improvement of the few opportunities thrown in their way, have rendered themselves, in like manner, useful to their fellow-men; the objects of admiration to those who witness their attainments, and of gratitude to those who reap the fruit of their labors.

On a late visit to New Haven, I saw exhibited a most beautiful work of art; two figures in marble, representing the affecting scene of the meeting of Jephthah and his daughter, as described in the Bible. The daughter, a lovely young woman, is represented as going forth, with the timbrel in her hand, to meet her father, as he returns in triumph from the wars. Her father had rashly vowed to sacrifice to the Lord the first living thing which he should meet, on his return; and, as his daughter runs forth to embrace him, he rends his garments, and turns his head in agony, at the thought of his vow. The young maiden pauses, astonished and troubled at the strange reception. This pathetic scene is beautifully represented in two marble figures of most exquisite taste, finished in a style which would do credit to a master in the art. They are the work of a self-taught artist, at New Haven, who began life, I have been informed, as a retailer of liquors. This business he was obliged to give up, under a heavy load of debt. He then turned his attention to carving in wood; and, by his skill and thrift in that pursuit, succeeded in paying off the debts of his former establishment, to the amount of several thousand dollars. Thus honorably placed at liberty, he has since devoted himself to the profession of a sculptor, and, without education, without funds, without instruction, he has risen, at once, to extraordinary proficiency in this difficult and beautiful art, and bids fair to enrol his name among the brightest geniuses of the day.

I scarce know if I may venture to adduce an instance, nearer home, of the most praiseworthy and successful cultivation of useful knowledge, on the part of an individual, without education, busily employed in mechanical industry. I have the pleasure to be acquainted, in one of the neighboring towns, with a person, who was brought up to the trade of a leather-dresser, and has all his life worked, and still works, at this business. He has devoted his leisure hours, and a portion of his honorable earnings, to the cultivation of useful and elegant learning. Under the same roof, which covers his store and workshop, he has the most excellent library of English books, for its size, with which I am acquainted. The books have been selected with a good judgment, which would do credit to the most accomplished scholar, and have been imported from England by himself. What is more important than having the books, their proprietor is well acquainted with their contents. Among them, are several volumes of the most costly and magnificent engravings. Connected with his library, is an exceedingly interesting series of paintings, in water-colors, which a fortunate accident placed in his possession, and several valuable pictures, purchased by himself. The whole forms a treasure of taste and knowledge, not surpassed, if equalled, by any thing of its kind in the country.

I should leave this part of my address too unjustly defective, did I not add, that we possess, within our own city, an instance of merit, as eminent as it is unobtrusive, in the person of one who has raised himself, from the humblest walks of life, to the highest scientific reputation. Little, perhaps, is it known to the intelligent mariner, who resorts to his Practical Navigator, for the calculations with which he finds his longitude in mid-ocean, that many of them are the original work of one, who started at the same low point in life with himself. Still less is it known to him, that this was but the commencement of a series of scientific productions, which have placed their author upon an equality with the most distinguished philosophers of Europe, and inscribed the name of Bowditch with those of Newton and La Place, upon that list of great minds, to which scarcely one is added in a century.

But why should I dwell on particular instances? Our whole country is a great and speaking illustration of what may be done by native force of mind, uneducated, without advantages, but starting up under strong excitement, into new and successful action. The statesmen, who conducted the Revolution to its honorable issue, were called, without experience, to the head of affairs. The generals, who commanded our armies, were most of them taken, like Cincinnatus, from the plough ; and the forces which they led, were gathered from the firesides of an orderly and peaceful population. They were arrayed against all the experience, talent, and resource of the elder world ; and came off victorious. They have handed down to us a country,—a constitution,—and a national career, affording boundless scope to every citizen, and calling every individual to do for himself, what our fathers unitedly did for the country. What man can start in life, with so few advantages as our country started with, in the race of independence? Over whose private prospects, can there hang a cloud, as dark as that which brooded over the cause of America? Who can have less to encourage, and more to appal and dishearten him, than the sages and chieftains of the Revolution? Let us, then, endeavor to follow in their steps ; and each, according to his means and ability, try to imitate their glorious example ; despising difficulties, grasping at opportunities, and steadily pursuing some honest and manly aim. We shall soon find, that the obstacles which oppose our

38

progress, sink into the dust before a firm and resolute step; and that the pleasures and benefits of knowledge are within the reach of all who seek it.

There are a few considerations, which I beg leave more particularly to address to the younger part of the audience, and which seem to call on them, peculiarly, with a loud voice, to exert themselves, according to their opportunities, to store their minds with useful knowledge.

The world is advanced to a high point of attainment in science and art. The progress of invention and improvement has been, especially of late years, prodigiously rapid; and now, whether we regard the science of nature or of art, of mind or of morals, of contemplation or of practice, it must be confessed, that we live in a wonderfully improved period.

Where is all this knowledge? where does it dwell? In the minds of the present generation of men. It is, indeed, recorded in books, or embodied in the various works and structures of man. But these are only the manifestations of knowledge. The books are nothing, till they are read and understood; and then they are only a sort of short-hand, an outline, which the mind fills up. The thing itself, the science, the art, the skill, are in the minds of living men,—of that generation which is now upon the stage.

That generation will die and pass away. This hour, which we have spent together, has been the last hour to many thousands throughout the world. About three thousand of our race have died since I began my lecture. Among them, of course, is a fair proportion of all the learned and the wise, in all the nations. In thirty years, all now living will be gone, or retired from the scene, and a new generation will have succeeded.

This mighty process does not take place at once, either throughout the world, or in any part of it; but it is constantly going on, —silently, effectually, inevitably; and all the knowledge, art, and refinement, now in existence, must be either acquired by those who are coming on the stage, or it perishes with those who are going off, and is lost for ever. There is no way, by which knowledge can be handed down, but by being learned over again; and of all the science, art, and skill in the world, so much only will survive, when those who possess it are gone, as shall be acquired by the succeeding generation. All the rest must perish.

The rising generation is now called upon to take up this mighty weight; to carry it along a little way; and then hand it over, in turn, to their successors.

The minds which, in their maturity, are to be the depositories of all this knowledge, are coming into existence every day and every hour, in every rank and station of life; all equally endowed with faculties; all, at the commencement, equally destitute of ideas; all starting with the ignorance and helplessness of nature; all invited to run the noble race of improvement. In the cradle there is as little distinction of persons as in the grave.

The great lesson which I would teach you is,—that it depends mainly on each individual, what part he will bear in the accomplishment of this great work. It is to be done by somebody. In a quiet order of things, the stock of useful knowledge is not only preserved, but augmented; and each generation improves on that which went before. It is true, there have been periods, in the history of the world, when tyranny at home, or invasion from abroad, has so blighted and blasted the condition of society, that knowledge has perished with one generation, faster than it could be learned by another; and whole nations have sunk from a condition of improvement, to one of ignorance and barbarity, sometimes in a very few years. But no such dreadful catastrophe is now to be feared. Those who come after us will not only equal, but surpass their predecessors. The existing arts will be improved, science will be carried to new heights, and the great heritage of useful knowledge will go down unimpaired and augmented.

But it is all *to be shared out anew*; and it is for each man to say what part he will gain in the glorious patrimony.

When the rich man is called from the possession of his treasures, he divides them as he will among his children and heirs. But an equal Providence deals not so with the living treasures of the mind. There are children just growing up in the bosom of obscurity, in town and in country, who have inherited nothing but poverty and health, who will, in a few years, be striving in stern contention with the great intellects of the land. Our system of free schools has opened a straight way from the threshold of every abode, however humble, in the village or in the city, to the high places of usefulness, influence, and honor. And it is left for each, by the cultivation of every talent; by watching, with an eagle's eye, for every chance of improvement; by bounding forward, like a greyhound, at the most distant glimpse of honorable opportunity; by grappling, as with hooks of steel, to the prize, when it is won; by redeeming time, defying temptation, and scorning sensual pleasure, to make himself useful, honored, and happy.

SPEECH

AT the annual meeting of the Colonization Society, on the 16th of January, 1832, in the hall of the House of Representatives, at Washington, Mr Mercer, of Virginia, being in the chair, Mr Edward Everett offered the following resolution :—

Resolved, That the colonization of the coast of Africa is the most efficient mode of suppressing the slave trade, and of civilizing the African continent.

In submitting the foregoing resolution, Mr Everett addressed the chair as follows :—

MR CHAIRMAN,

In obtruding myself, for a short time, upon your notice, this evening, I perform, in some sense, an official duty. The Legislature of the State, which I have the honor in part to represent in Congress, adopted, at its session last winter, a resolution, requesting its Senators and Representatives to lend their efforts, in co-operation with the American Colonization Society. This instruction, of course, referred to official exertions on this floor, in another capacity. But I have regarded it also as a motive of an imperative nature, in reference to the objects of this meeting, by which it is proposed to concentrate and apply the force of public opinion, in furtherance of the same great design.

In the part of the country in which I live, the presence of a colored population, co-existing with the whites, is not felt as an evil. They are few in proportion to the rest of the community. They contain among their numbers many respectable and useful persons. At the same time, it is true, as a class, they are depressed to a low point in the social scale. A single fact will illustrate this remark. They form, in Massachusetts, about one seventy-fifth part of the population; but one-sixth of the convicts in our prisons, are of this class. Allowing for some exaggeration in this statement, it is still a painful disproportion. What do I infer from it? Nothing, surely, as to any superior proneness of the colored population, as such, to crime. But I think it proves, that as a class, they are ignorant and needy; ignorance and want being the parents of crime. Among the whites, I have no doubt, that of that portion who are born to hopeless want and hopeless ignorance, —an inheritance of poverty, temptation, and absence of moral restraint,—an equal proportion become the subjects of our penal laws.

But though this population is not felt as an evil in New-England, we are able to enter into those considerations, which have led the venerable Chief Justice of the United States, in the letter just read to us, to speak of it as an evil of momentous character to the peace and welfare of the Union. That evil, however, we of the North have been, for the most part, willing to leave to those whom it more immediately concerns; some of whom, I trust, speaking under the lights of observation and experience, will favor this meeting with their views on this very important subject. There are, however, aspects of the influence and operations of this Society, universally interesting to the philanthropist and friend of humanity; prospects of discharging a moral duty of the most imperative character, and of achieving a work of great, comprehensive, and ever-during benevolence. In the resolution which I have had the honor to submit, I have alluded to these views of the operations and effects of the Society.

It is now somewhat more than half a century, since the abolition of the slave-trade began to be seriously agitated.* This work, I believe, sir, was begun by your native State. If I mistake not,

---

* See, on this subject, the very interesting tract,—Judge Tucker's Queries respecting Slavery, with Dr Belknap's Answers. Collections of Mass. Hist. Soc., Vol. IV, p. 191; First Series.

(speaking from general recollection), Virginia led the way before the American Revolution, in prohibiting the African slave-trade. The acts of her colonial legislature to that effect, were disallowed by the British crown,—a grievance set forth in the Declaration of Independence among the causes of the Revolution. In 1776, Mr David Hartley laid upon the table of the House of Commons, some of the fetters used in confining the unhappy victims of this traffic on board the slave-ships, and moved a resolution, that it was contrary to the laws of God, and the rights of man. The public sensibility had been strongly excited about this time, by the atrocious circumstance, that one hundred and thirty-two living slaves had been thrown overboard, from a vessel engaged in the trade. In 1787, Mr Wilberforce made his first motion in the House of Commons, on this subject. The same year, the Constitution of the United States fixed the period for its abolition in the United States, which accordingly took place, by a law passed at the time prescribed,—1808. In 1788, the slave-trade was abolished in Massachusetts. In 1792, Mr Pitt made his great speech in Parliament, which continued from that time for fifteen years a grand arena, where this question was strenuously contested, by the ablest statesmen of the day. Having carried the point at home, the British government, with praiseworthy zeal, directed its attention to procure from the continental powers, an abolition of this guilty traffic. At the Congress of Vienna, in 1815, the Sovereigns there present, and the States represented, pledged themselves to its suppression ; and at length, after a tedious succession of negotiations and conventions, not very creditable to some of the high parties concerned, on the 23d of March, 1830, the prosecution of the slave-trade ceased to be lawful, for the citizens or subjects of any Christian power in Europe or America.

And now, Mr Chairman, I must state the melancholy fact, that, notwithstanding all these exertions, and the success with which they seemed to be crowned, less has, at any period, been effected, than was hoped for and anticipated. Until the 23d of March, 1830, the Brazilians were allowed to carry on the trade south of the equator. There was but little difficulty thrown in the way of 'a very extensive prosecution of it. Slave ships of all countries, pursuing the traffic to every part of the coast, were provided with fabricated papers, to show that they were carrying on the permitted traffic, south of the equator. Dr Walsh, in his interesting work on Brazil, gives a very affecting account of the chase of a slave-ship by the British frigate in which he was sailing for Europe. After a keen pursuit of three hundred miles, the slave-ship was captured. She had taken in five hundred and sixty-two slaves on the coast of Africa, and had been out seventeen days, in which time fifty-five had died! The wretched crew, over five hundred in number, were liberated from their horrid confinement between decks, and for a short time flattered with the hope of liberty. But on examining the papers of the commander of the ship, although there was the strongest reason to suspect their want of genuineness, there was nothing to prove it; and it became necessary for the British officers to drive these unhappy beings back to their hold, and surrender them up to the wretch, who was dragging them from their native country, into perpetual slavery in Brazil.

Although the traffic is now denounced, and declared illegal or piratical, by every Christian government, it is supposed that it is still very extensively carried on. The regulations of the British service forbid the capture of vessels, however apparently they are fitted out for the pursuit of this trade, unless they actually have slaves on board. The slave-ships consequently hover about the coast, which is mostly low, sunken, and indented with numerous branching rivers, taking in their cargo in the night, escaping by one arm of a stream, while another is blockaded by a cruiser, and thus elude capture. In addition to this, the governments of France and America have not yet felt themselves authorized to admit a right of search by foreign cruizers.* These circumstances united, together with the enhanced value of slaves, occasioned by the obstacles thrown in the way of the accustomed pursuit of the slave-trade will, it is to be feared, for some time, have the effect of causing it to be conducted with greater keenness, ferocity, and waste of life. It will be carried on in swift-sailing vessels; on board of which, the wretched victims of

* Since the foregoing remarks were made, it has been stated in the papers, that, by a recent convention between England and France, the French Government has authorized the right of search on the coast of Africa, with a view to the suppression of the slave-trade.

the traffic will be more than ever crowded ; and barbarous expedients, in the event of search, will be resorted to, to escape detection. It has already happened that slaves have been enclosed in casks, and thrown overboard, in a chase, to be picked up when the danger of capture was over.* The want of a vigorous government, and of an enlightened sentiment in the Havana, the general growth of piracy, and the vicinity of Brazil to the coast of Africa, will, it is to be feared, under present circumstances, furnish but too many facilities for carrying on this wicked commerce. It is supposed, that nearly one hundred thousand human beings are still annually taken by violence from the coast of Africa, and carried into slavery.

If such be the facts of the case, and even with considerable allowance for exaggeration, it is plain that the methods hitherto pursued for the destruction of the slave-trade,—penal denunciation, enforced by armed cruisers,—have proved, in a high degree, ineffectual. Nor can it be hoped, that it will be found practicable to guard the coast of Africa, (an extent all round of eighty degrees of latitude), by any force competent to the suppression of the trade. Another mode, then, must be adopted, or the attainment of the object must be abandoned in despair. Such another mode happily presents itself, of efficacy already proved by experience ; and that is, the establishment of colonies on the African coast. In this way, a cordon is drawn along that continent, which the slave-trader cannot penetrate. The experience already had in the British colony of Sierra Leone, and in our own Liberia, abundantly authorizes this conclusion. In reference to Liberia, I take great pleasure in quoting an honorable testimony from a recent British publication,

---

* Shortly after these remarks were made, the following account appeared in the English papers :

' The Fair Rosamond and the Black Joke, tenders to the Dryad frigate, have captured three slave-vessels, which had originally eleven hundred slaves on board; but of which they succeeded in taking only three hundred and six to Sierra Leone. It appears, that the Fair Rosamond had captured a lugger with 160 Africans, and shortly after saw the Black Joke in chase of two other luggers. She joined in the pursuit; but the vessels succeeded in getting into Bonny river, and landed six hundred slaves, before the tenders could take possession of them. They found on board only two hundred, but ascertained that the rascals, in command of the slavers, had thrown overboard one hundred and eighty slaves, manacled together, of whom only four were picked up.'

entitled to additional credit, on the score of impartiality, from the source from which it proceeds. After an exceedingly favorable account of the colony, in all its aspects, the writer to whom I allude, continues : ' Nothing has tended more to suppress the slave-trade in this quarter, than the constant intercourse and communication of the natives with these industrious colonists. The American agent, Mr Ashmun, took every opportunity and means in his power, to extinguish a traffic, so injurious, in every way, to the fair trader.' ' Wherever the influence of this colony extends, the slave-trade has been abandoned by the natives, and the peaceful pursuits of legitimate commerce established in its place.'*

Wherever a civilized jurisdiction is established on the African coast, the slave-trade is destroyed, not merely by preventing and prohibiting the approach of the traders, but by instituting a lawful and lucrative commerce with the natives, and inducing them to seek the supply of their wants, in the exchange of the abundant products of their fertile soil for those articles of foreign product and manufacture, which are in request among them.

Not only is this the most effectual, I may say the only effectual, mode of suppressing the trade, but it is unfortunately true, that the other method, (the pursuit of the slave-traders by armed cruisers in the seas most infested by them,) is, even when successful in its operations, accompanied by some of the worst evils of the trade, in its undisturbed prosecution. A cruising ship of war perceives a suspicious vessel at a distance, and gives chase to her, for hours, perhaps days. It is evident, that in the crowded condition of such vessels, the sufferings of the wretched beings on board, must be greatly heightened by the neglect, perhaps the cruelties, attendant on being chased. Some of the slave-ships are, provided with false decks, below which the slaves are crowded, when about to fall into the hands of a cruiser, and casks and packages are piled above, to give the semblance of an ordinary trading voyage. Some of the slave-ships are strongly armed, and an action often takes place with the cruiser. This must add, of course, immeasurably to the suffer-

---

* Essay on the actual state of the slave-trade on the coast of Africa, in the Amulet for 1832, said to be ' extracted principally from the Journal of a gallant and distinguished naval officer, who passed three years on the African coast, from which he has just returned.'

ings and sacrifice of life of the miserable victims crowded between decks. When captured, what is their condition? They are in the mid ocean, perhaps. It is known to all, that the horrors of the middle passage form one of the most frightful features of the slave-trade. When a slave-ship is captured, that horrid voyage is yet to be performed, and with scarce any alleviation of its sufferings. The slaves still remain, of necessity, crowded to suffocation, on a miserable allowance of food, exposed to all the causes of disease and death. If captured by an American cruiser, they must be sent across the Atlantic, to be adjudicated in the United States. If captured by the cruisers of the other powers, they must be sent up to windward, to the seat of the mixed commission on the African coast; a voyage frequently of weeks, sometimes of months, during the whole of which they are suffering an amount of misery, and dying at a rate of mortality, probably without a parallel in any other condition of human nature. It would lead me too greatly into detail, to trace the situation of the captured Africans, after they are safely landed on the coast either of the United States or of Africa. As to the former, your memory, sir, can furnish you with facts, which I will not grieve this audience by repeating. But this I will say, that the situation of the re-captured African is too often one, that affords but little cause of congratulation, on the score of humanity. I do not go too far in saying, (for the public documents of this government bear me out in the assertion), that there have been cases of re-captured Africans, brought within the jurisdiction of the United States, who, for aught they have gained by their liberation, might as well have remained in the hands of the slave-trader!

To all these evils, so far as the influence of the civilized colonies on the coast of Africa extends, they furnish a complete remedy. They purify from the contamination of the slave-trade, the entire extent of coast within their jurisdiction. That our colony has borne its part in this happy work, is manifest from the Reports of the Managers, which have informed us, that, short as the annals of the colony are, they already present instances of native tribes, who, harassed and exhausted by this all-destroying traffic, have placed themselves under the American colony for protection. The same is true, and, of course, to a greater extent, of the more powerful British colony at Sierra Leone.

By the same process, by which the colonization of the coast tends to the suppression of the slave-trade, it promotes the civilization of the interior of the continent of Africa. This is a topic, which, as it seems to me, has not received its share of consideration. Of this mighty continent, four times as large as Europe, one third part, at least, is within the direct reach of influences, from the west of Europe and America,—influences, which, for three hundred years, have been employed, through the agency of the slave-trade, to depress and barbarize it; to chain it down to the lowest point of social degradation. I trust these influences are now to be employed in repairing the wrongs, in healing the wounds, in gradually improving the condition of Africa. I trust that a great reaction is at hand. Can it be believed, that this mighty region, most of it overflowing with tropical abundance, was created and destined for eternal barbarity? Is it possible, in the present state of the public sentiment of the world,—with the present rapid diffusion of knowledge,—with the present reduction of antiquated errors to the test of reason,—that such a quarter of the world will be permitted to derive nothing but barbarism, from intercourse with the countries which stand at the head of civilization? It cannot be.

I know it is said, that it is impossible to civilize Africa. Why? Why is it impossible to civilize man in one part of the earth more than in another? Consult history. Was Italy,—was Greece, the cradle of civilization? No. As far back as the lights of tradition reach, Africa was the cradle of science, while Syria, and Greece, and Italy, were yet covered with darkness. As far back as we can trace the first rudiments of improvement, they came from the very head waters of the Nile, far in the interior of Africa; and there are yet to be found, in shapeless ruins, the monuments of this primeval civilization. To come down to a much later period, while the west and north of Europe were yet barbarous, the Mediterranean coast of Africa was filled with cities, academies, museums, churches, and a highly civilized population. What has raised the Gaul, the Belgium, the Germany, the Scandinavia, the Britain of ancient geography, to their present improved and improving condition ? Africa is not now sunk lower, than most of those countries were eighteen centuries ago ; and the engines of social influence are increased a thousand fold in numbers and efficacy. It is not eighteen hundred years since Scotland, whose metropolis has been called the Athens of modern Europe, the country of Hume, of Smith, of Robertson, of Blair, of Stewart, of Brown, of Jeffrey, of Chalmers, of Scott, of Brougham, was a wilderness, infested by painted savages. It is not a thousand years, since the north of Germany, now filled with beautiful cities, learned universities, and the best educated population in the world, was a dreary, pathless forest.

Is it possible, that, before an assembly like this, an assembly of Americans, it can be necessary to argue the possibility of civilizing Africa, through the instrumentality of a colonial establishment, and that, in a comparatively short time ? It is but about ten years, since the foundations of the colony of Liberia were laid, and every one, acquainted with the early history of New-England, knows that the colony at Liberia has made much greater progress than was made by the settlement at Plymouth, in the same period. More than once were the first settlements in Virginia in a position vastly less encouraging than that of the American colony on the coast of Africa ; and yet, from these feeble beginnings in New-England and Virginia, what has not been brought about in two hundred years ? Two hundred years ago, and the continent of North America, for the barbarism of its native population, and its remoteness from the sources of improvement, was all that Africa is now. Impossible to civilize Africa ! Sir, the work is already, in no small part, accomplished. We form our ideas of Africa too much from the wasted and degraded state of the coast. There are numerous and powerful nations in the interior, who are familiar with the art of writing ; the great index and engine of civilization. You and I, sir, have seen a native African, carried into slavery in the West Indies in his youth, exposed, for more than forty years, to the labors and hardships of that condition, the greater part of the time in the field, and at the age of seventy years, writing his native Arabic with the elegance and fluency of a scribe !

I cannot but regard the colonizing of Africa, by a kindred race of African origin, as an enterprise, in all respects as hopeful, and in some respects far more promising, than that of settling and civilizing America, by an alien and hostile people. In the settlement and civilization of the American continent, either from the fatality of circumstances, or the incurable imperfection of man, the extermination of the native population has been the preliminary condition of the introduction of the civilized race. It has been found, or thought impossible, that the red man and the white man should subsist side by side.

In colonizing Africa, no such painful incongruity presents itself. The colored emigrants from this country will present themselves on the African shore, a people of kindred origin, bringing with them the arts of civilized life, unaccompanied with those fatal causes of separation, which have driven the aborigines of America before the approach of the white man. The gentle hand of nature will draw toward them the affections and confidence of the natives. The jealousies and suspicions, which diversity of race invariably produces, can have no foundation ; and it may reasonably be expected, if a vigorous impulse can now be given to the colony, that the work of civilization will proceed from it, as from a centre, with a rapidity unexampled in the history of other colonies.

I am aware, that the partial failure of the establishment at Sierra Leone may be quoted, in opposition to these encouraging views. But it must not be forgotten, that Sierra Leone is an establishment totally different, in its origin and character, from Liberia. It is formed from the crews of the re-captured slave-ships, helpless savages of a hundred different tribes, thrown, without preparation, upon the coast, and, without any principle of order or self-government, subjected to all the evils of a remote and neglected military establishment. The progress that has been made at Liberia, is, on the contrary, all that could have been hoped. A tract of coast two hundred miles north and south, and twenty or thirty east and west ; a population of two thousand emigrants, and several thousands of the native tribes who have voluntarily sought the protection of the colony ; with schools and churches, and all the institutions of civilized life,—a great state of prosperity, and every encouraging prospect,—this surely is not slow progress for ten years.

And is there any thing in the nature of the case, which makes the restoration of the descendants of Africa to their native land, necessarily more slow than the process of abduction ? It is supposed, that one hundred thousand slaves have been annually brought from Africa ; and that, too, at times when the trade has been pursued under great obstacles, illegally, piratically, by stealth, and under the watch of ships of war, stationed to intercept it. Can any man doubt, that if the governments of France, Great Britain, and the Netherlands, of the United States of America, and the several States, should apply their influence, their power, their resources to this great work, it might proceed with any desirable degree of rapidity ? The gentleman who preceded me (Rev. Mr Bacon, of New Haven), alluded to the prodigious influx of emigrants into this country. I have lately seen a statement, that, within the past year, over forty thousand emigrants from Great Britain alone, have arrived at the single port of Quebec. More than half as many more have arrived in the various ports of the United States, making an aggregate of sixty thousand persons, in the different ports of North America. It is by no means to be desired, at present, that any thing like this number of emigrants should be annually set down on the African coast ; but I much mistake the public feeling in those parts of the United States most interested in this question, if a weight of influence and a supply of means are not shortly applied. to this purpose, commensurate with the magnitude of the object to be effected.

The age seems favorable to the movement; it is in harmony with the great incidents of the time. From the east of Europe to the north of Africa, surprising changes, favorable to civilization, have taken place. Greece has been brought within the reach of the sympathies of the rest of Christendom. Temporary disorders, the natural fruit of revolution, will create but a brief delay in the advancement of that interesting country. The restoration of the northern coast of Africa to the domain of civilization has begun. The strongest of its barbarous regencies has been shaken ; and its power, which, for ages, seemed impregnable,—the scandal and the dread of Christendom,—has crumbled in a day. May we not hope, that a still more auspicious era is about to commence,—that a bloodless triumph is to be achieved on the western coast of Africa ?

Happy for America, if she shall take an honorable lead in this great and beneficent work! Happy, if, having presented to the world, on her own soil, a great model of popular institutions, she should now become an efficient agent in their diffusion over the ancient abodes of civilization, now relapsed into barbarity. Happy, if she shall be forward to acquit her share of the mighty debt, which is due to injured Africa, from the civilized nations of the world. Who that has contemplated the infernal horrors of the slave-trade ; that has seen, in his mind's eye, hundreds of men, women, and children, crowded between decks, into a space too low to stand up,—too short to lie down,—too narrow to turn,—chained, scourged, famished, parched, heaped together,—the old and the young, the languishing, the dying, and the dead,—who can dwell on this spectacle, and not turn, with a throbbing heart, to the sight of a company of emigrants, the children of Africa, wafted over the ocean, to the land of their fathers, bound toward the great and genial home of their race, commissioned to trample the slave-trade into the dust, returning from a civilized land, to scatter the seeds of civilization over the mighty extent of western Africa !

I know not but I may entertain an exaggerated impression of this matter ; that I may see it under lights too strong for practical life. But I must confess, I think there is opened to the colored population of this country, a career of broad and lasting usefulness, a destiny of honor and exaltation, unexampled in history.

There seem to be peculiar circumstances in the work, of which they are the chosen agents, to be found in no other similar enterprise in the annals of the world. A mighty continent is to be civilized : that is not without example in history ; but the restoration of the descendants of those who were torn as slaves from this ill-fated region, going back the heralds and missionaries of civilization, with freedom, the arts, and Christianity in their train ; returning to regenerate a continent,—to raise themselves from a depressed condition, to one of the loftiest in which man can be placed,—the condition of benefactors of an entire race, to the end of time ; this is the destiny of the colored population of the United States, who shall embark in the great enterprise of civilizing Africa ;—a destiny, as it seems to me, without a parallel in the history of mankind.

This glorious era has begun to dawn. Over a line of coast of nearly one thousand miles in extent, the purple streaks of the morning are beginning to appear; and

> jocund day
> Stands tiptoe on the misty mountain tops.

From the extreme north of the British territory of Sierra Leone, southward to the Cape of Palmas, the entire coast, with one or two exceptions, has thrown off the curse of the slave-trade. Many, I know, who hear me, have seen the numbers of the Liberia Herald, a respectable newspaper, printed at Monrovia, and edited by a colored emigrant, regularly educated at one of the colleges of the United States.* You and I, sir, and many gentlemen around me, have listened, in the committee rooms of this Capitol, to the animated and intelligent accounts of the prosperity of this colony, the fertility of the soil,—the salubrity of the climate,—the freedom and happiness of the mode of life in Liberia,—given by an emigrant from the United States,—a descendant of African slaves, who had amassed a fortune, by honest and successful industry, in the land of his fathers.

Sir, when men have a great, benevolent, and holy object in view, of permanent interest, *obstacles are nothing.* If it fails in the hands of one, it will be taken up by another. If it exceeds the powers of an individual, society will unite toward the desired end. If the force of public opinion in one country is insufficient, the kindred spirits of foreign countries will lend their aid. If it remain unachieved by one generation, it goes down, as a heritage of duty and honor, to the next; and, through the long chain of counsels and efforts, from the first conception of the benevolent mind, that planned the great work, to its final and glorious accomplishment, there is a steady and unseen, but irresistible cooperation of that divine influence, which orders all things for good.

Am I told, that the work we have in hand is too great to be done? Too great, I ask, to be done *when;* too great to be done *by whom?* Too great, I admit, to be done at once; too great to be done by this Society; too great to be done by this generation,

---

* At Bowdoin College, Brunswick, Maine.

40

perhaps; but not too great to be done.   Nothing is too great to be
done, which is founded on truth and justice, and which is pursued
with the meek and gentle spirit of Christian love.   When this objection was suggested in the British House of Commons, to the
measures proposed for the regeneration of the children of Africa,
Mr Pitt, in reply to it, exclaimed, ' We Britons were once as obscure
among the nations of the earth, as savage in our manners, as debased
in our morals, as degraded in our understandings, as these unhappy
Africans are at present.'   The work is doubtless too great to be
entirely effected by this Society, by the most ardent and zealous of
its friends, perhaps for the present and the next succeeding generation.   But is it too great for the enlightened public opinion of the
world?   Is it too great for the joint efforts of the United States, of
Great Britain, and of France, and the other Christian countries,
already pledged to the cause ?   Is it too great for the transmitted
purpose, the perpetuated concert of generations succeeding generations, for centuries to come ?   Sir, I may ask, without irreverence,
in a case like this, though it be too great for man, is it too great
for that AUGUST PROVIDENCE whose counsels run along the line
of ages, and to whom a thousand years are as one day ?

SPEECH

AT A PUBLIC MEETING, HELD AT ST PAUL'S CHURCH, BOSTON, 21ST MAY, 1833, ON BEHALF OF KENYON COLLEGE, OHIO.

THE lucid exposition, which has been made of the object of the meeting, by the right reverend bishop (McIlvaine), lightens the task of recommending it to an audience like this. I do not know but I should act more advisedly, to leave his cogent and persuasive statement to produce its natural effect, without any attempt on my part, to enforce it. But as we have assembled to communicate our mutual impressions on the subject ;—to consult with each other, whether we *can* do any thing, and whether we *will* do any thing, to promote the object in view, (which, I own, seems to me one of high moment), I will, with the indulgence of the meeting, and at the request of those by whom it is called, briefly state the aspect in which the matter presents itself to my mind.

I understand the object of the meeting to be, to aid the funds of a rising seminary of learning, in the interior of the State of Ohio, particularly with a view to the training up of a well-educated ministry of the gospel, in that part of the United States ;—and the claims of such an object on this community.

As to the general question of the establishment and support of places of education, there are principally *two courses,* which have been pursued in the practice of nations. One is, to leave them, so to say, as an after-thought,—the last thing provided for ;—to let the community grow up, become populous, rich, powerful ; an immense body of unenlightened peasants, artisans, traders, soldiers,

subjected to a small privileged class ;—and then let learning creep
in with luxury ; be esteemed itself a luxury, endowed out of the
surplus of vast private fortunes, or endowed by the state ; and, instead of diffusing a wholesome general influence, of which all partake, and by which the entire character of the people is softened
and elevated, forming itself but another of those circumstances of
disparity and jealous contrast of condition, of which too many were
in existence before ; adding the aristocracy of learning, acquired
at expensive seats of science, to that of rank and wealth.   This is,
in general, the course, which has been pursued with respect to the
establishment of places of education, in some countries of Europe.
The other method is, that introduced by our forefathers, viz., to
lay the foundations of the commonwealth on the corner-stone of
religion and education ;—to make the means of enlightening the
community go hand in hand with the means for protecting it against
its enemies, extending its commerce, and increasing its numbers ;
to make the care of the mind, from the outset, a part of its public
economy ; the growth of knowledge a portion of its public wealth.
This, sir, is the New-England system.   It is the system on which
the colony of Massachusetts was led, in 1647, to order that a school
should be supported in every town, and which, eleven years earlier,
caused the foundations of Harvard college to be laid, by an appropriation out of the scanty means of the country, and at a period of
great public distress, of a sum equal to the whole amount raised
during the year, for all the other public charges.   I do not know
in what words I can so well describe this system, as in those used
by our fathers themselves.   Quoted as they have been times innumerable, they will bear quoting again ; and seem to me peculiarly
apposite to this occasion :   ' After God had carried us safe to New-
England, and we had builded our houses, provided necessaries for
our livelihood, reared convenient places for God's worship, and settled the civil government, one of the next things we longed for
and looked after, was to advance learning, and perpetuate it to posterity ; dreading to leave an illiterate ministry to the churches,
when the present ministers shall be in the dust.'

Now, sir, it is proposed to assist our brethren in Ohio, to lay the
foundations of their commonwealth on this good old New-England
basis ; and if ever there was a region where it was peculiarly expe-

dient that this should be done, most assuredly the western part of America,—and the State of Ohio as much as any other portion of it,—is that region. It is two centuries since New-England was founded, and its population, by the last census, fell short of two millions. Forty years ago, Ohio was a wilderness, and by the same enumeration, its population was little less than a million. At this moment, the population of Ohio, (the settlement of which was commenced in 1788, by a small party from our counties of Essex and Middlesex), is almost twice as large as that of our ancient and venerable Massachusetts. I have seen this wonderful State, with my own eyes. The terraqueous globe does not contain a spot more favorably situated. Linked to New-Orleans on one side, by its own beautiful river, and the father of waters, and united to New York, on the other side, by the lake and the Erie canal, she has, by a stupendous exertion of her own youthful resources, completed the vast circuit of communication between them. The face of the country is unusually favorable to settlement. There is little waste or broken land. The soil is fertile, the climate salubrious; it is settled by as true-hearted and substantial a race, as ever founded a republic; and there they now stand, a million of souls, gathered into a political community, in a single generation !

Now it is plain, that this extraordinary rapidity of increase requires extraordinary means, to keep the moral and intellectual growth of the people on an equality with their advancement in numbers and prosperity. These last take care of themselves. They require nothing but protection from foreign countries, and security of property, under the ordinary administration of justice. But a system of institutions for education,—schools and colleges,— requires extra effort and means. The individual settler can fell the forest, build his log-house, reap his crops, and raise up his family in the round of occupations pursued by himself;—but he cannot, of himself, found or support a school, far less a college ; nor can he do as much toward it, as a single individual, in older States, where ampler resources and a denser population afford means, cooperation, and encouragement, at every turn. The very fact, therefore, that the growth of the country in numbers has been unexampled, instead of suggesting reasons why efforts in the cause of education are superfluous, furnishes an increased and increasing claim on the sympathy and good offices of all the friends of learning and education.

What, then, are the reasonable grounds of the claim, as made on us? I think I perceive several.

We live in a community comparatively ancient, possessed of an abundance of accumulated capital, the result of the smiles of Providence on the industry of the people. We profess to place a high value on intellectual improvement, on education, on religion, and on the institutions for its support. We habitually take credit that we do so. To whom should the infant community, destitute of these institutions, desirous of enjoying their benefits, and as yet not abounding in disposable means, to whom should they look? Whither shall they go, but to their brethren, who are able to appreciate the want, and competent to relieve it? Some one must do it; these institutions, struggling into existence, must be nurtured, or they sink. To what quarter can they address themselves, with any prospect of success, if they fail here? Where will they find a community more likely to take an interest in the object,—to feel a livelier sympathy in the want,—more liberal, more able to give, more accustomed to give?

It is not merely in the necessity of things, that young and rising communities, if assisted at all, should derive that assistance from the older and richer; but the period is so short, since we ourselves stood in that relation to the mother country, and derived from her bounty, benefactions to our institutions, that the obligation to requite these favors, in the only practicable way, is fresh and strong, and like that which requires a man to pay his debts. Dr Franklin was accustomed sometimes to bestow a pecuniary favor on a young man, and, instead of requiring payment, to enjoin the object of his bounty, when advanced in life, and in prosperous circumstances, to give the same sum of money, with a like injunction, to some other meritorious and needy young person. The early annals of our country contain many instances of liberality from beyond the ocean. Our own university and that of New Haven, were largely indebted,—particularly ours,—to pious and benevolent individuals in England. I know no mode of requiting these favors, (which we cannot repay to the country from which we received them;—she wants nothing we can give,—) more natural and more simple, than by imitating the liberality of which we have profited, and supplying the wants of others, at that stage of their social progress, at which our own were supplied.

The inducements to such an exercise of liberality on our part, toward our brethren in the West, are certainly stronger than those which could have influenced England to assist the rising institutions of America. The settlers of the western country are not the aggrieved and persecuted children of the older States. We have not driven them out from among us, by cruel star-chamber edicts, nor have they, in leaving us, shaken off from their feet the dust of an unfriendly soil. They have moved away from the paternal roof, to seek a new but not a foreign home. They have parted from their native land, neither in anger nor despair; but full of buoyant hope and tender regret. They have gone to add to the American family, not to dismember it. They are our brethren, not only after the flesh, but after the spirit also, in character and in feeling. We, in our place, regard them, neither with indifference, jealousy, nor enmity, but with fraternal affection, and true good will. Whom, in the name of Heaven, should we assist, if we refuse to assist them? What, sir, can we minister to the intellectual and spiritual wants of Syria, and of Greece, of Burmah, of Ceylon, and of the remotest isles of the Pacific;—have we enough and to spare for these remote nations and tribes, with whom we have no nearer kindred, than that Adam is our common parent, and Christ our common Saviour; and shall we shut our hands on the call for the soul's food, which is addressed to us, by these our brethren, our school-mates;—whose fathers stood side by side with ours, in the great crisis of the country's fortune;—whose forefathers rest, side by side, with ours, in the sacred soil of New-England? I say nothing, sir, in disparagement of the efforts made to carry the Gospel to the farthest corners of the earth. I bid them God-speed, with all my heart. But surely, the law of Christian love will not permit us, in our care for the distant heathen, to overlook the claims of our fellow citizens at home.

On a theme like this, I am unwilling to appeal to any thing like interest; nor will I appeal to an interest of a low and narrow character; but I cannot shut my eyes on those great considerations of an enlarged policy, which demand of us a reasonable liberality

toward the improvement of these western communities. In the year
1800, the State of Ohio sent one member to Congress ; and Massachusetts, (not then separated from Maine), sent twenty-one.
Now, Ohio sends nineteen, and Massachusetts,—recently, and, I
am constrained to add, in my judgment, unfairly,* deprived of one
of her members,—sends but twelve. Nor will it stop here. ' They
must increase, and we, in comparison, must decrease.' At the
next periodical enumeration, Ohio will probably be entitled to nearly thirty representatives, and Massachusetts to little more than a
third of this number. Now, sir, I will not, on this occasion, and
in this house of prayer, unnecessarily introduce topics and illustrations, better befitting other resorts. I will not descant on interests
and questions, which, in the divided state of the public councils,
will be decided, one way or the other, by a small majority of voices.
I really wish to elevate my own mind, and, as far as lies in me,
the minds of those I have the honor to address, to higher views.
I would ask you, not in reference to this or that question, but in
reference to the whole complexion of the destinies of the country,
as depending on the action of the general government ; I would
ask you as to that momentous future, which lies before us and our
children,—by whom, by what influence, from what quarter, is our
common country, with all the rich treasure of its character, its
hopes, its fortunes, to be affected, to be controlled, to be sustained,
and guided in the paths of wisdom, honor, and prosperity, or sunk
into the depth of degeneracy and humiliation ? Sir, the response
is in every man's mind,—on every man's lips. The balance of
the country's fortunes is in the West. There lie, wrapped up in
the folds of an eventful futurity, the influences, which will most
powerfully affect our national weal and woe. We have, in the
order of Providence, allied ourselves to a family of sister communities, springing into existence, and increasing with unexampled
rapidity. We have called them into a full partnership in the government ; the course of events has put crowns on their heads, and
sceptres in their hands ; and we must abide the result.

* By adopting a ratio of representation which left Massachusetts with an unrep-
esented fraction sufficient, within a few hundreds, for another member.

But has the power indeed departed from us ; the efficient ulti-mate power ? That, sir, is, in a great measure, as we will. The real government in this country is that of opinion. Toward the formation of the public opinion of the country, New-England, while she continues true to herself, will, as in times past, contribute vastly beyond the proportion of her numerical strength. But be-sides the general ascendancy which she will maintain, through the influence of public opinion, we can do two things to secure a strong and abiding interest in the West, operating, I do not say, in our favor, but in favor of principles and measures, which we think sound and salutary. The first is, promptly to extend toward the West, on every fitting occasion which presents itself consistently with public and private duty, either in the course of legislation or the current of affairs, those good offices, which of right pertain to the relative condition of the two parts of the country ;—To let the West know, by experience, both in the halls of Congress and the channels of commercial and social intercourse, that the East is truly, cordially, and effectively her friend ; not her rival nor enemy.

The kindly influence thus produced will prove of great power and value ; and will go far to secure a return of fraternal feeling and political sympathy ; but it will not of itself, on great and try-ing occasions of a supposed diversity of sectional interest, always prove strong enough to maintain a harmony of councils. But we can do another thing, of vastly greater moment. We can put in motion a principle of influence, of a much higher and more gener-ous character. We can furnish the means of building up institutions of education. We can, from our surplus, contribute toward the establishment and endowment of those seminaries, where the mind of the West shall be trained and enlightened. Yes, sir, we can do this ; and it is so far optional with us, whether the power to which we have subjected ourselves, shall be a power of intelligence or of ignorance ; a reign of reflection and reason, or of reckless strength ; a reign of darkness or of light. This, sir, is true states-manship,—this is policy, of which Washington would not be ashamed. While the partisan of the day plumes himself upon a little worthless popularity, gained by bribing the interest of one quarter, and falling in with the prejudices of another ; it is truly wor-thy of a patriot, by contributing toward the means of steadily, dif-

41

fusively, and permanently enlightening the public mind, as far as opportunity exists, in every part of the country, to secure it in a wise and liberal course of public policy.

Let no Bostonian capitalist, then,—let no man, who has a large stake in New-England, and who is called upon to aid this institution in the centre of Ohio, think that he is called upon to exercise his liberality at a distance, towards those in whom he has no concern. Sir, it is his own interest he is called upon to promote. It is not their work he is called upon to do ; it is his own work. It is my opinion, which, though it may sound extravagant, will, I believe, bear examination, that, if the question were propounded to us, this moment, whether it were most for the benefit of Massachusetts, to give fifty thousand dollars toward founding another college in Middlesex, Hampshire, or Berkshire, or for the support of this college in the Ohio, we should, if well advised, decide for the latter. We have Harvard, Amherst, Williams ;—we do not want another college. In the West, is a vast and growing population, possessing a great and increasing influence in the political system of which we are members. Is it for our interest, strongly, vitally for our interest, that this population should be intelligent, and well educated ; or ignorant, and enslaved to all the prejudices which beset an ignorant people ?

When, then, the right reverend bishop, and the friends of the West, ask you, on this occasion, to help them, they ask you, in effect, to spare a part of your surplus means, for an object, in which, to say the least, you have a common interest with them. They ask you to contribute to give security to your own property, by diffusing the means of light and truth throughout the region, where so much of the power to preserve or to shake it resides. They ask you to contribute to perpetuate the Union, by training up a well educated population, in the quarter which may hereafter be exposed to strong centrifugal influences. They ask you to recruit your waning strength in the national councils, by enlisting on your side their swelling numbers, reared in the discipline of sound learning and sober wisdom ; so that when your voice in the government shall become comparatively weak, instead of being drowned by a strange and unfriendly clamor from this mighty region, it may be re-echoed with increased strength and a sympathetic response, from the rising millions of the North-Western States.   Yes, sir, they do more.   They ask you to make yourselves rich in their respect, good will, and gratitude ;—to make your name dear and venerable in their distant shades.   They ask you to give their young men cause to love you, now in the spring-time of life, before the heart is chilled and hardened ;—to make their old men, who in the morning of their days went out from your borders, lift up their hands for blessings on you, and say, ' Ah, this is the good old-fashioned liberality of the land where we were born.'   Yes, sir, we shall raise an altar in the remote wilderness.   Our eyes will not behold the smoke of its incense, as it curls up to heaven.   But there the altar will stand ;—there the pure sacrifice of the spirit will be offered up ; and the worshipper who comes, in all future time, to pay his devotions before it, will turn his face to the Eastward, and think of the land of his benefactors.

SPEECH

DELIVERED IN FANEUIL HALL, 28TH MAY, 1833, ON THE SUBJECT
OF THE BUNKER-HILL MONUMENT.*

———

MR PRESIDENT, AND BRETHREN OF THE MASSACHUSETTS CHARITABLE
MECHANIC ASSOCIATION,

(FOR by your favor, I enjoy the privilege of being an honorary member of that institution,) when I consider the auspices under which this meeting is assembled, when I reflect upon the zeal evinced in this cause, by the Mechanic Association, and the moral power with which that body moves to the accomplishment of any object which it takes in hand, I feel a satisfaction which I want words to express. It was my fortune to be one of those who took an early interest in the erection of a monument upon Bunker-Hill. In the efforts made to bring forward and carry on this great work, I bore a very humble, but, I believe I may say, an assiduous and laborious part. I gave, sir, all I had to give,—a large portion of my time and my best efforts, in union with my valued associates, to recommend this object to the public favor. I shared with the friends of the enterprise, the satisfaction with which they witnessed the first burst of enthusiasm with which the project was welcomed, and their regret and mortification, at finding that the popular excitement and interest which were to furnish the resources to carry on this expensive work did not hold out to its completion. If it

* This meeting was called by the Massachusetts Charitable Mechanic Association, to take measures for the completion of the monument.

afford satisfaction, or is deemed a duty, in any quarter, to indicate faults committed by the early boards of directors, to point out errors of judgment into which it is supposed they fell,—(errors of intention will not, I think, be imputed to them),—I, for one, will, with meekness, submit to the rebuke, from any individual, who has given more of his time, attention, labor,—and money even, in proportion to their means,—than the members of these much censured boards of directors. Nay, sir, even from any one who has not done this, I will submit, for one, to any deserved rebuke, if he will, —now that the work is so far advanced that its completion is matter of calculation, and now that the state of the times admits and encourages a fresh appeal to the liberality of a prosperous community,—step forward and exert himself zealously and effectually in the cause. I do not rise to vindicate former boards of directors, nor former measures, but to congratulate you, sir, and my fellow citizens, on the prospect which is now opening upon the work ; and cheerfully, for one, to transfer to those who shall now take it up and complete it, the unshared and unqualified credit of the patriotic undertaking. The work, I am confident, will now be completed. It is taken in hand by those accustomed to finish what they undertake ;—and whatever we have done before, I am sure, sir, we are now hammering upon the nail that will go.

Sir, I suppose there can be but one opinion on the question, when it is fairly stated. It is not whether the monument shall be built, but whether it shall be left incomplete ;—not whether it shall be begun, but whether it shall be finished. Nay, not even exactly this. The question is not whether it shall be finished at all, but, whether it shall be finished by us, or, after remaining unfinished another half century, a memorial,—not to the renown of the great men we commemorate, but to the discredit of this generation of their descendants,—the honor of completing it shall be reserved to other times, when a more enduring patriotic sentiment shall be awakened in its favor.

That it will be completed,—whether by us or not,—is certain. What is already done is as substantial as the great pyramid of Egypt. The foundations have been laid with such depth and solidity, that nothing but an earthquake can shake them. The part already constructed will stand to the end of time ; and the real question which we have to settle is, will we leave it in its present state, an object unsightly to the eye, and painful to the mind; or will we, who assisted to lay the foundations, enjoy the satisfaction of beholding the noble shaft rising in simple majesty towards the heavens, where, in the language of that surpassing eloquence, which I would to heaven, Mr President, could rouse and animate us this afternoon, ' the earliest light of the morning shall gild it, and parting day linger and play on its summit.'

But, sir, I wrong myself, and I wrong my fellow citizens gathered around, in treating this subject, as if the strongest reason for completing the monument arose from mortification and regret, at leaving it in its present state. Far otherwise, I know, sir, do you view this question; far otherwise do I view it myself. Those great patriotic and moral inducements which originally prompted the enterprise, remain in unimpaired force, and must gather strength with each succeeding year. The idea which lay at the basis of this undertaking was, to redeem from all desecrating uses, and devote to the eternal remembrnce of the event of which it was the scene, the sacred summit of Bunker-Hill, and to erect upon its height a plain but majestic monumental structure, to identify the spot to the latest time. This idea was first conceived by an amiable and accomplished fellow citizen, now no more, (the late William Tudor), when the half century was near expiring, since the occurrence of the event. It was by him communicated to a circle of friends, and by them to the public, by whose favor the enterprise was so far advanced, that the corner stone was laid in the presence of such an assembly as was perhaps never before witnessed, on the jubilee anniversary of the battle,—the 17th of June, 1825. It was my misfortune, sir, not to be present on that auspicious day. I was absent on the public service, at a distance. But I know too well the feelings which animated the mighty multitude gathered together on that hallowed spot, in the presence of the nation's guest, returning from his triumphant progress through the Union, in the presence of the time-worn and revered remnants of the battle and of the war, and within the hearing of that all-eloquent voice, which poured forth its deepest and richest strains on the glorious occasion,—not to appeal fearlessly to all who heard it, —that they felt that it was good to be there. They felt that the event deserved to be commemorated ; that the spot ought, through all time, to be marked out and kept sacred ; and that this generation owed it to that which preceded us, and bought for us, with its blood, this great heritage of blessings, to erect upon this spot a monumental structure, which should last as long as our freedom shall last ;—as long as a happy posterity of Americans shall have cause to cherish, with pious gratitude, the memory of their fathers.

And do not these reasons still exist ? Is the spot less precious, now that eight more seasons have wept their dews over the dear and sacred blood, that has remained for eight more years uncommemorated beneath the sod ? Are the valor, the self-devotion of the heroes of that day,—of Warren, and Prescott, and Putnam, and Stark, and their gallant associates, less deserving of celebration ? Is this mighty and eventful scene in the opening drama of the revolution less worthy of celebration, now that eight more years, in the prosperous enjoyment of our liberties, contrasted as they have been with disastrous struggles in other countries, have given us fresh cause for gratitude to our fathers ?

But I am met with the great objection, *What good will the Monument do ?* I beg leave, sir, to exercise my birthright as a Yankee, and answer this question, by asking two or three more, to which I believe it will be quite as difficult to furnish a satisfactory reply. I am asked, What good will the Monument do ? And, I ask, What good does any thing do ? What is good? Does any thing do any good ? The persons who suggest this objection, of course, think that there are some projects and undertakings, that do good ; and I should therefore like to have the idea of *good,* explained, and analyzed, and run out to its elements. When this is done, if I do not demonstrate, in about two minutes, that the Monument does the same kind of good that any thing else does, I will consent that the huge blocks of granite, already laid, should be reduced to gravel, and carted off to fill up the mill-pond; for that I suppose is one of the good things. Does a rail-road or canal do good ? Answer, Yes. And how ? It facilitates intercourse,—opens markets,—and increases the wealth of the country. But what is this good for ? Why, individuals prosper and get rich. And what good does that do ? Is mere wealth, as an ultimate end,—gold and silver, without an inquiry as to their use,—are

these a good? Certainly not. I should insult this audience by
attempting to prove, that a rich man, as such, is neither better nor
happier, than a poor one? But as men grow rich, they live better.
Is there any good in this, stopping here? Is mere animal life,—
feeding, working, and sleeping like an ox,—entitled to be called
good? Certainly not. But these improvements increase the population. And what good does that do? Where is the good in
counting twelve millions instead of six of mere feeding, working,
sleeping animals? There is then no good in the mere animal life, except that it is the physical basis of that higher moral existence, which
resides in the soul, the heart, the mind, the conscience; in good
principles, good feelings, and the good actions, (and the more disinterested, the more entitled to be called good), which flow from
them. Now, sir, I say that generous and patriotic sentiments;
sentiments, which prepare us to serve our country, to live for our
country, to die for our country,—feelings like those, which carried
Prescott, and Warren, and Putnam to the battle-field, are good,—
good, humanly speaking, of the highest order. It is good to have
them, good to encourage them, good to honor them, good to commemorate them;—and whatever tends to cherish, animate and strength-
en such feelings, does as much right down practical good, as filling
up low grounds and building rail-roads. This is my demonstration.
I wish, sir, not to be misunderstood. I admit the connexion between enterprises, which promote the physical prosperity of the
country, and its intellectual and moral improvement: but I maintain, that it is only *this connexion* that gives these enterprises all
their value; and that the same connexion gives a like value to
every thing else, which, through the channel of the senses, the
taste, or the imagination, warms and elevates the heart.

But we are told that BOOKS will do all this; that HISTORY will
record the exploits we would commemorate, and carry them, with
the spot on which they were acted out, down to the latest posterity. Even my worthy friend, who has just addressed us, although
I am sure he agrees with me in substance, and although I admit
the superior efficacy of the art of printing over that of writing, in
perpetuating the remembrance of the past,—yet seemed to me to
give a little too much weight to this objection. I am inclined to
doubt whether it be sound in any sense; I am confident it is not,

to the extent to which it is made. That history will preserve the memory of the battle of Bunker-Hill, I certainly do not doubt ; but that history alone, without sensible monuments, would preserve the knowledge of the identity of the spot is not so certain. The fame of the immortal plain of Troy, commemorated by the first of bards in time and renown, is coeval with history, and embalmed in its earliest pages. But where the site of Troy is, I have the best reason to know is very doubtful. Books have surely done here, as much as they can ever do. A man may seek it with Strabo in his head and Homer in his heart, and he shall not find it. Even the still existing natural features of the scene are not sufficient to identify it. The 'broad Hellespont' still rolls into the Ægean. Tenedos, that rich and most famous island city,—which, when Æneas told his tale to Dido, had sunk into a treacherous port,—still keeps its station in front of the Troad ; but if the spot where Troy stood can be settled at all, it is principally by the simple mound, still standing, and, as is supposed, erected to Achilles. History tells us of the memorable pass of Thermopylæ, where Leonidas and his brave associates encountered the barbarous invader. I have searched in vain for the narrow pass between the foot of the mountain and the sea. It is gone. Time, which changes all things, has changed the great natural features of the spot,—in which not merely its geographical, but, if I may say so, its moral identity resided,—and has stretched out a broad plain in its place ; but a rude monumental pile still remains to designate the spot where the Spartan hero fell. History tells us of the field of Cannæ, where Hannibal overthrew the Roman consuls, and slaughtered forty thousand of their troops, till the Aufidus ran blood. Why, sir, you cannot, with your Livy in your hand, retrace the locality. History has preserved us the story of the battle of Pharsalia, where the star of Cæsar prevailed over the star of Pompey ; a battle which fixed the fortunes of the world for fifteen centuries. It is impossible, even with the Commentaries of Cæsar for your guide, precisely to fix the spot where it was fought. History tells us of the battle of Philippi, where Brutus and Cassius, and with them the last hopes of Roman liberty were cloven down ; but historians do not all agree, within two or three hundred miles, as to the precise scene of the action. Now, sir, I trust that the memory

42

of Bunker-Hill will be preserved in history as long as that of Troy, of Thermopylæ, of Cannæ, of Pharsalia, or of Philippi; but who is there, that would not wish that the identity of this precious spot should be transmitted with its name to posterity; so that when our children, in after times, shall visit these hallowed precincts, they may know and be assured, that they stand upon the very sod, that was moistened by the life-blood of the martyrs of that eventful day?

But I know and admit, that history will perform her duty to those who fought and fell at Bunker-Hill. Her duty, did I say? It will be her most glorious prerogative to record their deeds, in letters of light, on one of the brightest pages in the annals of freedom. There, when the tongues we now speak are forgotten, they will be read, as long and as widely, as though we

> ' Could write their names on every star that shines ;
> Engrave their story on the living sky,
> To be for ever read by every eye.'

But history would do this, though Bunker-Hill were surrendered to-morrow to the pick-axe and the spade ;—though it were levelled to its base ;—though it were torn from its roots, and cast into the sea. But, sir, though books will do what they can, they cannot do all things. There are some things which they cannot do; no, not if the muse of history herself, in bodily presentment, should take her stand on Bunker-Hill, to describe the scene. There are things not in the physical competence of books to effect. Can the dead letter of history present you the glowing lineaments of your Washington, as he looks down upon you from that wall? or reproduce to you his majestic form in the chiselled marble? Who does not gaze with delight on the portrait or the statue of the Father of his Country, where Stuart, and Chantrey, and Canova have wrought up the silent canvass and the cold marble into life and beauty? History would transmit the record of what he was and what he did, though with sacrilegious hands, we should tear his image from these walls, or grind his statue to powder. But shall we, for this reason, even while we stand within the light of his benignant countenance, find the heart to ask, what good does it do?

Sir, the man that asks such a question, takes a partial and super-ficial view of his own nature; he belies himself. There is an original element in our natures,—a connexion between the senses, the mind and the heart,—implanted by the Creator for pure and noble purposes, which cannot be reasoned away. You cannot ar-gue men out of their senses and feelings; and after you have wearied yourself and others, by talking about books and history, you cannot set your foot upon the spot where some great and mem-orable exploit was achieved, especially by those with whom you claim kindred, but your heart swells within you. You do not now reason; you feel the inspiration of the place. Your cold philoso-phy vanishes; and you are ready to put off the shoes from off your feet, for the place whereon you stand is holy ground. A language which letters cannot shape, which sounds cannot convey, speaks, not to the understanding, but to the heart.

Such a spot is the field of battle on Bunker-Hill, already rescued from impending desecration. It is now proposed to enclose this memorable spot; to restore it, as near as possible, to its condition on the 17th of June, 1775, so that all who shall make their pilgrimage to it, may be able to retrace, as on a map, each incident of the eventful day; to plant around its borders a few trees from our na-tive forests; and to complete the erection of the monumental shaft already begun, simple in its taste, grand in its dimensions and height, and of a solidity of structure, which shall defy the power of time.

And now, I appeal to you, Mr Chairman and fellow citizens, that such a work, on such a spot, is in accordance with the best principles and purest feelings of our nature. It speaks to the heart. The American who can gaze on it with indifference, does not deserve the name of American. I would say of such a one, if one could be found so cold and heartless, in the language of the great genius of the age, of a fancied being of kindred apathy;—

'Breathes there the man of soul so dead ?—
If such there breathe, go, mark him well ;
For him no minstrel raptures swell.
Proud though his title, high his fame,
Boundless his wealth, as wish could claim ;
In spite of title, power, and pelf,
The wretch, concentred all in self,

Living, shall forfeit fair renown,
And, doubly dying, shall go down
To the vile earth, from whence he sprung,
Unwept, unhonored, and unsung.'

I think I can bring this to a practical issue in every man's mind. Is there any one who hears me, and will figure to himself the aspect of the work, as it will appear when it is completed:—who will place himself, in imagination, on the summit of the beautiful hill where the battle was fought ; look out upon the prospect, of unsurpassed loveliness, that spreads before him, by land and by sea; the united features of town and country ; the long rows of buildings and streets in the city, rising one above another, upon the sides of her triple hills ; the surrounding sweep of country, checkered with prosperous villages ; on one side the towers of city churches, on the other the long succession of rural spires ; the rivers that flow on either side to the sea ; the broad expanse of the harbor and bay, spotted with verdant islands,—with a hundred ships, dancing in every direction over the waves ; the vessels of war, keeping guard with their sleeping thunders, at the foot of the hill ;—and on its top, within the shade of venerable trees, over the ashes of the great and good, the noble obelisk, rising to the heavens, and crowning the magnificent scene ;—is there any one who will look at this picture, with his mind's eye, and not be willing to contribute, in proportion to his means, to do the little, which remains to be done, to realize it ?

There have been times when I have desponded ; but I do so no longer. I am sure the work will be done. I hear good auguries and words of encouragement on all sides. I cannot mistake, when I think I perceive that the true spirit is awakened.

The time is well adapted to the deed. It is now eight years since the corner stone was laid, on the day that completed the half century from the battle. Let us this year urge the work to the close, with the completion of the half century, since the termination of the war. If we celebrated the grand commencement of hostilities, in the foundation ; let us bring forth the top-stone, in happy commemoration of the return of peace.

I believe, sir, as I have already said, that the work is in the proper hands. I mean no fulsome compliment ; I speak what history avouches, that the Mechanics, as a class, were prime agents, in all the measures of the Revolution. It was with them that Warren, and Hancock, and Adams took counsel in dark and trying hours. As a class, they contributed their full quota to the armies that fought the battles of our freedom :—and when the war was over, and it remained to be seen, whether we had reaped any substantial fruit from the contest ; when the Constitution was proposed,—when it was laboring,—when it was in imminent danger of miscarriage,—the Mechanics, as a class, put their shoulders to the wheel, and urged it into action. Who so fit to take an energetic and decisive lead, in achieving this great work of commemoration ?

I rejoice, above all, in this day's meeting ; and that the doors of Faneuil Hall have been thrown open to this great and patriotic assemblage ; a temple worthy the offering. The spirit of the Revolution is enshrined within its columns ; and old Faneuil Hall seems to respond to old Bunker-Hill ;—this with the ancient thunders of its eloquence, and that with the thunders of the battle ;—as deep calleth unto deep, with the noise of its water-spouts. It was beneath this roof that the spirits of our fathers were roused to that lofty enthusiasm, which led them up, calm and unresisting, to the flaming terrors of the mount of sacrifice ;—and well does it become us, their children, to gather beneath the venerable arches, and resolve to discharge the debt of gratitude and duty to their memory !

Two of the periods assigned to a generation of men have passed away, since the immortal Warren appeared before his fellow citizens, on the memorable anniversary of the 5th of March. He was, at that time, in the very dawn of manhood, and as you behold him in yonder delineation of his person. Amiable, accomplished, prudent, energetic, eloquent, brave ; he united the graces of a manly beauty to a lion heart, a sound mind, a safe judgment, and a firmness of purpose, which nothing could shake. At the period to which I allude, he was but just thirty-two years of age ;—so young, and already the acknowledged head of the cause ! He had never seen a battle-field, but the veterans of Louisburg and Quebec looked up to him as their leader ; and the hoary headed sages, who had guided the public councils for a generation, came to him for advice. Such he stood, the organ of the public sentiment, on the occasion just mentioned. At the close of his impassioned address, after having depicted the labors, hardships, and sacrifices endured by our ancestors, in the cause of liberty, he broke forth in the thrilling words, 'the voice of our fathers' blood cries to us from the ground!' Three years only passed away; the solemn struggle came on; foremost in council, he also was foremost in the battle-field, and offered himself a voluntary victim, the first great martyr in the cause. Upon the heights of Charlestown, the last that was struck down, he fell, with a numerous band of kindred spirits, the gray-haired veteran, the stripling in the flower of youth, who had stood side by side through that dreadful day, and fell together, like the beauty of Israel, on their high places!

And now, sir, from the summit of Bunker-Hill THE VOICE OF OUR FATHERS' BLOOD CRIES TO US FROM THE GROUND. It rings in my ears. It pleads with us, by the sharp agonies of their dying hour; it adjures us to discharge the last debt to their memory. Let us hear that awful voice; and resolve, before we quit these walls, that the long-delayed duty shall be performed; that the work SHALL BE DONE, SHALL BE DONE!

SPEECH

DELIVERED AT A TEMPERANCE MEETING IN SALEM, ON THE 14TH
OF JUNE, 1833.

—

MR EVERETT moved the following resolution :—

Resolved, That, while we behold, with the highest satisfaction, the success of the efforts which have been made for the suppression of intemperance, we consider its continued prevalence as affording the strongest motives for persevering and increased exertion.

Mr Everett then spoke substantially as follows :—

MR PRESIDENT,

WHEN I look around me, and see how many persons there are in the assembly, better entitled than myself to the privilege of addressing the audience, it is not without great diffidence that I present myself before you. But if there are occasions on which it is our duty to exert ourselves, in season and out of season, there are also objects we should endeavor to promote, in place and out of place, if, indeed, a man can ever be out of place, who rises, in a civilized and Christian community, to speak in behalf of Temperance. Emboldened by this reflection, and in compliance with your request, I have ventured to submit the resolution which I have just read, and of which, with your permission, I will briefly enforce the purport ;—and most sincerely can I say, that I never raised my voice with a clearer conviction of duty, nor a more cheerful hope of the ultimate success of the cause.

I am not insensible to the force of the objection which meets us on the threshold :—I mean the objection taken to the multiplication of what are called self-created societies, and, in general, to the free development and application of the social influence which have been witnessed in our day. But, though these objections have been urged in the most respectable quarter, I have never been able to feel their force. I think it will be found, on full examination of the matter, that societies are liable to precisely the same objections as the action of individual men, that is, they are liable to misapplication and abuse. But I believe it would be quite as easy, for a powerful and ingenious mind to point out the abuses to which individual effort is liable, as those to which societies are exposed ; quite as easy to show the good that might have been and has not been done ; the reforms which might have been and have not been accomplished ; the happiness which might have been and has not been enjoyed ;—had the social principle been brought out in a still earlier, ampler, and more cordial development. In a word, sir, though I am not over-fond of abstract generalities on questions of this nature, I cannot but think that the individual principle tends to selfishness, to weakness, to barbarism, to ignorance, and to vice ; and that the social principle is the principle of benevolence, civilization, knowledge, genial power, and expansive goodness. On this point, however, it would be safer to leave theoretical axioms aside. It is, perhaps, enough, to insist on good faith, good temper, and sound principle, on the part of societies and individuals. Where these prevail, there is little danger of abuse. Where they are absent, it little matters whether the public peace is disturbed, the cause of reform obstructed, and bad passion nourished, by associations or individuals. In fact, in the complicated structure of modern society, it is impossible to draw a line between them. It is powerful individuals that move societies ; it is listening multitudes, which give power to individuals.

If there is any cause, in which it is right and proper to employ the social principle, the promotion of temperance is that cause ; for intemperance, in its origin, is peculiarly a social vice. Although, in its progress, men may creep away, out of shame, to indulge the depraved appetite in secret, yet no man, in a state of civilization, is born, I imagine, with a taste so unnatural, that he would seek an intoxicating liquor, in the outset, for his ordinary or frequent drink. It is usually tasted, for the first time, as the pledge of hospitality, and the bond of good fellowship. Idle men, who meet casually together,—with kind feelings toward each other,—ask each other to step into the dram-shop, and 'take something to drink,' for want of any thing else to say or do ;—and there they swallow the liquid poison 'to each other's health.' The social circle, the stated club, the long protracted sitting at the board, on public occasions, the midnight festivities of private assemblies ;—these, nine cases out of ten, teach men the fatal alphabet of intemperance ; surprise them into their first excesses ; break down the sense of shame ; establish a sympathy of conscious frailty ; and thus lead them on, by degrees, to habitual, and, at length, craving, solitary, and fatal indulgence. The vice of intemperance, then, is social in its origin, progress, and aggravation ; and most assuredly authorizes us, by every rule of reason and justice, in exerting the whole strength of the social principle, in the way of remedy.

If it were possible to entertain a doubt on this point, as a matter of theory, that doubt would be removed by the safe test of experience. The maxims of temperance are not new ; they are as old as Christianity ; as old as any of the inculcations of personal and social duty. Every other instrument of moral censure had been tried, in the case of intemperance, as in that of other prevailing errors, vices, and crimes. The law had done something ; the press had done something ; the stated ministrations of religion had done something ; but altogether had done but little ; and intemperance had reached a most alarming degree of prevalence. At length, the principle of association was applied ; societies were formed, meetings were held, public addresses made, information collected and communicated, pledges mutually given, the minds of men excited, and their hearts warmed, by comparison of opinions, by concert and sympathy ; and within the space of twenty years, of which not more than ten have been devoted to strenuous effort, a most signal and unexampled reform has been achieved. The bubbling, and, as it seemed, perennial fountains of this vice have, in many cases, been dried up. The example alluded to by the gentleman who has already addressed us, (Dr Pierson), of villages absolutely regenerated, is by no means a solitary one. The aspect of many

43

entire communities has been changed ; and an incalculable amount
of vice and woe has been prevented. The statistical facts publicly
brought out at the National Temperance Convention, recently held
in Philadelphia, abundantly sustain this proposition.

But, if we are encouraged to continued and persevering efforts,
by the success which has thus far crowned the cause, we ought to
be still more so, by reflecting upon the extent to which the evil
still rages. If we are to obey the injunction of the Roman moralist, and ' think nothing done, while aught remains to do,' what new
motives to zealous exertion ought we not to find in the fact, that,
though much has been done, much, very much, remains to be effected ? I have recently seen it stated, on the authority of the highly
respectable warden of the state's prison in Maine, that ' three
fourths of all the convicts in that establishment were led to the
commission of the crimes, for which they are now suffering imprisonment, by intemperance,' in most cases directly, in others more
remotely. There are many gentlemen present, no doubt, able to
form an opinion, entitled to full confidence, whether this would be
an over-estimate for the other States in the Union. I am inclined,
myself, to think that it is not. If we carry the inquiry a little farther, from our state prisons to our county gaols and houses of correction, I am disposed to believe that the same proportion, also, of
their inmates is brought within their walls by intemperance. It is
well known, that a considerable portion of the small debts collected
or attempted to be collected by the law, are for spirituous liquors ;
and that the least evil this liquor has done its consumers, has been
to bring them within the poor debtors' ward of a gaol.

If we pass from vice to pauperism, we shall find a similar result.
Pauperism is another of the greatest public burdens ; and is, at this
moment, tasking the ingenuity of the statesman and philanthropist
in Europe and America, as a great and growing public evil, which
seems to derive a principle of increase from the measures necessary
to its alleviation. I believe we may, in like manner, set down
three fourths of the pauperism which prevails, to the direct or remote influence of intemperance. In fact, intemperance is peculiarly a principle of pauperism ; more directly so than of crime, though
it tends strongly enough to crime. But every man who depends
upon his industry for his support and that of his family, by becom-

ing intemperate, unavoidably becomes a pauper. His strength and health are impaired; his arm palsied; his energies stupified; his earnings squandered; his credit and character sacrificed;—all around him, except those who are unfortunately bound to him by ties that cannot be broken, are repelled;—and the man sinks into pauperism, almost as a matter of course. He cannot be rescued.

But it must not be forgotten, that, in addition to the crimes which people our prisons; in addition to the poverty which seeks a refuge in the alms-house; there is an untold amount, both of want and vice in the world, which, although not exposed to the public view, either in the prisons or poor-houses, exists, and inflicts the most cruel sufferings and sorrows on a large part of the human family; and of this vice and want, a very large proportion is produced by intemperance. Take the case of a man, in easy circumstances, in town or country, of intemperate habits, but yet retaining self-control enough to manage his property, and honesty enough to keep out of gaol. This man, of course, will be neither a convict nor a pauper; on the contrary, he may fill what is called a respectable station in society; and yet, under the influence of a daily indulgence in ardent spirits, he may be the very tyrant of his household; never pleased, never soothed, never gratified, when the utmost has been done by every body to gratify him; often turbulent and outrageous; sometimes cruel; the terror of those whom he is bound by every law of God and man to protect; the shame of those whom nature teaches to reverence and love him. Such a man falls not into the clutches of the law; but, in a moral point of view, I deem him much more criminal than the ignorant, weak-minded, needy, sorely tempted creature, who cannot resist the temptation of passing a counterfeit bill, for which he is sentenced, for two or three years, to the state's prison. Such a man does not take refuge in the alms-house, nor drive his family to it; but the coarsest and hardest bread that is broken within its walls, is a dainty, compared with the luxuries of his cheerless table.

Then,—as to poverty. I believe the poverty out of the alms-house, produced by intemperance, is greater in the amount of suffering which it occasions, than the poverty in the alms-house. To the victims of drunkenness, whom it has conducted to the alms-house, one bitter ingredient of the cup is spared. The sense of shame, and the struggles of honest pride are at length over. But take the case of a person, whose family is dependent on the joint labor of its heads. Suppose the man a hard-working mechanic or farmer, the woman an industrious housewife, and the family supported by their united labor, frugality, and diligence. The man, as the phrase is, 'takes to drink.' What happens? The immediate consequence is, that the cost of the liquor which he consumes, is taken from the fund which was before barely adequate for their support. They must, therefore, reduce some other part of their expenditure. They have no luxuries, and must, accordingly pinch in the frugal comforts and necessaries of life, in wholesome food, in decent clothing, in fuel, in the education of the children. As the habit of excess increases, there must be more and more of this melancholy retrenchment. The old clothes, already worn out, must be worn longer; the daily fare, none too good at the beginning, becomes daily more meagre and scanty; the leak in the roof, for want of a nail, a shingle, or a bit of board, grows wider every winter; the number of panes of broken glass, whose place is poorly supplied with old hats and rags, daily increases; but not so the size of the unreplenished wood-pile, which no longer furnishes an adequate defence against the piercing elements. Before long, the children are kept from school, for want of books and clothing; and, at length, the wretched family are ashamed to show their sordid tatters in the meeting-house, on the Sabbath day. Meantime, the fund for the support of the family, the labor of its head, although burdened with a constantly growing charge for liquor, is diminished, in consequence of the decline of his health, strength, and energy. He is constantly earning less, and of what he earns, constantly consuming more unproductively, —destructively. Let this process proceed a year or two, and see to what they are reduced, and how poverty passes into crime. Look into his hovel, for such, by this time, it is, when he comes home on Saturday evening;—the wages of his week's labor already squandered in excess. Not wholly intoxicated, he is yet heated with liquor, and craves more. Listen to the brutal clamors, accompanied by threats and oaths, with which he demands of his family the food, which they have been able to procure neither for themselves nor him. See the poor, grown-up children,—boys and girls, perhaps young men and women, old enough to feel the shame as well as the misery of their heritage,—without a tinge of health upon their cheeks, without a spark of youthful cheerfulness in their eyes, silent and terrified, creeping supperless for the night, to their wretched garret, to escape outrage, curses, and blows, from the author of their being. Watch the heart-broken wife, as, with a countenance haggard with care and woe, she seeks in vain to supply the wants of a half-starved, sickly, shrieking babe, out of the fountain which hunger, and ill-usage, and despair have exhausted; and then return in the morning, and find her blood, and the infant's, wet upon the hearth-stone. Do I paint from the imagination, or do I paint from nature? Am I sporting with your feelings, or might I heighten the picture, and yet spare you many a heart-sickening trait from real life?

In a word, sir, when we contemplate intemperance in all its bearings and effects on the ·condition and character of men, I believe we shall come to the conclusion, that it is the greatest evil, which, as beings of a compound nature, we have to fear: the greatest, because striking directly at *the ultimate principle of the constitution of Man.* Let us contemplate this point a moment, for within it is comprehended, if I mistake not, the whole philosophy of this subject. Our life exists in a mysterious union of the corporeal and intellectual principles, an alliance of singular intimacy, as well as of strange contrast, between the two extremes of being. In their due relation to each other, and in the rightful discharge of their respective functions, I do not know whether the pure ethereal essence itself, (at least as far as we can comprehend it, which is but faintly), ought more to excite our admiration than this most wondrous compound of spirit and matter. I do not know that it is extravagant to say, that there is as signal a display of the Divine skill in linking those intellectual powers, which are the best image of the Divinity, with the forms and properties of matter, as in the creation of orders of beings purely disembodied and spiritual. When I contrast the dull and senseless clod of the valley, in its unanimated state, with the curious hand, the glowing cheek, the beaming eye, the discriminating sense which dwells in a thousand nerves, I feel the force of that inspired exclamation, ' I am fearfully and wonderfully made!' And when I consider the action and

reaction of soul and body on each other, the impulse given to voli-
tion from the senses; and again to the organs by the will; when
I think how thoughts,—so exalted, that, though they comprehend
all else, they cannot comprehend the laws of their own existence,
—are yet able to take a shape in the material air, to issue and
travel from one sense in one man to another sense in another man;
—so that, as the words drop from my lips, the secret chambers of
the soul are thrown open, and its invisible ideas made manifest,—
I am lost in wonder. If to this I add the reflection, how the world
and its affairs are governed, the face of nature changed, oceans
crossed, continents settled, families of men gathered and kept together
for generations, and monuments of power, wisdom, and taste erected, which last for ages after the hands that reared them have turned
to dust,—and all this by the regency of that fine intellectual principle, which sits modestly concealed behind its veil of clay, and
moves its subject organs, I find no words to express my admiration
of that union of mind and matter, by which these miracles are
wrought. Who *can* thus contemplate the wonder, the beauty, the
vast utility, the benevolence, the indescribable fitness of this organization, and not feel that this vice of intemperance, which aims
directly to destroy it, is the *arch-abomination* of our natures ; tending not merely to create a conflict between the nicely adjusted
principles ; but to assure the triumph of that which is low, base,
sensual, and earthly, over the heavenly and pure ; to convert this
so curiously organized frame into a disordered, crazy machine, and
to drag down the soul to the slavery of grovelling lusts ?

In the first place, there is the shameful abuse of the bounties of
Providence, which, after making the substantial provision for the
supply of our daily wants,—after spreading out the earth, with its
vegetable stores, as a great table for our nutriment, and appointing
the inferior animals for our solid food, was pleased,—as it would
seem, of mere grace and favor,—to add unnumbered cordial spirits
to gratify and cheer us,—sweet waters and lively spices,—to fill the
fibres of the cane with its luscious sirups, the clusters of the vine,
with its cooling juices, and a hundred aromatic leaves, berries, and
fruits, with their refreshing and reviving essences :—and even to
infuse into the poppy an anodyne against the sharpest pains our
frail flesh is heir to ;—I say it is the first aggravation of the sin of

intemperance, that it seizes on all these kind and bountiful provisions, and turns them into a source not of comfort and health, but of excess,—indecently revelling at the modest banquet of nature, shamefully surfeiting at the sober table of Providence, and converting every thing that has a life and power, alike the exhilarating and the soothing, the stimulant and the opiate, into one accursed poison.

Next come the ravages of this all-destroying vice on the health of its victims. You see them resolved, as it were, to anticipate the corruption of their natures. They cannot wait to get sick and die. They think the worm is slow in his approach, and sluggish at his work. They wish to reconvert the dust, before their hour comes, into its primitive deformity and pollution. My friend, who spoke before me, (Dr Pierson), called it a *partial* death. I would rather call it a *double* death, by which they drag about with them, above the grave, a mass of diseased, decaying, aching clay. They will not only commit suicide, but do it in such a way as to be the witnesses and conscious victims of the cruel process of self-murder; doing it by degrees, by inches; quenching the sight, benumbing the brain, laying down the arm of industry to be cut off; and changing a fair, healthy, robust frame, for a shrinking, suffering, living corpse, with nothing of vitality but the power of suffering, and with every thing of death but its peace.

Then follows the wreck of property,—the great object of human pursuit; the temporal ruin, which comes, like an avenging angel, to waste the substance of the intemperate; which crosses their threshold, commissioned, as it were, to plague them with all the horrors of a ruined fortune and blasted prospect; and passes before their astonished sight, in the dread array of affairs perplexed, debts accumulated, substance squandered, honor tainted,—wife, children cast out upon the mercy of the world,—and he, who should have been their guardian and protector, dependent for his unearned daily bread on those to whom he is a burden and a curse.

Bad as all this is, much as it is, it is neither the greatest nor the worst part of the aggravations of the crime of intemperance. It produces consequences of still more awful moment. It first exasperates the passions, and then takes off from them the restraints of the reason and will; maddens and then unchains the tiger, ravening for blood ; tramples all the intellectual and moral man under the feet of the stimulated clay ; lays the understanding, the kind affections, and the conscience, in the same grave with prosperity and health ; and, having killed the body, kills the soul !

Such, faintly described, is the vice of intemperance. Such it still exists in our land ; checked, and, as we hope, declining, but still prevailing to a degree which invites all our zeal for its effectual suppression. Such as I have described it, it exists, I fear, in every city, in every town, in every village in our country. Such, and so formidable is its power. But I rejoice in the belief, that an antagonist principle of equal power has been brought into the field. Public opinion, in all its strength, is enlisted against it. Men, that agree in nothing else, unite in this. Religious divisions are healed and party feuds forgotten, in this good cause. Individuals and societies, private citizens and the government, have joined, in waging war against intemperance ; and, above all, the press,— the great engine of reform,—is thundering, with all its artillery, against it. It is a moment of great interest ; and also of considerable delicacy. That period in a moral reform, in which a great evil, that has long passed comparatively unquestioned, is overtaken by a sudden bound of Public Opinion, is somewhat critical. Individuals, as honest as their neighbors, are surprised in pursuits and practices, sanctioned by the former standard of moral sentiment, but below the mark of the reform. Tenderness and delicacy are necessary, to prevent such persons, by mistaken pride of character, from being made enemies of the cause. In our denunciations of the evil, we must take care not to include those whom a little prudence might bring into cordial cooperation with us in its suppression. Let us, sir, mingle discretion with our zeal ; and the greater will be our success in this pure and noble enterprise.

ORATION

———

FELLOW CITIZENS,

I HAVE accepted, with great cheerfulness, the invitation with which you have honored me, to address you on this occasion. The citizens of Worcester did not wait to receive a second call, before they hastened to the relief of the citizens of Middlesex, in the times that tried men's souls. I should feel myself degenerate and unworthy, could I hesitate to come, and, in my humble measure, assist you in commemorating those exploits which your fathers so promptly and so nobly aided our fathers in achieving.

Apprised by your committee, that the invitation, which has brought me hither, was given on behalf of the citizens of Worcester, without distinction of party, I can truly say, that it is also, in this respect, most congenial to my feelings. I have several times had occasion to address my fellow citizens on the fourth of July; and sometimes at periods when the party excitement,—now so happily, in a great measure, allayed,—has been at its height; and when custom and public sentiment would have borne me out, in seizing the opportunity of inculcating the political views of those on whose behalf I spoke. But of no such opportunity have I ever availed myself. I have never failed, as far as it was in my power, to lead the minds of those whom I have had the honor to address, to those common topics of grateful recollection, which unite the patriotic feelings of every American. It has not been my fault, if ever, on this auspicious national anniversary, a single individual

44

has forgotten that he was a brother of one great family, while he has recollected that he was a member of a party.

In fact, fellow citizens, I deem it one of the happiest effects of the celebration of this anniversary, that, when undertaken in the spirit which has animated you on this occasion, it has a natural tendency to soften the harshness of party, which I cannot but regard as the great bane of our prosperity. It was pronounced by the Father of his Country, in his valedictory address to the people of the United States, ' the worst enemy of popular governments;' and the experience of almost every administration, from his own down, has confirmed the truth of the remark. The spirit of party unquestionably has its source in some of the native passions of the heart; and free governments naturally furnish more of its aliment than those under which the liberty of speech and of the press is restrained by the strong arm of power. But so naturally does party run into extremes, so unjust, cruel, and remorseless is it in its excess,—so ruthless in the war which it wages against private character,—so unscrupulous in the choice of means for the attainment of selfish ends,—so sure is it, eventually, to dig the grave of those free institutions, of which it pretends to be the necessary accompaniment,—so inevitably does it end in military despotism and unmitigated tyranny, that I do not know how the voice and influence of a good man could, with more propriety, be exerted, than in the effort to assuage its violence.

We must be strengthened in this conclusion, when we consider that party controversy is constantly showing itself, as unreasonable and absurd, as it is unamiable and pernicious. If we needed illustrations of the truth of this remark, we should not be obliged to go far to find them. In the unexpected turns that continually occur in affairs, events arise, which put to shame the selfish adherence of resolute champions to their party names. No election of chief magistrate has ever been more strenuously contested, than that which agitated the country the last year; and I do not know that party spirit, in our time at least, has ever run higher, or the party press been more virulent on both sides. And what has followed? The election was scarcely decided; the President, thus chosen, had not entered upon the second term of his office, before the state of things was so entirely changed, as to produce, in reference to the most important question which has engaged the attention of the country since the adoption of the Constitution, a concert of opinion among those, who, two months before, had stood in hostile array against each other. The measures adopted by the President, for the preservation of the Union, met with the most cordial support in Congress and out of it, from those who had most strenuously opposed his election; and he, in his turn, depended upon that support, not only as auxiliary, but as indispensable, to his administration, in this great crisis. And what do we now behold? The President of the United States, traversing New-England, under demonstrations of public respect, as cordial and as united, as he would receive in Pennsylvania or Tennessee; and the great head of his opponents in this part of the country, the illustrious champion of the Constitution in the Senate of the United States, welcomed, with equal cordiality and equal unanimity, by men of all names and parties, in the distant West.

And what is the cause of this wonderful and auspicious change; —auspicious, however transitory its duration may unfortunately prove? That cause is to be sought in a principle so vital, that it is almost worth the peril to which the country's best interests have been exposed, to see its existence and power made manifest and demonstrated. This principle is, that the union of the States,— which has been in danger,—must, at all hazards, be preserved; that union, which, in the same parting language of Washington which I have already cited, 'is the main pillar in the edifice of our real independence, the support of our tranquillity at home, our peace abroad, our safety, our prosperity; of that very liberty which we so highly prize.' Men have forgotten their little feuds, in the perils of the Constitution. The afflicted voice of the country, in its hour of danger, has charmed down, with a sweet persuasion, the angry passions of the day; and men have felt that they had no heart to ask themselves the question, Whether their party were triumphant or prostrate? when the infinitely more momentous question was pressing upon them, Whether the Union was to be preserved or destroyed?

In speaking, however, of the preservation of the Union, as the great and prevailing principle in our political system, I would not have it understood, that I suppose this portion of the country to be more interested in it than any other. The intimation which is sometimes made, and the belief which, in some quarters, is avowed, that the Northern States have a peculiar and a selfish interest in the preservation of the Union ;—that they derive advantages from it, at the uncompensated expense of other portions ;—I take to be one of the grossest delusions ever propagated by men, deceived themselves, or willing to deceive others. I know, indeed, that the dissolution of the Union would be the source of incalculable injury to every part of it; as it would, in great likelihood, lead to border and civil war, and eventually to military despotism. But not to us would the bitter chalice be first presented. This portion of the Union,—erroneously supposed to have a peculiar interest in its preservation,—would be sure to suffer, no doubt, but it would also be among the last to suffer, from that deplorable event ; while that portion, which is constantly shaking over us the menace of separation, would be swept with the besom of destruction, from the moment an offended Providence should permit that purpose to reach its ill-starred maturity.

Far distant be all these inauspicious calculations. It is the natural tendency of celebrating the Fourth of July, to strengthen the sentiment of attachment to the Union. It carries us back to other days of yet greater peril to our beloved country, when a still stronger bond of feeling and action united the hearts of her children. It recalls to us the sacrifices of those who deserted all the walks of private industry, and abandoned the prospects of opening life, to engage in the service of their country. It reminds us of the fortitude of those who took upon themselves the perilous responsibility of leading the public councils in the paths of revolution ; in the sure alternative of that success, which was all but desperate, and that scaffold, already menaced as their predestined fate, if they failed. It calls up, as it were, from the beds of glory and peace where they lie,—from the heights of Charlestown to the southern plains,—the vast and venerable congregation of those who bled in the sacred cause. They gather in saddened majesty around us, and adjure us, by their returning agonies and reopening wounds, not to permit our feuds and dissensions to destroy the value of that birthright, which they purchased with their precious lives.

There seems to me a peculiar interest attached to the present anniversary celebration. It is just a half century, since the close of the revolutionary war. It is the jubilee of the restoration of peace between the United States and Great Britain. It has been sometimes objected to these anniversary celebrations, and to the natural tendency of the train of remark, in the addresses which they call forth, that they tend to keep up a hostile feeling toward the country from which we are descended, and with which we are at peace. Without denying that this celebration may, like all other human things, have been abused in injudicious hands, for such a purpose, I cannot, nevertheless, admit that, either as philanthropists or citizens of the world, we are required to renounce any of the sources of an honest national pride. A revolution like ours is a most momentous event in human affairs. History does not furnish its parallel. Characters like those of our fathers,—services, sacrifices, and sufferings like theirs, form a sacred legacy, transmitted to our veneration, to be cherished, to be preserved unimpaired, and to be handed down to after ages. Could we consent, on any occasion, to deprive them of their just meed of praise, we should prove ourselves degenerate children ; and we should be guilty, as a people, of a sort of public and collective self-denial, unheard of among nations, whose annals contain any thing of which their citizens have reason to be proud. Our brethren in Great Britain teach us no such lesson. In the zeal with which they nourish the boast of a brave ancestry, by the proud recollections of their history, they have,—so to speak,—consecrated their gallant and accomplished neighbors, the French,—(from whom they, also, are originally, in part descended),—as a sort of natural enemy, an object of hereditary hostile feeling, in peace and in war. That it could be thought ungenerous or unchristian to commemorate the exploits of the Wellingtons, the Nelsons, or the Marlboroughs, I believe is an idea that never entered into the head of an English statesman or patriot.

But, at the same time, I admit it to be not so much the duty as the privilege, of an American citizen, to acquit this obligation to the memory of his fathers, with discretion and generosity. It is true, that the greatest incident of our history,—that which lies at the foundation of our most important and most cherished national traditions,—is the revolutionary war. But it is not the less true, that there are many ties, which ought to bind our feelings to the land of our fathers. It is characteristic of a magnanimous people, to do justice to the merits of every other nation; especially of a nation with whom we have been at variance and are now in amity; and most especially of a nation of common blood. Where are the graves of our fathers? In England. The school of the free principles, in which, as the last great lesson, the doctrine of our independence, was learned,—where did it subsist? In the hereditary love of liberty of the Anglo-Saxon race. The great names which, —before America began to exist for civilization and humanity,— immortalized the language which we speak, and made our mother tongue a heart-stirring dialect, which a man is proud to take on his lips, whithersoever, on the face of the earth, he may wander, are English. If it be, in the language of Cowper,

> praise enough
> To fill the ambition of a private man,
> That Chatham's language is his mother tongue,
> And Wolfe's great name compatriot with his own,

let it not be beneath the pride nor beyond the gratitude of an American to remember, that Wolfe fell on the soil of this country, with some of the best and bravest of New-England by his side; and that it was among the last of the thrilling exclamations, with which Chatham shook the House of Lords:—'Were I an American, as I am an Englishman, I never would lay down my arms; never, never, never!'

There were, indeed, great and glorious achievements in America, before the Revolution, in which the colonies and the mother country were intimately and honorably associated. There lived brave men before the Agamemnons of seventy-six; and, thanks to the recording pen of history, their names are not and never shall be forgotten. Nothing but the noon-tide splendor of the revolutionary period could have sufficed to cast into comparative forgetfulness the heroes and the achievements of the old French war, and of that which preceded it in 1744. If we wished an effective admonition of the unreasonableness of permitting the events of the Revolution to engender a feeling of permanent hostility in our minds, toward the land of our fathers, we might find it in the fact, that the war of independence was preceded, by only twenty years, by that mighty conflict of the Seven Years' war, in which the best blood of England and the colonies was shed beneath their united banners, displayed on the American soil, and in a cause which all the colonies, and especially those of New-England, had greatly at heart. And this observation suggests the topic to which I beg leave to call your attention, for the residue of the hour.

It will not be expected of me, on this happy occasion,—(which seems more appropriately to be devoted to the effusion of kind and patriotic feeling, than to labored discussion,—to engage in a regular essay) ;—particularly as other urgent engagements have left me but a very brief period of preparation, for my appearance before you. I shall aim only, out of the vast storehouse of the revolutionary theme, to select one or two topics, less frequently treated than some others, but not inappropriate to the day. Among these, I think we may safely place *the civil and military education which the country had received, in the earlier fortunes of the colonies;* the great *præparatio libertatis*, which had fitted out our fathers to reap the harvest of independence on bloody fields, and to secure and establish it, by those wise institutions, in which the only safe enjoyment of freedom resides.

This subject, in its full extent, would be greatly too comprehensive for the present occasion, and the circumstances under which I have the honor to address you. I shall confine myself chiefly to the Seven Years' war, as connected with the war of the Revolution ;—a subject which has not, perhaps, received all the attention which it merits. The influence on the revolutionary struggle of the long civil contest which had been kept up with the Crown, and the effect of this contest in awakening the minds of men in the colonies, and forming them to the intelligent and skilful defence of their rights, have been often enough set forth. But the peculiar and extraordinary concurrence of facts, in the military history of the colonies; the manner in which the moving causes of the Revolution are interwoven with the great incidents of the previous wars; deserve a particular development. If I mistake not, they disclose a systematic connexion of events, which, for harmony, interest, and grandeur, will not readily be matched with a parallel in civil history.

When America was approached by the Europeans, it was in the occupancy of the Indian tribes; an unhappy race of beings, not able, as the event has proved, to stand before the advance of civilization;—feeble, on the whole, compared with the colonists, when armed with the weapons and arts of Europe; but yet capable of carrying on a most harassing and destructive warfare, for several generations; particularly after having learned the use of fire-arms, and provided themselves with steel tomahawks and scalping-knives from the French and English colonists. Between the two latter, the continent was almost equally divided. From Nova Scotia to Florida, the English possessed the sea-coast. From the St Lawrence to the Mississippi, the French had established themselves in the interior. The Indian tribes, who occupied the whole line of the frontier, and the intermediate space between the settlements, were alternately stimulated by the two parties, against each other; but more extensively and effectively, along the greater part of the line, by the French against the English, than by the English against the French. With every war in Europe, between England and France, the frontier was in flames, from the Savannah to the St Croix; and down to so late a period did this state of things last, that I have noticed, within eighteen months, the death of an aged person, who was tomahawked by the Canadian savages, on their last incursion to the banks of the Connecticut river, as low down as Northampton. There were periods, at which the expulsion of the English from the continent seemed inevitable;—and at other times, the French empire in America appeared equally insecure. But it was plain, that no thought of independence could suggest itself, and no plan of throwing off the colonial yoke could prosper, while a hostile power of French and Canadian savages, exasperated by the injuries inflicted and retaliated for a hundred years, was encamped along the frontier. On the contrary, the habit, so long kept up, of acting in concert with the mother country against their French and savage neighbors, was one of the strongest ties of interest which bound the colonies to the Crown.

At length, in the year 1754, the conflicting claims of the two Crowns to the jurisdiction of various portions of the Indian territory, belonging, perhaps, by no very good title to either of them, led to the commencement of hostilities between the English and the

French, in different parts of the colonies. Among the measures of strength which were adopted against the common foe, was the plan of uniting the colonies in a general confederation, not dissimilar to that which was actually formed in the revolutionary war. It is justly remarked by the historians, as a curious coincidence of dates and events, that, on the fourth of July, 1754, General Washington, then a colonel in the provincial service, under Virginia, should have been compelled to capitulate to the French, at Fort Necessity, and that Benjamin Franklin, as one of the commissioners assembled at Albany, should have put his name, on the same day, to the abortive plan of the confederation ; and that, on the very same day, twenty-two years afterwards, General Washington should be found at the head of the armies of Independent and United America, and Franklin in the Congress at Philadelphia, among the authors and signers of the Declaration.

It is obvious, that the necessary elements of a Union could not subsist in a state of dependence on a foreign government ; and the failure of the confederation of 1754 is another proof, that our Union is but the form in which our Independence was organized. One in their origin, there is little doubt that they will continue so in their preservation. The most natural event of a secession of a small part of the Union from the other States, would be its re-colonization by Great Britain. It was only the *United* States which were acknowledged to be independent by Great Britain, or declared to be independent by themselves.

Two years after the period last mentioned, namely, in 1756, the flames of the war spread from America to Europe, where it burst forth, and raged to an extent, and with a violence, scarcely surpassed by the mighty contests of Napoleon. The empress of Austria, and Frederic the Great, France and Spain,—not yet humbled, and united by the family compact in the closest alliance,—and above all, England,—then comprehending within her dominions the colonies that now form the United States, and at last roused and guided by the towering genius and the lion heart of the elder Pitt,—plunged, with all their resources, into the conflict. There were various subsidiary objects at heart, with the different powers ; but the great prize of the contest, between England and France, was the possession of America. That prize, by the fortune of war,

45

or rather by that Providence which, in this manner, was preparing
the way for American independence, was adjudged to the arms of
England. The great work was accomplished,—the decisive blow
was struck,—when Wolfe fell, in the arms of victory, on the heights
of Abraham ; furnishing, in his fate, no unapt similitude of the
British empire in America, which that victory had seemed to consummate. As Wolfe died in the moment of triumph, so the power
of the British on this continent received its death blow in the event
that destroyed its rival.

It is curious to remark, how instantly this effect began to develop itself. Up to this time, the utmost political energy of the
colonies, in conjunction with that of the mother country, had been
required to maintain a foothold on the continent. They were in
constant apprehension of being swept away, by the united strength
of the French and Indians. Their thoughts had never wandered
beyond the frontier line, marked as it was, in its whole extent, with
fire and blood. But the power of the French, once expelled from
the country, as it was, with a trifling exception at New Orleans,
and their long line of strong holds transferred to the British government, the minds of men immediately moved forward, over the
illimitable space that seemed opening to them. A political miracle was wrought ; the mountains sunk, the vallies rose, and the
portals of the West were burst asunder. The native tribes of the
forest still roamed the interior, but, in the imaginations of men,
they derived their chief terror from the alliance with the French.
The idea did not immediately present itself to the minds of the
Americans, that they might, in like manner, be armed and stimulated by the English against the colonies, whenever a movement
toward independence should require such a check. Hutchinson
remarks an altered tone in the state papers of Massachusetts, from
this period, which he ascribes, less distinctly than he might, to the
same cause. Governor Bernard, on occasion of the fall of Quebec, congratulates the General Court on ' the blessings they derive
from their *subjection* to Great Britain ;' and the Council, in their
echo to the speech, acknowledge that it is ' to their *relation* to
Great Britain, that they owe their freedom ;' and the same historian traces the rise of a vague idea of independency to the same
period and the same influence upon the imaginations of men, of
the removal of the barrier of the French power.

The subversion of this power required, or was thought to require, a new colonial system. Its principles were few and simple. An army was to be stationed, and a revenue raised, in America. The army was to enforce the collection of the revenue ; the revenue was to pay the cost of the army ; and by this army, stationed in the colonies and paid by them, the colonies were to be kept down and the French kept out. The policy was ingenious and plausible ; it wanted but one thing for its successful operation ; but that want was fatal. It needed to be put to practice among men who would submit to it. It would have done exceedingly well, in the new Canadian conquests ; but it was wholly out of place among the descendants of the Pilgrims and the Puritans. Up to this hour, although the legislative supremacy of England had not been contested in general terms, yet the government at home had never attempted to enact laws, simply for the collection of revenue. They had confined themselves to the indirect operation of the laws of trade, (which purported to be for the advantage of all parts of the empire, the colonies as well as the mother country), and those not rigidly enforced. The reduction of the French possessions was the signal, not merely for the infusion of new vigor into the administration of the commercial system, but for the assertion of the naked right to tax America.

When a great event is to be brought about, in the order of Providence, the first thing which arrests the attention of the student of its history in after times, is the appearance of the fitting instruments for its accomplishment. They come forward, and take their places on the great stage of action. They know not themselves, for what they are raised up ; but there they are. James Otis was then in the prime of manhood, about thirty-seven years of age. He was fully persuaded, that the measures adopted by the British government were unconstitutional, and he was armed with the genius, and learning ; the wit, and eloquence ; the vehemence of temper, the loftiness of soul ; the firmness of nerve, the purity of purpose, necessary to constitute a great popular leader in difficult times. The question was brought before a judicial tribunal, I must confess, in a small way,—on the petition of the Custom House officers of Salem, for writs of assistance to enforce the acts of trade. Otis appeared, as the counsel of the commercial interest, to oppose the granting of these writs. Large fees were tendered him; but his language was, 'In such a cause, I despise all fees.' His associate counsel, Mr Thacher, preceded him in the argument of the cause, with moderation and suavity; 'but Otis,' in the language of the elder President Adams, who heard him, 'was a flame of fire. With a promptitude of classical allusions, a depth of research, a rapid summary of historical events and dates, a profusion of legal authorities, a prophetic glance of his eye into futurity,' (that glorious futurity, which he lived not, alas, to enjoy), 'and a deep torrent of impetuous eloquence, he carried all before him. American independence was then and there born. Every man of an immense crowded audience appeared to me to go away, as I did, ready to take arms against writs of assistance. Then and there was the first scene of the first act of opposition to the arbitrary claims of Great Britain.'*

It would be travelling over a beaten road, to pursue the narrative of the parliamentary contest from this time to 1775. My object has merely been to point out the curious historical connexion between the consolidation and the downfall of the British empire in America, consequent upon the successful issue of the Seven Years' war. One consequence only may deserve to be specified, of a different character, but springing from the same source, and tending to the same end, and more decisive of the fate of the Revolution, than any other merely political circumstance. The event which wrested her colonial possessions on this continent from France, gave to our fathers a friend in that power which had hitherto been their most dreaded enemy, and prepared France,—by the gradual operation of public sentiment and the influence of reasons of state,—when the accepted time should arrive, to extend to them a helping hand to aid them in establishing their independency. Next to a re-conquest of her own possessions, or rather vastly more efficacious toward humbling Great Britain, than a re-conquest of the colonies of France, was the great policy of enabling the whole British empire in America, alike the recent acquisitions and the ancient colonies along the coast, (for to this length the policy of France extended), to throw off the English yoke. France played,

* Tudor's Life of Otis, page 61.

in this respect, on a much grander scale, that game of state, which gave Mr Canning so much *éclat* a few years since, in reference to the affairs of Spain. Perceiving Spain to be in the occupation of the French army, Mr Canning, with a policy, it must be owned, more effective as towards France than friendly toward Spain, determined, as he said, to redress the balance of power in the Spanish colonies; and in order to render the acquisition of Spain comparatively worthless to France, to use his own language, ' he called into being a new world in the West.' Much more justly might the Count de Vergennes have boasted, that, England having wrested from France her American colonies, he had determined to redress the balance of power in the quarter where it was disturbed; to wrest from the victorious arms of England their new acquisitions, —to strike their ancient foothold from beneath their feet; and call into being a new world in the West. On the score of generosity, the French minister had the advantage, that his blow was one of retaliation, aimed at his enemy, while the British minister struck at a power with which he was at peace, through the sides of his ally.

But all this wonderful conjunction of political causes does not sufficiently explain, in a practical way, the phenomenon of the Revolution, nor furnish a satisfactory account of the promptitude with which the feeble colonies made the decisive appeal to arms against the colossal power of England,—the boldness with which they plunged into the revolutionary struggle,—and the success with which, through a thousand vicissitudes, they conducted it to a happy close. Fully to comprehend this, we must again cast our eyes on the war of 1744, and still more on that of 1756, as forming a great school of military conduct and discipline, in which the future leaders of the Revolution were trained to the duties of the camp and the field. It was here that they became familiarized to the idea of great military movements, and accustomed to the direction of great military expeditions, conceived in the colonial councils, and often carried on, in the first instance, by the unaided colonial resources.

In the extent of their military efforts, the numbers of men enlisted in the New-England colonies,—the boldness and comprehension of the campaigns,—the variety and hardship of the service, and the brilliancy of the achievements, I could almost venture to say, that as much was effected in these two wars as in that of the Revolution. The military efforts of the colonies had, indeed, from the first, been remarkable. It was calculated, near the commencement of the last century, that every fifth man in Massachusetts, capable of bearing arms, had been engaged in the service, at one time. The more melancholy calculation was at the same time made, that, in the period of thirty years from king Philip's war, from five to six thousand of the youth of the colony had perished in the wars. In the second year of the war of 1744, the famous expedition against Louisburg was planned by the Governor of Massachusetts, and sanctioned by its General Court. Three thousand two hundred of her citizens, with ten armed ships, sailed against that place. This force, compared with the population of Massachusetts at that time, was equal to an army of twelve thousand men with our present numbers ; and the same immense force was kept up the following year. Louisburg, by an auspicious coincidence, fell on the 17th of June, just thirty years before the battle of Bunker-Hill. Colonel Gridley, who pointed the mortar, which, on the third trial, threw a shell into the citadel at Louisburg, marked out the lines of the redoubt on Bunker-Hill ;* and old Colonel Frye, who hastened to join his regiment on Bunker-Hill, after the fight had begun, recalling the surrender of Louisburg, at which he had been present thirty years before, declared that it was an auspicious day for America, and that he would take the risk of it. At the treaty of Aix-la-Chapelle, between the great powers of Europe, this poor little New-England conquest was all that Great Britain had to give, for the restitution of all the conquests made by France in the course of the war.

But in the war of 1756, the military efforts of the colonies were still more surprising. If it is said, that they were upheld by the resources of the mother country, let it not be forgotten, in making the comparison of their exertions in this war, with those in the Revolution, that in the latter they had the powerful support of France. The Seven Years' war was carried on in America, at the same time, in the extreme south, against the Cherokee Indians,

* For this, and some other facts in this Address, I am indebted to Colonel Swett's interesting and valuable history of the battle of Bunker-Hill.

then a formidable enemy, in the western part of Virginia and Pennsylvania, at Niagara, on the whole frontier line, from Albany to the St Lawrence and Quebec, in the extreme north-eastern corner of the country, where Nova Scotia and Cape Breton were retaken, in the West Indies and on the Spanish Main. The regiments of New-England and New-York, in this war, fought on lake Ontario and lake George, at Quebec, in Nova Scotia, in Martinico, Porto Bello, and at the Havana. From the year 1754 to 1762, there were raised, by the single province of Massachusetts, thirty-five thousand men ; and for three years successively, seven thousand men each year. This was in addition to large numbers of the sea-faring inhabitants, who enlisted or were impressed into the British navy ; and in addition to those who enlisted in the regular British army, who amounted, in one year, to near a thousand. Napoleon, at the summit of his power, did not carry an equal number of the French people into the field. An army of seven thousand, compared with the population of Massachusetts, in the middle of the last century, is considerably greater than an army of one million for France, in the time of Napoleon.

If I were to repeat the names of all the distinguished pupils in this great school of war, I should have to run over the list of a large proportion of the officers of the revolutionary army. Among them were Prescott, Putnam, Stark, Gridley, Pomroy, Gates, Montgomery, Mercer, Lee, and, above all, Washington. If I were to undertake to recount the heroic adventures, the incredible hardships, the privations and exposures, that were endured in the frontier wilderness, in the warfare with the savage foe,—on the dreary scouting parties in mid-winter,—I should unfold a tale of human fortitude and human suffering, to which it would make the heart bleed to listen. I should speak of the gallant Colonel Williams, the founder of the important institution which bears his name, in the western part of the Commonwealth, the accomplished, affable, and beloved commander, who fell at the head of his regiment, on the bloody eighth of September, 1755. Nor would I forget the faithful Mohawk chieftain, Hendrick, who fell at his side. I should speak of Putnam, tied to a tree by a party of savages who had surprised him at the commencement of an action in a subsequent campaign, and exposed, in this condition, to the fire of both par-

ties; afterwards bound again to the stake, and the piles kindled
which were to burn him alive, but, by the interference of an Indian
warrior, rescued from this imminent peril, and preserved by Providence to be one of the thunderbolts of the Revolution. I should
speak of Gridley,—whom I have already mentioned,—the engineer at Louisburg, the artillerist at Quebec, where his corps
dragged up the only two field-pieces which were raised to the
heights of Abraham, in the momentous assault on that city, and
who, as I have already said, planned the lines of the redoubt on
Bunker-Hill, with consummate ability. I should speak of Pomroy,
of Northampton, who, in the former war, wrote to his wife from
Louisburg, that, 'if it were the will of God, he hoped to see her
pleasant face again; but if God, in his holy and sovereign Providence, has ordered it otherwise, he hoped to have a glorious meeting with her in the kingdom of heaven, where there are no wars,
nor fatiguing marches, nor roaring cannons, nor cracking bomb-
shells, nor long campaigns, but an eternity to spend in perfect harmony and undisturbed peace;'* and who did not only live to see
his wife's pleasant face again, but to slay with his own hands, in
the year 1755, the commander of the French army, the brave
Baron Dieskau; and who, on the 17th of June, 1775, dismounted
and passed Charlestown Neck, on his way to Bunker-Hill, on foot,
in the midst of a shower of balls, because he did not think it con-
scionable to ride General Ward's horse, which he had borrowed,
through the cross fire of the British ships of war and floating batteries. I should speak of Rogers, the New Hampshire partisan,
who, in one of the sharp conflicts in which his corps of rangers
was continually engaged, was shot through the wrist, and having
had his queue cut off by one of his men to stop up the wound,
went on with the fight. I should speak of the superhuman endurance and valor of Stark, a captain in the same corps of rangers,
throughout the Seven Years' war,—a colonel at Bunker-Hill,—
and who, by the victory at Bennington, which he planned and
achieved almost by the unaided resources of his own powerful
mind and daring spirit, first turned the tide of disaster in the revolutionary war. I should speak of Frye, who was included as

* See the Note at the end.

commander of the Massachusetts forces, in the disastrous capitulation of Fort William Henry, in 1757, and escaping, stripped and mangled, from the tomahawk of the savages, who fell upon them the moment they were marched out of the fort, wandered about the woods several days, naked and starving, but who was one of the first to obey the summons that ran through the country, on the 19th of April, 1775, and who called to mind the 17th of June, 1745, as he hastened to join his regiment on Bunker-Hill. I should speak of Lord Howe, the youthful, gallant, and favorite British general. On the eve of the fatal assault on Ticonderoga, in 1758, he sent for Stark to sup with him, on his bear-skin in his tent, and talk over the prospects of the ensuing day. He fell the next morning, at the head of his advancing column, equally lamented by Britons and Americans. The General Court of Massachusetts erected a monument to his memory, in Westminster Abbey; and Stark, who never spoke of him without emotion, used to rejoice, since he was to fall, that he fell before his distinguished talents could be employed against America. Above all, I should speak of Washington, the youthful Virginian colonel, as modest as brave, who seemed to bear a charmed life amidst the bullets of the French and Indians at Braddock's defeat, and who was shielded, on that most bloody day, by the arm of Providence, to become the earthly saviour of his country.

Such were some of the incidents which connect the Seven Years' war with that of the Revolution. Such was the school in which, upon the then unexplored banks of the Ohio, by the roaring waters of Niagara, and in the pathless wilderness of the North-Western frontier, the men of 1776 were trained, in the strictest school of British military discipline and conduct. And if there were wanted one instance more signal than all others, of the infatuation which at that time swayed the councils of Great Britain, it would be the fact, that the British ministry not only attempted to impose their unconstitutional laws upon men who had drawn in the whole great doctrine of English liberty with their mothers' milk, but who, a few years before, had, for eight campaigns, stood side by side with the veterans of the British army; who had marched beneath the wings of the British eagle, and shared the prey of the British lion, from Louisiana to Quebec.

46

At length the Revolution, with all this grand civil and military preparation, came on ; and oh, that I could paint out in worthy colors, the magnificent picture! Such a subject as it presents, considered as the winding up of a great drama, of which the opening scene begins with the landing of our fathers, is nowhere else, I firmly believe, to be found in the annals of man. It is a great national *Epos* of real life,—unsurpassed in grandeur and attraction. It comprehends every kind of interest,—politics of the most subtile and expansive schools ; great concerns of state and humanity, mingled up with personal intrigues ; the passions of ministers, and the arts of cabinets, in strange contrast with the mighty developments of Providence, which seem to take in the fate of the civilized world for ages. On the one hand, the great sanctuary of the British power, the *adytum imperii*, is heard, as Tacitus says of the sanctuary at Jerusalem, to resound with the valediction of the departing gods. On the other hand, the fair temple of American independence is seen rising, like an exhalation from the soil,

> Not in the sunshine and the smile of heaven,
> But wrapt in whirlwinds, and begirt with woes.

The incidents, the characters, are worthy of the drama. What names, what men ! Chatham, Burke, Fox, Franklin, the Adamses, Washington, Jefferson, and all the chivalry and all the diplomacy of Europe and America. The voice of generous disaffection sounds beneath the arches of St Stephen's ; and the hall of Congress rings with an eloquence like that, which

> Shook the arsenal, and fulmined over Greece,
> To Macedon and Artaxerxes' throne.

Then contemplate the romantic groups that crowd the military scene ; all the races of men, and all the degrees of civilization, brought upon the stage at once. The English veteran, the plaided Highlander, the hireling peasantry of Hesse-Cassel and Anspach, the gallant chevaliers of Poland, the well-appointed legions of France, led by her polished *noblesse*, the hardy American yeoman, his leather apron not always thrown aside, the mountain rifleman, the painted savage. At one moment, we hear the mighty *armadas* of Europe thundering in the Antilles. Anon we behold the blue-eyed Brunswickers, whose banners told, in their tattered sheets, of the victory of Minden, threading the wilderness between the St Lawrence and Albany, under an accomplished British gentleman, and capitulating to the American forces, commanded by a naturalized Virginian, who had been present at the capture of Martinico, and was shot through the body at Braddock's defeat. While the grand drama is closed at Yorktown, with the storm of the British lines, by the emulous columns of the French and American army ; the Americans, led by the gallant scion of the oldest French nobility, the heroic Lafayette ; a young New York lawyer, the gallant and lamented Hamilton, commanding the advanced guard.

Nor let us turn from the picture, without shedding a tear over the ashes of the devoted men who laid down their lives in the cause, from Lexington and Concord to the farthest sands of the South. Warren was the first conspicuous victim. If ever a man went to an anticipated and certain death, in obedience to the call of duty, he was that man. Though he had no military education, he knew, from the first, that to hold Bunker-Hill, in the state of the American army, was impracticable. He was against fortifying it, but overruled in that, he resolved to assist in its defence. His associate, in the provincial Congress, Mr Gerry, besought him not to risk his life, for that its loss was inevitable. Warren thought it might be so, but replied,—that he dwelt within the sound of the cannon, and that he should die beneath his roof, if he remained at home, while his countrymen were shedding their blood for him. Mr Gerry repeated, that if he went to the hill, he would surely be killed ; and Warren's rejoinder was,—' *Dulce et decorum est pro patria mori.*' Montgomery moved to the assault of Quebec in the depth of a Canadian winter, at the end of December, under a violent snow-storm. One gun only was fired from the batteries, but that proved fatal to the gallant commander and his aids, who fell where he had fought by the side of Wolfe, sixteen years before. Mercer passed through the Seven Years' war with Washington. On one occasion in that war, he wandered through the wilderness, wounded and faint with the loss of blood, for one hundred miles, subsisting on a rattle-snake which he killed by the way. He was pierced seven times through the body with a bayonet, at Princeton. Scammel, severely wounded at Saratoga, fell on the eve of the glorious success at Yorktown ; and Laurens, the youthful prodigy of valor and conduct, the last lamented victim of the war, paid the forfeit of his brilliant prospects after those of the country were secured.

These were all men who have gained a separate renown; who have secured a place for their names in the annals of liberty. But let us not, while we pay a well-deserved tribute to their memory, forget the thousand gallant hearts which poured out their life-blood in the undistinguished ranks ; who followed the call of duty up to the cannon's mouth ; who could not promise themselves the meed of fame, and, Heaven knows, could have been prompted by no hope of money ; the thousands who pined in loathsome prison-ships, or languished with the diseases of the camp ; and, returning from their country's service with broken fortunes and ruined constitutions, sunk into an early grave.

> ' How sleep the brave, who sink to rest,
> With all their country's wishes blest.
> When spring, with dewy fingers cold,
> Returns to deck their hallowed mould,
> She there shall dress a sweeter sod
> Than fancy's feet have ever trod.
> There honor comes, a pilgrim gray,
> To bless the turf that wraps their clay ;—
> And freedom shall awhile repair,
> To dwell a weeping hermit there.'

Still less let us forget, on this auspicious anniversary, the venerable survivors of the eventful contest. Let us rejoice, that so many of them are spared to enjoy the fruits of their efforts and sacrifices. Let us behold, in their gray locks and honorable scars, the strongest incentives to the discharge of every duty of the citizen and patriot ; and, above all, let us listen to the strong appeal which the whole army of the Revolution makes to us, through these its aged surviving members, to show our gratitude to those who fell, by smoothing the pathway to the grave of their brethren, whom years and the early hardships of the service yet spare for a short time among us.

But it is time to turn from all these mingled contemplations, to the practical lesson which it becomes us to draw from our reflections on this great subject.

Momentous as the Revolution was in its origin and causes, its incidents and characters, it derives a still greater interest from its results.

Fifty years have elapsed since the termination of the war, and in that half century we have been reaping fruits of the precious seed then sown,—most costly and peculiar. One general Constitution of federal government has been framed; and connected with it, in most harmonious relation, twenty-four constitutions of government for the separate States. These, in their respective spheres, operating each to its assigned end,—have secured us in all the blessings of political independence and well-regulated liberty. The industry of the country has been protected and fostered, and carried to a wonderful point of skill,—the rights of the country have been triumphantly vindicated in a second war,—its boundaries pushed into the remote wilderness,—its population increased five fold, and its wealth augmented in still greater ratio,—avenues of communication, by land and by water, stretched across the plains and over the mountains, in every direction,—the most astonishing improvements made in all the arts of life,—and literature and science not less successfully cultivated.

Did time permit me to descend to particulars, I could point out five or six principles or institutions, each of the highest importance in civil society; for some of which the best blood of Europe has, from time to time, been shed, and mighty revolutions have been attempted in vain; and which have grown up, silently and unconsciously, in this country in the space of fifty years. I can but run over the names of the reforms which, in this connexion, have been achieved, or are in progress. The feudal accumulation of property in a few hands has been guarded against, and liberty has been founded on its only sure basis, equality; and with this all-important change, a multitude of minor reforms have been introduced into our system of law. The great question of the proper mode of disposing of crime has been solved, by the establishment of a penitentiary system, which combines the ends of penal justice with the interests of humanity; divests imprisonment of its ancient cruelties, without making it cease to be an object of terror;—affords the best chance for the reform of the convict, and imposes little or no burden on the state. A like success seems to be promised, in reference to the other great evil of pauperism, a burden of intoler-

able weight in every other country.   Experiments have pretty satisfactorily shown, that, by a judicious system carefully administered,
pauperism may be made to cease to be a school for crime, and, to
a considerable degree also, cease to be a burden to the public.   A
plan of popular education has been introduced, by which the elements of useful knowledge have been carried to every door.   Political equality has been established on the broadest footing, with
no other evils than those which are inseparable from humanity,—
evils infinitely less than those of despotic government.   In fine,
freedom of conscience has been carried to the highest point of practical enjoyment, without producing any diminution of the public
respect due to the offices of religion.

These, I take to be the real substantial fruits of our free institutions of government.   They are matters each of the highest moment.   Their importance would well occupy each a separate essay.
Time only has been left me thus to indicate them.

With these results of our happily organized liberty, we are starting, fellow citizens, on the second half century, since the close of
the revolutionary war.   Let us hope that we are to move with a
still accelerated pace on the path of improvement and happiness,
of public and private virtue and honor.   When we compare what
our beloved country now is,—or, to go no farther than our own
State,—when we compare what Massachusetts now is, with what
it was fifty years ago, what grounds for honest pride and boundless
gratitude does not the comparison suggest!   And if we wished to
find an example of a community as favored as any on earth with
a salubrious climate ;—a soil possessed of precisely that degree of
fertility which is most likely to create a thrifty husbandry ;—advantages for all the great branches of industry, commerce, agriculture,
the fisheries, manufactures, and the mechanic arts ;—free institutions
of government ;—establishments for education, charity, and moral
improvement ;—a sound public sentiment,—a widely diffused love
of order,—a glorious tradition of ancestral renown,—a pervading
moral sense,—and an hereditary respect for religion : if we wished
to find a land where a man could desire to live, to educate and
establish his children, to grow old and to die,—where could we
look, where need we wander, beyond the limits of our own ancient
and venerable State ?

Fellow citizens of Worcester,—words, after all, are vain. Do you wish to learn how much you are indebted to those who laid the foundation of these your social blessings,—do not listen to me, but look around you; survey the face of the country,—of the immediate neighborhood in which you live. Go up to the rising grounds that overlook this most beautiful village; contemplate the scene of activity, prosperity, and thrift spread out before you. Pause on the feelings of satisfaction with which you dismiss your children in the morning to school, or receive them home at evening; the assured tranquillity with which you lie down to repose at night, half of you, I doubt not, with unbolted doors, beneath the overshadowing pinions of the public peace. Dwell upon the sacred calm of the Sabbath morn, when the repose of man and of nature is awakened by no sound but that of the village bell, calling you to go up and worship God, according to the dictates of your conscience; and reflect that all these blessings were purchased for you by your high-souled fathers, at the cost of years of labor, trial, and hardship; of banishment from their native land, of persecution and bloodshed, of tyranny and war. Think, then, of Greece, and of Poland; of Italy, and Spain; aye, of France, and of England; of any, and of every country, but your own; and you will know the weight of obligation you owe your fathers; and the reasons of gratitude, which should prompt you to celebrate the Fourth of July.

NOTE.

I have thought that the reader, who is curious in the earlier history of our country, would be gratified with the whole of the letter of General Pomroy, of which a characteristic sentence is quoted in the text. It has never been printed, and is here subjoined from a copy furnished me by my much valued friend, Mr George Bancroft, of Northampton.

From ye Grand Battre 5 mile & haf North From ye City Louisbourg.
May ye 8, 1745.

My dear Wife, Altho ye many Dangers & hazards I have been in since I left you, yet I have been through ye goodness of God Preserved, tho much worried with ye grate business I have upon my hands. But I go cherefully on with it. I have much to write, but little time Shall only give some hints Tuesday ye Last day of April, ye fleet landed on ye Island of Cape Breton about 5 miles from Louisbourg. ye French saw our vessels and came out with a company to prevent our landing But as Fast as ye boats could git on shore ye men were landed. A warm ingagement with them: They sone retreated, we followed them, & drove them into ye woods but few of them able to git into ye city yt day 4 we killed yt were found many taken we lost not one man: We have taken & killed since many more, ye number I do not know, but not less than eighty parsons what is since killed. The grand Battre is ours: but before we entered it the people were fled out of it, and gon over to ye town But had stopt up ye Tutchhols of ye cannon——General Peppril gave me ye Charge & oversight of above twenty smiths in boaring of them out: Cannon boals & Bourns hundred of them were fired at us from ye city & ye Island Fort. Grate numbers of Them struck ye Fort: Some in ye parade among ye People But none of them hurt & as sone as' we could git ye cannon clear we gave them Fire for Fire & Bombarded them on ye west side. Louisbourg an exceeding strong handsom & well sittiated place with a fine harber it seams impregnable. But we have ben so succeeded heitherto yt I do not doubt But Providence will Deliver it into our hands.

Sunday What we have lost of our men I do not certinly know, But I fear near
May ye 20 men ye army in general have been in health: It looks as if our cam-
12 from pane would last long But I am willing to stay till God's time comes to
this deliver ye Citty Louisbourg into our hands, which do not doubt but
below will in good time be done: we have shut them up on every side and
writ still are making our works stronger against them. 42 pound shot they
have fired in upon them every day; one very large mortar we have with which we
play upon them upon there houses often braks among them: there houses are com-

pact, which ye boums must do a grate deal of hirt & distress them in a grate degree Small mortars we have with which we fire in upon them. I have had my health since I landed.

My dear wife I expect to be longer gon from home then I did when I left it : but I desire not to think of returning Till Louisbourg is taken: & I hope God will inable you to submit quietly to his will whatever it may be ; and inable you with courage & good conduct to go through ye grate business yt is now upon your hands & not think your time ill spent in teaching and governing your family according to ye word of God.

My company in general are well: Some few of them are Ill, But hope none dangerous.

The affairs at home I can order nothing But must wholly leave Hoping yt they will be well ordered & taken care of : My kind love to Mr Sweetland my duty to Mother Hunt & love to Brothers and sisters all

My Dear wife If it be the will of God I hope to see your pleasant face again : But if God in his Holy and Sovereign Providence has ordered it others wise, I hope to have a glorious meeting with you in ye Kingdom of heaven where there is no wars nor Fatiguing marches, no roaring cannon nor cracking Boum shells, nor long Campains; But an eternity to spend in Perfect harmony and undisturbed peace.

This is ye hartty Desire & Prayer
of him yt is your loving
Husband SETH POMROY.

To Mrs MARY POMROY at Northampton in New-England.

47

ADDRESS

DELIVERED BEFORE THE PHI BETA KAPPA SOCIETY IN YALE COL-
LEGE, NEW-HAVEN, AUGUST 20, 1833.

Mr President, and Gentlemen,

It has given me peculiar satisfaction to obey your call, and appear before you on this occasion. I take a sincere pleasure, as an affectionate and dutiful child of Harvard, and as an humble member of the branch of our fraternity there established, in presenting myself within the precincts of this ancient and distinguished seminary, for the discharge of the agreeable duty which you have assigned me. I rejoice in the confidence implied in your invitation, that I know neither sect nor party, in the republic of letters; and that I enter your halls with as much assurance of a kind reception, as I would enter those of my own revered and ever gracious Alma Mater. This confidence does me no more than justice. Ardently and gratefully attached to the institution in which I received my education, I could in no way so effectually prove myself its degenerate child, as by harboring the slightest feeling of jealousy at the great and growing reputation of this its distinguished rival. In no way could I so surely prove myself a tardy scholar of the school in which I have been brought up, as by refusing to rejoice in the prosperity and usefulness of every sister institution devoted to the same good cause; and especially of this the most eminent and efficient of her associates.

There are recollections of former times, well calculated to form a bond of good feeling between our universities. We cannot forget that, in the early days of Harvard, when its existence almost depended on the precarious contributions of its friends,—contributions not of munificent affluence, but of pious poverty,—not poured into the academic coffers in splendid dotations, but spared from the scanty means of an infant and destitute country, and presented in their primitive form,—a bushel of wheat, a cord of wood, and a string of Indian beads, (this last not a little to the annoyance of good old President Dunster, who, as the records of the Commissioners of the United Colonies tell us, was sorely perplexed, in sifting out from the mass of the genuine quahog and periwinkle, bits of blue glass and colored stones, feloniously intermixed, without the least respect for the purity of the Colony's wampum),* we cannot forget that, in that day of small things, the contributions of Connecticut and New-Haven,—as the two infant colonies were distinguished,—flowed as liberally to the support of Cambridge, as those of Plymouth and Massachusetts. Still less would I forget that, of the three first generations of the fathers of Connecticut, those who were educated in America received their education at Cambridge; that the four first Presidents of Yale were graduates of Harvard; and that of all your distinguished men in church and state, for nearly a hundred years, a goodly proportion were fitted for usefulness in life within her venerable walls. If the success of the child be the joy of the parent, and the honor of the pupil be the crown of the master, with what honest satisfaction may not our institutions reflect, that they stood to each other in this interesting relation, in this early and critical state of the country's growth, when the direction taken and the character impressed were decisive of interminable consequences. And while we claim the right of boasting of your character and institutions as in some degree the fruit of a good old Massachusetts' influence, we hope you will not have cause to feel ashamed of the auspices under which, to a certain extent, the foundation of those institutions was laid, and their early progress encouraged.

In choosing a topic on which to address you this morning, I should feel a greater embarrassment than I do, did I not suppose that your thoughts, like my own, would flow naturally into such a

* Hazard's State Papers, Vol. II, p. 124.

channel of reflection as may be presumed at all times to be habitual and familiar with men of liberal education or patriotic feeling. The great utility of occasions like this, and of the addresses they elicit, is not to impart stores of information laboriously collected,— not to broach new systems, requiring carefully weighed arguments for their defence, or a multitude of well-arranged facts for their illustration. We meet at these literary festivals, to promote kind feeling; to impart new strength to good purposes; to enkindle and animate the spirit of improvement in ourselves and others. We leave our closets, our offices, and our studies, to meet and salute each other in these pleasant paths; to prevent the diverging walks of life from wholly estranging those from each other, who were kind friends at its outset; to pay our homage to the venerated fathers, who honor with their presence the return of these academic festivals; and those of us who are no longer young, to make acquaintance with the ardent and ingenuous, who are following after us. The preparation for an occasion like this, is in the heart, not in the head; it is in the attachments formed, and the feelings inspired, in the bright morning of life. Our preparation is in the classic atmosphere of the place, in the tranquillity of the academic grove, in the unoffending peace of the occasion, in the open countenance of long-parted associates joyous at meeting, and in the kind and indulgent smile of the favoring throng, which bestows its animating attendance on these our humble academic exercises.

When I look around upon the assembled audience, and reflect, from how many different places of abode throughout our country the professional part of it is gathered, and in what a variety of pursuits and duties it is there occupied; and when I consider that this our literary festival is also honored with the presence of many from every other class of the community, all of whom have yet a common interest in one subject at least, I feel as if the topic on which I am to ask your attention, were imperatively suggested to me. It is the nature and efficacy of education, as the great human instrument of improving the condition of man.

Education has been, at some former periods, exclusively, and more or less, at all former periods, the training of a learned class; the mode in which men of letters or the members of the professions acquired that lore, which enabled them to insulate themselves from the community, and gave them the monopoly of rendering the services in church and state, which the wants or imaginations of men made necessary, and of the honors and rewards, which, by the political constitution of society, attached to their discharge.

I admit, that there was something generous and liberal in education; something popular, and, if I may so express it, republican, in the educated class,—even at the darkest period. Learning, even in its most futile and scholastic forms, was still an affair of the mind. It was not like hereditary rank, mere physical accident: it was not, like military power, mere physical force. It gave an intellectual influence, derived from intellectual superiority; and it enabled some minds, even in the darkest ages of European history, to rise from obscurity and poverty, to be the lights and guides of mankind. Such was Beda, the great luminary of a dark period, a poor and studious monk, who, without birth or fortune, became the great teacher of science and letters to the age in which he lived. Such, still more eminently, was his illustrious pupil Alcuin, who, by the simple force of mental energy, employed in intellectual pursuits, raised himself from the cloister, to be the teacher, companion, and friend of Charlemagne; and to whom it has been said, that France is indebted, for all the polite literature of his own and the succeeding ages.* Such, at a later period, was another poor monk, Roger Bacon, the precursor, and for the state of the times in which he lived, scarcely the inferior of his namesake, the immortal Chancellor.

But a few brilliant exceptions do not affect the general character of the education of former ages. It was a thing apart from the condition, the calling, the service, and the participation of the great mass of men. It was the training of a privileged class; and was far too exclusively the instrument by which one of the favored orders of society was enabled to exercise a tyrannical and exclusive control over the millions which lay wrapt in ignorance and super-

---

* ' *Ei* quicquid politioris literaturæ isto et sequentibus sæculis Gallia ostentat totum acceptum referri debet. Ei Academiæ Parisiensis, Turonensis, Fuldensis, Suessionensis, aliæque plures originem et incrementa debent, quibus, ille, si non præsens præfuit, aut fundamenta posuit, saltem doctrina præluxit, exemplo præivit, et beneficiis a Carolo impetratis adauxit.'—*Cave, Hist. Lit. Sæc. VII, An.* 780, cited in the *Life of Alcuin, in the Biographia Britannica.*

stition. It is the great glory of the age in which we live, that learning, once the instrument of this bondage, has become the instrument of reform; that instead of an educated class, we have made some good approach to an educated community. That intellectual culture, which gave to a few the means of maintaining an ascendency over the fears and weaknesses of their age, has now become the medium of a grand and universal mental equality, and, humanly speaking, the great concern of man. It has become the school of all the arts, the preparation for all the pursuits, the favorite occupation of leisure, the ornament of every age, office, vocation, and sex. In a word, education is now the preparation of a very considerable portion of the mass of mankind for the duties, which, in the present state of the world, devolve upon them.

Let us then dwell, for a moment, on what is to be effected by education, considered in its ultimate objects and most comprehensive sense, in which, of course, is included, as the most important element, the sound and enlightened influence of deep religious principle, to be cherished and applied, through the institutions existing for that sacred purpose.

A great work is to be done. What is it, in its general outline and first principles?

To answer this question, we must remember, that of the generation now on the stage, by which the business of the country, public and private, is carried on, not an individual, speaking in general terms, will be in a state of efficient activity, and very few in existence, thirty years hence. Not merely those by whom the government is administered and the public service performed, in its various civil and military departments, will have passed away; but all who are doing the great, multifarious, never-ending work of social life, from the highest teacher of spiritual wisdom and the profoundest expositor of the law, to the humblest artisan, will have ceased to exist. The work is to go on; the government is to be administered, laws are to be enacted and executed, peace preserved or war levied, the will of the people to be expressed by their suffrages, and the vast system of the industrious action of a great people, in all their thousand occupations, by sea and land, to be kept up and extended; but those now employed in all this great work, are to cease from it, and others are to take their places.

Like most of the great phenomena of life,—miracles, if I may so say, of daily occurrence,—this vast change, this surcease of a whole generation, loses, from its familiarity, almost all power of affecting the imagination. The political revolution which subverts one crowned family, which prostrates a king to elevate an emperor, and cements his throne with the blood of some hundreds, perhaps thousands, of the wretched victims of his ambition, is the wonder of the age; the perpetual theme of discourse; the standing topic of admiration. But this great revolution, which prostrates not one man nor one family in a single nation; but every man, in every family, throughout the world; which bids an entire new congregation of men to start into existence and action; which fills with new incumbents, not one blood-stained seat of royalty, but every post of active duty, and every retreat of private life;—this new creation steals on us silently and gradually, like all the primordial operations of Providence, and must be made the topic of express disquisition, before its extent and magnitude are estimated, and the practical duties to be deduced from it are understood.

Such a revolution, however, is impending,—as decisive, as comprehensive, as real, as if, instead of being the gradual work of thirty years, it were to be accomplished in a day or an hour: and so much the more momentous, for the gradual nature of the process. Were the change to be effected at once, were this generation swept off, and another brought forward, by one great act of creative energy, it would concern us only as speculative philanthropists, what might be the character of our successors. Whether we transmitted them a heritage honored or impaired; or whether they succeeded to it well trained to preserve and increase, or ready to waste it, would import nothing to our interests or feelings. But by the law of our nature, the generations of men are most closely interlaced with each other, and the decline of one and the accession of the other are gradual. One survives, and the other anticipates its activity. While in the decline of life, we are permitted to reap, on the one hand, a rich reward for all that we have attempted patriotically and honestly, in public or private, for the good of our fellow men; on the other hand, retribution rarely fails to overtake us, as individuals or communities, for the neglect of public duties, or the violation of the social trust.

We still have judgment here; that we but teach
Bloody instructions, which, being taught, return
To plague the inventor: this even-handed justice
Commends the ingredients of the poisoned chalice
To our own lips.

By this law of our natures, the places which we fill in the world
are to be taken from us; we are to be dispossessed of our share in
the honors and emoluments of life; driven from our resorts of business and pleasure; ousted from our tenements; ejected from our
estates; banished from the soil we called our own, and interdicted
fire and water in our native land; and those who ward off this destiny the longest, after holding on a little while with a convulsive
grasp, making a few more efforts, exposing their thin gray hairs in
another campaign or two, will gladly, of their own accord, before
a great while, claim to be exempts in the service.

But this revolution connects itself with the constitution of our nature, and suggests the great principles of education as the duty and
calling of man, precisely because it is not the work of violent hands,
but the law of our being. It is not an outraged populace, rising
in their wrath and fury, to throw off the burden of centuries of oppression. Nor is it an inundation of strange barbarians, issuing, nation after nation, from some remote and inexhaustible *officina
gentium*, lashed forward to the work of destruction by the chosen
scourges of God; although these *are* the means by which, when
corruption has attained a height beyond the reach of ordinary influences, a preparation for a great and radical revolution is made.
But the revolution of which I speak, and which furnishes the principles of the great duty of education,—all-comprehensive and un-
sparing as it is,—is to be effected by a gentle race of beings, just
stepping over the threshold of childhood, many of them hardly
crept into existence. They are to be found within the limits of
our own country, of our own community, beneath our own roofs,
clinging about our necks. Father, he whom you folded in your
arms, and carried in your bosom; whom, with unutterable anxiety,
you watched through the perilous years of childhood, whom you
have brought down to college, this very commencement, and are
dismissing from beneath your paternal guard, with tearful eyes and
an aching heart; it is he, who is destined, (if your ardent prayers

are heard), to outthunder you at the forum and in the Senate House! Fond mother, the future rival of your not yet fading charms, the *matre pulcra filia pulcrior*, is the rose bud, which is beginning to open and blush by your side! Destined to supersede us in all we hold dear, they are the objects of our tenderest cares. Soon to outnumber us, we spare no pains to protect and rear them; and the strongest instinct of our hearts urges us, by every device and appliance, to bring forward those who are to fill our places, possess our fortunes, wear our honors, snatch the laurel from our heads, the words from our lips, the truncheon of command from our hands, and at last gently crowd us, worn out and useless, from the scene.

I have dwelt on this connexion of nature and affection between the generations of men, because it is the foundation of the high philosophy of education. It places the duty of imparting it upon the broad eternal basis of natural love. It is manifest, that in the provident constitution of an intellectual order of beings, the trust of preparing each generation of which it was to consist, for the performance of its part on the great stage of life, was all-important, all-essential; too vitally so to be put in charge with any but the most intimate principles of our being. It has accordingly been interwoven with the strongest and purest passions of the heart. Maternal fondness; a father's thoughtful care; the unreasoning instincts of the family circle; the partialities, the prejudices of blood,—are all made to operate as efficient principles, by which the risen generation is urged to take care of its successor: and when the subject is pursued to its last analysis, we find that education in its most comprehensive form,—the general training and preparation of our successors,—is the great errand which we have to execute in the world. We either assume it as our primary business, or depute it to others, because we think they will better perform it, while we are engaged in occupations subsidiary to this. Much of the practical and professional part we direct ourselves. We come back to it as a relaxation or a solace. We labor to provide the means of supplying it to those we love. We retrench in our pleasures, that we may abound in this duty. It animates our toils, dignifies our selfishness, makes our parsimony generous, furnishes the theme for the efforts of the greatest minds; and directly or indirectly fills up our lives.

48

In a word, then, we have before us, as the work to be done by this generation, to train up that which is to succeed us.

This is a work of boundless compass, difficulty, and interest. Considered as brethren of the human family, it looks, of course, to the education of all mankind. If we confine ourselves to our duty, as American citizens, the task is momentous, almost beyond the power of description. Though the view which I would at this time take of the subject does not confine itself to the fortunes of a single nation, I will dwell upon it for a moment, exclusively in relation to this country. I will suppose that our Union is to remain unbroken for another generation ; a supposition which, I trust, I may safely make ; and if this should be the case, it is no violent presumption to suppose, that in all respects the country will continue to advance, with a rapidity equal to that which has marked its progress for the last thirty years. On this supposition, the close of another generation will see our population swelled to above thirty millions ; all our public establishments increased in the same ratio ; four or five new States added to the Union ; towns and villages scattered over regions now lying in the unbroken solitude of nature ; roads cut across pathless mountains ; rivers, now unexplored, alive with steamboats ; and all those parts of the country, which at this time are partially settled, crowded with a much denser population, with all its attendant structures, establishments, and institutions. In other words, besides replacing the present numbers, a new nation, more than fifteen millions strong, will exist within the United States. The wealth of the country will increase still more rapidly ; and all the springs of social life which capital moves, will, of course, increase in power ; and a much more intense condition of existence will be the result.

It is for this state of things, that the present generation is to educate and train its successors ; and on the care and skill with which their education is conducted, on the liberality, magnanimity, and single-heartedness with which we go about this great work,—each in his proper sphere, and according to his opportunities and vocation,—will, of course, depend the honor and success with which those who come after us will perform their parts on the great stage of life.

This reflection of itself, would produce a deep impression of the importance of the great work of education to be performed by the present generation of men. But we must farther take into consideration, in order to the perfect understanding of the subject, the quality of that principle which is to receive, and of that which is to impart, the education; that is, of the *mind of this age* acting upon the *mind of the next;* both natures indefinitely expansive, in their capacities of action and apprehension;—natures, whose powers have never been defined; whose depths have never been sounded; whose orbit can be measured alone by that superior intelligence which has assigned its limits, if limits it have. When we consider this, we gain a vastly extended and elevated notion of the duty which is to be performed. It is nothing less than to put in action the entire mental power of the present day, in its utmost stretch, consistent with happiness and virtue, and so as to develop and form the utmost amount of capacity, intelligence, and usefulness, of intellectual and moral power and happiness, in that which is to follow. We are not merely to transmit the world as we receive it; to teach, in a stationary repetition, the arts which we have received; as the dove builds this year just such a nest as was built by the dove that went out from the ark, when the waters had abated; but we are to apply the innumerable discoveries, inventions, and improvements, which have been successively made in the world,—and never more than of late years,—and combine, and elaborate them into one grand system of increased instrumentality, condensed energy, invigorated agency, and quickened vitality, in forming and bringing forward our successors.

These considerations naturally suggest the inquiry,—how much can be done, by a proper exertion of our powers and capacities, to improve the condition of our successors? Is there reason to hope, that any great advances can be made; that any considerable stride can be taken, by the moral and intellectual agency of this age, as exerted in influencing the character of the next?

I know of no way to deal practically with this great problem, but to ask more particularly, what is effected, in the *ordinary* course of intellectual action and reaction? What is the average amount of the phenomena of education, in their final result, which the inspection of society presents to us? How much is effected so frequently and certainly as to authorize a safe inference, as what may be done, in the ordinary progress of the mind, and conjectures as to its possible strides, bounds, and flights?

We can make this inquiry on no other assumed basis, but that of the natural average equality of all men, as rational and improvable beings. I do not mean that all men are created, with a physical and intellectual constitution capable of attaining, with the same opportunities, the same degree of improvement. I cannot assert that, nor would I willingly undertake to disprove it. I leave it aside; and suppose that, on an average, men are born with equal capacities. What then do we behold, as regards the difference resulting from education and training? Let us take examples, in the two extremes. On the one hand, we have the New Zealand savage; but little better in appearance, than the ourang outang, his fellow-tenant of the woods, which afford much the same shelter for both; almost destitute of arts, except that of horribly disfiguring the features, by the painful and disgusting process of tattooing, and that of preparing a rude war club, with which he destroys his fellow savage of the neighboring tribe, his natural enemy while he lives, his food, if he can conquer or kidnap him; laying up no store of provision, but one, which I scarce dare describe,—which consists in plunging a stick into the water, where it is soon eaten to honey comb by the worms, which abound in tropical climates, and which, then taken out, furnishes, in these worms, a supply of their most favorite food to these forlorn children of nature. Such is this creature from youth to age, from father to son,—a savage, a cannibal, a brute;—a human being, a fellow-man, a rational and immortal soul; carrying about under that squalid loathsome exterior, hidden under those brutal manners, and vices disgusting at once and abominable, a portion of the intellectual principle, which likens man to his Maker. This is one specimen of humanity; how shall we bring another into immediate contrast with it? How better than by contemplating what may be witnessed on board the vessel, which carries the enlightened European or American to these dark and dreary corners of the earth? You there behold a majestic vessel, bounding over the billows, from the other side of the globe; easily fashioned to float, in safety, over the bottomless sea; to spread out her broad wings, and catch the midnight breeze, guided by a single drowsy sailor at the helm, with two or three companions reclining listlessly on the deck, gazing into the depths of the starry heavens. The commander of this vessel, not surpassing thousands of his brethren in intelligence and skill, knows how, by pointing his glass at the heavens, and taking an observation of the stars, and turning over the leaves of his ' Practical Navigator,' and making a few figures on his slate, to tell the spot which his vessel has reached on the trackless sea :—and he can also tell it by means of a steel spring and a few brass wheels, put together in the shape of a chronometer. The glass with which he brings the heavens down to the earth, and by which he measures the twenty-one thousand six hundredth part of their circuit, is made of a quantity of flint, sand, and alkali,—coarse opaque substances, which he has melted together into the beautiful medium which excludes the air and the rain, and admits the light,—by means of which he can count the orders of animated nature in a dew-drop, and measure the depth of the vallies in the moon. He has, running up and down his mainmast, an iron chain, fabricated at home, by a wonderful succession of mechanical contrivances, out of a rock brought from deep caverns in the earth, and which has the power of conducting the lightning harmlessly down the sides of the vessel, into the deep. He does not creep timidly along, from headland to headland, nor guide his course across a narrow sea, by the north star ; but he launches bravely on the pathless and bottomless deep, and carries about with him in a box, a faithful little pilot, who watches when the eye of man droops with fatigue, a small and patient steersman, whom darkness does not blind, nor the storm drive from his post, and who points from the other side of the globe,— through the convex earth,—to the steady pole. If he falls in with a pirate, he does not wait to repel him, hand to hand ; but he puts into a mighty engine a handful of dark powder, into which he has condensed an immense quantity of elastic air, and which, when it is touched by a spark of fire, will instantly expand into its original volume, and drive an artificial thunderbolt before it, against the distant enemy. When he meets another similar vessel on the sea, homeward bound from a like excursion to his own, he makes a few black marks on a piece of paper, and sends it home, a distance of ten thousand miles ; and thereby speaks to his employer, to his family, and his friends, as distinctly and significantly as if they were seated by his side. At the cost of half the labor with which the savage procures himself the skin of a wild beast, to cover his nakedness, this child of civilized life has provided himself with the most substantial, curious, and convenient clothing,—textures and tissues of wool, cotton, linen, and silk,—the contributions of the four quarters of the globe, and of every kingdom of nature. To fill a vacant hour, or dispel a gathering cloud from his spirits, he has curious instruments of music, which speak another language of new and strange significance to his heart,—which make his veins thrill and his eyes overflow with tears, without the utterance of a word,— and with one sweet succession of harmonious sounds, send his heart back, over the waste of waters, to the distant home where his wife and his children are gathered around the fireside, trembling at the thought that the storm, which beats upon the windows, may perhaps overtake their beloved voyager on the distant seas. And in his cabin he has a library of volumes,—the strange production of a machine of almost magical powers,—which, as he turns over their leaves, enable him to converse with the great and good of every clime and age, and which even repeat to him, in audible notes, the laws of his God and the promises of his Saviour, and point out to him that happy land, which he hopes to reach, when his flag is struck, and his sails are furled, and the voyage of life is over.

The imaginations of those whom I have the honor to address, will be able to heighten this contrast, by a hundred traits on either side, for which I have not time; but even as I have presented it, will it be deemed extravagant, if I say, that there is a greater difference between the educated child of civilized life and the New Zealand savage, than between the New Zealand savage and the ourang outang?—And yet the New Zealander was born a rational being, like the civilized European and American; and the civilized European and American entered life, like the New Zealander, a helpless, wailing babe.

This, then, is the difference made by education;—made by education. I do not mean, that if a school were set up in New Zealand, you could convert the rising generation of savage children, in eight or ten years, into a civilized, well-educated, orderly society. I will not undertake to say, what could be done with an individual of that race, taken at birth and brought to a Christian country, and there reared, under the most favorable circumstances; nor do I know into what sort of a being one of our children would grow up,—supposing it could survive the experiment,—were it taken from the nurse's arms, and put in charge to a tribe of New Zealanders. But it is, upon the whole, education, in the most comprehensive sense, which makes the vast difference which I have endeavored to illustrate, and which actually, in the case of a civilized person, transforms his intellect from what it is at birth, into what it becomes in the mature, educated, consummate man.

These reflections teach us what education ordinarily accomplishes. They illustrate its power, as measured by its effects. Let us now make a single remark on its prodigious efficacy, measured by the shortness of the time within which it produces its wonders. When we contemplate the vast amount of the arts, useful and mechanical, elegant and literary;—the sciences, pure and mixed, and of the knowledge, practical and speculative, belonging to them;—a portion of which,—sometimes a very large portion,—is within the command of every well-educated person, the wonder we should naturally feel may be a little abated by the consideration, that this is the accumulated product of several thousand years of study,—the fruits of which have been recorded, or transmitted by tradition from age to age. But when we reflect again upon the subject, we find, that though this knowledge has been for four or five thousand years in the process of accumulation, and consists of the condensed contributions of great and gifted minds, or of the mass of average intellect, transmitted from race to race, since the dawn of letters and arts in Phœnicia and Egypt, it is nevertheless mastered by each individual, if at all, in the compass of a few years. It is in the world, but it is not inherited by any one. Men are born rich, but not learned. The La Place of this generation did not come into life, with the knowledge possessed and recorded by the Newtons, the Keplers, and the Pythagorases of other days. It is doubtful, whether, at three years old, he could count much beyond ten;—and if at six, he was acquainted with any other cycloidal curves, than those generated by the trundling of his hoop, he was a prodigy indeed. But by the time he was twenty-one, he had mastered all the discoveries of all the philosophers who preceded him, and was prepared to build upon them the splendid superstructure of his

own.   In like manner, the whole race of men, who thirty years
hence are to be the active members of society, and some of them
its guides and leaders, its Mansfields and Burkes, its Ellsworths,
Marshalls, and Websters,—the entire educated and intelligent population, which will have prepared itself with the knowledge requisite for carrying on the business of life is, at this moment, enacting
the part of

> the whining school-boy with his satchel
> And shining morning face, creeping like snail
> Unwillingly to school:—

our future Ciceros are mewling infants; and our Arkwrights and
Fultons, who are hereafter to unfold to our children new properties
of matter ;—new forces of the elements ;—new applications of the
mechanical powers, which may change the condition of things, are
now, under the tuition of a careful nurse, with the safeguard of a
pair of leading strings, attempting the perilous experiment of putting
one foot before the other.   Yes, the ashes that now moulder in
yonder grave-yard, the sole remains on earth of what was Whitney,
—are not more unconscious of the stretch of the mighty mind which
they once enclosed ;—than the infant understandings of those now
springing into life, who are destined to follow in the luminous track
of his genius, to new and still more brilliant results, in the service
of man !

When we consider, in this way, how much is effected by education, in how short a time, for the individual and the community,
and thence deduce some not inadequate conception of its prodigious
efficiency and power, we are led irresistibly to another reflection,
upon its true nature.   We feel that it cannot be so much an act of
the teacher, as an act of the pupil.   It is not, that the master, possessing this knowledge, has poured it out of his own mind into that
of the learner ;—but the learner, by the native power of apprehension, judiciously trained and wisely disciplined, beholds, comprehends, and appropriates what is set before him, in form and order ; and not only so, but with the first quickenings of the intellect,
commences himself the creative and inventive processes.   There
is not the least doubt, that the active mind, judiciously trained, in
reality sometimes invents for itself, not a little of that which,—

being already previously known and recorded,—is regarded as a part of the existing stock of knowledge. From this principle also, we are led to an easy explanation of those curious appearances of simultaneous discoveries in art and science, of which literary history records many examples ;—such as the rival pretensions of Newton and Leibnitz,—of Arkwright and Hargraves,—of Priestley and Lavoisier,—of Bell and Lancaster,—of Young and Champollion, which show, that at any given period, especially in a state of society favorable to the rapid diffusion of knowledge, the laws of the human mind are so sure and regular, that it is not an uncommon thing for different persons, in different countries, to fall into the same train of reflection and thought, and to come to results and discoveries, which,—injuriously limiting the creative powers of the intellect,—we are ready to ascribe to imitation or plagiarism.

It is indeed true, that one of the great secrets of the power of education, in its application to large numbers, is, that it is a mutual work. Man has three teachers,—the school-master,—himself,—his neighbor. The instructions of the two first commence together; and long after the functions of the school-master have been discharged, the duties of the two last go on together ; and what they effect is vastly more important than the work of the teacher, if estimated by the amount of knowledge self-acquired, or caught by the collision or sympathy of other minds, compared with that which is directly imparted by the school-master, in the morning of life. In fact, what we learn at school and in college, is but the foundation of the great work of self-instruction and mutual instruction, with which the real education of life begins, when what is commonly called the education is finished. The daily intercourse of cultivated minds,—the emulous exertions of the fellow-votaries of knowledge,—controversy,—the inspiring sympathy of a curious and intelligent public, are all powerful in putting each individual intellect to the stretch of its capacity. A hint,—a proposition,—an inquiry, proceeding from one mind, awakens new trains of thought in a kindred mind, surveying the subject from other points of view, and with other habits and resources of illustration ;—and thus truth is constantly multiplied and propagated, by the mutual action and reaction of the thousands engaged in its pursuit. Hence the phenomena of Periclean, Augustan, and Medicean ages, and

49

golden eras of improvement;—and hence the education of each individual mind, instead of being merely the addition of one to the well-instructed and well-informed members of the community, is the introduction of another member into the great family of intellects, each of which is a point not merely bright but radiant, and competent to throw off the beams of light and truth in every direction. Mechanical forces, from the moment they are put in action, by the laws of matter grow fainter and fainter, till they are exhausted. With each new application, something of their intensity is consumed. It can only be kept up by a continued or repeated resort to the source of power. Could Archimedes have found his place to stand upon, and a lever with which he could heave the earth from its orbit, the utmost he could have effected would have been to make it fall a dead weight into the sun. Not so the intellectual energy. If wisely exerted, its exercise, instead of exhausting, increases its strength; and not only this, but as it moves onward from mind to mind, it awakens each to the same sympathetic, self-propagating action. The circle spreads in every direction. Diversity of language does not check the progress of the great instructer, for he speaks in other tongues, and gathers new powers from the response of other schools of civilization. The pathless ocean does not impede, it accelerates his progress. Space imposes no barrier, time no period to his efforts; and ages on ages after the poor clay, in which the creative intellect was enshrined, has mouldered back to its kindred dust, the truths which it has unfolded,—moral or intellectual,—are holding on their pathway of light and glory, awakening other minds to the same heavenly career.

But it is more than time to apply these principles to the condition of the world as it now exists, and to inquire, what hope there is,—in the operation of this mighty engine,—of a great and beneficial progress in the work of civilization.

We certainly live in an enlightened age; one in which civilization has reached a high point of advancement and extension, in this and several other countries. There are several nations besides our own, where the Christian religion, civil government, the usual branches of industry, the diffusion of knowledge, useful and ornamental, and of the fine arts, have done and are doing great things for the happiness of man. But when we look a little more nearly, it must be confessed, that, with all that has been done in this cause, the work which still remains to be accomplished is very great. The population of the globe is assumed, in the more moderate estimates, to be seven hundred millions. Of these, two hundred and fifty millions are set down for America and Europe, and the residue for Asia and Africa. Two hundred and fifty millions again are assumed to be Christians; and of the residue three fourths are pagans. There is certainly a considerable diversity of condition among the various Asiatic and African,—who are also the unchristianized, —races, as there is also among the European and American, who belong to the family of civilization and Christianity. But, upon the whole, it must be admitted, that about two thirds of mankind are without the pale of civilization, as we understand it; and of these a large majority are pagan savages, or the slaves of the most odious and oppressive despotisms. The Chinese and Hindoos,— who make up two thirds of this division of mankind,—contain, within their vast masses, perhaps the most favorable specimens of this portion of the human family; and if we turn from them to the Turks, the Tartars, the Persians, the native races of the interior of Africa, the wretched tribes on the coast, or the degraded population of Australia or Polynesia, we shall find but little, (except in the recent successful attempts at civilization), on which the eye of the philanthropist can rest with satisfaction. Almost all is dark, cheerless, and wretched.

Nor, when we look into what is called the civilized portion of the globe, is the prospect as much improved- as we could wish. The broad mantle of civilization, like that of charity, covers a great deal, which, separately viewed, could claim no title to the name. Not to speak of the native tribes of America, or the nomadic races of the Russian empire, how vast and perilous is the inequality of mental condition among the members of the civilized states of the earth. Contemplate the peasantry of the greater part of the north of Europe, attached as property to the soil on which they were born. The same class in the Austrian dominions, in Spain, in Portugal, in Italy,—if not held in precisely the same state of political disability,—are probably, to a very slight degree, more improved in their mental condition. In the middle and western states of

Europe,—France, Holland, Germany, and Great Britain,—although
the laboring population is certainly in a more elevated and happier
state than in the countries just named, yet how little opportunity
for mental improvement do even they possess! We know that
they pass their lives in labors of the most unremitted character,
from which they derive nothing but the means of a most scanty
support; constantly relapsing into want, at the slightest reverse of
fortune, or on the occurrence of the first severe casualty.

Then consider the character of a large portion of the population
of the great cities of all countries,—London, St Petersburg, Vienna ; where the extremes of human condition stand in painful juxtaposition ;—and by the side of some specimens of all that adorns
and exalts humanity,—the glory of our species,—we find the large
mass of the population profoundly ignorant, and miserably poor,
and no small part of it sunk to the depths of want and vice. It is
painful to reflect, in this age of refinement, how near the two opposite conditions of our nature may be brought, without the least
communication of a direct genial influence from one to the other.
If any thing were necessary, beyond the slightest inspection of obvious facts, to show the artificial structure of the society in which
we live, and the need of some great and generous process of reno-
vation, it would be the reflection, that, if a man wished to explore
the very abyss of human degradation,—to find how low one could
get in the scale of nature, without going beneath the human race,
—if he wished to find every want, every pang, every vice, which
can unite to convert a human being into a suffering, loathsome
brute,—he would not have to wander to the cannibal tribes of
Australia, already described, or to the dens of the bushmen of
the Cape of Good Hope. He would need only to take a ten
steps' walk from Westminster Abbey, or strike off for half a quarter
of a mile, in almost any direction, from the very focus of all that is
elegant and refined,—the pride and happiness of life,—in London
or Paris.

The painful impressions produced by these melancholy truths,
are increased by the consideration, that in some parts of the region
of civilization, the cause of the mind has seemed to go backward.
Who can think of the former condition of the coasts of the Mediterranean, and not feel a momentary anxiety for the fortunes of

the race? In ancient times, the shores of the Mediterranean, all around, were civilized after the type of that day, flourishing and happy. In this favored region, the human mind was developed, in many of its faculties, to an extent, and with a beauty, never surpassed, and scarcely ever equalled. Greece was the metropolis of this great intellectual republic; and through her letters and her arts extended the domain of civilization to Asia Minor and Syria, to Egypt and Africa, to Italy and Sicily, and even to Gallia and Iberia. What a state of the world it was, when all around this wide circuit, whithersoever the traveller directed his steps, he found cities filled with the beautiful creations of the architect and the sculptor; marble temples in the grandest dimensions and finest proportions; statues, whose miserable and mutilated fragments are the models of modern art! Wheresoever he sojourned, he found the schools of philosophy crowded with disciples, and heard the theatres ringing with the inspirations of the Attic muse, and the forum thronged by orators of consummate skill and classic renown. We are too apt, in forming our notions of the extent of Grecian civilization, to confine our thoughts to one or two renowned cities,—to Athens alone. But not only all Greece, but all the islands, Sicily and Magna Græcia, round all their coasts, the Ionian shore, the remote interior of Asia Minor and Syria, almost to the Euphrates, the entire course of the Nile up to its cataracts, and Libya far into the desert, were filled with populous and cultivated cities. Places, whose names can scarcely be traced, but in an index of ancient geography, abounded in all the stores of art, and all the resources of instruction, in the time of Cicero. He makes one of the chief speakers in the Orator say, ' At the present day, all Asia imitates Menecles of Alabanda and his brother.' Who was Menecles, and where was Alabanda? Cicero himself studied not only under Philo the Athenian, but Milo the Rhodian, Menippus of Stratonice, Dionysius of Magnesia, Æschylus of Cnidus, and Xenocles of Adramyttium. These were the masters,—the schools of Cicero! Forgotten names, perished cities, abodes of art and eloquence, of which the memory is scarcely preserved!

What then is the hope, that much can be effected in the promotion of the great object of the improvement of man, by the instrumentality of education, as we have described it? And here, I am willing to own myself an enthusiast, and all I ask is, that men will have the courage to follow the light of general principles, and patience for great effects to flow from mighty causes. If, after establishing the great truths of the prodigious power of the principles, by which the education of the world is to be achieved, men suffer themselves to be perplexed by apparent exceptions ;—and especially, if they will insist upon beginning, carrying on, and completing themselves every thing which they propose or conceive for human improvement,—forgetful that humanity, religion, national character, literature, and the influence of the arts,—are great concerns,— spreading out over a lapse of ages, and infinite in their perfectibility ; then indeed the experience of one short life can teach nothing but despair.

But if we will do justice to the power of the great principles which I have attempted to develop, that are at work for the education of man,—if we will study the causes which in other times have retarded his progress,—which seem in some large portions of the globe to doom him even now to hopeless barbarity,—and if we will duly reflect, that what seems to be a retrograde step in the march of civilization, is sometimes, (and most memorably in the downfall of the Roman empire), the peculiar instrumentality with which a still more comprehensive work of reform is carried on, we shall have ample reason to conceive the brightest hopes for the progress of our race ; for the introduction within the pale of civilization of its benighted regions, and the effective regeneration of all. We have now in our possession, three instruments of civilization unknown to antiquity, of power separately to work almost any miracle of improvement, and the united force of which is adequate to the achievement of any thing not morally and physically impossible. These are the art of printing,—a sort of mechanical magic for the diffusion of knowledge ;—free representative government,—a perpetual regulator and equalizer of human condition, the inequalities of which are the great scourge of society ;—and lastly a pure and spiritual religion,—the deep fountain of generous enthusiasm,—the mighty spring of bold and lofty designs,—the great sanctuary of moral power. The want of one or all of these, satisfactorily explains the vicissitudes of the ancient civilization ; and the possession of them all as satisfactorily assures the permanence of that, which has been for some centuries, and is now going on, and warrants the success of the great work of educating the world. Does any one suppose, that if knowledge among the Greeks, instead of being confined to the cities, and, in them, to a few professional sophists, and rich slave-holders, had pervaded the entire population in that and the neighboring countries, as it is made to do in modern times, by the press —if, instead of their anomalous, ill-balanced, tumultuary republics and petty military tyrannies, they had been united, in a well-digested system of representative government, or even constitutional monarchy,—they and the states around them, Persia, Macedonia, and Rome ;—and if, to all these principles of political stability, they had, instead of their corrupting and degrading superstitions, been blessed with the light of a pure and spiritual faith ;— does any one suppose that Greece and Ionia, under circumstances like these, would have relapsed into barbarism ? Impossible. The Phœnicians invented letters, but what did they do with them ? Apply them to the record, the diffusion, transmission, and preservation of knowledge ? Unhappily for them, that was the acquisition of a far subsequent period. The wonderful invention of alphabetical writing,—after all, perhaps, the most wonderful of human inventions,—was probably applied by its authors to no other purpose, than to carve the name of a king on his rude statue, or perhaps to record some simple catalogue of titles on the walls of a temple. So it was with the Egyptians, whose hieroglyphics have recently been discovered to be an alphabetical character ; but which were far too cumbrous to be employed for an extensive and popular diffusion of knowledge, and which, with all the wisdom of their inventors, are not certainly known to have been applied to the composition of books. It was the freer use of this flexible instrument of knowledge, which gave to Greece her eminence,—which created so many of the objects of her national pride ; and redeemed the memory of her distinguished sons from that forgetfulness, which has thrown its vast pall over the great and brave men and noble deeds of the mighty but unlettered states of antiquity. No one thinks that the powerful and prosperous nations which flourished for two thousand years, on the Nile and the Euphrates, were destitute of heroes, patriots, and statesmen. But, for want of a popular literature, their merits and fame did not, at the time, incorporate themselves with the popular character; and now, that they are no more, their memory lies crushed with their ashes beneath their mausoleums and pyramids. The mighty cities they built, the seats of their power, are as desolate as the cities they wasted. The races of men, whom they ruled and arrayed in battle, bound in an iron servitude,—degraded by mean superstitions,—sunk before the first invader,—and now the very languages, on whose breath their glory was wafted from the Atlas to the Indus, are lost and forgotten, because they were never impressed on the undying page of a written literature.

The more diffusive and popular nature of the Grecian literature was evidently the cause of the preservation of the national spirit of the Greeks, and with it of their political existence. Greece, it is true, fell, and with it the civilization of the ancient world. In this, it may seem to present us rather an illustration of the inefficiency than of the power of the preservative principle of letters. But let us bear in mind, in the first place, that greatly as the Greeks excelled the eastern nations in the diffusion of knowledge, they yet fell infinitely below the modern world, furnished as it is, with the all-efficacious art of printing. Still more, let us recollect, that if Greece, in her fall, affords an example of the insufficiency of the ancient civilization, her long, glorious, and never wholly unsuccessful struggles, and her recent recovery from barbarism, furnish the most pleasing proof, that there is a life-spring of immortality in the combined influence of letters, freedom, and religion. Greece indeed fell. But how did she fall? Did she fall like Babylon? Did she fall ' like Lucifer, never to hope again ?' Or did she not rather go down, like that brighter luminary of which Lucifer is but the herald ?

> So sinks the day-star in the ocean's bed,
> And yet anon repairs his drooping head,
> And tricks his beams, and, with new-spangled ore,
> Flames in the forehead of the morning sky.

What, but the ever living power of literature and religion, preserved the light of civilization and the intellectual stores of the past, undiminished in Greece, during the long and dreary ages of the decline and downfall of the Roman empire? What preserved these sterile provinces and petty islets from sinking, beyond redemption, in the gulf of barbarity, in which Cyrene, and Egypt, and Syria, were swallowed up? It was Christianity and letters, retreating to their fastnesses on mountain tops, and in secluded vallies,—the heights of Athos, the peaks of Meteora, the caverns of Arcadia, the secluded cells of Patmos. Here, while all else in the world seemed swept away, by one general flood of barbarism, civil discord, and military oppression, the Greek monks of the dark ages preserved and transcribed their Homers, their Platos, and their Plutarchs. There never was, strictly speaking, a dark age in Greece. Eustathius wrote his admirable commentaries on Homer, in the middle of the twelfth century. That surely, if ever, was the midnight of the mind; but it was clear and serene day in his learned cell; and Italy, proud already of her Dante, her Boccaccio, and Petrarch,—her Medicean patronage, and her reviving arts,—did not think it beneath her to sit at the feet of the poor fugitives from the final downfall of Constantinople.

What, but the same causes, enforced by the power of the press, and by the sympathy with Greece, which pervaded the educated community of the modern world, has accomplished the political restoration of that country? Thirteen years ago, it lay under a hopeless despotism: its native inhabitants, as such, marked out for oppression and plunder,—tolerated in their religion for the sake of the exactions, of which it furnished the occasion,—shut out from the hopes and honors of social life,—agriculture, and all the visible and tangible means of acquisition, discountenanced,—commerce, instead of lifting her honored front, like an ocean queen, as she does here, creeping furtively from islet to islet, and concealing her precarious gains,—the seas infested with pirates, and the land with robbers,—the population exhibiting a strange mixture of the virtues of the bandit and the vices of the slave, but possessing, in generous transmission from better days, the elements of a free and enlightened community. Such was Greece thirteen years ago, and the prospect of throwing off the Turkish yoke, in every respect but this last, was as wild and chimerical, as the effort to throw off the Cordilleras from this continent. In all respects but one, it would have been as reasonable to expect to raise a harvest of grain from the barren rock of Hydra, as to found a free and prosperous state in this abject Turkish province. But the standard of liberty

50

was raised on the soil of Greece, by the young men who returned from the universities of western Europe, and the civilized world was electrified at the tidings. It was the birth-place of the arts,—the cradle of letters. Reasons of state held back the governments of Europe and of America from an interference in their favor, but intellectual sympathy, religious and moral feeling, and the public opinion of the age, rose in their might, and swept all the barriers of state logic away. They were feeble, unarmed, without organization, distracted by feuds; an adamantine wall of neutrality on the west; an incensed barbarian empire,—horde after horde,—from the confines of Anatolia to the cataracts of the Nile,—pouring down upon them on the east. Their armies and their navies were a mockery of military power, their resources calculated to inspire rather commiseration than fear. But their spirits were sustained, and their wearied hands upheld, by the benedictions and the succors of the friends of freedom. The memory of their great men of old went before them to battle, and scattered dismay in the ranks of the barbarous foe, as he moved, like Satan in hell, with uneasy steps, over the burning soil of freedom. The sympathy of all considerate and humane persons was enlisted in behalf of the posterity, however degenerate, of those who had taught letters and humanity to the world. Men could not bear with patience, that Christian people, striking for liberty, should be trampled down by barbarian infidels, on the soil of Attica and Sparta. The public opinion of the world was enlisted on their side,—and Liberty herself, personified, seemed touched with compassion, as she heard the cry of her venerated parent, the guardian genius of Greece. She hastened to realize the holy legend of the Roman daughter, and send back from her pure bosom the tide of life to the wasting form of her parent :—

> The milk of his own gift;—it is her sire
> To whom she renders back the debt of blood,
> Born with her birth;—no, he shall not expire.

Greece did not expire. The sons of Greece caught new life from desperation; the plague of the Turkish arms was stayed; till the governments followed, where the people had led the way, and the war, which was sustained by the literary and religious sympathies of the friends of art and science, was brought to a triumphant close, by the armies and navies of Europe :—and there they now stand, the first great re-conquest of modern civilization.

Many, I doubt not, who hear me, have had the pleasure, within a few weeks, of receiving a Greek oration, pronounced in the temple of Theseus, on the reception at Athens of the first official act of the young Christian prince, under whom the government of this interesting country is organized. What contemplations does it not awaken, to behold a youthful Bavarian prince, deputed by the great powers of Europe to go, with the guaranties of letters, religion, and the arts, to the city of Minerva, which had reached the summit of human civilization ages before Bavaria had emerged from the depths of the Black Forest ! One can almost imagine the shades of the great of other days, the patriots and warriors, the philosophers and poets, the historians and orators, rising from their renowned graves, to greet the herald of their country's restoration. One can almost fancy that the sacred dust of the Ceramicus must kindle into life, as he draws near; that the sides of Delphi and Parnassus, and the banks of the Ilissus, must swarm with the returning spirits of ancient times. Yes! Marathon and Thermopylæ are moved to meet him at his coming. Martyrs of liberty, names that shall never die,— Solon and Pericles, Socrates and Phocion, not now with their cups of hemlock in their hands, but with the deep lines of their living cares effaced from their serene brows,—at the head of that glorious company of poets, sages, artists and heroes, which the world has never equalled, descend the famous road from the Acropolis to the sea, to bid the deliverer welcome to the land of glory and the arts. 'Remember,' they cry, ' Oh, Prince ! the land thou art set to rule ; it is the soil of freedom. Remember the great and wise of old, in whose place thou art called to stand,—the fathers of liberty ; remember the precious blood which has wet these sacred fields ; pity the bleeding remnants of what was once so grand and fair ; respect these time-worn and venerable ruins ; raise up the fallen columns of these beautiful fanes, and consecrate them to the Heavenly Wisdom ; restore the banished muses to their native seat ; be the happy instrument, in the hand of Heaven, of enthroning letters, and liberty, and religion, on the summits of our ancient hills ; and pay back the debt of the civilized world to reviving, regenerated Greece. So shall the blessing of those ready to perish come upon thee, and ages after the vulgar train of conquerors and princes is forgotten, thou shalt be remembered, as the youthful restorer of Greece!'

This is a most important step in the extension of civilization; what is to hinder its farther rapid progress, I own, I do not perceive. On the contrary, it seems to me, that political causes are in operation, destined, at no very distant period, to throw open the whole domain of ancient improvement to the great modern instruments of national education,—the press, free government, and the Christian faith. The Ottoman power,—a government, which, till lately, has shown itself hostile to all improvement,—is already dislodged from its main positions in Europe, and will, no doubt, before long, be removed from that which it still retains. The Turk, who four centuries ago threatened Italy, and long since that period carried terror to the gates of Vienna, will soon find it no easy matter to sustain himself in Constantinople. His empire is already, as it were, encircled by that of Russia, a government despotic indeed, but belonging to the school of European civilization, acknowledging the same law of nations, connected with the intellectual family of western Europe and America, and making most rapid advances in the education of the various races which fill her vast domain. It is true, that some prejudices exist against that government, at the present time, in the minds of the friends of liberal institutions. But let it not be forgotten, that within the last century, as great a work of improvement has been carried on in the Russian empire as was ever accomplished, in an equal period, in the history of man; and that it is doubtful whether, in any other way, than through the medium of such a government, the light of the mind could penetrate to a tenth part of the heterogeneous materials of which that empire is composed.

It is quite within the range of political probability, that the extended dominion of the czar will be the immediate agent of regenerating western Asia. If so, I care not how soon the Russian banner is planted on the walls of Constantinople. No man can suppose that an instantaneous transition can be made in Asiatic Turkey, from the present condition of those regions to one of pure republican liberty. The process must be gradual, and may be slow.

If the Russian power be extended over them, it will be a civilized and a Christian sway. Letters, law, and religion will follow in the train ; and the foundation will be laid for further progress,—in the advancing intelligence of the people.

On the African coast, the great centre of barbarism has fallen ; and the opportunity seems to present itself of bringing much of that interesting region within the pale of civilization, under the auspices of one of the politest nations in Europe. The man who, but fifteen years ago, should have predicted that within so short a period of time, Greece would be united into an independent state under a European prince ;—that a Russian alliance should be sought, to sustain the tottering power of the Ottoman porte ;—that Algiers, which had so long bid defiance to Christendom, would be subjected ; that a flourishing colony of the descendants of Africa should be planted on its western coast ; and that the mystery of the Niger would be solved, and steamboats be found upon its waters, would have been deemed a wild enthusiast. And now, when we reflect, that, at so many different points, the whole power of modern civilization is turned upon western Asia and Africa ;—that our printing presses, benevolent institutions, missionary associations, and governments, are exerting their energies, to push the empire of improvement into the waste places,—when we consider, that the generation coming forward in these regions, will live under new influences, and, instead of the Mussulman barbarism, repressing every movement toward liberty and refinement, that the influence and interest of the leading powers of Europe will be exerted to promote the great end ; is it too sanguine to think, that a grand and most extensive work of national education is begun, not destined to stand still, or go backward ? Go backward, did I say ; what is to hinder its indefinite progress ? Why should these regions be doomed to perpetuated barbarity ? Hitherto they have been kept barbarous by the influence of an anti-christian, despotic, illiterate government. At present, vast regions, both of eastern and western Asia, and portions of Africa, on the Mediterranean and Atlantic coasts, are under the protection of enlightened, civilized and Christian governments, whose interest and genius are alike pledged to promote the improvement of their subjects. Why should they not improve, and improve with rapidity ? They occupy a soil, which once bore an

intelligent population. They breathe a climate, beneath which
the arts and letters once flourished. They inhabit the coasts of
that renowned sea, whose opposite shores of old seemed to respond
to each other, in grand intellectual concert, like the emulous choirs
of some mighty cathedral, sending back to each other, from the re-
sounding galleries, the alternate swell of triumph and praise. They
are still inhabited by men,—rational, immortal men,—men of no
mean descent,—whose progenitors enrolled their names high on the
lists of renown.

For myself, I see nothing to prevent, and little finally to retard
the work. The causes are adequate to its achievement,—the times
are propitious,—the indications are significant,—and the work itself,
though great indeed, is in no degree chimerical or extravagant.
What is it ?—To teach those who have eyes, to see ; to pour instruction into ears open to receive it ; to aid rational minds to think ;
to kindle immortal souls to a consciousness of their faculties ; to cooperate with the strong and irrepressible tendency of our natures ;
to raise, out of barbarity and stupidity, men, who belong to the
same race of beings as Newton and Locke, as Shakspeare and
Milton, as Franklin and Washington. Let others doubt the possibility of doing it ; I cannot conceive the possibility of its remaining
much longer undone. The difficulty of civilizing Asia and Africa ?
I am more struck with the difficulty of keeping them barbarous.
When I think what man is, in his powers and improvable capacities ;—when I reflect on the principles of education, as I have already attempted in this address to develop them, my wonder is at
the condition to which man is sunk, and with which he is content,
and not at any project or prophecy of his elevation. On the contrary, I see a thousand causes at work, to hasten the civilization of
the world. I see the interest of the commercial nations enlisted
in the cause of humanity and religion. I see refinement, and the
arts, and Christianity, borne on the white wings of trade, to the
farthest shores, and penetrating, by mysterious rivers, the hidden
recesses of mighty continents. I behold a private company, beginning with commercial adventure, ending in a mighty association of
merchant princes, and extending a government of Christian men
over a hundred millions of benighted heathens in the barbarous
East ; and thus opening a direct channel of communication between

the very centre of European civilization and the heart of India. I see the ambition of extended sway, carrying the eagles of a prosperous empire, and with them, the fruitful rudiments of a civilized rule, over the feeble provinces of a neighboring despotism. I see the great work of African colonization auspiciously commenced, promising no scanty indemnity for the cruel wrongs which that much injured continent has endured from the civilized world, and sending home to the shores of their fathers an intelligent well-educated colored population, going back with all the arts of life to this long oppressed land ; and I can see the soldiers of the cross beneath the missionary banner, penetrating the most inaccessible regions, reaching the most distant islands, and achieving, in a few years, a creation of moral and spiritual education, for which centuries might have seemed too short. When I behold all these active causes, backed by all the power of public sentiment, Christian benevolence, the social principle, and the very spirit of the age, I can believe almost any thing of hope and promise. I can believe every thing sooner, than that all this mighty moral enginery can remain powerless and ineffectual. It is against the law of our natures, fallen though they be, which tend not downwards but upwards. To those who doubt the eventual regeneration of mankind, I would say, in the language which the wise and pious poet has put into the mouth of the fallen angel,

> Let such bethink them,—
> That in our proper motion we ascend
> Up to our native seat. Descent and fall
> To us are adverse.

Let him who is inclined to distrust the efficiency of the social and moral causes which are quietly at work for the improvement of the nations, reflect on the phenomena of the natural world. Whence come the waters, which swell the vast current of the great rivers, and fill up the gulfs of the bottomless deep ?—Have they not all gone up to the clouds, in a most thin and unseen vapor, from the wide surface of land and sea ?—Have not these future billows, on which navies are soon to be tossed, in which the great monsters of the deep will disport themselves, been borne aloft on the bosom of a fleecy cloud,—chased by a breeze,—with scarce enough of substance to catch the hues of a sunbeam ;—and have they not de-

scended, sometimes indeed, in drenching rains,—but far more diffusively in dew-drops, and gentle showers, and feathery snows,
over the expanse of a continent, and been gathered successively
into the slender rill, the brook, the placid stream, till they grew, at
last, into the mighty river, pouring down his tributary floods into
the unfathomed ocean ?

Yes! let him who wishes to understand the power of the principles at work for the improvement of our race,—if he cannot comprehend their vigor in the schools of learning,—if he cannot see
the promise of their efficiency in the very character of the human
mind ;—if, in the page of history, sacred and profane, checkered
with vicissitude as it is, he cannot, nevertheless, behold the clear
indications of a progressive nature, let him accompany the missionary bark to the Sandwich Islands.   He will there behold a people
sunk, till within fifteen years, in the depths of savage and of heathen barbarity,—indebted to the intercourse of the civilized world
for nothing but wasting diseases and degrading vices: placed by
Providence in a garden of fertility and plenty, but by revolting
systems of tyranny and superstition, kept in a state of want, corruption, war, and misery.   The Christian benevolence of a private
American association casts its eyes upon them.   Three or four individuals, without power, without arms, without funds, except such
as the frugal resources of private benevolence could furnish them,
—strong only in pious resolutions, and the strength of a righteous
cause,—land on these remote islands, and commence the task of
moral and spiritual reform.   If ever there was a chimerical project
in the eyes of worldly wisdom, this was one.   If this enterprise is
feasible, tell me what is not!   Within less than half the time usually assigned to a generation of men, sixty thousands of individuals,
in a population of one hundred and fifty thousands, have been
taught the elements of human learning.   Whole tribes of savages
have demolished their idols, abandoned their ancient cruel superstitions and barbarous laws, and adopted some of the best institutions of civilization and Christianity.   It would, I think, be difficult to find, in the pages of history, the record of a moral improvement, of equal extent, effected in a space of time so inconsiderable,
and furnishing so striking an exemplification of the power of the
means at work at the present day, for the education and improvement of man.

If I mistake not, we behold, in the British empire in the East, another most auspicious agency for the extension of moral influences over that vast region. It is true, that hitherto, commercial profit and territorial aggrandizement have seemed to be the only objects, which have been pursued by the government. But when we look at home, at the character of the British people, an enlightened, benevolent and liberal community ; when we consider the power of the press and the force of public sentiment in that country, and the disposition to grapple with the most arduous questions, evinced by its rulers, we may hope, without extravagance, that a glorious day of improvement is destined to dawn on India, under the patronage and auspices of Great Britain. The thoughts of her public-spirited and benevolent men have long been bent on this great object. Some of the finest minds that have adorned our nature, have labored in this field. I need not recall to you the boundless learning, the taste, and the eloquence of Sir William Jones, nor the classical elegance, the ardent philanthropy, the religious self-devotion of Heber ; nor repeat a long list of distinguished names, who, for fifty years, have labored for the diffusion of knowledge in the East.—Nor labored in vain. Cheering indications are given in various quarters, of a great moral change in the condition of these vast and interesting regions, once the abode of philosophy and the arts. The bloodiest and most revolting of the superstitions of the Hindoo paganism has been suppressed by the British government. The widow is no longer compelled, by the fanatical despotism of *caste*, to sacrifice herself on the funeral pile of her husband. The whole system of the castes is barely tolerated by the government ; and being at war with the fundamental principles of the British law, as it is with the interest of the great part of the population, must, at no distant period, crumble away. The consolidation of the British empire in India promises a respite from the wars hitherto perpetually raging among the native states of India, and forming of themselves an effectual barrier to every advance out of barbarism. The field seems now open to genial influences. It is impossible to repress the hope, that out of the deep and living fountains of benevolence, in the land of our fathers, a broad and fertilizing current will be poured over the thirsty plains of India,—the abodes of great geniuses in the morning of the world ;—and that

51

letters, arts, and religion will be extended to a hundred millions of these mild and oppressed fellow beings.

But it is time to relieve your patience ; I will do it, after a reflection on the relation which this country bears to the work of general education ; and all I wish to say will be comprised in one word of encouragement, and one of warning.

The recent agitations of the country have a bearing on the great moral questions we have been discussing, more important, as it seems to me, than their immediate political aspect. In its present united condition, that of a state already large and powerful, and rapidly increasing,—its population more generally well-educated, than that of any other country, and imbued with an unusual spirit of personal, social, and moral enterprise, it presents in itself the most effective organization imaginable, for the extension of the domain of improvement at home and abroad. The vital principle of this organization is the union of its members. In this, they enjoy an exemption from the heavy burden of great local establishments of government, and still more from the curse of neighboring states,— eternal border war. In virtue of this principle, they are enabled to devote all their energies, in peace and tranquillity, to the cultivation of the arts of private life, and the pursuit of every great work of public utility, benevolence, and improvement. To attack the principle of union, is to attack the prosperity of the whole and of every part of the country ; it is to check the outward development of our national activity ; to turn our resources and energies, now exerted in every conceivable manner, for public and private benefit, into new channels of mutual injury and ruin. Instead of roads and canals to unite distant States, the hill tops of those which adjoin each other, would be crowned with fortresses ; and our means would be strained to the utmost in the support of as many armies and navies as there were rival sovereignties. Nor would the evil rest with the waste of treasure. The thoughts and feelings of men would assume a new direction ; and military renown, and rank, plunder and revenge, be the ruling principles of the day. Destroy the Union of the States, and you destroy their character, change their occupations, blast their prospects. You shut the annals of the republic, and open the book of kings. You shut the book of peace, and you open the book of war. You unbar the gates of hell to the legion of civil discord, ambition, havoc, bloodshed, and ruin!

Let these considerations never be absent from our minds. But if the question is asked, What encouragement is there, that a vast deal can be done, in a short time, for the improvement of man? I would say to him who puts the question, Look around you. In what country do you live? under what state of things has it grown up? Do you bear in mind, that in a space of time, one half of which has been covered by the lives of some yet in existence, in two hundred years, these wide-spread settlements, with so many millions of inhabitants,—abounding in all the blessings of life, more liberally and equally bestowed than in any other country, have been built up in a remote and savage wilderness? Do you recollect, that it is not half a century, since, with a population comparatively insignificant, she vindicated her independence, in a war against the oldest and strongest government on earth? Do you consider, that the foundations of these powerful and prosperous States were laid by a few persecuted and aggrieved private citizens, of moderate fortune, unsupported, scarcely tolerated, by the government? If you will go back to the very origin, do you not perceive, that, as if to consecrate this country, from the outset, as a most illustrious example of what a man can do, it was owing to the fixed impression on the heart of one friendless mariner, pursued through long years of fruitless solicitation, and fainting hope, that these vast American continents are made a part of the heritage of civilized men? Look around you again, at the institutions which are the pride and blessing of the country. See our entire religious establishments,—unendowed by the state, supported by the united efforts of the individual citizens. See the great literary institutions of our country, especially those in New-England,—Dartmouth, Williams, Bowdoin, Brown, Amherst, and others,—founded by the liberality of citizens of moderate fortune, or by the small combined contributions of public-spirited benefactors, aided, at the most, by moderate endowments from the public treasury;—and 'the two twins of learning,' if I may, without arrogance, name them apart from the rest; this most efficient and respected seminary, within whose walls we are now convened, and my own ancient and beloved Harvard; to whom and what do they trace their origin?—

Yale, to the ten worthy fathers, who assembled at Branford, in 1700, and laying each a few volumes on the table, said, ' I give these books for the founding of a college in this colony ;' and Harvard, to the dying munificence of an humble minister of the gospel, who landed on the shores of America, but to lay his dust in its soil ; but who did not finish his brief sojourn, till he had accomplished a work of usefulness, which, we trust, will never die. Whence originated the great reform in our prisons, which has accomplished its wonders of philanthropy and mercy, in the short space of eight years, and made the penitentiaries of America the model of the penal institutions of the world ?   It had its origin in the visit of a missionary, with his Bible, to the convict's cell.— Whence sprang the mighty temperance reform, which has already done so much to wipe off a great blot from the character of the country ?   It was commenced on so small a scale, that it is not easy to assign its effective origin to a precise source.   And counsels and efforts, as humble and inconsiderable at the outset, gave the impulse to the missionary cause of modern times, which, going forth, with its devoted champions, conquering and to conquer, beneath

> the great ensign of Messiah,—
> Aloft by angels borne, their sign in Heaven,

has already gained a peaceful triumph over the farthest islands, and added a new kingdom to the realms of civilization and Christianity.

ADDRESS

DELIVERED AT BRIGHTON, BEFORE THE MASSACHUSETTS AGRICUL-
TURAL SOCIETY, 16TH OCTOBER, 1833.

IT is generally admitted, that since the institution of cattle-
shows in this country, the condition of our agriculture has been
manifestly improved. Before their establishment, our husbandmen
seemed to want those means of improvement, and encouragements
to action, which are enjoyed by their fellow citizens engaged in several other pursuits. Instead of living together in large towns, they
are scattered over the surface of the country. Instead of having two
thirds of every newspaper which appears, filled with advertisements
or information relative to their occupation,—as is the case with the
merchants,—the most they could promise themselves was, that the
weight of an enormous vegetable should be faithfully recorded;
and the memory of some calf, with two heads and six legs, be
handed to posterity. They held no conventions and assemblies,
like the clergy and physicians;—were not brought together like
the lawyers, at the periodical terms of court, to take sweet counsel
with each other, for the public good; and seemed not to possess,
in any way, the means of a rapid comparison and interchange of
opinion and feeling.

Since the establishment of the cattle-show of the Massachusetts
Agricultural Society, and those of the several county societies, this
state of things has been greatly amended; and to a considerable
degree, I imagine, through the agency of these institutions. The
cultivators of the soil are now brought together. Their agricultu-

ral improvements,—their superior animals,—their implements of husbandry,—the products of their farms,—their methods of cultivation, are all subjects of inquiry, comparison, and excitement. The premiums proposed, have given a spring to the enterprise of the cultivators; not on account of the trifling pecuniary reward which is held out, but under the influence of a generous spirit of emulation. The agricultural magazines and newspapers take up the matter in this stage, and give notoriety and permanency to all that is done or doing. The knowledge of every improvement is widely diffused. Increased prosperity begins to show itself, as the reward of increased skill and knowledge; and thus the condition of the husbandman is rendered more comfortable and more honorable.

A word of exhortation has become by usage a part of the ceremonial on these occasions:—and it has been thought not unseasonable, that the husbandmen's festival should afford some brief opportunity for the expression of opinions on important interests connected with their pursuits, and for the inculcation of the sentiments which belong to the vocation, standing, and usefulness of the farmer. You have just left the exhibition grounds, where you have been eye-witnesses of the dexterity of our ploughmen; where you have admired the display of the strength and docility of the well-trained draught cattle; where you have examined the animals brought forward as specimens of the improvement of their various races. You have not, of course, retired from this animated and interesting scene,—thronged as it is by the assembled yeomanry of the Commonwealth,—the living masters of the great art of agriculture,— to come together here, with the view of gaining additional knowledge of matters of practical husbandry. This, I am well persuaded, at all events, is not expected from me, and I shall have fulfilled the object for which I have been invited to appear before you, on this occasion, if I shall succeed, in any degree, in bringing home to the minds of those whom I have the honor to address, the importance and respectability of the occupation of the farmer, and his comparative condition in this and other countries.

In the first place, then, let us say a word of the importance of the pursuit of the husbandman. What rank does agriculture hold, in the scale of usefulness among the pursuits of men in civilized communities? We shall arrive at a practical answer to this question, by considering, that it is agriculture which spreads the great and bountiful table, at which the mighty family of civilized man receives his daily bread. Something is yielded by the chase, and much more by the fisheries ; but the produce of the soil constitutes the great mass of the food of a civilized community, either directly in its native state, or through the medium of the animals fed by it, which become, in their turn, the food of man. In like manner, agriculture furnishes the material for our clothing. Wool, cotton, flax, silk, leather, are the materials, of which nearly all our clothing is composed ; and these are furnished by agriculture. In producing the various articles of clothing, the manufacturing arts are largely concerned, and commerce, in the exchange of raw materials and fabrics. These, therefore, to a considerable degree, rest on agriculture, as their ultimate foundation ; especially as it feeds all the other branches of industry.

If we suppose the population of this State to consume in food and clothing, on an average, half a dollar a week each, (and that is about half the cost of supporting a slave in the Southern States), it will give nearly fifty-two millions of agricultural produce consumed in Massachusetts in a year. In addition to this, is all that is consumed by the domestic animals, and all that is raised and not consumed, but exported, or otherwise given in exchange for articles of value, which are preserved and accumulated.

Agriculture seems to be the first pursuit of civilized man. It enables him to escape from the life of the savage, and the wandering shepherd, into that of social man, gathered into fixed communities, and surrounding himself with the comforts and blessings of neighborhood, country, and home. The savage lives by the chase, —a precarious and wretched independence. The Arab and the Tartar roam, with their flocks and herds, over a vast region, destitute of all those refinements, which require for their growth the features of a permanent residence, and a community organized into the various professions, arts, and trades. They are found now, after a lapse of four thousand years, precisely in the same condition in which they existed in the days of Abraham. It is agriculture alone, that fixes men in stationary dwellings, in villages, towns, and cities, and enables the work of civilization, in all its branches, to go on.

Agriculture was held in honorable estimation, by the most enlightened nations of antiquity. In the infancy of commerce and
manufactures, its relative rank among the occupations of men was
necessarily higher than now. The patriarchs of the ancient Scripture times cultivated the soil. Abraham was very rich in cattle, in
gold, and in silver. Job farmed on a very large scale : he had seven
thousand sheep, three thousand camels, five hundred yoke of oxen,
and five hundred she-asses. In Greece, the various improvements
in husbandry, the introduction of the nutritive grains, and the invention of convenient instruments for tilling the soil, were regarded as the immediate bounties of the gods. At a later period, land
was almost the only article of property ; and those who cultivated
it, if they were freemen, were deemed a more respectable class
than manufacturers and mechanics, who were mostly slaves. Among
the Romans, agriculture was still more respected than among the
Greeks. In the best and purest times of the republic, the most
distinguished citizens, the proudest patricians, lived on their farms,
and labored with their own hands. Cato the censor was both a
practical and scientific farmer, and wrote a treatise on the art ;—
and who has not heard of Cincinnatus ? When the Sabines had
advanced with a superior army to the walls of the city, the people,
although at that period greatly disaffected toward the patricians, demanded that Lucius Quinctius Cincinnatus, one of that unpopular
class, should be created Dictator,—that is, that all the laws, and
the power of all the magistrates should be suspended, and despotic
authority vested in his hands. Livy, in relating the occurrence,
cannot help breaking out in the exclamation, ' That it is well worth
the attention of those who despise every thing on earth but money,
and think that there is no place for honor or virtue, except where
wealth abounds. The sole hope of the Roman empire, (adds he),
in this the day of her extremity, L. Quinctius, was cultivating, at
this time, a farm beyond the Tiber, which still bears his name, and
which consisted of four acres. There he was found by the messengers who were sent to hail him as Dictator, leaning on his spade, or
holding his plough. After having raised an army and defeated the
enemy, he laid down, in sixteen days, the dictatorship, which he
was authorized to hold for six months, and on the seventeenth day,
got back to his farm.'*

* Liv. lib. III, § 26.

In the progress of wealth and luxury, in the Roman empire, the class of husbandmen sunk from their original estimation, in consequence of the employment of vast numbers of slaves on the estates of the great landholders. Still, however, there was a large and respectable class of rural tenantry, who cultivated at the halves the lands of the rich proprietors ; and the free and independent citizens who tilled their own small farms, like the great men of better days, never wholly disappeared till the overthrow of the Roman empire, by the invasion of the barbarous tribes.

On the destruction of the Roman empire, the feudal system arose in Europe, a singularly complicated plan of military despotism. In this system, the possession of the land was made the basis of the military defence of the country. The king was the ultimate proprietor ; and apportioned the territory among the great lords, his retainers. Those who cultivated the soil were slaves, the property of their lord, and were bought and sold with the cattle which they tended. Sir Walter Scott, in describing, with his graphic pen, one of this class of the former population of England, after depicting the other peculiarities of his costume, adds, a trait which speaks volumes as to their condition,—' One part of his dress only remains, but it is too remarkable to be suppressed ; it was a brass ring, resembling a dog's collar, but without any opening, and soldered fast round his neck ; so loose as to form no impediment to his breathing ; yet so tight as to be incapable of being removed, excepting by the use of the file. On this singular gorget was engraved in Saxon characters, " Gurth, the son of Beowulph, is the born thrall of Cedric." ' There is but one reflection wanting, to give us the full conception of the degradation of the peasantry of this period, which is, that these ' born thralls ' were the original rightful masters of the soil, subjected to foreign conquerors.

If the estimate of Dr Lingard can be trusted, two thirds of the population of England, under the Anglo-Saxons, were of this class. They were either the native race, enslaved by their conquerors, or free born Anglo-Saxons, reduced to slavery for debt,—(a crime still punished by imprisonment),—for offences against the laws, or by a voluntary surrender of their liberty, as a refuge from want. Their occupations were, of course, as various as the wants or will of their masters might dictate; but their persons, families, and goods of every description were the property of their lord. He could dispose of them as he pleased, by gift or sale ; he could annex them to the soil, or remove them from it ; he could transfer them with it to a new proprietor, or leave them by will to his heirs. Many such devises are still on record. Even the slave-trade existed in all its horrors, and in a form scarcely less abominable than in modern times. Slaves were sold openly in the market, during the whole of the Anglo-Saxon period, and it is supposed that the value of a slave was fourfold that of an ox. The importation of foreign slaves was unrestrained, but the exportation of natives was strictly forbidden. The Northumbrians, however, in their eager pursuit of gain, despised the prohibition, and are said to have carried off, not merely their countrymen, but their friends and relatives, and sold them as slaves, in the ports of the continent. Bristol, as in modern times, was infamous for the zeal with which her merchants prosecuted this detestable traffic. It was abandoned at length, with slavery itself, under the mild and humanizing influence of Christianity.*

What reflections are not awakened by the fact, that, ten centuries ago, two thirds of the population of England, the land of our forefathers, were born slaves, who wore dogs' collars soldered round their necks, and were bought and sold like slaves in the market !

But these are times long since past. Let us proceed to the next topic, which invites our attention,—the condition of the cultivators of the soil, at the present day, and especially their comparative condition in Europe and America. I do not know in what way so effectually, the New-England yeoman can be made proud of his calling, and happy in its pursuit, as by instituting this comparison.

There are, then, *four* principal states or conditions, in which the agricultural population of modern Europe and America is found :— and among these four states, I do not include that of the West Indian and North American slaves.

* Lingard's History of England, Vol. I, p. 502.

First and lowest in the scale of those, by whom the soil is cultivated in Europe, are the *serfs* of Russia. In the different provinces of this vast empire, about thirty millions of souls, (nearly the
entire population employed in husbandry), are found almost exactly in the state which has already been described, under the feudal
system. Some ameliorations have been introduced in some provinces, and not in others; and in the south-western portions of the
empire, as Courland and Livonia, principally settled by Germans,
the system of actual slavery has been abolished by law. But with
these local exceptions, the Russian peasantry continue the property
of the land owner, and may be sold by him with or without the
land, as he pleases. He has power to give or to sell them their
freedom, and power to keep them in slavery; the power to chastise them, and to imprison them; and in all respects to dispose
of them, with the exception of taking life, or preventing their
being enlisted into the army. But when a draft is ordered by the
government, the landlord directs who shall march. The wealth of
a great landholder is estimated by the number of his peasants; and
individuals in the Russian empire are named, who possess a hundred thousand and even a hundred and twenty thousand slaves.
Each individual peasant, of either sex, is bound, from the age of
fifteen, to pay the avrock, or capitation tax, of about four dollars
per annum. This is taken in lieu of performing three days' labor,
in each week, to which the landlord is entitled by the law. In
addition to this, the serf has to account to his lord for a certain
part of all his produce; and besides all, he is subject to the government taxes. If the peasant chooses to make an effort to rise above
his condition, he must apply to his lord for permission to leave the
spot where he was born, and pursue some other trade. If this occupation be a more lucrative one, his annual tax is proportionably
increased.* Such is the condition of the entire civilized portion of
the Russian empire; and it is needless to state, that it places this
portion far below the wild Tartars, who own a nominal subjection
to the Russian sceptre, and pay a trifling tribute for the privilege
of roaming their remote steppes, unmolested and free.

* Clark's Travels in Russia, Vol. I, p. 218, where will be found, in a note, a
very interesting extract on this subject, from Bishop Heber's MS. Journal.

I have already remarked, that the condition in which the agricultural population exists in Russia, is but little if any better than that of the vassals, under the feudal system. When this system was undermined, the character of the peasantry assumed a new form, in which it still exists, in a considerable part of Europe. The sovereigns found it for their interest to weaken the power of the great barons, by granting privileges to their small retainers; and either from the same motives of policy, or from higher considerations of Christian charity, the church of Rome united with the kings in elevating the condition of the peasantry. Pope Alexander III, in the twelfth century, published a bull for the general emancipation of slaves.* By degrees the *villains*, (for such was the ill-omened name given by our forefathers to the cultivators of the soil), rose to the possession of some of the rights of freemen; but it was not till the reign of Charles II, that villenage was virtually suppressed by statute.† On the continent of Europe, when the abject servitude of the feudal system was broken up, the peasants became *tenants at the halves;* and such are a considerable portion of the cultivators of the soil, at the present day. It was calculated that in France, before the revolution, seven eighths of the agricultural population were *Métayers*, that is, tenants at the halves. The revolution has greatly increased the number of small proprietors, in consequence of the sale of the estates of emigrants, and of the public domain; but one half of the cultivators of the soil, it is supposed, are still *tenants at the halves.* Such a tenancy is not wholly unheard of in this country. The estates in Lombardy, and in some other parts of Italy, are cultivated in this way. The terms of the contract between the landlord and the tenant are not uniform; in some cases a third, and in others a half of the produce belongs to the landlord. In some cases, the landlord finds the whole of the stock and the seed, in others, the half. In some cases, the tenant has a property in the lease, which descends to his children; in others, he is a tenant at will; in others, the leases are periodically renewed at short intervals. But, however the details

---

* Smith's Wealth of Nations, Vol. II, p. 91.   London, 1822.

† 2 Blackstone, 96.

may vary, the system resolves itself, in the main, into a general system of tenancy at the halves. It is considered highly unfavorable to the improvement of agriculture. There is a constant struggle, on the side of each party, to get as much as possible out of the land, with the least possible outlay. The tenant has no interest in using the stock with care and prudence, as this is to be replaced by the landlord. In France, the effect of this system is acknowledged by the best writers in that country to be pernicious.* A better account of it is given in Lombardy. There the tenant has the whole of the clover, and divides only the wheat, Indian corn, flax, wine, and silk. The landlord advances nothing but the taxes.

This mode of occupying the land was formerly common in England, but is little known there at the present day. The great majority of farms are there the property of large landholders; and are cultivated by tenants, who take them on leases, the terms of which vary according to circumstances, both as to the amount of the rent and the duration of the lease.

It has been a question much debated in England, whether a system of this kind, by which the land is principally held in large farms belonging to the aristocracy of the country, and cultivated by tenants on lease, is more favorable to the improvement of agriculture than the multiplication of small farms. It has been urged, that great and expensive improvements in farming, cannot take place without great capital, which can only be furnished by large proprietors. It is these alone, who can reclaim wastes,—convert sandy plains into fertile fields,—drain extensive fens,—or shut out the sea from large tracts of meadow. All this is true; but where great improvements are made by the application of large amounts of capital; the return is not to the tenant, but to the capitalist. A judicious operation upon a poor soil may turn it into a good one: the soil may produce twice as much as it did before; but the rent,

---

* Say, Tom. II, p. 174. See, also, Arthur Young's Tour.—The views taken, in this address, of all the subjects alluded to are necessarily superficial. A very instructive discussion of the condition of the cultivators of the soil in the different states of modern Europe, may be found in Sismondi's *Nouveaux Principes d'Economie politique*, Tom. I, p. 186.

in that case, will be doubled. The landlord has doubled his capital; but it will depend on other circumstances, whether any beneficial change is produced in the condition of the tenant. The neighborhood, it is true, will be improved by the new creation of property,—the population will increase,—and, indirectly, every individual's condition will be improved, by living in a larger community; but directly, I cannot perceive that the tenant is benefitted; inasmuch as it is plain, that precisely as the land is rendered more productive, the rent increases. As the landed interest in England is the main interest of the country, and the accumulation of large estates in land is the most important element in their system, every thing is made to favor this mode of cultivating the land, and the small proprietor labors under great disadvantages. Wherever he moves, he has a wealthy rival to contend with, able to overbid and to undersell him; and as things now are in England, it is very possible that the condition of the tenant in that country is more desirable than that of the small farmer. But this, I conceive, proves nothing in the argument, whether the condition of the tenant or the proprietor of a small farm is to be preferred. It is, in fact, justly made a leading objection to the English system of tenancy, by the learned French writer already quoted, (M. de Sismondi),* that it tends to the extermination of the small proprietors, and to reduce the cottagers, peasants, and all those by whom, under whatever name, the labor of cultivation is performed, to a state of abject and servile dependence.

This brings me to the consideration of the fourth and last state, in which the cultivator of the soil is found; and that is, the condition which almost universally obtains in the non-slave-holding States of this country, and especially in New-England, in which the farmer is the proprietor of the soil;—and I cannot but express my decided conviction, that this condition is the most favorable to the prosperity of the state and the happiness of the individual. It will immediately be perceived, that it is not inconsistent with the possession of some very ample landed estates by individuals. In a

---

* Nouveaux Principes, Tom. I, p. 217.

country like ours, where every man's capacity, industry, and good fortune are left free, to work their way without prejudice, as far as possible; there will be among the agricultural, as well as among the commercial population, fortunes of all sizes; from that of the man who owns his thousand acres,—his droves of cattle,—his flocks of sheep,—his range of pastures,—his broad fields of mowing and tillage,—down to the poor cottager who can scarce keep his cow over winter. There will always be, in a population like ours, opportunities enough for those who cannot own a farm, to hire one; and for those who cannot hire one, to labor in the employment of their neighbors, who need their services; and when we maintain that it is for the welfare of the society, that the land should be cultivated by an independent yeomanry, who own the soil they till, we mean only that this should be the general state and condition of things, and not that there should be no such thing as a wealthy proprietor, whose lands, in whole or in part, are cultivated by a tenant;—no such thing as a prudent husbandman taking a farm on a lease;—or an industrious young man,—without any capital but his hands,—laboring in the employ of his neighbor. These all are parts of the system, as it exists among us. And we maintain that it is a better system than the division of the country into a few vast domains cultivated by a dependent tenantry, to the almost total exclusion of the class of small independent farmers.

Am I asked, Why is it better? This is a question not easy to bring down to a dry argument. It involves political and moral considerations;—it trenches on the province of the feelings;—it concerns the whole character of a people.

In a pecuniary point of view, it is not, of course, maintained, that because it is desirable that the cultivator should own a farm, it is therefore expedient that he should, in all cases, attempt to purchase one. It cannot, as a general rule, be assumed, that it is better for a young man to buy a farm than to hire one, supposing him to have no more capital than is necessary to stock his farm, and purchase implements of husbandry. If he buys, he must mortgage his farm for the payment; and the interest on the purchase money will, perhaps, be greater than the rent he would have to pay for a farm equally good. Whether it is good policy, for a man, not having capital enough at once to pay for his farm, to buy one, depends upon his energy and talent,—the situation and quality of the farm,—and the prospect that, within a reasonable period of time, and the enjoyment of an average success, he can pay for it. If he cannot do this, he can in no sense become the owner of a farm ;—he can only encumber himself with the responsibility of it, paying more in the shape of interest, than he would have to pay in that of rent. But, supposing a young man, at the commencement of life, and desirous of passing his days on the soil which gave him birth, possessing so much capital, that besides stocking a farm, he can do something toward its purchase at the outset, with a reasonable expectation that, in the course of time, with industry, perseverance, and temperance, he can make it his own, then it is better that he should purchase than hire. He has then, the strongest inducements to be industrious, frugal, and temperate ; for every dollar he can save, passes silently into investment, in paying off his debt. The earnings of the tenant are in danger of being needlessly spent or lost, for want of a safe and ready investment. The owner makes improvements with zeal and spirit, for he makes them on his own soil ; in the assurance that he or his children will reap the benefit of them, and every new improvement furnishes a new stimulus to those efforts which are necessary to pay off the debt. But no person takes a genuine pleasure in improving another man's property. It is the interest of the tenant to get as much out of the soil as he can, and to give as little back to it. When he has exhausted one farm, he can take another. Thus the land, as far as it is cultivated in this way, is undergoing a gradual decay ; but not more surely than the generous principle in the heart of him who thus occupies it, and who is perpetually, though perhaps unconsciously, under the influence of his interest, engaged in deteriorating his neighbor's property. The owner is under precisely the opposite influence, and especially while it is necessary to make his farm as productive as possible. He strives to render back to it as much as possible in return for what he takes from it. For he feels that he is making it the depository of all that his youth and manhood can lay up for the decline of life, for his family, and his children.

Whatever, in this way, is true, with respect to the young farmer who has purchased his farm on credit, is still more applicable to him who happily begins life, the proprietor of the soil which he cultivates. It is particularly in reference to him, that the subject presents itself in other relations than those of pecuniary calculation, and assumes the aspect not merely of an economical, but also of a political question. In general, the inquiry, how the land is cultivated, derives great consequence from its connexion with the political condition of the cultivators. A very considerable portion of the political power of every country must be vested in the landholders; for they hold a large part of the property of the country. They do so even in England, where there is such a vast amount of commercial and manufacturing wealth. Although the land is, to a considerable degree, in England, monopolized by rich proprietors, yet attempts have been made, and with success, to give political privileges and consequence to the tenantry. Still, however, the greatest landholder, in most of the countries, is generally able to carry the elections as he pleases. I have read, and that too, since the passage of the Reform Bill, in the English newspapers, of voters being refused a renewal of leases, which had been in the family two generations, in consequence of voting against their landlord's candidate. There is no way in which a calm, orderly and intelligent exercise and control of political power can be assured to the people, but by a distribution among them, as equally as possible, of the property of the country; and I know no manner, in which such a distribution can be effected, legally, permanently, and peacefully, but by keeping the land in small farms, suitable to be cultivated by their owners. Under such a system, and under no other, the people will exercise their rights with independence. The assumption of a right to dictate, will be frowned at, if attempted; and even the small portion of the population who may be tenants, will possess the spirit and freedom of the proprietors. But when the great mass of the land is parcelled out into a few immense estates, cultivated by a dependent tenantry, the unavoidable consequence is a sort of revival of the feudal ages, when the great barons took the field against each other at the head of their vassals.*

* Story's Commentaries, I, p. 160.—p. 166.

53

But, I own, it is not even on political grounds, that I think our
system of independent rural freeholders is most strongly entitled to
the preference. Its moral aspects, its connexion with the character and feelings of the yeomanry give it, after all, its greatest value.
The man who stands upon his own soil ; who feels, that by the
laws of the land in which he lives,—by the law of civilized nations,—he is the rightful and exclusive owner of the land which he
tills, is, by the constitution of our nature, under a wholesome influence, not easily imbibed from any other source. He feels,—
other things being equal,—more strongly than another, the character of man as the lord of the inanimate world. Of this great and
wonderful sphere, which, fashioned by the hand of God, and upheld by his power, is rolling through the heavens, a portion is his :
—his, from the centre to the sky. It is the space, on which the
generations before him moved in its round of duties ; and he feels
himself connected, by a visible link, with those who preceded him,
as he is, also, to those who will follow him, and to whom he is to
transmit a home. Perhaps his farm has come down to him from
his fathers. They have gone to their last home ; but he can trace
their footsteps over the daily scene of his labors. The roof which
shelters him, was reared by those to whom he owes his being.
Some interesting domestic tradition is connected with every enclosure. The favorite fruit tree was planted by his father's hand. He
sported, in his boyhood, by the side of the brook, which still winds
through his meadow. Through that field, lies the path to the village school of his earliest days. He still hears from his window,
the voice of the Sabbath bell, which called his fathers and his forefathers to the house of God ; and near at hand is the spot where
he laid his parents down to rest, and where he trusts, when his
hour is come, he shall be dutifully laid by his children. These are
the feelings of the owner of the soil. Words cannot paint them ;
gold cannot buy them ;—they flow out of the deepest feelings of
the heart ;—they are the life-spring of a fresh, healthy, generous
national character.

The history and experience of the world illustrate their power.
Whoever heard of an enlightened race of serfs, slaves, or vassals ?
How can we wonder at the forms of government which prevail in
Europe, with such a system of monopoly in the land, as there ex-

ists? Nothing but this explains our own history,—clears up the mystery of the Revolution,—and makes us fully comprehend the secret of our own strength. Austria or France must fall, whenever Vienna or Paris is seized by a powerful army. But what was the loss of Boston or New-York, in the revolutionary war, to the people of New-England? The moment the enemy set his foot in the country, he was like the hunter going to the thicket, to rob the tigress of her young. The officers and soldiers of the Revolution were farmers and sons of farmers, who owned the soil for which they fought; and many of them, like the veteran Putnam, literally left their ploughs in the furrow, to hasten to the field. The attempt to conquer such a population, is as chimerical, as it would be to march an army down to the sea-shore, in the bay of Fundy, when the tide is rolling in seventy feet high, in order to beat back the waves with their bucklers.

But it is time to conclude. When the civil wars of Rome were over, Virgil was requested, by the emperor Augustus, to write a poem on agriculture, in order to encourage the Italian husbandmen to return to the culture of their wasted fields. The farmers in Italy, at that time, were mostly *tenants at the halves;** but the philosophic poet could not help pronouncing even them *too happy, did they but know their blessings.* After having compared, with some attention, the various conditions in which man is found, in the principal countries of Europe and in America, I have come to the undoubting conclusion, that there is not a population on earth, taken as a whole, so highly favored in the substantial blessings of life, as the yeomanry of New-England. There are other countries that surpass us in wealth and power; in military strength; in magnificence, and the display of the expensive arts;—but none, which can so justly lay claim to that glorious character,—a free and happy commonwealth;—none in which the image of a state, sketched by the fancy of the philosophic poet, is so beautifully realized:—

' What constitutes a state ?
Not high-raised battlement, and labored mound,
Thick wall or moated gate;
Not cities proud, with spires and turrets crowned;

* Coloni Partiarii.

Not bays and broad-armed ports,
Where, laughing at the storm, proud navies ride;
Not starred and spangled courts,
Where low-browed baseness wafts perfumes to pride.—
No! men! high-minded men,
Men who their duties know,
But know their rights;—and, knowing, dare maintain;—
Prevent the long-aimed blow,
And crush the tyrant, while they rend the chain;—
These constitute a state,
And sovereign law, that state's collected will,
O'er thrones and globes elate,
Sits empress, crowning good, repressing ill.'

EULOGY

ON LAFAYETTE, DELIVERED IN FANEUIL HALL, AT THE REQUEST
OF THE YOUNG MEN OF BOSTON, SEPTEMBER 6TH, 1834.*

———

WHEN I look round upon this vast audience, and reflect upon
the deep interest manifested by so many intelligent persons in the
occasion which has called us together,—when I consider the variety,
the importance, and singularity of the events which must pass in
review before us, and the extraordinary character of the man
whom we commemorate,—his connexion with Europe and America, in the most critical periods of their history,—his intercourse in
both hemispheres with the master spirits of the age,—his auspicious,
long protracted, and glorious career, alternating, with fearful rapidity, from one extreme of fortune to the other,—and when I feel
that I am expected, by the great multitude I have the honor to ad-

———

* To avoid the necessity of frequent marginal references, I would observe, that
the account of Lafayette's first visit to America is chiefly taken from a very interesting article on that subject, communicated by Mr Sparks to the Boston Daily Ad-
vertiser, of 26th June, 1834, from his edition of Washington's Works, now in the
press. Among the other authorities which I have consulted, are the well-known
works of Sarrans, the Memoirs of Lafayette and the Constitutional Assembly, by
Regnault-Warin, Montgaillard's History of France, from the close of the reign of
Louis XVI, to the year 1825, and Mr Ticknor's beautiful sketch of the Life of Lafayette; originally published in the North American Review. But I owe a more
particular acknowledgment to Mr Sparks, who not only furnished me with the sheets
of those parts of the unpublished volumes of Washington's Works, which throw
light on the military services of Lafayette in the war of the American Revolution,
but placed in my hands a great mass of original papers, of the highest interest and

dress,—the flower of this metropolis,—to say something not inappropriate to such an occasion, nor wholly beneath the theme, I am oppressed with the weight of the duty I am to perform.   I know not how, in the brief space allotted to me, to take up and dispose of a subject so vast and comprehensive.   I would even now, were it possible, retire from the undertaking ; and leave to your own hearts, borne upwards with the swelling strains of yonder choir,— whose pious and plaintive melody is just dying on the ear,—to muse, in expressive silence, the praise of him we celebrate.   But since this may not be,—since the duty devolved upon me must, however feebly, be discharged,—let me, like the illustrious subject of our contemplation, gather strength from the magnitude of the task.   Let me calmly trace him through those lofty and perilous paths of duty, which he trod with serenity, while empires were toppling round him ;—and, trampling under foot the arts of the rhetorician, as he trampled under foot all the bribes of vanity, avarice, and ambition, and all the delights of life, let me, in the plainness of history, and the boldness of truth, not wholly uncongenial to the character of the man I would reproduce to your admiration and love, discharge as I may, the great duty which you have assigned to me.

There is, at every great era of the history of the world, a leading principle, which gives direction to the fortunes of nations, and the characters of distinguished men.   This principle, in our own time, is that of the action and reaction upon each other, of Europe and America, for the advancement of free institutions, and the promotion of rational liberty.   Ever since the discovery of America,

---

value, relating to the career of Lafayette, and furnished to Mr Sparks by the General himself, from his own collections, and the public offices at Paris.   These papers contain the Correspondence of Lafayette with Washington, from the year 1778 to his death; his Correspondence and Notes of his Conferences with the Count de Vergennes and other French ministers ; his Correspondence with his family and friends, from America and from his prisons in Germany; Notes and Commentaries on the most important incidents of his life; his Correspondence with the Governor of Virginia and officers of the army, especially during the campaign of 1781, and miscellaneous papers bearing on the main subject.   They form altogether ample materials for a history of the life and services of Lafayette ; a work which no one is so well qualified as Mr Sparks to execute, and which, it is greatly to be wished, he might be induced to undertake.

this principle has been in operation, but naturally and necessarily with vastly increased energy, since the growth of an intelligent population this side the water. For the formation of a man of truly great character, it is necessary that he should be endowed with qualities to win respect and love ;—that he should be placed in circumstances favorable to a powerful action on society ;—and then, that with a pure affection, a strong, disinterested, glowing zeal,—a holy ambition of philanthropy,—he should devote himself to the governing principle of the age. Such a combination, humanly speaking, produces the nearest approach to perfection which the sphere of man admits. Of such characters the American Revolution was more than commonly fertile, for it was the very crisis of that action and reaction, which is the vocation of the age. Such a character was Washington ; such was Lafayette.

Lafayette was born at Chavaniac, in the ancient province of Auvergne, in France, on the sixth day of September, 1757, seventy-seven years ago this day. His family was one of the most ancient in the country, and of the highest rank in the French nobility. As far back as the fifteenth century, one of his ancestors, a marshall of France, was distinguished for his military achievements ;—his uncle fell in the wars of Italy, in the middle of the last century ;—and his father lost his life in the seven years' war, at the battle of Minden. His mother died soon after, and he was thus left an orphan, at an early age, the heir of an immense estate, and exposed to all the dangers incident to youth, rank, and fortune, in the gayest and most luxurious city on earth, at the period of its greatest corruption. He escaped unhurt. Having completed the usual academical course, at the college of Duplessis in Paris, he married, at the age of sixteen, the daughter of the Duke d'Ayen, of the family of Noailles, somewhat younger than himself ;—and at all times the noble encourager of his virtues,—the heroic partner of his sufferings,—the worthy sharer of his great name and of his honorable grave.

The family to which he thus became allied, was then, and for fifty years had been, in the highest favor at the French court. Himself the youthful heir of one of the oldest and richest houses in France, the path of advancement was open before him. He was offered a brilliant place in the royal household. At an age and in a situation most likely to be caught by the attraction, he declined the proffered distinction, impatient of the attendance at court which it required. He felt, from his earliest, years, that he was not born to loiter in an ante-chamber. The sentiment of liberty was already awakened in his bosom. Having, while yet at college, been required, as an exercise in composition, to describe the well-trained charger, obedient even to the shadow of the whip; he represented the noble animal, on the contrary, as rearing at the sight of it, and throwing his rider. With this feeling, the profession of arms was, of course, the most congenial to him; and was, in fact, with the exception of that of courtier, the only one open to a young French nobleman before the Revolution.

In the summer of 1776, and just after the American declaration of independence, Lafayette was stationed at Metz, a garrisoned town on the road from Paris to the German frontier, with the regiment to which he was attached, as a captain of dragoons, not then nineteen years of age. The duke of Gloucester, the brother of the king of England, happened to be on a visit to Metz, and a dinner was given to him, by the commandant of the garrison. Lafayette was invited, with other officers, to the entertainment. Despatches had just been received by the duke, from England, relating to American affairs,—the resistance of the colonists, and the strong measures adopted by the ministers to crush the rebellion. Among the details stated by the duke of Gloucester, was the extraordinary fact, that these remote, scattered, and unprotected settlers of the wilderness *had solemnly declared themselves an independent people.* That word decided the fortunes of the enthusiastic listener; and not more distinctly was the great declaration a charter of political liberty to the rising States, than it was a commission to their youthful champion to devote his life to the sacred cause.

The details which he heard were new to him. The American contest was known to him before, but as a rebellion,—a tumultuary affair in a remote transatlantic colony. He now, with a promptness of perception which, even at this distance of time, strikes us as little less than miraculous, addressed a multitude of inquiries to the duke of Gloucester on the subject of the contest. His imagination was kindled at the idea of a civilized people struggling for political liberty. His heart was warmed with the possibility of drawing his sword in a good cause. Before he left the table, his course was mentally resolved on; and the brother of the king of England, (unconsciously, no doubt), had the singular fortune to enlist, from the French court and the French army, this gallant and fortunate champion in the then unpromising cause of the Colonial Congress.

He immediately repaired to Paris, to make further inquiries and arrangements, toward the execution of his great plan. He confided it to two young friends, officers like himself, the Count Segur and Viscount de Noailles, and proposed to them to join him. They shared his enthusiasm, and determined to accompany him, but, on consulting their families, they were refused permission. But they faithfully kept Lafayette's secret. Happily, shall I say, he was an orphan,—independent of control, and master of his own fortune, amounting to near forty thousand dollars per annum.

He next opened his heart to the Count de Broglie, a marshall in the French army. To the experienced warrior, accustomed to the regular campaigns of European service, the project seemed rash and quixotic, and one that he could not countenance. Lafayette begged the count at least not to betray him;—as he was resolved, (notwithstanding his disapproval of the project), to go to America. This the count promised, adding, however, 'I saw your uncle fall in Italy, and I witnessed your father's death, at the battle of Minden, and I will not be accessary to the ruin of the only remaining branch of the family.' He then used all the powers of argument which his age and experience suggested to him, to dissuade Lafayette from the enterprise, but in vain. Finding his determination unalterable, he made him acquainted with the Baron de Kalb, who,—the count knew,—was about to embark for America;—an officer of experience and merit, who, as is well known, fell at the battle of Camden.

The Baron de Kalb introduced Lafayette to Silas Deane, then agent of the United States in France, who explained to him the state of affairs in America, and encouraged him in his project. Deane was but imperfectly acquainted with the French language, and of manners somewhat repulsive. A less enthusiastic temper than that of Lafayette might have been somewhat chilled by the

54

434 EVERETT'S ORATIONS.

style of his intercourse. He had, as yet, not been acknowledged, in any public capacity ; and was beset by the spies of the British ambassador. For these reasons, it was judged expedient that the visit of Lafayette should not be repeated, and their further nego-tiations were conducted through the intervention of Mr Carmichael, an American gentleman, at that time in Paris. The arrangement was at length concluded, in virtue of which, Deane took upon him-self, without authority, but by a happy exercise of discretion, to engage Lafayette to enter the American service, with the rank of Major General. A vessel was about to be despatched with arms and other supplies for the American army, and in this vessel it was settled that he should take passage.

At this juncture, the news reached France, of the evacuation of New York, the loss of Fort Washington, the calamitous retreat through New Jersey, and the other disasters of the campaign of 1776. The friends of America in France were in despair. The tidings, bad in themselves, were greatly exaggerated in the British gazettes. The plan of sending an armed vessel with munitions, was abandoned. The cause, always doubtful, was now pronounced desperate ; and Lafayette was urged by all who were privy to his project, to give up an enterprise so wild and hopeless. Even our commissioners, (for Deane had been joined by Dr Franklin and Arthur Lee), told him they could not in conscience urge him to proceed. His answer was, ' My zeal and love of liberty have per-haps hitherto been the prevailing motive with me, but now I see a chance of usefulness which I had not anticipated. These supplies I know are greatly wanted by Congress. I have money ; I will purchase a vessel to convey them to America ; and in this vessel, my companions and myself will take passage.'

Yes, fellow citizens, that I may repeat an exclamation, uttered ten years ago, by him who has now the honor to address you, in the presence of an immense multitude, who welcomed ' the Nation's Guest' to the academic shades of Harvard, and by them received with acclamations of approval and tears of gratitude ;—when he was told by our commissioners, ' that they did not possess the means nor the credit to provide a single vessel in all the ports of France,' then, exclaimed the gallant and generous youth, ' I will provide my own ;' and it is a literal fact, that when our beloved country was too poor to offer him so much as a passage to her shores, he left, in his tender youth, the bosom of home, of happiness, of wealth, and of rank, to plunge in the dust and blood of our inauspicious struggle.

In pursuance of the generous purpose thus conceived, the secretary of the Count de Broglie was employed by Lafayette, to purchase and fit out a vessel at Bordeaux; and while these preparations were in train, with a view of averting suspicion from his movements, and passing the tedious interval of delay, he made a visit with a relative, to his kinsman, the Marquis de Noailles, then the French ambassador in London. During their stay in Great Britain, they were treated with kindness by the king and persons of rank; but having, after a lapse of three weeks, learned that his vessel was ready at Bordeaux, Lafayette suddenly returned to France. This visit was of service to the youthful adventurer, in furnishing him an opportunity to improve himself in the English language; but a nice sense of honor forbade him to make use of the opportunity which it afforded, for obtaining military information, that could be of utility to the American army. So far did he carry this scruple, that he declined visiting the naval establishment at Portsmouth.

On his return to France, he did not even visit Paris; but after three days passed at Passy, the residence of Dr Franklin, he hastened to Bordeaux. Arrived at this place, he found that his vessel was not yet ready; and had the still greater mortification to learn that the spies of the British ambassador had penetrated his designs, and made them known to the family of Lafayette, and to the king, from whom an order for his arrest was daily expected. Unprepared as his ship was, he instantly sailed in her to Passage, the nearest port in Spain, where he proposed to wait for the vessel's papers. Scarcely had he arrived in that harbor, when he was encountered by two officers, with letters from his family, and from the ministers, and a royal order, directing him to join his father-in-law at Marseilles. The letters from the ministers reprimanded him for violating his oath of allegiance and failing in his duty to his king. Lafayette, in some of his letters to his friends about court, replied to this remark, that the ministers might chide him with failing in his duty to the king when they learned to discharge theirs to the people. His family censured him for his desertion of his domestic duties ;—but his heroic wife, instead of joining in the reproach, shared his enthusiasm, and encouraged his enterprise.   He was obliged to return with the officers to Bordeaux, and report himself to the commandant.   While there, and engaged in communicating with his family and the court, in explanation and defence of his conduct, he learned from a friend at Paris, that a positive prohibition of his departure might be expected from the king.   No farther time was to be lost, and no middle course pursued.   He feigned a willingness to yield to the wishes of his family, and started as for Marseilles, with one of the officers who was to accompany him to America.   Scarcely had they left the city of Bordeaux, when he assumed the dress of a courier, mounted a horse and rode forward to procure relays.   They soon quitted the road to Marseilles, and struck into that which leads to Spain.   On reaching Bayonne, they were detained two or three hours.   While the companion of Lafayette was employed in some important commission in the city, he himself lay on the straw in the stable.   At St Jean de Luz, he was recognized by the daughter of the person who kept the post house ;—she had observed him a few days before, as he passed from Spain to Bordeaux.   Perceiving that he was discovered, and not daring to speak to her, he made her a signal to keep silence.   She complied with the intimation ; and when, shortly after he had passed on, his pursuers came up, she gave them an answer which baffled their penetration, and enable Lafayette to escape into Spain.   He was instantly on board his ship and at sea, with eleven officers in his train.

It would take me beyond the limits of the occasion, to repeat the various casualties and exposures of his passage, which lasted sixty days.   His vessel had cleared out for the West Indies ; but Lafayette directed the captain to steer for the United States, which, especially as he had a large pecuniary adventure of his own on board, he declined doing.   By threats to remove him from his command, and promises to indemnify him for the loss of his property, should they be captured, Lafayette prevailed upon the captain to steer his course for the American coast, where at last they happily arrived, having narrowly escaped two British vessels of war which were cruising in that quarter.   They made the coast near Georgetown, South Carolina.   It was late in the day before they could approach so near land as to leave the vessel. Anxious to tread the American soil, Lafayette, with some of his fellow officers, entered the ship's boat, and were rowed at nightfall to shore. A distant light guided them in their landing and advance into the country. Arriving near the house from which the light proceeded, an alarm was given by the watch-dogs, and they were mistaken by those within for a marauding party from the enemy's vessels, hovering on the coast. The Baron de Kalb, however, had a good knowledge of the English language, acquired on a previous visit to America, and was soon able to make known who they were and what was their errand. On this, they were, of course, readily admitted, and cordially welcomed. The house in which they found themselves, was that of Major Huger, a citizen of worth, hospitality, and patriotism, by whom every good office was performed to the adventurous strangers. He provided the next day the means of conveying Lafayette and his companions to Charleston, where they were received with enthusiasm by the magistrates and the people.

As soon as possible, they proceeded by land to Philadelphia. On his arrival there, with the eagerness of a youth anxious to be employed upon his errand, he sent his letters to our townsman, Mr Lovell, chairman of the committee of foreign relations. He called the next day at the hall of Congress, and asked to see this gentleman. Mr Lovell came out to him,—stated that so many foreigners offered themselves for employment in the American army, that Congress was greatly embarrassed to find them commands,—that the finances of the country required the most rigid economy,—and that he feared, in the present case, there was little hope of success. Lafayette perceived that the worthy chairman had made up his report, without looking at the papers ;—he explained to him, that his application, if granted, would lay no burden upon the finances of Congress, and addressed a letter to the President, in which he expressed a wish to enter the American army, on the condition of serving without pay or emolument, and on the footing of a volunteer. These conditions removed the chief obstacles alluded to, in reference to the appointment of foreign officers ;—the letters brought by Lafayette made known to Congress his high connexions, and his large means of usefulness, and without an hour's delay he received from them a commission of Major General in the American army, a month before he was twenty years of age.

A month before he is twenty years of age, he is thought worthy
by that august body, the revolutionary Congress, to be placed in
the highest rank of those, to whom the conduct of their arms was
entrusted in this hour of their extremest peril. What a commencement of life! None of the golden hours of youth wasted on its
worthless, but tempting vanities ;—none of those precious opportunities are lost for him, which, once lost, neither gold, nor tears, nor
blood can buy back, and which, for the mass of men, are lost, irre-
trievably, and for ever! None of the joyous days of youthful vigor
exhausted even in the praiseworthy but cheerless vigils with which,
in the present artificial state of society, it is too often the lot of advancing merit to work its way toilsomely up the steeps of usefulness and fame! It pleased a gracious Providence, in disposing
the strange and various agency by which the American independence was to be established, to place in the company of its defend-
ers a youthful champion from the highest circle of the gayest court
of Europe. By the side of Washington from his broad plantations,
—of Greene, from his forge,—of Stark, from his almost pathless
forests and granite hills,—of Putnam, from his humble farm, there
is a place, at the war council of the Revolution, for a young nobleman from France. He is raised at once, above the feverish
appetite for advancement,—the pest of affairs,—for he is born to
the highest station society can bestow. He comes from the bosom
of the domestic endearments, with which he has surrounded himself, before any of the accursed poisons of pleasure have been poured
into his heart ; and youth as he is, he brings the chaste and manly
virtues of the husband and the father to the virtuous cause which
he has embraced. The possessor of an immense estate, he is beyond the reach of mercenary motives ; and is enabled even to confer favors on the Congress whose confidence he receives.

But though his enterprise is one which requires, for its very conception, a rare enthusiasm ;—although, considering his position at
home, he must be all but a madman to persevere in such an adventure ; yet the nature of the cause to which he consecrates himself,
and of the duties which he undertakes to perform, implies a gravity of character, and sound judgment, belonging to mature years,
and long experience ; and that gravity and good judgment, young
and inexperienced as he is, he possesses in an eminent degree. To

succeed in the undertaking, he seems to need qualities of character not merely different from those which alone could prompt him to embark in it; but he must have the opposite and contradictory qualities. He must be cool, prudent, and considerate, at the very moment that he enters a career, from which every cool, prudent, and considerate man would have dissuaded him;—and arduous as it is, he enters it, without preparation or training.

But let him enter it, the noble and fortunate youth; let him enter it, without preparation or training! Great as the work is, and completely as he is to succeed in it, it is itself but a work of preparation. This is not yet the province of duty assigned him. He comes without training, for this is the school in which he is to be trained. He comes unprepared, because he comes to a great preparation of liberty. Destined, when, with full success and spotless honor, he shall have gone through the American Revolution, to take the lead in a mighty work of political reform in his native land,—he comes, in his youth, to the great monitorial school of Freedom; —to imbibe its holy doctrines from an authentic source, before his heart is hardened and his mind perverted; to catch its pure spirit, —living and uncorrupted,—from the lips of a pure master!

Before that master he is yet to appear. The youthful adventurer has a test of character at hand more severe than any to which he has yet been subjected. He has stood from his youth before princes and kings, and felt that his clay is as good as theirs. But he has yet to stand before that face, where, more than ever yet in the face of mere man, the awful majesty of virtue abode, in visible personation: the serene but melancholy countenance which now looks down upon us from that canvass, which no smile of light-hearted gladness illuminated, from the commencement to the close of his country's struggle. Washington was at head-quarters, when Lafayette reached Philadelphia, but he was daily expected in the city. The introduction of the youthful stranger to the man, on whom his career depended, was therefore delayed a few days. It took place in a manner peculiarly marked with the circumspection of Washington, at a dinner party, where Lafayette was one among several guests of consideration. Washington was not uninformed of the circumstances connected with his arrival in the country. He knew what benefits it promised the cause, if his character and

talents were adapted to the course he had so boldly struck out ;—
and he knew, also, how much it was to be feared, that the very
qualities which had prompted him to embark in it, would make
him a useless and even a dangerous auxiliary. We may well suppose, that the piercing eye of the Father of his Country was not
idle during the repast. But that searching glance, before which
pretence or fraud never stood undetected, was completely satisfied.
When they were about to separate, Washington took Lafayette
aside,—spoke to him with kindness,—paid a just tribute to the
noble spirit which he had shown, and the sacrifices he had made in
the American cause; invited him to make the head-quarters of the
army his home, and to regard himself, at all times, as one of the
family of the commander-in-chief.

Such was the reception given to Lafayette, by the most sagacious and observant of men ; and the personal acquaintance thus
commenced, ripened into an intimacy, a confidence, and an affection without bounds, and never for one moment interrupted. If
there lived a man whom Washington loved, it was Lafayette. The
proofs of this are not wanted by those who have read the history
of the Revolution,—but the private correspondence of these two
great men, hitherto unpublished, discloses the full extent of the
mutual regard and affection which united them. It not only shows
that Washington entertained the highest opinion of the military
talent, the personal probity, and the general prudence and energy
of Lafayette, but that he regarded him with the tenderness of a
father ; and found in the affection which Lafayette bore to him in
return, one of the greatest comforts and blessings of his own life.
Whenever the correspondence of Washington and Lafayette shall
be published, the publication will do, what perhaps nothing else
can, raise them both in the esteem and admiration of mankind.

On the 31st of July, 1777, Lafayette received, by a resolution
of Congress, his commission as a Major General in the American
army. Not having at first a separate command, he attached himself to the army of the commander-in-chief, as a volunteer. On
the 11th of the following September, he was present at the unfortunate battle of Brandywine. He there plunged, with a rashness,
pardonable in a very youthful commander, into the hottest of the
battle, exposed himself to all its dangers, and exhibited a conspicu-

ous example of coolness and courage. When the troops began to retreat in disorder, he threw himself from his horse, entered the ranks, and endeavored to rally them. While thus employed, he was shot by a musket ball through the leg. The wound was not perceived by himself, till he was told by his aid that the blood was running from his boot. He fell in with a surgeon, who placed a slight bandage on his limb, with which he rode to Chester. Regardless of his situation, he thought only of rallying the troops, who were retreating in disorder through the village; and it was not till this duty was performed, that the wound was dressed. It was two months before it was sufficiently healed to enable him to rejoin the army. This was the first battle in which he was ever engaged, and such was his entrance into the active service of America.

It would obviously be impossible to do more than glance at the military services of Lafayette during the revolutionary war, but it seems to belong to a proper treatment of the subject, that they should not be wholly omitted.

In the winter of 1778, he was designated to the command of an expedition into Canada, a project formed without consulting Washington, by the members of Congress and the cabal in the army, opposed to the commander-in-chief. Lafayette was placed at the head of it, partly, no doubt, with a view of detaching him from the support, and thereby impairing the influence of Washington. But his veneration for Washington, his good feeling, his sound military judgment, and, above all, his correct perception of the character of the great man aimed at, enabled him to escape the snare. On repairing to Albany, he found no preparations made to carry the expedition into effect. He perceived its impracticability, and it was abandoned. His retreat at Barren-Hill, from a very critical and dangerous situation, into which he was thrown by the abandonment of their post on the part of a detachment of militia stationed to protect his position, received the highest commendations of Washington. On General Lee's declining the command of the advance of the army at Monmouth, it was given to Lafayette. Lee, perceiving the importance of the command, and the unfavorable appearance which his waiver of it might wear, prevailed with great difficulty, on Lafayette, the day before the battle, to allow him to assume it. The conduct of Lafayette on that important day was marked with bravery and skill. On the very day that the British effected their entrance into New York, the French fleet, under the Count d'Estaing, appeared in the American waters. Rhode Island having been fixed upon, as the theatre of operations, Lafayette was detached with two brigades, to join the army under General Sullivan. During all the perilous incidents of this critical and unsuccessful campaign, the most important services were rendered by Lafayette. He exerted the happiest influence in restoring harmony between the officers and soldiers of the French and American armies, which had been seriously interrupted, in consequence of the unfortunate issue of the expedition. This was of infinite importance to the cause, as a permanent disgust on the part of the French troops, in this the first expedition sent out in virtue of the alliance, might have effectually damped the further efforts of France. His services on the occasion were acknowledged by express resolutions of Congress.

France being now in a state of declared hostility against England, and Lafayette being still an officer in the French army, he deemed it his duty, at the close of the campaign, to return to his native country, and place himself at the disposal of his government.

He united with this object that of exerting his influence in favor of America, by his personal conferences with the French ministry. He accordingly applied to Congress for a furlough, which on the particular recommendation of General Washington was granted. This permission was accompanied by resolutions expressing, in flattering terms, the sense which was entertained by Congress, of the importance of his services, and by a letter recommending him to the good offices of the American minister in France. At the same time also, Congress ordered that a sword should be presented to him, adorned with emblematic devices, appropriate to its object.

Lafayette embarked for France, at Boston, in January, 1779, on board an American frigate. Just before arriving on the coasts of France, he happily discovered and assisted in subduing a mutiny on the part of some British prisoners of war, whom he had been induced to admit as a portion of the crew of the frigate, from his aversion to impressment, which must otherwise have been resorted to, in order to make up the ship's complement of men. He was now twenty-two years of age, and returned, after two years of absence, marked with honorable scars, and signalized by the thanks of Congress, the admiration of America, and the friendship of Washington. He was received with enthusiasm by the people, and even at court. As he had left the country in disobedience to a royal mandate, etiquette demanded that he should for a few days be required to keep his house, and to see no persons but the members of his family. This, however, embraced within its circle nearly every person of distinction about the court. His name had already been introduced into several dramatic performances, and hailed with acclamations in the theatres ; and a beautiful apostrophe to him in one of these performances, was copied by the queen, and long preserved in her hand-writing, by her confidential attendant, Madame Campan. On a journey to one of his estates in the south of France, the whole population came out to meet him, and the *fêtes* of the city of Orleans, in honor of his return, were prolonged for a week.

The entire effect of the enthusiasm of which he was thus the object, was turned by Lafayette to the advantage of America. He was the confidential adviser of Dr Franklin ; he was in unbroken correspondence with Washington, and he was sure to be approached by every American arriving in France, and by every European repairing to America. A Major General in her armies, he was clothed with an official right to interfere in her cause ; and his country being now at war with England, no reasons of state interposed to check his activity. He was, as a French officer, attached to the staff of the Marshall Vaux, at that time commander-in-chief of the French army. In this capacity, having direct access to the court, the personal and warmly-devoted friend of the Count de Vergennes, and the popular favorite, he did for America what no other man could have done, and rendered services to the cause not yet sufficiently appreciated,—and worthy a moment's reflection.

The alliance with France was the great turning point in the fortunes of the Revolution. I do not, of course, say, that without it, our independence could not have been established. Had this failed, other means would, no doubt, in some wholly different train of affairs, have been disclosed. I would not say of any thing, not even of the character of Washington, that without it, the country could not have been carried through the war. But, in looking back upon the history of the times, I cannot now perceive that in the series of events by which the independence of the United States was achieved, the alliance with France could have been dispensed with. Her recognition of our independence inspirited our own councils and disheartened England. The loans of money and military supplies derived from France, were a vital resource, for which I know not what substitute could have been found ;— and, finally, the cooperation of her fleets and armies, involving, as it did eventually, that of the Spanish forces, brought down upon the British ministry a burden which they could not bear, and compelled them to abandon the struggle.

At the same time, the greatest difficulties opposed themselves to the practical development of the benefits of the treaty of alliance. In the first place, it required of an old European monarchy to countenance a colonial revolt. France had colonies. Spain, the kindred sovereignty, had a colonial world in America, where the formidable and all but successful revolt of Tupac-Amaru was already in secret preparation. It was the last moment, which France or Spain would have voluntarily chosen, to sanction an example of transatlantic independence. The finances of France were any thing but prosperous, and she had to support, unaided, the expense of the fleets and armies which she sent to our assistance. Great difficulties, it was supposed, would attend the cooperation of a French army with American forces on land. Congress was jealous of the introduction of a foreign soldiery into the interior of the country, and Washington himself gave but a reluctant consent to the measure. Considerable discontent had arisen in connexion with Count d'Estaing's movements in Rhode Island, which,—had it not been allayed by the prudent and effectual mediation of Lafayette,—would, as has been already stated, probably have prevented a French army from being sent over to the United States. Such were the feelings, on both sides of the ocean, when Lafayette went back to France, in 1779 ; and during the whole of that year, he exerted himself unceasingly, in his correspondence and conferences with the French ministry, to induce them to send out an army. The difficulties to be overcome were all but insurmountable, acting, as he was, not only without the instructions, but against the sense of Congress, and scarcely sanctioned by Washington. He, however, *knew* that success would attend the measure. He had that interior conviction, which no argument or authority can subdue, that the proposed expedition was practicable and expedient, and he succeeded in imparting his enthusiasm to the ministers. He knew that the anticipated difficulties could be overcome. He had proved, in his own experience, that cooperation was practicable. Military subordination made it impossible to put him, a young man of twenty-two, holding in the king's army only the commission of a subaltern, in the command of a large force; but he relied, with a just confidence, on the services which his standing in America, and his possession of the confidence of Washington would enable him to render. He accordingly pursued the object with an ardor, an industry, and an adroitness, which nothing could surpass. When his correspondence with the French ministers, particularly the Count de Vergennes, shall be published, it will appear that it was mainly the personal efforts and personal influence of Lafayette,—idol of the French people as he had made himself,—which caused the army of Rochambeau to be sent to America. It was pleasantly remarked by the old Count de Maurepas, who, at the age of seventy-nine, still stood at the head of the French ministry, that ' it was fortunate for the king, that Lafayette did not take it into his head to strip Versailles of its furniture to send to his dear Americans ;—as his Majesty would have been unable to refuse it.' In addition to his efforts to obtain the army of Rochambeau, Lafayette was actively employed, during the year 1779, in conjunction with our ministers, in procuring a large pecuniary subsidy for the United States.

Having thus contributed to the accomplishment of these great objects, he returned to America, in the spring of 1780. He landed at Boston, where, though nothing was as yet known of the all-important services he had rendered to us, he was received with every mark of attachment and admiration. He immediately repaired to the head-quarters of the army ; but soon left them to arrange with Count Rochambeau the interview between him and the commander-in-chief, in which the future operations of the campaign were concerted, at which also he was present. He was at West Point, at the period of the ever memorable scene of the treachery of Arnold. The following winter he marched at the head of his division, to Portsmouth, in Virginia, to cooperate in an attack on the British forces, by the combined French and American troops. This plan failed, in consequence of the reverses experienced by the French squadron under Destouches. On his march backward to the north, Lafayette received a courier from Washington, informing him of the concentration of the troops under Lord Cornwallis, Phillips, and Arnold, in Virginia, and directing him to watch their movements, and prevent this great State, whose fortunes involved that of the whole southern country, from falling into their hands. This order found him at the head of Elk, in Maryland. He instantly put in train the requisite measures of preparation. His scanty force was in a state of perfect destitution. In all his army, there was not a pair of shoes fit for service. But the love and confidence which the country bore him, supplied the place of credit; and he was able, in his own name, to raise a loan in Baltimore, sufficient to supply the most urgent wants of his little command. Thus furnished, he hastened into Virginia, and during the whole summer of 1781, he conducted the campaign with a vigor, discretion, and success, which saved the State of Virginia, and proved himself to be endowed with the highest qualities of generalship. While Lord Cornwallis, to whom he was opposed, —a person not less eminent for talent and experience, than for rank and political influence,—was boasting, in derision of his youthful adversary, that 'the boy should not escape him,' the boy was preparing a pit, into which his lordship plunged, with all his forces.

My limits do not allow me to sketch the history of this great campaign, nor even its final glorious consummation, the closing scene of the war. But I may with propriety pause to say, that it evinced, on the part of our venerable Washington, now at length favored with an opportunity of acting with ample means on a broad scale, a power of combination and a reach of mind, with a promptitude and vigor of execution which, exhibited at the head of mighty armies, gave to Napoleon his reputation, as the greatest captain of the age. I cannot but think, that in the manœuvres, by which Lord Cornwallis was detained in Virginia;—by which Sir Henry Clinton was persuaded, in New York, that a siege of that city was the great object of Washington;—by which the French forces were brought up from Rhode Island;—the armies of Washington and

Rochambeau moved, by a forced march across the country, to Yorktown, at the moment that the French squadron from Newport, under the Count de Barras, and the great fleet under the Count de Grasse, effected their junction in the Chesapeake,—there is displayed as much generalship, as in any series of movements in the wars of the last thirty years. The operations of Lafayette in Virginia, in the preceding summer, were the basis of them all; as his untiring efforts in France the preceding season, had mainly occasioned the despatch of the army of Count Rochambeau, without which, the great exploit at Yorktown, could not have been achieved.

And who, that has a sense for all that is beautiful in military display, grand and eventful in political combinations, and auspicious to the cause of liberty,—but must linger a moment on the plain of Yorktown! Before you, stretches the broad expanse of York river, an arm of Chesapeake bay. Beyond it, to the north, the British general has left a force at Gloucester point, for his support, should he be compelled to retreat across the river; and there the Duke de Lauzun, with his legion united with the Virginia militia, effectually encloses the British force within their lines. The intervening expanse of water is covered with the British vessels of war. But it is around the lines of Yorktown, that the interest of the scene is concentrated. Above the town, are stationed the French; below, the Americans. The royal regiments of Deux Ponts, of Touraine, and Saintonge, on the one side, and the troops of Pennsylvania and Virginia, of New-Jersey and New-England, on the other. The Marquis de St Simon commanded on the extreme left, and General Lincoln on the extreme right. Before the former, we behold the position of the two Viomenils, and near the latter, the post of Lafayette. At the point of junction between the two lines, the head-quarters of Count Rochambeau and those of Washington are placed, in harmony of council and of action, side by side. Two redoubts are to be carried. To excite the generous emulation of the combined forces, one is committed to the French, and the other to the Americans. Lafayette, with Hamilton at his side, commands the latter, and both redoubts are carried at the point of the bayonet. Cornwallis attempts, but without success, to escape. He is reduced, after a siege of thirteen days, to enter into capitulation ; and the last British army of the revolutionary war surrenders to the united forces of America and France.

At the close of the campaign, to the successful issue of which he had so essentially contributed, Lafayette again asked the permission of Congress to return to France. Well might they permit him, for he went to rouse France and Spain, with all their fleets, armies, and treasures, to strike a last and an overwhelming blow. A committee of Congress, of which Charles Carroll was chairman, and James Madison was a member, reported a series of resolutions of the most honorable character, which were adopted by that body. They directed all the ministers of the United States, in Europe, to confer and correspond with Lafayette ; they invited him to correspond with Congress, and they recommended him, in the most affectionate terms, to the especial favor of his sovereign.

He returned to his native country, with these new laurels and new titles to admiration, and France rose up as one man to receive him. His welcome, before enthusiastic, was now rapturous ; it was prompted before by admiration of a chivalrous adventure, but the national pride and patriotic spirit of Frenchmen were now aroused. The heavy reproach of the seven years' war was rolled away ; and the stains of Quebec washed white at Yorktown. The government, as well as the people of France, was elated at the success of the campaign ;—all doubts as to the possibility of a combined action were removed ; and to Lafayette, as the prime mover of the enterprise, proportionate credit was justly given for his forecast and sagacity. He could now ask for nothing that was deemed extravagant; or, however extravagant, he could ask for nothing which could be refused. The enthusiasm caught from France to Spain. The Castilian coldness was melted ; and although the mountains of Peru were bristling with the bayonets of the last of the Incas, king Charles III could not resist the temptation of humbling Great Britain, and resolved at last, that Spain and the Indies should go, with all their resources, for the Congress. A mighty plan of campaign was resolved on. An expedition such as Europe has rarely witnessed, was projected. The old armada seemed almost to rise from the depths of the ocean, in mightily augmented array, to avenge the ancient disasters of Spain.

The preparations commenced at Cadiz. Count d'Estaing, as generalissimo, with sixty vessels of the line and smaller ships in proportion, with twenty-four thousand troops, was to make a descent on Jamaica, and thence strike at New-York. Lafayette was the first at the rendezvous: he had already proceeded with eight thousand men from Brest to Cadiz. He was placed at the head of the staff of the combined armies, and after New-York had fallen, was to have moved with his division into Canada. But these magnificent and formidable preparations effected their object at a cheaper cost than that of rivers of blood. The British government learned wisdom, before it was too late;—and the peace was concluded. It was the wish of Lafayette to bear in person the joyous tidings to America. Just as he was about stepping on board a frigate for that purpose, he returned to Madrid, to render an important service to our minister there. But his despatches were sent by the frigate, and conveyed to Congress the first intelligence of the peace.

In the course of the following year, he yielded to the invitation of Washington and his other friends, and revisited America. He was received with acclamations of joy and gratitude from one end of the country to the other; but nowhere with a more cordial welcome than in this ancient metropolis. On the 19th of October, 1784, in the hall in which we are now assembled to pay the last tribute to his memory, surrounded by his fellow soldiers, by the authorities of the commonwealth, the magistracy of the town, and the grateful and admiring citizens of Boston, he celebrated the third anniversary of the capture of Cornwallis, in which he had himself so efficiently cooperated. Fifty years have passed away. The pillars of this venerable hall, then twined with garlands, are hung with mourning. The cypress has taken the place of the rose bud; the songs of patriotic rejoicing are hushed; and the funeral anthem is heard in their stead; but the memory of the beloved champion, the friend of America and of freedom, shall bloom in eternal remembrance.*

* The incidents of Lafayette's visit to America in 1784, are succinctly related in the 'Letters of an American Farmer.' The narrative is highly interesting, and but for the more recent and still more extraordinary events of 1824, would well merit a more detailed reference.

56

The year after his return to France, Lafayette made a tour in Germany. He was received throughout that country with the attention due to his rank and the *éclat* of his services in America. At Vienna, he met the duke of York, at the table of the emperor Joseph, and employed the opportunities which such an interview afforded him, to inculcate the policy of a liberal course, on the part of the powers of Europe, and particularly Great Britain, toward the rising States of America. He was received with distinction by Frederic the Great, and accompanied him on a tour of inspection and review of his armies. On this occasion, he became acquainted with the flying artillery, which Frederic had just organized, and formed the purpose of introducing it into the service of France, on the first opportunity;—an intention which he carried into effect, when, at the commencement of the French Revolution, he was placed at the head of an army.

On his return to Paris, he united with M. de Malsherbes in endeavoring to ameliorate the political condition of the Protestants. In concert with the minister of the Marine, the Marshall de Castries, he expended a large sum from his private fortune, in an experiment towards the education and eventual emancipation of slaves. To this end, he purchased a plantation in Cayenne, intending to give freedom to the laborers, as soon as they should be in a condition to enjoy it without abuse. In the progress of the Revolution, this plantation, with the other estates of Lafayette, was confiscated, and the slaves sold back to perpetual bondage, by the faction which was drenching France in blood, under the motto of liberty and equality.

On the breaking out of the troubles in Holland, in 1787, the patriotic party made overtures to Lafayette to place himself at the head of a popular government in that quarter; but the progress of the Revolution was arrested by the invasion of Prussia, and the policy of England and France. Besides this, greater events were preparing at home.

As far as the United States were concerned, during all the period which intervened from the peace of 1783 to the organization of the federal government, Lafayette performed, in substance, the functions of their minister. He was engaged with indefatigable industry, and a zeal that knew no bounds, in promoting the interests of America at the courts of France and Spain. The published works of Mr Jefferson, which are before the country, and the Diplomatic Correspondence of our ministers abroad, during this period, abundantly show that not one of the accredited ministers of the United States abroad, able and faithful as they were, was more assiduously devoted to the service of the country and the promotion of its political and commercial interests, than Lafayette. New and most convincing proofs of this have recently come before the public.*

At length the mighty crisis came on. The French Revolution draws near;—that stupendous event of which it is impossible to be silent;—next to impossible to speak. Louis XV once said to a courtier, 'this French monarchy is fourteen hundred years old : it cannot last long.' Such was the terrific sentiment, which, even in the bosom of his base pleasures, stole into the conscience of the modern Sardanapalus. But in that mysterious and bewildering chain of connexion which binds together the fortunes of states and of men, the last convulsive effort of this worn out and decrepit monarchy, in which the spasmodic remains of her strength were exhausted, and her crazy finances plunged into irretrievable confusion, was the American alliance. This corrupt and feeble despotism, trembling on the verge of an abyss, toward which time and events were urging it, is made to hold out a strong and helping hand, to assist the rising republic into the family of nations. The generous spirits whom she sent to lead her armies to the triumphs of republicanism in America, came back to demand, for their own country, and to assert, on their own soil, those political privileges, for which they had been contending in America. The process of argument was short. If this plan of government, administered by responsible agents, is good for America, it is good for France. If our brethren in the United States will not submit to power assumed by men not accountable for its abuse, why should we? If we have done wisely and well in going to shed our blood for this constitutional liberty beyond the Atlantic, let us be ready to shed it in the same great cause, for our fathers, for our friends, for ourselves,

---

* In the two collections published under the authority of Congress,—the Diplomatic Correspondence of the Revolution; and its Continuation to the Peace of 1789.

in our native land. Is it possible to find, I will not say a sound
and sufficient answer to this argument, but an answer which would
be thought sound and sufficient, by the majority of ardent tempers
and inquisitive minds?

The atrocious, the unexampled, the ungodly abuses of the reign
of terror have made the very name of the French Revolution hateful to mankind. The blood chills, the flesh creeps, the hair stands
on end, at the recital of its horrors; and no slight degree of the
odium they occasion is unavoidably reflected on all, who had any
agency in bringing it on. The subsequent events in Europe have
also involved the French Revolution in a deep political unpopularity. It is unpopular in Great Britain, in the rest of Europe, in
America, in France itself; and not a little of this unpopularity
falls on every one whose name is prominently connected with it.
All this is prejudice,—natural prejudice, if you please,—but still
prejudice. The French Revolution was the work of sheer necessity.
It began in the act of the court, casting about, in despair, for the
means of facing the frightful dilapidation of the finances. Louis
XV was right,—the monarchy could not go on. The Revolution
was as inevitable as fate.

I go farther. Penetrated as I am to heart-sickness, when I pe-
ruse the tale of its atrocities, I do not scruple to declare, that the
French Revolution, as it existed in the purposes of Lafayette and
associates, and while it obeyed their impulse, and so long as it was
controlled by them, was, notwithstanding the melancholy excesses
which stained even its early stages, a work of righteous reform;—
that justice, humanity, and religion demanded it. I maintain this
with some reluctance, because it is a matter, in respect to which,
all are not of one mind, and I would not willingly say any thing,
on this occasion, which could awaken a single discordant feeling.
But I speak from a sense of duty; and standing as I do over the
grave of Lafayette, I may not, if my feeble voice can prevent it,
allow the fame of one of the purest men that ever lived to be sacrificed to a prejudice; to be overwhelmed with the odium of abuses which he did not foresee, which, if he had foreseen, he could
not have averted, and with which he had himself no personal connexion, but as their victim. It is for this reason I maintain, that
the French Revolution, as conceived by Lafayette, was a work

of righteous reform. Read the history of France, from the revocation of the edict of Nantes downward. Reflect upon the scandalous influence which dictated that inhuman decree to the dotage of Louis XIV,—a decree which cost France as much blood as flowed under the guillotine. Trace the shameful annals of the regency, and the annals not less shameful, of Louis XV. Consider the overgrown wealth and dissoluteness of the clergy, and the arrogance and corruption of the nobility, possessing together a vast proportion of the property, and bearing no part of the burdens of the state. Recollect the abuses of the law,—high judicial places venal in the market,—warrants of arrest issued to the number of one hundred and fifty thousand in the single reign of Louis XV, oftentimes in blank, to court favorites, to be filled up with what names, for what prisons, for what times they pleased. Add to this the oppression of the peasantry by iniquitous taxes that have become proverbial in the history of misgovernment, and the outlawry of one twenty-fourth part of the population as Protestants;—who were forbidden to leave the kingdom, subject to be shot if they crossed the frontier, but deprived of the protection of the government at home, their contracts annulled, their children declared illegitimate, and their ministers,—who might venture, in dark forests and dreary caverns, to conduct their prohibited devotions,—doomed to the scaffold. As late as 1745, two Protestant ministers were executed in France, for performing their sacred functions. Could men bear these things in a country like France, a reading, inquiring country, with the success of the American Revolution before their eyes, and at the close of the eighteenth century? Can any man who has Anglo-Saxon blood in his veins, hesitate for an answer? Did not England shake off less abuses than these, a century and a half before? Had not a paltry unconstitutional tax, neither in amount nor in principle to be named with the *taille* or the *gabelle*, just put the continent of America in a flame; and was it possible that the young officers of the French army should come back to their native land, from the war of political emancipation waged on this continent, and sit down contented, under the old abuses, at home? It was not possible. The Revolution was as inevitable as fate, and the only question was, by whose agency it should be brought on.

The first step in the French Revolution was, as is well known, the assembly of Notables, February 22d, 1787. Its last convocation had been in 1626, under the Cardinal Richelieu. It was now convoked by the minister Calonne, the controller general of the finances, from the utter impossibility, without some unusual resources, of providing for the deficiency in the finances, which had, for the preceding year, amounted to 181,000,000 livres, and was estimated at the annual average of 140,000,000. This assembly consisted of one hundred and thirty-seven persons, of whom scarcely ten were in any sense the representatives of the people. Lafayette was of course a distinguished member, then just completing his thirtieth year. In an assembly called by direction of the king, and consisting almost exclusively of the high aristocracy, he stepped forth, at once, the champion of the people. It was the intention of the government to confine the action of the assembly to the discussion of the state of the finances, and the contrivance of means to repair their disorder. It was not so that Lafayette understood his commission. He rose to denounce the abuses of the government. The Count d'Artois,—since Charles X, the brother of the king,—attempted to call him to order, as acting on a subject not before the assembly. 'We are summoned,' said Lafayette, 'to make the truth known to his Majesty. I must discharge my duty.' He accordingly, after an animated harangue on the abuses of the government, proposed the abolition of private arrests and of the state prisons, in which any one might be confined on the warrant of the minister;—the restoration of Protestants to the equal privileges of citizenship, and the convocation of the States General, or representatives of the people. 'What!' said the Count d'Artois, 'do you demand the States General?' 'Yes,' replied Lafayette, 'and something better than that.'

The assembly of Notables was convoked a second time in 1788, and Lafayette was again found in his place, pleading for the representation of the people. As a member of the provincial assemblies of Auvergne and Britanny, he also took the lead in all the measures of reform that were proposed by those patriotic bodies.

But palliatives were vain : it became impossible to resist the impulse of public opinion, and the States General were convened.

This body assembled at Versailles, on the 3d of May, 1789.—
According to Mr Jefferson, writing from personal observation on
the spot, its initiatory movements were concerted by Lafayette and
a small circle of friends, at the hotel of Mr Jefferson himself, who
calls Lafayette, at this momentous period of its progress, the Atlas of
the Revolution.* He proposed and carried through the assembly, of
which he was vice-president, a declaration of rights similar to those
contained in the American constitutions. He repeated the demand
which he had made in the assembly of the Notables, for the suppression of *lettres de cachet,* and the admission of Protestants to all the
privileges of citizens. For the three years that he sustained the command of the National Guard, he kept the peace of the capital, rent
as it was by the intrigues of the parties, the fury of a debased populace, and the agitations set on foot by foreign powers ; and so long
as he remained at the head of the Revolution, with much to condemn
and more to lament, and which no one resisted more strenuously
than Lafayette, it was a work of just reform, after ages of frightful
corruption and abuse.

Before the National Guard was organized, but while he filled
the place of commander of the city guard of Paris, he was the
great bulwark of the public peace, at the critical period of the
destruction of the Bastile. From his position at the head of
the embodied militia of the capital and its environs, Lafayette was
clothed in substance with the concentrated powers of the state.
These, it is unnecessary to say, were exercised by him for the preservation of order and the repression of violence. Hundreds of those
threatened, at this unsettled period, as victims of popular violence,
were saved by his intervention. But when at length he found himself unable to rescue the unfortunate Foulon and Berthier from the
hands of the infuriated populace, he refused to retain a power which
he could not make effective, and resigned his post. The earnest
entreaties of the friends of order, assuring him that they deemed
the public peace to be safe in no hands but his, persuaded him to
resume it ; but not till the electoral districts of Paris had confirmed the appointment, and promised to support him in the discharge of his duty.

* Jefferson's Correspondence. Vol. I, pp. 75, 84.

It was a short period after this event, that Lafayette proposed the organization of the National Guard of France. The ancient colors of the city of Paris were blue and red. To indicate the union, which he wished to promote between a king governing by a constitution and a people protected by laws, he proposed to add, —the white,—the royal color of France ; and to form of the three the new ensign of the nation. ' I bring you, gentlemen,' said he, ' a badge, which will go round the world ;—an institution at once civil and military ; which will change the system of European tactics, and reduce the absolute governments to the alternative of being conquered, if they do not imitate it, and overturned if they do.' The example of Paris was followed in the provinces, and the National Guard, three millions seven hundred thousand strong, was organized throughout France, with Lafayette at its head.

These are occurrences, which arrest the attention, as the eye runs down the crowded page of the chronicles of the time. But we are too apt to pass over unnoticed, the humbler efforts, by which Lafayette endeavored, from the first moment of the Revolution, to make it produce the fruits of practical reform in the institutions of the country. Under his influence, and against strong opposition,—a deputation was sent by the city of Paris to the national assembly, demanding an immediate reform in criminal jurisprudence,—the publicity of trials,—the confrontation of witnesses,— the privilege of counsel for the accused, and free intercourse between the prisoner and his family. These privileges were enjoyed by the accused, in the only three state trials which took place while Lafayette retained his popularity ; and the credit of having obtained them was justly ascribed to him, by the counsel of one of the individuals by whom they were enjoyed.

On the 5th of October, 1789, occurred the only incident in the life of Lafayette, upon which calumny has ventured to rely, as having affixed a blot upon his fair fame. Even Sir Walter Scott, in relating the history of this occurrence, has afforded some countenance to the imputations against Lafayette. I trust, therefore, I shall not seem to descend too much into particulars, if I briefly repeat the incidents of that night of terror.

Paris, during the whole of this memorable season, was in a state of the greatest excitement. All the elements of confusion were in the highest action. A great political revolution in progress,—the king feeble and irresolute, but already subdued by the magnitude of the events,—his family and court divided, corrupt, and laboring, by intrigue and treachery, to arrest the progress of the Revolution, —the duke of Orleans lavishing immense sums to sow dissension, and urge the Revolution to a point, at which, as he hoped, it would transfer the crown from the head of his unhappy kinsman to his own ;—the fiercest conflicts among the different orders of the state, and a wild consciousness of power in the mass of the people, late awakened for the recovery of long lost rights, and the revenge of centuries of oppression ;—these were some of the elements of disorder. The match was laid to the train, at a festival at the palace of Versailles, at which the national cockade was trampled under foot by the body guard, in presence of the queen and her infant son, and the Revolution denounced in terms of menace and contumely. The news spread to Paris,—already convulsed by the intrigues of the duke of Orleans, and exasperated by a want of bread. The hungry populace were told that the famine which they suffered was intentionally produced by the king and his ministry, for the purpose of starving them back to slavery. Riots broke out at an early hour on the 5th of October, around the city hall. For eight hours, Lafayette exerted himself, and not without success, to restrain the frantic crowds which constantly reassembled, as soon as dispersed, with cries, 'to Versailles for bread.' Hearing, at length, that from other points of the capital, infuriated mobs were moving toward Versailles, with muskets and cannons, he asked the orders of the municipality to hasten himself, with a detachment of the National Guard, to the defence of the royal family. On his arrival at Versailles, he administered to the troops the oath of fidelity to the nation, the law, and the king. He entered the court of the palace, accompanied only by two commissioners of the city. It was filled with Swiss guards, and the terrified inmates of the palace ; and as he advanced, the gloomy silence was broken by the exclamation of some person present, 'Here comes Cromwell.' 'Cromwell,' replied Lafayette, 'would not have come here alone.' Admitted to the presence of the king, whom he treated with the deference due to his rank, Lafayette asked that the posts in and about the palace might be confided to him. This

57

request was refused, as contrary to etiquette. In consequence, the palace itself, the interior court, and the approach by the garden remained, as usual, protected only by the body guard and the Swiss. At two o'clock in the morning, Lafayette made the round of the posts under his command, and asked another interview with the king ; but was told that he was asleep. After five o'clock in the morning, while all was quiet, exhausted by nearly twenty-four hours of unremitted and anxious labor, he repaired to his quarters, in the immediate vicinity of the palace, to receive the reports of his aids,—to prepare despatches for Paris,—and to take food and repose. Scarcely had he reached his quarters for these purposes, when an officer ran to apprize him that a band of ruffians, concealed in the shrubbery of the garden, had burst into the palace, and forced their way over two of the body guards, to the chamber of the queen ; who was barely enabled, by the brave resistance of the guards at her door, to escape with her life.

Lafayette rushed to the scene of action, with the detachment of his force nearest at hand, and took the proper steps to arrest the progress of the disorder. The royal family were protected, and several of the body guards rescued from the mob. Happening to be left alone, at one moment, in the midst of the lawless crowd, an individual among them raised a cry for the head of Lafayette. The imminent danger in which he stood was averted by the coolness, with which he ordered the madman to be seized by his fellows around him. The king deemed it necessary to yield to the clamors of the populace, and return with them to Paris. Lafayette was alarmed at the symptoms of disaffection toward the queen, which still prevailed in the throng. At once to make trial of the popular feeling, and to extend to her the protection of his unbounded popularity, he had the courage to propose to her, to appear with him alone on the balcony of the castle, with her son the dauphin on her arm. Leading her forward towards the people, it was his purpose to make an appeal to them on her behalf. The confused acclamations of the vast throng prevented his being heard ; and unable, in any other manner, to convey to the immense and agitated assemblage in motion beneath them, the sentiments which he wished to inspire in their bosoms, towards the defenceless person of the queen, and the innocent child whom she held in her arms, he stooped and kissed her hand. A cry of 'Long live the queen! Long live Lafayette!' responded to the action. Returning to the royal cabinet, he was embraced by its inmates as the saviour of the king and his family, and till the last hour of their unfortunate existence, the king and the queen never failed to do him the justice to acknowledge, that on this terrific day he had saved their lives.

From the commencement of the Revolution, Lafayette refused all pecuniary compensation, and every unusual appointment or trust. Not a dignity known to the ancient monarchy, or suggested by the disorder of the times, but was tendered to him and refused. More than once, it was proposed to create him field marshal, grand constable, lieutenant general of the kingdom. The titles of dictator and commander-in-chief of the armies of France, were successively proposed to him, but in vain. Knowing that the representatives of the great federation of the National Guards, who repaired to Paris in 1790, designed to invest him with the formal command of this immense military force, he hastened the passage of a decree of the assembly forbidding any person to exercise the command of more than one district. And having, at the close of a review, been conducted to the national assembly by an immense and enthusiastic throng, he took that occasion to mount the tribune, and announce the intention of returning to private life, as soon as the preparation of the constitution should be completed.

When the feudal system was established in Europe, and its entire population, in the several countries into which it was divided, was organized on a military principle, the various posts of command were dignified with appropriate names. All the great lords were barons, and according to their position at the head of armies, in the immediate train of the king, or on the frontier, they were dukes, counts, and marquises. These were titles, significant when first given, and in themselves harmless, when considered apart from the hereditary transmission of estates and rank, which in process of time went with them. But having long since ceased to possess their original significance, with the first steps of the Revolution, their frivolity was too apparent to be endured. There was a sort of theatrical insipidity in these curious gradations of unmeaning titles among men, who, in difficult times, were met together on serious business; and among the early measures of the assembly was the decree pronouncing their abolition. Lafayette, whose patent of nobility had at least the merit of four centuries of antiquity, was among the first to support the proposition, and lay down his title of Marquis, never again to be resumed. In the lapse of a few years, the member of assembly who proposed the abolition, became a count under Bonaparte, and those who were the most zealous to procure its adoption, lived to see themselves blazing in the decorations of the imperial court. But neither under Napoleon nor the restoration, did it enter into the head of Lafayette, to be guilty of this weakness, and the only title which he wore till his death, was that which he first derived from his commission in the American army.

On the recurrence of the anniversary of the destruction of the Bastile, on the 14th of July, 1790, the labors of the assembly in the formation of the constitution, were so far advanced, that it was deemed expedient, by a solemn act of popular ratification, to give the sanction of France to the principles on which it was founded. The place assigned for the ceremony was the Champ de Mars, and the act itself was regarded as a grand act of federation, by which the entire population of France, through the medium of an immense representation, engaged themselves to each other by oaths and imposing rites, to preserve the constitution, the monarchy, and the law. In front of the military school at Paris, and near the river Seine, a vast plain is marked out for the imposing pageant. Innumerable laborers are employed, and still greater multitudes of volunteers cooperate with them, in preparing a vast embankment disposed on terraces, and covered with turf. The entire population of the capital and its environs, from the highest to the lowest condition of life, of both sexes, and of every profession, is engaged from day to day, and from week to week, in carrying on the excavation. The academies and schools,—the official bodies of every description,—the trades and the professions, and every class and division of the people repair, from morning to night, to take a part in the work, cheered by the instruments of a hundred full orchestras, and animated with every sport and game in which an excited and cheerful populace gives vent to its delight. It was the perfect saturnalia of liberty;—the meridian of the Revolution, when its great and unquestioned benefits seemed established on a secure basis, with as little violence and bloodshed as could be reasonably expected in the tumultuous action of a needy, exasperated, and triumphant populace. The work at length is completed,—the terraces are raised,—and three hundred thousand spectators are seated in the vast amphitheatre. A gallery is elevated in front of the military school, and in its centre a pavilion above the throne. In the rear of the pavilion is prepared a stage, on which the queen, the dauphin, and the royal family are seated. The deputed members of the federation, eleven thousand for the army and navy, and eighteen thousand for the National Guard of France, are arranged in front,—within a circle, formed by eighty-three lances planted in the earth, adorned with the standards of the eighty-three departments. In the midst of the Champ de Mars, the centre of all eyes, with nothing above it, but the canopy of heaven,—arose a magnificent altar,—the loftiest ever raised on earth. Two hundred priests in white surplices, with the tri-color as a girdle, are disposed on the steps of the altar ; on whose spacious summit mass is performed by the bishop of Autun. On the conclusion of the religious ceremony, the members of the federation and the deputies of the assembly advance to the altar, and take the oath of fidelity to the nation, the constitution, and the king. The king himself assumes the name and rank of chief of the federation, and bestows the title of its major general on Lafayette. The king took the oath on his throne, but Lafayette, as the first citizen of France, advancing to the altar, at the head of thirty thousand deputies, and in the name of the mighty mass of the National Guard, amidst the plaudits of near half a million of his fellow citizens, in the presence of all that was most illustrious and excellent in the kingdom, whose organized military power he represented as their chief, took the oath of fidelity to the nation, the constitution, and the king. Of all the oaths that day taken, by the master spirits of the time, his was, perhaps, the only one kept inviolate. It sealed his fidelity to the doubtful fortunes of the monarch, and in the onward march of the Revolution,—destined to wade through seas of blood,—it raised an inseparable barrier between Lafayette and the remorseless innovators who soon appeared on the scene. It decided his own fortunes, and in no inconsiderable degree the fortunes of the Revolution.

The beauty of this great festival was impaired by a drenching rain, and the general joy with which it was celebrated was a last gleam of sunshine through the gathering clouds of the Revolution. The flight of the king, which occurred the following summer, placed Lafayette in an embarrassing position. He was determined to maintain the sanctity of his oath of fidelity to this unfortunate prince. The king had given his word of honor to Lafayette, that he would not attempt to leave the capital; and Lafayette had, in consequence, pledged his own honor,—his head even,—to the assembly, that no attempt to carry off the king should succeed. Nevertheless, on the night of the 21st of June, the king and royal family succeeded in making their escape from Paris, and Lafayette was denounced the same day, by Danton, at the club of Jacobins, as being either a traitor who had allowed the king to escape;—or as incompetent to his trust, in not knowing how to prevent it. With the moral courage which carried him safe through so many fearful days of peril, Lafayette presented himself, calm and fearless, before the incensed multitude, and made his good faith to the public apparent. But the difficulties of his position daily increased. He was alternately compelled to strain his popularity to the utmost, in repressing the violence of the populace, and controlling the intrigues of the partisans of the ancient order of things. Weary of this situation, he deemed the definitive adoption of the constitution a justifiable occasion for laying down his ungracious command, and, on the 8th of October, 1791, he took his leave of the National Guard, in a letter which would have done no discredit,—for its patriotic spirit and enlightened counsels,—to the great American exemplar, whom he had adopted as the object of his respectful imitation.

Hitherto the powers of Europe had looked with astonishment and apparent inactivity, upon the portentous events that were crowding upon each other in France; and France herself, rent with factions, and distracted with the embarrassments incident to such mighty changes, had scarcely turned her attention to the foreign relations of the country. In this manner, five years from the meeting of the assembly of Notables passed away, during which there was unconsciously forming and organizing itself at home and abroad, the principle of those mighty wars which were to signalize the next thirty years. From the commencement of 1792, the questions which arose between the French and Austrian governments, relative to the territorial jurisdiction of the empire on the border of France, ripened towards a rupture; and, strange as it may now appear, an open declaration of hostilities was the desire of all the numerous parties, interests, and governments, concerned in the issue. The king of France, the queen and the partisans of the old *régime* generally at home; the emperor and the other sovereigns of Europe, the emigrant princes and nobles, and their friends, desired a war as the means of pouring down upon the popular party of France, the combined military powers of the ancient government. On the other hand, the leaders of all the factions in France desired not less ardently a declaration of war, as the means of strengthening their power by the organization and control of standing armies, and gratifying the ambitious, the avaricious, the needy, and the adventurous in their ranks, with promotion and plunder. The zealots burned with the vision of revolutionizing Europe. The honest constitutional party alone deprecated the measure; but even they were bound by their oaths to take arms against the preposterous *ultimatum* of the Austrian cabinet, which required France to renounce the constitution of 1791, a constitution which the king and people had alike sworn to defend. And thus all parties strangely rushed into a war, destined, in turn, to subvert, crush, and revolutionize, with indiscriminate fury, every interest, party, and government drawn into its vortex.

The formal declaration of war was made by Louis XVI, on the 20th of March, 1792. Three armies, each nominally consisting of fifty thousand men, were raised to guard the frontier of the Netherlands, and placed under the command of Luckner, an ancient chieftain of the seven years' war, Lafayette, and Rochambeau. The plan of operations was decided by the king in council, at Paris, in conference with the three generals, who immediately took the field. The political intrigues of the capital were not slow in reaching the camp. The Jacobins at Paris, not yet the majority, but rapidly becoming so, had long marked out Lafayette as their victim. Orders were sent by the minister of war designedly to embarrass and disgust him; and he soon found that it was necessary for him openly to denounce the Jacobins to the legislative assembly and the nation, as the enemies of the country. He accordingly, on the 16th of June, addressed a letter to the assembly, in which he proclaimed this faction to be the enemy of the constitution and the people ; and called on all the friends of liberty to unite for its suppression. The voice of reason for a moment prevailed ;—a majority of the assembly received with approbation the letter of Lafayette, and seventy-five of the departments of France, in their local assemblies, gave their formal sanction to its sentiments. Braving the enemy in his strong hold, he followed up his letter, by hastening to Paris,—appearing at the bar of the assembly, and demanding the punishment of the wretches who had forced the Tuilleries, and menaced and insulted the king the preceding week. Anxious for the safety of the king's person, he proposed to him to retire to Compiègne, under the protection of his army, and there await the issue of the efforts for the suppression of the Jacobins. Incredible as it may appear, these proposals were rejected, from an unwillingness on the part of the queen, to owe her life a second time to Lafayette, and in consequence of the advice secretly conveyed to the court by the duke of Brunswick, then concentrating his army on the frontiers ; who recommended to the king to remain in tranquillity at the Tuilleries, till the allied forces should hasten to his relief.

Lafayette accordingly returned to his army, defeated in the last efforts which afforded a shadow of hope for the safety of the royal family or the preservation of the constitution. On the 8th of August, he was formally denounced in the assembly, as an enemy of his country, and a motion made for his arrest and trial. After vehement debates, it was put to vote, and resulted in his acquittal, by a majority of 407 to 224. But many of those who voted in his favor were, on the following day, insulted by the populace. Baffled in the attempt to destroy him, and in him the last support of the constitutional monarchy, and weary of the tardy march of their infernal policy, the Jacobins at Paris resolved, without further delay, to strike a blow which should intimidate the majority of the assembly, and the constitutional party throughout the country, and, by a frightful measure of violence and blood, establish the reign of terror. Accordingly the horrid tragedy of the 10th of August is enacted,—the palace forced by the army of assassins,—its guards massacred, and the king and the royal family driven to take refuge in the assembly, by which, after suffering every thing that was distressing, humiliating, and cruel, he is deposed, and ordered to be imprisoned in the temple. The news of these events reached Lafayette at his head-quarters in Sedan. He had sworn to support the constitution, and to be faithful to the king. The assembly,— the capital,—the people,—the army, were struck with dismay ;— the horrid scenes of Paris were acted over in the departments, and the reign of terror was established. Commissioners were sent by the assembly to the army, to arrest the generals ;—it remained for Lafayette to anticipate them by an attack on the enemy, which, if successful, would but put new strength in the hands of Robespierre and his associates,—to march on Paris, which, in the present state of feeling in the nation and in the army, was to deliver himself up to his executioners,—or to save himself by flight. Happily, he adopted the latter course, and, having placed his army in the best condition possible, to receive no injury from his leaving it, he passed, with a few of his friends and aids, across the frontier, intending to repair to Holland or England, countries not as yet engaged in the war. While in the territory of Liége, he fell into the hands of an Austrian military force, and notwithstanding the circumstances under which he had left his army and France, was treated as a prisoner. Various unworthy attempts were made, to engage Lafayette in the service of the armies marching against France, and to draw from him information which would be of use in the approaching campaign. Refusing to act the treacherous part proposed to him, he was handed over to the Prussian government, and dragged from fortress to fortress, till he was thrown into the dungeons of Magdeburg. The secrets of that horrid prison-house have been laid open to the world. Lafayette was there confined in a subterraneous vault,—dark,—damp,—and secured by four successive doors, loaded with bolts and chains. But the arms of the duke of Brunswick were unsuccessful in France. On the heights of Valmy, the first of those victories of revolutionary fame, which astonished and terrified the world, was gained over the Prussian army. Negotiations for peace were concluded, and an exchange of prisoners was proposed. To evade the necessity of including Lafayette in the exchange, he was transferred by the king of Prussia to the emper-

58

or of Germany, and immured in the castle of Olmütz, in Moravia. On entering this prison, Lafayette and his fellow sufferers were told, that, ' from that time forward, they would see nothing but the four walls within which they were enclosed ; that no tidings would reach them of what was passing without; that not even their gaolers would pronounce their names; that when mentioned in the despatches of the government, it would only be by their numbers on the register ; that no intelligence would pass from them to their families, nor from their families to them ; and that, to prevent their seeking relief from the slow agonies of this torture, they would be interdicted the use of knives or forks, and every other instrument of self-destruction.

It is scarcely necessary to state, that the health of Lafayette sunk, in no long time, under this barbarous treatment. After a thrice repeated opinion on the part of his physician, that he could not live, unless permitted to breathe a purer air than that of his dungeon, and after answering the first application by the remark, that ' he was not yet sick enough,' the court of Vienna, either touched with remorse, or shaking before the outcry of public indignation, in Europe and America, granted him permission to take exercise abroad under an armed escort, but not on condition that he would not attempt his escape, as was falsely asserted by his calumniators.

This opportunity of taking the air abroad, gave occasion for a bold and generous effort to effect his liberation. His friends, from the first moment of his captivity, had had this object at heart ; but after his removal to Olmütz, they remained for a long time ignorant of the place of his captivity. The count Lally Tolendal, who, notwithstanding their difference of opinion in politics, had ever preserved his personal respect and attachment for Lafayette, spared no pains to discover the place of his seclusion. He employed for this purpose, a young Hanoverian physician, Dr Eric Bollmann, afterwards a naturalized citizen of the United States. Dr Bollmann immediately undertook a voyage of inquiry into Germany, but could learn only that Lafayette had been transferred from the Prussian, to the Austrian dominions. On a second visit to Germany, made in the same benevolent object, he succeeded in ascertaining that there were four state prisoners confined, with extreme rigor, in separate cells at Olmütz, which he had no reason to doubt were Lafayette and his companions. He immediately devoted himself to the object of effecting his liberation. He established himself for six months as a physician at Vienna, to prevent the suspicions, which might be awakened by an unprepared appearance in the Austrian dominions, in the immediate neighborhood of Olmütz. While engaged in concerting his plans, Mr Huger, of South Carolina, the son of the gentleman under whose roof Lafayette passed his first night in America, happened to arrive at Vienna on his travels, and engaged with cordiality in the generous enterprise of Dr Bollmann.

They repaired at length to Olmütz. Dr Bollmann had contrived to obtain letters at Vienna, which obtained him the means, in his professional character, of secretly communicating with Lafayette, and agreeing upon a signal, by which he might be recognized by the two friends,—and ascertaining the day when he would be permitted to take exercise abroad. On that day they repaired, on their horses, to a place under the ramparts of the city, on the road by which Lafayette and his guard would pass. The carriage soon arrives, containing Lafayette, an officer, and a soldier. The friends allow it to pass them, that they may exchange the signal agreed upon. This being done, they again pass forward in advance of the carriage, toward a spot where Lafayette was accustomed to descend and walk. The moment he set his foot on the ground, Lafayette, unarmed as he was, fell upon his two guards. The soldier, disarmed and terrified, instantly fled to the city, to report what had happened. The contest with the officer was violent. Lafayette succeeded in depriving him of his sword, but in the contest, the officer, with his teeth, tore the hand of Lafayette to the bone. He also suffered a violent strain in his back, in consequence of his exertions. The two friends came up at the moment of the struggle, and placing Lafayette on one of their horses, Mr Huger told him in English to go to *Hoff*. This was a post town about twenty miles from Olmütz, where they had prepared a travelling carriage. He mistook the expression, as merely a direction to go *off*, and failed to take the proper road.

One of the horses of Messrs Bollmann and Huger was trained to carry two persons ; the other horse, on which Lafayette was to be mounted, unfortunately escaped in the confusion of the struggle. It became necessary, therefore, that he should mount the horse destined for the two friends; and, on their urgent solicitation, he rode forward alone, while they remained behind, to retake their horse. Some time was lost in effecting this object, and when mounted by Messrs Bollmann and Huger, he proved intractable, and it was found impossible to make him proceed. Mr Huger generously insisted on Dr Bollmann's riding off alone, while he should make his escape, as well as he could, on foot. Mr Huger was soon stopped by some peasants who had witnessed the scene, and handed over to the officers and guards, who hastened in pursuit. Dr Bollmann arrived with ease at Hoff, but there had the mortification to find that Lafayette was prevented by some cause, at that time unknown, from joining him. He passed the Prussian frontier, but was arrested in a day or two, as an Austrian fugitive.

It was almost night when these events took place. Lafayette was oppressed with pain and fatigue. Being left alone, from the causes mentioned, he was not only at a loss what direction to take, but was in a state of the most painful anxiety for the fate of his generous liberators. He proceeded towards the frontier, on the road by which he had entered Moravia, intending to secrete himself there; and if Messrs Bollmann and Huger should be in prison, to give himself up, on condition of their release. Not well knowing the road, he requested a peasant to guide him. His broken German, the blood with which he was covered, and the condition of his clothing, sufficiently betrayed his character. The peasant left him, pretending to go in search of a horse, on which to accompany him, but in reality to give the alarm at the next town, where he was arrested. The following day he was brought back to Olmütz.*

Bollmann and Huger were thrown into close dungeons, and chained by the neck to the floor. Mr Huger asked permission to send an open letter to his mother, containing the words 'I am alive,' and nothing else, but he was refused. He was left in the

* A portion of these details are from an unpublished letter of Latour-Maubourg, one of the companions of Lafayette in captivity, preserved among the Washington papers. See, also, the highly interesting 'Story of the Life of Lafayette, as told by a father to his children.'

most distressing uncertainty as to the fate of Lafayette and his companion, and could form only the darkest anticipations of his own. His food was bread and water. His cell was dark;—and once in six hours it was entered by the gaoler, to see that his chain was sound. After six months' confinement, their case was adjudged, and owing to the kind interference of count Metrowsky, a nobleman of liberal character and great influence, who found in their crime but a new title to respect, they were released with a nominal punishment, and ordered to quit the Austrian dominions. Scarcely were they at liberty, when an order was issued for the re-investigation of their case; but they were already in safety beyond the frontier.

The treatment of Lafayette, after his re-capture, was doubly severe. On his first entrance into the prison at Olmütz, he had been plundered of his watch and shoe-buckles, the only articles of value which the Prussians had left in his possession. But on his return to his dungeon, he was stripped of the few comforts of life, which he had before been permitted to enjoy. He was kept in a dark room, denied a supply of decent clothing, and fed on bread and water. He was constantly told, as he was the first day of his capture by the Austrians, that he was reserved for the scaffold.

But whatever anxiety he might feel on his own account, was merged in his cruel solicitude for his family. No tidings were permitted to reach him from his wife and children, and the last intelligence he had received from her was, that she was confined in prison at Paris. There she had been thrown during the reign of terror. Her grandmother, the duchess de Noailles, her mother, the duchess d'Ayen, and her sister, the countess de Noailles, had perished in one day on the scaffold. She was herself reserved for the like fate; but the downfall of Robespierre preserved her. During her imprisonment, her great anxiety was for her son, George Washington Lafayette, then just attaining the age, at which he was liable to be forced by the conscription into the ranks of the army. The friendly assistance of two of our fellow citizens, whom I have the pleasure to see before me, Mr Joseph Russell and Colonel Thomas H. Perkins, was exerted in his behalf; and in consequence of their influence with Boissy d'Anglas, then a member of the committee of safety, they succeeded in obtaining permission for his departure. He was

conveyed by Mr Russell to Havre, whence he took passage to
Boston, and after a month spent in this city, was received into the
family of General Washington at Mount Vernon, where he remained till the liberation of his father.*

Relieved from anxiety on account of her son, the wife of Lafayette was resolved, with her daughters, if possible, to share his
captivity. Just escaped from the dungeons of Robespierre, she
hastened to plunge into those of the German emperor. This admirable lady, who, in the morning of life, had sent her youthful
hero from her side, to fight the battles of constitutional freedom,
beneath the guidance of Washington, now goes to immure herself
with him in the gloomy cells of Olmütz. Born, brought up, accustomed to all that was refined, luxurious, and elegant, she goes
to shut herself up in the poisonous wards of his dungeon,—to partake his wretched fare ;—to share his daily repeated insults ;—to
breathe an atmosphere so noxious and intolerable, that the gaolers
who bring them their daily food, are compelled to cover their faces,
as they enter their cells.

Landing at Altona, on the 9th of September, 1795, she proceeded with an American passport, under the family name of her
husband (Motier), to Vienna. Having arrived in that city, she
obtains, through the compassionate good offices of count Rosem-
berg, an interview with the emperor. Francis II is not a cruel
man. At the age of twenty-five, he has not yet been hardened by
long training in the school of state policy. He is a husband and a
father. The heroic wife of Lafayette, with her daughters, is admitted to his presence. She demands only to share her husband's
prison, but she implores the emperor to restore to liberty the father
of her children. ' He was indeed, sire, a general in the armies of
republican America ; but it was at a time when the daughter of
Maria Theresa was foremost in his praise. He was indeed a leader
of the French Revolution, but not in its excesses, not in its crimes ;
and it was owing to him alone, that on the dreadful 5th of October, Marie Antoinette and her son had not been torn in pieces by
the blood-thirsty populace of Paris. He is not the prisoner of your
justice, nor your arms, but was thrown by misfortune into your

* The letter of Lafayette to Colonel Perkins, written in acknowledgment of these
services, immediately after his liberation, is before me.

power, when he fled before the same monsters of blood and crime, who brought the king and queen of France to the scaffold. Three of my family have perished on the same scaffold,—my aged grandparent, my mother, and my sister. Will the emperor of Germany close the dark catalogue, and doom my husband to a dungeon worse than death? Restore him, sire, not to his army, to his power, to his influence, but to his shattered health, his ruined fortunes,— to the affections of his fellow citizens in America, where he is content to go and close his career,—to his wife and children.'

The emperor is a humane man. He hears, considers, reasons, hesitates ;—tells her 'his hands are tied,'* by reasons of state, and permits her to shut herself up, with her daughters, in the cells of Olmütz! There her health soon fails ; she asks to be permitted to pass a month at Vienna, to recruit it, and is answered, that she may leave the prison whenever she pleases ; but if she leaves it, she is never again to return. On this condition, she rejects the indulgence with disdain, and prepares herself to sink, under the slow poison of an infected atmosphere, by her husband's side. But her brave heart,—fit partner for a hero's,—bore her through the trial ; though the hand of death was upon her. She prolonged a feeble existence for ten years, after their release from captivity, but never recovered the effects of this merciless imprisonment.

The interposition of the friends of Lafayette, in Europe and America, to obtain his release, was unsuccessful. On the floor of the House of Commons, General Fitzpatrick, on the 16th of December, 1796, made a motion in his behalf. It was supported by Colonel Tarleton, who had fought against Lafayette in America, by Wilberforce and Fox. The speech of the latter is one of the most admirable specimens of eloquence ever heard in a deliberative assembly. But justice remonstrated, and humanity pleaded in vain. General Washington, then President of the United States, wrote a letter to the emperor of Germany. What would not the emperor afterwards have given, to have had the wisdom to grant

---

* This remark of the emperor was the subject of severe reflection in the admirable speech in which Mr Fox endeavored to induce the British ministry to interfere for the liberation of Lafayette; for while the emperor had given this reason for not releasing him, the British minister pleaded his inability to interfere with the internal concerns of the German empire.

the liberty of Lafayette to the entreaty of Washington! An advocate was at hand, who would not be refused. The Man of Destiny was in the field. The archduke Charles was matched against him, during the campaign of 1797. The eagles of Bonaparte flew from victory to victory. The archduke displayed against him all the resources of the old school ;—but the days of strategy were past. Bonaparte stormed upon his front, threw his army across deep rivers, and burst upon his rear,—and annihilated the astonished archduke in the midst of his manœuvres. He fought ten pitched battles in twenty days, drove the Austrians across the Julian Alps, approached within eleven days' march of Vienna, and then granted the emperor, just preparing for flight into the recesses of Hungary, the treaty of Campio Formio, having demanded, in the preliminary conferences of Leoben, the release of Lafayette.* Napoleon was often afterwards heard to say, that in all his negotiations with foreign powers, he had never experienced so pertinacious a resistance, as that which was made to this demand. The Austrian envoys, at the French head-quarters, asserted that he was not in confinement in the imperial territories. But Bonaparte distrusted this assertion, and sent a former aid-de-camp of Lafayette to Vienna, to communicate directly with the Austrian minister on the subject. He was finally released on the 23d of September, 1797. But while his liberation was effected by the interference of the army of the republic abroad, the confiscation and sale of the residue of his property went on at home.

Included in the general decree of outlawry, as an emigrant, Lafayette did not go back to France, till the directory was overturned. On the establishment of the consular government, being restored to his civil rights, though with the loss of nearly all his estates, he returned to his native country, and sought the retirement of Lagrange. He was indebted to Napoleon for release from captivity, probably for the lives of himself and family. He could not but see that all hope of restoring the constitution of 1791, to which he had pledged his faith, was over, and he had every reason of interest and gratitude, to compound with the state of things as it

* Sir Walter Scott, by a somewhat singular inadvertence, states that Lafayette was released 19th December, 1795, in exchange for the daughter of Louis XVI, afterwards duchess of Angouleme.—Life of Napoleon, Vol. I, ch, 13.

existed. But he never wavered for a moment. Bonaparte endeavored, in a personal interview, to persuade him to enter the senate, but in vain. When the question was submitted to the people of France, whether Bonaparte should be first consul for life, Lafayette gave his vote in the negative, in a letter to Napoleon, which has been published. Of all the ancient nobility, who returned to France, Lafayette and the young Count de Vaudreuil were the only individuals, who refused the favors, which Napoleon was eager to accord to them. Of all to whom the cross of the legion of honor was tendered, Lafayette alone had the courage to decline it. Napoleon is said to have exclaimed, when they told him that Lafayette refused the decoration, 'What, will nothing satisfy that man, but the chief command of the National Guard of the empire?' Yes, much less abundantly satisfied him;—the quiet possession of the poor remnants of his estate, enjoyed without sacrificing his principles.

From this life nothing could draw him. Mr Jefferson offered him the place of governor of Louisiana, then just become a territory of the United States; but he was unwilling, by leaving France, to take a step, that would look like a final abandonment of the cause of constitutional liberty on the continent of Europe. Napoleon ceased to importune him, and he lived at Lagrange, retired and unmolested, the only public man, who had gone through the terrible Revolution, with a character free from every just impeachment. He entered it with a princely fortune;—in the various high offices which he had filled he had declined all compensation; —and he came out poor. He entered it, in the meridian of early manhood, with a frame of iron. He came out of it, fifty years of age, his strength impaired by the cruelties of his long imprisonment. He had filled the most powerful and responsible offices; and others, still more powerful,—the dictatorship itself,—had been offered him;—he was reduced to obscurity and private life. He entered the Revolution, with a host of ardent colleagues of the constitutional party; of those who escaped the guillotine, most had made their peace with Napoleon. Not a few of the Jacobins had taken his splendid bribes;—the emigrating nobility came back in crowds, and put on his livery; fear, interest, weariness, amazement, and apathy, reigned in France and in Europe;—kings, emperors, armies, nations, bowed at his footstool ;—and one man alone,—a private man, who had tasted power, and knew what he sacrificed ;—who had inhabited dungeons, and knew what he risked ;—who had done enough for liberty in both worlds, to satisfy the utmost requisitions of her friends,—this man alone stood aloof in his honor, his independence,—and his poverty. And if there is a man in this assembly, that would not rather have been Lafayette to refuse, than Napoleon to bestow his wretched gew-gaws ; that would not rather have been Lafayette in retirement and obscurity, and just not proscribed, than Napoleon with an em-peror to hold his stirrup ;—if there is a man, who would not have preferred the honest poverty of Lagrange to the bloody tinsel of St Cloud ;—that would not rather have shared the peaceful fire-side of the friend of Washington, than have spurred his triumphant courser over the crushed and blackened heaps of slain, through the fire and carnage of Marengo and Austerlitz, that man has not an American heart in his bosom. That man is a slave, and fit to be the father of slaves. He does not deserve to breathe the pure air, to drink the cold springs, to tread the green fields, and hear the Sabbath bells of a free country. He ought, with all his garters, ribbons, and stars upon him, to be bolted, with a golden chain, to the blazing pavement of a palace court yard, that when his lord and master goes out to the hunt of beasts or of men, he may be there,—the slave,—to crouch down, and let his majesty vault from his shoulders to the saddle.

But the time at length arrived which was to call Lafayette from his retirement, and place him again,—the veteran pilot,—at the helm. The colossal edifice of empire, which had been reared by Napoleon, crumbled by its own weight. The pride, the interests, the vanity, the patriotism, of the nations were too deeply outraged and wounded by his domination. In the ancient world,—or in the middle ages,—whose examples he too much studied, his dynasty would have stood for centuries. He would have founded an em-pire, as durable as that of Cæsar or Mahomet, had he, like them, lived in an age, when there was but one centre of civilization, and when it was possible for one mighty vortex of power, to draw into itself all the intelligence and capacity of the world. But the division of civilized man into several co-existing national systems,

—all, in the main, equally enlightened and intelligent,—each having its own pride,—its own patriotism,—its own public opinion, —created an obstacle too powerful for the genius of Napoleon;— too strong for his arm; too various, too widely complicated for his skill;—too sturdy for his gold. Accordingly his mighty system went to pieces. The armies of insulted and maddened Europe poured down like an inundation on France. It was then that Lafayette appeared again upon the scene. His 'well known voice,' never silent when there was danger and hope for the cause of liberty, is heard, clear and strong, amidst the tumult of invading armies and contending factions. When, after the disaster of Waterloo, Napoleon came back in desperation to Paris, and began to scatter dark hints of dissolving the representative chamber, repeating at Paris the catastrophe of Moscow, and thereby endeavoring to rouse the people of France to one universal and frantic crusade of resistance, Lafayette was the first to denounce the wild suggestion. He proposed a series of resolutions, setting forth that the independence of the nation was threatened, declaring the chambers a permanent body, and denouncing the instant penalties of high treason against all attempts to dissolve it. The same evening he proposed, in the secret assembly of the council of state, the abdication of Napoleon. The subject was again pressed the following day; but the voluntary act of the Emperor anticipated the decision. Thus, true to the cause, to which his life was sacred, Lafayette was found at the tribune, in the secret council, before the assembled populace, and as the deputed representative of his distracted country in the camp of the invading enemy,—every where, in short, except where places of precedence were courted, —and money greedily clutched. Unhappily for France, all, who were thrown in the troubled state of the times to the head of affairs, were not of the same stamp. Men, who in the horrible national convention had voted for the death of Louis XVI,—men, who had stimulated and executed the worst measures of Napoleon, —who had shot the arrows of his police in the dark, and whetted the glittering sabre of his conquests; and now that he was in the dust, bravely trod upon his neck; these were the instruments, the confidants, the favorites of the allied powers, and of the monarch whom they installed over reluctant France. There was of course, no place for Lafayette among men like these. He was not with them in the Revolution, and could not be with them in the Restoration. He was too old to make new acquaintances. There was room in the cabinet and palace of Louis XVIII for men, that were stained with the best blood of France, not excepting his brother's ; but there was no room for the man to whom it was more than once owing, that his brother's blood and his own had not flowed together in the streets of Paris.

But when, under the Restoration, the representative system was established in France, there was a place, a fitting place, for him, at the tribune ; a faithful representative of the people, a friend of liberty regulated and protected by law, an enemy of usurpation at home and abroad, not less than of the bloody reactions to which it leads. From his first appearance in the chamber, to the last hour of his life, he is found at his post, the able, the eloquent, the consistent champion of the principles, to which from his youth he had been devoted.

His re-appearance on the scene, as the active expounder and champion of constitutional liberty, was not unobserved by the people of the United States. A generation had arisen, who had read the story of his services, and heard their fathers speak with affection of his person. They were anxious themselves to behold the friend of their fathers ; and to exhibit to him the spectacle of the prosperity he had done so much to establish. A resolution passed the two houses of Congress unanimously, requesting the President to invite him to visit the United States. In conveying this invitation, Mr Monroe informed Lafayette that the North Carolina ship of the line, was ordered to bring him to America. With characteristic modesty, he declined the offer of a public vessel, and with his son and secretary, took passage on board one of the packet ships, between New-York and Havre. He arrived at New-York on the 15th of August, 1824, just forty years from the time of his landing in the same city, on occasion of his visit to the United States, after the close of the revolutionary war.

You need not, fellow citizens, that I should repeat to you the incidents of that most extraordinary triumphal progress through the country. They are fresh in your recollection ; and history may be searched in vain for a parallel event. His arrival in the United States seemed like the re-appearance of a friendly genius, on the theatre of his youthful and beneficent visitations. He came back to us from long absence, from exile and from dungeons, almost like a beloved parent rising from the dead. His arrival called out the whole population of the country to welcome him, but not in the stiff uniform of a parade, or the court dress of a heartless ceremony. Society, in all its shades and gradations, crowded cordially around him, all penetrated with one spirit,—the spirit of admiration and love. The wealth and luxury of the coast, the teeming abundance of the west ;—the elegance of the town, the cordiality of the country ;—the authorities, municipal, national, and state ; the living relics of the Revolution, honored in the honors paid to their companion in arms ;—the scientific and learned bodies, the children at the schools, the associations of active life and of charity ; the exiles of Spain, France and Switzerland ;—banished kings ;—patriots of whom Europe was not worthy ; and even the African and Indian ; —every thing in the country, that had life and sense, took a part in this auspicious drama of real life.

Had the deputed representatives of these various interests and conditions been assembled, at some one grand ceremonial of reception, in honor of the illustrious visitor, it would, even as the pageant of a day, have formed an august spectacle. It would even then have outshone those illustrious triumphs of Rome, where conquered nations and captive princes followed in the train, which seemed with reason almost to lift the frail mortal thus honored, above the earth, over which he was borne. But when we consider, that this glorious and purer triumph was co-extensive with the Union,—that it swept majestically along, from city to city and from state to state,—one unbroken progress of rapturous welcome ; —banishing feuds, appeasing dissensions, hushing all tumults but the acclamations of joy,—uniting in one great act of public salutation, the conflicting parties of a free people, on the eve and throughout the course of a strenuous contest,—with the *aura epileptica* of the canvass already rushing over the body politic,— that it was continued near a twelvemonth, an *annus mirabilis* of rejoicing, auspiciously commenced, successfully pursued, and happily and gracefully accomplished, we perceive in it a chapter in human

affairs equally singular, delightful, instructive, and without example.

But let no one think it was a light and unreflecting movement of
popular caprice.   There was enough in the character and fortunes
of the man, to sustain and justify it.   In addition to a rare endowment of personal qualities, sufficient for an ample assignment of merit, to a dozen great men of the common stamp,—it was necessary
toward the production of such an effect on the public mind, that
numberless high and singular associations should have linked his
name, with all the great public movements of half a century.   It
was necessary that, in a venerable age, he should have come out
of a long succession of labors, trials, and disasters, of which a much
smaller portion is commonly sufficient to break down the health
and spirits, and send the weary victim, discouraged and heart-sick,
to an early retreat.   It was necessary that he should, in the outset, taking age, and circumstances, and success into consideration,
have done that for this far distant land, which was never done for
any country in the world.   Having performed an arduous, a dangerous, an honorable and triumphant part in our Revolution,—itself an event of high and transcendent character,—it was necessary,
that, pursuing at home the path of immortal renown on which his
feet had laid hold in America, he should have engaged among the
foremost, in that stupendous Revolution, in his own country, where
he stood sad but unshaken, amidst the madness of an empire ; faithful to liberty when all else were faithless ; true to her holy cause,
when the crimes and horrors committed in her name made the
brave fear and the good loathe it ; innocent and pure in that ' open
hell, ringing with agony and blasphemy, smoking with suffering
and crime.'   It was necessary to the feeling, with which Lafayette
was received in this country, that the people should remember how
he was received in Prussia and Austria ; how, when barely escaping from the edge of the Jacobin guillotine at Paris, he was generously bolted down into the underground caverns of Magdeburg ;
and shut up to languish for years with his wife and daughter, in a
pestiferous dungeon, by an emperor who had to thank him alone,
that his father's sister had not been torn limb from limb, by the
poissardes of Paris.   It was necessary to justify the enthusiasm,
with which Lafayette was welcomed to republican America, that

when another catastrophe had placed the Man of Fate on the throne of France, and almost of Europe, Lafayette alone, not in a convulsive effort of fanatical hardihood, but in the calm consciousness of a weight of character which would bear him out in the step, should, deliberately and in writing, refuse to sanction the power, before which the contemporary generation quailed. When again the wheel of empire had turned, and this dreadful colossus was about to be crushed beneath the weight of Europe, (mustered against him more in desperation than self-assured power,) and in falling had dragged down to earth the honor and the strength of France, —it was necessary, when the dust and smoke of the contest had blown off, that the faithful sentinel of liberty should be seen again at his post, ready once more to stake life and reputation in another of those critical junctures, when the stoutest hearts are apt to retire, and leave the field to desperate men,—the forlorn hope of affairs,— whom recklessness or necessity crowds up to the breach. But to refute every imputation of selfishness,—of a wish to restore himself to the graces of restored royalty,—himself the only individual of continental Europe, within the reach of Napoleon's sceptre, who refused to sanction his title,—it was necessary that he should be coldly viewed by the reappearing dynasty, and that he should be seen and heard,—not in the cabinet or the antechamber, swarming with men whom Napoleon had spangled with stars, but at the tribune; the calm, the rational, the ever consistent advocate of liberty and order, a representative of the people, in constitutional France. It was there I first saw him. I saw the marshals of Napoleon gorged with the plunder of Europe, and stained with its blood, borne on their flashing chariot wheels through the streets of Paris. I saw the ministers of Napoleon filling the highest posts of trust and honor under Louis XVIII; and I saw the friend of Washington, glorious in his noble poverty, looking down from the dazzling height of his consistency and his principles, on their paltry ambition and its more paltry rewards.

But all this,—much as it was,—was not all that combined to insure to Lafayette the respect, the love, the passionate admiration of the people, to whom he had consecrated the bloom of his youth; —for whom he had lavished his fortune and blood. These were the essentials, but they were not all. In order to give even to the common mind a topic of pleasing and fanciful contrast, where the strongest mind found enough to command respect and astonishment ; in order to make up a character, in which even the ingredients of romance were mingled with the loftiest and sternest virtues, it was necessary that the just and authentic titles to respect which we have considered, should be united in an individual, who derived his descent from the ancient chivalry of France ;—that he should have been born within the walls of a feudal castle ; that the patient volunteer who laid his head contentedly on a wreath of snow, beneath the tattered canvass of a tent at Valley Forge, should have come fresh from the gorgeous canopies of Versailles ; that he should abandon all that a false ambition could covet, as well as attain all that a pure ambition could prize ; and thus begin life by trampling under foot that which Chatham accepted, which Burke did not refuse,—and for which the mass of eminent men in Europe barter health, comfort, and conscience.

Such was the man whom the Congress of the United States invited to our shores, to gather in the rich harvest of a people's love. Well might he do it.   He had sown it in weakness,—should he not reap it in power ? He had come to us, a poor and struggling colony, and risked his life and shed his blood in our defence,—was it not just, that he should come again in his age, to witness the fruits of his labors, to rejoice with the veteran companions of his service, and to receive the benediction of the children, as he had received that of the fathers ?

But the delightful vision passes.   He returns to France to reappear in the chamber of deputies, the still consistent champion of reform, both at home and throughout Europe.   His extraordinary reception in the United States had given an added weight to his counsels, which nothing could withstand.   It raised him into a new moral power in the state :—an inofficial dictator of principle ; a representative of the public opinion of the friends of liberty in the whole world,—a personation of the spirit of reform.   At the close of the session of 1829, on occasion of a visit to the place of his birth, in the ancient province of Auvergne, his progress through the country was the counterpart of his tour through the United States.   In the towns and villages on his way, he was received in triumph. Arches arose over his venerable head,—the population gathered round him at the festive board, and the language of the addresses made to him, and of his replies, was of startling significance. It was a moment, you may remember, in France, when the tide of reform seemed flowing backwards. Some of the worst abuses of the ancient *régime* were openly re-established. The ministry was filled with some of the most obnoxious of the emigrant nobility. The expedition to Algiers gave no small *éclat* to the administration, feeble and odious as it was ;—and on a superficial view it seemed, that the entire fruit of the immense sacrifices, which France had made for constitutional liberty, was about to be wrested from her. Such, I own, for a short time, was my own apprehension. But the visit of Lafayette to the south of France convinced me, that there was no ground for despondence. I saw plainly, that either by way of awakening the slumbering spirit of resistance, or because he saw that it was awakened and demanded sympathy and encouragement ; either to excite or guide the public mind, the sagacious veteran was on the alert ; and that language, such as he was daily addressing to the people,—received in willing ears,—was the award of fate to the administration. In some remarks, submitted to the public on the 1st of January 1830, I ventured to express myself, in the following manner :

'When we read, in the last papers from France, the account of the present state of things in that kingdom ; when we notice the irresistible onset made upon the ministry and the visible perturbation of its ranks, it is impossible wholly to suppress the idea, that another great change is at hand. When we see the spontaneous movement of the people toward the person of Lafayette, the glowing zeal with which they have turned an excursion of business into another triumphant progress, strewing his way with honors, such as loyal France never paid to her most cherished princes, we cannot but think, that, in the language of the venerable Spanish priest at New-Orleans, he is still reserved for great achievements. The feelings of men inspire their actions ; public sentiment governs states ; and revolutions are the out-breakings of mighty, irrepressible passions. It is in vain to deny, that these passions are up in France, and happy is it that they have concentrated themselves upon a patriot, whom prosperity has been as little able to corrupt, as adversity to subdue.'

What was vague foreboding on the first of January, was history by the last of July. On that day, Charles X and his family, who had learned nothing, and forgotten nothing, in thirty years of banishment and exclusion, were on their way to the frontier, and Lafayette was installed at the Hôtel de Ville, chief of the National Guards,—at the head of a new revolution.

At the head of a new revolution? Not so. He lives, the fortunate man, to see the first revolution,—emerging from years of abuse and seas of blood,—and approaching its peaceful consummation. A weak and besotted prince, who had attempted, by one monstrous act of executive usurpation, to repeal the entire charter, and had thus produced a revolt, in which six thousand lives were lost, —is permitted, unmolested, and in safety, to leave the city, where, twenty-seven years before, his innocent brother had been dragged to the scaffold. A dynasty is changed, with the promptitude and order of an election. And when the critical period comes on, for the trial of the guilty ministers,—the responsible advisers of the measures which had drenched Paris in blood,—Lafayette is able, by the influence of his venerable authority, and the exercise of his military command, to prevent the effusion of blood, and save their forfeited lives.

In these, his successful efforts, to prevent the late revolution from assuming a sanguinary character, I own I cannot but think, that our revered Lafayette did as much for the cause of liberty, as by all his former efforts and sacrifices. There is nothing more efficacious in reconciling men to the continued existence of corrupt forms of government, than the fear, that when once the work of revolution is undertaken, blood of necessity begins to flow in torrents. It was the reign of terror which reconciled men to the reign of Napoleon,—and it is the dread of seeing its scenes reacted in Austria, in Prussia, and in Russia, which prevents the intelligence of those countries from engaging in earnest, in the work of radical reform.

In all the steps of the recent revolution in France, so long as there was responsibility to be assumed or danger to be braved, Lafayette was its leader. It is plain, from documents before the world, that he could have organized the government on the republican model, and placed himself at its head. Although, in refraining from this, it may be justly said, that he abstained from a course for which his advanced age,—his pledged disinterestedness,—and the consistency of his whole life unfitted him; it is not the less true, that in deciding for an hereditary executive, with a legislature chosen by the people, or, in his own language, a monarchy surrounded by republican institutions, he acted up to the principles, with which he commenced his political course. There is as much truth as point in the remark ascribed to Charles X, on his way to the sea-coast, ' that he and Lafayette were the only consistent men of the day.'

Born for mighty constitutional movements, for the support of great principles, to take the direction in critical junctures of affairs, —but absolutely insensible to the love of power or money, or the passion for place, Lafayette's functions were exhausted, as soon as the new government was organized. He re-created the National Guard, which he had called into being in 1789, and in which lay the germ of the victories of Napoleon,—placed a constitutional crown, without commotion or bloodshed, on the head of the duke of Orleans,—and carried the government through the crisis of the trial of the ministers. Having performed these great services to the country,—and disdaining to enter into the petty politics which succeed a great movement,—the scramble for office and the rivalries of small men,—he laid down his commission as commander-in-chief of the National Guards, and confined himself to his duties, as a representative of the people, and to the exercise of his moral influence, as the acknowledged chief of the constitutional party on the continent of Europe.

In the course of the last spring, our beloved benefactor, in attending the funeral of a colleague in the chamber of deputies, from long exposure to the dampness of the air and ground, contracted a cold, which settled on his lungs; and which, though deemed slight at first, gradually assumed a serious aspect. After a protracted struggle with the remains of a once vigorous constitution, the disease became alarming; but not, as was supposed, critical, till the 19th of May. On that day, by a mark of public sympathy never perhaps paid before to a private citizen, the chamber of deputies directed their president to address a note to Mr G. W. Lafayette, inquiring after the health of his venerable parent. At the time of this inquiry, the symptoms of the disease were less alarming, but an unfavorable change soon took place; and on the following day, the illustrious sufferer,—the patriarch of liberty,— died, in the seventy-seventh year of his age.   He was buried, by his own direction, not within the vaults of the Pantheon,—not among the great and illustrious that people the silent alleys of Père la Chaise, but in a rural cemetery near Paris, by the side of her who had shared his pure love of liberty, his triumphs, his dungeon, and his undying renown.   In a secluded garden, in this humble retreat, beneath the shade of a row of linden trees, between his wife and his daughter, the friend of Washington and America, has lain down to his last repose.

I attempt not, fellow citizens, to sketch his character.   I have no space, no capacity, for the task.   I have endeavored to run over,—superficially, of necessity,—the incidents of his life; his character is contained in the recital.

There have been those who have denied to Lafayette the name of *a great man*.   What is greatness?   Does goodness belong to greatness, and make an essential part of it?   If it does, who, I would ask, of all the prominent names in history, has run through such a career, with so little reproach, justly or unjustly, bestowed? Are military courage and conduct the measure of greatness?   Lafayette was entrusted by Washington with all kinds of service;— the laborious and complicated, which required skill and patience, the perilous that demanded nerve;—and we see him keeping up a pursuit, effecting a retreat, out-manœuvring a wary adversary with a superior force, harmonizing the action of French regular troops and American militia, commanding an assault at the point of the bayonet; and all with entire success and brilliant reputation.   Is the readiness to meet vast responsibility a proof of greatness?   The memoirs of Mr Jefferson show us, as we have already seen, that there was a moment in 1789, when Lafayette took upon himself, as the head of the military force, the entire responsibility of laying down the basis of the Revolution.   Is the cool and brave adminis- tration of gigantic power, a mark of greatness?   In all the whirl- wind of the Revolution, and when as commander-in-chief of the National Guard, an organized force of three millions of men, who, for any popular purpose, needed but a word, a look, to put them in motion,—and he their idol,—we behold him ever calm, collected, disinterested; as free from affectation as selfishness, clothed not less with humility than with power. Is the fortitude required to resist the multitude pressing onward their leader to glorious crime, a part of greatness? Behold him, the fugitive and the victim, when he might have been the chief of the Revolution. Is the solitary and unaided opposition of a good citizen to the pretensions of an absolute ruler, whose power was as boundless as his ambition, an effort of greatness? Read the letter of Lafayette to Napoleon Bonaparte, refusing to vote for him as consul for life. Is the voluntary return, in advancing years, to the direction of affairs, at a moment like that, when in 1815, the ponderous machinery of the French empire was flying asunder,—stunning, rending, crushing thousands on every side,—a mark of greatness? Contemplate Lafayette at the tribune, in Paris, when allied Europe was thundering at its gates, and Napoleon yet stood in his desperation and at bay. Are dignity, propriety, cheerfulness, unerring discretion in new and conspicuous stations of extraordinary delicacy, a sign of greatness? Watch his progress in this country, in 1824 and 1825, hear him say the right word at the right time, in a series of interviews, public and private, crowding on each other every day, for a twelvemonth, throughout the Union, with every description of persons, without ever wounding for a moment the self-love of others, or forgetting the dignity of his own position. Lastly, is it any proof of greatness, to be able, at the age of seventy-three, to take the lead in a successful and bloodless revolution;—to change the dynasty,—to organize, exercise, and abdicate a military command of three and a half millions of men;—to take up, to perform, and lay down the most momentous, delicate, and perilous duties, without passion, without hurry, without selfishness? Is it great, to disregard the bribes of title, office, money;—to live, to labor, and suffer for great public ends alone;—to adhere to principle under all circumstances;—to stand before Europe and America conspicuous, for sixty years, in the most responsible stations, the acknowledged admiration of all good men?

But I think I understand the proposition, that Lafayette was not a great man. It comes from the same school which also denies greatness to Washington, and which accords it to Alexander and

Cæsar, to Napoleon and to his conqueror. When I analyze the greatness of these distinguished men, as contrasted with that of Lafayette and Washington, I find either one idea omitted, which is essential to true greatness, or one included as essential, which belongs only to the lowest conception of greatness. The moral, disinterested, and purely patriotic qualities are wholly wanting in the greatness of Alexander and Cæsar; and on the other hand, it is a certain splendor of success, a brilliancy of result, which, with the majority of mankind, marks them out as the great men of our race. But not only are a high morality and a true patriotism essential to greatness,—but they must first be renounced before a ruthless career of selfish conquest can begin. I profess to be no judge of military combinations; but, with the best reflection I have been able to give the subject, I perceive no reason to doubt that, had Lafayette, like Napoleon, been by principle, capable of hovering on the edges of ultra-revolutionism; never halting enough to be denounced; never plunging too far to retreat;—but with a cold and well-balanced selfishness, sustaining himself at the head of affairs, under each new phase of the Revolution, by the compliances sufficient to satisfy its demands,—he might have anticipated the career of Napoleon. At three different periods, he had it in his power, without usurpation, to take the government into his own hands. He was invited, urged to do so. Had he done it, and made use of the military means at his command, to maintain and perpetuate his power,—he would then, at the sacrifice of all his just claims to the name of great and good, have reached that which vulgar admiration alone worships,—the greatness of high station and brilliant success.

But it was of the greatness of Lafayette, that he looked down on greatness of the false kind. He learned his lesson in the school of Washington, and took his first practice in victories over himself. Let it be questioned by the venal apologists of time-honored abuses, —let it be sneered at by national prejudice and party detraction; let it be denied by the admirers of war and conquest;—by the idolaters of success,—but let it be gratefully acknowledged by good men; by Americans,—by every man, who has sense to distinguish character from events; who has a heart to beat in concert with the pure enthusiasm of virtue.

But it is more than time, fellow citizens, that I commit the memory of this great and good man to your unprompted contemplation. On his arrival among you, ten years ago,—when your civil fathers, your military, your children, your whole population poured itself out, as one throng, to salute him,—when your cannons proclaimed his advent with joyous salvos,—and your acclamations were responded from steeple to steeple, by the voice of festal bells, with what delight did you not listen to his cordial and affectionate words ;—' I beg of you all, beloved citizens of Boston, to accept the respectful and warm thanks of a heart which has for nearly half a century been devoted to your illustrious city !' That noble heart,—to which, if any object on earth was dear, that object was the country of his early choice,—of his adoption, and his more than regal triumph,—that noble heart will beat no more for your welfare.   Cold and motionless, it is already mingling with the dust.   While he lived, you thronged with delight to his presence, —you gazed with admiration on his placid features and venerable form, not wholly unshaken by the rude storms of his career ; and now that he is departed, you have assembled in this cradle of the liberties for which, with your fathers, he risked his life, to pay the last honors to his memory.   You have thrown open these consecrated portals to admit the lengthened train, which has come to discharge the last public offices of respect to his name.   You have hung these venerable arches, for the second time since their erection, with the sable badges of sorrow.   You have thus associated the memory of Lafayette in those distinguished honors, which but a few years since you paid to your Adams and Jefferson ; and, could your wishes and mine have prevailed, my lips would this day have been mute, and the same illustrious voice which gave utterance to your filial emotions over their honored graves, would have spoken also, for you, over him who shared their earthly labors, —enjoyed their friendship,—and has now gone to share their last repose, and their imperishable remembrance.

There is not, throughout the world, a friend of liberty, who has not dropped his head, when he has heard that Lafayette is no more. Poland, Italy, Greece, Spain, Ireland, the South American republics, —every country where man is struggling to recover his birthright,— has lost a benefactor, a patron, in Lafayette.   But you, young men, at whose command I speak, for you a bright and particular lodestar is henceforward fixed in the front of heaven. What young man that reflects on the history of Lafayette,—that sees him in the morning of his days the associate of sages,—the friend of Washington,— but will start with new vigor on the path of duty and renown?

And what was it, fellow citizens, which gave to our Lafayette his spotless fame? The love of liberty. What has consecrated his memory in hearts of good men? The love of liberty. What nerved his youthful arm with strength, and inspired him in the morning of his days, with sagacity and counsel? The living love of liberty. To what did he sacrifice power, and rank, and country, and freedom itself? To the horror of licentiousness ;—to the sanctity of plighted faith ;—to the love of liberty protected by law. Thus the great principle of your revolutionary fathers, of your pilgrim sires, the great principle of the age, was the rule of his life : *The love of liberty protected by law.*

You have now assembled within these celebrated walls, to perform the last duties of respect and love, on the birth day of your benefactor, beneath that roof which has resounded of old with the master voices of American renown. The spirit of the departed is in high communion with the spirit of the place ;—the temple worthy of the new name which we now behold inscribed on its walls. Listen, Americans, to the lesson which seems borne to us on the very air we breathe, while we perform these dutiful rites! Ye winds, that wafted the Pilgrims to the land of promise, fan, in their children's hearts, the love of freedom ;— Blood, which our fathers shed, cry from the ground ;—Echoing arches of this renowned hall, whisper back the voices of other days ;—Glorious Washington, break the long silence of that votive canvass ;—Speak, speak, marble lips, teach us THE LOVE OF LIBERTY PROTECTED BY LAW!

ORATION

DELIVERED AT LEXINGTON, ON THE 19TH (20TH) OF APRIL, 1835,

BY REQUEST OF THE CITIZENS OF THAT PLACE.

FELLOW CITIZENS,

AT the close of sixty years, we commemorate the eventful scenes of the opening Revolution. We have come together, to celebrate the affecting incidents, which have placed the name of this beautiful village on the first page of the history of our independence. The citizens of a free, prosperous, and powerful republic, we come to pay the last honors to the memory of those who offered themselves up, on this spot, the first costly sacrifice in the cause of American liberty. In the day of our peace and safety, in the enjoyment of the richest abundance of public and private blessings, we have met together to summon up, in grateful recollection, the images of that night of trial, of fearful anticipation, of high and stern resolve,—and of that morning of blood, which, to the end of time, will render the name of Lexington sacred to the heart of the American freeman.

Sixty years have passed away :—two full returns of the period assigned by the common consent of mankind to one of our transitory generations. I behold around me a few,—alas! how few,— of those who heard the dismal voice of the alarm bell, on the 19th of April, 1775, and the sharp angry hiss of the death vollies from the hostile lines. Venerable men! we gaze upon you with respectful emotion. You have reached an age allotted to the smallest po rtionof our race, and your gray hairs, under any circumstances,

61

would be entitled to our homage. As the survivors of the militia of Lexington, who, on the 19th of April, 1775, were enrolled in defence of the rights of America, and obeyed the alarm which called you to protect them, we regard you as objects at once of admiration and gratitude. But when we reflect that you, a small and venerable remnant of those who first took the field in the dawn of the Revolution which wrought out the liberty of the country, have been spared, not merely to see that Revolution brought to a triumphant close, but to witness the growth of that country to its present palmy height of prosperity and power, we feel that you are marked out by a peculiar Providence, above all the rest of your fellow citizens. But where, oh, where are your brave associates? Seven of them, who, full of life, and vigor, and patriotic daring, stood side by side with you, sixty years ago, on this ever memorable spot, are gathered,—what is mortal of them,—in that mournful receptacle. Others laid down their lives for their country, in the hard fought and honorable fields of the revolutionary war. The greater part have stolen away, one by one, and in silence, and lie beneath the scattered hillocks of yonder grave-yard. Twelve only survive,—ten alone are present,—to unite with us in the touching rites of this honored anniversary. May the happy contrast in your own existence on the great day we commemorate, and on this its sixtieth return, and in the position and fortunes of our beloved and common country, prove an ample compensation for your anxieties and perils, and fill the close of your days with peace and joy.*

Fellow citizens of Lexington, you are discharging your duty;— a filial, pious duty. The blood which wet these sods on the day you celebrate, must not sink uncommemorated into the soil. It is your birth-right; your heritage; the proudest you possess. Its sacred memory must be transmitted by your citizens, from father to son, to the end of time. We come to join you in this solemn

---

* See, in note A, the roll of Capt. Parker's company of Lexington militia. The following are the names of the survivors, four of whom were seated on the platform from which this address was spoken :—Dr Joseph Fiske, Messrs Daniel Mason, Benjamin Locke, William Munroe, Jonathan Harrington, Ebenezer Simonds, Jonathan Loring, John Hosmer, Isaac Durant, Josiah Reed. Mr Solomon Brown and Ebenezer Parker were absent.

act of commemoration. Partakers of the blessings, for which your fathers laid down their lives, we come to join you in these last affecting obsequies. And when all now present shall be passing, —passed,—from the stage ; when sixty years hence we, who have reached the meridian of life, shall have been gathered to our fathers, and a few only of these little children shall survive, changed into what we now behold in the gray heads and venerable forms before us, let us hope that it may at least be said of us, that we felt the value of the principles to which the day is consecrated, and the cost at which they were maintained.

We perform a duty which is sanctioned by reason and justice. It is the spontaneous impulse of the heart, to award the tribute of praise and admiration to those who have put every thing to risk, and sacrificed every thing in a great public cause,—who have submitted to the last dread test of patriotism, and laid down their lives for their country. In the present case, it is doubly warranted, by the best feelings of our nature. We do not come to weave fresh laurels for the hero's wreath, to flatter canonized pride, to extol the renowned, or to add new incense to the adulation, which is ever offered up at the shrine of the conqueror :—but to give the humble man his due, to rescue modest and untitled valor from oblivion ;— to record the names of those, whom neither the ambition of power, the hope of promotion, nor the temptation of gain,—but a plain, instinctive sense of patriotic duty,—called to the field.

Nor is it our purpose to rekindle the angry passions, although we would fain revive the generous enthusiasm of the day we celebrate. The boiling veins,—the burning nerves,—the almost maddened brain, which alone could have encountered the terrors of that day, have withered into dust, as still and cold as that with which they have mingled. There is no hostile feeling in that sacred repository. No cry for revenge bursts from its peaceful enclosure. Sacred relics ! Ye have not come up, from your resting-place in yonder grave-yard, on an errand of wrath or hatred. Ye have but moved a little nearer to the field of your glory ; to plead that your final resting-place may be on the spot where you fell; to claim the protection of the sods which you once moistened with your blood. It is a reasonable request. There is not an American who hears me, I am sure, who would profane the touching harmony of the scene, by an unfriendly feeling ;—and if there is an Englishman present, who carries an Anglo-Saxon heart in his bosom, he will be among the last to grudge to these poor remains of gallant foes, the honors we this day pay to their memory. Though they fell in this remote transatlantic village, they stood on the solid rock of the old liberties of Englishmen, and struck for freedom in both hemispheres.

Fellow citizens ! The history of the Revolution is familiar to you. You are acquainted with it, in the general and in its details. You know it as a comprehensive whole, embracing, within its grand outline, the settlement and the colonization of the country, —the development, maturity, and rupture of the relations between Great Britain and America. You know it, in the controversy carried on for nearly a hundred and fifty years between the representatives of the people and the officers of the crown. You know it in the characters of the great men, who signalized themselves as the enlightened and fearless leaders of the righteous and patriotic cause. You know it in the thrilling incidents of the crisis, when the appeal was made to arms. You know it,—you have studied it,—you revere it, as a mighty epoch in human affairs ; a great era in that order of Providence, which, from the strange conflict of human passions and interests, and the various and wonderfully complicated agency of the institutions of men in society,—of individual character,—of exploits,—discoveries,—commercial adventure,—the discourses and writings of wise and eloquent men,— educes the progressive civilization of the race. Under these circumstances, it is scarcely possible to approach the subject in any direction, with a well grounded hope of presenting it in new lights, or saying any thing in which this intelligent and patriotic audience will not run before me, and anticipate the words before they drop from my lips. But it is a theme that can never tire nor wear out. God grant that the time may never come, when those who, at periods however distant, shall address you on the 19th of April, shall have any thing wholly new to impart. Let the tale be repeated, from father to son, till all its thrilling incidents are as familiar as household words ; and till the names of the brave men who reaped the bloody honors of the 19th of April, 1775, are as well known to us, as the names of those who form the circle at our fire-sides.

The events of the day we commemorate, of course, derive their interest from their connexion with that struggle for constitutional liberty, which dates from the settlement of the country ; and which is beyond question the most important topic, in the history of free government. It presents to us a spectacle worthy of the deepest meditation,—full of solemn warning, and of instruction not yet exhausted. We are, at times, almost perplexed, with the phenomena which pass before us. We see our ancestors ;—a people of singular gravity of character, not turbulent nor impracticable, imbued with an hereditary love of order and law, and of a temper signally loyal ; engaged in a course of almost uninterrupted opposition to the authority of a government, which they professed themselves at all times bound to obey. On the other hand, we see the British government, under all administrations,—whether animated by liberal principles or the reverse,—adopting measures and pursuing a policy toward the North American colonies, which excited discontent and resistance. It is not till after careful scrutiny, that we find the solution of the problem, in a truth, which,—though our fathers, some of them at least, unquestionably felt its reality,—was never professed in any stage of the contest, till the declaration of independence, and then not as a general axiom, but as a proposition true in the then present case, viz., the inherent incongruity of colonial government with the principles of constitutional liberty. Such a government,—involving, as it almost of necessity does, the distance of the seat of power from the colony,—a *veto* on the colonial legislation,—an appeal from the colonial justice,—a diversion of the colonial resources to objects not necessarily connected with the welfare of the people,—together with the irritation produced by the presence of men in high office, not appointed by those who are obliged to submit to their authority,—seems, in its very nature, inconsistent with the requirements of constitutional liberty, either in the colony or the mother country. It is but half the mischief of the colonial system, that it obstructs the growth of freedom in the colony ; it favors the growth of arbitrary power in the mother country. It may be laid down as the moral of the long and varied struggle, which was brought to a crisis on this spot, on the 19th of April, 1775, that a colonial government can neither be exercised on principles of constitutional liberty, without gross inconsistency, nor submitted to by a free people, possessing numbers and resources which authorize resistance.

The truth of this doctrine shines brighter and brighter, from each successive page of our colonial history. The very genius of the British constitution,—the love of liberty, which was our fathers' inheritance, the passionate aversion to arbitrary power, which drove them into banishment from the pleasant fields of England,— unfitted them for their colonial position and its duties. For this reason, the cares of the mother country were as wisely bestowed on the colonies, as those of the huntsman in the ancient drama, who nursed the lion's whelp in his bosom, and brought him up as the playmate of his children. It was the nature, not the vice of the noble animal, that, tame and gentle as a lamb at the beginning, he grew up to the strength and boldness of a lion, impatient of restraint, indignant at injury, and ready, at the first opportunity, to bound off to his native woods.*

From this condition of things it resulted, that the statesmen on both sides the water,—as well in England as in America,—who took a lead in public affairs, were, to use the language of modern politics, in a false position, striving to do what could not be done ; —to tax constitutionally without a representation, and to preserve allegiance in despite of everlasting opposition. It was one consequence of this unnatural state of things, that the real ground of the discontents was continually misapprehended,—that they were ascribed to temporary, local, and personal causes,—and not to the inherent nature of the process which was going on, and of the impossibility of a cordial union of elements so discordant. This is peculiarly visible in the writings of Governor Hutchinson. This valuable historian was on the stage for the entire generation preceding the Revolution. For more than thirty years before it broke out, he was a political leader in Massachusetts. From the close of the French war to the year 1775, he was probably the most confidential adviser of the crown ; and for the chief part of the time the incumbent of the highest offices in its gift. He has brought the history of his native State down to the very moment, when, on the eve of the war, he left America, never to return. Learned, sagacious, wary, conciliatory, and strongly disposed, as far as pos-

* Æschyl. Agamemn., 720.

sible, to evade the difficulties of his position ; no man had better opportunities of knowing the truth, and after making proper allowance for his prejudices, few are entitled to greater credit in their statements. And yet, with all the sources of information in his reach, and all the opportunities enjoyed by him to arrive at an enlarged conception of the nature of the controversy, Governor Hutchinson seriously traces the origin of the Revolution to the fact that he himself was appointed chief justice, instead of James Otis, who aspired to the place.*

But a more signal instance of this delusion was of much older date, than the opposition to the stamp act. The government party never understood the character of the people nor the nature of the contest ; and a most memorable proof of this is found, in an act of provincial legislation, at the early period of 1694. In that year a step was taken by the court party, which showed, in a most extraordinary manner, the extent of their infatuation. Before this time, it had been the practice in many of the country towns to elect, as their representatives to the General Court, citizens of Boston, who, either from being natives of the towns or for any other cause, possessed the confidence of those, by whom they were thus chosen. A number of members of this class, having voted against an address to his Majesty, praying the continuance of Sir William Phips in office, the Court party immediately brought forward and carried a law, forbidding the election of any person as a representative, who did not reside in the town, by which he was chosen. Provision was thus made by law to compel the towns, even if otherwise disinclined to do so, to take an interest in public affairs; and to secure from their own bosom a constant and faithful representation of the yeomanry. This was a court measure, designed to disqualify a few popular citizens of Boston, who had been elected for the country ; but it may be doubted whether any thing else contributed more, to carry the great constitutional controversy home to the doors of every citizen of the community, and to link together the town and country, by the strongest bonds of political sympathy.

I need but allude to the measures, by which the Revolution was

---

* From an anecdote preserved by Dr Eliot, (Biograph. Dict. Art. Hutchinson), it would appear, on the authority of Judge Trowbridge, that Otis also viewed the question in the same connexion with his own personal relations to it.

at last brought on. The Boston Port Bill was a proof, that the British ministry had determined to force matters to extremities ; and it awakened the liveliest sympathy, in the fate of Boston, from one end of the continent to the other. The acts of Parliament passed in 1774, for altering the mode of summoning juries and transporting obnoxious persons to England for trial, were direct violations of the charter ; and indicated the dangerous policy of striking at the lives of individuals, under color of legal procedure. Nothing produces so great an exasperation, as this policy, and no policy is so weak ; for the most insignificant individual is made important by proscription, while few are so gifted, but their blood will prove more eloquent than their pens or their tongues. These threatening steps, on the part of the ministry, did but hasten the preparations for resistance, on the part of the people of America. A continental Congress was organized in 1774, and a provincial Congress met, about the same time, in Massachusetts. Before the close of that year, the latter body had made arrangements for a levy of twelve thousand men in Massachusetts, as her share of twenty thousand to be raised by the New England colonies, and one fourth of the number to act as *minute* men. By the same authority, magazines were established,—arms and munitions of war procured, and supplies of all kinds provided for a state of actual service. The greatest attention was paid to drilling and exercising the troops, particularly in the portions of the province, immediately contiguous to Concord and Worcester, where the military *depots* were established. A committee of safety and a committee of supplies were clothed with the chief executive power. General officers,—principally the veterans of the French war,—were appointed to command the troops. As the royal forces in Boston were in the habit of making excursions into the neighboring country, for parade and exercise, it became necessary to decide the question, when they should be met with forcible resistance. It was resolved by the provincial Congress, that this should be done, whenever the troops came out with baggage, ammunition, and artillery, and other preparations for hostile action. Having thus made provision for the worst, the provincial Congress of Massachusetts adjourned early in December, 1774, to give the members an opportunity to keep the stated thanksgiving with their families ;—and among the causes of gratitude to Almighty God, even at this dark and anxious period, which are set forth in the proclamation of the provincial Congress, they call upon the people to be devoutly thankful for the union of sentiment, which prevailed so remarkably in the colonies.

The situation of Massachusetts, at that time, presents a most striking and instructive spectacle. It contained a population, not far from three hundred thousand ; arrested in the full career of industrious occupation in all the branches of civilized pursuit. Their charter was substantially abrogated by the new laws. Obedience was every where withheld from the arbitrary powers assumed by the government. The proclamations of the governor were treated with silent disregard. The port of Boston is shut, and with it much of the commerce of the province is annihilated ; for the neighboring seaport towns vie with each other, in a generous refusal to take advantage of the distresses of Boston. The courts are closed, and the innumerable concerns, which, in an ordinary state of things, require the daily and hourly interposition of the law, are placed under the safe guardianship of the public sentiment of a patriotic community. The powers assumed by the committees of safety and supplies, and by the provincial Congress, are obeyed, with a ready deference, never yielded, in the most loyal times, to the legal commands of the king's governors. The community, in a word, is reduced,—no, is elevated,—to a state of nature :—to a state of nature, in a high and solemn sense, in which the feeling of a great impending common danger, and the consciousness of an exalted and resolute common purpose, take the place, at once and with full efficacy, of all the machinery of constitutional government. It is thus that a people, fit for freedom, may get the substance before the forms of liberty. Luxury disappears ; a patriotic frugality accumulates the scattered elements of the public wealth ;—feuds are reconciled ;—differences compromised ;—the creditor spares his debtor ;—the debtor voluntarily acquits his obligations ;—an unseen spirit of order, resource, and power walks, like an invisible angel, through the land ;—and the people, thoughtful, calm, and collected, await the coming storm.

The minds of the people throughout the country, had become thoroughly imbued with the great principles of the contest. These principles had for years been discussed at the primary meetings in

Massachusetts; and the municipal records of many of the towns, at that period, are filled with the most honorable proofs of the intelligence and patriotism of their citizens. The town of Lexington stands second to none, in an early, strenuous, and able vindication of the rights of the colonies. In the year 1765, a very conclusive exposition of the question on the stamp act was adopted by the town, in the form of instructions to their representative in the General Court. It is a paper not inferior to the best of the day. In 1767, the town expressed its unanimous concurrence, in the measures adopted by Boston, to prevent the consumption of foreign commodities. In 1768, a preamble and resolutions were adopted by the town, in which the right of Great Britain to tax America is argued with extraordinary skill and power. In 1772, their representative was furnished with instructions, expressed in the most forcible terms, to seek a redress of the daily increasing wrongs of the people. The object of these instructions is declared to be, that ' thus, whether successful or not, succeeding generations may know that we understood our rights and liberties, and were neither afraid nor ashamed to assert or maintain them; and that we ourselves may have at least this consolation, in our chains, that it was not through our neglect, that this people were enslaved.'*
In 1773, resolutions of the most decided and animated character, were unanimously passed, relative to the duty on tea. At numerous town meetings toward the close of 1774, measures were taken for a supply of ammunition, the purchase and distribution of arms, and other measures of military defence. A representative was chosen to the provincial Congress, and the town's tax directed to be paid, not to the royal receiver general, but to the treasurer appointed by the provincial Congress.

Although the part thus taken by Lexington was in full accordance with the course pursued by many other towns in the province, there is nothing invidious in the remark, that the documents to which I have referred, and in which the principles and opinions of the town are embodied, have few equals and no superiors, among the productions of that class. They are well known to have proceeded from the pen of the former venerable pastor of the church

---

* Lexington Town Records, Fol. 209.

in this place, the Reverend Jonas Clark, who for many years previous to the Revolution, and to the close of his life, exercised a well-deserved ascendency in the public concerns of the town. To the older part of the citizens of Lexington it were needless to describe him :—they remember too well the voice, to which, within these walls, they listened so long with reverence and delight. Even to those who are too young to have known him, the tradition of his influence is familiar. Mr Clark was of a class of citizens, who rendered services second to no other, in enlightening and animating the popular mind on the great questions at issue,—I mean the patriotic clergy of New-England. The circumstances under which this portion of the country was settled, gave a religious complexion to the whole political system. The vigorous growth of transatlantic liberty was owing, in no small degree, to the fact, that its seed was planted at the beginning, by men, who deemed *freedom of conscience* a cheap purchase at any cost ; and that its roots struck deep into the soil of Puritanism. Mr Clark was eminent in his profession,—a man of practical piety,—a learned theologian,—a person of wide, general reading,—a writer perspicuous, correct, and pointed, beyond the standard of the day,—and a most intelligent, resolute, and ardent champion of the popular cause. He was connected by marriage with the family of John Hancock. To this circumstance, no doubt, may properly be ascribed some portion of his interest in the political movements of the time ;— while on the mind of Hancock, an intimacy with Mr Clark was calculated to have a strong and salutary influence. Their connexion led to a portion of the interesting occurrences of the 19th of April, 1775. The soul-stirring scenes of the great tragedy which was acted out on this spot, were witnessed by Mr Clark, from the door of his dwelling hard by. To perpetuate their recollection, he instituted, the following year, a service of commemoration. He delivered himself, an historical discourse of great merit, which was followed on the returns of the anniversary, till the end of the revolutionary war, in a series of addresses in the same strain, by the clergy of the neighboring towns. Mr Clark's instructive and eloquent narrative, in the appendix to the discourse, remains to this day one of the most important authorities for this chapter, in the history of the Revolution.

It may excite some surprise, that so great alacrity was evinced in the work of military preparation, by the town of Lexington, and other towns similarly situated in the colonies. How are we to account for the extraordinary fact, that a village not of the first class in size, and not in any respect so circumstanced as to require its citizens to stand forth, in the position of military resistance, should have taken such prompt and vigorous measures of a warlike character? This is a fact to be explained by a recurrence to the earlier history of the colonies. It is a truth, to which sufficient attention has not, perhaps, been given, in connexion with the history of the Revolution, that in the two preceding wars between Great Britain and France, the colonies had taken a very active and important part. The military records of those wars, as far as the province of Massachusetts Bay are concerned, are still in existence. The original muster rolls are preserved in the State House at Boston. I have examined a great many of them. They prove that the people of Massachusetts, between the years 1755 and 1763, performed an amount of military service, probably never exacted of any other people, living under a government professing to be free. Not a village in Massachusetts, but sent its sons to lay their bones in the West Indies, in Nova Scotia, and the Canadian wilderness. Judge Minot states, that in the year 1757, one third part of the effective men of Massachusetts were, in some way or other, in the field, and that the taxes imposed on real property in Boston, amounted to two thirds of the income. In 1759, the General Court, by way of excusing themselves to Governor Pownall for falling short of the military requisitions of that year, informed him, that the military service of the preceding year had amounted to one million of dollars. They nevertheless raised that year six thousand eight hundred men ; a force which contributed most essentially to the achievement of the great object of the campaign,— the reduction of Quebec. The population of Massachusetts and Maine, at that time, might have been half the present population of Massachusetts ; the amount of taxable property beyond all proportion less. Besides the hardships of voluntary service, the most distressing levies were made on the towns by impressment, enforced by all the rigors of martial law.

These are not the most affecting documents in our archives, to

show the nature of that school of preparation, in which the men of
1775 were reared. Those archives are filled with the tears of
desolate widows and bereaved parents. After the disastrous capitulation of Fort William Henry, in 1757, the governor of Massachusetts invited those who had relatives carried into captivity among
the Canadian Indians, to give information to the colonial secretary,
that order might be taken for their redemption. Many of the
original returns to this invitation are on file. Touching memorials!
Here an aged parent in Andover, transmits the name of his 'dear
son,' that he may have the benefit of 'the gracious design' of the
government. A poor widow at Newbury, states that her child,
who was made captive at what she calls 'Rogers' great fight,' was
but seventeen years old, when he left her. And old Jonathan
Preble of Maine, whose son and daughter-in-law were killed by
the Indians at Arrowsick Island, and six of their children, from the
age of twelve years down to three months, carried into captivity,
the same day, 'makes bold,' as he says, to send up the sad catalogue of their names. He apologizes for this freedom, on the
ground of 'having drank so deep' of this misery; and then apparently reflecting, that this was too tender an expression for an official paper, he strikes out the words, and simply adds, 'having been
deprived of so many of my family.' The original paper, with the
erasure and the correction, is preserved.

In fact, the land was filled, town and country,—and in proportion to its population, no town more than Lexington,—with men
who had seen service,—and such service too! There were few
villages in this part of the province which had not furnished re-
cruits for that famous corps of rangers which was commanded by
Rogers, and in which Stark served his military apprenticeship;—a
corps, whose duties went as far beyond the rigors of ordinary warfare, as that is more severe than a holiday parade. Their march
was through the untrodden by-paths of the Canadian frontier;—
the half-tamed savage, borrowing from civilization nothing but its
maddening vices and destructive weapons, was the ranger's sworn
enemy. Huntsman at once and soldier, his supply of provisions,
on many of his excursions, was the fortune of the chase, and a
draught from the mountain stream, that froze as it trickled from
the rocks. Instead of going into quarters, when the forest put on

its sere autumnal uniform of scarlet and gold,—winter,—Canadian winter,—dreary mid winter,—on frozen lakes, through ice-bound forests, from which the famished deer, chased by the gaunt wolf, was fain to fly to the settlements, called the poor ranger to the field of his duties. Sometimes he descended the lake on skates; sometimes he marched on snow-shoes, where neither baggage-wagon nor beast of burden could follow him, and with all his frugal store laden on his back. Not only was the foe he sought, armed with the tomahawk and scalping-knife, but the tortures of the fagot and the stake were in reserve for the prisoner, who, for wounds, or distance, or any other cause, could not readily be sold into an ignominious slavery among the Canadian French. Should I relate all the hardships of this service, I should expect almost to start the lid of that coffin ;—for it covers the remains of at least one brave heart, who could bear witness to their truth. Captain Spikeman, who fell on the 21st of January, 1757, raised his company, in which Stark, I believe, was a lieutenant, principally in this neighborhood. The journal of General Winslow contains the muster roll, and I find there the names of several inhabitants of Lexington. Edmund Munroe, (afterwards, with another of the same name, killed by one cannon ball at the battle of Monmouth), was of the staff in Rogers' regiment; and Robert Munroe, whose remains are gathered in that receptacle, was an ensign at the capture of Louisburg, in 1758. There could not have been less than twenty or thirty of the citizens of Lexington, who had learned the art of war in some department or other of the military colonial service. They had tasted its horrors in the midnight surprise of the savage foe, and they had followed the banners of victory under the old provincial leaders, Gridley, and Thomas, and Ruggles, and Frye, up to the ramparts of Quebec. No wonder that they started again at the sound of the trumpet; no wonder that men, who had followed the mere summons of allegiance and loyalty to the shores of lake Champlain, and the banks of the St Lawrence, should obey the cry of instinct, which called them to defend their homes. The blood which was not too precious to be shed upon the plains of Abraham, in order to wrest a distant colony from the dominion of France, might well be expected to flow like water, in defence of all that is dear to man.

From the commencement of 1775, a resort to extremities was manifestly inevitable ;—but the time and mode, in which it should take place, were wrapped in solemn uncertainty. The patriots of the highest tone, well knowing that it could not be avoided, did not wish it postponed. Warren burned for the decisive moment ;—young, beloved, gifted for a splendid career,—he was ready,—impatient for the conflict. The two Adamses and Hancock, bore, with scarcely suppressed discontent, the less resolute advances of some of their associates ;—and Quincy wrote from London, in December, 1774, in the following strain of devoted patriotism ; ' Let me tell you one very serious truth, in which we are all agreed, —your countrymen must seal their cause with their blood. They must now stand the issue ;—they must preserve a consistency of character ; THEY MUST NOT DELAY ; they must [resist to the death], or be trodden into the vilest vassalage,—the scorn, the spurn of their enemies, a by-word of infamy among all men !'

In anticipation of this impending crisis, the measures of military preparation, to which I have alluded, were taken. The royal governor of Massachusetts had served in the old French war, and did not undervalue his adversary, but adopted his measures of preparation as against a resolute foe. Officers in disguise were sent to Concord and Worcester, to explore the roads and passes, and gain information relative to the provincial stores. At Medford, the magazine was plundered. An unsuccessful attempt was made to seize the artillery at Salem. On the 30th of March, General Gage sent eleven hundred men out of Boston, and threw down the stone walls which covered some of the passes in the neighborhood. These indications sufficiently showed that an attempt to destroy the provincial stores at Concord and Worcester, might be expected ; a hostile excursion from Boston, on that errand, was daily anticipated, for some time before it took place ;—and proper measures were taken, by stationing two persons on the look out, in all the neighboring towns, to obtain and propagate the earliest intelligence of the movement.

In anxious expectation of the crisis, a considerable part of the people of Boston sought refuge in the country. Inclination prompted them to withdraw themselves from beneath the domination of what was now regarded as a hostile military power ; and patriotism suggested the expediency of diminishing, as far as possible, the number of those who, while they remained in Boston, were at the mercy of the royal governor ; and held as hostages for the submission of their countrymen.

In conjunction with the seizure of the province stores, the arrest of some of the most prominent of the patriotic leaders was threatened.   Hancock and Adams had been often designated by name, as peculiarly obnoxious, and on the adjournment of the provincial Congress, a strong opinion had been expressed by their friends that they ought not to return to the city.   Hancock yielded to the advice, and took up his abode in this place,—the spot where his father was born,—where he had himself passed a portion of his childhood, and where he found in his venerable connexion, Mr Clark, an associate of congenial temper.   Beneath the same hospitable roof, Samuel Adams also found a cordial welcome. Thus, my friends, your village became the place of refuge, and your fathers were constituted the guardians of these distinguished patriots, at a moment when a price was believed to be set on their heads.

Samuel Adams and John Hancock !—Do you ask why we should pause at their names ?   Let the proclamation of General Gage furnish the answer : ' I do hereby, in his Majesty's name, promise his most gracious pardon to all persons who shall forthwith lay down their arms, and return to the duties of peaceable subjects, excepting only from the benefit of such pardon, Samuel Adams and John Hancock, whose offences are of too flagitious a nature to admit of any other consideration than that of condign punishment.'

The flagitious offences of Hancock and Adams were their early unrelaxing, and fearless efforts, in defence of the rights of American freemen ; and the cordial cooperation of these men, in that great cause, unlike as they were in every thing else, is one of the most pleasing incidents of the history of the Revolution.   John Hancock would have been the spoiled child of fortune, if he had not been the chosen instrument of Providence.   His grandfather was for fifty-four years the pastor, with great authority, of this church, and his father, afterwards minister of Braintree, was born in Lexington.   John Hancock was left an orphan at the age of seven years, and from that period, passed much of his time in this village, and received a part of his education at the town school. After leaving college, he entered the family, and became associated in the business of his uncle, a distinguished citizen and a wealthy merchant in Boston, who shortly afterwards died, bequeathing to John Hancock a fortune of seventy thousand pounds sterling;— the largest estate, probably, which had ever been amassed in the colonies. He was thus left, at twenty-seven years of age, without parents, brought up in luxury, distinguished for personal appearance, voice, manners, and address, the master of a princely estate. He seemed, as it were, marked out by destiny, to pursue the tempting path of royal favor. He *was* accused of ambition. But what had he to gain by joining the austere ranks of those who were just commencing the great battle of liberty? He was charged with a love of display. But no change of public affairs could improve his private fortunes; and he had but to seek them through the paths of loyalty, and all the honors of the empire, pertaining in any measure to his position, are at his command, on either side of the Atlantic. The tempter did whisper to him, that he might lead a gay and luxurious existence, within the precincts of the court. But his heart was beneath yonder roof where his father was born. In the midst of all the enjoyments and temptations of London, he remembered the school where he had first learned to read his Bible; and exclaimed, amidst the seductions of the British metropolis, 'If I forget thee, O New-England, may my right hand forget her cunning.'

He witnessed the coronation of George III, and it was the immediate spectacle of a life of court attendance, that taught John Hancock to prize the independence of a Boston merchant,—of an American citizen. He returned from England, to plunge, heart and soul, into the contest for principle and for liberty. He scattered his princely wealth like ashes. He threw his property into the form in which it would be least productive to himself, and most beneficial to the industrious and suffering portion of the community. He built ships at a time, not when foreign trade was extending itself, but when new restrictions were daily laid upon the commerce of America, and the shipwrights were starving; and he built houses when real estate was rapidly sinking in value. He shunned personal danger as little as he spared his purse. On the retire-

63

ment of Peyton Randolph from the chair of Congress in May, 1775, he was called by the members of that venerable body to preside in their councils; and in that capacity, he had the singular good fortune to sign the commission of George Washington, and the immortal honor to affix his name first to the Declaration of Independence. To the solid qualities of character, he added all the graces of the old school; and as if to meet the taunts which were daily pointed at the rustic simplicity of the American cause, the enemies of the country beheld in its patriotic president an elegance of appearance and manners unsurpassed at their own court. When the rapid depreciation of continental paper had greatly increased the distresses of the people, Hancock instructed his agents at home to receive that poor discredited currency, with which his country was laboring to carry on the war, in payment of every thing due to him; and when asked his opinion in Congress, of the policy of an assault upon Boston, he recommended the measure, although it would lay half his property in ashes. During all the distresses, which preceded the commencement of hostilities, while Boston was sinking under the privations of the Port Bill, Hancock not only forbore the enforcement of his debts, but literally shared his diminished income with his suffering townsmen. Providence rewarded his warm-hearted and uncalculating patriotism with the highest honors of the country;—enabled him to build up his impaired estate out of the ashes of the Revolution; and gave him a place as bright and glorious, in the admiration of mankind, ' as if,' to use the words of Daniel Webster, ' his name had been written in letters of light on the blue arch of heaven, between Orion and the Pleiades.'

Samuel Adams was the counterpart of his distinguished associate in proscription. Hancock served the cause with his liberal opulence, Adams with his incorruptible poverty. His family, at times, suffered almost for the comforts of life, when he might have sold his influence over the councils of America for uncounted gold,— when he might have emptied the British treasury, if he would have betrayed his country. Samuel Adams was the last of the Puritans;—a class of men to whom the cause of civil and religious liberty on both sides of the Atlantic, is mainly indebted, for the great progress which it has made for the last two hundred years;

and when the Declaration of Independence was signed, that dispensation might be considered as brought to a close. At a time when the new order of things was inducing laxity of manners, and a departure from the ancient strictness, Samuel Adams clung with greater tenacity, to the wholesome discipline of the fathers. His only relaxation from the business and cares of life, was in the indulgence of a taste for sacred music, for which he was qualified by the possession of a melodious voice, and of a soul solemnly impressed with religious sentiment. Resistance of oppression was his vocation. On taking his second degree, he maintained the noble thesis, that it is ' lawful to resist the supreme magistrate, if the commonwealth cannot otherwise be preserved.' Thus, at the age of twenty-one, twenty years before the stamp act was thought of, Samuel Adams, from the cloisters of Harvard college, announced in two lines, the philosophy of the American Revolution. His after life showed that his practice was not below his theory. On leaving college, he devoted himself for some years to the profession of divinity ; but he gave himself afterwards wholly to the political service of the country. He was among the earliest and ablest writers on the patriotic side. He caught the plain, downright style of the commonwealth in Great Britain. More than most of his associates, he understood the efficacy of personal intercourse with the people. It was Samuel Adams, more than any other individual, who brought the question home to their bosoms and firesides, —not by profound disquisitions and elaborate reports,—though these in their place were not spared,—but in the caucus, the club-room, at the green-dragon, in the ship-yards, in actual conference, man to man, and heart to heart. He was forty-six years of age, when he first came to the House of Representatives. There he was, of course, a leader ; a member of every important committee ; the author of many of the ablest and boldest state papers of the time. But the throne of his ascendency was in Faneuil Hall. As each new measure of arbitrary power was announced from across the Atlantic, or each new act of menace and violence, on the part of the officers of the government or of the army, occurred in Boston,—its citizens, oftentimes in astonishment and perplexity, rallied to the sound of his voice, in Faneuil Hall ; and there, as from the crowded gallery or the moderator's chair, he animated, enlightened, fortified, and roused the admiring throng, he seemed to gather them together beneath the ægis of his indomitable spirit, as a hen gathereth her chickens under her wings, With his namesake, John Adams, Warren, and Hancock, he perceived the inevitable necessity of striking for independence, a considerable time before it was generally admitted. In some branches of knowledge he was excelled by other men ; but one thing he knew thoroughly, and that was liberty. He began with it early, studied it long, and possessed the whole science of it. He knew it, class and order,—genus and species,—root and branch. With him it was no matter of frothy sentiment. He knew it was no gaudy May-day flower, peeping through the soft verdant sods of spring, and opening its painted petals as a dew cup for midnight fairies to sip at. He knew it was an austere and tardy growth,—the food of men, long hungering for their inalienable rights,—a seed scattered broad cast on a rough, though genial soil,—ripening beneath lowering skies and autumnal frosts,—to be reaped with a bloody sickle. Instead of quailing, his spirit mounted and mantled with the approach of the crisis. Chafed and fretted with the minor irritations of the early stages of the contest, he rose to a religious tranquillity, as the decisive hour drew nigh. In all the excitement and turmoil of the anxious days that preceded the explosion, he was of the few, who never lost their balance. He was thoughtful,—serious almost to the point of sternness,—resolute as fate ; but cheerful himself, and a living spring of animation to others. He stood among the people a pillar of safety and strength :—

> As some tall cliff, that lifts its awful form,
> Swells from the vale, and midway leaves the storm ;
> Though round its breast the rolling clouds are spread,
> Eternal sunshine settles on its head.

And so he looked forward to the impending struggle, as the consummation of a great design, of which not man but God had laid the foundation stone on the rock of Plymouth ; and when on the morning of the day you now commemorate, the vollies of fire-arms from this spot, announced to him and his companion, in the neighboring field, that the great battle of liberty had begun, he threw up his arms, and exclaimed, in a burst of patriotic rapture, ' O, what a glorious morning is this !'

Yes, fellow citizens, such was the exclamation of Samuel Adams, when a thousand British troops were in possession of your village, and seven of your citizens were struggling in the agonies of death. His prophetic soul told him, that the divine form of his country's liberty would follow on, the next personage in that fearful but all-glorious pageant. He saw that the morning sun, whose first slanting beams were dancing on the tops of the hostile bayonets, would not more surely ascend the heavens, than the sun of independence would arise on the clouded fortunes of his country. The glory he foresaw has come to pass. Two generations attest the truth of his high-souled prophecy. And you, 'village Hampdens, who, with dauntless breast' withstood, not 'the petty tyrant of your fields,' but the dread and incensed sovereign of a mighty empire, when he came in his embattled hosts to subdue you; you, who sealed your devotion to the cause by the last great attestation of sincerity, your blood has not sunk unprofitably into the ground! If your spirits are conscious of the honors we now pay your relics, you behold in the wide-spread prosperity of the growing millions of America, the high justification of that generous impulse, which led you, on that glorious morning, to the field of death!

On Saturday, the 15th of April, the provincial Congress, then in session at Concord, adjourned to meet again on the 10th of May. It is probable that the intelligence of this event had not reached General Gage in Boston, when on the same day, he commenced his arrangements for the projected expedition. The grenadiers and light infantry were relieved from their several stations in Boston, and concentrated on the common, under pretence of learning a new military exercise. At midnight following, the boats of the transport ships, which had been previously repaired, were launched, and moored under the sterns of the men-of-war in the harbor. Dr Warren, on his way home from the Congress on Saturday, had expressed to the family of Mr Clark his firm persuasion, that the moment was at hand when blood would flow. He justly regarded the military movements of the following night, as a confirmation of this opinion, and despatched Colonel Paul Revere the next day to this place, to bring the intelligence to Messrs Hancock and Adams. They naturally inferred from the magnitude of the preparations, that their own seizure could not be the sole object, and advised the committee of safety, then sitting at West Cambridge, to order the distribution, into the neighboring towns, of the stores collected at Concord. Colonel Paul Revere, on his return to town on Sunday, concerted with his friends in Charlestown, that two lights should be shown from the steeple of the North Church, if the British troops should cross in boats to Cambridge, and one, if they should march out, over Boston neck.

Wednesday, the 19th, was fixed upon as the eventful day. Ten or twelve British officers were sent out the day before, on horseback, who dined at Cambridge; and at nightfall scattered themselves on the roads to Concord, to prevent the communication of intelligence from the town. Early information of this fact was brought to this place by Solomon Brown,* of Lexington, who returned late from Boston market on the afternoon of the 18th, and passed them and was passed by them several times, as they sometimes rode forward or fell back on the road. A despatch to the same effect was also sent by Mr Gerry, of the committee of safety, at West Cambridge, to Mr Hancock, whose answer, still preserved, evinces the calmness and self-possession which he maintained at the approaching crisis. In consequence of this information, a guard of eight men, under the late Colonel William Munroe, then a sergeant in the Lexington company, was marched, in the course of the evening, to Mr Clark's house, for the protection of Messrs Adams and Hancock. At the same time, Messrs Sanderson, Loring,† and Brown, were sent up towards Concord, to watch the movement of the officers. They came upon them unawares in Lincoln, and fell into their hands. About midnight, Colonel Paul Revere, who had left Boston, by direction of Dr Warren, as soon as the movement of the troops was discovered, and had passed by the way of Charlestown, (where he narrowly escaped two British officers,) through Medford and West Cambridge, giving the alarm at every house on the way,—arrived at Mr Clark's with despatches from Dr Warren for Hancock and Adams. Passing on towards Concord, Revere also fell into the hands of the British officers in Lin-

* Mr Brown is still living, but from the distance of his place of residence, was not able to attend with the other survivors of Captain Parker's company, (eleven in number), the celebration of the anniversary.

† Mr Loring was present on the stage, at the delivery of this address.

coln, but not till he had had an opportunity of communicating his errand to young Dr Prescott of Concord, whom he overtook on the road. At the moment Revere was arrested by the officers, Prescott succeeded in forcing his way through them, and thus carried the alarm to Concord. The intelligence sent by Dr Warren to Messrs Hancock and Adams, purported that 'a large body of the king's troops, (supposed to be a brigade of 1200 or 1500 men), had embarked in boats from Boston.'

After the detention of an hour or two in Lincoln, the British officers were informed by Colonel Revere, of all the measures he had taken to alarm the country ; and deemed it expedient for their own safety to hasten back toward Boston. On their way toward Lexington, they put many questions to their prisoners, as to the place where Messrs Adams and Hancock were residing. As they approached Lexington, the alarm bell was ringing, and a volley was fired by some of the militia, then assembling on the green. Upon this, they hastened their flight, and just as they entered the village, their prisoners escaped from them. Colonel Revere repaired to the house of Mr Clark, and the general apprehensions relative to his distinguished guests having been confirmed by the interrogatories of the British officers, Messrs Hancock and Adams were persuaded with great difficulty to withdraw from the immediate vicinity of the road. On the return of Colonel Revere to the centre of the village, he met Captain Thaddeus Bowman coming up the road, in full gallop, with the news that the British troops were at hand.

It was at this time between four and five o'clock in the morning. Three messengers had been sent down the road, to ascertain the approach of the British army. The two first brought no tidings, and the troops were not discovered by the third, Captain Bowman, till they were far advanced into the town. They had been put in motion about seven hours before on Boston common. They crossed in boats, near the spot where the court house now stands in East Cambridge ; and there took up their march, from eight hundred to one thousand strong, grenadiers, light infantry, and marines. They crossed the marshes, inclining to their right, and came into the Charlestown and West Cambridge road, near the foot of Prospect hill. It was a fine, moonlight, chilly night. No hostile movement was made by them, till they reached West Cambridge. The committee of safety had been in session in that place, at Wetherbee's tavern; and three of its distinguished members, vice-president Gerry, Colonel Lee, and Colonel Orne, had taken up their lodgings for the night at the same house. The village having been alarmed by Colonel Revere, was on the alert at the approach of the army; and Messrs Gerry, Lee, and Orne had risen from their beds and gone to their windows to contemplate the strange spectacle. As the troops came up on a line with the house, a sergeant's guard was detached to search it; and the members of the committee had but a moment to escape by flight into the adjacent fields.

It was now perceived by Colonel Smith, who commanded the British detachment, that the country, on all sides, was in a state of alarm. The news had spread in every direction, both by the way of Charlestown and Roxbury. The lights in the North Church steeple had given the signal before the troops had fairly embarked. It was propagated by the alarm bell, from village to village; volleys from the minute men were heard in every direction;—and as fast as light and sound could travel, the news ran through Massachusetts, I might say through New-England; and every man as he heard it sprang to his arms. As a measure of precaution, under these circumstances, Colonel Smith detached six companies of light infantry and marines, to move forward under Major Pitcairne and take possession of the bridges at Concord, in order to cut off the communication with the interior of the country. At the same time, also, he sent back to General Gage and asked a reinforcement, a piece of forethought which saved all that was saved of the fortunes of that day. Before these detached companies could reach Lexington, the officers already mentioned were hastening down the road; and falling in with Major Pitcairne, informed him that five hundred men were assembling on Lexington green to resist the troops. In consequence of this exaggerated account, the advance party was halted, to give time for the grenadiers to come up.

And thus, fellow citizens, having glanced at all the other movements of this memorable night, we are prepared to contemplate that which gives interest to them all. The company assembled on this spot, and which had been swelled by the British officers to five hundred, consisted in reality of sixty or seventy of the militia of Lexington. On the receipt of the information of the excursion of the officers and the movement of the troops, a guard had been set, as we have seen, at the house of Mr Clark, the evening before. After the receipt of the intelligence brought by Revere, the alarm bell was rung; and a summons sent round to the militia of the place, to assemble on the green. This was done by direction of the commander of the company, Captain John Parker,—an officer of approved firmness and courage. He had probably served in the French war, and gave many proofs, on this trying occasion, of a most intrepid spirit. About two o'clock in the morning, the drum beat to arms, the roll was called, and about one hundred and thirty answered to their names;—some of them, alas,—whose ashes, now gathered in that depository, invoke the mournful honors of this day,—for the last time on earth. Messengers were sent down the road, to bring intelligence of the troops; and the men were ordered to load with powder and ball. One of the messengers soon returned with the report, that there were no troops to be seen. In consequence of this information, as the night was chilly, in order to spare the men, already harassed by the repeated alarms which had been given, and to relieve the anxiety of their families, the militia were dismissed; but ordered to await the return of the other expresses sent down to gain a knowledge of the movements of the enemy, and directed to be in readiness, at the beat of the drum. About half the men sought refuge from the chill of the night, in the public house still standing on the edge of the green; the residue retired to their homes in the neighborhood. One of the messengers was made prisoner by the British, who took effectual precautions to arrest every person on the road. Benjamin Wellington, hastening to the centre of the village, was intercepted by their advanced party, and was the first person seized by the enemy in arms, in the revolutionary war. In consequence of these precautions, the troops remained undiscovered till within a mile and a half of this place, and when there was scarce time for the last messenger, Captain Thaddeus Bowman, to return with the tidings of their certain approach.

A new, the last alarm, is now given:—the bell rings,—guns are

64

fired in haste on the green,—the drum beats to arms. The militia, within reach of the sound, hasten to obey the call, sixty or seventy in number, and are drawn up in order, a very short distance in rear of the spot on which we stand. The British troops, hearing the American drum, regard it as a challenge, and are halted at the distance of one hundred and sixty rods, to load their guns. At the sight of this preparation, a few of the militia, on the two extremities of the line, naturally feeling the madness of resisting a force outnumbering their own, ten to one, and supposed to be near twice as large as it was, showed a disposition to retreat. Captain Parker ordered them to stand their ground, threatened death to any man who should fly,—but directed them not to fire unless first fired upon. The commanders of the British forces advance some rods in front of their troops. With mingled threats and oaths, they bid the Americans lay down their arms and disperse, and call to their own troops, now rushing furiously on,—the light infantry on the right of the church in which we are now assembled, and the grenadiers on the left,—to fire. The order not being followed with instant obedience, is renewed with oaths and imprecations,—the officers discharge their pistols,—and the foremost platoon fires over the heads of the Americans. No one falls, and John Munroe, standing next to a kinsman of the same family name, calmly observed that they were firing nothing but powder. Another general volley, aimed with fatal precision, succeeds. Ebenezer Munroe replied to the remark just made, that something more than powder was then fired, as he was shot himself, in the arm. At the same moment, several dropped around them, killed and wounded. Captain Parker now felt the necessity of directing his men to disperse; but it was not till several of them had returned the British fire, and some of them more than once, that this handful of brave men were driven from the field.

Of this gallant little company, seven were killed and ten wounded, a quarter part at least of the number drawn up, and a most signal proof of the firmness with which they stood the British fire. Willingly would I do justice to the separate merit of each individual of this heroic band; but tradition has not furnished us the means. A few interesting anecdotes have, however, been preserved. Jedediah Munroe was one of the wounded. Not disheartened by this circumstance, instead of quitting the field, he marched with his company, in pursuit of the enemy, to Concord, and was killed in the afternoon. Ebenezer Munroe, Jr, received two wounds, and a third ball through his garments. William Tidd, the second in command of the company, was pursued by Major Pitcairne, on horseback up the north road, with repeated cries to stop, or he was a dead man. Having leaped the fence, he discharged his gun at his pursuer, and thus compelled him in turn to take flight. Robert Munroe was killed with Parker, Muzzy, and Jonathan Harrington, on or near the line where the company was formed. Robert Munroe had served in the French wars. He was the standard-bearer of his company at the capture of Louisburg, in 1758. He now lived to see set up for the first time, the banner of his country's independence. He saw it raised amidst the handful of his brave associates ; alas, that he was struck down, without living, like you, venerable survivors of that momentous day, to behold it, as it dallies with the wind, and scorns the sun, blest of heaven and of men, —at the head of the triumphant hosts of America! All hail to the glorious ensign! Courage to the heart and strength to the hand, to which, in all time, it shall be entrusted! May it for ever wave in honor, in unsullied glory, and patriotic hope, on the dome of the capitol, on the country's strong holds, on the tented plain, on the wave-rocked top-mast. Wheresoever on the earth's surface, the eye of the American shall behold it, may he have reason to bless it. On whatsoever spot it is planted, there may freedom have a foot-hold, humanity a brave champion, and religion an altar. Though stained with blood in a righteous cause, may it never, in any cause, be stained with shame. Alike, when its gorgeous folds shall wanton in lazy holiday triumph, on the summer breeze, and its tattered fragments be dimly seen through the clouds of war, may it be the joy and pride of the American heart. First raised in the cause of right and liberty, in that cause alone, may it for ever spread out its streaming blazonry to the battle and the storm. First raised in this humble village, and since borne victoriously across the continent and on every sea, may virtue, and freedom, and peace for ever follow, where it leads the way! The banner which was raised on this spot, by a village hero,* was not that whose glorious

* Joseph Simonds was the ensign of the Lexington company on the 19th of April, 1775.

folds are now gathered round the sacred depository of the ashes of his brave companions. He carried the old provincial flag of Massachusetts Bay. As it had once been planted in triumph, on the walls of Louisburg, Quebec, and Montreal, it was now raised in a New-England village, among a band of brave men, some of whom had followed it to victory in distant fields, and now rallied beneath it, in the bosom of their homes, determined, if duty called them, to shed their blood in its defence. May Heaven approve the omen. The ancient standard of Massachusetts Bay was displayed for the confederating colonies, before the STAR-SPANGLED BANNER OF THE UNION had been flung to the breeze. Should the time come, (which God avert), when that glorious banner shall be rent in twain, may Massachusetts, who first raised her standard in the cause of United America, be the last by whom that cause is deserted; and as many of her children, who first raised that standard on this spot, fell gloriously in its defence, so may the last son of Massachusetts, to whom it shall be entrusted, not yield it but in the mortal agony!

Harrington's was a cruel fate. He fell in front of his own house, on the north of the common. His wife, at the window, saw him fall, and then start up, the blood gushing from his breast. He stretched out his hands towards her, as if for assistance, and fell again. Rising once more on his hands and knees, he crawled across the road towards his dwelling. She ran to meet him at the door, but it was to see him expire at her feet. Hadley and Brown were pursued, and fell, after they had left the common. Porter, of Woburn, was unarmed. He had been taken prisoner on the road, before the British army reached Lexington. Attempting to make his escape, when the firing commenced, he was shot within a few rods of the common. Four of the company went into the meeting-house which stood on this spot, for a supply of ammunition. They had brought a cask of powder from an upper loft into the gallery, and removed its head. At this moment, the house was surrounded by the British force, and the discharge of musketry and the cries of the wounded announced that the work of death was begun. One of the four secreted himself in the opposite gallery. Another, Simonds, cocked his gun, and lay down by the open cask of powder, determined never to be taken alive. Comee and Harrington resolved to force their way from the house, and in this desperate attempt, Comee was wounded and Harrington killed. History,—Roman history,—does not furnish an example of bravery that outshines that of Jonas Parker. A truer heart did not bleed at Thermopylæ. He was the next door neighbor of Mr Clark, and had evidently imbibed a double portion of his lofty spirit. Parker was often heard to say, that be the consequences what they might, and let others do what they pleased, he would never run from the enemy. He was as good as his word,—better. Having loaded his musket, he placed his hat, containing his ammunition, on the ground between his feet, in readiness for a second charge. At the second fire he was wounded, and sunk upon his knees; and in this condition discharged his gun. While loading it again, upon his knees, and striving in the agonies of death to redeem his pledge, he was transfixed by a bayonet; and thus died on the spot where he first stood and fell.

These were a portion of the terrors of this blood-stained field; but how shall I describe the agonizing scene which presented itself, that fearful night and the following day, to every family in Lexington?—The husband, the father, the brother, the son, gone forth on the errand of peril and death. The aged, the infirm, the unprotected, left, without a guardian, at the desolate fireside, at this dismal moment, awaiting the instant intelligence of some fatal disaster;—fainting under the exaggerated terrors of a state of things so new and trying;—or fleeing, half clad and bewildered, to the covert of the neighboring woods, there to pass the ensuing day,—famished,—exhausted,—distracted,—the prey of apprehensions worse than death. The work of destruction had begun. Who could assure them that their beloved ones were not among the first victims? The British force had moved on towards Concord, and the citizens of Lexington had joined in the pursuit. What new dangers awaited them on the march? The enemy was to return through their village,—exasperated with opposition,—what new horrors might not be expected from his vengeance?

While a considerable portion of the unarmed population of Lexington, dispersed through the nearest villages, or wandering in the open air, behind the neighboring hills, and in the adjacent woods, were at the mercy of these apprehensions, the British column moved on toward Concord. The limits of the occasion put it out of my power to dwell, as I would gladly do, on the gallant resistance made at Concord,—the heroic conduct of Davis, Hosmer, and Buttrick, and their brave companions,—the rapid and formidable gathering of the population, the precipitate and calamitous retreat of the enemy. On the return of this anniversary ten years ago, I endeavored, at the request of our fellow citizens of Concord, as far as I was able, to do justice to this interesting narrative, and to the distinguished and honorable part borne by the people of Concord, in the memorable transactions of the day. Time will only permit me now to repeat in brief, that the country poured down its population in every direction. They gathered on the hills that overlooked the road, like dark lowering clouds. Every patch of trees, every stream, covert, building, stone wall, was lined, to use the words of a British officer, with an unintermitted fire. A skirmish engaged the enemy at every defile and cross road. Through one of them Governor Brooks led up the men of Reading. At another, Captain Parker, with the Lexington militia, although seventeen of his number had been killed or wounded in the morning, returned to the conflict. Before they reached Lexington, the rout of the invaders was complete; and it was only by placing themselves in the front, and threatening instant death to their own men, if they continued their flight, that the British officers were able in some degree to check their disorder. Their entire destruction was prevented, by the arrival of reinforcements under Lord Percy, who reached Lexington in time to rescue the exhausted troops, on their flight from Concord. Lord Percy brought with him two pieces of artillery, which were stationed on points commanding the road. A cannon shot from one of them passed through the meeting-house which stood on this spot. These pieces were diligently served, and kept the Americans at bay; but the moment the retreat was resumed, the whole country was again alive.* It was a season of victory for the cause,—auspicious of the fortune of the Revolution;—but purchased with accumulated sacrifices on the part of Lexington. To cover their retreat, the British army set fire to the houses on the road; some were burned to the ground;

* See note B, at the end.

several injured; and three more of the brave citizens of Lexington were killed.

At length the eventful day is passed,—the doleful tocsin is hushed,—the dreadful voice of the cannon is still,—the storm has passed by. It has spent its fury on your devoted village,—your houses have been wrapped in flames,—your old men, women, and children have fled in terror from their firesides,—your brave sons have laid down their lives at the threshold of their dwellings, and the shades of evening settle down upon your population, worn with fatigue,—heavy with bereavement and sorrow. What is the character, and what are the consequences of the day?—It was one of those occasions, in which the duration of ages is compressed into a span. What was done and suffered on that day, will never cease to be felt, in its ulterior consequences, till all that is America has perished. In the lives of individuals, there are moments which give a character to existence;—moments too often through levity, indolence, or perversity, suffered to pass unimproved; but sometimes met with the fortitude, vigilance, and energy due to their momentous consequences. So, in the life of nations, there are all-important junctures, when the fate of centuries is crowded into a narrow space,—suspended on the results of an hour. With the mass of statesmen, their character is faintly perceived,—their consequences imperfectly apprehended,—the certain sacrifices exaggerated,—the future blessings dimly seen;—and some timid and disastrous compromise,—some faint-hearted temperament is patched up, in the complacency of short-sighted wisdom. Such a crisis was the period which preceded the 19th of April. Such a compromise the British ministry proposed, courted, and would have accepted most thankfully,—but not such was the patriotism nor the wisdom of those who guided the councils of America, and wrought out her independence. They knew, that in the order of that Providence, in which a thousand years are as one day, a day is sometimes as a thousand years. Such a day was at hand. They saw,—they comprehended,—they welcomed it;—they knew it was an era. They met it with feelings like those of Luther, when he denounced the sale of indulgences, and pointed his thunders at once —poor Augustine monk,—against the civil and ecclesiastical power of the church, the Quirinal and the Vatican. They courted the storm of war, as Columbus courted the stormy billows of the glorious ocean, from whose giddy curling tops he seemed to look out, as from a watch-tower, to catch the first hazy wreath in the west, which was to announce that a new world was found. The poor Augustine monk knew and was persuaded, that the hour had come, and he was elected to control it, in which a mighty revolution was to be wrought in the Christian church. The poor Genoese pilot knew in his heart, that he had, as it were, but to stretch out the wand of his courage and skill, and call up a new continent from the depths of the sea;—and Hancock and Adams, through the smoke and flames of the 19th of April, beheld the sun of their country's independence arise, with healing in his wings.

And you, brave and patriotic men, whose ashes are gathered in this humble place of deposit, no time shall rob you of the well-deserved meed of praise! You too perceived not less clearly than the more illustrious patriots whose spirit you caught, that the decisive hour had come. You felt with them, that it could not,—must not be shunned. You had resolved it should not. Reasoning, remonstrance had been tried; from your own town-meetings, from the pulpit, from beneath the arches of Faneuil Hall, every note of argument, of appeal, of adjuration, had sounded to the foot of the throne, and in vain. The wheels of destiny rolled on;—the great design of Providence must be fulfilled;—the issue must be nobly met, or basely shunned. Strange it seemed, inscrutable it was, that your remote and quiet village should be the chosen altar of the first great sacrifice. But so it was;—the summons came and found you waiting; and here in the centre of your dwelling places, within sight of the homes you were to enter no more, between the village church where your fathers worshipped, and the graveyard where they lay at rest, bravely and meekly, like Christian heroes, you sealed the cause with your blood. Parker, Munroe, Hadley, the Harringtons, Muzzy, Brown :—alas, ye cannot hear my words ;—no voice, but that of the archangel, shall penetrate your urns; but to the end of time your remembrance shall be preserved! To the end of time, the soil whereon ye fell is holy; and shall be trod with reverence, while America has a name among the nations !

And now ye are going to lie down beneath yon simple stone, which marks the place of your mortal agony. Fit spot for your last repose !

Where should the soldier rest, but where he fell !

For ages to come, the characters graven in the enduring marble shall tell the unadorned tale of your sacrifice; and ages after that stone itself has crumbled into dust, as inexpressive as yours, history,—undying history,—shall transmit the record! Aye, while the language we speak retains its meaning in the ears of men ;— while a sod of what is now the soil of America shall be trod by the foot of a freeman, your names and your memory shall be cherished !

65

NOTES.

Note A, to page 490.

The following is the list of Captain Parker's company, as they stood enrolled on the 19th of April, 1775.

Those marked with an asterisk, were present at the celebration on the 20th of April, 1835.

Blodget Isaac
Bowman Francis
Bridge John
Bridge Joseph
Brown Francis, sergeant, wounded
Brown James
Brown John, killed
Brown Solomon, living
Buckman John
Chandler John
Chandler John, Jr
Child Abijah
Comee Joseph, wounded
Cutter Thomas
*Durant Isaac, living
Eastabrook Joseph
Farmer Nathaniel, wounded
Fessenden Nathan
Fessenden Thomas
*Fisk Dr Joseph, living
Green Isaac
Grimes William
Hadley Benjamin
Hadley Ebenezer
Hadley Samuel, killed
Hadley Thomas
Harrington Caleb, killed
Harrington Daniel, clerk
Harrington Ebenezer
Harrington Jeremiah
Harrington John

Harrington Jonathan
Harrington Jonathan, Jr, killed
Harrington Jonathan, 3d, living
Harrington Moses
Harrington Thaddeus
Harrington Thomas
Harrington William
Hastings Isaac
*Hosmer John, living
Lock Amos
Lock Benjamin, living
*Loring Jonathan, living
Loring Joseph
Marrett Amos
*Mason Daniel, living
Mason Joseph
Mead Abner
Merriam Benjamin
Merriam William
Mulliken Nathaniel
Munroe Asa
Munroe Ebenezer
Munroe Ebenezer, Jr, wounded
Munroe Edmund, lieutenant
Munroe George
Munroe Isaac, Jr, killed
Munroe Jedediah, wounded in morning, killed in the afternoon.
Munroe John
Munroe John, Jr
Munroe Philemon

Munroe Robert, killed
Munroe William, orderly sergeant
*Munroe William, Jr, living
Muzzy Amos
*Parker Ebenezer, living
Parker John, captain,
Parker Jonas, killed
Parker Thaddeus
Parkhurst John
Pierce Solomon, wounded
Porter Asahel, of Woburn, killed
Prince, a negro, wounded
Raymond John, killed
Reed Hammond
Reed Josiah, living
Reed Joshua
Reed Nathan
Reed Robert
Reed Thaddeus
Reed William
Robbins John, wounded
Robbins Thomas
Robinson Joseph
Sanderson Elijah
Sanderson Samuel
*Simonds Ebenezer, living
Simonds Joseph, ensign

Simonds Josiah
Simonds Joshua
Smith Abraham
Smith David
Smith Ebenezer
Smith Jonathan
Smith Joseph
Smith Phineas
Smith Samuel
Smith Thaddeus
Smith William
Stearns Asahel
Stone Jonas
Tidd John, wounded
Tidd Samuel
Tidd William
Viles Joel
White Ebenezer
Williams John
Wellington Benjamin
Wellington Timothy
Winship John
Winship Simeon
Winship Thomas
Wyman James
Wyman Nathaniel

Note B, to page 518.

The proper limits of the occasion precluded a detail of the interesting occurrences of the retreat and pursuit from Lexington to Charlestown. One portion of these were commemorated at Danvers, on the 20th of April, 1835. Next to Lexington, Danvers suffered more severely than any other town. Seven of the Danvers company were killed. On the late return of the anniversary, the corner-stone of a monument to their memory was laid at Danvers, with affecting ceremonies, and a highly interesting address was delivered by Daniel P. King, Esq., of that place.

The following return of all the killed and wounded, is taken from the Appendix to Mr Phinney's pamphlet :

LEXINGTON. *Killed in the morning.*—Jonas Parker, Robert Munroe, Samuel Hadley, Jonathan Harrington, Jr, Isaac Muzzy, Caleb Harrington, John Brown.—7.

Killed in the afternoon.—Jedediah Munroe, John Raymond, Nathaniel Wyman.
—3.

Wounded in the morning.—John Robbins, Solomon Pierce, John Tidd, Joseph Comee, Ebenezer Munroe, Jr, Thomas Winship, Nathaniel Farmer, Prince Estabrook, Jedediah Munroe.—9.

Wounded in the afternoon.—Francis Brown.—1.

CAMBRIDGE. *Killed.*--Wm. Marcy, Moses Richardson, John Hicks, Jason Russell, Jabez Wyman, Jason Winship.—6.

Wounded.--Samuel Whittemore.—1.

Missing.—Samuel Frost, Seth Russell.—2.

CONCORD. *Wounded.*—Charles Miles, Nathan Barnet, Abel Prescott.—3.

NEEDHAM.—Lieut. John Bourn, Elisha Mills, Amos Mills, Nathaniel Chamberlain, Jonathan Parker.—5.

Wounded.—Eleazer Kinsbury,   Tolman.—2.

SUDBURY. *Killed.*—Josiah Haynes, Asahel Reed.—2.

Wounded.—Joshua Haynes, Jr.--1.

ACTON. *Killed.*—Capt. Isaac Davis, Abner Hosmer, James Hayward.—3.

BEDFORD. *Killed.*—Jonathan Wilson.—1. *Wounded.*—Job Lane.—1.

WOBURN. *Killed.*—Asahel Porter, Daniel Thompson.—2.

Wounded.—George Reed, John Bacon,   Johnson.—3.

MEDFORD. *Killed.*—Henry Putnam, William Polly.—2.

CHARLESTOWN. *Killed.*—James Miller, C. Barber's son.—2.

WATERTOWN. *Killed.*—Joseph Coolidge.—1.

FRAMINGHAM. *Wounded.*—Daniel Hemmenway.—1.

DEDHAM. *Killed.*—Elias Haven. *Wounded.*—Israel Everett.

STOW. *Wounded.*—Daniel Conant.

ROXBURY. *Missing.*—Elijah Seaver.

BROOKLINE. *Killed.*—Isaac Gardner, Esq.—1.

BILLERICA. *Wounded.*—John Nickols, Timothy Blanchard.

CHELMSFORD. *Wounded.*—Aaron Chamberlain, Oliver Barron.—2.

SALEM. *Killed.*—Benjamin Pierce.

NEWTON. *Wounded.*—Noah Wiswell.

DANVERS. *Killed.*—Henry Jacobs, Samuel Cook, Ebenezer Goldthwait, George Southwick, Benjamin Daland, Jotham Webb, Perley Putnam.—7.

Wounded.—Nathan Putnam, Dennis Wallace.—2.

Missing.—Joseph Bell.—1.

BEVERLY. *Killed.*—Reuben Kenyme.—1.

Wounded.—Nathaniel Cleves, Samuel Woodbury, William Dodge, 3d.—3.

LYNN. *Killed.*—Abednego Ramsdell, Daniel Townsend, William Flint, Thomas Hadley.—4.

Wounded.—Joshua Felt, Timothy Munroe.—2.

Missing.—Josiah Breed.—1.

TOTAL. *Killed, 49.— Wounded, 36.—Missing, 5.*

ORATION

DELIVERED ON THE FOURTH DAY OF JULY, 1835, BEFORE THE CIT-
IZENS OF BEVERLY, WITHOUT DISTINCTION OF PARTY.

—

WHEN our fathers united in resistance to the oppressive measures of the British ministry, a few only of the leading patriots, and
those principally of Massachusetts, contemplated the establishment
of an independent government. They were unanimously determined to assert their rights, and to stand or fall in their defence;
but the mass of the people desired and expected a reconciliation.
There is preserved a letter of Washington, written from Philadelphia, on the 9th of October, 1774, at which place he was in attendance, as a member of the first revolutionary Congress. It is
addressed to Captain McKenzie, an officer of the British army in
Boston, with whom Washington had served in the former war. It
probably gives the precise state of the feelings of the patriots, both
in and out of Congress, with the exception of a very few bold,
far-reaching,—and I might almost say inspired,—individuals, who
went far beyond their age, and knew that separation and independence were inevitable. It contains unquestionably the feelings and
opinions of Washington himself. 'I think,' says he, 'I can announce it as a fact, that it is not the wish nor the interest of the
government of Massachusetts, or any other government upon this
continent, separately or collectively, to set up for independence;
but this you may rely upon, that none of them will ever submit to
the loss of those valuable rights and privileges, which are essential
to the inhabitants of every free state, and without which life, liberty,

and property are rendered totally insecure.'* The address to the king, which was adopted by Congress a short time after this letter was written, contains the most solemn protestations of loyalty ;—and after setting forth, in strong language, the views entertained in America of the ministerial policy, it adds, ' these sentiments are extorted from hearts that would much more willingly bleed in your Majesty's service.'

I have no doubt these and numerous other like protestations were entirely sincere ; and I quote them to show, in the clearest manner, that the revolutionary struggle was a contest for principle, in which our fathers engaged with reluctance, and that the torch of independence was not kindled by the unholy fire of personal ambition. But the measures of the British ministry were conceived in the lofty spirit of offended power, dealing with disaffected colonial subjects. The sovereign considered the prerogatives of majesty to be invaded. The crisis was beyond the grasp of common minds. The government and people of England,—and perhaps I should add the people of America,—were unconscious that a state of things existed, vastly transcending the sphere of ordinary politics.

It was not possible, that the great controversy should be settled by any common mode of adjustment. A change in the British constitution, by which the colonies should have been admitted to a full representation in parliament, would probably have restored harmony. But this was rejected even by the most enlightened friends of America in the British parliament. After alternate measures of inadequate conciliation and feeble and irritating coercion, the sword is drawn. The wound of which Chatham spoke, —the *vulnus immedicabile*, the wound for which, in all the British Gilead, there was not one drop of balm,—the wound, which a child, a madman, a thoughtless moment might inflict, and did inflict,—a wretched project to knock the trunnions off a half a dozen iron six-pounders, and throw a few barrels of flour into the river at Concord,—this incurable wound, which not parliaments, nor ministers, nor kings, to the end of time, could heal,—is struck. When

---

* Washington's Works, Vol. II, p. 401. In making this citation, I would acknowledge my obligations to Mr Sparks' invaluable collection of the Writings of Washington, particularly the Appendix to the second volume, for the greater portion of the historical materials made use of in this address.

the sun went down on the 18th of April, 1775, England and America, inflamed as they were, might yet, under a great and generous constitutional reform, have been led by an infant's hand, in the silken bonds of union. When the sun rose on the 19th of April, hooks of steel could not have held them together. And yet, even yet, the hope of an amicable adjustment is not wholly abandoned. The armies of America, under the command of her beloved Washington, are in the field; but near a month after he was appointed, another petition to the king, breathing the warmest spirit of loyalty, was adopted by Congress. But a twelvemonth passes by,—that petition is unavailing,—war, flagrant war, rages from Carolina to Maine,—the heights of Charlestown had already flowed with blood,—Falmouth is wrapped in flames,—seventeen thousand German troops, in addition to twenty-five thousand British veterans, are organized into an army destined to trample the spirit of the Revolution into bloody dust, and the people of America are declared to be out of the protection, though subject to the power of the crown, abandoned to a free hunt, by all the dogs of war. It was then, that the hope of accommodation was abandoned; and the cup of reconciliation, drained to its dregs, was cast away. A son of Massachusetts, to use his own language, ' crossed the Rubicon.'

In the measures touching the final renunciation of allegiance to Great Britain, John Adams took the lead; the first individual, as it seems to me, who formed and expressed a distinct idea of American independence. In a letter written in the month of October, 1754, when he was himself but twenty years old, while France and her Indian allies stood, like a wall of fire, against the progress of the Americans westward, he predicted the expulsion of the French from the continent, and the establishment of an independent government, on the basis of the union of the colonies, fortified by a controlling naval power. Such was the vision of Adams, before the open commencement of the war which removed the French from the continent; long before the new financial policy of Great Britain had woke the thunders of James Otis and Patrick Henry; twenty-one years before the blood of Lexington was shed. For twenty-one years at least, John Adams had cherished the vision of independence. He had seen one war fought through in singular

528EVERETT'S ORATIONS.

accordance with the destiny he had foretold for his country. He had caught and fanned the first sparks of patriotic disaffection. His tongue,—his pen,—in thoughts that breathe and words that burn,—had discoursed to the understandings and hearts of his fellow citizens. He had spurned the bribes of office; he had burst the bonds of friendship; and identifying himself, as well he might, with his beloved country, he had said to the friend of his heart,— who unhappily differed from him in politics,—in the moment of their last separation: 'I know that Great Britain has determined on her system, and that very fact determines me on mine. You know that I have been constant and uniform in opposition to all her measures. The die is now cast; I have passed the Rubicon; swim or sink, live or die, with my country, is my unalterable determination.'

On the 6th of May, 1776, John Adams moved a resolution, in Congress, that the colonies, which had not already done so, should establish independent systems of government; and this resolution, after having been strenuously debated for nine days, passed. The deed was done,—but the principle must be asserted. On the 7th of June, by previous concert, resolutions to that effect were moved by Richard Henry Lee, of Virginia, and seconded by John Adams of Massachusetts. They were debated in committee of the whole, on Saturday, the 8th, and again on Monday, the 10th, on which last day the first resolution was reported to the House, in the following form; 'That these united colonies are, and of right ought to be, free and independent States; that they are absolved from all allegiance to the British crown; and that all political connexion between them and the state of Great Britain is, and ought to be, totally dissolved.' The final decision of this resolution was postponed till the first day of July, but in the meanwhile it was, with characteristic simplicity, resolved, in order 'that no time be lost, in case the Congress agree thereto, that a committee be appointed to prepare a Declaration, to the effect of the first resolution.' The following day, a committee of five was chosen. Richard Henry Lee, who had moved the resolutions for independence, and would of course have been placed at the head of the committee, had been obliged, by sickness in his family, to go home, and Thomas Jefferson, of Virginia, the youngest member of the Congress, was elected first on the committee in his place. John Adams stood second on the committee; the other members were Benjamin Franklin, Roger Sherman, and Chancellor Livingston. Jefferson and Adams were, by their brethren on the committee, deputed to draw the Declaration, and the immortal work was performed by Jefferson.

Meantime the resolution had not yet been voted in Congress. The first day of July came, and at the request of a colony, the decision was postponed till the following day. On that day, July the 2d, it passed. The discussion of the Declaration continued for that and the following day. On the 3d of July, John Adams wrote to his wife, in the following memorable strain: 'Yesterday, the greatest question was decided, which was ever debated in America; and greater perhaps never was nor will be decided among men. A resolution was passed, without one dissenting colony,— That these United States are, and of right ought to be, free and independent States.' In another letter the same day, he wrote, 'The day is passed; the second of July, 1776, will be a memorable epoch in the history of America. I am apt to believe it will be celebrated by succeeding generations, as the great anniversary festival. It ought to be commemorated as the *Day of Deliverance*, by solemn acts of devotion to Almighty God. It ought to be solemnized with pomp, shows, games, sports, guns, bells, bonfires, and illuminations from one end of the continent to the other, from this time forward for ever. You will think me transported with enthusiasm; but I am not. I am well aware of the toil, blood, and treasure, that it will cost to maintain this Declaration, and support and defend these States; yet through all the gloom I can see rays of light and glory; I can see that the end is worth more than all the means; that posterity will triumph, although you and I may rue, which I hope we shall not.'

On the following day, the 4th, the Declaration was formally adopted by Congress, and proclaimed to the world;—the most important document in the political history of nations. As the day on which this solemn manifesto was made public, rather than that on which the resolution was adopted in private, was deemed the proper date of the country's independence, the Fourth of July has been consecrated as the National Anniversary; and will thus be celebrated, with patriotic zeal and pious gratitude, by the citizens of America, to the end of time.

Such it was ever regarded,—as such, for half a century, it had been hailed throughout the Union, in conformity with the prediction of the illustrious Adams. But what new sanctity did it not acquire, when nine years ago, and on the fiftieth return of the auspicious anniversary, it pleased Heaven to signalize it by the most remarkable and touching Providence, which merely human history records!

Who among us, fellow citizens, of years to comprehend the event, but felt an awe-struck sense of direct interposition, when told that Jefferson and Adams,—one the author of the immortal Declaration,—the other his immediate associate in preparing it,— 'the Colossus who sustained it in debate,' had departed this life together on the day, which their united act had raised into an era in the history of the world! Whose heart was not touched at beholding these patriarchs,—after all their joint labors,—their lofty rivalry,—their passing collisions,—their returning affections,—their long enjoyment of the blessings they had done so much to procure for their country,—closing their eventful career, on that day which they would themselves have chosen as their last,—that day which the kindest friend could not have wished them to survive!

This is the day, fellow citizens of Beverly, which we have met to commemorate ;—which you have done me the honor,—an humble stranger, known but to a very few of you,—to invite me to join you in celebrating. Had I looked only to my personal convenience, I could have found a justification for excusing myself from the performance of the duty you have assigned me. Had I followed my strong inclination, I should have been a listener to-day. A single consideration has induced me to obey your call ; and that is, that it proceeds from my fellow citizens, without distinction of party. I have ever been of opinion, that the anniversary of our national independence is never so properly celebrated, as when it brings us all together, as members of one great family. Our beloved and venerated Washington, in his farewell address, has declared party spirit to be 'the worst enemy' of a popular government ; and that 'the effort ought to be, by the force of public opinion, to mitigate and assuage it.'

It is of little avail, to agitate the question, whether the existence of parties, in a free state, is an unmingled evil, or an evil in some measure compensated by a mixture of good. It is unavailing, because it may be taken for granted, that in all free states,—in all countries in which representative governments exist, and places of honor, trust, and emolument are elective, where the press is free, and thought is free, and speech is free,—there parties must and will arise, by the very necessity of our nature. They cannot be avoided, while the state remains a free one ;—and no force or influence could be applied to control them, that would not be at the same time, destructive of liberty. There are no parties in Turkey, and none in China, though there are frequent rebellions in both. There were no parties in France, under Louis XIV. But wherever the constitution gives to the people a share in the government, —there parties spring up, under the influence of the different interests, opinions, and passions of men. The zeal and violence with which the party controversies are waged, will depend on the habits and temper of the people ; the nature of the questions at stake ; the mode in which they are decided ; the facility with which the will of the majority takes effect. In some countries, the dissensions of party have been kept almost always within comparatively reasonable limits ; and have never or rarely proceeded so far as to endanger the peace of society, shake the security of property, or bring upon the community the terrors of bloodshed and civil war. In other countries, the operation of causes too numerous to be detailed, has made the pages of their domestic annals a bloody record of violence and crime, of remorseless and maddening convulsions, in which peace, property, and life, have made common shipwreck.

In our own country, and in that from which, for the most part, we are descended,—but especially in our own country,—party dissensions have probably been attended with as little evil as is compatible with the frailty of our natures. It is generally admitted, that the opposite parties have acted as watchful sentinels of each other. It would not be easy to point out any free country in history, where so few of those deplorable acts of violence which go to the destruction of peace and life,—which constitute that most frightful of all despotisms, a *reign of terror*,—are set down to the reproach of a people. It has never happened in New-England,—and God grant it never may happen,—that lawless assemblages, inflamed by party rage, have encountered each other, with murderous weapons, in the streets ; and never, that a triumphant faction, feeling power and forgetting right, has made the sword of public justice to wreak the vengeance of party feeling.

Many causes might be assigned for an effect, which is so honorable to the character of the people, and which has contributed so much to the prosperity of the country. I take it a main cause has been the thoroughly popular organization of the government, and the frequent recurrence of the elections. When the majority of the people, at regularly returning periods of one, two, four, or six years, have it in their honor to bestow, wherever they please, all the places of trust and power, there is little temptation to proceed by violence against the opposite party. There is no need of resorting to banishment or the scaffold, to displace an obnoxious ruler or an odious opponent, when a single twelvemonth will reduce him to the level of the rest of the community. It is true the community is kept agitated and excited ; but it is not kept armed. Electioneering takes the place of all the other forms and manifestations of party spirit ;—and though the paroxysm of a contested election is not in itself a condition of society favorable to its peace or prosperity, it is far better than cruel hereditary feuds, and bloody contests of rival states, like those which stain the annals of ancient Greece, and of the Italian republics.

Other causes that assuage the violence of party, are the general diffusion of knowledge and the multiplication of liberal pursuits. Ignorance is the hotbed of party prejudice, and party detraction. A people who read little, and that little exclusively the production of the partisan press, may be grossly duped as to the condition and interests of the country,—the designs and actions of parties,—and the characters of men. But an enlightened people, whose minds are stored with knowledge,—who read, observe, and reflect ;—who know the history of the country, and as a portion of it, the history of parties, instead of being a prey to the exaggerated statements of the political press, form an independent opinion of men and things, and are able to correct misstatements and rejudge prejudices. The well-informed mind has other objects of interest and pursuit. In proportion to the intelligence of a community, will be the diversity of its occupations and the variety of the objects, which invite and receive the attention of active minds. Political interests are less keenly pursued in such a community, than where they form the exclusive object of attention. Other great questions connected with religious and moral improvement, social progress, the cause of education, and the advancement of the elegant and useful arts engage the thoughts of the active and the inquisitive. These liberal pursuits bring those together, whom politics separate ; and show men that their opponents are neither the knaves, nor the fools they might otherwise have thought them.

But especially the spirit of patriotism may be looked to, as the great corrective of party spirit. Whatsoever revives the recollections of exploits and sacrifices, of which all share the pride as all partake the benefits,—the memory of the pilgrim fathers and revolutionary patriots,—the common glories of the American name,— serves to moderate the growing bitterness of party animosity. The unkind feelings kindled by present struggles are subdued, by the generous emotions with which we contemplate the glorious events of our history and the illustrious characters with which it is adorned. It is scarcely possible for men who have just united in an act of patriotic commemoration ;—who have repeated to each other, with mutual pride, the names of a common ancestry ;—who have trod together the field of some great and decisive struggle,—who have assembled to join in recalling the merits of some friend and ornament of his country,—to go away and engage with unmitigated rancor, in the work of party defamation. The spirit of party, which yields nothing to these humanizing influences, is not the laudable spirit of political independence, but malignant and selfish passion ;—and that patriotism, which expires in wordy commendation of the acts or principles of our forefathers, without softening the asperities which exist between their children at the present day, is hollow-hearted pretence.

Of all the occasions rightfully redeemed from the contamination of party feeling and consecrated to union, harmony, and patriotic affection, the day we celebrate stands first,—for on what day can we meet as brothers, if the fourth of July sunders us as partisans ? It is an occasion toward which no man, and no party can feel indifferent ;—in which no man and no party can arrogate an exclusive interest; for which every American citizen, in proportion as he has sense to perceive the blessings which have fallen to his lot, and sagacity to mark the connexion of the independence of America with the progress of liberty throughout the world, must feel the same profound reverence. It is for this reason that I ever rejoice, when it is proposed to celebrate the Fourth of July, without distinction of party; for this reason, that on this day,—and I hope not on this day alone,—I have a hand of fellowship and a heart warm with kind feeling, for every patriotic brother of the great American family. I would devote this day, not to the discussion of topics which divide the people, but to the memory of the events and of the men which unite their affections. I would call up, in the most imposing recollection, the venerated images of our patriotic ancestors. I would strive to place myself in the actual presence of that circle of sages, whose act has immortalized the day. As they rise one by one to the eye of a grateful imagination, my heart bows down at the sight of their venerable features, their gray hairs, and their honorable scars; and every angry feeling settles into reverence and love.

It has seemed to me, fellow citizens, that I could select no topic more appropriate to the occasion,—none more in harmony with the spirit of the day, and the feelings, which have led you to unite in celebrating it,—than the character of Washington. Considered as the great military leader of the Revolution, it is admitted, on every side, that his agency in establishing the independence of the country, was more important than that of any other individual. It is not less certain, that, but for the cooperation of Washington, in the federal convention, and the universal understanding that he was to fill the chief magistracy, under the new government, the Constitution of these United States would not have been adopted. Let me not seem unjust to others. The perils and trials of the times,—the voice of a bleeding country,—the high tone of public feeling, —the sympathy of an astonished and delighted age,—the manifest indications of a providential purpose to raise up a new state in the family of nations, called into action a rare assemblage of wise, courageous, and patriotic men. To numbers of them the meed of well-deserved applause has been, and in all time will be, gratefully accorded. My own poor voice has never been silent in their praise, and when hushed on that theme, may it never be listened to on any other. But of Washington alone it has been said, with an aptitude which all feel, and an emphasis which goes to the heart, that he was 'First in war, first in peace, and first in the hearts of his countrymen.'

Nor let it be thought, fellow citizens, that this is an exhausted subject. It can never be exhausted, while the work of his hands, —the monuments of his achievements,—and the fruits of his counsels, remain. On the contrary, it is a subject which every age will study, under new lights; which has enduring relations, not only with the fortunes of America, but the general cause of liberty. I have, within a few weeks, seen an official declaration of General Santander, the enlightened chief magistrate of the republic of New Grenada, in which he avows his intention to decline a re-election, and assigns the example of Washington as the cause. I do not believe it within the compass of the most active imagination to do full justice to the effect on mankind of having embodied, in the conspicuous living illustration of the character of Washington, the great principles which should govern the conduct of a patriotic chief magistrate, in a representative government. For myself, I am well persuaded that the present generation is better able to do justice to this character, than that in which he lived. We behold it more nearly than our predecessors, entire, in all its parts. We approach it free from the prejudices, of which, under the influence of the passions of the day, even the purest and most illustrious men are the subjects while they live. Every day furnishes new proofs of the importance of his services, in their connexion with American liberty;—and I am sure, that instead of sinking into comparative obscurity, with the lapse of time, the character of Washington, a century hence, will be the subject of a warmer and a more general enthusiasm, on the part of the friends of liberty, than at the present day. The great points in his character are living centres of a self-diffusive moral influence, which is daily taking effect, and which is destined still more widely to control the minds and excite the imaginations of men.

It is, in all cases, difficult for contemporaries, or the next generation, to do full justice to the riches of a character, destined to command the respect of all time. It is a part of the character,

that it contained within it, qualities so true, that, while they conflict, perhaps, with the interests, passions, and prejudices of the
day, they justify themselves in the great experience of ages. The
planets, as we behold them, are sometimes stationary, and sometimes seem to retrograde. But it is only to the imperfect sense of
man, that they stand still, and move backward ; while, in reality,
they are ever rolling in majesty along their orbits, and will be found,
at the appointed season, to have compassed the heavens. Instead
of expecting at once to sound the depths of a character like Washington's, it requires all our study and all our vigilance, not to measure such a character on the scale of our own littleness ; not to estimate it from a partial development of its influence. A great
character, founded on the living rock of principle, is, in fact, not a
solitary phenomenon, to be at once perceived, limited, and described.
It is a dispensation of Providence, designed to have not merely an
immediate, but a continuous, progressive, and never-ending agency.
It survives the man who possessed it ; survives his age,—perhaps
his country,—his language. These, in the lapse of time, may
disappear, and be forgotten. Governments, tribes of men, chase
each other, like the shadows of summer clouds, on a plain. But
an earthly immortality belongs to a great and good character. History embalms it ; it lives in its moral influence ; in its authority ;
in its example ; in the memory of the words and deeds in which
it was manifested ; and as every age adds to the illustrations of its
efficacy, it may chance to be the best understood by a remote posterity.

There is, however, but a single point of view, in which the limits of the occasion will allow me to dwell on this great theme,—
more suitable for a volume than the address of an hour ;—and that
is, *the early formation of the character of Washington.* It must
have occurred to you all, in reading the history of the Revolution,
that from the period at which Washington assumed the chief command, he was not merely the head of the army, but to all practical
purposes, the chief magistrate of the country. Congress, in fact,
conferred on him, by one of their resolutions, powers that may,
without exaggeration, be called *dictatorial.* The point, then, on
which I would dwell, is this, that it was absolutely necessary for
the prosperous issue of the Revolution,—*not,* that a character like

Washington's, perfectly qualified for the duties of the camp and the council, should have gradually formed itself; this would not have sufficed for the salvation of the country, in the critical, embarrassed, often disastrous, state of affairs. It was necessary, *not* that, after having for some years languished or struggled on, beneath incompetent, unsuccessful, unpopular, and perhaps faithless chieftains, the country should at last have found her Washington, when her spirit was broken,—her resources exhausted,—her character discredited,—her allies disgusted,—in short, when Washington himself could not have saved her. No, it strikes the reflecting mind to have been necessary, absolutely necessary, at the very outset of the contest, to have a leader possessed of all the qualities, which were actually found in him. He cannot be waited for, even if by being waited for, he is sure to be found. The organization of the army may be a work of difficulty and time,—the plan of confederation may drag tardily along,—the finances may plunge from one desperate expedient to another,—expedition after expedition may fail;—but it is manifestly indispensable, that from the first, there should be one safe governing mind, one clear, unclouded intellect, one resolute will,—one pure and patriotic heart,—placed at the head of affairs by common consent. One such character there must be, for the very reason that all other resources are wanting;—and with one such character, all else in time will be supplied. The storm sails may fly in ribbons to the wind; mast and top-mast may come down,—and every billow of the ocean boil through the gaping seams;—and the brave ship, by the blessing of Heaven, may yet ride out the tempest. But when the winds, in all their fury, are beating upon her, and the black and horrid rocks of a lee shore are already hanging over the deck, and all other hope and dependence fail, if then the chain cable gives way, she must, with all on board, be dashed to pieces. I own I regard it, though but a single view of the character of Washington, as one of transcendent importance, that the commencement of the Revolution found him already prepared and mature for the work; and that on the day on which his commission was signed by John Hancock,—the immortal 17th of June, 1775,—a day on which Providence kept an even balance with the cause, and while it took from us our Warren, gave us our Washington,—he was just as consummate a leader for peace or for war, as when, eight years after, he resigned that commission at Annapolis.

His father, a Virginia gentleman in moderate circumstances of fortune, died when George Washington was but ten years old. His surviving parent,—a woman fit to be the mother of Washington,—bestowed the tenderest care upon the education of her oldest and darling son ; and instilled into his mind those moral and religious principles, that love of order, and what is better, that love of justice, and devout reliance on Providence, which formed the basis of his character. His elder brother, Lawrence, the child of a former marriage, was a captain in the British army. He was ordered with his company to Jamaica, in 1741, and was present at the capture of Porto Bello, and at the disastrous attack on Carthagena, to which Thompson so pathetically alludes in the Seasons. In honor of Admiral Vernon, who commanded those expeditions, Captain Lawrence Washington gave the name of Mount Vernon to the beautiful estate which he purchased on the banks of the Potomac, and which, at his death, he bequeathed to his brother George. Influenced no doubt by the example of his brother, but led by his advice to engage in the other branch of the service, George Washington, at the age of fourteen years, sought and obtained a midshipman's warrant in the British navy. Shall he engage in this branch of the military service, on which his heart is bent? Shall his feet quit the firm soil of his country? Shall he enter a line of duty and promotion, in which, if he escape the hazards and gain the prizes of his career, he can scarce fail to be carried to distant scenes,—to bestow his energies on foreign expeditions, in remote seas, perhaps in another hemisphere ; in which he will certainly fail of the opportunity of preparing himself, in the camp and field of the approaching war, to command the armies of the Revolution ; and not improbably sink under the pestilential climate of the West Indies and the Spanish Main? Such, indeed, seems almost inevitably his career. He desires it ; his brother, standing in the place of a parent, approves it ; the warrant is obtained. But nothing could overcome the invincible repugnance of his widowed mother. She saw only the dangers which awaited the health, the morals, and the life of her favorite child,—and her influence prevailed. Thus the voice of his high destiny first spoke to the affections of the youthful hero, through the fond yearnings of a mother's heart. He abandoned his commission, remained beneath the paternal roof, and was saved to the country.

The early education of Washington was confined to those branches of useful knowledge commonly taught in English grammar schools. But he soon entered upon a course of practical education singularly adapted to form him for his future career. He is to lead an active and a laborious life, and he must carry to it a healthy frame. Destined for the command of armies, to direct the movement and the supply of troops,—to select the routes of march and the points of attack and defence,—to wrestle with privation, hunger, and the elements;—raised up, above all, to perform the part of a great and patriotic chieftain, in the revolutionary councils of a new country, where the primeval forest had just begun to yield to the settler's axe, and most of the institutions of society, and the thoughts and prejudices of a good part of the population are those of an early stage of improvement, and, so to express it, to some extent, of frontier life;—with this destiny, how shall he be educated? A great extent and variety of literary accomplishments are evidently not the things most required.

It is impossible to read the account of his early years, without feeling that he was thrown upon an occupation, which, without carrying on its outside any thing particularly attractive to a young man, able to indulge his taste in the choice of a pursuit, was unquestionably of all pursuits, the best adapted to form the youthful Washington. At the period when he came forward into life, the attention of men of adventure, in Virginia, had begun to turn toward the occupation of the regions west of the Blue Ridge and Alleghany mountains;—a region now filled with a dense population, with all the works of human labor, and all the bounties of a productive soil; then shaded by the native forest,—infested with its savage inhabitants, and claimed as the domain of France. The enterprise of the English colonists of the Atlantic coast was beginning to move boldly forward into the interior. The destiny of the Anglo-Saxon race, transplanted to this continent, had too long awaited its fulfilment. The charter of Virginia, as well as of several other of the colonies, extended from sea to sea;—but of the broad region, which lay to the south and east of the Ohio, a country as highly favored of nature, as any on which heaven sends rain and sunshine, the comparatively narrow belt to the east of the Blue Ridge, was all that was yet occupied by compact settlements. But the bold huntsman had followed the deer to the upper waters of the Potomac; and trapped the beaver in his still, hereditary pool, among the western slopes of the Alleghany. The intrepid woodsman, in a few instances, had fixed his log cabin on the fertile meadows which are watered by the tributaries of the Ohio. Their reports of the riches of the unoccupied region excited the curiosity of their countrymen, and just as Washington was passing from boyhood to youth, the enterprise and capital of Virginia were seeking a new field for exercise and investment, in the unoccupied public domain beyond the mountains. The business of a surveyor immediately became one of great importance and trust, for no surveys were executed by the government. To this occupation, the youthful Washington, not yet sixteen years of age, and well furnished with the requisite mathematical knowledge, zealously devoted himself. Some of his family connexions possessed titles to large portions of public land, which he was employed with them in surveying. Thus, at a period of life, when, in a more quiet and advanced stage of society, the intelligent youth is occupied in the elementary studies of the schools and colleges, Washington was running the surveyor's chain through the fertile valleys of the Blue Ridge and the Alleghany mountains; passing days and weeks in the wilderness, beneath the shadow of eternal forests;—listening to the voice of the waterfalls, which man's art had not yet set to the healthful music of the saw-mill or the trip-hammer;—reposing from the labors of the day on a bear-skin, with his feet to the blazing logs of a camp-fire; and sometimes startled from the deep slumbers of careless hard-working youth, by the alarm of the Indian war whoop. This was the gymnastic school, in which Washington was brought up; in which his quick glance was formed, destined to range hereafter across the battle field, through clouds of smoke, and bristling rows of bayonets;—the school in which his senses, weaned from the taste for those detestable indulgences miscalled pleasures, in which the flower of adolescence so often languishes and pines away, were early braced up to the sinewy manhood, which becomes the

Lord of the lion heart and eagle eye.

There is preserved, among the papers of Washington, a letter written to a friend, while he was engaged on his first surveying tour, and when he was consequently but sixteen years of age. I quote a sentence from it, in spite of the homeliness of the details, for which I like it the better, and because I wish to set before you not an ideal hero wrapped in cloudy generalities and a mist of vague panegyric, but the real, identical man, with all the peculiarities of his life and occupation. ' Your letter,' says he, ' gave me the more pleasure, as I received it among barbarians and an uncouth set of people. Since you received my letter of October last, I have not slept above three or four nights in a bed ; but after walking a good deal all the day, I have lain down before the fire, upon a little hay, straw, fodder, or a bear-skin, whichever was to be had,—with man, wife, and children, like dogs and cats ; and happy is he who gets the berth nearest the fire. Nothing would make it pass off tolerably, but a good reward. A doubloon is my constant gain every day that the weather will permit my going out, and sometimes six pistoles. The coldness of the weather will not allow of my making a long stay, as the lodging is rather too cold for the time of year. I have never had my clothes off, but have lain and slept in them, except the few nights I have been in Fredericksburg.' If there is an individual in the morning of life, in this assembly, who has not yet made his choice, between the flowery path of indulgence and the rough ascent of honest industry,—if there is one, who is ashamed to get his living by any branch of honest labor,— let him reflect, that the youth who was carrying the theodolite and surveyor's chain, through the mountain passes of the Alleghanies, in the month of March,—sleeping on a bundle of hay before the fire, in a settler's log cabin, and not ashamed to boast, that he did it for his doubloon a day, is George Washington ;—that the life he led trained him up to command the armies of United America ;— that the money he earned was the basis of that fortune which enabled him afterwards to bestow his services, without reward, on a bleeding and impoverished country !

For three years was the young Washington employed, the greater part of the time, and whenever the season would permit, in this laborious and healthful occupation ;—and I know not if it would be deemed unbecoming, were a thoughtful student of our history to say, that he could almost hear the voice of Providence, in the language of Milton, announce its high purpose :—

> To exercise him in the wilderness;—
> There he shall first lay down the rudiments
> Of his great warfare, ere I send him forth
> To conquer!

At this period, the military service, in all countries, was sorely infested by a loathsome disease, not known to the ancients,—supposed to have been generated in some pestilential region of the East ;—and brought back to Europe by the crusaders, an ample revenge for the desolation of Asia. Long since robbed of its terrors, by the sublime discovery of Jenner, it is now hardly known, except by the memory of its ravages. But before the middle of the last century, it rarely happened that a large body of troops was brought together, without the appearance among them of this terrific malady, whose approach was more dreaded, often more destructive, than that of the foe. Shortly before the career of Washington commenced, this formidable disease had been brought within the control of human art, by the practice of inoculation, which was introduced into England from Turkey, by the wife of the British ambassador, and into this neighborhood, by Dr Zabdiel Boylston, in the first quarter of the eighteenth century. An unfortunate prejudice, however, arose in many minds against the practice of inoculation. It was believed to be an unwarrantable tempting of Providence, voluntarily to take into the frame so dangerous a disease. In many places, its introduction was resisted by all the force of popular prejudice and sometimes of popular violence ; and in the colony of Virginia, it was prohibited by law. At the age of nineteen, George Washington accompanied his elder brother, already mentioned, and whose health was now infirm, to the island of Barbadoes. Here he was attacked by this terrific malady, in the natural way ; but skilful medical attendance was at hand, the climate mild, the season favorable, and on the twenty-fifty day from the commencement of the disease, he had passed through it in safety. He was thus, before his military career commenced, placed beyond the reach of danger from this cause. In the very first campaign of the revolutionary war, the small pox was one of the most dangerous enemies with which the troops under Washington were obliged to contend. It broke out in the British army in Boston, and was believed by General Washington to have been propagated in the American camp, by persons purposely inoculated and sent into the American lines. However this might be, it was necessary to subject the American army to the process of inoculation, at a period, when, destitute as they were of powder, an attack was daily expected from the royal army. But the beloved commander was safe.

The time had now arrived, when the military education of Washington, properly so called, was to commence. And in the circumstances of this portion of his life, if I am not greatly deceived, will be found a connexion of the character and conduct of this illustrious man, with the fortunes and prospects of his country, which cannot be too much admired, nor too gratefully acknowledged. The struggle between the governments of France and England, for the exclusive possession of the American continent, was a principal source of the European wars of the last century. The successes of each contest furnished new subjects of jealousy, and peace was but a cessation of arms, preparatory to another struggle. The English colonies, favored by the maritime superiority of the mother country, had possessed themselves of the Atlantic shore. The French adventurers, who excelled in the art of gaining the affections of the aborigines, having entrenched themselves at the mouth of the St Lawrence and the Mississippi, aimed, by a chain of posts through the whole interior, at all events, to prevent the progress of the English westward, and as circumstances should favor the design, to confine them within constantly reduced limits ;—ultimately, if possible, to bring the whole coast into subjection to France. This struggle retarded for a century the progress of civilization on this continent. During that period, it subjected the whole line of the frontier to all the horrors of a remorseless border and savage war. It resulted, at last, in the entire expulsion of the French from the continent ; in the reduction of the British dominion to a portion of that territory which had been wrested from the French ; and in the establishment of the independence of the United States of America. Every thing preceding the year 1748, when the treaty of Aix-la-Chapelle was concluded, may be considered as preliminary to that grand series of events, which makes the day we celebrate an era in the history of the world, and in which the first part was performed by Washington.

Previous to this period, the fertile region west of the Alleghany mountains, and now containing a third part of the population of the United States, was unoccupied by civilized man. In the western part of Pennsylvania and Virginia, in Kentucky and all the States directly south of it, in the entire region north-west of the Ohio, and west of the Mississippi, there did not, less than ninety years ago, arise the smoke of a single hamlet, in which the descendants of Englishmen dwelt. On the return of peace between France and England, in the year 1748, the Ohio company was formed. Its object was the occupation and settlement of the fertile district southeast of the Ohio and west of the Alleghany mountains. It consisted of a small number of gentlemen in Virginia and Maryland, with one associate in London, Mr Thomas Hanbury, a distinguished merchant of that city. The elder brothers of George Washington were actively engaged in the enterprise. A grant of five hundred thousand acres of land was obtained from the crown, and the company were obliged, by the terms of the grant, to introduce a hundred families into the settlement within seven years, to build a fort, and provide a garrison adequate to its defence. Out of this small germ of private enterprise, sprung the old French war, and by no doubtful chain of cause and effect, the war of American independence.

The Ohio Company proceeded to execute the conditions of the grant. Preparations for opening a trade with the Indians were commenced,—a road across the mountains was laid out, substantially on the line of the present national road, and an agent was sent to conciliate the Indian tribes, on the subject of the new settlement. In 1752, the tribes entered into a treaty with the Virginia commissioners, in which they agreed not to molest any settlements, which might be formed by the company on the south-eastern side of the Ohio. On the faith of this compact, twelve families of adventurers from Virginia, headed by Captain Gist, immediately established themselves, on the banks of the Monongahela.

The French colonial authorities in Canada viewed these movements with jealousy. Although Great Britain and France had lately concluded a treaty of peace, emissaries were sent from Canada to the Indians on the Ohio, to break up the friendly relations just established with Virginia. Some of the traders were seized and sent to France ; and, by order of the French ministry, a fort was immediately commenced on Buffalo river, as a position, from which the Indians could be controlled and the Virginians held in check. These proceedings were promptly reported to Governor Dinwiddie, by the agents of the Ohio company ; and the Governor immediately determined to make them the subject of remonstrance to the commandant of the French fort.

To transmit such a remonstrance from Williamsburg in Virginia to the shores of lake Erie, was, in the state of the country at that time, no easy matter. A distance of three or four hundred miles was to be travelled, the greater part of the way through a wilderness. Mountains were to be climbed and rivers crossed. Tribes of savages were to be passed, by the way ; and all the hazards of an unfriendly Indian frontier, in a state of daily increasing irritation, were to be encountered. To all these difficulties the season of the year, (it was now the month of November), added obstacles all but insuperable. It is scarcely matter of reproach therefore, that the mission was declined, by those, to whom Governor Dinwiddie at first tendered it.

But there was one at hand, by whom no undertaking was ever declined, however severe or perilous, which was enjoined by duty, or which promised benefit to the country. On his return from Barbadoes in 1752, George Washington, then in the twentieth year of his age, received his commission as adjutant of militia in the northern neck of Virginia. The colony was divided into four military districts, the following year, and Washington received the same appointment in one of them. An expectation of approaching hostilities prevailed, and the militia were every where drilled, as in preparation for actual service. In this state of things, Governor Dinwiddie proposed to Major Washington, to undertake the mission to the French commandant. Washington had just received by bequest the fine estate of Mount Vernon ; but he accepted the

68

tendered appointment with alacrity, and started on his journey the following day.

At the frontier settlements on the Monongahela above alluded to, he was joined by Captain Gist, an intelligent and brave pioneer of civilization, and by some Indians of rank in their tribe, who were to add their remonstrances to those of the Governor of Virginia. After encountering all the hardships of the season and the wilderness, and various embarrassments arising from the policy of the French, Washington penetrated to their post and performed his errand. On the return of the party, their horses failed, from the inclemency of the weather and the severity of the march ; and Washington and his companion Gist, (left by their friendly Indians), with their packs on their shoulders and guns in their hands, were compelled to make the dreary journey on foot. They were soon joined by Indians in the French interest, who had dogged them, ever since they left the French fort. One of them exerted all the arts of savage cunning, to get possession of the arms of Washington, and lead him and his companion astray in the forest. Baffled by their wariness and self-possession, and when he perceived them, at night-fall, worn down, by the fatigue of the march, the savage turned deliberately, and at a distance of fifteen steps, fired at Washington and his companion. The Indian's rifle missed its aim. Washington and Gist immediately sprang upon and seized him. Gist was desirous of putting him to death, but Washington would not permit his life to be taken, justly forfeited as it was. After detaining him to a late hour, they allowed him to escape ; and pursued their own journey, worn and weary as they were, through the livelong watches of a December night.

Well knowing that the savages were on their trail, they dared not stop, till they reached the Alleghany, a clear and rapid stream, which they hoped to be able to cross on the ice ;—the only poor consolation which they promised themselves from the stinging severity of the weather. The river unfortunately was neither frozen across nor wholly open ; but fringed with broken ice for fifty yards on each shore, and the middle stream filled with cakes of ice, furiously drifting down the current. With one poor hatchet, to use Washington's own expression, they commenced the construction of a raft. It was a weary day's work, and not completed till sunset. They launched it upon the stream, but were soon so surrounded and crushed, by drifting masses of ice, that they expected every moment, that their raft would go to pieces, and they themselves perish. Washington put out his pole to stop the raft, till the fields of ice should float by ; but the raft was driven forward so furiously upon his pole, that he himself holding to it, was violently thrown into the river, where it was ten feet deep. He saved his life by clinging to a log, but, unable to force the raft to either shore, Washington and his companion left it, and passed the night on an island in the middle of the river. So intense was the cold, that the hands and feet of Captain Gist, hardy and experienced woodsman as he was, were frozen. Happily, however, they were enabled, on the following morning, to cross to the opposite bank of the river, on the ice,—a circumstance which no doubt saved them from the tomahawk of the unfriendly Indians.

Such was the commencement of the public services of the youthful hero, as related with admirable simplicity by himself, in his journal of the expedition. That of his companion Gist, though never yet printed, is still preserved ;* and states, much more particularly than it is done by Washington, the murderous attempt of the Indian. Such was the journey undertaken by Washington at a season of the year, when the soldier goes into quarters,—in a state of weather, when the huntsman shrinks from the inclemency of the skies ; amidst perils, from which his escape was all but miraculous : and this, too, not by a pennyless adventurer, fighting his way, through desperate risks, to promotion and bread ; but by a young man, already known most advantageously in the community, and who, by his own honorable industry and the bequest of a deceased brother, was already in possession of a fortune. In this his first official step, taken at the age of twenty-one, Washington displayed a courage, resolution, prudence, disinterestedness, and fortitude, on a small scale, though at the risk of his life, which never afterwards failed to mark his conduct. He seemed to spring at once into public life, considerate, wary, and fearless; and that

---

* It will appear in the next volume of the Collections of the Massachusetts Historical Society.

Providence, which destined him for other and higher duties, manifestly extended a protecting shield over his beloved head.

The answer of the French commandant to the remonstrance of the Governor of Virginia was evasive and unsatisfactory. A regiment was immediately enlisted; Major Washington, on the ground of youth and inexperience, declined being a candidate for the place of colonel, but solicited and accepted the second command. He hastened with two companies to the scene of action, beyond the Alleghanies; and, by the death of Colonel Fry, was soon left in full command of the regiment. He had never served a campaign nor faced an enemy. The French and Indians were in force on the Ohio. They had already commenced the erection of Fort Duquesne, on the site of Pittsburgh; and, hearing of the approach of Washington, sent forward a detachment of French and Indians, to reconnoitre his position. Informed by friendly Indians of the secret advance of this detachment, Washington, who was never taken by surprise, forced a march upon them in the night, and overtook them in their place of concealment. A skirmish ensued, in which, with the loss of one man killed and two or three wounded, the party of French and Indians were defeated; ten of them being killed, including their commander Jumonville, and twenty-one made prisoners.

This bold advance, however, was necessarily followed by a hasty retreat. The regiment of Washington counted but three hundred; —the force of the French and Indians exceeded a thousand. Washington reluctantly fell back to *Fort Necessity*, a hasty work on the meadows, at the western base of the mountains, whose name sufficiently shows the feelings, with which the youthful commander found himself compelled to occupy it. Here he entrenched himself and waited for reinforcements. But before they came up, the joint French and Indian army arrived in the neighborhood of the fort. A sharp action took place, on the 3d of July, 1754, which was kept up the whole day, till late in the evening. The American force was considerably reduced; but the French commander saw that he had to do with men, who were determined, if pushed to extremities, to sell their lives dear. He proposed a capitulation: a parley was held to settle its terms. A captain in the Virginia regiment, and the only man in it who understood the French language, was sent by Colonel Washington to treat with the French commander. The articles of capitulation drawn up in French, and treacherously assented to by the Virginian captain, contained the assertion, that Jumonville, who, as was just observed, fell in the late skirmish, was *assassinated.* These articles were interpreted to Washington at midnight, under a drenching rain, among the wrecks of the battle, amidst heaps of the dead and dying, and after a severe engagement of ten hours. By a base mistranslation of the French word that signifies assassination, Washington was made to subscribe an article, in which the death of Jumonville was called by that revolting name. It was not until his return to Virginia, that this fraud was detected. On the following day, THE FOURTH OF JULY, in virtue of this capitulation, Washington led out the remains of his gallant regiment, grieved but not dishonored. He conducted them with consummate skill, through the ill-restrained bands of Indians, who hovered around his march, and brought them safely to Fort Cumberland. Heaven had in reserve for him a recompense for the disasters of this mournful fourth of July, when, on the return of that day, after a lapse of twenty-two years, it found him the Commander-in-Chief of the armies of independent and United America !

These incidents aroused the attention of France and England, who yet stood glaring at each other, in an attitude of defiance; reluctant to plunge again into the horrors of a general war, but deeply conscious that peace could not be preserved. No formal declaration of war was made in Europe, but both governments prepared for vigorous action in America. Two veteran regiments were sent from Great Britain, destined to dislodge the French from Ohio. They were placed under the command of the brave, headstrong, self-sufficient, and unfortunate Braddock. By an extraordinary fatality of the British councils,—and as if to sow the seeds of division and weakness, at a moment when every nerve of strength required to be strained,—an ordinance for settling the rank of the army was promulgated, in virtue of which, all officers holding British commissions were to take rank of all holding provincial commissions; and provincial general and field officers were to lose their commands, when serving with those commissioned by the

crown. Colonel Washington, on the promulgation of this ill-con-
ceived order, resigned his commission in disdain ;—but to show that
no unworthy motive had prompted that step, and happily resolved
to persevere in the arduous school of dear-bought experience, he
offered his services to General Braddock, as an aid,—and they
were gladly accepted. Washington fell dangerously sick on the
march toward the field of slaughter, beyond the mountains ;—but
consented to be left behind, at the positive instances of the surgeon,
only on the solemn pledge of the general, that he should be sent
for before an action.

Time would fail me to recount the horrors of the 9th of July,
1755. Washington, emaciated, reduced by fatigue and fever,
had joined the army. He implored the ill-starred general to send
forward the Virginia Rangers to scour the forest in advance : he
besought him to conciliate the Indians. His counsels were un-
heeded ; the wretched commander moved forward to his fate.
Washington was often heard to say, in the course of his life-time,
that the most beautiful spectacle he had ever witnessed, was that
of the British troops on this eventful morning. The whole detachment was clad in uniform, and moved as in a review, in regular
columns, to the sound of martial music. The sun gleamed upon
their burnished arms, the placid Monongahela flowed upon their
right, and the deep, native forest overshadowed them with solemn
grandeur, on their left.* It was a bright midsummer's day, and
every bosom swelled with the confident expectation of victory. A
few hours pass, and the forest rings with the yell of the savage
enemy ;—the advance of the British army under Colonel Gage,
afterwards the governor of Massachusetts, is driven back on the
main body ;—the whole force, panic-struck,—confounded,—and
disorganized, after a wild and murderous conflict of three hours,
falls a prey to the invisible foe. They ran before the French and
Indians " like sheep before the dogs." Of eighty-six officers, sixty-
one were killed and wounded. The wretched general had four
horses shot under him, and received at last his mortal wound,
probably from an outraged provincial, in his own army. The
Virginia Rangers were the only part of the force, that behaved with

* Sparks' Writings of Washington, Vol. II. p. 469.

firmness ; and the disordered retreat of the British veterans was actually covered by these American militia men. Washington was the guardian angel of the day. He was every where, in the hottest of the fight. " I expected every moment," said Dr Craik, his friend, " to see him fall." His voice was the only one, which commanded obedience. Two horses were killed under him, and four bullets passed through his garments. No common fortune preserved his life. Fifteen years after the battle, Washington made a journey to the great Kenhawa, accompanied by Dr Craik. While exploring the wilderness, a band of Indians approached them, headed by a venerable chief. He told them, by an interpreter, the errand on which he came. " I come, said he, to behold my great father Washington. I have come a long way, to see him. I was with the French, in the battle of the Monongahela. I saw my great father on horseback, in the hottest of the battle. I fired my rifle at him many times, and bade my young men also fire their rifles at him. But the Great Spirit turned away the bullets ;—and I saw that my great father could not be killed in battle." This anecdote rests on the authority of Dr Craik, the comrade and friend of Washington, the physician who closed his eyes. Who needs doubt it ? Six balls took effect on his horses and in his garments. Who does not feel the substantial truth of the tradition ?—Who, that has a spark of patriotic or pious sentiment in his bosom, but feels an inward assurance that a heavenly presence overshadowed that field of blood, and preserved the great instrument of future mercies ?—Yes, gallant and beloved youth, ride safely as fearlessly through that shower of death ! Thou art not destined to fall in the morning of life, in this distant wilderness. That wan and wasted countenance shall yet be lighted up with the sunshine of victory and peace !—The days are coming and the years draw nigh, when thy heart, now bleeding for thy afflicted country, shall swell with joy, as thou leadest forth her triumphant hosts, from a war of independence !

From this period, the relation of Washington to his country was sealed. It is evident that his character, conduct, and preservation, —though he was scarcely twenty-three years of age,—had arrested the public attention, and awakened thoughtful anticipations of his career. I confess, there is something which I am unable to

fathom, in the hold which he seems already to have gained over
the minds and imaginations of men.   Never did victorious consul
return to republican Rome, loaded with the spoils of conquered
provinces, with captive thousands at his chariot wheels, an object
of greater confidence and respect,—than Washington, at the close
of two disastrous campaigns, from one of which he was able to
save his regiment only by a painful capitulation,—in the other,
barely escaping with his life and the wrecks of his army.   He had
formed to himself, on fields of defeat and disaster, a reputation for
consummate bravery, conduct, and patriotism.   A sermon was
preached to the volunteers of Hanover county, in Virginia, by the
Rev. Samuel Davies, afterwards president of Princeton college, in
which he uses this memorable language:—'As a remarkable instance of patriotism, I may point out to the public that heroic
youth, Colonel Washington, whom I cannot but hope Providence
has hitherto preserved, in so signal a manner, for some important
service to his country.'

The entire completion of this extraordinary prediction was,
of course, reserved for a future day ; but from the moment of its
utterance, its fulfilment began.   Terror and havoc followed at the
heels of Braddock's defeat.   The frontier settlements were broken
up,—the log cabins were burned,—their inmates massacred, or
driven in dismay across the mountains.   A considerable force was
raised in Virginia, and Washington was appointed its commander-
in-chief.   But the councils of England were weak and irresolute,
and no efficient general head as yet controlled those of the colonies.   The day-star of Pitt was near, but had not yet ascended
above the horizon.—Disaster followed disaster, on the frontiers of
Virginia, and Washington, for two years and a half, was placed in
precisely the position which he was afterwards to fill, in the revolutionary war.   A reluctant and undisciplined militia was to be
kept embodied by personal influence,—without pay,without clothes,
without arms.   Sent to defend an extensive mountain frontier, with
forces wholly inadequate to the object,—the sport of contradictory
orders from a civil governor, inexperienced in war,—defrauded by
contractors,—tormented with arrogant pretensions of subaltern officers in the royal army,—weakened by wholesale desertions in the
hour of danger,—misrepresented by jealous competitors,—traduced,
—maligned,—the youthful commander-in-chief was obliged to

foresee every thing,—to create every thing,—to endure every thing, —to effect every thing, without encouragement, without means, without cooperation. His correspondence during the years 1756 and 1757 is, with due allowances for the difference of the field of operations, the precise counterpart of that of the revolutionary war, twenty years later. You see it all,—you see the whole man,— in a letter to Governor Dinwiddie, of the 22d April, 1756:—

' Your honor may see to what unhappy straits the inhabitants and myself are reduced. I am too little acquainted, sir, with pathetic language, to attempt a description of the people's distresses, though I have a generous soul, sensible of wrongs, and swelling for redress. But what can I do? I see their situation, know their danger, and participate their sufferings, without having it in my power to give them farther relief than uncertain promises. In short, I see inevitable destruction, in so clear a light, that unless vigorous measures are taken by the assembly, and speedy assistance sent from below, the poor inhabitants that are now in forts must unavoidably fall, while the remainder are flying before a barbarous foe. In fine, the melancholy situation of the people,—the little prospect of assistance,—the gross and scandalous abuse cast upon the officers in general,—which is reflecting on me in particular for suffering misconduct of such extraordinary kinds,—and the distant prospect, if any, of gaining honor or reputation in the service, cause me to lament the hour that gave me a commission, and would induce me, at any other time than this of imminent danger, to resign without one hesitating moment, a command from which I never expect to reap either honor or benefit; but on the contrary, have an almost absolute certainty of incurring displeasure below, while the murder of helpless families may be laid to my account here! The supplicating tears of the women, the moving petitions of the men, melt me into such deadly sorrow, that I solemnly declare, if I know my own mind, I could offer myself a willing sacrifice to the butchering enemy, provided that would contribute to the people's ease!'

And here I close the detail. You behold in this one extract your Washington, complete, mature, ready for the salvation of his country. The occasion that calls him out may come soon, or it may come late, or it may come both soon and late;—whenever it

69

comes, he is ready for the work.   A misguided ministry may accelerate, or measures of conciliation retard, the struggle ; but its hero is prepared. His bow of might is strung, and his quiver hangs from his shoulders, stored with three-bolted thunders.   The summons to the mighty conflict may come the next year,—the next day ; it will find the rose of youth on his cheek, but it will find him wise, cautious, prudent, and grave ; it may come after the lapse of time, and find his noble countenance marked with the lines of manhood, but it will find him alert, vigorous, unexhausted.   It may reach him the next day, on the frontiers, in arms for the protection of the settlement ; it may reach him at the meridian of life, in the retirement of Mount Vernon ; it may reach him as he draws near to the grave ; but it will never take him by surprise.   It may summon him to the first Congress at Philadelphia ; it will find him brief of speech, in matter weighty, pertinent, and full ; in resolution firm as the perpetual hills, in personal influence absolute.   It may call him to the command of armies ; the generous rashness of youth alone will be chastened by the responsibility of his great trust, but in all else he will exhibit unchanged that serene and godlike courage, with which he rode unharmed through the iron sleet of Braddock's field.   It may call him to take part in the convention, assembled to give a constitution to the rescued and distracted country.   The soldier has disappeared, the statesman, the patriot, is at the post of duty ; he sits down in the humblest seat of the civilian, till in the assembly of all that is wisest in the land, he, by one accord is felt the presiding mind.   It will call him to the highest trust of the new-formed government ; he will conciliate the affections of the country in the dubious trial of the constitution ; and he will organize, administer, and lay down the arduous duties of a chief magistracy unparalleled in its character, without even the suspicion of swerving in a single instance from the path of rectitude.   Lastly, the voice of a beloved country may call him for a third time, on the verge of threescore years and ten, to the field.   The often sacrificed desire for repose, —the number and variety of services already performed ;—his declining years might seem to exempt him, but he will obey the sacred call of his country in his age, as he obeyed it in his youth.   He gave to his fellow citizens the morning, he will give them the evening, of his existence ;—he will exhaust the last hour of his being, and breathe his dying breath, in the service of his country.

ADDRESS

DELIVERED BEFORE THE LITERARY SOCIETIES OF AMHERST COL-
LEGE, AUGUST 25, 1835.

THE place of our meeting, the season of the year, and the occasion which has called us together, seem to prescribe to us the general topics of our discourse. We are assembled within the precincts of a place of education. It is the season of the year, at which the seminaries of learning throughout the country are dismissing to the duties of life that class of their students, whose collegiate course is run. The immediate call which has brought us together at this time, is the invitation of a portion of the members of the literary societies of this highly respectable and fast rising institution, who, agreeably to academical usage, on the eve of their departure from a spot endeared to them, by all the pleasant associations of collegiate life, are desirous, by one more act of literary communion, to strengthen the bond of intellectual fellowship and alleviate the regrets of separation. In the entire uncertainty of all that is before us, for good or for evil, there is nothing so nearly certain, as that we, who are here assembled to-day, shall never, in the Providence of God, be all brought together again in this world. Such an event is scarcely more within the range of probability, than that the individual drops, which, at this moment, make up the rushing stream of yonder queen of the valley, mounting in vapor to the clouds, and scattered to the four winds, will, at some future period, be driven together and fall in rains upon the hills, and flow down and recompose the identical river that is now spreading abundance and beauty before our eyes. To say nothing of the dread summons which comes to all when least expected, you will scarce step out of this sanctuary of your intellectual worship, before you will find how widely the paths of life diverge, not more so in the literal sense of the word, than in the estrangement which results from variety of pursuit, opinion, party, and success. Influenced by the feelings which this reflection inspires, it is natural that we should pause;—that we should give our minds up to the meditations which belong to the place, to the occasion, and the day;—that we should inquire into the character of that general process, in which you are now taking so important a step;—that we should put our thoughts in harmony with the objects that surround us, and thus seek from the hour as it flies, from the occasion, which once passed will never in all its accidents and qualifications return, to extract some abiding good impression, and to carry away some memorial, that will survive the moment.

The multiplication of the means of education and the general diffusion of knowledge, at the present day, are topics of universal remark. There are twelve collegiate institutions in New-England, whose commencement is observed during the months of August and September, and which will send forth, the present year, on an average estimate, about four hundred graduates. There are more than fifty other institutions of the same general character, in other parts of the United States. The greater portion of them are in the infancy of their existence and usefulness, but some of them compare advantageously with our New-England institutions. Besides the colleges, there are the schools for theological, medical, and legal education, on the one hand; and on the other, the innumerable institutions for preparatory or elementary instruction, from the infant schools, to which the fond and careful mother sends her darling lisper, not yet quite able to articulate, but with the laudable purpose of getting him out of the way, up to the high schools and endowed academies, which furnish a competent education for all the active duties of life. Besides these establishments for education of various character and name,—societies for the promotion of useful knowledge, mechanics' institutes, lyceums, and voluntary courses of lectures, abound in many parts of the country, and perform a very important office in carrying on the great work of instruction. Lastly, the press, by the cheap multiplication of books, and especially by the circulation of periodical works of every form and description, has furnished an important auxiliary to every other instrument of education, and turned the whole community, so to say, into one great monitorial school. There is probably not a newspaper of any character, published in the United States, which does not, in the course of the year, convey more useful information to its readers, than is to be found in the twenty-one folios of Albertus Magnus,—light as he was of the thirteenth century. I class all these agencies under the general name of the means of education, because they form one grand system, by which knowledge is imparted to the mass of the community, and the mind of the age, —with the most various success, according to circumstances,—is instructed, disciplined, and furnished with its materials for action and thought.

These remarks are made in reference to this country; but in some countries of Europe, all the means of education enumerated, with an exception perhaps in the number of newspapers, exist to as great an extent as in our own. Although there are portions of Europe where the starless midnight of the mind still covers society with a pall as dreary and impervious as in the middle ages, yet it may be safely said, upon the whole, that not only in America, but in the elder world, a wonderfully extensive diffusion of knowledge has taken place. In Great Britain, in France, in Germany, in Holland, in Sweden, in Denmark, the press is active, schools are numerous, higher institutions for education abound, associations for the diffusion of knowledge flourish, and literature and science, in almost every form, are daily rendered more cheap and accessible. There is, in fact, no country in Europe, from which the means of light are wholly shut out. There are universities in Austria and Russia, and newspapers at Madrid and Constantinople.

It is the impulse of the liberal mind to rejoice in this manifest progress of improvement, and we are daily exchanging congratulations with each other, on the multiplication, throughout the world, of the means of education. There are not wanting, however, those who find a dark side even to such an object as this. We ought not, therefore, either to leave a matter so important exposed to vague prejudicial surmises, on the one hand; nor, on the other,

should we rest merely in the impulses of liberal feeling and unreflecting enthusiasm. We should fortify ourselves, in a case of such
magnitude, in an enlightened conviction. We should seek to reduce to an exact analysis the great doctrine, that the extension of
the means of education and the general diffusion of knowledge are
beneficial to society. It is the object of the present address to
touch briefly,—and in the somewhat desultory manner required on
such an occasion,—on some of the prominent points involved in
this great subject; and to endeavor to show that the diffusion of
knowledge, of which we have spoken, is favorable to liberty, to
science, and virtue ;—to social, intellectual, and spiritual improvement; the only three things which deserve a name below.

I. Although liberty, strictly speaking, is only one of the objects
for which men have united themselves in civil societies, it is so intimately connected with all the others, and every thing else is so
sunk in value when liberty is taken away, that its preservation may
be considered, humanly speaking, the great object of life in civilized communities. It is so essential to the prosperous existence of
nations, that even where the theory of the government,—as in many absolute monarchies,—seems to subvert its very principle, by
making it depend on the will of the ruler, yet usage, prescription,
and a kind of beneficent instinct of the body politic, secure to the
people some portion of practical liberty. Where political interests
and passions do not interfere, (which they rarely do in respect to
the private rights of the mass of the community), the subjects of
the absolute monarchies of the north and east of Europe enjoy almost as large a share of liberty, as under some of what are called
the constitutional governments, in their neighborhood. Where this
is not the case,—where a despotic theory of the government is
carried out into a despotic administration,—and life, rights, and
property are habitually sacrificed to the caprice and passions of
men in power, as in all the despotisms which stretch across Asia,
from the Euxine to the Pacific, there the population is kept permanently degenerate, barbarous, and wretched.

Whenever we speak of liberty, in this connexion, we comprehend under it, legal security for life, personal freedom, and property.
As these are equally dear to all men ; as all feel, with equal keenness and bitterness, the pang which extinguishes existence, the

chain which binds the body, the coercion which makes one toil for another's benefit, it follows, as a necessary consequence, that all governments which are hostile to liberty are founded on force; that all despotisms are, what some by emphasis are occasionally called, *military despotisms*. The degree of force required to hold a population in subjection, other things being equal, is in direct ratio to its intelligence and skill; its acquaintance with the arts of life; its sense of the worth of existence; in fine, to its spirit and character. There is a point, indeed, beyond which this rule fails, and at which even the most thoroughly organized military despotism cannot be extended over the least intellectual race of subjects, serfs or slaves. History presents us with the record of numerous servile wars and peasants' wars, from the days of Spartacus to those of Tupac-Amaru and Pugatschef; in which, at the first outbreak, all the advantages of authority, arms, concert, discipline, skill, have availed the oppressor nothing against humanity's last refuge, the counsel of madness, and the resources of despair.

There are two ways in which liberty is promoted by the general diffusion of knowledge. The first is by disabusing the minds of men of the theoretical frauds, by which arbitrary governments are upheld. It is a remark almost, if not quite, without exception, that all governments unfriendly to well-regulated liberty, are founded on the basis of some religious imposture; the arm of military violence is clothed with the enervating terrors of superstition. The Oriental nations, as far back as our accounts run, worshipped their despots as divinities, and taught this monstrous adulation to the successors of Alexander. The Roman emperors, from the time of Julius Cæsar, were deified; and the thrones of modern European absolutism rest on a basis a little more refined, but not more rational. The divine right of Henry VIII, or of Charles V, was no better, in the eye of an intelligent Christian, than that of their contemporary, Solyman the Magnificent.

Superstitions like these, resting, like all other superstitions, on ignorance, vanish with the diffusion of knowledge, like the morning mists on yonder river before the rising sun; and governments are brought down to their only safe and just basis,—the welfare and will of the governed. The entire cause of modern political reform has started in the establishment of this principle, and no example

is more conspicuous than that which, for the magnitude of the rev
olution and the immensity of its consequences is called *The Reformation;* and which, on account of the temporal usurpations of
the Church of Rome, the intrusion of its power into the affairs of
foreign countries, and the right claimed by the Pope to command
the obedience of subject and sovereign,—was not less a political
than a religious revolution. Throughout this great work, the course
and conduct of Luther present a most illustrious example of the
efficacy of a diffusion of knowledge,—of an appeal to the popular
mind,—in breaking the yoke of the oppressor, and establishing a
rational freedom. When he commenced the great enterprise, he
stood alone. The governments acknowledged the supremacy of
the Roman pontiff. The teachers of the universities and schools
were, for the most part, regular priests, bound not only by the
common tie of spiritual allegiance, but by the rules of the monastic
orders to which they belonged. The books of authority were exclusively those of the schoolmen, implicitly devoted to the church,
filled with fantastical abstractions, with a meagre and unprofitable
logic, and written in a dead language. In this state of things, says
Lord Bacon, 'Martin Luther, conducted, no doubt, by a higher
Providence, but in a discourse of reason, finding what a province
he had undertaken against the bishop of Rome and the degenerate
traditions of the church, and finding his own solitude, being no
ways aided by the opinions of his own time, was enforced to awake
all antiquity, and to call former times to his succor, to make a party
against the present time. So that the ancient authors, both in
divinity and humanity, which had long time slept in libraries, began generally to be read and revolved. This, by consequence,
did draw on a necessity of a more exquisite travel in the languages
original, wherein those authors did write, for a better understanding
of those authors, and the better advantages of pressing and applying their words. And thereof grew again a delight in their manner and style of phrase, and an admiration of that kind of writing;
which was much furthered and precipitated by the enmity and opposition that the propounders of those primitive, but seeming new,
opinions had against the schoolmen, who were generally of the
contrary part, and whose writings were altogether in a different
style and form, taking liberty to coin and frame new terms of art,

to express their own sense, and to avoid circuit of speech, without regard to the pureness, pleasantness, and, as I may call it, lawfulness of the phrase or word. And again, because the great labor then was with the people, of whom the Pharisees were wont to say, *execrabilis ista turba, quæ non novit legem;* for the winning and persuading them, there grew, of necessity, in chief price and request, eloquence and variety of discourse, as the fittest and forciblest access into the capacity of the vulgar sort.'*

With the greatest reverence for the authority of Lord Bacon, I would say, that he seems to me to have somewhat mistaken the relative importance of the great instruments of the Reformation. In the solemn loneliness, in which Luther found himself, he called around him not so much the masters of the Greek and Latin wisdom, through the study of the ancient languages, as he did the mass of his own countrymen, by his translation of the Bible. It would have been a matter of tardy impression and remote efficacy, had he done no more than awake from the dusty alcoves of the libraries the venerable shades of the classic teachers. He roused up a population of living sentient men, his countrymen, his brethren. He might have written and preached in Latin to his dying day, and the elegant Italian scholars, champions of the church, would have answered him in Latin better than his own;—and with the mass of the people, the whole affair would have been a contest between angry and loquacious priests. ' Awake all antiquity from the sleep of the libraries?' He awoke all Germany and half Europe from the scholastic sleep of an ignorance worse than death. He took into his hands not the oaten pipe of the classic muse; he moved to his great work, not

———————to the Dorian mood
Of flutes and soft recorders :—

He grasped the iron trumpet of his mother tongue,—the good old Saxon from which our own is descended, the language of noble thought and high resolve,—and blew a blast that shook the nations from Rome to the Orkneys. Sovereign, citizen, and peasant, started at the sound; and, in a few short years, the poor monk,

* Lord Bacon's Works, Vol. I, p. 14, quarto ed.

who had begged his bread for a pious canticle, in the streets of
Eisenach,*—no longer friendless, no longer solitary,—was sustained by victorious armies, countenanced by princes, and, what is a
thousand times more precious than the brightest crown in Christendom, revered as a sage, a benefactor, and a spiritual parent, at the
firesides of millions of his humble and grateful countrymen.

Nor do we less plainly see in this, as in numerous other examples in the modern history of liberty, the more general operation of
the influences by which the diffusion of knowledge promotes rational freedom. Simply to overturn the theoretical sophisms upon
which any particular form of despotism may rest, is but to achieve
a temporary work. While the mass of the people remain ignorant,—to undermine the system of oppression, political or ecclesiastical, under which, at any time they may labor, is but to stagger
darkling from one tyranny to another. It is for this reason,—a
truth too sadly exemplified in the history of the world for the last
fifty years,—that countries in which the majority of the people have
grown up without knowledge, stung to madness by intolerable oppression, may make a series of plunges, through scenes of successive
revolution and anarchy, and come out at last drenched in blood,
and loaded with chains.

We must therefore trace the cause of political slavery beyond
the force which is the immediate instrument;—beyond the superstition which is its puissant ally;—beyond the habit and usage, the
second nature of governments as of men,—and we shall find it in
that fatal inequality which results from hereditary ignorance. This
is the ultimate, the broad, the solid foundation of despotism. A
few are wise, skilful, learned, wealthy; millions are uninformed,
and consequently unconscious of their rights. For a few are concentrated the delights, the honors, and the excitements of life;—
for all the rest remains a heritage of unenlightened subjection and
unrewarded toil.

Such is the division of the human race in all the Oriental despotisms, at the present day. Such it was in all Europe, in the
middle ages. Such, in some parts of Europe, it still is: such it
naturally must be every where, under institutions which keep the

* Luther's Werke, Th. X, 524.

mass of the people ignorant. A nation is numerically reckoned at its millions of souls. But they are not souls ; the greater part are but bodies. God has given them souls, but man has done all but annihilate the immortal principle :—its life-spring, its vigor, its conscious power, are broken down, and the people lie buried in subjection, till, through the medium of the understanding, a new creation takes place. The physical creation began with light ; the intellectual and moral creation begins with light also. Chosen servants of Providence are raised up to speak the word ; power is given to political or religious reformers to pronounce the decree ; it spreads like the elemental beam, by the thousand channels of intelligence, from mind to mind, and a new race is created. Let there be light ; let those rational intellects begin to think. Let them but look in upon themselves and see that they are men, and look upon their oppressors and see if they are more. Let them look round upon nature :—'it is my Father's domain ; shall not my patient labor be rewarded with its share ?' Let them look up to the heavens ;—' has He that upholds their glorious orbs, and who has given me the capacity to trace and comprehend their motions, designed me to grovel, without redemption, in the dust beneath my feet, and exhaust my life for a fellow man no better than myself ?'

These are the truths, which in all ages shoot through the understandings to the hearts of men : they are what our revolutionary fathers called " first principles ;" and they prepared the way for the revolution. All that was good in the French revolution was built upon them. They are the corner-stone of modern English liberty ; they emancipated the Netherlands and the Swiss Cantons ; and they gave to republican Greece and Rome that all but miraculous influence in human affairs,—which succeeding ages of civil discord, of abuse, and degeneracy have not yet been able to countervail. They redress the inequalities of society. When, penetrated with these great conceptions, the people assert their native worth and inherent rights, it is wonderful to behold how the petty badges of social inequality, the emblems of rank and of wealth, are contemned. Cincinnatus, who saved Rome from the Sabines, was found ploughing his own land, a farm of four acres, when created dictator ; and Epaminondas, who rescued his country from the domination of Sparta, and was implored by the emissaries of the king of Persia to do their master the honor to take his bribes, possessed no other property, when he fell gloriously at Mantinæa, than the humble utensils for cooking his daily food. A single bold word, heroic exploit, or generous sacrifice, at the fortunate crisis, kindles the latent faculties of a whole population, turns them from beasts of burden into men ; excites to intense action and sympathetic counsel millions of awakened minds, and leads them forth to the contest. When such a development of mental energy has fairly taken place, the battle is fought and won. It may be long and deadly, it may be brief and bloodless. Freedom may come quickly in robes of peace, or after ages of conflict and war ; but come it will, and abide it will, so long as the principles by which it was acquired are held sacred.

Nor let us forget, that the dangers to which liberty is exposed are not all on the side of arbitrary power. That popular intelligence, by which the acquisition of rational freedom is to be made, is still more necessary to protect it against anarchy. Here is the great test of a people, who derserve their freedom. Under a parental despotism, the order of the state is preserved, and life and property are protected, by the strong arm of the government. A measure of liberty,—that is, safety from irregular violence,—is secured by the constant presence of that military power, which is the great engine of subjection. But beneath a free government, there is nothing but the intelligence of the people to keep the people's peace. Order must be preserved, not by a military police or regiments of horse-guards ; but by the spontaneous concert of a well-informed population, resolved that the rights, which have been rescued from despotism, shall not be subverted by anarchy. As the disorder of a delicate system and the degeneracy of a noble nature are spectacles more grievous than the corruption of meaner things, so if we permit the principle of our government to be subverted, havoc, terror and destruction, beyond the measure of ordinary political catastrophes will be our lot. This is a subject of intense interest to the people of the United States at the present time. To no people since the world began, was such an amount of blessings and privileges ever given in trust. No people was ever so eminently made the guardians of their own rights ; and if this great experiment of rational liberty should here be permitted to fail, I know not where or when among the sons of Adam, it will ever be resumed.

II. But it is more than time to proceed to the second point, which I proposed briefly to illustrate,—the favorable influence of the extension of the means of education and the diffusion of knowledge, on the progress of sound science. It is a pretty common suggestion, that while the more abundant means of popular education, existing at the present day, may have occasioned the diffusion of a considerable amount of superficial knowledge, the effect has been unfavorable to the growth of profound science. I am inclined to think this view of the subject entirely erroneous ;—an inference by no means warranted by the premises from which it is drawn. It is no doubt true, that, in consequence of the increased facilities for education, the number of students of all descriptions, both readers and writers, is almost indefinitely multiplied, and with this increase in the entire number of persons who have enjoyed, in a greater or less degree, advantages for improving their minds, the number of half-taught and superficial pretenders has become proportionably greater. Education, which, at some periods of the world, has been a very rare accomplishment of a highly gifted and fortunate few ; at other times, an attainment attended with considerable difficulty, and almost confined to professed scholars,—has become, in this country at least, one of the public birthrights of freemen, and, like every other birthright, is subject to be abused. In this state of things, those, who habitually look at the dark side of affairs,—often witnessing the arrogant displays of superficial learning,—books of great pretension and little value, multiplied and circulated, by all the arts and machinery of an enterprising and prosperous age, and in all things much forwardness and show, often unaccompanied by worth and substance,—are apt to infer a decline of sound learning, and look back, with a sigh, to what they imagine to have been the more solid erudition of former days. But I deem this opinion without real foundation, in truth.

It is an age, I grant, of cheap fame. A sort of literary machinery exists, of which the patent paper-mill, the power-press, the newspapers, magazines and reviews ; the reading clubs and circulating libraries, are some of the principal springs and levers, by means of which almost any thing, in the shape of a book, is thrown into a sort of notoriety, miscalled reputation. The weakest distillation of soft sentiment from the poet's corner flows round a larger circle of admirers, than Paradise Lost, when first ushered to the world; and the most narcotic infliction of the quarterly critical press, (*absit invidia verbo*), no doubt far excels the *Novum Organum* in the number of its contemporary readers. But nothing is to be inferred from this state of things, in disparagement of the learning and scholarship of the age. All that it proves is, that, with a vast diffusion of useful knowledge,with an astonishing multiplication of the means of education, and, as I firmly believe, with a prodigious growth of true science, there has sprung up, by natural association, a host of triflers and pretenders, like a growth of rank weeds, with a rich crop, on a fertile soil.

But there were surely always pretenders in science and literature, in every age of the world; nor must we suppose, because their works and their names have perished, that they existed in a smaller proportion formerly than now. Solomon intimates a complaint of the number of books in his day, which he probably would not have done, if they had been all good books. The sophists in Greece were sworn pretenders and dealers in words,—the most completely organized body of learned quacks that ever existed. Bavius and Mævius were certainly not the only worthless poets in Rome; and from the age of the grammarians and critics of the Alexandrian school, through that of the monkish chroniclers and the schoolmen of the middle ages, and the mystics of the sixteenth and seventeenth centuries, the kingdom of learned dulness and empty profession has been kept up, under an unbroken succession of leaden or brazen potentates. If the subjects at the present day seem more numerous than formerly, it is only in proportion to the increase in the entire numbers of the reading and writing world; and because the sagacious hand of time brushes away the false pretensions of former days, leaving real talent and sound learning the more conspicuous for standing alone.

But, as in elder days, notwithstanding this unbroken sway of false lore and vain philosophy, the line of the truly wise and soundly learned was also preserved entire; as the lights of the world have in all former ages successively risen, illuminating the deep darkness, and outshining the delusive meteors; so, at the present day, I am firmly convinced that there is more patient learning, true philosophy,

fruitful science, and various knowledge, than at any former time.
By the side of the hosts of superficial, arrogant, and often unprin-
cipled pretenders, in every department, there is a multitude innumerable of the devoted lovers of truth, whom no labor can exhaust, no obstacles can discourage, no height of attainment dazzle ;
and who, in every branch of knowledge, sacred and profane, moral,
physical, exact, and critical, have carried and are carrying the
glorious banner of true science, into regions of investigation wholly
unexplored in elder times. Let me not be mistaken. I mean not
arrogantly to detract from the fame of the few great masters of the
mind,—the gifted few, who, from age to age, after long centuries
have intervened, have appeared ; and have risen, as all are ready
to allow, above all rivalry. Aftertime alone can pronounce whether
this age has produced minds worthy to be classed in their select
circle. But this aside,—I cannot comprehend the philosophy by
which we assume as probable, nor do I see the state of facts, by
which we must admit as actually existing, an intellectual degeneracy at the present day, either in Europe or in this country. I see
not why the multiplication of popular guides to partial attainments,
—why the facilities, that abound for the acquisition of superficial
scholarship, should, in the natural operation of things, either diminish the number of powerful and original minds, or satisfy their ardent
thirst for acquisition, by a limited progress. There is no doubt
that many of these improvements in the methods of learning,—many
of the aids to the acquisition of knowledge, which are the product
of the present time, are, in their very nature, calculated to help the
early studies even of minds of the highest order. It is a familiar
anecdote of James Otis, that, when he first obtained a copy of
Blackstone's Commentaries, he observed with emphasis, that if he
had possessed that book when commencing his studies of the law,
it would have saved him seven years' labor. Would those seven
years have borne no fruit to a mind like that of James Otis ?
Though the use of elementary treatises of this kind may have the
effect to make many superficial jurists, who would otherwise have
been no jurists at all, I deem it mere popular prejudice to suppose,
that the march of original genius to the heights of learning has been
impeded, by the possession of these modern facilities to aid its progress. To maintain this, seems to be little else than to condemn as

worthless the wisdom of the ages, which have gone before us.   It
is surely absurd to suppose that we can do no more with the assistance of our predecessors, than without it ; that the teachings of one
generation, instead of enlightening, confound and stupify that which
succeeds ; and that 'when we stand on the shoulders of our ancestors, we cannot see so far as from the ground.'   On the contrary, it is unquestionably one of the happiest laws of intellectual
progress, that the judicious labors, the profound reasonings, the
sublime discoveries, the generous sentiments of great intellects,
rapidly work their way into the common channel of public opinion,
find access to the general mind, raise the universal standard of attainment, correct popular errors, promote arts of daily application, and
come home at last to the fireside, in the shape of increased intelligence, skill, comfort and virtue ; which, in their turn, by an instantaneous reaction, multiply the numbers and facilitate the efforts
of those who engage in the farther investigation and discovery of
truth.   In this way, a constant circulation, like that of the life-
blood, takes place in the intellectual world.   Truth travels down
from the heights of philosophy to the humblest walks of life, and up
from the simplest perceptions of an awakened intellect to the discoveries, which almost change the face of the world.   At every
stage of its progress it is genial, luminous, creative.   When ˙first
struck out by some distinguished and fortunate genius, it may address itself only to a few minds of kindred power.   It exists then
only in the highest forms of science ; it corrects former systems,
and authorizes new generalizations.   Discussion, controversy begins ; more truth is elicited, more errors exploded, more doubts
cleared up, more phenomena drawn into the circle, unexpected
connexions of kindred sciences are traced, and in each step of the
progress, the number rapidly grows of those who are prepared to
comprehend and carry on some branches of the investigation,—till, in
the lapse of time, every order of intellect has been kindled, from
that of the sublime discoverer to the practical machinist ; and every
department of knowledge been enlarged, from the most abstruse
and transcendental theory to the daily arts of life.

     I presume it would not be difficult to deduce, from the discovery
and demonstration of the law of gravity, attainments in useful
knowledge, which come home every day to the business and

bosoms of men ; enlightening the mass of the community, who
have received a common education, on points, concerning which
the greatest philosophers of former times were at fault. Bold as
the remark sounds, there is not a young man who will to-morrow
receive his degree on this stage, who could not correct Lord Bacon
in many a grave point of natural science. His lordship questioned
the rotation of the earth on its axis, after it had been affirmed by
Copernicus, Kepler, and Galileo. He states positively, that he
judges the work of making gold possible,* and even goes so far,
after condemning the procedure of the alchemists, as to propound
his own. Finally, he says, it 'is not impossible, and I have heard
it verified, that upon cutting down of an old timber tree, the stub
hath put out sometimes a tree of another kind, as that beech hath
put forth birch ;' ' which, if it be true,' the immortal chancellor
discreetly adds, ' the cause may be, for that the old stub is too
scanty of juice to put forth the former tree, and therefore putteth
forth a tree of a smaller kind, that needeth less nourishment.' †
Surely no man can doubt that the cause of true science has been
promoted by such a diffusion of knowledge, as has eradicated even
from the common mind such enormous errors as these, from which,
notwithstanding their enormity, the greatest minds of other times
could not emancipate themselves. It is extremely difficult even
for the boldest intellects to work themselves free of all those popular
errors, which form a part as it were of the intellectual atmosphere,
in which they have passed their lives. Copernicus was one of the
boldest theorists that ever lived, but was so enslaved by the existing popular errors, as even while proposing his own simple and
magnificently beautiful theory of the heavens, to retain some of the
most absurd and complicated contrivances of the Ptolemaic
scheme.‡ Kepler was one of the most sagacious and original of
philosophers, and the laws which bear his name have been declared,

---

* 'The world hath been much abused by the opinion of making gold. The
work itself I judge to be possible, but the means hitherto propounded to effect it are
in the practice full of error and imposture, and in the theory full of unsound imaginations.' Lord Bacon's Works, Vol. I, p. 204.

  † Lord Bacon's Works, Vol. I, p. 241.

  ‡ Dr Small's Account of the Astronomical Discoveries of Kepler, chap. III
and VIII.

on respectable authority, ' the foundations of the whole theory of Newton ;' but he believed that the planets were monstrous animals, swimming in the ethereal fluid, and speaks of storms and tempests as the pulmonary heavings of the great Leviathan, the earth, breathing out hurricanes from its secret spiracles, in the valleys and among the hills.   It may raise our admiration of this extraordinary man, that with notions so confused and irrational, he should, by a life of indefatigable research, discover some of the sublimest laws of nature ; but no one can so superstitiously reverence the past,— no one so blindly undervalue the utility of the diffusion of knowledge,—as not to feel that these absurdities must have hung like a millstone about the necks of the strongest minds of former ages, and dragged them, in the midst of their boldest flights, to the dust.   When I behold minds like these, fitted to range, with the boldest step, in the paths of investigation, bound down by subjection to gross prevailing errors ; but at length, by a happy effort of native sense or successful study, grasping at the discovery of some noble truth, it brings to my mind Milton's somewhat fantastical description of the creation of the animals, in which the great beasts of the forest, not wholly formed, are striving to be released from their native earth,

> now half appeared
> The tawny lion, struggling to get free
> His hinder parts. then springs, as burst from bonds,
> And rampant shakes his brinded mane.

In short, when we consider the laws of the human mind, and the path by which the understanding marches to the discovery of truth, we must see that it is the necessary consequence of the general diffusion of knowledge, that it should promote the progress of science.   Since the time of Lord Bacon, it has been more and more generally admitted, that the only path to true knowledge is the study and observation of nature, either in the phenomena of the external creation, or in the powers and operations of the human mind.   This does not exclude the judicious use of books which record the observations and the discoveries of others, and are of inestimable value in guiding the mind in its own independent researches. They are, in fact, not its necessary, but its most usual instruments ; and as the book of nature is never so well perused, as with the assistance of the learned and prudent, who have studied it before us, so the true and profitable use of books is to furnish materials, on which other minds can act, and to facilitate their observation of nature.

I know not where I could find a better illustration of their value and of their peculiar aptitude to further the progress of knowledge, than in the admirable report on the geology of Massachusetts, which has recently emanated from this place.* Under the enlightened patronage of the commonwealth, a member of the faculty of this institution has set before the citizens of the State such a survey of its territory,—such an inventory of its natural wealth,—such a catalogue of its productions in the animal, the vegetable, and, still more, in the mineral world, as cannot be contemplated without gratification and pride. By one noble effort of learned industry and vigorous intellectual labor, the whole science of geology,—one of the great mental creations of modern times,—has been brought home, and applied to the illustration of our native State. There is not a citizen who has learned to read, in the humblest village of Massachusetts, from the hills of Berkshire to the sands of Nantucket, who has not now placed within his reach, the means of beholding, with a well-informed eye, either in his immediate neighborhood, or in any part of the State to which he may turn his attention, the hills and the vales, the rocks and the rivers, the soil and the quarries that lie beneath it. Who can doubt, that out of the hundreds,—the thousands,—of liberal minds, in every part of the commonwealth, which must thus be awakened to the intelligent observation of nature, thus helped over the elementary difficulties of the science, not a few will be effectually put upon the track of independent inquiries, and original attainments in science!

We are confirmed in the conclusion that the popular diffusion of knowledge is favorable to the growth of science, by the reflection, that, vast as the domain of learning is, and extraordinary as is the progress which has been made in almost every branch, it may be assumed as certain,—I will not say that we are in its infancy, but as truth is as various as nature, and as boundless as creation,—that the discoveries already made, wonderful as they are, bear but a small

* Report on the geology, mineralogy, botany, and zoology of Massachusetts, by Professor Hitchcock.

proportion to those that will hereafter be effected. In the yet unexplored wonders and yet unascertained laws of the heavens,—in
the affinities of the natural properties of bodies,—in magnetism,
galvanism, and electricity,—in light and heat,—in the combination
and application of the mechanical powers,—the use of steam,—
the analysis of mineral products, of liquid and äeriform fluids,—in
the application of the arts and sciences to improvements in husbandry, to manufactures, to navigation, to letters, and to education ;
—in the great department of the philosophy of the mind, and the
realm of morals ;—and, in short, to every thing that belongs to the
improvement of man, there is yet a field of investigation broad
enough to satisfy the most eager thirst for knowledge, and diversi-
fied enough to suit every variety of taste, order of intellect, or degree of qualification. For the peaceful victories of the mind, that
unknown and unconquered world, for which Alexander wept, is
for ever near at hand ; hidden, indeed, as yet, behind the veil with
which nature shrouds her undiscovered mysteries, but stretching all
along the confines of the domain of knowledge, sometimes nearest
when least suspected. The foot has not yet pressed, nor the eye
beheld it ; but the mind, in its deepest musings, in its widest excursions, will sometimes catch a glimpse of the hidden realm,—a
gleam of light from the Hesperian island,—a fresh and fragrant
breeze from off the undiscovered land,

Sabæan odors from the spicy shore,

which happier voyagers in aftertimes, shall approach, explore, and
inhabit. Who has not felt, when, with his very soul concentred
in his eyes, while the world around him is wrapped in sleep, he
gazes into the holy depths of the midnight heavens, or wanders in
contemplation among the worlds and systems that sweep through
the immensity of space,—who has not felt as if their mystery
must yet more fully yield to the ardent, unwearied, imploring research of patient science ? Who does not, in those choice and
blessed moments, in which the world and its interests are forgotten,
and the spirit retires into the inmost sanctuary of its own meditations, and there, unconscious of every thing but itself and the infinite Perfection, of which it is the earthly type, and kindling the
flame of thought on the altar of prayer,—who does not feel, in mo-

ments like these, as if it must at last be given to man, to fathom the great secret of his own being; to solve the mighty problem

Of providence, foreknowledge, will, and fate !

When I think in what slight elements the great discoveries, that have changed the condition of the world, have oftentimes originated; on the entire revolution in political and social affairs, which has resulted from the use of the magnetic needle; on the world of wonders, teeming with the most important scientific discoveries, which has been opened by the telescope ; on the all-controlling influence of so simple an invention as that of movable metallic types ; on the effects of the invention of gunpowder, no doubt the casual result of some idle experiment in alchemy ; on the consequences that have resulted, and are likely to result from the application of the vapor of boiling water to the manufacturing arts, to navigation, and transportation by land ; on the results of a single sublime conception in the mind of Newton, on which he erected, as on a foundation, the glorious temple of the system of the heavens ;—in fine, when I consider how, from the great master-principle of the philosophy of Bacon,—the induction of truth from the observation of fact,—has flowed, as from a living fountain, the fresh and still swelling stream of modern science, I am almost oppressed with the idea of the probable connexion of the truths already known, with great principles which remain undiscovered ;—of the proximity in which we may unconsciously stand, to the most astonishing though yet unrevealed mysteries of the material and intellectual world.

If after thus considering the seemingly obvious sources from which the most important discoveries and improvements have sprung, we inquire into the extent of the field, in which farther discoveries are to be made, which is no other and no less than the entire natural and spiritual creation of God,—a grand and lovely system, even as we imperfectly apprehend it ; but no doubt most grand, lovely, and harmonious, beyond all that we now conceive or imagine ;— when we reflect that the most insulated, seemingly disconnected, and even contradictory parts of the system are, no doubt, bound together as portions of one stupendous whole ;—and that those, which are at present the least explicable, and which most completely defy the penetration hitherto bestowed upon them, are as intelligible, in reality, as that which seems most plain and clear ; that as every atom in the universe attracts every other atom, and is attracted by it, so every truth stands in harmonious connexion with every other truth ;—we are brought directly to the conclusion, that every portion of knowledge now possessed, every observed fact, every demonstrated principle, is a clew, which we hold by one end in the hand, and which is capable of guiding the faithful inquirer farther and farther into the inmost recesses of the labyrinth of nature. Ages on ages *may* elapse, before it conduct the patient intellect to the wonders of science, to which it will eventually lead him ; and, perhaps, with the next step he takes, he will reach the goal, and principles, destined to affect the condition of millions, beam in characters of light upon his understanding. What was at once more unexpected and more obvious, than Newton's discovery of the nature of light ? Every living being, since the creation of the world, had gazed on the rainbow ; to none had the beautiful mystery revealed itself. And even the great philosopher himself, while dissecting the solar beam, while actually untwisting the golden and silver threads that compose the ray of light, laid open but half its wonders. And who shall say that to us, to whom, as we think, modern science has disclosed the residue, truths more wonderful than those now known, will not yet be revealed ?

It is, therefore, by no means to be inferred, because the human mind has seemed to linger for a long time around certain results, —as ultimate principles,—that they and the principles closely connected with them, are not likely to be pushed much farther ; nor, on the other hand, does the intellect always require much time to bring its noblest fruits to seeming perfection. It was, I suppose, about two thousand years from the time when the peculiar properties of the magnet were first observed, before it became, through the means of those qualities, the pilot which guided Columbus to the American continent. Before the invention of the compass could take full effect, it was necessary that some navigator should practically and boldly grasp the idea that the globe is round. The two truths are apparently without connexion ; but in their application to practice, they are intimately associated. Hobbes says that Dr Harvey the illustrious discoverer of the circulation of the blood, is the only author of a great discovery, who ever lived to see it universally adopted. To the honor of subsequent science, this remark could not now, with equal truth, be made. Nor was Harvey himself without some painful experience of the obstacles arising from popular ignorance, against which truth sometimes forces its way to general acceptance. When he first proposed the beautiful doctrine, his practice fell off; people would not continue to trust their lives in the hands of such a dreamer. When it was firmly established, and generally received, one of his opponents published a tract, *de circulo sanguinis Salomoneo*, and proved from the twelfth chapter of Ecclesiastes, that the circulation of the blood was no secret, in the time of Solomon. The whole doctrine of the Reformation may be found in the writings of Wiclif; but neither he nor his age felt the importance of his principles, nor the consequences to which they led. Huss had studied the writings of Wiclif in manuscript, and was in no degree behind him, in the boldness with which he denounced the papal usurpations. But his voice was not heard beyond the mountains of Bohemia;—and he expired in agony at the stake, and his ashes were scattered upon the Rhine. A hundred years passed away. Luther, like an avenging angel, burst upon the world, and denounced the corruptions of the church, and rallied the host of the faithful, with a voice which might almost call up those ashes from their watery grave, and form and kindle them again into a living witness to the truth.

Thus Providence, which has ends innumerable to answer, in the conduct of the physical and intellectual, as of the moral world, sometimes permits the great discoverers fully to enjoy their fame; sometimes to catch but a glimpse of the extent of their achievements; and sometimes sends them, dejected and heart-broken, to the grave, unconscious of the importance of their own discoveries, and not merely undervalued by their contemporaries, but by themselves. It is plain that Copernicus, like his great contemporary, Columbus, though fully conscious of the boldness and the novelty of his doctrine, saw but a part of the changes it was to effect in science. After harboring in his bosom for long, long years, that pernicious heresy,—the solar system,—he died on the day of the appearance of his book from the press. The closing scene of his life, with a little help from the imagination, would furnish a noble subject for an artist. For thirty-five years, he has revolved and

matured in his mind, his system of the heavens. A natural mild-
ness of disposition, bordering on timidity, a reluctance to encounter
controversy, and a dread of persecution, have led him to withhold
his work from the press ; and to make known his system but to a
few confidential disciples and friends. At length he draws near
his end ; he is seventy-three years of age, and he yields his work
on ' the revolutions of the heavenly orbs ' to his friends for publication. The day, at last, has come, on which it is to be ushered
into the world. It is the twenty-fourth of May, 1543. On that
day,—the effect, no doubt, of the intense excitement of his mind,
operating upon an exhausted frame,—an effusion of blood brings
him to the gates of the grave. His last hour has come ; he lies
stretched upon the couch, from which he will never rise, in his
apartment at the Canonry at Frauenberg, in East Prussia. The
beams of the setting sun glance through the gothic windows of his
chamber ; near his bed-side is the armillary sphere, which he has
contrived, to represent his theory of the heavens,—his picture,
painted by himself, the amusement of his earlier years, hangs before him ; beneath it his astrolabe and other imperfect astronomical
instruments ; and around him are gathered his sorrowing disciples.
The door of the apartment opens ;—the eye of the departing sage
is turned to see who enters : it is a friend, who brings him the first
printed copy of his immortal treatise. He knows that in that book
he contradicts all that had ever been distinctly taught by former
philosophers ;—he knows that he has rebelled against the sway of
Ptolemy, which the scientific world had acknowledged for a thousand years ;—he knows that the popular mind will be shocked by
his innovations ;—he knows that the attempt will be made to press
even religion into the service against him ;—but he knows that his
book is true. He is dying, but he leaves a glorious truth, as his
dying bequest, to the world. He bids the friend who has brought
it, place himself between the window and his bed-side, that the
sun's rays may fall upon the precious volume, and he may behold
it once, before his eye grows dim. He looks upon it, takes it in
his hands, presses it to his breast, and expires. But no, he is not
wholly gone ! A smile lights up his dying countenance ;—a beam
of returning intelligence kindles in his eye ;—his lips move ;—and
the friend, who leans over him, can hear him faintly murmur the

beautiful sentiments, which the Christian lyrist, of a later age, has so finely expressed in verse ;—

Ye golden lamps of heaven, farewell, with all your feeble light!
Farewell, thou ever-changing moon, pale empress of the night!
And thou, refulgent orb of day, in brighter flames arrayed,
My soul, which springs beyond thy sphere, no more demands thy aid.
Ye stars are but the shining dust of my divine abode,
The pavement of those heavenly courts, where I shall reign with God!

So died the great Columbus of the heavens.* His doctrine, at first, for want of a general diffusion of knowledge, forced its way with difficulty against the deep-rooted prejudices of the age. Tycho Brahe attempted to restore the absurdities of the Ptolemaic system ; but Kepler, with a sagacity, which more than atones for all his strange fancies, laid hold of the theory of Copernicus, with a grasp of iron, and dragged it into repute. Galileo turned his telescope to the heavens, and observed the phases of Venus, which Copernicus boldly predicted must be discovered, as his theory required their appearance ; and lastly Newton arose, like a glorious sun, scattering the mists of doubt and opposition, and ascended the heavens full-orbed and cloudless, establishing at once his own renown and that of his predecessors, and crowned with the applauses of the world ; but declaring, with that angelic modesty which marked his character, ' I do not know what I may appear to the world ; but to myself I seem to have been only like a boy, playing on the sea-shore, and diverting myself in finding now and then a pebble, or a prettier shell than ordinary, while the great ocean of truth lay all undiscovered before me.'†

* "Ceterum editio jam perfecta erat, illiusque exemplum Rheticus ad ipsum mittebat, cum ecce, (ut optimus Gysius ad ipsum Rheticum rescripsit) qui vir fuerat totâ ætate valetudine satis firmâ, laborare cepit sanguinis profluvio et insequuta ex improviso paralysi ad dextrum latus. Per hoc tempus memoria illi vigorque mentis debilitatus. Habuit nihilominus, unde ad hanc vitam et dimittendam et cum meliore commutandam se compararet. Contigit autem, ut eodem die ac horis non multis priusquam animam efflaret, operis exemplum, ad se destinatum sibique oblatum, et viderit quidem et contigerit ; sed erant jam tum alia ipsi cura. Quare ad hoc compositus, animam Deo reddidit, die Maii xxiv anno MDXLIII, cum foret tribus jam mensibus et diebus quinque septuagenario major. Atque hujus modi quidem vita, hujusmodi mors Copernici fuit. *Nicolai Copernici Vita.* Opera Petri Gassendi, Tom. v, p. 451.

† Brewster's Life of Sir Isaac Newton, p. 301.

72

But whether the progress of any particular discovery toward a general reception be prompt or tardy, it is one of the laws of intellectual influence, as it is one of the great principles, on which we maintain, that the general diffusion of knowledge is favorable to the growth of science, that whatsoever be the fortune of inventors and discoverers, the invention and discovery are immortal,—the teacher dies in honor or neglect, but his doctrine survives. Fagots may consume his frame, but the truths he taught, like the spirit it enclosed, can never die. Partial and erroneous views may even retard his own mind, in the pursuit of a fruitful thought; but the errors of one age are the guides of the next; and the failure of one great mind but puts its successor on a different track, and teaches him to approach the object from a new point of observation.

In estimating the effect of a popular system of education upon the growth of science, it is necessary to bear in mind a circumstance, in which the present age and that which preceded it, are strongly discriminated from former periods; and that is the vastly greater extent, to which science exists among men, who do not desire to be known to the world as authors. Since the dawn of civilization on Egypt and Asia Minor, there never have been wanting individuals,—sometimes many flourishing at the same time,—who have made the most distinguished attainments in knowledge. Such, however, has been the condition of the world, that they formed a class by themselves. Their knowledge was transmitted in schools, often under strict injunctions of secrecy; or if recorded in books,—for want of the press, and owing to the constitution of society,—it made but little impression on the mass of the community and the business of life. As far as there is any striking exception to this remark, it is in the *free states* of antiquity, in which, through the medium of the popular organization of the governments, and the necessity of constant appeals to the people, the cultivated intellect was brought into close association with the understandings of the majority of men. This fact may perhaps go far to explain the astonishing energy and enduring power of the Grecian civilization, which remains to this day, after all that has been said to explain it, one of the most extraordinary facts in the history of the human mind. But from the period of the downfall of the Roman republic, and more especially after the establishment of the feudal system, the

division of the community into four classes, viz., the landed aristocracy, or nobles and gentry ; the spiritual aristocracy, or priesthood ;
the inhabitants of the cities ; and the peasantry ; (a division, which
has in modern Europe been considerably modified,—in some countries more, and in some less,—but in none wholly obliterated),—the
action and manifestation of knowledge were, till a comparatively
recent period, almost monopolized by the two higher classes ; and
in their hands it assumed in a great degree a literary, by which 1
mean, a book form. Such, of course, must ever, with reasonable
qualifications, continue to be the case ; and books will always be, in
a great degree, the vehicle, by which knowledge is to be communicated, preserved and transmitted.

But it is impossible to overlook the fact,—it is one of the most
characteristic features of the civilization of the age, that this is far
less *exclusively* the case, than at any former period. The community is filled with an incalculable amount of unwritten knowledge, of science which never will be committed to paper by the
active men who possess it, and which has been acquired on the
basis of a good education, by observation, experience, and the action
of the mind itself. A hundred and fifty years ago, it is doubtful
whether, out of the observatories and universities, there were ten
men in Europe who could ascertain the longitude by lunar observation. At the present day, scarce a vessel sails to foreign lands, in
the public or mercantile service, in which the process is not understood. In like manner, in our manufacturing establishments, in the
construction and direction of railroads and canals, on the improved
farms throughout the country, there is possessed, embodied, and
brought into action, a vast deal of useful knowledge, of which its
possessors will never make a literary use, for the composition of a
book, but which is daily employed to the signal advantage of the
country. Much of it is directly derived from a study of the great
book of nature, whose pages are written by the hand of God ; and
which, in no part of the civilized world, has been more faithfully or
profitably studied than in New-England. The intelligent population
of the country, furnished with the keys of knowledge at our institutions of education, have addressed themselves to the further acquisition of useful science,—to its acquisition at once, and applica-

tion,—with a vigor, a diligence, a versatility, and a success, which are the admiration of the world.

Let it not be supposed, that I wish to disconnect this diffusive science, from that which is recorded and propagated in books ; to do this, would be to reverse the error of former ages. It is the signal improvement of the present day, that the action and reaction of book-learning and general intelligence are so prompt, intense, and all-pervading. The moment a discovery is made, a principle demonstrated, a proposition advanced through the medium of the press, in any part of the world, it finds immediately a host, num- berless as the sands of the sea, prepared to take it up, to canvass, confirm, refute, or pursue it. At every waterfall, on the line of every canal and railroad, in the counting-room of every factory and mercantile establishment, on the quarter-deck of every ship which navigates the high seas, on the farm of every intelligent husband- man, in the workshop of every skilful mechanic, at the desk of the schoolmaster, in the office of the lawyer, the study of the physician and clergyman, at the fireside of every man, who has had the elements of a good education, not less than in the professed retreats of learning, there is an intellect to seize, to weigh, and appropriate the suggestion, whether it belong to the world of science, of taste, or of morals.

In some countries there may be more, and in some less, of this *latent* intellectual power ; latent I call it, in reference not to its action on life, but to its display in books. In some countries, the books are in advance of the people, in others greatly behind them. In Europe, as compared with America, the advantage is in favor of the books. The restraint imposed upon the mind, in reference to all political questions, has had the effect of driving more than a pro- portion of the intellect of that part of the world into the cultivation of science and literature, as a profession ; and if we were to judge merely from the character of a few great works published at the expense of the government, and the attainments of a few individ- uals, Italy and Austria would stand on a level with Great Britain and France. The great difference between nation and nation, in reference to knowledge, is in fact, in no small degree, in this very distinction. In reference to the attainments of scholars and men of science by profession, of which some few are found in every civilized country, all nations may be considered as forming one intellectual republic; but in reference to the diffusion of knowledge among the people, its action on the character of nations, its fruitful influence on society,—the most important differences exist between different countries.

III. There remains to be discussed the last topic of our address,—the influence of a general diffusion of knowledge on morals, a point which, if it were debatable, would raise a question of portentous import;—for if the diffusion of knowledge is unfriendly to goodness, shall we take refuge in the reign of ignorance? What is the precise question on which, in this connexion, rational scruples may be started, deserving a serious answer?

The merits of the case may, I believe, be stated somewhat as follows:—that there seems, in individuals, no fixed proportion between intellectual and moral growth. Eminent talent and distinguished attainment are sometimes connected with obliquity of character. Of those who have reached the heights of speculative science, not all are entitled to the commendation bestowed on Sir William Jones,—that he was 'learned, without pride; and not too wise to pray;' and one entire class of men of letters and science, the French philosophers of the last century, were, as a body,—though by no means without honorable exceptions,—notorious for a disbelief of revealed religion; an insensibility to the delicacies of moral restraint; a want of that purity of feeling and character, which we would gladly consider the inseparable attendant of intellectual cultivation. It is a question of deep interest, whether, from these facts, and others like them, any thing can be fairly deduced, unfavorable to the moral influence of a diffusion of knowledge.

No country in Europe had retained more of the feudal divisions than France before the Revolution. A partition of the orders of society, but little less rigid than the oriental economy of *castes*, was kept up. Causes, which time would fail us to develop, had rendered the court and capital of France signally corrupt, during the last century. It is doubtful whether, in a civilized state, the foundations of social morality were ever so totally subverted. It was by no means one of the least active causes of this corruption,

that all connexion between the court and capital, and the higher
ranks in general, on the one hand, and the people on the other,
was cut off by the constitution of society, and the hopeless depression, degradation, and ignorance of the mass of the people. Under
these influences, the school of the encyclopedists was trained.
They did not make, they found the corruption. They were
reared in it. They grew up in the presence and under the patronage of a most dissolute court, surrounded by the atmosphere of an
abandoned metropolis, without the constraint, the corrective, or the
check of a wholesome public sentiment, emanating from an intelligent and virtuous population. The great monitors of society
were hushed. The pulpit, not over active at that time as a moral
teacher in the Catholic church in Europe, was struck dumb, for
some of the highest dignitaries were stained with all the vices of the
rest of their order, that of the nobility; and some of the most
virtuous and eloquent of the prelates had been obliged to exhaust
their talents in panegyrics of the frail but royal dead. The press
was mute on every thing which touched the vices of the time. It
was not then the diffusion of knowledge, from the philosophical
circles of Paris, that corrupted France; it was the gross darkness
of the provinces, and the deep degradation every where of the
majority of the people, which left unrebuked the depravity of the
capital. It was precisely a diffusion of knowledge that was wanted. And if, as I doubt not, France at this time is more virtuous,
(notwithstanding the demoralizing effects of the Revolution and its
wars), than at any former period, it is owing to the diffusion of
knowledge, which has followed the subversion of feudalism, and
the regeneration of the provinces. Paris has ceased to be France.
A dissolute court has ceased to give the tone of feeling to the
entire kingdom; for an intelligent class of independent citizens and
husbandmen has sprung up on the ruins of a decayed landed
aristocracy, and the reformation of France is rapidly going on, in
the elevation of the intellectual, and with it the political, social, and
moral character of the people.

I do not deem it necessary to argue, at length, against any
general inference from individual cases, in which intellectual
eminence has been associated with moral depravity. The question
concerns general influences and natural tendencies, and must be

considered mainly in reference to the comparative effects of ignorance and knowledge on communities, nations, and ages. In this reference, nothing is more certain than that the diffusion of knowledge is friendly to the benign influence of religion and morals. The illustrations of this great truth are so abundant, that I know not where to begin nor where to end with them. Knowledge is the faithful ally both of natural and revealed religion. Natural religion is one grand deduction made by the enlightened understanding, from a faithful study of the great book of nature; and the record of revealed religion, contained in the Bible, is not merely confirmed by the harmony which the mind delights to trace between it and the 'elder Scripture writ by God's own hand;' but Revelation, in all ages, has called to its aid the meditations and researches of pious and learned men; and most assuredly, at every period, for one man of learning, superficial or profound, who has turned the weapons of science against religion or morals, hundreds have consecrated their labors to their defence. Christianity is revealed to the mind of man, in a peculiar sense. To what are its hopes, its sanctions, its precepts addressed; to the physical or the intellectual portion of his nature; to the perishing or the immortal element? Is it on ignorance or on knowledge, that its evidences repose? Is it by ignorance or knowledge, that its sacred records are translated from the original tongues, into the thousands of languages, spoken in the world?—and if, by perverted knowledge, it has sometimes been attacked, is it by ignorance or knowledge that it has been and must be defended? What but knowledge is to prevent us, in short, from being borne down and carried away, by the overwhelming tide of fanaticism and delusion, put in motion by the moon-struck impostors of the day? Before we permit ourselves to be agitated with painful doubts as to the connexion of a diffusion of knowledge with religion and morals, let us remember that, in proportion to the ignorance of a community, is the ease with which their belief can be shaken and their assent attained to the last specious delusion of the day,—till you may finally get down to a degree of ignorance, on which reason and Scripture are alike lost; which is ready to receive Joe Smith as an inspired prophet, and Matthias as —— but shame and horror forbid me to complete the sentence.

But this topic must be treated in a higher strain. The diffusion
of knowledge is not merely favorable to religion and morals, but,
in the last and highest analysis, they cannot be separated from each
other. In the great prototype of our feeble ideas of perfection, the
wise and the good are so blended together, that the absence of one
would enfeeble and impair the other. There can be no real knowledge of truth which does not tend to purify and elevate the affections. A little knowledge,—much knowledge,—may not, in individual cases, subdue the passions of a cold, corrupt, and selfish
heart. But if knowledge will not do it, can it be done by the
want of knowledge?

What is human knowledge? It is the cultivation and improvement of the spiritual principle in man. We are composed of two
elements; the one, a little dust caught up from the earth, to which
we shall soon return; the other, a spark of that divine intelligence,
in which and through which we bear the image of the great Creator. By knowledge, the wings of the intellect are spread;—by
ignorance, they are closed and palsied; and the physical passions
are left to gain the ascendancy. Knowledge opens all the senses
to the wonders of creation; ignorance seals them up, and leaves
the animal propensities unbalanced by reflection, enthusiasm, and
taste. To the ignorant man, the glorious pomp of day, the sparkling mysteries of night, the majestic ocean, the rushing storm, the
plenty-bearing river, the salubrious breeze, the fertile field, the do-
cile animal tribes, the broad, the various, the unexhausted domain
of nature, are a mere outward pageant, poorly understood in their
character and harmony, and prized only so far as they minister to
the supply of sensual wants. How different the scene to the
man whose mind is stored with knowledge! For him the mystery
is unfolded, the veils lifted up, as one after another he turns the
leaves of that great volume of creation, which is filled in every
page with the characters of wisdom, power, and love; with lessons
of truth the most exalted; with images of unspeakable loveliness
and wonder; arguments of Providence; food for meditation; themes
of praise. One noble science sends him to the barren hills, and
teaches him to survey their broken precipices. Where ignorance
beholds nothing but a rough inorganic mass, instruction discerns
the intelligible record of the primal convulsions of the world; the

secrets of ages before man was; the landmarks of the elemental struggles and throes of what is now the terraqueous globe. Buried monsters, of which the races are now extinct, are dragged out of deep strata, dug out of eternal rocks, and brought almost to life, to bear witness to the power that created them. Before the admiring student of nature has realized all the wonders of the elder world, thus, as it were, re-created by science, another delightful instructress, with her microscope in her hand, bids him sit down and learn at last to know the universe in which he lives; and contemplate the limbs, the motions, the circulations of races of animals, disporting in *their* tempestuous ocean,—a drop of water. Then, while his whole soul is penetrated with admiration of the power which has filled with life, and motion, and sense, these all but non-existent atoms,—O, then, let the divinest of the muses, let astronomy approach, and take him by the hand; let her

> Come, but keep her wonted state,
> With even step and musing gait,
> And looks commercing with the skies,
> Her rapt soul sitting in her eyes:—

Let her lead him to the mount of vision; let her turn her heaven-piercing tube to the sparkling vault : through that, let him observe the serene star of evening, and see it transformed into a cloud-encompassed orb, a world of rugged mountains and stormy deeps; or behold the pale beams of Saturn, lost to the untaught observer amidst myriads of brighter stars, and see them expand into the broad disk of a noble planet,—the seven attendant worlds,—the wondrous rings,—a mighty system in itself, borne at the rate of twenty-two thousand miles an hour, on its broad pathway through the heavens; and then let him reflect that our great solar system, of which Saturn and his stupendous retinue is but a small part, fills itself, in the general structure of the universe, but the space of one fixed star; and that the power which filled the drop of water with millions of living beings, is present and active, throughout this illimitable creation!—Yes, yes,

> The undevout astronomer *is* mad !

But it is time to quit these sublime contemplations, and bring this address to a close. I may seem to have undertaken a superfluous labor, in pleading the cause of education. This institution, consecrated to learning and piety ; these academic festivities ; this favoring audience, which bestows its countenance on our literary exercises ; the presence of so many young men, embarking on the ocean of life, devoted to the great interests of the rational mind and immortal soul, bear witness for me, that the cause of education stands not here in need of champions. Let it be our pride, that it has never needed them, among the descendants of the Pilgrims ; let it be our vow, that, by the blessing of Providence, it never shall need them, so long as there is a descendant of the Pilgrims to plead its worth. Yes, let the pride of military glory belong to foreign regions ; let the refined corruptions of the older world attract the traveller to its splendid capitals ; let a fervid sun ripen, for other states, the luxuries of a tropical clime. Let it be ours to boast that we inherit a land of liberty and light ; let the school-house and the church continue to be the landmarks of the New-England village ; let the son of New-England, whithersoever he may wander, leave that behind him, which shall make him home-sick for his native land ; let freedom, and knowledge, and morals, and religion, as they are our birthright, be the birthright of our children to the end of time !

ADDRESS

DELIVERED AT BLOODY BROOK, IN SOUTH DEERFIELD, SEPTEMBER
30, 1835, IN COMMEMORATION OF THE FALL OF THE 'FLOWER
OF ESSEX,' AT THAT SPOT, IN KING PHILIP'S WAR, SEPTEMBER
18, (o. s.) 1675.

GATHERED together in this temple not made with hands, to
unroll the venerable record of our fathers' history, let our first thoughts
ascend to Him, whose heavens are spread out, as a glorious canopy, above our heads. As our eyes look up to the everlasting hills
which rise before us, let us remember that in the dark and eventful
days we commemorate, the hand that lifted their eternal pillars to
the clouds, was the sole stay and support of our afflicted sires.
While we contemplate the lovely scene around us,—once covered
with the gloomy forest and the tangled swamps, through which the
victims of this day pursued their unsuspecting path to the field of
slaughter,—let us bow in gratitude to Him, beneath whose paternal care a little one has become a thousand, and a small one a strong
nation. Assembled under the shadow of this venerable tree, let
us bear in thankful recollection, that at the period when its sturdy
limbs which now spread over us, hung with nature's rich and verdant tapestry, were all folded up within the narrow compass of
their seminal germ,—the thousand settlements of our beloved country, teeming with the life, energy, and power of prosperous millions,
were struggling with unimagined hardships for a doubtful existence,
in a score of feeble plantations scattered through the hostile wilder-

ness.   Alas, it was not alone the genial showers, and the gentle dews, and the native richness of the soil, which nourished the growth of this stately tree.   The sod from which it sprung, was moistened with the blood of brave men who fell for their country, and the ashes of peaceful dwellings are mingled with the consecrated earth.   In like manner, it is not alone the wisdom and the courage, the piety and the virtue of our fathers,—not alone the prudence with which they laid the foundations of the state, to which we are indebted for its happy growth and all-pervading prosperity. No, we ought never to forget, we ought this day especially to remember, that it was in their sacrifices and trials, their heart-rending sorrows, their ever-renewed tribulations, their wanderings, their conflicts, their wants, and their woes,—that the corner-stone of our privileges and blessings was laid.

As I stand on this hallowed spot, my mind filled with the traditions of that disastrous day, surrounded by these enduring natural memorials, impressed with the touching ceremonies we have just witnessed,—the affecting incidents of the bloody scene crowd upon my imagination.   This compact and prosperous village disappears, and a few scattered log cabins are seen, in the bosom of the primeval forest, clustering for protection around the rude blockhouse in the centre.   A corn-field or two has been rescued from the all-surrounding wilderness, and here and there the yellow husks are heard to rustle in the breeze, that comes loaded with the mournful sighs of the melancholy pine woods.   Beyond, the interminable forest spreads in every direction, the covert of the wolf, of the rattle-snake, of the savage ; and between its gloomy copses, what is now a fertile and cultivated meadow, stretches out a dreary expanse of unreclaimed morass.   I look,—I listen.   All is still,— solemnly,—frightfully still.   No voice of human activity or enjoyment breaks the dreary silence of nature, or mingles with the dirge of the woods and water-courses.   All *seems* peaceful and still : —and yet there *is* a strange heaviness in the fall of the leaves in that wood that skirts the road ;—there is an unnatural flitting in those shadows ;—there is a plashing sound in the waters of that brook, which makes the flesh creep with horror.   Hark ! it is the click of a gun-lock from that thicket ;—no, it is a pebble, that has dropped from the over-hanging cliff, upon the rock beneath.   It is, it is the gleaming blade of a scalping-knife;—no, it is a sun-beam, thrown off from that dancing ripple. It is, it is the red feather of a savage chief, peeping from behind that maple tree;—no, it is a leaf, which September has touched with her many-tinted pencil. And now a distant drum is heard; yes, that is a sound of life,— conscious, proud life. A single fife breaks upon the ear,—a stirring strain. It is one of the marches, to which the stern warriors of Cromwell moved over the field at Naseby and Worcester. There are no loyal ears, to take offence at a puritanical march in a transatlantic forest; and hard by, at Hadley, there is a gray-haired fugitive, who followed the cheering strain, at the head of his division in the army of the great usurper. The warlike note grows louder;—I hear the tread of armed men:—but I run before my story.

Before we proceed to the details of the catastrophe, which forms the subject of this day's commemoration, let us pause, for a moment, on the state of things at that time existing in New-England, and the previous events of the war, of which this was so prominent an occurrence.

Although the continent of America, when discovered by the Europeans, was in the possession of the native tribes, it was obviously the purpose of Providence, that it should become the abode of civilization, the arts, and Christianity. How shall these blessings be introduced? Obviously by no other process,—none other is practicable,—than an emigration to the new-found continent from the civilized communities of Europe. This is doubly necessary, not only as being the only process adequate to produce the desired end, but in order to effect another great purpose connected with the relief and regeneration of mankind, namely, the establishment of a place of refuge for the children of persecution, and the opening of a new field of action, where principles of liberty and improvement could be developed, without the restraints imposed on the work of reform, by the inveterate abuses of the established order of things abroad.

There was, therefore, a moral necessity, that the two races should be brought into contact, in the newly-discovered region; the one, ignorant, weak in every thing that belongs to intellectual strength, feebly redeeming the imperfections of the savage, by the stern and

cheerless virtues of the wilderness ;—the other, strong in his powerful arts, in his weapons of destruction, in his capacity of combination ;—strong in the intellectual and moral elevation of his character and purposes :—the two thus separated, alas, by a chasm,
which seems all but impassable !—A fearful approach ;—a perilous
contiguity ! But how shall it be avoided ? Shall this fair continent,
adequate to the support of civilized millions,—on which nature has
bestowed her bounties,—on which Providence is ready to shower its
blessings,—lie waste, the exclusive domain of the savage and the wild
beast ? Heaven forbid. How shall it be settled ? The age of miracles
is past ; the emigrants must be brought hither, and sustained here,
by the usual motives and impulses which operate on the minds of
men, and under the various working of the circumstances of the
first discovery and occupation. If things are left to second causes,
the passion for adventure, the lust of power, the thirst for gold, will
spur on the remorseless bands of Pizarro and Cortes. Prospects
of political aggrandizement and commercial profit must actuate the
planters of Virginia. The sword of spiritual persecution must
drive out the suffering Puritan, in search of a place of rest. In
correspondence with the motives which prompt the separate expeditions or the individual leaders, will be the relations established
with the natives. In Spanish America, a wild and merciless crusade will be waged against them ; they will be hunted by the war-
horse and the bloodhound ; vast multitudes will perish, the residue
will be enslaved, their labor made a source of profit, and they will
thereby be preserved from annihilation. In the Anglo-American
settlements, treaties will be entered into, mutual rights acknowledged ; the artificial relations of independent and allied states will
be established ; and as the civilized race rapidly multiplies, the native tribes will recede, sink into the wilderness, and disappear.
Millions of Mexicans, escaping the exterminating sword of the conquerors, subsist in a miserable vassalage to the present day ;—of
the tribes that inhabited New-England,· not an individual, of unmixed blood, and speaking the language of his fathers, remains.

Was this an unavoidable consequence ? However deplorable,
there is too much reason to think that it was. We cannot perceive
in what way the forest could have been cleared, and its place taken
by the cornfield, without destroying the game ; in what way the

meadows could be drained, and the beaver-dams broken down, without expelling their industrious little builders ;—nor in what way the uncivilized man, living from the chase, and requiring a wide range of forest for his hunting-ground, destitute of arts and letters,—belonging to a different variety of the species, speaking a different tongue, suffering all the disadvantages of social and intellectual inferiority, could maintain his place, by the side of the swelling, pressing population,—the diligence and dexterity,—the superior thrift, arts, and arms,—the seductive vices, of the civilized race. I will not say, that imagination cannot picture a colonial settlement, where the emigrants should come in such numbers, with such resources, with such principles, dispositions, and tempers, as instantly to form a kindly amalgamation with the native tribes ; and from the moment of setting foot on the new-found soil, commence the benign work of brotherhood and assimilation, moving forward to a peaceful conquest, beneath the banner of charity. I would not stint the resources, or sound the depths of godlike benevolence. But in a practical survey of life on both sides, such a consummation seems impossible. The new comers are men,—men of all tempers and characters. Their society may be formed on the platform of religion ; their principles may be pure, lofty, austere ; their dispositions peaceful ; their carriage mild and gentle ; but their judgments will be fallible, and they cannot be expected to rise far above the errors and prejudices of their age. Our fathers regarded the aboriginal inhabitants as heathen. They bestowed unwearied pains to christianize them, and with much greater success, than is generally supposed. Still the mass remained unconverted, and an ominous inference was drawn from the expulsion of the native races of Canaan. Scarcely, moreover, were the first colonists settled in Plymouth, when licentious adventurers followed in their train ; who not only introduced among the Indian tribes the destructive vices of the Europeans, and furnished them with fire-arms and weapons of steel ; but by acts of violence and injustice gave provocation for their use. Then, too, we must look on the Indian, not with the eye of sentiment and romance, but of truth and reality. Seen as he really is, he stands low in the scale of humanity. His vices were not all learned of the white settlers. Before the European was known on the continent, he was perpetually engaged in exterminating conflicts with the neighboring tribes. His merciless mode of waging war,—the horrors of the scalping-knife and the stake, are of his own invention. Within the bosom of his tribe he leads an indolent, a squalid, and a cheerless exist-ence, alternating from repletion to starvation,—without law to pro-tect his property, or restrain his passions ;—and between tribe and tribe he is unacquainted with those blessings of an international code, which do so much to soften the horrors of war. The supe-rior race approaches, jealousies arise, conflicts succeed, acts of vio-lence are committed, and war rages. It is, in its nature, a de-structive war, for the savage rarely gives quarter. Is the blame all on one side? Does reason require us to trace all the evils to the corruption of the civilized race,—to suppose that no malignant feelings, no acts of barbarity, no outbreakings of savage rage or savage fraud, are to be laid to the account of the untutored child of nature ?

There are other considerations, which must not be overlooked in this connexion. When we contemplate the mighty throngs in the civilized settlements that now line the coast, and fill the interior regions adjacent to it, we must not conclude that vast aboriginal tribes, once occupying them, were exterminated by the hand of violence, to make room for the white race. This portion of the continent was very thinly peopled on the arrival of our fathers. There never were any large towns inhabited by the natives of New-England, like those which were found by the Spaniards, in Mexico and Peru. It was probably not practicable, without the aid of the arts of civilized life, without the use of iron, and without agricul-ture, to support a dense population, in so cold a climate, on a comparatively hard soil, covered with forests. In addition to this, the population, not crowded at best, had been greatly reduced by a pestilence a few years before the commencement of the planta-tion at Plymouth. A constant and uniform statement was made by the Indians to the first settlers, that an epidemic disease ran through all their tribes a few years before the landing of the Pil-grims, baffling their simple skill, and in some cases reducing large clans almost to the point of extinction. In this state of things, the settlers at Plymouth, and afterwards those of Massachusetts, landed on the coast, and fifty-five years,—a period longer than that which has elapsed since the peace of 1783,—passed away, before the commencement of hostilities in either colony, between the settlers and the natives. It is true that in 1636 and 1637, the Pequot war broke out in Connecticut ;—a war in which all the New-England colonies took part. But the Pequots were themselves an invading race. They had dispossessed the tribes, which previously occupied the eastern portion of Connecticut ; and when the war with the English commenced, the remnants of those tribes, cut off or subjugated, promptly seized the opportunity of revenging the injuries inflicted on themselves, by the great war-chiefs of the Pequots. In the disastrous campaigns of 1636 and 1637, in which that tribe was destroyed, one thousand persons are said to have perished, and the warriors of Sassacus were computed at seven hundred. As every able-bodied savage was a warrior, the whole number of his tribe could not have exceeded three thousand,—a large community to be subjugated by their own or others' wrong, but a small number to lay claim to the perpetual reservation of a region like Connecticut.

There is still another circumstance of very considerable interest in reference to the melancholy fate of the New-England Indians. To barbarous tribes, who stand as low in the scale of humanity as the Pequots and Narragansets, the Wampanoags or the Nipmucks, who live by hunting and fishing, with scarce any thing that can be called agriculture, and wholly without arts, the removal from one tract of country to another is comparatively easy. A change of abode implies no great sacrifice of private interest or social prosperity. No fixed property is destroyed, no pursuits deserted not to be resumed, no venerable establishments broken up, none of the great and costly structures of a civilized state of society abandoned. Nor is this all. The extreme simplicity of savage life favors the amalgamation of tribes, forced by circumstances upon each other. As far as we can trace the relations of the North American tribes with each other, both before and since the settlement of the country, an absorption of the fragments of once powerful communities, by more prosperous tribes, is constantly going on. In no part of the human family is war so much the business of life, as among the native races of our continent ; nowhere are wars more sanguinary and fatal ; and in proportion to the simplicity of their mode of life

74

is the ease, with which the feeble remnants of once powerful but subjugated tribes are swallowed up by the victor, or forced into union with neighboring friendly clans. On the same principle, with the advance of civilization, the native tribes receded. No wars, literally, of extermination, at any time, were waged. The battles were stern, decisive, and to those engaged in them, fatal. Prisoners of war were reduced to slavery, and sometimes sold into foreign bondage. But no general and indiscriminate slaughter took place. The number of Indians slain in the early wars, I take to have been not much greater than that of the whites, in the same period. The great majority of the Indians did, what the settlers of Deerfield, Hadley, Northampton, and Springfield were at times tempted to do, and would have done, had the war continued; they fell back upon their kindred. As the English colonists, if the fortune of war had been adverse, would have gone back from the Connecticut river to the coast, the Indians, that hunted and fished on the river, retired before the advancing settlements, united themselves with their brethren farther west and north, supplying the waste of their continual wars, and easily incorporated among them.*

I dwell the more on this point, because it is one of vague reproach to the memory of our fathers; and yet I am not sure, that, unless we deny altogether the rightfulness of settling the continent, —unless we maintain that it was from the origin unjust and wrong to introduce the civilized race into America, and that the whole of what is now our happy and prosperous country ought to have been left, as it was found, the abode of barbarity and heathenism,—I am not sure, that any different result could have taken place. Had the colonists and the Indians been men without interests, passions, and vices, occasions of collisions and bloodshed on both sides might have been avoided; but, taking white men as they are and savages as they are, looking on the one hand not for faultless perfection of

---

* It can be scarcely necessary to state, that considerations of this kind have no applicability to the questions recently agitated in the United States, relative to the rights acquired by Indian tribes, under solemn compacts, voluntarily entered into by the United States, at the instance and for the benefit of an individual State, and for considerations deemed advantageous, at the time, both to the individual State and the general government. The author's opinion of those questions was fully expressed, in the House of Representatives of the United States, in 1830 and 1831.

counsel or policy, on the part of governments or individuals, but allowing for the occasional operation of human weaknesses in both, and expecting of the Indians that they will display toward the new settlers the violence and barbarity, which mark their intercourse with each other, and which belong to uncivilized heathen,—I am unable to see, that there was on either side great matter of reproach. On the contrary, I see much deserving of the highest commendation, in the humanity and forbearance of the colonists, and in the hospitality and magnanimity of the Indian chiefs, who for an entire generation maintained the peace of the country, in the new and critical condition of affairs in which they were placed.* The colonies of Plymouth and Massachusetts both commenced their settlements in amity with the Indians. They were welcomed, in both cases, by the tribes with which they came immediately in contact. It was the established policy of the colonists to purchase the Indian title to the land, at a price regarded as satisfactory by those who disposed of it, and by prohibiting private purchases, to protect the natives from being overreached by adventurers. I believe that it was with perfect justice, as it evidently was with entire sincerity, that Governor Winslow declared, in the spring of 1676, that ' before these present troubles broke out, the English did not possess one foot of land in the colony of Plymouth, but what was fairly obtained by honest purchase of the Indian proprietors.'

But, however justly we may defend the memory of our fathers, against the charge of wantonly pursuing a policy of extermination, it is not the less certain, that the march of events was well calculated to excite the jealousy of the native tribes. Every day's experience of the growing power of the whites gave force to this jealousy; and as war is the mad resort to which, in the blindness of his passions, savage as well as civilized man instinctively flies, for the redress of all sorts of public injuries, real or threatened, it was perfectly natural, that the bold and impatient chiefs of the native races should at length begin to contemplate the possibility of arresting by force the progress of the dangerous intruders. They

* See some judicious remarks on this subject in Mr Upham's Artillery Election Sermon, delivered June, 1832, page 8.

had learned the use of fire-arms, and obtained a supply of them from the French in Nova Scotia, the Dutch in New-York, and from illicit traders in New-England. It required but little discernment to perceive, that, in every thing, but the undefined resources of civilized communities, (the extent of which they had not yet learned fully to appreciate), the Indians greatly overbalanced the colonists. In addition to the general sense of encroachment and danger, it is easy to conceive, that a thousand individual provocations, on both sides, must have taken place between parties like the whites and the Indians; by which a great amount of private irritation and bitterness was infused into the public sentiment between the two races.

Their relations toward each other reached their crisis in 1675. Thirty-eight years had elapsed, since the destruction of Sassacus and his Pequots. A race of young warriors had grown up, on whom the lesson of wisdom taught by that catastrophe was lost. As has been just observed, they had learned to use and repair the guns, which they had obtained from various quarters. They were well acquainted with the numbers and habits of the settlers, and had found out, that the proportion of non-combatants to fighting men was vastly greater than among themselves. The Narragansets and Pokanokets were now the most powerful of the New-England tribes. They occupied the old colony of Plymouth, and the State of Rhode Island. The latter was the tribe, with which the settlers of Plymouth first entered into amicable relations, under their friendly chief Massassoit, and these relations remained unimpaired to his death. He was the firm, the considerate, the unwavering friend of the settlers, and adhered with fidelity to the compact which he had formed with them, in the very infancy of the colony. Massassoit died about 1660. He left two sons, who, at their own request, and during their father's lifetime, received the English names of Alexander, and Philip. Alexander was the elder, and exercised the authority of sachem on his father's death, not without suspicion, how well founded it is now impossible to say, of entertaining hostile designs toward the colony. On his death, he was succeeded by his brother Philip, a person greatly the superior both of his elder brother and his father, in reach of policy, capacity, vigor, and resource. With his accession to power in his tribe, the suspicion of unfriendly purposes toward the whites rapidly increased. The government of Plymouth colony entertained serious fears that he meditated mischief to the settlement. The government of Massachusetts seems at first to have thought these fears without foundation. Under its mediation, an interview between the two parties was brought about in the meeting-house at Taunton, in 1671. The commissioners of Plymouth and Massachusetts, and their armed attendants, being arrayed on one side of the church; and Philip, and his chieftains, on the other. In this conference, Philip made the submission which was required of him, renewed the compact with Plymouth, and agreed to give up his fire-arms.

These measures, however they may have delayed the execution of his projects, no doubt confirmed him, by the sense of new injury, in his ultimate design; and from this period, he is supposed to have meditated the dangerous project of a union of all the tribes in New-England against the colonists.

And here let us pause for a moment, to reflect on the respective condition and strength of the parties. Accustomed to what we see around us of the power and resources of our own prosperous states, and with only a fading tradition of the strength of the Indians, and with our minds habitually penetrated with the impression of the essential superiority of the white race, we are in danger of greatly mistaking the relative strength of the parties. Very different was an Indian war, a century and a half ago, from those which are waged at the present day, in which, from the bosom of the overswarming population of the States, regiments of infantry, artillery, and dragoons are sent out, to trample down the enervated remnants of once warlike races, with the certainty, on both sides, if that force should fail, that another, twice as powerful, would instantly take its place. The population of New-England at this period, 1675, is not accurately known. It is conjecturally stated by Chalmers, at one hundred and twenty thousand. But Dr Trumbull, by an accurate deduction from the known number of the militia of Connecticut, and the proportion it bore in the levies of the United Colonies, reduces it to one third of that amount, which I am inclined to think much nearer the truth. The whole interior of the country was unsettled. The region west of Connecticut was a pathless wilderness, and that portion of it now within the States of Massachusetts and Vermont was unoccupied even by savages. There were a few feeble settlements on the coasts of Maine and New-Hampshire. In Massachusetts, there were small settlements at Westfield, Springfield, Northampton, Hadley, Hatfield, Deerfield, and Northfield;—some of them rather stations than settlements. After leaving the river to go to the east, Brookfield was the first settlement, and this with Lancaster was the only settlement in Worcester county. Medfield, Sudbury, Marlborough, Groton, Chelmsford, formed the frontier, and were all attacked by the Indians, in the course of Philip's war. The danger of the settlements was so great, that all the male inhabitants were required to be armed, and although the country was penetrated with the liveliest sense of peril, and numerous volunteers marched against the enemy,—men, horses, and provisions were continually called for, by the severest exercise of the power of impressment.

The numbers of the Indians are not more accurately known, than those of the colonists. The warriors under the immediate command of Philip are supposed to have numbered seven hundred. Those of the Narragansets, who joined him in the course of the war, are estimated at two thousand. The tribes which occupied the central portions of the State and the banks of the river, and who were drawn by Philip into the contest, cannot be estimated at less than seven or eight hundred more; making the entire hostile force about thirty-five hundred.

Many of the advantages of the contest were on the side of the Indians. War was their hereditary pursuit:—boldness and fortitude, the capacity of effort and fatigue their chief virtues. The generation of colonists then on the stage was wholly unused to war. Thirty-eight years had passed, since the conquest of the Pequots; and the military forces now raised, were drawn, to a great extent, by conscription, from the various walks of industrious, peaceful life. The Indians had been in the habit of constant intercourse with the settlers. They knew the position of their towns, and even of their houses, fields, and places of worship. They knew the persons of the leading men; and were able to choose the best place for an ambuscade, and the best time for an assault. Sundays and fast days were the chosen times for an attack; for then observation had taught them, though the men went armed to meeting, that the aged and the defenceless, the women and the children were led, by the strong sense of religious duty, to venture abroad. On the other hand, the colonists had, of necessity, but a limited acquaintance with the haunts of the Indians, in the forests and the swamps. The Indians, though not as well furnished with arms, were better marksmen than the English. The state of the roads, and the nature of Indian warfare, excluded the use of artillery, and the peculiar weapons of the savage, the tomahawk and the scalping-knife, with the inhuman tortures inflicted on the prisoners, carried terrors to hearts unshaken by common perils. Cæsar tells us that when, for the first time, he was about to come into conflict with the barbarous Germans,—a race which stood at about the same point, on the scale of civilization, as the North American Indians,—many of the young officers who had followed him from Rome, panic-struck with the thought of a battle with the dreaded barbarians, sought excuses for asking a furlough ; and those whose pride forbade their quitting the army, hid themselves in their tents and wept. It is not to be wondered at, if the horrors of Indian warfare were felt by the young men of Massachusetts, who were dragged from the plough and the workshop, and forced to plunge into pathless woods and frightful swamps, in search of the ferocious savage.

Both parties concentrated their strength, as for a decisive struggle. The confederation among the colonies, of which defence against the Indians was the main object, had experienced some interruption, but was revived at the commencement of the war. A little more than half the troops raised in the United Colonies were apportioned on Massachusetts. Philip, on the other hand, had, as is supposed, for some years labored to effect a general confederacy of the Indian tribes. There are not wanting even suggestions, that he endeavored to rouse the native tribes as far south as Virginia ; but these suggestions are chiefly entitled to notice, as indications of the opinion formed by the English writers of the reach of his policy, and activity of his movements. I see in the contemporary accounts, no proof of any such remote operations. But the events of the war showed, that he had labored with success among all the Indians in New-England, with the exception of the Mohegans, and that he narrowly failed to engage the Mohawks in the contest. It deserves remark, that in this fearful struggle for life and death, not a dollar nor a man was furnished by the mother country, to prevent the colonies from being turned into one heap of bloody ashes.

The designs of Philip were penetrated by his secretary Sausamon, a converted Indian well acquainted with the English language, and by this channel they were disclosed to the English. Sausamon was immediately after murdered on the ice on Middleborough pond, by order of Philip, and the agency of some of his chief men. The murder took place within the jurisdiction of Plymouth, and those concerned in it, three in number, were immediately brought to justice. This happened in the spring of 1675, and hastened the commencement of hostilities, which had been reserved by Philip for the following year. He was now compelled to plunge into the contest, without the aid of the Narragansets, who were not yet prepared. The Indians had a superstition, that the party which struck the first blow would be defeated. For this reason, they took pains, by repeated insults and threats, by killing their cattle, and plundering their houses, to bring on an actual commencement of hostilities, on the part of the settlers. Irritated by these provocations, an Englishman at last fired at and mortally wounded an Indian. The alarm spread; intelligence of the state of things reached Plymouth and Boston, and troops were put in motion. The Indians anticipated their arrival, by an attack on the town of Swansea, on the 24th of June, 1675. The inhabitants were fired upon, on their return from public worship, and ten were killed in different parts of the town on that day.

Thus was the blow struck, and a war commenced not inferior in magnitude, compared with the population of the parties engaged in it, to the revolutionary war; nor of minor importance, if we contemplate the consequences, had the Indians prevailed. Among the romantic traits, with which his biographers have adorned the character of Philip, they have described him as shedding tears, when told that his young men had begun the war. Fifty years after his fall, the neighboring inhabitants of Bristol and the aged Indians who had survived the war, pointed out the spring where Philip was seated when he received the news of the tragedy at

Swansea, and wept at the thoughts of the destruction which impended over his race.*

But the die was cast. Sorrowful or joyous, Philip roused himself, with all his energies, to the war. Retreating before the embodied forces of Plymouth and Massachusetts, his warriors were divided into bands, and scattered along the frontier settlements, carrying terror and havoc before them. Swansea was destroyed, Taunton was attacked, Middleborough and Dartmouth burned, and all Plymouth filled with alarm. Surrounded in a swamp at Pocasset, the iron grasp of Church almost upon him, the flames of Brookfield announce that the theatre of the war is changed, and thither the chieftain and his principal warriors repaired. From the smoking ashes of Brookfield the scene is shifted to Connecticut river; and Hadley, Hatfield and Deerfield are in arms.

While the Indians hovered about Brookfield, a considerable force from the eastern part of the State, from Springfield, and Connecticut, was concentrated there, under the skilful command of Major Willard. When the Indians disappeared from Brookfield, and showed themselves in this region, Major Willard marched, with a part of his forces, to Hadley. Here the principal station of defence was assumed, and the companies of Captain Lothrop and Captain Beers, of Watertown, were left in garrison. Major Willard returned to the eastern part of the State, and the chief command devolved on Major Pynchon, of Springfield. The Indians, at Hadley, already in secret understanding with Philip, on his arrival in their neighborhood, threw off the mask. By professions of friendly intentions, they had obtained a supply of arms, and had been entrusted with the defence of a fort about a mile above Hatfield. The English received intelligence that they were preparing to desert the fort, and join the enemy. Determined that they should not carry with them the weapons, with which they had been furnished for the defence of the settlement, Captains Lothrop and Beers, with one hundred men, were sent to disarm them. The Indians had already fled in the night to Deerfield. Lothrop and Beers came up with them in the morning, in a swamp, a short distance south of the sugar-loaf hill, when an action ensued, in which

---

* Callendar's Sermon, page 73.

ten of the English and twenty-six of the Indians were slain. This
was on the 25th of August, old style, 1675.

The 1st of September following, was a day of alarm and blood.
The woods from Hadley to Northfield were filled with lurking bands
of savages. Deerfield was attacked on that day, and many of the
houses and barns in the settlement were burned. Hadley was assailed on the same day. It was a day observed as a fast by the
church in that place. While the inhabitants were engaged in the
religious services, the savages burst in upon the village. Although
it was the practice to go armed to church, yet, taken by surprise
at the sudden inroad, the inhabitants were thrown into confusion.
The savage foe rushes on ; the citizens are about to disperse and
fly. At the moment of greatest confusion and danger, a venerable
stranger appeared, of commanding aspect, clothed in black apparel
of unusual fashion, his hair white from age. With sword in hand,
he places himself at the head of the flying inhabitants, encourages
them to stand and resist the enemy, animates them at once by his
example and his voice, disposes them in the most advantageous
manner, fights valiantly at their head, and repulses the enemy. This
done, he vanishes as promptly as he appeared. The superstitious
Indians, not less than the devout and awe-struck English, believed
it was an angel. The wish to conceal the place of refuge of the
fugitives, for a long time prevented an explanation of the fact. In
the course of time it was discovered to have been General Goffe,
one of the judges who sat in the trial of Charles I, and who, taking refuge on this the very frontier of the British empire, with one
of his colleagues, Whalley, had for many years lived in concealment in the house of Mr Russell, the minister at Hadley.

The inhabitants of the settlements on the river, and indeed in
the frontier towns generally, were obliged either wholly to confine
themselves to the garrisoned houses, as they were called, or to flee
to them on the first alarm, abandoning their homes and property to
pillage and conflagration. On the day following the assaults on
Deerfield and Hadley, a party went out from the garrison at Northfield, then called Squakeag, to work in the fields. Eight of their
number were shot down, by the invisible foe. Order had been already taken to remove the settlers from Northfield, it being considered too exposed a position. On the 3d of September, not having

heard of the tragedy of the preceding day, Captain Beers, of Watertown, was despatched from Hadley, with a detachment of between thirty and forty mounted men, to bring off the inhabitants of Northfield. He passed in safety through the forest, which stretched along the eastern bank of the river; the tract of country now occupied by Sunderland, Montague, and Erving's grant. He had crossed Miller's river, before he saw any traces of the enemy. Having passed the night about three miles from the place of his destination, on the morning of the 4th, they were attacked by a large body of Indians before they could regain their horses. Captain Beers and several men were killed at the commencement of the action. Attempting to reach their horses, twelve more fell; a small remnant only found their way back to Hadley. On the following day, the 5th, Major Treat, who commanded the Connecticut troops, was detached from Hadley, with a hundred men, to chastise the Indians. But they fled before the approach of a commanding force, into the forest. The heads of Captain Beers' unfortunate men exposed on stakes, where they fell, and their mangled bodies suspended from the trees, bore witness to the fatal issue of the battle. Major Treat continued his march without interruption, though his troops were fired upon by the concealed foe, and he himself struck with a spent ball; but no one was killed, and the inhabitants in garrison at Northfield, were brought off in safety. On his way back, he fell in with Captain Appleton, who, in expectation of a serious conflict, had followed him from Hadley, with a reinforcement ; and who was desirous of pursuing the enemy to his hiding places. But it was judged inexpedient, without more accurate information of their numbers, to plunge into the forest, and the united force returned to Hadley. Northfield, thus abandoned by the inhabitants, was immediately burned by the Indians.

Among the papers preserved in the public archives, I have found a list of the unfortunate men who were killed with Captain Beers, or made prisoners when he fell. He was an officer of sterling valor, a public servant of approved patriotism and usefulness. At the time when he fell, in the service of his country, he was, as he had been, for thirteen years, the representative of Watertown, in the General Court, and deserves that his name should be held in honorable remembrance. No monument,—the work of men's hands,—-marks the spot where he fell; but tradition has affixed his name to the plain where the death-struggle began, and to the mountain where he sunk before the savage foe, and will hand it down, in grateful remembrance, to the latest posterity.

By the destruction of Northfield, Deerfield became the frontier settlement on Connecticut river; and as such was again doomed to bear the brunt of savage warfare. On the 12th, as a portion of the inhabitants, twenty-two in number, were passing from one of the garrisoned houses, to attend worship in the other, they were fired upon, but no one was slain. The empty garrison house was set on fire, and one man left in it was heard of no more. Aid was despatched from Hadley, under Captain Lothrop, who, with the men at Deerfield, under Captain Appleton, engaged in an unsuccessful pursuit of the flying enemy. The master genius who guided them, had taught them to carry on exclusively a warfare of ambuscade and surprise.

While these events transpired on Connecticut river, those parts of the country where the war broke out were comparatively tranquil. No man had seen king Philip on Connecticut river; he constantly went disguised even from his friends, and never passed the night twice in the same spot. He was known at this time to be in this neighborhood by the transfer of the war to this quarter, by the report of friendly Indians, who acted as spies, and by those who occasionally came in as deserters. In the following winter, Mrs Rowlandson, who was made prisoner at Lancaster, saw him frequently in this region. The terror of his name wrought powerfully on weaker minds, and as he was never encountered in the field, nor identified among those exposed to the chances of war, the boldest began to regard him with something of that undefined dread, inspired by an invisible and malignant spirit of evil, ranging the gloomy forest, lighting up the darkness of night by the blaze of peaceful hamlets, pointing the death-volley from the ambuscade, at the wayfarer and husbandman, and vanishing with the light of day, or at the approach of a powerful force.

Having thus sketched the progress of the war in its preliminary scenes, we are brought to the affecting tragedy, which is the more immediate object of this day's commemoration. The presence of

Philip on the river made it necessary to establish a formidable force in some convenient position. Hadley, which had been selected for this purpose by Massachusetts, was adopted by the commissioners of the United Colonies, as the most suitable place for the head-quarters of the little army. Small detachments were posted at the other settlements, but here was concentrated the greater part of the troops assigned to this quarter. It of course became necessary to increase the supply of provisions at Hadley. A considerable quantity of wheat being preserved in stacks at Deerfield, it was deemed expedient to have it threshed, and brought down to Hadley. Captain Lothrop and his company volunteered to proceed to Deerfield, and protect the convoy. His march from Hadley was effected without interruption; the wheat was threshed, placed in eighteen wagons, with a portion of the effects of the inhabitants of Deerfield, disposed to remove, and the train moved down the road, towards its destination. Captain Moseley, who had arrived on Connecticut river three days before, was at this time stationed with his company at Deerfield, and proposed, while Captain Lothrop was on the march downward, to range the woods in search of the enemy.

Moseley was a partisan of great skill and courage; he had commanded a privateer in the West Indies. It is not improbable that Captain Lothrop and his men, relying too much on Moseley's co-operation, proceeded with less caution than their safety required. Having passed with safety through a level and closely-wooded country, well calculated for a surprise, and deeming themselves in some degree sheltered by the nature of the ground they had reached, the tradition is, that on their arrival at the spot near which we are now assembled, their vigilance relaxed. The forest that lines the narrow road, on which they were marching, was hung with clusters of grapes, and, as the wagons dragged through the heavy soil, it is not unlikely that the teamsters, and possibly a part of the company, may have dispersed to gather them. Such is the contemporary account. At this moment of fatal security, and just as they had reached the brook which winds through the village, a band of savages, outnumbering Captain Lothrop's company ten to one, pours in upon them a murderous fire, from their place of ambuscade on the right of the line of march. A considerable number drop at the first volley. The Indians spring from their covert, upon the survivors, who, broken and scattered by the overwhelming attack, fly to the shelter of the forest, on the spot where we stand. Here ensued the murderous death-struggle : escape was impossible. The young men fled, each to his tree, imitating the barbarous foe, in his mode of warfare, and determined to sell their lives as dearly as possible. But the enemy amounted to seven hundred ; the force of Captain Lothrop, weakened by the first fatal fire, fell below a tenth of that number. His men were consequently surrounded, singled out, shot down, crushed by overwhelming numbers, and finally sunk, one great and fearful sacrifice, to the tomahawk. Lothrop fell at the commencement of the action, ' a godly and courageous commander :' the loss of their leader added new horrors to the scene, and before its close, the whole company, with the exception of a few who escaped, was destroyed.

The cruel fate of these unfortunate young men did not remain long unavenged. While the Indians were employed in mangling, scalping, and stripping the dying and the dead, Captain Moseley, who, as has been observed, was ranging the woods, hearing the report of musketry, hastened, by a forced march, to the relief of his brethren. The Indians, confiding in their superior numbers, taunted him as he advanced, and dared him to the contest. Moseley came on with firmness, repeatedly charged through them, and destroyed a large number, with the loss on his side, of but two killed and eleven wounded. His lieutenants, Savage and Pickering, greatly distinguished themselves on this occasion. He was, however, so greatly outnumbered, that though he sustained the action from eleven o'clock till evening, he did not succeed in driving the enemy from the field. At this juncture, Major Treat arrived, with a hundred soldiers, and sixty Mohegan Indians, and, joining his forces with Captain Moseley's, drove the enemy from the field of the hard-fought and murderous action. They fled across the brook, about two miles to the westward, closely pursued by the American force, and here the action was probably suspended by the night. A quantity of bones recently found in that quarter, are very probably the remains of the Indians who fell there at the close of the action.

The united English force encamped for the night at Deerfield.

They returned, in the morning, to bury the dead, and found a part of the Indians upon the field, stripping the bodies of the victims. These they quickly dispersed, and the remains of the brave young men, or some portion of them, were committed to the earth, near the spot, which we have this day consecrated anew to their memory.

A list of the brave men who fell with Lothrop, with the names of the towns to which they belonged, has been preserved in the public archives.* They were fifty-nine in number, and three of Captain Moseley's shared the same fate. The accounts vary as to the number who escaped. Hubbard states them as not above seven or eight; a letter written by Mr Cotton, five days after the event, reduces the number to two. A tradition still preserved at Newbury, gives us the name of two out of three reputed survivors. An individual who died at Newbury, in the year 1824, at the age of ninety-seven, was well acquainted with Henry Bodwell and John Tappan, two of Captain Lothrop's soldiers. Bodwell was a man of great strength. His left arm was broken by a musket ball; but, forcing his way with the but-end of his musket, through a band of Indians, who endeavored to surround him, he got safe to Hadley. John Tappan crept into the channel of a water-course, and drew the grass and shrubs over his head.† The Indians passed near him repeatedly, but he was not discovered. The escape of a third, Robert Dutch, of Ipswich, was still more extraordinary. He received a musket-shot in the head, was wounded by a tomahawk, stripped of his clothing, and left for dead. On the approach of Captain Moseley, he revived and was rescued.

The tidings of this disastrous day spread alarm and sorrow through the colony. Essex felt the bereavement in almost every family. The flower of her population,—her hopeful young men, 'all culled out of the towns belonging to that county,' called by the voice of duty, in the morning of life, to leave their homes and kindred, and encounter all the horrors of savage warfare, were cut down. By the records of the ancient town of Newbury, it ap-

---

* See note at the end of this address.

† There is some reason to think, that this tradition refers to another action in this neighborhood.

pears, that on the 5th of August there were impressed to go against
the Indian enemy, nine men ; on the 6th, seven more ; on the
27th, seven more. From August 5th to September 27th, there
were impressed, in the single town of Newbury, thirty men and
forty-six horses ; facts that show the prodigious severity of the
military service of the colony at that period,—vastly greater than
at any subsequent period in the history of the country.

The catastrophe of the 18th of September, the day we commemorate, was the heaviest which had befallen the colony. ' It
was a sadder rebuke of Providence,' says Dr Increase Mather,
' than any thing that hitherto hath been,'—' a black and fatal day,
wherein there were eight persons made widows, and six-and-twen-
ty children made fatherless, and about sixty persons buried in one
fatal grave.' *

Time would fail me to recount in detail the succeeding incidents
of the war ; but they ought not to be dismissed without an allusion. Deerfield was soon deserted by the inhabitants, and burned
by the Indians. Springfield was next assaulted, and a considerable portion of it was sacked and burned. On the 19th of October, Hadley was again attacked by a powerful force, but by the
vigorous and successful resistance of the troops then under the
chief command of Captain Samuel Appleton, was rescued. A
predatory warfare was kept up, during the rest of the autumn, on
the remaining settlements on Connecticut river, but the storm of
war was carried back to the place of its origin. The great Narraganset expedition, in which the combined forces of Massachusetts,
Plymouth, and Connecticut, were placed under Governor Winslow, of Plymouth, as commander-in-chief, took place in December. On the 19th of that month, the great battle of Petaquam-
scot was fought, which, for the zeal with which the men, after a
march of fifteen miles in a snow-storm, went into the action,—the
bravery with which it was fought,—the destruction of the enemy,
and the hardships endured by the troops, in a night march of
eighteen miles, in the depth of winter, after the battle, has no parallel in our history. Six captains fell at the head of their compa-

---

* The spot has recently been identified by excavation, on the road side, directly
in front of the house of Stephen Whitney, Esq., of South Deerfield.

nies. By this battle the power of the Narragansets was effectually broken. Among the plunder of the day, were muskets which had belonged to Captain Lothrop's men. The Indians, who escaped from the slaughter, fled to the Nipmuck country.

Winter gave no respite to this tremendous war. In February, Lancaster fell, and, in appalling succession, Medfield, Weymouth, Groton, Warwick, Marlborough, Rehoboth, Providence, Chelmsford, Sudbury, Scituate, Bridgewater, Plymouth, and Middleborough, were assaulted and wholly or in part destroyed before the middle of May. No period of the revolutionary war was to the interior of any part of the United States so disastrous. In May, from the lower part of the state, the scene of action again shifted to Connecticut river. On the 18th of May, a large body of Indians concentrated at Deerfield was surprised by an English force from the lower towns, and several hundreds were destroyed. The fortune of the day was unhappily clouded at its close, by the loss of Captain Turner, and a considerable number of men. On the 12th of June, another furious attack was made on Hadley, but successfully resisted by the troops.

Again the main body of the enemy disappears from this region, and emerges in the Narraganset country. He is keenly pursued, and in the months of July and August sustains several vigorous defeats. The tide of fortune turns at once. About a twelvemonth from the commencement of the war, the Indians become disheartened and spiritless, and make their submission in great numbers to the colonial governments.

Philip still stood at bay. He had endeavored, by an artifice of cruel treachery, to enlist the Mohawks in the war. But his murderous fraud was discovered, and the Mohawks, instead of joining, swore enmity to him. He was accordingly driven back to the neighborhood of Mount Hope, and abandoned by the greater part of those, whom he had so lately roused and united in the cause. On the 2d of August, he was surprised by Captain Church,—a man who, if his province had equalled his intrepidity and skill, would have possessed a name in the world, as distinguished as that of any of Napoleon's generals. One hundred and thirty of Philip's men were slain ; his wife and his son made prisoners. He himself escaped. Some of the Indian prisoners said to Church, ' You have now made Philip ready to die, for you have made him as poor and as miserable, as he used to make the English. You have now killed or taken all his relations,—and this bout has almost broken his heart.'

He makes one more plunge into the swamps. An Indian, whose brother Philip had killed for proposing peace, discovered to Church the place of his concealment. This intrepid officer, with a few brave volunteers, is instantly at the spot. The swamp is invested under cover of darkness, and an Englishman and an Indian planted behind every tree, at the outlet. At break of day the attack commences. The ill-starred chieftain, who, hunted to his last retreat, had dropped asleep, started from a troubled dream, seized his gun, and, half naked, ran directly toward a tree, behind which were posted an Englishman and the very Indian whose brother he had killed. The Englishman's gun missed fire ; the Indian fires, and shoots the fallen chief through the heart. ' He fell upon his face in the mud and water, with his gun beneath him.'

Such was the fate of Philip, which was immediately followed by a termination of the war, in every quarter, except the eastern frontier. It was a war of extermination between his followers and the whites ; happy, if the kindred tribes had learned wisdom from the fatal lesson. Thus fell king Philip ! The ground on which we stand is wet with the blood, which flowed beneath the tomahawk of his young men ; and the darkness of night in these peaceful vales was often lighted up, in days of yore, by the flames of burning villages, kindled by his ruthless warriors. But that blood has sunk, not forgotten, but forgiven, into the ground. Havoc and dismay no longer stalk through these happy meadows ;—and as we meet to-day to perform the simple and affecting rites of commemoration over the grave of the gallant victims of the struggle, let us drop a compassionate tear also for these the benighted children of the forest,—the orphans of Providence,—whose cruelties have long since been expiated by their fate. It could not be expected of them, to enter into the high counsels of Heaven. It was not for them,—dark and uninstructed even in the wisdom of man,—to comprehend the great design of Providence, of which their wilderness was the appointed theatre. It may well have exceeded their sagacity, as it baffles ours, that this benign work should so often have moved forward through pathways dripping with blood. Yes! the savage fought a relentless war; but he fought for his native land, for the mound that covered the bones of his parents; he fought for his squaw and pappoose;—no, I will not defraud them of the sacred names, which our hearts understand;—he fought for his wife and children. He would have been, not a savage,—he would have been a thing, for which language has no name,—for which neither human nor brute existence has a parallel,—if he had not fought for them. Why, the very wild-cat, the wolf, will spring at the throat of the hunter, that enters his den;—the bear, the catamount, will fight for his hollow tree. The Indian was a man; —a degraded, ignorant savage, but a human creature,—aye, and he had the feelings of a man. President Mather, in relating the encounter of the 1st of August, 1676, the last but one of the war, says, 'Philip hardly escaped with his life also. He had fled and left his *peage* behind him; also his squaw and his son were taken captive, and are now prisoners at Plymouth. Thus hath God brought that grand enemy into great misery, before he quite destroy him. It must needs be bitter as death to him, to lose his wife and only son, (for the Indians are marvellous fond and affectionate towards their children), besides other relations, and almost all his subjects, and country also.'

And what was the fate of Philip's wife and his son? This is a tale for husbands and wives, for parents and children. Young men and women, you cannot understand it. What was the fate of Philip's wife and child? She is a woman, he is a lad. They did not surely hang them. No, that would have been mercy. The boy is the grandson, his mother the daughter-in-law of good old Massassoit, the first and the best friend the English ever had, in New-England. Perhaps,—perhaps, now Philip is slain and his warriors scattered to the four winds, they will allow his wife and son to go back,—the widow and the orphan,—to finish their days and sorrows, in their native wilderness. They were sold into slavery, West Indian slavery!—an Indian princess and her child, sold from the cool breezes of Mount Hope, from the wild freedom of a New-England forest, to gasp under the lash, beneath the blazing sun of the tropics!* 'Bitter as death;' aye, bitter as hell!

* Morton's New-England Memorial. Judge Davis's edition, p. 353, &c.

Is there any thing,—I do not say in the range of humanity;—is there any thing animated, that would not struggle against this? Is there,—I do not say a man,—who has ever looked in the face of his sleeping child;—a woman,

> ————— that has given suck, and knows
> How tender 'tis to love the babe, that milks her;

is there a dumb beast, a brute creature, a thing of earth or of air, the lowest in creation, so it be not wholly devoid of that mysterious instinct which binds the generations of beings together, that will not use the arms, which nature has given it, if you molest the spot where its fledglings nestle, where its cubs are crying for their meat?

Then think of the country, for which the Indians fought! Who can blame them? As Philip looked down from his seat on Mount Hope, that glorious eminence, that

> ————throne of royal state, which far
> Outshone the wealth of Ormus or of Ind,
> Or where the gorgeous east, with richest hand,
> Showers on her kings barbaric pomp and gold,—

as he looked down and beheld the lovely scene which spread beneath, at a summer sunset,—the distant hill-tops blazing with gold, the slanting beams streaming along the waters, the broad plains, the island groups, the majestic forest,—could he be blamed, if his heart burned within him, as he beheld it all passing, by no tardy process, from beneath his control into the hands of the stranger? As the river chieftains—the lords of the waterfalls and the mountains—ranged this lovely valley, can it be wondered at, if they beheld with bitterness the forest disappearing beneath the settler's axe; the fishing place disturbed by his sawmills? Can we not fancy the feelings with which some strong-minded savage, the chief of the Pocomtuck Indians, who should have ascended the summit of the sugar-loaf mountain,—(rising as it does before us, at this moment, in all its loveliness and grandeur),—in company with a friendly settler, contemplating the progress already made by the white man, and marking the gigantic strides, with which he was advancing into the wilderness, should fold his arms and say, 'White man, there is eternal war between me and thee! I quit not the land of my fathers, but with my life. In those woods, where I bent my youthful bow, I will still hunt the deer; over yonder waters I will still glide unrestrained in my bark canoe. By those dashing waterfalls I will still lay up my winter's store of food; on these fertile meadows I will still plant my corn. Stranger, the land is mine! I understand not these paper rights. I gave not my consent, when, as thou sayest, these broad regions were purchased for a few baubles, of my fathers. They could sell what was theirs; they could sell no more. How could my father sell that which the Great Spirit sent me into the world to live upon? They knew not what they did. The stranger came, a timid suppliant,—few and feeble, and asked to lie down on the red man's bear-skin, and warm himself at the red man's fire, and have a little piece of land, to raise corn for his women and children;—and now he is become strong, and mighty, and bold, and spreads out his parchment over the whole, and says, it is mine. Stranger! there is not room for us both. The Great Spirit has not made us to live together. There is poison in the white man's cup; the white man's dog barks at the red man's heels. If I should leave the land of my fathers, whither shall I fly? Shall I go to the south, and dwell among the graves of the Pequots? Shall I wander to the west;—the fierce Mohawk, —the man-eater,—is my foe. Shall I fly to the east, the great water is before me. No, stranger; here I have lived, and here will I die; and if here thou abidest, there is eternal war between me and thee. Thou hast taught me thy arts of destruction; for that alone I thank thee; and now take heed to thy steps, the red man is thy foe. When thou goest forth by day, my bullet shall whistle by thee; when thou liest down at night, my knife is at thy throat. The noon-day sun shall not discover thy enemy, and the darkness of midnight shall not protect thy rest. Thou shalt plant in terror, and I will reap in blood; thou shalt sow the earth with corn, and I will strew it with ashes; thou shalt go forth with the sickle, and I will follow after with the scalping-knife; thou shalt build, and I will burn, till the white man or the Indian shall cease from the land. Go thy way for this time in safety,—but remember, stranger, there is eternal war between me and thee!'

Such were the feelings, which influenced the native tribes, at the period of king Philip's war. But let not our generous sympathies with them betray us into injustice toward our fathers. The right, by which the Pilgrims settled down upon the soil, was better than that, by which a great part of the native tribes (as far as we know) laid claim to the possession of it. The tribes along the coast were originally, and, at no remote period, conquerors. The fathers of Massachusetts and Plymouth, of Rhode Island, and Connecticut, purchased the land of those who claimed it, and often paid for it more than once. They purchased it for a consideration trifling to the European, but valuable to the Indian. An iron hatchet, or a kettle, or a piece of woollen cloth was worth a square mile of unproductive forest. There is no overreaching in giving but little, for that which, in the hands of the original proprietors, is worth nothing. Then as to the conduct of the settlers towards the savages,—pains as unwearied as unsuccessful were taken to instruct them in the arts of civilized life and Christianity. Since the death of the apostle Paul, a nobler, truer, and warmer spirit, than John Eliot, never lived; and, taking the state of the country,—the narrowness of the means,—the rudeness of the age, into consideration, the history of the Christian church does not contain an example of resolute, untiring, successful labor, superior to that of translating the entire Scriptures into the language of the native tribes of Massachusetts; a labor performed, not in the flush of youth, nor within the luxurious abodes of academic ease, but under the constant burden of his duties, as a minister and a preacher, and at a time of life when the spirits begin to flag. Eliot was over forty-two years of age, when he began to learn the Indian tongue and preach to the Indian tribes. 'It is incredible,' says his biographer, 'how much time, toil, and hardship, he underwent in the prosecution of his undertaking; how many weary days and nights rolled over him ; how many tiresome journeys he endured, and how many terrible dangers he experienced. If you would know what he felt and what carried him through all, take it in his own words, in a letter to Mr Winslow : "I have not been dry, night nor day, from the third day of the week to the sixth ; but so travelled, and at night pull off my boots, wring my stockings, on with them again, and so continue. But God steps in and helps." ' These were the circumstances, under which the herculean labor was performed of translating the entire Scriptures into a dialect probably as imperfect, as unformed, as remote from the analogy of our own tongue, as unmanageable, as any spoken on earth.

That the settlers made as near an approach to the spirit of the gospel, in their dealings with the Indians, as the frailty of our nature admits, under the circumstances in which they were placed, is clear, I think, from the circumstances already stated. The commencement of the death-struggle was postponed longer than, in the nature of human affairs, might have been expected ; and when it came on, he must have a sensibility of a morbid cast, whose sympathies are enlisted but on one side. I hope I compassionate the sufferings of the Indian ; Heaven forbid I should be indifferent to the sufferings of the fathers. When Philip's war began, the coast of New-England, to a depth of eighteen or twenty miles, and the banks of Connecticut river to the northern boundary of this State, were the abode of some of the most interesting communities ever gathered in the world. I know not, in human history or on the face of the globe, a period or a spot, where dearer hopes and richer prospects for the cause of liberty and truth were ever centred. It was the second generation of settlers; the wrong of the first comers (if wrong it was) could not be laid at their door. They formed a group of Christian settlements, a family of youthful republics,—a germ of civilization, enclosing all that now spreads around,—all that for our children and a late posterity shall rise on this foundation,—as the acorn encloses the trunk and branches of the future oak. Can the philosopher, the statesman, the Christian, be indifferent to their fate ? can he contemplate with calmness the approach of the catastrophe, that is to sweep these springing towns, and cities, and villages,—the elements of future states,—the cradles of rising millions, into ruin ? Can we, who have received this precious heritage, coolly weigh in the scales of a fastidious criticism the counsels and acts, by which our fathers, in the convulsive struggle for life, waged the war of extermination, that burst forth around them ? That war was brief ; but its havoc, and its terrors worse than death, no tongue can describe. Six hundred of the inhabitants, the greatest part of whom were the very flower of the country, fell in battle, or were murdered, oftentimes with circumstances of the most revolting cruelty. This is the number officially

reported at the time as falling. We may well suppose that half
as many more fell victims in the progress of the war. It was a
loss of her children to New-England, not inferior to twenty thousand at the present day. What havoc for a single year! Twelve
towns in Massachusetts, Plymouth, and Rhode Island were utterly
destroyed; and many more were greatly injured. Six hundred
buildings, mostly dwelling-houses, are known to have been burned;
and, according to Dr Trumbull's calculation, one man in eleven of
the arms-bearing population was killed, and one house in eleven
laid in ashes.

Then contemplate the details of Indian warfare;—they are
almost too much for the heart of man to bear, even as a tale that
is told;—what must they not have been to those who were daily
and nightly exposed to them! It is almost enough to make one
faint, to read the simple narrative of Mrs Rowlandson, the wife of
the minister at Lancaster. It was mid-winter, about five months
after the catastrophe of Bloody Brook,—her husband was absent
in Boston, soliciting the means of defence,—when her dwelling-
house, which had been fortified as a garrison, was assaulted by
several hundred Indians. The house is soon set on fire, to compel
the wretched inmates to flee; and yet the bullets, pouring in upon
them like hail, threaten instant death, if they come out. Driven at
last, by the flames, they venture out, men, women, and children.
Many instantly fall, under the death-shower. Mrs Rowlandson,
with a child of six years old in her arms, is shot in the side by a
bullet, which has first passed through her child's body; her other
children are torn from her. She is compelled to join the flight of
the savages, into the wilderness, scarcely clad, unprotected against
the wintry winds and the night frosts, her mortally wounded child
in her arms, perpetually moaning, *Mother, I shall die, I shall die;*
passing a night in the month of February on the snow, with her
dying child in her arms, parched with fever, crying for water,
which no one would bring it; without food for herself, from Wednesday night till Saturday night, till the child died. ' I cannot but
take notice,' says the heart-broken mother, ' how, at another time,
I could not bear to be in a room with a dead person;—but now
the case is changed. I must and could lie down with my dead
babe, all the night after. In the morning, when they understood

that my child was dead, they sent me home to my master's wigwam. I went to take up my dead child in my arms, to carry it, but they bid me let it alone.   There was no resisting, but go I must, and leave it.'   There are other horrors in that narrative, which I dare not repeat.   The cruel captivity of Mr Williams, the minister of Deerfield, is familiar to you all.   It makes the flesh creep, to read it. It was not till the year 1759, till Quebec fell, that the settlements on Connecticut river were safe from the incursions of the savage foe.   There are men, I presume, living in Deerfield, who remember the time when it was not safe from their incursions.

No, fellow citizens, let us not, in our commiseration of the fate of the native tribes, be insensible to the sufferings, or unjust to the memory, of our fathers.   Their claims to our reverence, as patriots and men, must not be disparaged nor qualified.   In this day of abundance and prosperity, while we are reaping the fruits of the labors and sufferings of our ancestors, it is easy to point out their errors, and rebuke their faults.   But are we sure, that the great work which was given them to do, and which they did, could be performed by different men, and in a different way ?   I speak not tauntingly, but in sober earnest, when I say, that it is one thing, in an age like this, of peace and prosperity,—in an age of high refinement, and enlightened public sentiment, when the alarms of a savage frontier are no longer felt, the hardships of an infant settlement forgotten, the austerities of a struggling sect have passed away, and the dreary delusions of a benighted age are exploded,— calmly, from our happy firesides, to theorize on the means by which the settlement of the country could have been effected ; and a very different thing, in times of persecution and terror, for men, pursued by the vengeance of an incensed hierarchy,—thrown upon a dreary and savage coast,—beset not merely by the savage tribes of the wilderness, but, as they believed, by the legions of darkness, —to go forth into the forest, to dare, to endure, and to die.   We revolt at some of the features of the method in which the war was carried on, by the Moseleys and Churches, and other stern and unrelenting partisans of the day ; but they were made of those elements which seem demanded in the composition of a successful chieftain, in such a warfare ; and I am not sure that men of milder tempers, or softer frames, would have been adequate to the work

77

of a winter's campaign, through frozen swamps, where it was necessary to creep on your face, through the morass, till you came
within sight of the enemy, and then, after the first discharge, spring
up and close with him, in the death-grapple. In the account of
one of his conflicts with a savage on the ice, Church states, that
'the Indian seized him fast by the hair of his head, and endeavored, by twisting, to break his neck. But though Mr Church's
wounds had somewhat weakened him, and the Indian a stout fellow, yet he held him in play, and twisted the Indian's neck as well,
and, taking the advantage, while they hung by each other's hair,
gave him notorious bunts in the face, with his head. But in the
heat of the scuffle, they heard the ice break with somebody coming apace to them. Church concluded there was help for one or
the other of them, but was doubtful which of them must now receive the fatal blow. Anon, somebody comes up, who proves to
be a friendly Indian. Without speaking a word, he felt them out,
(for it was so dark he could not distinguish them by sight, but one
was clothed and the other naked), and feeling where Mr Church's
hands were fastened in the Indian's hair, with one blow settled his
hatchet in between them, and thus ended the strife.' Such was
the price at which victory was to be bought;—the horrors that
waited on defeat and captivity, must not here be told.

    If we turn our thoughts to the grand design with which America
was colonized, and the success with which, under Providence, that
design has been crowned, I own I find it difficult to express myself in terms of moderation. When I compare our New-England,
at the present day, with the New-England of our fathers, a century and a half ago; the New-England on which this morning's sun
rose, with that of the day we commemorate; when I consider this
abundance and prosperity,—these fertile fields, these villages, crowded with a population instinct with activity, hope, and enjoyment;
when I look at the hills cultivated, or covered with flocks, to their
summits, and only so much of the forest remaining as ministers to
the convenience and use of man; when I see the roads, the bridges,
the canals, the railways, which spread their busy net-work over
the face of the country, quickening into intensity the exchanges of
business, and the intercourse of men; when I see the intellectual,
moral, and religious growth of the community,—its establishments,

its institutions, its social action, and reflect that all this life, enjoyment and plenty are placed under the invisible protection of the
public peace; when I consider, further, that what we see, and
hear, and feel, and touch, of all these blessings, is perhaps the
smallest part of them; that, by the force of our example, by the
blessed sympathy of light and truth, the glad tidings of political,
of moral, and religious revival are destined to spread to distant
regions, and flow down to the remotest generations, out of the living fountain which has been opened here;—my heart melts within
me for grief, that they, the high-souled and long-suffering fathers,
—they, the pioneers of the mighty enterprise,—they, the founders
of the glorious temple, must die before the sight of all these blessings. Oh, that we could call them back, to see the work of their
hands! Oh, that our poor strains of gratitude could penetrate their
tombs! Oh, that we could quicken into renewed consciousness
the brave and precious dust that moulders beneath our feet.—Oh,
that they could rise up in the midst of us, the hopeful, the valiant,
the self-devoted, and graciously accept these humble offices of
commemoration! But though they tasted not the fruit, they shall
not lose the praise of their sacrifice and toils. I read in your eyes,
that they shall not be defrauded of their renown. This mighty
concourse bears witness to the emotions of a grateful posterity.
Yon simple monument shall rise a renewed memorial of their
names. On this sacred spot, where the young, the brave, the patriotic, poured out their life-blood in defence of that heritage which
has descended to us, we this day solemnly bring our tribute of
gratitude. Ages shall pass away; the majestic tree which over-
shadows us shall wither and sink before the blast, and we, who are
now gathered beneath it, shall mingle with the honored dust we
eulogize; but the 'Flower of Essex' shall bloom in undying remembrance; and with every century, these rites of commemoration shall be repeated, as the lapse of time shall continually develop,
in richer abundance, the fruits of what was done and suffered by
our fathers!

Note to page 607.

I have been favored with the following list of those who fell with Captain Lothrop, kindly furnished me by Rev. Joseph B. Felt, whose profound acquaintance with the antiquities of Massachusetts is known to the public. Mr Felt observes, that the names in the list are given by him as spelt in the original, which appears to be from the hand of an illiterate writer. The list was copied two or three years ago, from a paper in the Secretary of State's office in Boston.

List of those slain at Bloody Brook, 18th *September*, (*O. S.*) 1675.

Capt. Thomas Laythrop, Sergeant Thomas Smith, Samuel Stevens, John Hobs, *Ipswich ;* Daniel Button, *Salem ;* John Harriman, Thomas Bayley, Ezekiel Sawier, *Salem ;* Jacob Kilborne, Thomas Manning, *Ipswich ;* Jacob Waynwritt, *Ipswich ;* Benjamin Roper *do. ;* John Bennett, *Manchester ;* Thos. Menter, Caleb Kimball, *Ipswich ;* Thomas Hobs, *Ipswich ;* Robert Homes, Edward Traske, *Salem ;* Richard Lambert, *Salem ;* Josiah Dodge, *Beverly ;* Peter Woodberry, *Beverly ;* Joseph Balch, *Beverly ;* Samuel Whitteridge, *Ipswich ;* William Dew, Serg't Samuel Stevens, Samuel Crumpton, John Plum, Thomas Buckley, *Salem ;* George Ropes, *Salem ;* Joseph King, Thomas Alexander, Francis Friende, Abel Oseph, John Litheate, Samuel Hudson, Adam Clarke, Ephraim Fearah, Robert Wilson, *Salem ;* Stephen Welman, *Salem ;* Benjamin Farnell, Solomon Alley, *Lynn ;* John Merrik, Robert Hinsdall, Samuel Hinsdall, Barnabas Hinsdall, John Hinsdall, Joseph Gilbert, John Allin, *Manchester ;* Joshua Carter, *Manchester ;* John Barnard, James Tufts, *Salem ;* Jonathan Plympton, Philip Barsham, Thomas Weller, William Smeade, Zebediah Williams, Eliakim Marshall, James Mudge, George Cole.——

Three of Captain Moseley's men, when he went to relieve Captain Lothrop, were killed; only two of their names are legible, Peter Barron and John Oates.—The same day two were killed at Northampton, Praiswer Turner, Uzacaboy *Shackspeer.*

APPENDIX.*

Commemoration of the Massacre of Capt. Lothrop's Company at Bloody Brook, in Deerfield.

This massacre, by Philip's Indians, on the 18th of September, 1675 (old style,) has long excited the attention of the antiquarian traveller, as well as the people of Deerfield and its vicinity; and many have been desirous that a monument should be erected to the memory of the fallen heroes. With this object in view, a number of inhabitants of Deerfield, Conway, Shelburn, Greenfield, and Gill, which now cover the territory formerly embraced by the original township of Deerfield, held a meeting, at which it was voted to commemorate the approaching anniversary of Lothrop's battle on the 30th of September, 1835.

A committee was then appointed to make the necessary arrangements, and another to examine the battle-ground, and, if possible, to ascertain the place of interment of Lothrop and his men, who, by some historians, as well as traditional accounts, are said to have been deposited in one grave, by the corps under Major Treat and Captain Moseley, the day after the disaster.

A small monument had been erected near the spot, by the early settlers of Deerfield, which had nearly disappeared ; but the *spot* was still known. Guided by this, and information obtained from an elderly gentleman of an adjacent town, the committee had the satisfaction to discover the grave. The bones were found much decayed, or rather changed to terrene substances, still retaining their primitive forms, with some degree of solidity, yet easily crumbled to dust by pressure of the fingers, and generally exhibiting a chocolate color, and often that of a bright scarlet, in masses of dark earth.

The cap-stone of the old monument had been preserved, and a dwelling-house built near the spot, by Stephen Whitney, Esq.

* Abridged from the original edition.

The grave found is directly in front of this house, on the east side of the stage road through Bloody Brook street; and is to be marked by a stone laid level with the surface of the ground.

The site selected for the new monument is a small distance north of the grave, on the west side of the street, near the margin of a morass, in which the Indians formed their ambuscade, and at the point where the attack on Lothrop commenced. The ground has been purchased, and a deed in trust obtained by several patriotic gentlemen of Bloody Brook village. When the monument is completed, it is to be surrounded by ornamental trees, and the ground will then present an open space, replete with interesting associations.

The Committee of Arrangements having engaged the Hon. Edward Everett to deliver the address, on Wednesday, the 30th of September, 1835, the day of the anniversary of the battle, the village of Bloody Brook was early thronged with people from Deerfield and the adjacent towns, and some from the neighboring States. At 11 o'clock, A. M., a procession was formed in front of Russell's hotel, headed by a military escort, with a band of music, and proceeded to the ground assigned for the monument, where a volley was fired by the escort.

After the corner-stone was laid, the Rev. Mr Fessenden, of Deerfield, addressed the throne of grace, and the following brief address was delivered by Gen. E. Hoyt:

FELLOW CITIZENS,—The practice of erecting monuments to commemorate the exploits of the heroes who have shed their blood in the service of their country, is now common wherever refinement of intellect has kept pace with other improvements. In Europe, when her gallant sons have strewed the ground in martial strife, often, indeed in a cause no better than the inordinate ambition of her kings,

> ' Fame spreads her broad pinions their exploits to tell,
> While the smooth chiseled bust their resemblance cherished,
> And well sculptured urns mark the place where they fell.'

And shall Americans—free-born *enlightened* Americans, bestow less honors on the heroes who gallantly shed their blood in defence of their *border-men*, at a time when their military efforts were feeble, and their numbers few ? Forbid it, Patriotism !— Forbid it, Justice !

Too long have the valuable men, who fell on this ground, slumbered in obscurity—lost to the world. This day, (I rejoice to see it,) will remove the ingratitude which cold apathy has so long suffered to exist. The *corner-stone* of a monument to their memory is now laid, and may it be the foundation of a pile, firm as yonder peak ; *imperishable*, so long as bravery and noble exploits shall be revered.

We assemble, my fellow citizens, not only to lay this stone, but to commemorate an event which occurred on this ground on the 18th of September, 1675, old style, which, according to the Georgian calendar, corresponds with the 30th of the present month. At that time the country here was wild and waste, thickly covered with its native woods, and no settlements had been made by the English, within the present county of Franklin, excepting at the north village of Deerfield and at Northfield; and in both places the inhabitants were few, and exposed to the attacks of the Indians.

During Philip's war, military operations were frequent in this part of the State, and in some instances disastrous. The massacre of Capt. Lothrop's company on this ground, by the fierce chief and his merciless allies, was of this description. A detail of the horrid scene, I leave to the orator, who is to favor us with an address from the centre of the ground, on which the young men of Essex met their tragic fate. But a short notice of the commanding officer, which has been obtained from various sources, I trust, will not be deemed intrusive.

Capt. Thomas Lothrop was one of the early emigrants from England, who took up his residence in Beverly, then a part of Salem, in the county of Essex. Of his early employments I am not informed ; but in 1634 he was made a freeman ; in 1644 he was a lieutenant under Capt. Hawthorn, and in 1654, a captain under Major Sedgwick, at the capture of St Johns and Port Royal.

Before Beverly was set off from Salem, he was a representative to the General Court from the latter town, for the years 1647 —1653 and 1664, and held other important offices. In 1668, when Beverly was incorporated, he was chosen a selectman, and re-elected to that office from year to year until his death ; and was also the representative from that town for several years, and extensively employed in almost all its public affairs, both civil and ecclesiastical. He became a member of the church in Salem as early as 1636, and was one who founded the church in Beverly in 1667. He had a sister Ellen who came with him from England, and married the noted schoolmaster, Ezekiel Cheever, who was the preceptor of most of the principal gentlemen of Boston, then on the stage.

Capt. Lothrop left a widow, but no children, and at his decease, about the age of 65 years, his estate, consisting of a house and thirty acres of land, granted to him by the government, situated in that part of Beverly called *Mackerel Cove*, was inherited by his sister and her husband, Mr Cheever. The estate is said now to be possessed by the descendants of Thomas Woodbury.

In the early part of Philip's war, Lothrop was selected to command a company of infantry, in the Massachusetts forces, and ordered to the western frontier of the then province. The company was *raised*, or, as the historian, Hubbard, expresses it, *culled* out of the towns in the county of Essex, and consisted of young men from the most respectable families. At this time the country now embraced within the county of Worcester was infested by the hostile Indians, and Lothrop's company performed much hard service at and in the vicinity of Brookfield, and made extensive marches through the northern woods, in search of the enemy. When Philip, driven from that part of the country, fell back to Connecticut river, and took up his quarters at and about Northfield, Lothrop's company and Capt. Beers', another from the eastern part of the province, were ordered to Hadley to protect the inhabitants in that quarter. A few days previous to the catastrophe at this place, these companies were ordered to pursue a body of Hatfield Indians, who had suddenly left their fort, in the north part of the town, to join Philip on the river above. Coming up with them in a swamp, near the south point of Sugarloaf hill, a skirmish ensued, in which the Indians were defeated and a number slain, with the loss of ten on the part of the English. Beers soon after fell into an ambuscade in the southerly part of Northfield, and was killed, with most of his men.

In the expedition from Hadley to Deerfield, to bring off the stores at the latter place, Lothrop volunteered his services, and on his return, fell into an ambuscade of 700 or 800 Indians at this place, and was slain, with the principal part of his men. The details of the action, though but faint pictures of the horrid scene, may be found in the histories of Philip's war.

Not long after the massacre of Lothrop's company, our fathers, impelled by a laudable sympathy, erected a rude monument near this spot, intended to perpetuate the memory of the slain; but time has dilapidated it, and *this stone* is its only vestige.

The recent discovery of the grave of the unfortunate men, and the erection of a new monument, will excite the sympathy of the traveller ; and the antiquary, while he shudders at the tragedy here acted, will find much to gratify his avidity at this BLOODY BROOK. Here he will behold the spot, where nearly *one hundred* young men, '*the flower of the county of Essex,*' with their brave commander, crimsoned the ground with their blood, in the hazardous service of their country, and left their bones to mingle with their mother earth, and their names—sad fate of the warrior—to perish from recollection.

Long have the residents of this soil traversed over the hallowed spot, unconscious that they were treading upon the ashes of the fallen heroes. The story of the sufferers, though often repeated by their fathers, had nearly lost its thrilling effects, and the peaceful aspect of the adjacent fields tells not, that once they were moistened with the precious blood of brave men. New inquiries will now be excited, and future generations will point to this ground, and their children will know where their fathers bled and died to secure to them the rich boon they possess; where the nightly howl of the wolf, the scream of the panther, and the yell of the red warrior, pierced the ear from the dark tangled woods, and the shuddering mother with fearful hands barred the door of her log hut, and clasped her little ones to her bosom, imploring protecting aid, which man could not interpose.

The men who fell on this ground, though unfortunate, fell not without a manly struggle. But assailed by a vast superiority of numbers, rushing furiously from their '*couched ambuscade,*' with savage yells and bloody intent, vain was military prowess. Strewed with dead and dying, the surrounding woods sent back the shrill war-whoop, intermingled with the last shrieks of the wounded heroes, writhing under the relentless tomahawk and scalping-knife, ' and shuddering pity ' left the sanguine field to the cannibal riots and frantic revels of the hirsute foe.

From this day the heroes of Essex will be remembered by all ' who are not indifferent and unmoved, when conducted over

78

ground that has been dignified by bravery and virtue.' Yes, my friends, the memory of these long lost heroes will be indelibly engraved on our hearts ; and

> ' Still, still, as they sleep, freed from war's dread commotion,
>   Their offspring for ages around them shall weep ;
> And the tears of their sons, as they kneel in devotion,
>   Shall hallow the turf where their forefathers sleep.'

SPEECH

ON THE SUBJECT OF THE WESTERN RAIL-ROAD, DELIVERED IN
FANEUIL HALL, 7TH OCTOBER, 1835.*

——

Mr E. Everett observed that nothing would have induced
him to present himself before his fellow citizens, at so late an hour,
but his engagement to the committee charged with the preparations
for holding the meeting. The gentlemen who had preceded him,
had exhausted the subject, and his fellow citizens in this vast assembly satisfied, he was well persuaded, with what they had heard,
were now desirous, by an earnest and unanimous vote, to prepare
for action. But he had been requested to address them on the
subject, and he was unaffectedly of the opinion, that, next to the
great questions of liberty and independence, the doors of Faneuil
Hall were never thrown open on an occasion of greater moment to
the people of the city and the State.

But, sir, continued Mr E., I do not approach this subject of an
enterprise which promises great and beneficial changes to the community, with feelings of despondency in reference to our present
condition. I would, on the contrary, speak the language of confidence, hope, and self-assured resource. The people of Massachusetts and the citizens of Boston, as the capital of the Common-

* The object of the meeting was to take measures to complete the subscription
to the capital stock of the rail-road, to the amount of two millions of dollars. The
object was effected; and in the course of the ensuing winter, an act passed the Legislature of Massachusetts, authorizing an additional subscription of one million of
dollars, on behalf of the State.

wealth, have been favored with as large a share of blessings as
ever fell to the lot of any people;—and the greatest of all these
blessings is the sagacity with which they are accustomed to perceive,—what industry, and energy, and enterprise can do, to supply that which nature leaves to the cooperation of man. For
carrying on the foreign trade and the fisheries, we have every thing
that the heart of man can desire;—for agriculture, we have the
soil and the climate best adapted,—not to the raising for exportation of the great agricultural staples,—but for the support of a frugal and industrious yeomanry; for manufactures, we are 'by this
last circumstance admirably prepared, as we are, in all other respects, able to compete, in many branches of manufacturing industry, with any other people on earth. In short, sir, we want nothing but what we are able ourselves, with enterprise, energy, and
the wise application of capital, to acquire;—and I have greatly
mistaken the character of the people of Massachusetts, town or
country, if any *such* wants remain long unsupplied. On the contrary, it is their peculiar characteristic, by the use of capital, by
energy, and enterprise, not merely to supply what are commonly
called natural defects, but to open mines of wealth, where others
see only the marks of barrenness. This trait of our character
strikes all observers. It was observed by the President of the
United States, on his visit to this part of the country a year or two
since, that what struck him most in New-England, were the marks
of plenty and comfort on a soil, which in some places seemed little
else than a mass of rocks. It is even so; and if (over no small part
of our beloved native State) nature, like an unkind step-dame, when
her children ask for bread, has given them a stone, by their frugality, industry, and enterprise, they have turned the very stones back
into bread. I speak literally. The gentleman from Springfield,
before me, (Hon. G. Bliss, President of the Senate), was good
enough to send me a pamphlet this morning, from which it appears,
that thousands of tons of the marbles of Berkshire are sent to Philadelphia, and sold to advantage, although their own quarries lie
within sixteen miles; and the City Hall in New-York is chiefly
built from the same Berkshire marble. In like manner, the granite from the quarries of Quincy, by the almost magical virtue of
three miles of rail-road, is now building up the stately piles of New-

York, Philadelphia, and New-Orleans. Look at the outside of Cape Ann,—Sandy Bay, Pigeon Cove, Halibut Point, and Squam, —a region, where the very genius of sterility has taken his abode, if there is such a genius,—(there ought to be, for nothing so sharpens the ingenuity of man),—and behold it converted, in the same way, by the industry, energy, frugality, of its substantial population, and the judicious application of capital, into a region of thrift and plenty !

But the great thing wanting to the prosperity of Massachusetts is COMMUNICATION WITH THE WEST. The internal commerce of this country is prodigious ; and of all that part which is accessible to us, on the present system of communication, we have an ample share. With the South, we have, in our freighting and coasting trade, every thing that can be asked. With the South-West, in reference to all that part of commerce which is calculated to seek the route by sea to New-Orleans, we have nothing more to desire ; —and the intercourse already established in this way, with the whole region drained by the Mississippi and its tributaries, is most extensive, various, and mutually profitable. In ascending the Mississippi and its tributaries, in 1829, on which occasion I was on board several boats, I continually saw casks, packages, and bales, in all of them, which I knew came from New-England, by their marks,—by the mode of doing up,—by a certain indescribable something, in which to a true Yankee eye there is no mistake. A distinguished gentleman, of Pittsburgh, told me there was a regular battle between the Boston nails and the Pittsburgh nails, on the Ohio river ;—the Boston nails coming all the way round, and the Pittsburgh made on the spot, from Juniata iron ; and that, though the Pittsburgh nails sometimes fought their way down the river to Louisville, the Bostonians, at times, had driven them up as far as Wheeling. I was informed by a respectable trading house in Pittsburgh, that they had, in the year preceding, imported two thousand barrels of pickled mackerel ; and I think I did not enter a public house in the West, to take a meal, morning, noon, or night, without seeing a pickled mackerel on the table. I remember, a year or two ago, that one of my neighbors from Charlestown, who had emigrated to the north-west corner of Arkansas,— a spot not then even laid out into counties,—told me, that in that re-

mote region,—the last foothold of civilization, where you have but
one more step to make, to reach the domain of the wild Indian
and the buffalo,—a settler did not think himself well accoutred,
without a *Leominster axe.* But, give him that,—give him, sir,
that weapon which has brought a wider realm into the pale of civilization than the sword of Cæsar or the sceptre of Justinian,—
give him a narrow Yankee axe,—he'll hew his way with it to a
living, in a season ; though I shrewdly suspect, without the least
disparagement of emigrants from other quarters, that after sending
the Yankee axe into the country, the best way to give it full effect
would be to send a little Yankee bone and sinew, to facilitate its
use.

But, sir, though by the way of New-Orleans, we have a considerable trade with the South-West, there is a vast region, which that
channel does not reach. A *direct communication* is greatly wanted. This is THE *want*, daily becoming more serious, and which
must be supplied. The destinies of the country, if I may use a
language which sounds rather mystical, but which every one, I
believe, understands,—the destinies of the country run East and
West. Intercourse between the mighty interior West and the sea-
coast, is the great principle of our commercial prosperity and political strength. Nature, in the aggregate, has done every thing that
could be desired, to promote this intercourse, and art has done
much to second her ; but, as far as the single State of Massachusetts is concerned, the course of the rivers from North to South,
and of the mountains between which they flow, deprives us of the
share of the benefits of this intercourse which we should otherwise
enjoy. And this operation of natural causes has been aided by
several important works of artificial communication, enumerated in
the able report of the committee. The consequence is, that a very
considerable part of the territory of Massachusetts has its commercial interests in one direction, and its political and social relations
in another ; so much so, that, as we all, I am sure, heard with pain
from the distinguished gentleman from Springfield, (Mr Calhoun),
the feeling of State pride, which ought of all feelings that end in
temporal affairs, to be among the dearest and deepest in the bosom
of a Massachusetts man, was daily growing weaker among the
people of one of the most intelligent and substantial portions of the
State.

This commercial alienation has gone to a length, which I suspect the citizens of Boston are not generally aware of. The entire region west of the hills of Berkshire communicates with New-York through the Hudson,—and the whole valley of the Connecticut, in and out of Massachusetts, communicates with Long Island Sound. I am afraid to say, in how large a part of Massachusetts I think a complete non-intercourse reigns with the capital ; but I will state to you a fact, that lately fell beneath my personal observation. Having occasion, last week, to go to Deerfield, I took the north road from Worcester, through Templeton, Athol, and the country watered by Miller's river. If there is a spot in Massachusetts where one would feel himself entrenched, shut up, land-locked, in the very bosom of the Commonwealth, Athol Green, surrounded with its rising grounds, is that spot. And what, Mr President, do you think I saw ? We had scarce driven out of the village and were making our way along through South Orange and Erving's Grant, when I saw two wagons straining up a hill,—the horses' heads to the east,—the wagons laden with crates, casks, and bales of foreign merchandize, which had come from Liverpool, by the way of Hartford, from New-York ! I hold that, sir, a little too much for a Massachusetts man to contemplate without pain.

Now, Mr President, this is the matter which we wish to put to rights. We do not wish to deprive New-York of her trade ; but to regain our own. It is the object of this meeting to remedy principally this evil. To open a great route of communication between the East and the West, by means of a rail-road from Boston to Albany, which with lateral routes, afterwards to be constructed, shall replace Boston in its natural position toward the trade of the interior.

And here, perhaps, we shall be met by the general vague objection, that it is impossible, by artificial works, to divert commerce from its *great natural channels*. Abstractions prove nothing. There are two kinds of natural channels,—one sort made directly by the hand which made the world ; the other, constructed by man, in the intelligent exercise of the powers which his Creator has given him. It is as natural for a civilized man to make a rail-way or canal, as for a savage to descend a river in a bark canoe, or to cross from one fishing place to another, by a path through the woods.

The city of New-York, no doubt, owes much to the noble river that unites her to Albany ; but she owes vastly more to her great artificial works of internal communication. The Hudson and the Mohawk, of themselves, unaided by art, so far from gathering in the commerce of the far West, would not monopolize that of one half the region west of Albany, within the State of New-York. How far is it from the head waters of the eastern branch of the Susquehannah, in Otsego lake, to the Mohawk? Perhaps fifteen miles ! I have stood on the high grounds, that overlook Harris-burgh in Pennsylvania, at a season of the year, before the Hudson was open, and seen the rafts, the flatboats, the canoes, the batteaux, the craft of undescribed shapes and unutterable names, following each other, on the broad bosom of the Susquehannah, from morn-ing to night, bearing the produce of the interior of New-York, to a market in Chesapeake Bay ! The same holds of the south-west-ern corner of New-York, which naturally is drained by the tributaries of the Ohio. I recollect that at New-Orleans, I saw a flat-bottomed boat loaded with shingles. I asked its steersman whence he came. He answered, from Olean. Perhaps I ought to be ashamed to confess, that, at that time, I did not know where Olean was. I found, to my astonishment, it was a settlement in Cattaraugus county, New-York, on the Alleghany river, a hundred and seventy or eighty miles north-east of Pittsburgh ! But, sir, to bring this wandering commerce back to herself, New-York has constructed her great artificial works. In this respect, Massachu-setts is naturally little, if any, worse off than New-York. If New-York has a great navigable river, Massachusetts has, what New-York wants, a vast sea-coast. What both wanted was a great line of artificial communication, running inward to the West. New-York has constructed hers, and has other mighty works of the same character in progress ; and all that Massachusetts needs is, by a work of very moderate extent, not merely to recover the trade of her own territory, but to acquire a fair share, a large, a growing share, of the commerce of the boundless West.

This, sir, is the object ; to take our share, at some seasons of the year the first share, at all seasons a proportionate share of the whole business, not merely of the interior of the State of New-York, but of that almost interminable region farther west, which now derives its supplies from the city of New-York. A great object surely ;—to a commercial eye in this community, the greatest that can be proposed. This, I repeat, is the object ;—and now what are the means which must be employed to effect it? *What are the means? What are we to do?* Are *we* to construct a canal from Albany to Buffalo? *No*, it is made, and with it the Champlain canal to the north, and the numerous lateral works, on either side of the Erie canal; as those which communicate with the Oneida and Ontario lakes on the north of the line; with the Seneca, the Cayuga and the Crooked lakes on the south ; the Chemung and the Chenango canals, also on the south, and designed to rescue the commerce of that region from the grasp of the eastern branch of the Susquehannah, and the extensive artificial works, with which Pennsylvania has strengthened it. Are *we*, perhaps, for the more rapid transportation of passengers, obliged to construct a railroad, parallel to the canal, from Albany to Buffalo? *No*, it is done in part, and the rest is doing. Are we, by great and expensive works, to open the far and mighty west beyond Buffalo? Not a mile of it, by land or water. Nature and man have done, or are doing it all. The great lakes stretch westward, the grand base line of operations. Then comes in, first, the Ohio canal from the mouth of the Scioto to Cleveland, wholly across the State. A parallel line of communication in Ohio, by canal and rail-road, through the Miami and Mad river country to Sandusky bay, comes next ; the canal, to Dayton, or beyond, is finished, the rail-road begun. Indiana, in the noble tier of the north-western States, comes next, with her projected canal to connect the Wabash with lake Erie ; and Illinois follows, with a similar communication, undertaken with the patronage of Congress and the state, to unite the Illinois river and through it the Mississippi with the southern extremity of lake Michigan. All, all is done or doing. The country, by nature or art, is traversed, crossed, reticulated, (pardon me, sir, this long word; the old ones are too short to describe these prodigious works), with canals and rail-roads, rivers and lakes. The entire west is moving to meet us ; by water, land, and steam, they ride, they sail, they drive, they paddle, they whiz—they do all but fly down toward us. They are even now gathering at Albany, a mighty host, with all their goods, looking over into good old Massa-

79

chusetts, desirous, eager to come. They have sent these most respectable gentlemen, to ask if we will take them. They have dug their own canals, built their own rail-roads, come at their own charges, and there they are, an overshadowing army, waiting to hear, if we are willing they should make a peaceful crusade, a profitable inroad into our domain, bringing the fruits of their industry and taking ours in return. I, for one, sir, am prepared to go and meet them, and I am sure my fellow citizens are of the same mind.

But is there *nothing* left for us to do? Next to nothing, sir; I am almost ashamed to state how little, when I consider how long the work has remained undone. It is not to open a rail-road from our western frontier to Albany. That is doing by the citizens of New-York. Charters of incorporation have been obtained from Albany and from Hudson to West Stockbridge, and the work (I believe) commenced; and another charter is solicited from Troy to the same point. That piece therefore is provided for; it is about forty miles. On the other end of the line, from Boston to Worcester, forty-two miles, the rail-road is in high operation. All that remains for us now to do is to complete this little part which lies between Worcester and Stockbridge. This is the question: Shall we make this little piece of road, for the sake of giving to Massachusetts, to Berkshire, to Old Hampshire, to Worcester, to Middlesex, to Boston, to our whole manufacturing, commercial, fishing interest, the benefit of a direct connection with the illimitable West? Shall we make these few miles of rail-road, for the sake of setting down every western trader from lake Erie to the head waters of the Missouri, who wants a bale of domestic goods, in Commercial street, Kilby street, or Liberty square? Don't talk of reaching to Buffalo, sir; talk of the falls of St Anthony and the Council Bluffs. Sir, if we had been told that we must construct the line of artificial communication, the whole way, we should have thought, that (could we possibly command the capital), the benefits which would flow from the expenditure would well warrant the outlay. New-York has practically shown that she thinks so; and the western country, which is looking to us to take up and complete our small part of the work, may well apply to us the words of the servant of the Syrian Captain—'If the prophet had bid thee do *some great thing*, wouldest thou not have done it?'

Suppose these hundred and eighteen miles, (for that is all which remains), completed, how shall we stand? Albany and every point of the United States west of it, and communicating through it with the Atlantic, are equi-distant from New-York city and Boston. Remember that, Mr Chairman:—when we are discouraged by the comparison of natural and artificial means of communication, let us bear in mind that, by nature, it is no *farther* from Boston to all this field of business,—this world of population and trade,—than from New-York. Secondly, let us reflect, that, the distance being equal, it will be travelled in one case by a river, navigated by steamboats; in the other, by rail-road cars, moved by locomotive steam-engines. In speed, the advantage in favor of the latter, may be taken at one third; which will be decisive as to passengers, other things being equal. For merchandise, the river will have an advantage in freight, not overbalancing the advantage of an additional market, and that the first market for all that part of business of which Boston is the natural emporium. This will be the state of things while the river is open. While, for three or four months, at least, of the year, the river is closed, the rail-road will monopolize the travel and the trade; and Boston will be New-York. I am as far, however, from thinking, as from wishing, that New-York should be injured. As for destroying the commerce of New-York, it will be destroyed when the Atlantic ocean evaporates, and the Hudson river dries up. It will be no detriment to her, that the commercial world behind her should be in full exercise and healthy action, in the winter season, rather than lie dormant and torpid;—and with her advantageous position, both for foreign and domestic trade, whatsoever benefits her neighbors, and particularly whatsoever benefits the great interior behind her, will benefit her. It would be of no advantage to New-York, to have Boston droop and decline.

Sometimes, sir, the best mode of judging of the value of a work is to ask how we should be affected by its loss, if, after possessing it, it should be taken away. Suppose we had at this moment a navigable river from Boston to Albany, or a canal, and it should, by some convulsion of nature, sink or dry up. Would it not be thought the direst of calamities? Suppose we had a railway,—a natural railway,—a level ridge from Boston bay to the confluence of the Mohawk and the Hudson, laid down by the hand of Providence, and ready for use ; and the philosophers had been able, by their tables and instruments, to predict some great catastrophe, which would destroy it, and had foretold the day when the earth would open and swallow it up. Should we not regard it almost as the day of approaching doom, and be ready to open our churches, and fall on our knees, and implore a merciful Providence to avert the calamity ? And how does the case differ, sir, in a practical point of view, between the loss of a great blessing, proceeding from an overwhelming natural convulsion, and its want, arising from our own neglect and apathy ?

Sir, I have almost done. I have trespassed much too long on your patience ; but I will add a few words more on another aspect of the question ;—one to which, *in this place*, in Faneuil Hall, although it is a view of the subject remote from financial questions, I may, in common with the gentlemen who have preceded me, with propriety allude. The great political basis of all our prosperity is *Union ;* the great political danger that menaces us is *Disunion.* All else can be borne, if we can avoid this calamity ; and if this is fated to befal us, all our other blessings will turn to dust and ashes in our grasp. The rapid growth of our country, the prodigious population and resources of single sections, tend to disunion. I am sorry to say, that on the floor of Congress, I have heard calculations of the capacity of individual States to support themselves as independent governments. I know of nothing so well calculated to counteract the centrifugal tendency, as to increase the facilities for intercourse. They will prove not merely avenues of business, but pathways of intelligence and social feeling. They will make the distant near and the many one, for all the purposes of defence, strength, and good neighborhood. It is the great prerogative of science and art, applied to the business of life, to conquer the obstacles of time and place ; to redress the wrongs of nature. By promoting the rapid circulation of knowledge, the prompt communication of intelligence, we shall carry on and perfect the noble work HERE begun by men, some of whose portraits are now looking down upon us. No subject, after the liberty of his country, lay nearer to the heart of Washington, than the opening of a great line of communication between the East and West. It was the very first subject to which he turned his attention, at the close of the revolutionary war.

I hold in my hand an extract from a letter, written by the Father of his Country, in 1784. I would not, while the bell is ringing for nine o'clock, obtrude with any lighter authority, on the audience. But who will not listen to the counsels of Washington, on the question before us?

'I have lately,' says he, 'made a tour through the lakes George and Champlain, as far as Crown Point; then returning to Schenectady, I proceeded up the Mohawk river to Fort Schuyler, crossed over to Wood Creek, which empties into Oneida lake, and affords a water communication with Ontario. I then traversed the country to the head of the eastern branch of the Susquehannah, and viewed the lake of Otsego, and the portage between that lake and the Mohawk river, at Canajoharie. Prompted by these actual observations, I could not help taking a more contemplative and extensive view of the vast inland navigation of these United States, and could not but be struck with the immense diffusion and importance of it; and with the goodness of that Providence which has dealt his favors to us with so profuse a hand. *Would to God, we may have wisdom enough to improve them!*'

Such, sir, is the voice of him, whose sagacity in all the civil concerns of life, was equal to his patriotism in council, and conduct in the field;—and to this affecting prayer of Washington, who can deem it irreverent to add, *Let all the people say* AMEN!

ERRATUM.—Page 426, seventh line from the bottom, for *feelings* read *fountains*.

The Romantic Tradition in American Literature

An Arno Press Collection

Alcott, A. Bronson, editor. **Conversations with Children on the Gospels.** Boston, 1836/1837. Two volumes in one.

Bartol, C[yrus] A. **Discourses on the Christian Spirit and Life.** 2nd edition. Boston, 1850.

Boker, George H[enry]. **Poems of the War.** Boston, 1864.

Brooks, Charles T. **Poems, Original and Translated.** Selected and edited by W. P. Andrews. Boston, 1885.

Brownell, Henry Howard. **War-Lyrics** and Other Poems. Boston, 1866.

Brownson, O[restes] A. **Essays and Reviews Chiefly on Theology, Politics, and Socialism.** New York, 1852.

Channing, [William] Ellery (The Younger). **Poems.** Boston, 1843.

Channing, [William] Ellery (The Younger). **Poems of Sixty-Five Years.** Edited by F. B. Sanborn. Philadelphia and Concord, 1902.

Chivers, Thomas Holley. **Eonchs of Ruby:** A Gift of Love. New York, 1851.

Chivers, Thomas Holley. **Virginalia;** or, Songs of My Summer Nights. (Reprinted from *Research Classics,* No. 2, 1942). Philadelphia, 1853.

Cooke, Philip Pendleton. **Froissart Ballads,** and Other Poems. Philadelphia, 1847.

Cranch, Christopher Pearse. **The Bird and the Bell,** with Other Poems. Boston, 1875.

[Dall], Caroline W. Healey, editor. **Margaret and Her Friends.** Boston, 1895.

[D'Arusmont], Frances Wright. **A Few Days in Athens.** Boston, 1850.

Everett, Edward. **Orations and Speeches,** on Various Occasions. Boston, 1836.

Holland, J[osiah] G[ilbert]. **The Marble Prophecy,** and Other Poems. New York, 1872.

Huntington, William Reed. **Sonnets and a Dream.** Jamaica, N. Y., 1899.

Jackson, Helen [Hunt]. **Poems.** Boston, 1892.

Miller, Joaquin (Cincinnatus Hiner Miller). **The Complete Poetical Works of Joaquin Miller.** San Francisco, 1897.

Parker, Theodore. **A Discourse of Matters Pertaining to Religion.** Boston, 1842.

Pinkney, Edward C. **Poems.** Baltimore, 1838.

Reed, Sampson. **Observations on the Growth of the Mind.** *Including,* **Genius** (Reprinted from *Aesthetic Papers,* Boston, 1849). 5th edition. Boston, 1859.

Sill, Edward Rowland. **The Poetical Works of Edward Rowland Sill.** Boston and New York, 1906.

Simms, William Gilmore. **Poems:** Descriptive, Dramatic, Legendary and Contemplative. New York, 1853. Two volumes in one.

Simms, William Gilmore, editor. **War Poetry of the South.** New York, 1866.

Stickney, Trumbull. **The Poems of Trumbull Stickney.** Boston and New York, 1905.

Timrod, Henry. **The Poems of Henry Timrod.** Edited by Paul H. Hayne. New York, 1873.

Trowbridge, John Townsend. **The Poetical Works of John Townsend Trowbridge.** Boston and New York, 1903.

Very, Jones. **Essays and Poems.** [Edited by R. W. Emerson]. Boston, 1839.

Very, Jones. **Poems and Essays.** Boston and New York, 1886.

White, Richard Grant, editor. **Poetry:** Lyrical, Narrative, and Satirical of the Civil War. New York, 1866.

Wilde, Richard Henry. **Hesperia:** A Poem. Edited by His Son (William Wilde). Boston, 1867.

Willis, Nathaniel Parker. **The Poems, Sacred, Passionate, and Humorous, of Nathaniel Parker Willis.** New York, 1868.